Weiss Ratings' Guide to Banks

Weiss Ratings' Guide to Banks

A Quarterly Compilation of Financial Institutions Ratings and Analyses

Fall 2020

GREY HOUSE PUBLISHING

Weiss Ratings
4400 Northcorp Parkway
Palm Beach Gardens, FL 33410
561-627-3300

Published by Grey House Publishing, Inc., located at 4919 Route 22, Amenia, NY 12501; telephone 518-789-8700. Grey House Publishing neither guarantees the accuracy of the data contained herein nor assumes any responsibility for errors, omissions or discrepancies. Grey House Publishing accepts no payment for listing; inclusion in the publication of any organization, agency, institution, publication, service or individual does not imply endorsement of the publisher.

4919 Route 22
PO Box 56
Amenia, NY 12501-0056

Edition No. 119, Fall 2020

ISBN: 978-1-64265-550-6
ISSN: 2158-5962

Contents

Terms and Conditions

This document is prepared strictly for the confidential use of our customer(s). It has been provided to you at your specific request. It is not directed to, or intended for distribution to or use by, any person or entity who is a citizen or resident of or located in any locality, state, country or other jurisdiction where such distribution, publication, availability or use would be contrary to law or regulation or which would subject Weiss Ratings or its affiliates to any registration or licensing requirement within such jurisdiction.

No part of the analysts' compensation was, is, or will be, directly or indirectly, related to the specific recommendations or views expressed in this research report.

This document is not intended for the direct or indirect solicitation of business. Weiss Ratings, LLC and its affiliates disclaims any and all liability to any person or entity for any loss or damage caused, in whole or in part, by any error (negligent or otherwise) or other circumstances involved in, resulting from or relating to the procurement, compilation, analysis, interpretation, editing, transcribing, publishing and/or dissemination or transmittal of any information contained herein.

Weiss Ratings has not taken any steps to ensure that the securities or investment vehicle referred to in this report are suitable for any particular investor. The investment or services contained or referred to in this report may not be suitable for you and it is recommended that you consult an independent investment advisor if you are in doubt about such investments or investment services. Nothing in this report constitutes investment, legal, accounting or tax advice or a representation that any investment or strategy is suitable or appropriate to your individual circumstances or otherwise constitutes a personal recommendation to you.

The ratings and other opinions contained in this document must be construed solely as statements of opinion from Weiss Ratings, LLC., and not statements of fact. Each rating or opinion must be weighed solely as a factor in your choice of an institution and should not be construed as a recommendation to buy, sell or otherwise act with respect to the particular product or company involved.

Past performance should not be taken as an indication or guarantee of future performance, and no representation or warranty, expressed or implied, is made regarding future performance. Information, opinions and estimates contained in this report reflect a judgment at its original date of publication and are subject to change without notice. Weiss Ratings offers a notification service for rating changes on companies you specify. For more information visit WeissRatings.com or call 1-877-934-7778. The price, value and income from any of the securities or financial instruments mentioned in this report can fall as well as rise.

Date of Data Analyzed: March 31, 2020

Data Source: Call Report data provided by SNL Financial.

Welcome to Weiss Ratings'
Guide to Banks

Most people automatically assume their bank will survive, year after year. However, prudent consumers and professionals realize that in this world of shifting risks, the solvency of financial institutions can't be taken for granted. After all, your bank's failure could have a heavy impact on you in terms of lost time, lost money (in cases of deposits exceeding the federal insurance limit), tied-up deposits, lost credit lines, and the possibility of being shifted to another institution under not-so-friendly terms.

If you are looking for accurate, unbiased ratings and data to help you choose a commercial bank, savings bank, or savings and loan for yourself, your family, your company or your clients, Weiss Ratings' Guide to Banks gives you precisely what you need.

Weiss Ratings' Mission Statement

Weiss Ratings' mission is to empower consumers, professionals, and institutions with high quality advisory information for selecting or monitoring a financial services company or financial investment.

In doing so, Weiss Ratings will adhere to the highest ethical standards by maintaining our independent, unbiased outlook and approach to advising our customers.

Why rely on Weiss Ratings?

Weiss Ratings provides fair, objective ratings to help professionals and consumers alike make educated financial decisions.

At Weiss Ratings, integrity is number one. Weiss Ratings never takes a penny from rated companies for issuing its ratings. And, we publish Weiss Safety Ratings without regard for institutions' preferences. Our analysts review and update Weiss ratings each and every quarter, so you can be sure that the information you receive is accurate and current – providing you with advance warning of financial vulnerability early enough to do something about it.

Other rating agencies focus primarily on a company's current financial solvency and consider only mild economic adversity. Weiss Ratings also considers these issues, but in addition, our analysis covers a company's ability to deal with severe economic adversity in terms of a sharp decline in the value of its investments and a drop in the collectability of its loans.

Our use of more rigorous standards stems from the viewpoint that a financial institution's obligations to its customers should not depend on favorable business conditions. A bank must be able to honor its loan and deposit commitments in bad times as well as good.

Weiss's rating scale, from A to F, is easy to understand. Only a few outstanding companies receive an A (Excellent) rating, although there are many to choose from within the B (Good) category. A large group falls into the broad average range which receives C (Fair) ratings. Companies that demonstrate marked vulnerabilities receive either D (Weak) or E (Very Weak) ratings. So, there's no numbering system, star counting, or color-coding to keep track of.

How to Use This Guide

The purpose of the *Guide to Banks* is to provide consumers, businesses, financial institutions, and municipalities with a reliable source of banking industry ratings and analysis on a timely basis. We realize that the financial safety of a bank is an important factor to consider when establishing a relationship. The ratings and analysis in this Guide can make that evaluation easier when you are considering:

- A checking, merchant banking, or other transaction account
- An investment in a certificate of deposit or savings account
- A line of credit or commercial loan
- Counterparty risk

The rating for a particular company indicates our opinion regarding that company's ability to meet its obligations – not only under current economic conditions, but also during a declining economy or in an environment of increased liquidity demands.

To use this Guide most effectively, we recommend you follow the steps outlined below:

Step 1 To ensure you evaluate the correct company, verify the company's exact name as it was given to you. It is also helpful to ascertain the city and state of the company's main office or headquarters since no two banks with the same name can be headquartered in the same city. Many companies have similar names but are not related to one another, so you will want to make sure the company you look up is really the one you are interested in evaluating.

Step 2 Turn to Section I, the Index of Banks, and locate the company you are evaluating. This section contains all federally-insured commercial banks and savings banks. It is sorted alphabetically by the name of the company and shows the main office city and state following the name for additional verification.
If you have trouble finding a particular institution or determining which is the right one, consider these possible reasons:

- You may have an incorrect or incomplete institution name. There are often several institutions with the same or very similar names. So, make sure you have the exact name and proper spelling, as well as the city in which it is headquartered.
- You may be looking for a *bank holding company*. If so, try to find the exact name of the main bank in the group and look it up under that name.

Step 3 Once you have located your specific company, the first column after the state shows its current Weiss Safety Rating. Turn to *About Weiss Safety Ratings* for information about what this rating means. If the rating has changed since the last edition of this Guide, a downgrade will be indicated with a down triangle ▼ to the left of the company name; an upgrade will be indicated with an up triangle ▲.

Step 4 Following the current Weiss Safety Rating are two prior ratings for the company based on year-end data from the two previous years. Use this to discern the longer-term direction of the company's overall financial condition.

Step 5 The remainder of Section I; provides insight into the areas our analysts reviewed as the basis for assigning the company's rating. These areas include size, capital adequacy, asset quality, profitability, liquidity, and stability. An index within each of these categories represents a composite evaluation of that particular facet of the company's financial condition. Refer to the Critical Ranges In Our Indexes table for an interpretation of which index values are considered strong, good, fair, or weak. In most cases, lower-rated companies will have a low index value in one or more of the indexes shown. Bear in mind, however, that Weiss Safety Rating is the result of a complex qualitative and quantitative analysis which cannot be reproduced using only the data provided here.

Step 6 If the company you are evaluating is not highly rated and you want to find a bank with a higher rating, turn to the page in Section II that has your state's name at the top. This section contains Weiss Recommended Banks by State (rating of A+, A, A- or B+) that have a branch office in your state. If the main office telephone number provided is not a local telephone call or to determine if a branch of the bank is near you, consult your local telephone Yellow Pages Directory under "Banks," "Savings Banks," or "Savings and Loan Associations." Here you will find a complete list of the institution's branch locations along with their telephone numbers.

Step 7 Once you've identified a Weiss Recommended Company in your local area, you can then refer back to Section I to analyze it.

Step 8 In order to use Weiss Safety Ratings most effectively, we strongly recommend you consult the *Important Warnings and Cautions* listed. These are more than just "standard disclaimers." They are very important factors you should be aware of before using this Guide. If you have any questions regarding the precise meaning of specific terms used in the Guide, refer to the Glossary.

Step 9 Make sure you stay up to date with the latest information available since the publication of this Guide. For information on how to set up a rating change notification service, acquire follow-up reports, check ratings online or receive a more in-depth analysis of an individual company, call 1-877-934-7778 or visit www.weissratings.com.

About Weiss Safety Ratings

The Weiss Ratings are calculated based on a complex analysis of hundreds of factors that are synthesized into five indexes: capitalization, asset quality, profitability, liquidity and stability. Each index is then used to arrive at a letter grade rating. A weak score on any one index can result in a low rating, as financial problems can be caused by any one of a number of factors, such as inadequate capital, non-performing loans and poor asset quality, operating losses, poor liquidity, or the failure of an affiliated company.

Our **Capitalization Index** gauges the institution's capital adequacy in terms of its cushion to absorb future operating losses under adverse business and economic scenarios that may impact the company's net interest margin, securities' values, and the collectability of its loans.

Our **Asset Quality Index** measures the quality of the company's past underwriting and investment practices based on the estimated liquidation value of the company's loan and securities portfolios.

Our **Profitability Index** measures the soundness of the company's operations and the contribution of profits to the company's financial strength. The index is a composite of five sub-factors: 1) gain or loss on operations; 2) rates of return on assets and equity; 3) management of net interest margin; 4) generation of noninterest-based revenues; and 5) overhead expense management.

Our **Liquidity Index** evaluates a company's ability to raise the necessary cash to satisfy creditors and honor depositor withdrawals.

Finally, our **Stability Index** integrates a number of sub-factors that affect consistency (or lack thereof) in maintaining financial strength over time. These include 1) risk diversification in terms of company size and loan diversification; 2) deterioration of operations as reported in critical asset, liability, income and expense items, such as an increase in loan delinquency rates or a sharp increase in loan originations; 3) years in operation; 4) former problem areas where, despite recent improvement, the company has yet to establish a record of stable performance over a suitable period of time; and 5) relationships with holding companies and affiliates.

In order to help guarantee our objectivity, we reserve the right to publish ratings expressing our opinion of a company's financial stability based exclusively on publicly available data and our own proprietary standards for safety.

Each of these indexes is measured according to the following range of values.

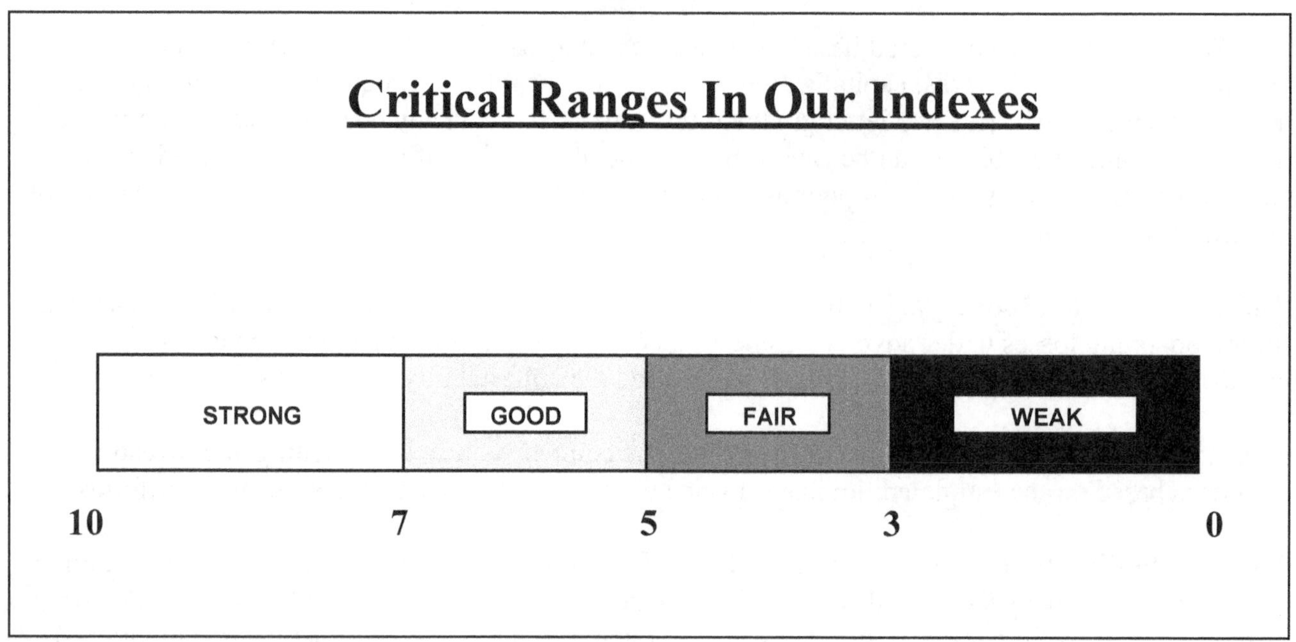

Finally, the indexes are combined to form a composite company rating which is then verified by one of our analysts. The resulting distribution of ratings assigned to all banks looks like this:

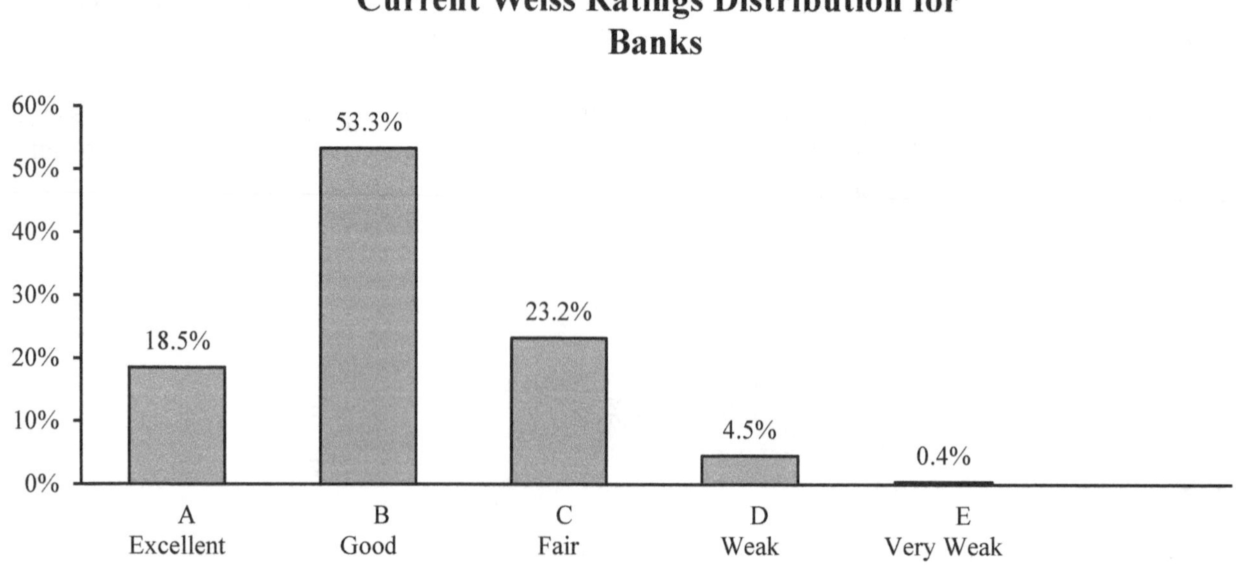

What Our Ratings Mean

A **Excellent.** The institution offers excellent financial security. It has maintained a conservative stance in its business operations and underwriting practices as evidenced by its strong equity base, high asset quality, steady earnings, and high liquidity. While the financial position of any company is subject to change, we believe that this institution has the resources necessary to deal with severe economic conditions.

B **Good.** The institution offers good financial security and has the resources to deal with a variety of adverse economic conditions. It comfortably exceeds the minimum levels for all of our rating criteria, and is likely to remain healthy for the near future. Nevertheless, in the event of a severe recession or major financial crisis, we feel that this assessment should be reviewed to make sure that the company is still maintaining adequate financial strength.

C **Fair.** The institution offers fair financial security, is currently stable, and will likely remain relatively healthy as long as the economic environment remains relatively stable. In the event of a severe recession or major financial crisis, however, we feel this company may encounter difficulties in maintaining its financial stability.

D **Weak.** The institution currently demonstrates what, in our opinion, we consider to be significant weaknesses which could negatively impact depositors or creditors. In the event of a severe recession or major financial crisis, these weaknesses could be magnified.

E **Very Weak.** The institution currently demonstrates what we consider to be significant weaknesses and has also failed some of the basic tests that we use to identify fiscal stability. Therefore, even in a favorable economic environment, it is our opinion that depositors or creditors could incur significant risks.

F **Failed.** The institution has been placed under the custodianship of regulatory authorities. This implies that it will be either liquidated or taken over by another financial institution.

\+ The **plus sign** is an indication that the institution is in the upper third of the letter grade.

\- The **minus sign** is an indication that the institution is in the lower third of the letter grade.

U **Unrated.** The institution is unrated due to the absence of sufficient data for our ratings.

Peer Comparison of Bank Safety Ratings

Weiss Ratings	Veribanc	Bauer Financial	IDC Financial	Bankrate.com	Lace Financial
A+, A, A-	Green, Three Stars w/ Blue Ribbon recognition	5 stars, 4 stars	201-300	1, Five stars	A+, A
B+, B, B-	Green, Three Stars w/out Blue Ribbon recognition	3 ½ stars	166-200	2, Four stars	B+
C+, C, C-	Green Two Stars, Yellow Two Stars	3 stars	126-165	3, Three stars	B, C+
D+, D, D-	Green one star, Yellow one star, Green no stars	2 stars	76-125	4, Two stars	C, D
E+, E, E-	Yellow no stars, Red no stars	1 star	1-75	5, One star	E

Important Warnings and Cautions

1. **A rating alone cannot tell the whole story.** Please read the explanatory information contained here, in the section introductions and in the appendix. It is provided in order to give you an understanding of our rating philosophy as well as to paint a more complete picture of how we arrive at our opinion of a company's strengths and weaknesses. In addition, please remember that our safety rating is not an end-all measure of an institution's safety. Rather, it should be used as a "flag" of possible troubles, suggesting a need for further research.

2. **Safety ratings shown in this directory were current as of the publication date.** In the meantime, the rating may have been updated based on more recent data. Weiss Ratings offers a notification service for ratings changes on companies that you specifiy. For more information call 1-877-934-7778 or visit www.weissratings.com.

3. **When deciding to do business with a financial institution, your decision should be based on a wide variety of factors in addition to Weiss Safety Rating**. These include the institution's pricing of its deposit instruments and loans, the fees you will be charged, the degree to which it can help you meet your long-term planning needs, how these costs/benefits may change over the years, and what other choices are available to you given your current location and financial circumstances.

4. **Weiss Safety Ratings represent our opinion of a company's insolvency risk.** As such, a high rating means we feel that the company has less chance of running into financial difficulties. A high rating is not a guarantee of solvency nor is a low rating a prediction of insolvency. Weiss Safety Ratings are not deemed to be a recommendation concerning the purchase or sale of the securities of any bank that is publicly owned.

5. **All firms that have the same Weiss Safety Rating should be considered to be essentially equal in safety.** This is true regardless of any differences in the underlying numbers which might appear to indicate greater strengths. Weiss Safety Rating already takes into account a number of lesser factors which, due to space limitations, cannot be included in this publication.

6. **A good rating requires consistency.** If a company is excellent on four indicators and fair on one, the company may receive a fair rating. This requirement is necessary due to the fact that fiscal problems can arise from any *one* of several causes including poor underwriting, inadequate capital resources, or operating losses.

7. **Our rating standards are more conservative than those used by other agencies.** We believe that no one can predict with certainty the economic environment of the near or long-term future. Rather, we assume that various scenarios – from the extremes of double-digit inflation to a severe recession – are within the range of reasonable possibilities over the next one or two decades. To achieve a top rating according to our standards, a company must be adequately prepared for the worst-case reasonable scenario, without impairing its current operations.

8. **We are an independent rating agency and do not depend on the cooperation of the companies we rate**. Our data are derived, from quarterly financial statements filed with federal regulators. Although we seek to maintain an open line of communication with the companies being rated, we do not grant them the right to influence the ratings or stop their publication. This policy stems from the fact that this Guide is designed for the protection of our customers.

9. **Inaccuracies in the data issued by the federal regulators could negatively impact the quality of a company's Safety Rating.** While we attempt to find and correct as many data errors as possible, some data errors inevitably slip through. We have no method of intercepting fraudulent or falsified data and must take for granted that all information is reported honestly to the federal regulatory agencies.

10. **Institutions that operate exclusively or primarily as a trust company may have skewed financial information.** Due to the nature of their business, these companies often record high profit levels compared to other more "traditional" banks. Trust companies can usually be recognized by the initials "TC" or "& TC" in their names.

11. **This Guide does not cover nonbank affiliates of banking companies.** Although some nonbank companies may be affiliated with the banks cited in this Guide, the firms are separate corporations whose financial strength is only partially dependent on the strength of their affiliates.

12. **There are many companies with the same or similar sounding names, despite no affiliation whatsoever.** Therefore, it is important that you have the exact name, city, and state of the institution's headquarters before you begin to research the company in this Guide.

13. **Affiliated companies do not automatically receive the same rating.** We recognize that a troubled institution may expect financial support from its parent or affiliates. Weiss Safety Ratings reflect our opinion of the measure of support that may become available to a subsidiary bank, if the subsidiary were to experience serious financial difficulties. In the case of a strong parent and a weaker subsidiary, the affiliate relationship will generally result in a higher rating for the subsidiary than it would have on a stand-alone basis. Seldom, however, would the rating be brought up to the level of the parent.

    This treatment is appropriate because we do not assume the parent would have either the resources or the will to "bail out" a troubled subsidiary during a severe economic crisis. Even when there is a binding legal obligation for a parent corporation to honor the obligations of its subsidiary banks, the possibility exists that the subsidiary could be sold and lose its parental support. Therefore, it is quite common for one affiliate to have a higher rating than another. This is another reason why it is especially important that you have the precise name of the company you are evaluating.

14. **This publication does not include foreign banking companies, or their U.S. branches.** Therefore, our evaluation of foreign banking companies is limited to those U.S. chartered domestic banks owned by foreign banking companies. In most cases, the U.S. operations of a foreign banking company are relatively small in relation to the overall size of the company, so you may want to consult other sources as well. In any case, do not be confused by a domestic bank with a name which is the same as – or similar to – that of a foreign banking company. Even if there is an affiliation between the two, we have evaluated the U.S. institution based on its own merits.

Section I

Index of Banks

An analysis of all rated

U.S. Commercial Banks and Savings Banks

Institutions are listed in alphabetical order.

Section I Contents

This section contains Weiss Safety Ratings, key rating factors, and summary financial data for all U.S. federally-insured commercial banks and savings banks. Companies are sorted in alphabetical order, first by company name, then by city and state.

Left Pages

1. Institution Name	The name under which the institution was chartered. If you cannot find the institution you are interested in, or if you have any doubts regarding the precise name, verify the information with the bank itself before proceeding. Also, determine the city and state in which the institution is headquartered for confirmation. (See columns 2 and 3.)
2. City	The city in which the institution's headquarters or main office is located. With the adoption of intrastate and interstate branching laws, many institutions operating in your area may actually be headquartered elsewhere. So, don't be surprised if the location cited is not in your particular city. Also use this column to confirm that you have located the correct institution. It is possible for two unrelated companies to have the same name if they are headquartered in different cities.
3. State	The state in which the institution's headquarters or main office is located. With the adoption of interstate branching laws, some institutions operating in your area may actually be headquartered in another state.
4. Safety Rating	Weiss rating assigned to the institution at the time of publication. Our ratings are designed to distinguish levels of insolvency risk and are measured on a scale from A to F based upon a wide range of factors. See *About Weiss Safety Ratings* for specific descriptions of each letter grade. Highly rated companies are, in our opinion, less likely to experience financial difficulties than lower rated firms. See *About Weiss Safety Ratings* for more information. Also, please be sure to consider the warnings regarding the ratings' limitations and the underlying assumptions.
5. Prior Year Safety Rating	Weiss rating assigned to the institution based on data from December 31 of the previous year. Compare this rating to the company's current rating to identify any recent changes.
6. Safety Rating Two Years Prior	Weiss rating assigned to the institution based on data from December 31 two years ago. Compare this rating to the ratings in the prior columns to identify longer term trends in the company's financial condition.

Asset Quality Index	Adjusted Non-Performing Loans as a % of Total Loans	Adjusted Non-Performing Loans as a % of Capital	Net Charge-Offs Avg Loans	Profitability Index	Net Income ($Mil)	Return on Assets (R.O.A.)	Return on Equity (R.O.E.)	Net Interest Spread	Overhead Efficiency Ratio	Liquidity Index	Liquidity Ratio	Hot Money Ratio	Stability Index
2.7	2.72	na	0.34	**4.2**	0.2	0.87	7.52	4.84	74.8	**3.1**	18.2	10.8	**6.2**
9.3	0.00	na	0.06	**5.4**	0.3	1.73	14.97	3.79	55.1	**6.4**	78.3	8.8	**6.7**
3.1	1.41	7.3	2.85	**10.0**	567.5	1.82	16.83	7.60	57.7	**2.0**	30.0	2.1	**10.0**
5.8	0.24	na	0.00	**5.5**	1.7	1.10	12.63	4.23	67.9	**1.8**	5.7	13.4	**7.1**
6.4	0.39	na	0.21	**6.3**	5.8	1.19	10.98	3.38	49.9	**0.6**	12.2	55.1	**9.7**
6.5	0.95	na	-0.03	**6.1**	0.3	1.34	10.78	4.13	65.9	**3.0**	41.9	21.0	**7.7**
8.8	1.82	na	0.04	**4.4**	3.5	1.18	12.29	3.17	72.0	**2.9**	13.8	14.8	**7.8**
8.3	0.29	1.0	-0.01	**6.6**	1.1	1.12	9.18	3.52	58.6	**4.6**	24.7	6.0	**8.1**
8.6	0.00	0.0	0.00	**10.0**	0.8	3.12	15.79	4.99	36.0	**4.5**	26.0	6.9	**10.0**
9.8	0.01	na	-0.45	**3.8**	0.1	0.60	5.09	3.61	80.6	**1.6**	20.8	25.1	**6.5**
6.5	2.34	na	-0.04	**2.5**	0.0	0.23	1.98	3.80	92.1	**0.7**	18.2	54.7	**5.5**
4.8	0.92	na	0.04	**6.3**	4.3	0.83	5.65	4.22	60.9	**4.2**	24.0	11.0	**10.0**
5.3	0.22	na	0.01	**5.2**	1.6	1.42	14.12	3.37	57.9	**1.4**	32.6	45.4	**6.4**
7.6	0.00	na	0.00	**5.8**	0.7	0.90	6.10	3.86	64.6	**4.9**	34.7	8.6	**8.5**
6.3	0.77	na	0.16	**6.5**	15.5	1.57	15.42	3.61	56.2	**3.0**	16.9	8.4	**9.2**
4.7	0.63	4.2	0.00	**5.2**	2.3	1.01	8.88	3.66	65.9	**1.6**	13.8	9.9	**8.1**
7.5	0.19	1.0	0.01	**6.2**	9.1	1.47	10.64	3.60	54.4	**2.7**	13.8	15.5	**9.8**
5.9	0.87	5.0	0.00	**4.2**	0.9	1.14	10.52	4.18	72.6	**0.7**	12.0	27.9	**7.3**
8.4	0.00	na	0.17	**5.3**	0.3	1.22	9.82	3.84	71.8	**2.2**	36.4	28.6	**8.3**
8.5	0.44	1.6	0.09	**5.6**	8.7	1.01	10.48	3.51	68.6	**4.2**	10.0	6.9	**8.2**
7.7	1.01	na	-0.02	**7.6**	1.3	1.65	11.52	3.29	53.2	**1.0**	26.7	22.6	**9.5**
7.2	0.00	na	0.00	**7.5**	1.2	0.87	5.88	3.55	38.9	**0.5**	10.8	54.7	**9.8**
4.5	2.19	na	0.00	**5.0**	0.4	0.87	5.91	4.02	74.7	**0.8**	17.9	38.4	**9.1**
6.7	1.51	na	0.00	**4.6**	1.6	0.88	7.34	3.76	61.0	**4.1**	24.1	9.5	**8.0**
7.2	0.05	na	-0.01	**4.5**	1.2	0.65	6.11	4.27	69.3	**4.0**	16.0	8.8	**7.1**
5.8	1.09	na	0.06	**6.2**	0.2	1.44	7.04	3.40	52.1	**4.6**	59.1	15.1	**9.1**
5.9	1.38	7.7	0.44	**5.1**	15.8	0.87	9.06	3.70	61.9	**4.3**	15.5	7.3	**8.2**
5.5	0.68	na	0.03	**7.7**	0.9	1.64	16.60	4.16	61.3	**1.6**	18.2	23.2	**7.6**
3.0	1.14	na	0.42	**6.9**	4.0	1.67	13.78	3.42	50.0	**1.2**	6.9	21.6	**8.3**
4.3	0.62	na	0.40	**3.5**	1.0	0.87	8.74	4.27	81.1	**1.1**	16.0	31.2	**5.2**
5.0	3.10	na	0.01	**9.5**	3.9	2.53	21.26	3.49	43.5	**6.0**	43.3	4.5	**9.4**
4.4	1.21	na	-0.01	**4.8**	1.4	0.88	6.20	3.70	67.9	**3.5**	17.3	11.6	**8.4**
4.4	1.67	na	0.00	**4.8**	0.2	1.35	12.37	3.73	65.3	**5.5**	34.9	4.1	**6.2**
9.4	0.18	na	-1.03	**1.9**	0.0	0.05	0.25	2.94	98.4	**6.5**	83.0	8.6	**6.7**
3.2	1.59	na	-0.07	**3.7**	0.2	0.60	6.95	3.65	78.4	**2.4**	19.6	13.8	**4.8**
5.8	1.36	4.4	0.00	**3.6**	0.3	0.65	6.06	4.07	77.5	**1.7**	17.9	22.0	**6.1**
10.0	0.22	na	3.70	**6.6**	13.6	1.12	17.40	2.12	34.4	**8.6**	94.3	0.0	**8.0**
5.0	0.75	3.3	0.12	**5.2**	24.9	0.55	3.82	3.80	67.3	**3.0**	8.7	11.5	**9.8**
8.2	0.26	na	0.05	**3.5**	1.6	0.55	6.00	3.40	79.3	**2.6**	7.7	15.5	**7.1**
2.3	2.63	na	0.13	**5.7**	1.2	1.70	19.10	4.16	66.9	**1.0**	23.5	30.9	**6.4**
9.0	0.00	na	0.00	**9.2**	2.2	1.59	17.14	2.09	67.4	**7.3**	56.2	0.2	**7.7**
7.5	0.03	na	0.00	**7.9**	0.1	1.60	11.16	4.93	68.0	**4.8**	28.9	6.5	**7.6**
7.2	0.67	na	0.15	**0.4**	-0.1	-0.42	-3.19	1.86	118.1	**1.7**	37.1	54.7	**5.5**
8.9	0.02	na	-0.02	**4.0**	0.5	0.95	11.30	3.17	74.4	**4.1**	22.0	9.1	**6.7**
7.4	0.81	5.1	-0.02	**5.8**	9.7	1.47	17.28	3.83	67.3	**5.5**	24.9	3.2	**8.3**
6.6	0.05	na	-0.01	**3.2**	0.0	0.01	0.14	4.02	99.9	**0.8**	14.5	36.3	**5.3**
6.4	0.34	na	0.05	**5.4**	1.0	1.72	16.01	3.45	67.7	**0.8**	17.6	36.6	**7.2**
8.8	0.00	na	0.00	**3.1**	0.0	0.41	1.71	3.15	79.6	**4.7**	62.4	13.5	**6.4**
3.3	1.07	7.9	1.34	**8.3**	3.3	1.52	15.68	7.38	60.9	**1.4**	16.3	23.6	**6.5**
9.2	0.22	na	-0.01	**4.2**	0.2	1.01	6.47	2.96	59.7	**5.8**	69.5	10.8	**8.0**
3.8	8.36	na	0.19	**2.8**	0.0	0.54	4.59	3.12	77.5	**2.5**	53.7	28.9	**4.5**
7.3	0.80	na	-0.02	**3.8**	0.8	0.73	7.18	2.90	76.9	**4.8**	35.8	9.6	**5.8**
6.3	0.37	na	0.00	**4.3**	0.3	0.87	11.06	3.79	72.4	**3.4**	19.4	12.5	**4.9**
6.3	0.74	4.0	0.00	**6.4**	1.2	1.18	10.83	4.38	63.1	**3.5**	19.3	12.2	**7.1**
5.9	1.23	na	0.00	**3.5**	1.7	0.63	5.68	3.44	75.6	**1.4**	13.8	10.0	**8.5**
4.7	1.98	na	0.09	**4.8**	0.1	0.86	9.08	4.49	75.6	**5.1**	37.4	8.2	**5.0**
7.8	1.18	na	0.02	**4.4**	0.2	0.90	6.04	3.09	64.2	**3.2**	47.6	20.8	**8.0**
7.0	1.47	na	0.09	**4.9**	0.6	1.04	7.10	3.96	62.0	**2.8**	30.5	17.9	**6.9**
5.8	0.43	na	0.01	**5.3**	2.2	1.20	12.46	3.88	62.8	**1.4**	11.3	25.1	**7.2**
5.0	1.71	na	0.00	**3.1**	0.3	0.64	6.10	3.85	85.3	**1.1**	17.9	30.7	**6.3**

Name	City	State	Rating	2019 Rating	2018 Rating	Total Assets ($Mil)	One Year Asset Growth	Asset Mix (As a % of Total Assets) Commercial Loans	Consumer Loans	Mortgage Loans	Securities	Capitalization Index	Leverage Ratio	Risk-Based Capital Ratio
Antwerp Exchange Bank Co.	Antwerp	OH	B-	B-	B	125.8	15.33	7.5	3.3	24.3	18.4	8.4	9.9	14.8
▼ ANZ Guam, Inc.	Hagatna	GU	C+	B-	C+	328.7	3.48	4.9	0.2	6.7	0.0	9.8	15.0	0.0
▼ Apex Bank	Camden	TN	C+	B-	C-	598.5	3.50	2.8	1.6	50.2	0.3	9.8	14.4	0.0
Apollo Bank	Miami	FL	B-	B-	C	740.1	5.22	8.2	2.3	15.2	17.4	8.1	9.7	14.7
Apollo Trust Co.	Apollo	PA	B+	B+	B	158.3	-2.03	5.3	1.8	44.9	18.9	10.0	11.3	20.1
▼ Apple Bank for Savings	New York	NY	C+	B-	C+	15600.9	8.83	32.2	0.1	0.7	25.0	5.3	7.3	14.4
Apple Creek Banking Co.	Apple Creek	OH	B-	B-	C+	142.6	2.43	7.8	0.4	25.2	12.7	6.2	8.2	12.4
Apple River State Bank	Apple River	IL	A-	A-	B	372.8	11.69	7.7	2.9	12.2	28.5	9.3	10.5	17.3
Applied Bank	Wilmington	DE	A	A	A	165.2	-0.51	0.2	0.0	3.0	0.0	10.0	23.9	57.7
▼ Aquesta Bank	Cornelius	NC	B-	B	B-	525.9	10.68	9.8	0.0	6.9	10.0	9.6	10.8	14.7
Arbor Bank	Nebraska City	NE	C	C	C-	386.4	12.85	17.1	1.3	13.8	6.8	4.7	8.2	10.8
▼ Arcola First Bank	Arcola	IL	C+	B-	B-	112.9	3.16	1.0	0.4	3.2	80.0	9.7	11.0	0.0
Argentine Federal Savings	Kansas City	KS	C	C	C	56.3	0.53	0.0	0.4	51.7	29.2	10.0	13.7	30.7
Arizona Bank & Trust	Phoenix	AZ	B+	B+	B+	866.1	29.31	20.0	1.0	7.5	26.3	5.1	9.1	11.1
▲ Arkansas County Bank	De Witt	AR	B+	B	B-	159.4	-2.78	5.6	2.3	20.0	29.0	10.0	11.4	19.6
Arlington State Bank	Arlington	MN	B+	B+	C+	52.3	1.05	4.3	1.9	3.3	31.5	10.0	11.3	24.9
Armed Forces Bank, N.A.	Fort Leavenworth	KS	A-	A-	B+	1105.6	-1.00	11.2	0.5	9.3	17.6	10.0	16.9	23.6
Armor Bank	Forrest City	AR	C	C	C	162.5	71.54	9.6	0.9	9.2	16.1	9.3	10.6	16.0
Armstrong Bank	Muskogee	OK	B-	B-	B-	1673.2	63.77	6.0	3.8	18.2	22.2	9.3	10.5	15.5
Armstrong County Building and Loan Assn.	Ford City	PA	C	C	C	88.5	4.49	0.0	0.6	52.7	30.3	10.0	14.8	36.0
Aroostook County Federal S&L Assn.	Caribou	ME	C+	C+	B-	139.4	7.84	13.6	11.5	50.8	11.8	9.5	10.7	17.5
Arrowhead Bank	Llano	TX	A-	A-	B	190.2	3.23	5.1	4.1	22.6	8.2	9.7	10.8	18.4
Arthur State Bank	Union	SC	B+	B+	B	521.6	3.29	5.3	1.4	30.9	15.4	7.8	9.5	14.5
Artisans' Bank	Wilmington	DE	C	C	C	559.1	1.96	6.4	0.1	17.0	19.9	6.9	9.2	12.4
▼ Arundel Federal Savings Bank	Glen Burnie	MD	C-	C	C+	425.8	-2.70	0.0	0.1	65.1	11.9	9.8	15.6	0.0
Arvest Bank	Fayetteville	AR	B-	B-	B-	20503.7	7.61	11.4	8.4	17.7	18.6	7.0	9.0	12.7
Ascent Bank	Helena	MT	B	B	C+	57.8	13.01	19.3	2.0	20.2	3.1	10.0	13.0	20.0
Ashton State Bank	Ashton	IA	B	B	B+	49.3	-0.73	7.6	2.6	9.5	24.9	9.8	13.1	0.0
Ashton State Bank	Ashton	NE	D-	D-	D-	18.5	-13.02	3.0	1.6	0.2	0.5	7.9	11.1	13.3
Asian Bank	Philadelphia	PA	B-	B-	C+	244.7	13.53	1.1	0.0	15.1	2.8	6.6	8.6	12.8
▼ Asian Pacific National Bank	San Gabriel	CA	C-	C	C+	55.1	-0.87	0.2	0.0	6.1	7.3	9.8	17.7	0.0
▲ Aspire Bank	Fargo	ND	C-	D+	C	40.5	20.73	15.6	0.9	11.1	0.3	6.1	8.1	12.1
▼ Associated Bank, N.A.	Green Bay	WI	B-	B	B-	33859.0	0.61	17.5	1.0	25.2	15.3	6.1	8.7	11.8
Associated Trust Co., N.A.	Milwaukee	WI	U	U	U	62.6	1.33	0.0	0.0	0.0	1.7	10.0	81.2	149.7
Astra Bank	Scandia	KS	B-	B-	C+	303.0	1.67	8.4	0.9	11.2	29.4	7.9	9.6	13.3
Atascosa Bank	Pleasanton	TX	B	B	B-	89.6	-1.88	3.2	2.4	3.2	52.8	8.9	10.4	0.0
▼ Athol Savings Bank	Athol	MA	C+	B-	C+	450.6	0.44	1.6	2.4	43.7	22.7	10.0	13.3	22.4
Atkins Savings Bank & Trust	Atkins	IA	B+	B+	B+	99.7	5.59	8.5	3.7	11.8	26.7	9.8	12.8	0.0
Atlanta National Bank	Atlanta	IL	B-	B-	C+	60.7	3.88	2.4	2.9	11.1	58.5	10.0	13.4	34.0
Atlantic Capital Bank, N.A.	Atlanta	GA	B+	B+	B	2719.3	-4.78	28.0	1.9	1.2	17.3	9.3	12.2	14.4
Atlantic Community Bankers Bank	Camp Hill	PA	B-	B-	B	805.5	4.37	1.6	0.1	2.6	15.8	10.0	13.0	22.8
Atlantic Union Bank	Richmond	VA	B+	B+	B+	17802.2	5.53	12.2	4.0	9.3	14.5	6.6	10.1	12.2
Auburn Banking Co.	Auburn	KY	B	B	C+	87.1	9.26	4.7	4.4	22.2	22.1	7.4	9.3	13.8
Auburn Savings Bank, FSB	Auburn	ME	C	C	C	84.6	6.38	5.4	0.8	55.6	7.9	6.9	8.9	14.6
▼ Auburn State Bank	Auburn	NE	B+	A-	A-	181.9	6.12	2.8	1.2	9.2	37.8	9.8	17.6	0.0
▼ AuburnBank	Auburn	AL	B+	A-	B+	856.9	2.42	4.3	1.0	10.3	32.7	10.0	11.2	18.7
Audubon State Bank	Audubon	IA	B+	B+	B	121.8	3.28	4.2	2.7	12.4	5.0	8.3	9.9	14.1
Austin Bank, Texas N.A.	Jacksonville	TX	A	A	A-	1903.1	3.63	8.0	5.8	22.9	13.0	9.8	14.5	0.0
Austin Capital Bank SSB	Austin	TX	B+	B+	B+	152.3	45.30	2.7	20.0	35.9	1.3	8.1	9.7	24.5
Austin County State Bank	Bellville	TX	B+	B+	B+	198.9	12.72	19.1	1.3	23.0	12.5	8.1	9.7	13.6
Auto Club Trust, FSB	Dearborn	MI	D-	D-	D	567.2	5.91	0.0	21.2	22.6	43.7	7.5	9.4	15.7
Availa Bank	Carroll	IA	B+	B+	B+	1099.5	20.41	7.8	0.6	9.9	17.4	7.4	9.4	0.0
AVB Bank	Broken Arrow	OK	B	B	B	403.6	4.75	14.9	0.4	24.0	9.8	8.2	10.1	13.5
Avidbank	San Jose	CA	B+	B+	B	1203.9	19.01	33.6	0.1	0.5	3.7	6.3	11.3	12.0
▼ Avidia Bank	Hudson	MA	B-	B	B	1798.9	10.52	23.6	0.7	19.6	13.4	7.6	9.4	13.5
▼ Axiom Bank, N.A.	Maitland	FL	C	C+	B-	689.5	5.02	7.7	15.6	20.9	7.3	9.8	12.4	0.0
Axos Bank	San Diego	CA	A-	A-	A-	11543.8	13.55	8.5	3.7	38.7	2.0	6.7	8.7	12.6
b1Bank	Baton Rouge	LA	B	B	B-	2289.2	8.92	16.8	1.0	10.2	12.0	9.6	10.9	0.0
BAC Community Bank	Stockton	CA	B	B	B	637.4	-1.15	4.4	1.5	6.2	20.6	9.7	10.9	0.0
BAC Florida Bank	Coral Gables	FL	B+	B+	B	2305.3	1.34	2.4	0.4	51.7	5.1	9.0	10.4	17.2

Asset Quality Index	Adjusted Non-Performing Loans as a % of Total Loans	Adjusted Non-Performing Loans as a % of Capital	Net Charge-Offs Avg Loans	Profitability Index	Net Income ($Mil)	Return on Assets (R.O.A.)	Return on Equity (R.O.E.)	Net Interest Spread	Overhead Efficiency Ratio	Liquidity Index	Liquidity Ratio	Hot Money Ratio	Stability Index
4.3	1.60	na	0.02	**3.4**	0.1	0.42	4.24	3.50	86.2	**3.8**	23.0	10.8	**5.9**
5.7	5.30	na	0.09	**1.7**	-0.4	-0.47	-3.14	2.59	113.0	**7.1**	90.2	7.5	**7.7**
2.7	1.47	16.4	0.06	**10.0**	4.1	2.80	17.90	7.28	47.5	**0.7**	20.3	38.4	**9.8**
5.5	0.80	na	0.02	**4.3**	1.2	0.62	6.32	3.13	70.7	**3.7**	30.9	13.5	**6.8**
8.8	0.10	na	0.00	**5.1**	0.4	1.03	9.55	4.26	71.6	**4.5**	14.2	3.8	**6.8**
7.9	0.01	0.1	0.00	**3.1**	14.0	0.37	4.25	1.95	70.4	**1.5**	16.2	25.4	**6.6**
6.5	0.35	2.9	0.65	**4.8**	0.4	0.98	12.14	4.55	70.1	**4.7**	13.7	3.7	**4.6**
8.5	0.28	na	0.00	**5.8**	1.3	1.38	13.23	3.13	64.4	**2.8**	26.3	16.5	**6.6**
9.4	0.00	na	0.00	**6.5**	0.4	0.98	4.12	3.09	77.7	**8.0**	80.8	0.2	**9.8**
3.8	1.47	14.0	0.06	**4.0**	0.9	0.71	6.70	3.52	69.9	**3.6**	13.0	10.5	**5.9**
5.6	1.48	na	0.07	**4.5**	0.8	0.91	11.09	3.86	78.5	**1.6**	9.0	14.5	**4.8**
10.0	0.00	na	0.00	**2.8**	0.2	0.58	4.79	2.29	76.1	**5.8**	58.4	10.7	**7.0**
10.0	0.22	na	0.00	**2.3**	0.0	0.25	1.85	2.87	87.7	**1.7**	35.3	37.4	**7.0**
5.7	0.45	2.6	0.16	**6.6**	1.9	0.95	9.66	4.24	58.6	**5.7**	33.1	2.2	**7.1**
5.2	2.30	na	0.10	**5.6**	0.6	1.43	12.62	4.18	70.6	**3.3**	23.4	13.5	**7.7**
6.6	0.56	na	0.35	**4.9**	0.2	1.22	10.46	3.56	65.7	**5.7**	60.1	9.6	**6.7**
7.3	0.58	na	0.13	**7.6**	3.0	1.12	6.31	3.53	73.2	**5.5**	29.4	6.3	**8.8**
5.1	1.09	na	0.16	**1.3**	-0.1	-0.23	-1.94	3.29	87.4	**2.7**	28.9	17.9	**5.5**
4.1	2.63	15.2	0.09	**5.5**	4.1	1.00	10.97	3.42	64.3	**3.1**	31.9	19.8	**10.0**
9.8	0.37	na	-0.03	**2.3**	0.1	0.40	2.73	1.48	77.0	**2.1**	45.4	39.8	**6.8**
5.0	0.77	na	0.00	**3.4**	0.3	0.76	7.18	2.98	74.0	**1.7**	22.9	24.1	**5.9**
8.5	0.01	1.2	0.00	**6.8**	0.8	1.70	16.02	4.27	57.9	**5.1**	29.5	4.6	**6.6**
5.8	1.31	5.2	0.04	**4.9**	1.2	0.90	9.33	4.24	74.2	**4.9**	20.3	3.6	**6.7**
5.1	1.15	na	-0.01	**2.6**	0.4	0.26	2.70	3.15	85.9	**2.8**	26.8	16.8	**6.5**
5.2	2.42	na	-0.30	**2.1**	0.2	0.17	1.08	2.16	95.5	**1.6**	24.7	25.7	**7.4**
4.3	1.22	5.6	0.26	**2.6**	-50.6	-1.03	-9.03	3.68	115.8	**5.4**	23.9	3.5	**8.6**
6.7	1.31	na	0.00	**5.0**	0.1	0.89	6.18	4.55	72.0	**2.8**	23.4	15.6	**7.0**
4.3	2.04	11.0	-0.10	**5.1**	0.1	0.97	7.38	2.96	62.0	**2.6**	32.4	19.6	**7.8**
0.0	8.18	na	-0.06	**0.0**	0.0	-0.79	-7.10	3.92	110.4	**2.2**	22.1	17.8	**2.9**
4.8	0.78	na	0.00	**4.7**	0.5	0.90	10.66	3.18	61.2	**0.8**	19.2	39.3	**5.8**
9.4	0.00	na	0.00	**1.8**	0.0	0.06	0.37	2.61	97.5	**2.4**	58.1	56.5	**7.3**
8.0	0.00	na	0.00	**2.3**	0.0	0.31	3.27	3.17	82.6	**2.8**	24.8	16.1	**4.3**
5.7	0.66	3.6	0.29	**3.8**	48.3	0.59	5.08	2.85	69.4	**3.5**	13.1	4.9	**9.7**
7.1	na	0.0	na	**9.5**	3.7	22.83	26.90	1.84	76.2	**4.0**	286.0	0.0	**5.7**
4.7	1.01	na	0.08	**4.3**	0.8	1.08	10.21	4.04	72.9	**4.4**	16.6	5.9	**6.4**
8.7	0.00	na	0.00	**4.7**	0.2	1.01	9.73	2.69	54.6	**6.7**	94.0	9.5	**5.4**
8.6	0.67	3.3	0.03	**1.6**	-2.9	-2.55	-18.92	2.84	86.5	**2.6**	34.6	17.0	**7.3**
2.7	0.93	na	0.75	**6.0**	0.4	1.49	11.38	3.32	51.5	**2.4**	36.2	24.7	**8.1**
8.9	0.00	na	-0.06	**3.4**	0.1	0.64	4.77	2.87	76.4	**5.9**	65.2	9.7	**6.7**
7.3	0.86	2.1	0.04	**4.3**	3.1	0.46	3.32	3.51	52.5	**5.3**	24.5	0.4	**9.4**
9.0	0.05	0.2	0.00	**2.7**	0.3	0.18	1.40	2.14	84.5	**2.6**	41.6	24.2	**7.7**
5.9	0.43	2.2	0.16	**4.3**	11.3	0.26	1.65	3.62	59.1	**3.2**	14.4	11.9	**9.6**
5.5	1.08	na	-0.07	**6.9**	0.3	1.47	16.02	3.98	65.3	**1.7**	22.4	23.3	**6.8**
4.4	2.77	na	-0.01	**2.8**	0.1	0.48	5.38	3.38	84.1	**0.8**	11.3	34.7	**5.0**
8.8	0.44	na	0.00	**5.1**	0.5	1.04	5.96	3.35	57.8	**2.3**	24.5	18.2	**8.4**
8.9	0.03	na	-0.07	**4.4**	1.6	0.78	6.72	3.24	67.6	**3.4**	29.2	14.4	**8.0**
7.1	0.48	na	0.05	**7.5**	0.5	1.65	13.69	3.71	52.6	**1.7**	18.8	18.1	**8.8**
6.4	1.10	4.6	0.20	**8.4**	6.5	1.39	9.35	4.52	60.3	**3.7**	14.8	11.0	**10.0**
7.9	0.07	na	0.00	**2.7**	0.0	0.02	0.26	3.62	99.2	**1.3**	26.6	31.7	**5.6**
8.6	0.02	na	-0.03	**5.4**	0.6	1.21	12.29	4.53	68.7	**0.8**	17.4	41.4	**6.8**
5.6	0.80	3.6	0.01	**0.0**	-2.4	-1.67	-16.05	1.04	169.0	**0.8**	26.1	42.2	**5.0**
7.1	0.30	1.9	-0.01	**5.2**	2.5	0.93	8.31	3.43	67.8	**2.4**	19.3	16.7	**9.1**
5.9	0.56	na	-0.01	**4.0**	0.7	0.66	6.58	4.16	75.0	**1.6**	5.2	20.7	**7.0**
6.5	0.40	2.8	0.00	**6.2**	2.5	0.91	8.15	4.39	68.4	**2.0**	18.9	19.6	**9.2**
6.1	1.44	na	0.43	**2.5**	-1.5	-0.34	-3.28	3.71	81.6	**1.8**	27.1	7.8	**7.8**
3.4	2.16	na	0.17	**0.8**	-2.7	-1.57	-10.64	3.12	120.2	**1.0**	26.1	45.8	**7.7**
6.2	0.55	4.8	0.03	**10.0**	60.1	2.03	22.26	5.11	33.0	**1.1**	8.5	15.3	**8.9**
6.5	0.52	3.2	0.04	**5.2**	5.6	1.00	7.54	4.04	64.4	**1.3**	13.5	28.2	**9.2**
5.0	0.65	na	-0.09	**5.5**	2.1	1.32	11.66	4.07	67.2	**5.1**	26.3	3.3	**8.0**
6.1	1.91	9.9	0.00	**6.2**	6.2	1.11	10.88	3.00	53.9	**1.1**	21.9	41.3	**8.8**

Name	City	State	Rating	2019 Rating	2018 Rating	Total Assets ($Mil)	One Year Asset Growth	Asset Mix (As a % of Total Assets) Comm-ercial Loans	Cons-umer Loans	Mort-gage Loans	Secur-ities	Capital-ization Index	Lever-age Ratio	Risk-Based Capital Ratio
Badger Bank	Fort Atkinson	WI	**A-**	A-	B+	137.8	1.05	4.4	1.2	34.1	11.7	**9.8**	13.4	0.0
Baker-Boyer National Bank	Walla Walla	WA	**B+**	B+	B	630.6	4.96	8.5	1.0	11.4	24.0	**7.5**	9.4	18.6
Balboa Thrift and Loan Assn.	Chula Vista	CA	**B-**	B-	B-	329.8	5.83	0.0	75.3	0.6	0.0	**9.8**	12.6	0.0
Baldwin State Bank	Baldwin City	KS	**C+**	C+	B-	83.2	4.19	5.3	2.8	25.6	25.8	**9.3**	10.6	26.6
Ballston Spa National Bank	Ballston Spa	NY	**B-**	B-	C+	623.5	15.00	6.4	4.5	32.4	11.6	**7.0**	9.0	13.1
▼ Baltic State Bank	Baltic	OH	**C**	C+	B+	80.6	21.50	6.5	2.9	38.4	3.5	**5.5**	7.9	11.4
Banc of California, N.A.	Santa Ana	CA	**C**	C	B-	7633.8	-22.73	6.8	0.1	19.3	12.7	**10.0**	12.7	18.2
BancCentral, N.A.	Alva	OK	**C**	C	C	498.9	-10.85	14.6	1.5	3.4	32.2	**6.6**	8.6	12.3
BancFirst	Oklahoma City	OK	**A-**	A-	A-	7812.5	1.60	17.9	4.6	12.2	7.2	**8.9**	10.4	14.1
Banco Do Brasil Americas	Miami	FL	**C+**	C+	C+	657.9	-0.63	1.7	0.8	49.6	2.9	**8.5**	10.0	19.4
Banco Popular de Puerto Rico	San Juan	PR	**C-**	C-	D+	42267.0	9.01	5.9	13.0	14.6	34.8	**6.4**	8.4	17.6
Banco Santander Puerto Rico	San Juan	PR	**B-**	B-	C	5931.5	11.91	3.2	4.2	14.5	34.2	**10.0**	17.6	43.5
Bancorp Bank	Wilmington	DE	**B**	B	B-	5461.0	18.02	5.1	19.7	1.2	24.8	**6.7**	8.7	17.1
BancorpSouth Bank	Tupelo	MS	**B+**	B+	B+	21045.4	14.88	8.9	1.1	18.0	21.2	**6.9**	8.9	13.8
Bandera Bank	Bandera	TX	**B+**	B+	B	71.3	-0.79	3.0	4.1	31.8	12.8	**10.0**	11.1	27.9
Banesco USA	Coral Gables	FL	**B-**	B-	B-	1804.9	37.19	10.8	0.0	18.3	17.3	**6.7**	8.7	13.1
Bangor Savings Bank	Bangor	ME	**B-**	B-	B-	4886.6	9.88	5.7	0.5	24.6	22.6	**7.2**	9.2	13.8
▲ BANK	Wapello	IA	**B-**	C+	C+	98.8	10.16	9.5	6.1	17.9	0.0	**10.0**	12.5	16.6
Bank & Trust Co.	Litchfield	IL	**B**	B	B-	356.8	7.57	8.1	6.0	14.1	25.5	**9.1**	10.4	15.4
Bank 1st	West Union	IA	**A**	A	A-	123.7	3.05	4.0	2.8	17.2	21.0	**9.8**	15.5	0.0
▲ Bank 21	Carrollton	MO	**B-**	C+	B-	143.2	-8.31	7.9	1.1	35.3	3.3	**6.4**	8.4	12.6
BANK 34	Alamogordo	NM	**C+**	C+	C+	407.9	9.26	7.2	0.1	10.5	15.1	**8.8**	10.4	14.0
Bank and Trust, SSB	Del Rio	TX	**B+**	B+	B+	437.1	3.66	5.1	2.9	37.3	17.9	**7.8**	9.6	17.2
Bank First, N.A.	Manitowoc	WI	**B**	B	B	2198.6	21.88	12.9	1.3	17.9	10.0	**5.2**	9.9	11.1
Bank Five Nine	Oconomowoc	WI	**C+**	C+	B-	1180.6	-1.41	4.9	0.1	17.0	10.0	**8.4**	9.9	14.0
▲ Bank Forward	Hannaford	ND	**B+**	B	B	710.5	10.03	9.5	2.8	10.1	4.1	**7.7**	9.6	0.0
Bank Independent	Sheffield	AL	**B**	B	B	1737.3	3.37	19.6	1.3	13.1	2.2	**7.5**	9.3	13.0
▼ Bank Iowa	West Des Moines	IA	**B-**	B	B	1481.4	13.54	6.8	0.8	7.9	22.9	**7.0**	9.7	12.5
Bank Leumi USA	New York	NY	**B**	B	B	7610.7	9.14	25.2	0.0	0.4	18.3	**8.2**	11.5	13.5
▼ Bank Michigan	Brooklyn	MI	**D+**	C-	D	105.6	-1.16	9.5	0.2	14.4	6.6	**7.0**	9.0	12.8
Bank Midwest	Spirit Lake	IA	**B-**	B-	B-	977.2	5.97	24.3	0.6	5.6	9.9	**5.7**	9.3	11.5
Bank Northwest	Hamilton	MO	**A-**	A-	A-	163.0	-4.36	8.6	2.2	12.7	10.9	**6.2**	8.2	12.2
Bank of Abbeville & Trust Co.	Abbeville	LA	**B-**	B-	B-	175.1	-2.20	7.9	1.9	15.3	33.3	**9.8**	17.2	0.0
▲ Bank of Advance	Advance	MO	**A**	A-	B+	350.2	6.16	7.4	5.9	29.4	12.0	**10.0**	12.5	17.8
Bank of Akron	Akron	NY	**B-**	B-	C	406.5	13.28	8.3	0.4	25.3	8.8	**7.9**	9.7	13.2
Bank of Alapaha	Alapaha	GA	**B+**	B+	B+	185.0	9.46	22.0	7.4	17.9	14.8	**9.6**	10.8	17.1
▲ Bank of Alma	Alma	WI	**A+**	A	A-	280.6	20.73	3.9	0.7	5.8	24.9	**10.0**	39.1	65.9
Bank of America California, N.A.	San Francisco	CA	**A-**	A-	A-	18802.0	26.99	0.0	0.0	49.3	0.0	**10.0**	13.6	37.9
Bank of America, N.A.	Charlotte	NC	**B+**	B+	B	2031940.0	14.45	17.0	8.1	11.6	22.5	**6.5**	8.5	13.0
Bank of Anguilla	Anguilla	MS	**C-**	C-	C-	149.1	8.74	5.6	4.8	7.8	18.9	**8.6**	10.3	0.0
Bank of Ann Arbor	Ann Arbor	MI	**A-**	A-	A-	1845.8	12.24	16.9	0.7	6.1	5.3	**7.9**	10.7	13.3
Bank of Austin	Austin	TX	**D+**	D+	D	202.7	37.79	24.8	0.0	5.2	10.7	**10.0**	17.6	22.2
▼ Bank of Baker	Baker	MT	**C**	B-	C	155.5	12.71	12.5	1.0	2.3	12.9	**9.8**	12.1	0.0
▼ Bank of Bartlett	Bartlett	TN	**C**	C+	C	362.7	2.91	5.6	3.0	24.6	19.9	**6.4**	8.5	14.3
Bank of Bearden	Bearden	AR	**B+**	B+	B	55.3	5.49	10.6	5.8	9.0	17.2	**9.8**	12.4	0.0
▼ Bank of Beaver City	Beaver	OK	**B-**	B	B	128.2	-7.32	11.9	2.6	14.2	33.2	**9.8**	11.7	0.0
Bank of Belle Glade	Belle Glade	FL	**B-**	B-	C+	110.0	5.10	3.6	0.4	11.4	32.1	**7.3**	9.3	0.0
Bank of Belleville	Belleville	IL	**C+**	C+	C+	240.8	15.18	14.0	1.6	12.1	15.9	**5.3**	8.2	11.3
Bank of Bennington	Bennington	NE	**B-**	B-	C	140.8	1.19	18.9	1.8	13.3	10.9	**9.4**	12.4	14.5
▼ Bank of Bennington	Bennington	VT	**B-**	B	B	426.5	3.18	2.3	0.2	57.9	12.3	**9.8**	11.3	0.0
Bank of Benoit	Benoit	MS	**C-**	C-	C-	16.6	-9.73	3.1	8.5	0.5	33.9	**10.0**	11.1	30.8
Bank of Billings	Billings	MO	**B-**	B-	C+	60.2	2.60	15.5	3.8	28.4	0.0	**8.5**	10.2	0.0
Bank of Bird-in-Hand	Bird in Hand	PA	**B**	B	B	468.8	23.35	7.3	0.1	23.0	0.0	**8.9**	12.1	14.1
Bank of Blue Valley	Overland Park	KS	**B+**	B+	B	1228.9	117.56	16.5	1.4	3.2	23.8	**10.0**	11.5	15.4
▼ Bank of Bluffs	Bluffs	IL	**C+**	B-	B-	54.1	-2.15	3.2	5.3	16.9	23.7	**9.8**	14.2	0.0
▲ Bank of Bolivar	Bolivar	MO	**B**	B-	C+	318.9	5.37	5.3	3.9	26.2	6.6	**2.9**	8.0	9.9
Bank of Botetourt	Buchanan	VA	**B**	B	C+	513.1	12.09	5.7	4.1	29.5	3.6	**8.8**	10.4	0.0
Bank of Bourbonnais	Bourbonnais	IL	**A-**	A-	B+	73.8	25.18	3.4	3.4	10.4	0.8	**10.0**	11.9	20.3
Bank of Bozeman	Bozeman	MT	**C+**	C+	C+	82.1	4.45	16.1	0.7	20.0	1.5	**6.3**	9.7	11.9
Bank of Brenham, N.A.	Brenham	TX	**B**	B	B+	500.7	16.59	2.4	0.8	6.8	80.0	**9.1**	10.6	0.0

Asset Quality Index	Adjusted Non-Performing Loans as a % of Total Loans	Adjusted Non-Performing Loans as a % of Capital	Net Charge-Offs Avg Loans	Profitability Index	Net Income ($Mil)	Return on Assets (R.O.A.)	Return on Equity (R.O.E.)	Net Interest Spread	Overhead Efficiency Ratio	Liquidity Index	Liquidity Ratio	Hot Money Ratio	Stability Index
5.9	1.05	na	-0.01	6.6	0.4	1.18	8.71	3.96	67.9	4.1	21.6	8.7	8.3
7.2	1.00	na	0.14	5.2	1.4	0.93	9.92	3.69	79.3	6.7	50.4	2.0	6.9
4.4	0.49	na	2.19	4.0	0.4	0.47	3.74	6.16	51.6	0.4	9.0	76.7	6.5
6.3	0.77	na	0.01	3.6	0.2	0.98	9.10	2.89	69.3	5.2	40.4	8.5	5.6
6.9	0.25	na	0.00	3.9	1.2	0.77	8.97	3.34	72.4	3.9	9.6	8.9	5.6
8.8	0.02	na	0.00	2.5	0.0	0.20	2.49	4.14	93.5	1.2	15.9	29.5	4.1
6.4	1.19	5.7	0.12	1.8	-1.7	-0.09	-0.71	3.09	77.1	2.1	20.4	15.7	7.6
4.1	1.50	12.5	0.05	3.0	1.0	0.79	7.96	3.62	84.5	0.8	18.1	36.0	5.9
6.2	0.86	5.0	0.04	7.2	20.4	1.06	9.32	3.87	55.7	4.9	21.1	4.8	9.4
8.7	0.13	na	0.01	3.9	1.3	0.79	6.96	3.38	72.4	1.6	24.9	26.3	7.1
1.7	9.37	30.0	1.19	5.8	80.0	0.78	7.85	4.22	59.4	3.8	20.9	11.0	8.2
6.1	6.35	8.4	0.41	3.7	1.9	0.13	0.75	3.19	69.1	5.1	32.9	9.2	6.8
5.9	1.09	4.3	0.16	7.0	14.2	1.07	12.25	3.51	64.0	1.8	29.6	0.0	5.8
5.5	0.83	3.6	0.38	4.6	24.3	0.46	3.62	3.52	68.8	3.6	11.2	10.6	10.0
8.9	0.44	na	-0.04	5.9	0.2	1.33	12.03	3.90	68.2	5.5	48.9	8.7	7.3
8.0	0.55	2.5	0.00	3.6	2.1	0.47	5.26	3.32	77.7	1.4	23.6	33.2	7.5
8.2	0.45	2.3	-0.01	3.9	9.5	0.80	7.76	3.04	76.4	3.7	14.1	5.2	8.4
6.0	1.01	na	0.00	3.6	0.2	0.63	5.09	4.00	79.2	1.9	15.5	18.0	6.5
6.1	0.80	3.4	0.03	4.8	0.8	0.93	8.69	3.43	65.7	1.7	22.3	23.3	6.6
5.5	0.05	na	0.04	7.3	0.5	1.63	10.92	3.97	58.3	4.3	29.4	9.9	9.4
5.8	0.18	na	0.94	4.9	0.4	1.11	13.18	3.59	71.0	2.7	13.3	15.1	5.9
6.1	1.11	na	0.00	2.8	0.3	0.32	3.05	4.13	78.4	2.2	18.0	13.6	6.5
8.2	0.28	na	0.03	5.4	1.5	1.46	14.40	4.03	69.5	3.6	15.9	11.3	6.6
7.1	0.37	2.8	-0.14	7.6	8.4	1.53	12.96	3.84	50.2	3.7	6.3	8.9	9.1
3.4	1.81	na	-0.06	5.4	4.5	1.51	14.92	3.50	69.5	1.4	7.4	21.5	8.3
5.8	0.40	2.7	-0.01	7.1	2.8	1.54	14.95	4.15	73.1	1.5	10.7	15.4	8.4
4.9	0.62	8.6	0.24	5.6	3.6	0.83	8.66	4.94	75.9	2.0	20.7	18.2	8.7
7.5	0.51	3.2	0.17	3.7	2.5	0.69	7.12	3.49	69.4	1.8	13.8	20.8	8.4
5.1	1.28	7.9	0.16	5.0	18.1	1.04	8.50	3.66	61.3	1.7	27.2	25.6	8.8
3.8	1.32	na	0.49	0.0	-0.4	-1.38	-14.06	3.45	148.0	0.9	22.5	36.7	3.9
5.8	0.19	na	0.03	6.0	2.9	1.27	12.72	4.19	66.6	1.7	12.8	15.2	7.8
5.9	0.30	6.7	0.01	9.6	0.9	2.19	23.57	4.37	47.8	3.8	18.2	10.3	7.2
6.8	3.47	na	0.00	3.6	0.3	0.78	4.59	3.12	75.4	4.0	41.4	15.4	7.6
6.5	0.92	na	0.15	9.8	1.8	2.12	17.09	4.62	55.6	1.8	13.8	19.9	9.2
5.2	1.29	na	0.03	4.4	0.7	0.66	6.76	3.78	75.5	1.9	9.3	14.1	5.7
4.7	0.89	na	0.30	3.7	0.2	0.50	4.62	3.11	75.9	1.0	22.6	34.0	6.8
8.8	3.09	na	0.00	9.8	1.8	2.39	6.15	3.66	13.1	7.0	73.5	5.5	9.5
6.7	3.31	10.3	-0.04	9.5	66.0	1.79	13.29	3.09	15.9	7.3	56.5	0.0	8.7
5.9	0.87	3.5	0.45	6.0	3498.0	0.76	6.67	2.90	52.7	6.4	41.9	2.5	9.0
1.9	3.23	na	0.08	2.9	0.2	0.50	5.27	4.49	75.3	1.0	8.9	30.6	3.6
8.2	0.14	0.8	0.15	9.2	7.2	1.58	13.97	4.13	51.8	4.6	18.7	5.7	10.0
8.4	0.00	na	0.00	1.2	0.1	0.17	0.98	3.34	88.4	5.5	36.5	5.3	2.7
1.3	6.35	na	2.37	7.4	0.5	1.34	11.74	3.88	52.0	5.3	31.4	4.3	7.8
2.6	2.74	na	0.27	3.5	0.5	0.54	5.90	4.00	83.5	4.6	19.9	5.6	4.8
8.2	0.16	na	-0.01	5.6	0.2	1.30	10.40	3.84	62.8	3.7	38.1	15.6	7.7
3.7	4.33	na	0.74	3.9	0.2	0.68	5.83	3.72	80.4	2.1	29.1	22.0	6.0
8.6	0.00	na	0.00	3.6	0.2	0.61	6.46	2.52	71.4	5.9	63.8	10.9	5.2
8.5	0.00	na	0.00	2.9	0.2	0.38	4.69	2.74	79.1	1.2	15.4	26.4	4.5
8.1	0.00	na	-0.08	4.0	0.4	1.13	8.59	4.46	70.8	4.7	14.1	3.9	6.5
7.4	0.74	3.5	0.51	2.8	0.3	0.23	2.06	2.98	76.6	2.7	16.0	15.8	6.6
6.2	0.63	na	0.09	1.9	0.0	0.31	2.81	3.40	88.4	3.1	77.4	32.4	4.2
3.0	1.35	6.8	-0.03	4.3	0.1	0.37	2.55	5.45	87.6	3.5	17.3	11.9	6.9
8.7	0.03	na	0.00	4.1	0.8	0.70	5.89	2.77	59.6	2.8	10.9	14.5	6.7
7.3	0.43	1.5	0.01	4.9	4.2	1.35	8.87	3.90	45.7	4.7	17.8	5.1	8.2
5.6	1.08	na	0.16	2.5	0.0	0.18	1.24	3.75	86.2	3.9	31.5	11.9	6.7
7.3	0.18	na	0.01	3.6	0.3	1.01	9.49	3.89	61.3	1.6	7.7	18.4	6.3
5.6	0.22	na	0.09	4.6	1.0	0.83	8.19	3.63	67.0	1.2	11.4	28.3	6.0
7.4	0.00	na	0.18	2.5	0.0	0.14	1.17	2.70	92.0	2.1	35.4	29.6	6.5
4.0	1.55	10.8	-0.01	3.3	0.1	0.52	4.63	4.49	86.1	1.1	8.9	29.3	7.3
8.8	0.95	1.0	0.08	4.6	3.1	2.55	18.05	2.32	50.8	2.6	53.6	48.7	7.7

Name	City	State	Rating	2019 Rating	2018 Rating	Total Assets ($Mil)	One Year Asset Growth	Asset Mix (As a % of Total Assets) Commercial Loans	Consumer Loans	Mortgage Loans	Securities	Capitalization Index	Leverage Ratio	Risk-Based Capital Ratio
Bank of Brewton	Brewton	AL	**C+**	C+	B	48.4	-4.27	8.5	11.5	5.4	49.1	**9.8**	24.2	0.0
Bank of Bridger, N.A.	Bridger	MT	**B**	B	B	606.9	16.43	5.3	2.5	7.9	45.0	**7.4**	9.3	18.4
Bank of Brodhead	Brodhead	WI	**B+**	B+	B+	216.8	41.89	7.7	2.2	14.2	23.1	**9.8**	16.2	0.0
Bank of Brookfield-Purdin, N.A.	Brookfield	MO	**B-**	B-	B-	89.0	-6.44	1.1	1.4	5.6	51.0	**10.0**	12.7	36.1
Bank of Brookhaven	Brookhaven	MS	**B+**	B+	B+	176.6	7.75	7.9	2.5	14.4	30.7	**10.0**	11.0	18.4
Bank of Buffalo	Buffalo	KY	**B**	B	B	75.0	1.59	1.4	5.6	27.0	39.0	**10.0**	11.3	19.8
Bank of Burlington	Burlington	CO	**B+**	B+	B	65.7	7.81	12.1	0.9	0.0	13.9	**9.8**	14.4	0.0
Bank of Cadiz and Trust Co.	Cadiz	KY	**B-**	B-	B-	120.0	10.92	3.3	2.8	23.5	29.1	**6.8**	8.8	16.9
Bank of Calhoun County	Hardin	IL	**C+**	C+	C	66.9	0.92	1.1	2.5	30.8	13.5	**7.7**	9.5	18.6
Bank of Camilla	Camilla	GA	**B+**	B+	B+	105.4	-0.71	12.0	1.2	14.7	27.3	**9.8**	15.8	0.0
Bank of Canton	Canton	MA	**B**	B	B	670.5	6.00	1.0	0.2	28.8	9.7	**10.0**	12.0	16.2
Bank of Carbondale	Carbondale	IL	**B+**	B+	B+	231.8	1.91	9.2	2.0	18.1	29.9	**9.8**	13.3	0.0
▼ Bank of Cashton	Cashton	WI	**B+**	A-	A-	100.8	11.94	20.3	2.1	13.4	12.8	**5.3**	11.0	11.2
Bank of Castile	Castile	NY	**B**	B	B	1518.7	0.59	11.8	0.6	16.6	18.2	**6.6**	9.1	12.2
Bank of Cattaraugus	Cattaraugus	NY	**D+**	D+	D+	28.9	2.07	5.8	6.2	15.9	29.6	**6.5**	8.5	19.8
Bank of Cave City	Cave City	AR	**B-**	B-	C+	131.3	13.41	5.8	4.3	17.3	16.8	**7.2**	9.1	16.3
Bank of Central Florida	Lakeland	FL	**B+**	B+	B	596.0	15.75	14.6	2.0	12.7	15.0	**6.7**	8.7	12.3
Bank of Charles Town	Charles Town	WV	**B-**	B-	B-	540.5	8.90	3.6	1.5	31.6	9.1	**9.1**	10.4	14.8
Bank of Charlotte County	Phenix	VA	**A-**	A-	A-	144.0	2.41	6.1	3.2	36.2	14.1	**10.0**	15.5	22.6
Bank of Cherokee County	Hulbert	OK	**C+**	C+	C+	119.5	6.47	3.8	9.3	24.2	1.6	**6.9**	8.9	13.3
Bank of Chestnut	Chestnut	IL	**D**	D	D	17.6	0.42	4.3	9.9	33.8	11.7	**8.1**	9.9	0.0
Bank of Clarendon	Manning	SC	**A**	A	A-	284.3	1.09	5.3	2.8	11.9	28.4	**10.0**	13.6	23.2
Bank of Clarke County	Berryville	VA	**B+**	B+	B	893.7	11.48	6.0	1.7	21.8	17.5	**8.9**	10.3	14.4
Bank of Clarks	Clarks	NE	**C+**	C+	C+	40.4	12.45	5.6	12.3	4.2	3.2	**7.9**	10.6	13.2
Bank of Clarkson	Clarkson	KY	**B+**	B+	B+	121.4	-0.48	1.7	5.9	27.8	16.9	**10.0**	14.1	18.7
Bank of Cleveland	Cleveland	TN	**A-**	A-	C+	304.3	9.51	3.9	0.5	16.7	1.2	**10.0**	14.7	20.7
Bank of Clovis	Clovis	NM	**A-**	A-	B+	226.9	11.77	10.7	3.0	13.2	31.9	**10.0**	12.6	26.8
Bank of Colorado	Fort Collins	CO	**A-**	A-	A-	4560.8	10.07	3.5	0.8	11.6	31.3	**7.4**	9.3	14.9
Bank of Columbia	Columbia	KY	**B**	B	C+	148.9	5.19	11.3	5.4	19.0	15.7	**8.8**	10.3	14.0
Bank of Commerce	Ammon	ID	**A**	A	A	1273.5	7.44	15.2	0.8	2.1	8.4	**10.0**	16.0	19.0
▲ Bank of Commerce	Chanute	KS	**B**	B-	B-	326.9	85.52	8.1	3.5	17.7	25.4	**8.2**	9.8	16.6
Bank of Commerce	White Castle	LA	**B-**	B-	B-	62.1	-0.59	12.7	2.9	9.9	23.1	**9.8**	12.0	0.0
Bank of Commerce	Greenwood	MS	**A-**	A-	B	601.1	26.53	7.0	2.4	17.1	35.7	**8.4**	10.0	15.6
Bank of Commerce	Chelsea	OK	**B+**	B+	B	153.4	5.38	10.5	8.3	17.3	10.4	**10.0**	12.9	17.7
Bank of Commerce	Chouteau	OK	**C+**	C+	C	39.9	-5.06	6.0	3.3	15.6	30.1	**6.8**	8.8	20.0
▼ Bank of Commerce	Duncan	OK	**D+**	C-	D+	315.2	2.24	16.3	1.4	4.2	3.6	**9.8**	12.0	0.0
Bank of Commerce	Rawlins	WY	**A-**	A-	A-	144.4	9.96	7.4	1.8	17.6	33.7	**10.0**	12.0	21.8
▼ Bank of Commerce & Trust Co.	Crowley	LA	**C+**	B-	B-	327.8	3.33	3.9	2.0	5.4	70.3	**9.8**	12.5	0.0
Bank of Commerce and Trust Co.	Wellington	KS	**B-**	B-	B-	85.1	6.15	4.9	5.0	17.8	31.7	**6.7**	8.7	16.0
Bank of Cordell	Cordell	OK	**B+**	B+	B-	38.6	-3.02	11.6	1.1	38.6	0.0	**10.0**	11.4	17.4
Bank of Coushatta	Coushatta	LA	**B**	B	B	238.5	1.88	2.5	1.5	14.8	52.1	**7.7**	9.6	0.0
Bank of Crocker	Waynesville	MO	**C+**	C+	B-	124.9	0.25	3.2	1.7	13.3	30.4	**9.8**	11.6	0.0
Bank of Crockett	Bells	TN	**B+**	B+	B+	186.8	10.69	6.7	2.8	5.4	53.0	**8.0**	9.9	0.0
Bank of Dade	Trenton	GA	**A-**	A-	B+	117.3	6.14	1.6	4.3	24.8	45.1	**9.3**	10.5	23.4
Bank of Dawson	Dawson	GA	**A-**	A-	B+	127.1	3.74	4.6	3.0	16.7	15.7	**9.8**	18.3	0.0
Bank of Deerfield	Deerfield	WI	**A-**	A-	B+	159.9	9.20	6.2	1.0	29.9	6.3	**9.3**	12.2	14.5
Bank of Delight	Delight	AR	**A-**	A-	B+	145.6	9.01	7.6	2.1	15.7	8.2	**10.0**	13.2	17.7
Bank of Delmarva	Salisbury	MD	**C**	C	C-	793.6	4.55	8.5	0.2	15.7	7.1	**7.2**	9.4	12.7
Bank of Denton	Denton	KS	**C**	C	C	18.3	1.73	4.3	10.2	32.8	15.8	**9.8**	18.8	0.0
▲ Bank of Denver	Denver	CO	**B-**	C+	B-	237.1	1.58	0.4	5.9	11.0	21.5	**8.5**	10.0	15.7
Bank of DeSoto, N.A.	Desoto	TX	**A-**	A-	B	192.7	8.26	7.8	13.6	19.0	1.2	**10.0**	11.0	17.9
▼ Bank of Dickson	Dickson	TN	**B-**	B	B	239.5	4.66	3.1	2.1	38.0	35.3	**9.8**	12.2	0.0
Bank of Dixon County	Ponca	NE	**B+**	B+	B-	98.3	5.30	10.0	5.5	15.5	12.3	**10.0**	12.3	18.8
Bank of Doniphan	Doniphan	NE	**B**	B	B-	117.2	5.32	9.4	2.7	8.8	20.5	**7.8**	9.7	0.0
Bank of Dudley	Dublin	GA	**A-**	A-	B	230.4	1.55	8.5	4.0	14.3	12.1	**9.8**	13.0	0.0
Bank of Eastern Oregon	Heppner	OR	**D+**	D+	C	485.7	3.83	12.8	0.8	4.4	3.2	**4.6**	9.9	10.8
▲ Bank of Eastman	Eastman	GA	**C+**	C	D+	160.4	-3.75	8.7	5.6	25.1	7.5	**9.8**	12.0	0.0
Bank of Easton	North Easton	MA	**B-**	B-	B-	162.4	9.68	0.1	0.5	42.8	22.3	**9.8**	11.4	0.0
Bank of Edison	Edison	GA	**C**	C	C	53.2	8.25	3.9	5.4	11.5	35.9	**7.0**	9.0	18.5
▲ Bank of Edmonson County	Brownsville	KY	**B+**	B	B-	221.0	1.29	2.4	3.4	28.4	13.5	**10.0**	12.1	19.6

Asset Quality Index	Adjusted Non-Performing Loans as a % of Total Loans	Adjusted Non-Performing Loans as a % of Capital	Net Charge-Offs Avg Loans	Profitability Index	Net Income ($Mil)	Return on Assets (R.O.A.)	Return on Equity (R.O.E.)	Net Interest Spread	Overhead Efficiency Ratio	Liquidity Index	Liquidity Ratio	Hot Money Ratio	Stability Index
6.8	1.58	2.6	0.05	**3.0**	0.1	0.49	2.07	4.35	93.3	**6.1**	57.2	6.6	**6.7**
7.1	1.47	na	0.05	**4.8**	1.5	1.00	9.68	3.40	60.4	**4.3**	34.2	11.6	**6.8**
7.1	1.09	na	0.04	**4.8**	0.4	0.93	6.30	3.29	65.1	**2.8**	42.0	23.7	**7.8**
9.6	0.00	na	0.00	**3.7**	0.2	0.79	6.04	2.80	71.0	**6.2**	65.0	7.6	**6.7**
8.3	0.29	na	0.03	**4.5**	0.5	1.10	9.95	3.32	65.8	**2.5**	32.8	20.2	**6.9**
6.5	1.09	na	0.20	**5.1**	0.2	0.93	8.06	3.14	56.9	**1.8**	38.3	33.8	**7.6**
8.7	0.00	na	0.00	**5.2**	0.2	1.29	8.96	3.96	64.6	**2.8**	40.8	23.2	**8.0**
6.5	0.62	3.5	0.44	**3.3**	0.2	0.63	7.05	3.32	80.8	**3.1**	41.9	20.5	**4.5**
8.6	0.87	na	0.00	**3.4**	0.1	0.59	5.82	3.04	74.5	**4.3**	34.3	11.8	**5.0**
5.9	2.38	na	-0.17	**5.1**	0.4	1.37	8.46	4.14	70.5	**1.7**	24.6	25.0	**8.5**
7.8	0.13	na	0.00	**3.5**	0.9	0.52	4.50	3.67	83.0	**4.2**	13.2	4.4	**7.4**
2.3	5.12	na	0.00	**5.3**	0.7	1.15	8.67	3.30	55.6	**4.9**	22.9	3.7	**7.3**
8.4	0.09	na	0.01	**6.2**	0.4	1.46	12.95	3.61	58.4	**3.0**	28.9	15.7	**8.1**
8.5	0.19	1.5	-0.01	**5.6**	2.2	0.57	6.41	3.61	54.6	**3.8**	5.1	8.4	**7.1**
7.8	0.17	na	0.00	**3.4**	0.0	0.57	6.75	4.57	86.6	**6.2**	36.9	0.9	**3.6**
4.4	1.69	na	0.26	**3.6**	0.2	0.54	5.88	3.90	72.0	**1.4**	14.3	22.6	**5.7**
8.5	0.03	na	-0.01	**5.5**	1.3	0.96	10.84	3.53	60.2	**4.4**	30.4	5.5	**6.0**
6.7	0.54	na	-0.01	**3.7**	0.8	0.61	6.07	3.41	73.7	**2.1**	14.9	17.9	**6.2**
8.0	0.92	2.9	0.00	**6.2**	0.4	1.21	7.74	4.40	69.5	**3.2**	19.2	13.2	**8.6**
4.5	0.85	na	0.00	**3.1**	0.2	0.50	5.80	4.27	89.4	**2.0**	19.6	19.6	**5.1**
3.0	2.16	13.6	0.00	**2.7**	0.0	0.15	1.54	3.74	83.6	**4.5**	17.9	4.0	**3.6**
8.8	0.47	na	-0.02	**6.3**	0.9	1.31	9.44	3.55	60.4	**4.6**	32.8	9.2	**8.2**
7.2	0.64	na	-0.31	**5.6**	2.5	1.11	10.52	3.84	70.8	**3.3**	22.1	13.4	**7.6**
4.3	0.34	3.5	0.41	**5.3**	0.1	0.96	9.13	4.48	72.1	**4.2**	19.2	8.0	**6.2**
6.1	2.44	6.5	-0.02	**8.7**	0.6	1.90	13.67	4.43	52.6	**2.7**	20.9	16.0	**8.5**
7.6	0.68	na	0.31	**7.5**	0.9	1.23	8.38	3.96	60.3	**4.1**	22.2	8.9	**9.4**
8.3	0.97	na	-0.17	**6.5**	0.8	1.35	10.93	4.12	60.6	**2.0**	27.5	22.5	**6.9**
8.3	0.42	2.2	0.01	**5.9**	12.1	1.08	10.54	3.31	61.2	**4.8**	29.9	10.9	**8.8**
5.3	0.62	na	0.00	**8.8**	0.8	2.07	19.82	4.45	56.6	**1.5**	15.5	25.1	**8.3**
8.3	0.30	1.3	-0.01	**10.0**	6.8	2.15	13.62	4.72	38.8	**4.3**	33.2	14.3	**10.0**
8.3	0.31	na	0.00	**4.8**	1.1	1.36	18.12	3.56	62.3	**2.7**	14.5	15.6	**5.4**
4.8	2.53	7.3	0.01	**3.4**	0.1	0.61	5.01	3.77	84.1	**2.7**	24.2	16.3	**6.2**
7.2	0.05	na	0.12	**7.5**	2.5	1.77	15.73	3.24	40.9	**2.3**	28.5	19.7	**7.2**
7.7	0.46	na	0.07	**5.3**	0.5	1.25	9.88	5.24	72.4	**2.8**	17.8	15.4	**7.0**
9.3	0.04	na	-0.05	**3.6**	0.1	0.57	6.52	3.98	85.6	**4.8**	32.3	8.0	**4.5**
1.5	2.44	na	0.36	**5.4**	1.1	1.43	11.62	4.19	62.3	**1.4**	17.9	27.5	**7.5**
8.9	0.06	na	0.00	**6.1**	0.5	1.27	10.49	3.95	60.0	**1.5**	20.0	25.4	**7.9**
5.4	5.22	na	0.04	**3.2**	0.4	0.53	4.43	2.33	71.9	**5.1**	45.4	10.9	**6.1**
6.8	0.49	na	0.00	**3.6**	0.2	0.98	10.79	3.76	84.2	**2.4**	28.9	19.4	**5.4**
8.8	0.00	na	-0.04	**9.0**	0.2	2.22	19.53	5.41	58.6	**0.8**	13.2	33.2	**7.0**
5.0	3.68	na	-0.22	**4.8**	0.7	1.17	12.54	3.13	63.3	**1.9**	15.5	19.7	**5.8**
5.0	3.05	9.8	-0.45	**2.8**	0.1	0.36	3.00	3.17	88.4	**3.1**	42.5	20.5	**6.5**
9.0	0.07	na	0.05	**6.3**	0.6	1.37	12.34	3.48	50.0	**2.5**	34.7	22.2	**7.1**
5.4	2.00	na	-0.08	**7.3**	0.5	1.77	16.19	4.05	60.8	**4.8**	32.8	8.1	**8.1**
4.5	3.09	na	1.15	**6.8**	0.5	1.50	8.17	4.25	61.6	**1.5**	22.4	27.2	**8.8**
8.2	0.00	na	0.00	**9.3**	0.9	2.16	17.84	3.76	55.1	**0.5**	14.7	48.0	**9.4**
7.6	1.55	na	0.00	**6.3**	0.5	1.41	10.82	3.25	55.6	**1.2**	21.2	31.1	**9.3**
3.4	1.75	9.4	0.08	**5.1**	2.0	1.00	9.97	3.92	64.8	**1.6**	16.0	20.3	**6.2**
5.3	1.54	na	0.00	**3.4**	0.0	0.75	4.01	3.40	76.3	**4.8**	26.8	4.6	**6.6**
7.2	0.05	na	0.25	**4.3**	0.5	0.88	8.83	4.00	75.1	**3.9**	12.4	9.1	**6.6**
7.4	0.38	na	0.67	**9.0**	0.9	1.85	16.85	6.50	61.4	**2.6**	41.1	26.5	**7.9**
4.4	3.86	na	0.01	**3.8**	0.4	0.60	4.80	3.03	76.5	**3.7**	34.7	14.9	**7.4**
7.1	0.54	na	0.08	**6.0**	0.3	1.17	9.60	3.78	60.5	**2.3**	14.9	17.6	**7.4**
8.0	0.00	na	0.00	**4.5**	0.3	0.94	8.90	4.09	74.5	**1.7**	18.2	22.9	**6.6**
5.2	1.16	na	0.18	**5.2**	0.5	0.91	7.03	4.49	67.8	**3.8**	17.8	10.1	**7.7**
1.0	2.53	na	-0.01	**5.5**	1.2	1.00	10.01	5.56	74.7	**4.5**	7.8	4.5	**6.4**
3.8	2.17	na	0.29	**3.9**	0.4	0.92	7.64	5.36	81.7	**2.8**	25.3	16.2	**6.2**
8.9	0.44	na	0.00	**4.0**	0.4	0.89	7.74	2.56	55.8	**3.0**	45.9	24.2	**6.6**
6.5	0.85	3.7	0.26	**2.6**	0.1	0.57	6.46	3.35	89.3	**2.8**	37.1	20.4	**4.5**
6.1	2.16	na	0.00	**6.0**	0.7	1.36	11.33	3.62	64.8	**1.2**	21.6	31.6	**8.3**

Name	City	State	Rating	2019 Rating	2018 Rating	Total Assets ($Mil)	One Year Asset Growth	Asset Mix (As a % of Total Assets) Commercial Loans	Consumer Loans	Mortgage Loans	Securities	Capitalization Index	Leverage Ratio	Risk-Based Capital Ratio
▲ Bank of Elgin	Elgin	NE	**A-**	B+	B+	57.6	-2.76	3.4	1.2	0.6	4.2	**9.8**	13.7	0.0
Bank of Elk River	Elk River	MN	**B+**	B+	B	470.8	8.12	16.7	2.2	9.0	28.3	**7.4**	9.3	14.6
Bank of England	England	AR	**B+**	B+	B	519.5	50.03	3.8	0.7	53.1	8.3	**7.5**	12.6	12.9
▼ Bank of Erath	Erath	LA	**B-**	B	B	101.0	-2.13	8.6	2.8	19.3	12.5	**10.0**	13.5	21.6
Bank of Estes Park	Estes Park	CO	**A-**	A-	B+	132.0	5.38	2.1	0.1	16.4	24.1	**9.4**	10.8	0.0
Bank of Eufaula	Eufaula	OK	**C+**	C+	B-	99.2	2.42	2.6	6.3	14.4	48.3	**9.8**	13.5	0.0
Bank of Evergreen	Evergreen	AL	**B-**	B-	C+	60.4	2.09	9.3	3.3	21.3	27.6	**9.8**	12.9	0.0
Bank of Farmington	Farmington	IL	**B-**	B-	B-	180.4	2.58	12.1	3.2	14.2	22.5	**10.0**	11.4	17.1
Bank of Fayette County	Piperton	TN	**B-**	B-	B-	678.1	7.26	6.2	6.9	31.5	5.7	**7.3**	9.4	0.0
Bank of Feather River	Yuba City	CA	**A-**	A-	B+	146.3	15.93	10.4	0.1	3.6	0.0	**9.4**	10.8	0.0
▲ Bank of Fincastle	Fincastle	VA	**C-**	D+	D-	223.9	4.40	9.8	0.6	19.1	9.5	**10.0**	11.9	16.5
Bank of Forest	Forest	MS	**B+**	B+	B+	212.2	6.73	5.8	4.3	10.2	27.2	**10.0**	13.3	19.5
Bank of Frankewing	Frankewing	TN	**B+**	B+	B+	313.2	5.80	10.1	4.3	18.8	4.6	**10.0**	11.4	15.6
Bank of Franklin	Meadville	MS	**A-**	A-	B+	151.7	5.52	7.3	4.5	21.3	23.1	**9.8**	11.6	0.0
Bank of Franklin County	Washington	MO	**C+**	C+	C	267.2	0.61	11.9	2.2	17.9	13.1	**7.2**	9.3	0.0
Bank of George	Las Vegas	NV	**A**	A	B+	346.0	36.58	3.9	0.0	1.7	1.0	**10.0**	12.7	21.5
Bank of Gibson City	Gibson City	IL	**C+**	C+	C	91.4	10.69	5.4	4.3	11.5	16.2	**6.3**	8.3	13.6
Bank of Gleason	Gleason	TN	**B+**	B+	B+	113.8	2.49	4.5	7.0	12.5	48.7	**10.0**	23.3	44.2
Bank of Glen Burnie	Glen Burnie	MD	**C**	C	C	380.5	-3.19	4.3	25.6	20.8	18.4	**7.5**	9.3	13.3
▼ Bank of Glen Ullin	Glen Ullin	ND	**C-**	C	D+	59.8	4.87	5.1	1.5	2.5	9.1	**9.8**	11.2	0.0
Bank of Grain Valley	Kansas City	MO	**A-**	A-	A-	91.1	0.01	14.0	1.1	18.4	13.7	**10.0**	22.8	40.0
Bank of Grand Lake	Grove	OK	**B-**	B-	B-	174.2	-1.90	5.7	2.9	26.6	12.3	**6.2**	8.2	12.0
Bank of Grandin	Grandin	MO	**B-**	B-	B-	175.2	8.46	12.1	7.1	12.7	26.1	**10.0**	15.5	16.1
Bank of Gravette	Gravette	AR	**C+**	C+	C+	128.0	-4.70	6.5	2.5	17.9	14.1	**7.1**	9.2	0.0
Bank of Greeley	Greeley	KS	**B**	B	B	38.4	-1.92	4.8	3.8	18.5	9.9	**9.8**	13.3	0.0
Bank of Greeleyville	Greeleyville	SC	**B+**	B+	C+	93.4	3.09	12.0	8.4	13.6	20.0	**9.8**	12.2	0.0
Bank of Greene County	Catskill	NY	**B+**	B+	B+	1581.4	24.42	5.6	0.3	21.9	38.5	**6.1**	8.1	15.2
Bank of Guam	Hagatna	GU	**C+**	C+	C+	1985.6	3.33	12.3	11.4	7.6	21.9	**6.7**	8.7	13.8
▼ Bank of Gueydan	Gueydan	LA	**B-**	B	B-	76.9	-2.97	4.7	6.7	1.0	61.3	**9.8**	20.6	0.0
Bank of Halls	Halls	TN	**B**	B	B	96.0	13.13	9.4	2.3	6.1	34.7	**7.6**	9.6	0.0
▼ Bank of Hamilton	Hamilton	ND	**C**	C+	C-	20.2	2.57	2.9	3.3	0.0	3.0	**9.8**	13.6	0.0
Bank of Hancock County	Sparta	GA	**B+**	B+	B+	76.4	0.88	4.3	5.3	14.8	58.5	**9.8**	21.0	0.0
Bank of Hartington	Hartington	NE	**B-**	B-	C+	104.9	11.22	9.5	1.6	6.0	15.2	**6.8**	9.4	12.4
Bank of Hawaii	Honolulu	HI	**B**	B	B	18513.2	6.28	5.6	6.0	25.0	31.2	**4.9**	6.9	12.7
Bank of Hays	Hays	KS	**B**	B	B-	260.6	0.96	11.7	2.1	9.0	30.3	**9.0**	10.5	0.0
Bank of Hazelton	Hazelton	ND	**B**	B	B-	50.9	3.50	1.4	0.6	0.8	22.4	**8.9**	10.3	20.6
Bank of Hazlehurst	Hazlehurst	GA	**D+**	D+	D	125.9	-6.53	8.6	2.4	7.6	23.1	**10.0**	12.4	24.1
▲ Bank of Hemet	Riverside	CA	**A**	A-	B+	680.4	-2.66	1.5	0.1	0.2	9.5	**9.6**	11.8	14.6
Bank of Herrin	Herrin	IL	**B-**	B-	B-	253.2	2.45	9.9	2.1	14.2	21.3	**9.0**	10.3	15.0
▲ Bank of Hillsboro, N.A.	Hillsboro	IL	**B+**	B	B-	391.4	10.09	6.3	0.8	8.0	19.1	**9.8**	11.0	0.0
Bank of Hindman	Hindman	KY	**C+**	C+	C	250.0	23.84	5.7	1.3	12.1	36.9	**7.2**	9.3	0.0
Bank of Holland	Holland	NY	**B-**	B-	B-	148.5	7.87	2.7	1.7	42.8	19.2	**6.3**	8.3	13.6
▼ Bank of Holly Springs	Holly Springs	MS	**B-**	B	B-	257.1	10.29	10.4	6.8	21.2	13.3	**9.8**	13.6	0.0
Bank of Holyrood	Holyrood	KS	**B**	B	B+	63.1	1.20	19.1	6.2	22.0	9.6	**10.0**	14.8	23.2
Bank of Hope	Los Angeles	CA	**B**	B	B	16020.3	4.04	16.0	0.3	5.3	10.7	**9.3**	12.1	14.4
Bank of Houston	Houston	MO	**D-**	D-	D-	32.3	5.71	8.5	0.7	6.6	9.0	**9.5**	10.6	18.3
Bank of Houston, N.A.	Houston	TX	**D+**	D+	C	175.9	133.40	12.4	1.5	7.7	1.2	**10.0**	24.2	27.1
Bank of Hydro	Hydro	OK	**A**	A	B+	126.3	-0.88	4.7	1.9	31.3	0.6	**9.8**	11.7	0.0
Bank of Iberia	Iberia	MO	**C**	C	D+	55.7	-1.08	2.2	5.6	25.1	16.3	**7.6**	9.4	18.0
Bank of Idaho	Idaho Falls	ID	**B-**	B-	B-	420.7	26.21	10.6	1.9	5.5	21.1	**10.0**	12.3	15.4
Bank of Jackson	Jackson	TN	**B-**	B-	B-	199.2	7.40	5.3	1.9	7.6	63.6	**8.2**	9.9	0.0
▲ Bank of Jackson Hole	Jackson	WY	**B+**	B	C+	938.4	11.90	5.5	0.3	17.6	5.3	**8.3**	9.9	15.0
Bank of Jamestown	Jamestown	KY	**B-**	B-	B-	205.7	2.59	5.1	1.0	10.1	26.7	**9.8**	11.5	14.8
Bank of Kampsville	Kampsville	IL	**B**	B	B	113.6	5.84	2.9	6.7	18.2	37.1	**9.8**	17.4	0.0
▲ Bank of Kaukauna	Kaukauna	WI	**C+**	C	D+	99.4	3.85	17.5	1.7	12.2	4.5	**7.5**	9.4	13.7
Bank of Kilmichael	Kilmichael	MS	**B+**	B+	B+	198.4	10.89	10.5	5.2	13.1	24.0	**7.9**	9.8	0.0
Bank of Kirksville	Kirksville	MO	**B+**	B+	B	431.6	-3.81	3.1	0.6	14.4	40.1	**10.0**	12.2	41.4
Bank of Kremlin	Kremlin	OK	**B-**	B-	C+	322.3	4.00	8.9	1.9	6.7	8.3	**7.8**	9.6	13.1
Bank of Labor	Kansas City	KS	**C**	C	C	679.5	9.99	20.1	0.1	2.9	45.6	**5.9**	7.9	13.1
Bank of LaFayette, Georgia	Lafayette	GA	**B**	B	B	287.9	3.57	1.1	6.0	19.1	57.8	**10.0**	12.4	44.0

Arrows denote recent upgrades ▲ or downgrades ▼

Asset Quality Index	Adjusted Non-Performing Loans as a % of Total Loans	Adjusted Non-Performing Loans as a % of Capital	Net Charge-Offs Avg Loans	Profitability Index	Net Income ($Mil)	Return on Assets (R.O.A.)	Return on Equity (R.O.E.)	Net Interest Spread	Overhead Efficiency Ratio	Liquidity Index	Liquidity Ratio	Hot Money Ratio	Stability Index
6.8	0.00	na	0.00	**9.4**	0.3	2.19	14.31	4.07	50.5	**4.4**	13.1	5.8	**9.5**
7.4	0.13	na	0.01	**5.7**	1.3	1.10	11.10	3.81	70.2	**4.7**	34.0	9.4	**6.9**
6.4	1.07	na	0.00	**3.7**	-0.7	-0.57	-4.47	2.89	100.1	**0.9**	19.8	33.7	**9.2**
5.1	2.10	10.8	-0.03	**2.9**	0.1	0.36	2.64	4.30	89.9	**1.9**	23.1	20.2	**7.0**
9.3	0.00	0.0	0.01	**5.6**	0.4	1.30	11.70	3.85	67.3	**6.6**	49.0	2.6	**7.6**
6.7	0.74	na	0.18	**2.7**	0.2	0.85	5.99	3.68	70.4	**3.0**	40.8	20.4	**5.8**
4.0	3.24	na	5.87	**3.7**	0.1	0.58	4.31	4.10	68.3	**2.3**	36.6	26.4	**5.8**
7.3	2.37	na	-0.02	**3.6**	0.2	0.49	4.33	3.58	80.7	**1.8**	21.6	22.1	**6.6**
4.8	0.65	na	0.07	**6.1**	2.1	1.29	13.93	4.02	59.8	**0.5**	6.8	39.2	**6.2**
8.4	0.00	na	-0.02	**6.6**	0.4	1.10	10.31	4.42	63.0	**1.5**	17.3	25.0	**7.3**
7.1	1.46	na	-0.49	**2.3**	0.1	0.16	1.23	3.77	96.0	**3.3**	15.8	12.8	**4.9**
6.4	0.82	3.8	0.26	**5.1**	0.6	1.22	8.84	3.98	71.4	**2.4**	34.4	22.9	**8.3**
6.2	0.93	na	-0.01	**6.2**	0.8	1.03	9.15	3.89	67.4	**0.9**	21.1	36.3	**8.0**
6.8	0.55	na	0.03	**5.5**	0.4	1.07	9.33	4.26	71.6	**2.6**	26.1	17.2	**7.1**
4.5	2.30	10.0	0.00	**3.9**	0.4	0.65	7.00	3.58	75.3	**3.1**	15.6	13.4	**5.3**
7.1	0.00	na	0.00	**7.6**	0.9	0.97	7.89	4.26	71.8	**3.7**	31.2	13.4	**9.3**
6.4	1.09	na	-0.02	**5.0**	0.3	1.09	9.70	3.38	55.7	**3.4**	22.3	13.0	**6.1**
8.8	0.52	na	0.23	**4.8**	0.4	1.53	6.51	3.43	67.4	**4.7**	74.8	18.4	**8.1**
2.9	1.48	10.9	0.10	**2.7**	0.3	0.34	3.60	3.34	90.0	**4.0**	25.4	10.0	**4.5**
1.9	2.52	na	0.00	**9.5**	0.4	2.50	20.96	4.65	44.2	**0.7**	12.8	44.8	**8.5**
8.9	0.00	na	0.02	**7.2**	0.4	1.72	7.57	4.01	57.6	**5.0**	35.7	8.0	**9.5**
4.9	1.28	na	0.00	**4.9**	0.5	1.17	14.39	3.70	68.7	**1.2**	14.8	24.4	**5.6**
4.0	8.98	na	0.19	**5.4**	0.6	1.32	8.55	3.74	59.1	**1.5**	25.5	27.6	**8.3**
3.6	1.08	na	-0.01	**2.4**	0.1	0.28	1.98	3.75	87.2	**1.5**	21.4	25.9	**7.0**
8.8	0.00	na	0.00	**5.4**	0.1	1.30	9.86	3.25	61.3	**4.6**	43.4	12.5	**7.3**
5.7	1.94	na	0.23	**5.6**	0.3	1.17	9.03	4.30	73.7	**3.5**	34.8	15.6	**7.4**
9.0	0.51	3.1	0.09	**5.2**	3.7	0.99	12.58	3.16	56.6	**5.0**	5.9	0.9	**7.1**
3.9	1.78	12.7	0.31	**4.1**	3.2	0.65	7.48	4.66	80.6	**2.3**	13.9	17.7	**6.8**
5.7	5.28	5.8	-2.30	**3.6**	0.1	0.72	3.50	2.88	71.0	**4.2**	84.7	22.8	**6.7**
4.4	4.10	na	0.00	**4.9**	0.2	0.99	9.69	3.23	62.7	**2.0**	32.2	27.4	**6.5**
9.6	0.00	na	0.00	**1.6**	0.0	0.26	1.95	2.33	88.0	**7.6**	98.4	2.6	**5.3**
9.0	0.49	na	0.14	**3.5**	0.1	0.65	2.96	4.04	88.1	**5.8**	71.5	11.0	**8.0**
8.2	0.00	na	0.00	**5.3**	0.3	1.32	14.53	4.15	66.9	**3.7**	23.0	11.2	**5.9**
7.7	0.65	3.9	0.13	**5.0**	35.2	0.78	11.24	2.98	55.2	**4.0**	17.0	9.4	**6.7**
6.0	2.02	4.2	0.00	**6.0**	0.8	1.22	11.15	3.67	54.5	**2.0**	26.4	21.3	**6.0**
8.9	0.00	na	0.00	**5.2**	0.2	1.30	12.24	3.40	61.0	**4.3**	54.1	16.1	**6.3**
1.1	9.75	na	-0.07	**3.2**	0.2	0.50	3.49	4.04	69.8	**5.4**	33.8	4.5	**6.1**
7.2	0.00	na	0.01	**9.8**	4.2	2.44	20.52	4.47	43.9	**4.8**	5.2	2.2	**9.8**
4.6	1.70	na	0.01	**5.3**	0.8	1.35	12.57	4.07	63.7	**4.6**	14.9	4.8	**6.5**
6.1	4.02	na	-0.02	**5.5**	1.0	1.06	9.40	3.55	60.5	**2.2**	14.2	17.9	**6.5**
3.8	3.45	na	0.07	**3.4**	0.4	0.63	5.43	2.63	68.1	**2.7**	43.6	26.9	**6.4**
5.8	0.74	na	0.00	**4.3**	0.3	0.80	9.66	3.78	71.2	**3.4**	15.2	11.8	**5.3**
4.0	2.29	na	0.30	**6.8**	1.0	1.62	11.97	4.38	59.4	**1.3**	15.4	27.0	**9.2**
4.3	1.97	12.1	0.25	**5.9**	0.2	1.18	7.94	3.67	55.6	**1.2**	28.3	31.4	**7.4**
5.1	1.15	3.1	0.11	**5.2**	29.5	0.77	5.15	3.42	51.8	**0.9**	16.5	27.5	**10.0**
6.3	0.00	na	0.00	**0.0**	-0.2	-2.96	-23.54	3.95	176.8	**5.7**	49.1	7.6	**3.3**
7.2	0.00	na	0.00	**1.0**	0.0	0.06	0.26	4.73	88.2	**2.3**	28.3	19.5	**6.5**
5.5	0.02	na	0.00	**9.6**	0.7	2.19	18.78	4.49	52.6	**1.2**	15.2	29.4	**8.8**
4.9	2.18	na	-0.06	**3.0**	0.1	0.72	7.64	4.24	87.7	**4.0**	43.1	15.6	**4.3**
5.5	1.86	na	0.12	**3.8**	0.4	0.38	3.05	4.69	88.0	**4.9**	20.1	1.8	**6.6**
8.6	0.86	na	0.20	**3.9**	0.4	0.91	8.10	2.83	70.5	**3.2**	54.3	28.3	**6.3**
6.7	1.17	na	0.00	**5.7**	2.3	0.95	9.63	3.38	64.6	**4.4**	26.3	8.0	**7.8**
8.0	0.69	na	0.01	**4.5**	0.5	1.02	8.84	3.43	62.6	**1.6**	17.0	23.1	**6.6**
5.6	1.88	na	-0.02	**4.1**	0.2	0.83	4.69	3.02	65.4	**4.7**	50.9	14.2	**8.1**
4.1	4.04	na	0.00	**6.1**	0.5	1.96	20.58	3.28	79.3	**3.1**	20.8	5.5	**6.2**
4.6	1.19	na	0.00	**6.9**	0.9	1.80	18.95	4.12	57.8	**2.2**	28.2	20.3	**6.1**
7.1	3.82	na	0.60	**4.0**	1.0	0.87	7.02	2.10	62.7	**4.7**	42.5	12.3	**7.8**
4.6	0.94	na	0.00	**4.8**	1.1	1.36	11.27	4.29	54.1	**0.8**	14.8	32.6	**7.4**
4.2	4.13	16.2	5.80	**1.1**	-2.8	-1.81	-22.59	3.39	97.8	**5.9**	47.8	6.7	**4.5**
6.9	2.07	na	0.04	**3.5**	0.4	0.53	4.23	2.78	73.2	**3.7**	28.7	13.0	**6.8**

Asset Quality Index	Adjusted Non-Performing Loans as a % of Total Loans	Adjusted Non-Performing Loans as a % of Capital	Net Charge-Offs Avg Loans	Profitability Index	Net Income ($Mil)	Return on Assets (R.O.A.)	Return on Equity (R.O.E.)	Net Interest Spread	Overhead Efficiency Ratio	Liquidity Index	Liquidity Ratio	Hot Money Ratio	Stability Index
7.3	1.16	na	0.27	**3.2**	-0.1	-0.89	-3.39	3.58	125.7	**2.0**	37.7	33.2	**4.8**
6.6	1.68	na	1.13	**4.5**	0.5	1.02	6.71	2.67	49.2	**2.8**	45.0	24.8	**8.3**
5.0	2.98	na	-0.08	**3.8**	0.1	0.67	6.04	3.57	75.2	**4.0**	36.6	13.9	**5.6**
6.1	2.07	na	-0.01	**2.7**	0.1	0.30	3.01	3.39	91.2	**4.7**	46.3	13.1	**6.1**
3.7	1.50	na	0.31	**5.6**	1.4	1.01	9.90	3.92	68.0	**3.7**	16.4	10.7	**6.7**
5.3	0.58	na	0.14	**4.1**	1.2	0.50	4.75	3.81	84.5	**1.4**	11.6	23.5	**7.0**
5.6	0.58	na	-0.03	**5.4**	1.0	1.08	10.15	4.47	70.9	**1.1**	25.0	30.3	**8.2**
8.7	0.05	na	0.00	**5.8**	0.7	1.13	8.62	3.86	57.5	**1.2**	14.1	19.2	**8.0**
6.5	2.02	na	0.00	**8.3**	0.8	2.94	14.80	4.59	53.0	**3.9**	18.0	9.7	**9.9**
4.7	1.41	6.3	0.40	**3.4**	166.0	0.48	3.89	2.59	62.6	**4.1**	31.0	8.7	**10.0**
10.0	na	0.0	na	**2.7**	0.0	0.05	0.06	0.00	0.0	**4.0**	na	0.0	**6.8**
5.6	0.12	0.6	0.17	**8.2**	39.6	1.46	9.78	2.19	24.7	**1.5**	29.2	1.9	**10.0**
6.7	1.41	5.1	0.07	**6.5**	1.9	1.39	11.24	3.29	53.9	**3.6**	30.9	14.2	**8.6**
4.8	0.97	4.5	0.02	**4.5**	10.3	0.82	7.20	3.31	57.6	**3.9**	11.3	5.3	**9.0**
8.0	0.46	na	0.17	**6.5**	4.7	1.93	17.58	3.31	67.1	**2.1**	22.7	10.8	**8.6**
4.1	15.09	2.9	0.00	**9.5**	1.4	4.50	6.65	1.99	39.8	**8.7**	111.4	0.0	**8.3**
6.9	0.09	0.3	0.00	**5.5**	73.0	0.99	7.53	1.09	63.7	**2.3**	41.0	63.4	**8.3**
8.8	0.00	na	-0.01	**7.2**	0.2	1.27	6.76	4.20	63.1	**3.5**	49.0	19.2	**7.0**
4.5	1.66	na	0.00	**4.0**	0.1	0.46	4.65	3.79	53.4	**0.8**	20.9	50.3	**5.9**
8.6	0.00	0.0	0.00	**4.1**	0.0	0.75	5.11	2.40	55.9	**3.8**	68.7	19.2	**6.7**
9.7	0.24	na	0.00	**1.4**	-1.3	-0.74	-5.99	1.79	158.2	**0.7**	18.5	46.7	**7.1**
5.9	0.87	3.4	0.31	**4.7**	74.3	0.66	6.28	2.76	55.3	**3.5**	13.2	5.8	**9.1**
5.2	0.15	na	0.54	**7.2**	2.1	1.60	14.66	4.81	63.7	**3.8**	10.9	9.6	**7.7**
6.2	0.38	na	0.11	**5.2**	0.2	1.27	14.14	4.11	66.7	**3.8**	14.4	9.4	**5.0**
8.9	0.33	na	0.00	**7.1**	0.4	2.36	10.62	3.43	35.8	**6.0**	64.8	8.8	**8.5**
9.0	0.10	0.4	-0.01	**4.4**	0.2	0.69	7.02	2.94	62.1	**2.8**	32.1	17.6	**6.8**
7.7	0.00	na	0.13	**1.8**	0.0	0.19	2.10	3.26	89.7	**1.0**	26.1	29.9	**3.6**
4.1	1.41	8.1	0.30	**4.2**	1.3	0.80	8.15	3.64	76.0	**1.4**	16.6	14.9	**6.9**
7.9	0.44	2.9	0.02	**2.9**	2.6	0.12	1.21	2.92	74.6	**2.9**	11.5	7.7	**8.3**
6.5	0.00	0.0	0.00	**10.0**	5.1	43.49	50.63	11.33	57.0	**2.3**	63.9	100.0	**10.0**
4.6	1.33	na	1.46	**3.2**	-0.1	-0.38	-2.91	4.37	90.9	**1.5**	15.7	25.2	**7.0**
6.3	2.70	na	0.52	**5.6**	1.2	1.28	9.81	3.60	59.7	**2.3**	44.8	21.7	**7.5**
3.8	3.54	na	0.00	**4.5**	0.5	1.38	15.14	3.09	65.2	**4.7**	39.2	11.0	**5.2**
5.8	0.44	na	0.00	**0.6**	0.0	0.20	2.83	3.32	97.3	**1.2**	11.6	15.1	**2.3**
6.3	1.34	na	0.00	**7.3**	2.3	1.65	25.24	3.55	57.7	**5.8**	47.3	7.2	**6.0**
5.6	0.72	na	0.01	**4.5**	0.4	0.74	7.32	3.90	76.2	**2.6**	8.7	14.8	**6.8**
8.1	0.24	na	-0.12	**5.9**	0.2	1.10	8.06	4.59	64.7	**4.1**	50.2	16.4	**6.9**
6.4	0.28	na	0.11	**2.1**	0.1	0.16	1.86	3.30	93.6	**3.4**	11.5	11.5	**5.2**
8.3	0.05	na	0.00	**10.0**	0.2	2.74	8.06	4.93	89.0	**1.3**	30.9	53.2	**8.0**
8.8	0.00	na	0.00	**7.2**	0.3	1.94	16.60	3.67	49.5	**4.4**	36.1	11.8	**8.1**
6.7	0.76	3.8	0.04	**5.5**	36.3	1.11	11.21	3.40	59.0	**2.9**	17.8	7.0	**9.0**
6.2	3.70	na	0.01	**5.9**	1.7	1.81	15.91	3.62	62.2	**5.2**	53.6	12.3	**7.6**
8.1	0.32	na	0.00	**2.9**	0.8	0.47	3.79	2.92	72.2	**2.8**	15.4	14.2	**7.5**
5.5	2.62	na	0.05	**2.3**	0.1	0.39	3.42	2.94	87.4	**1.7**	36.8	41.5	**5.7**
6.1	2.04	na	0.00	**4.4**	0.5	0.90	8.46	3.27	65.8	**6.6**	58.6	5.3	**5.8**
8.4	0.00	na	-0.05	**5.7**	0.3	1.18	10.50	3.65	63.6	**2.4**	19.7	17.5	**7.1**
7.3	0.06	0.3	0.01	**7.5**	7.6	1.32	12.00	3.68	44.0	**0.9**	17.0	27.1	**7.0**
8.8	0.00	na	0.00	**2.7**	0.6	0.35	3.53	3.05	88.9	**3.4**	25.8	13.1	**6.4**
1.7	3.62	35.4	-0.22	**0.4**	-0.1	-0.44	-6.61	4.64	106.7	**3.6**	13.0	10.7	**0.3**
6.2	2.70	na	0.00	**10.0**	1.3	2.35	18.73	5.15	55.9	**6.0**	35.4	1.4	**9.3**
6.8	0.69	3.1	0.02	**1.8**	-34.7	-5.91	-47.49	3.04	76.2	**3.1**	19.4	12.1	**10.0**
7.0	0.10	na	0.02	**1.4**	0.0	0.00	0.03	3.60	97.4	**1.6**	20.7	22.6	**5.3**
6.1	1.06	na	0.00	**1.8**	0.2	0.13	1.20	2.52	93.4	**0.6**	13.8	47.2	**5.2**
8.5	0.11	na	0.07	**4.6**	9.9	1.04	9.12	3.32	71.8	**5.6**	34.3	7.2	**9.7**
5.4	0.71	4.7	0.19	**3.7**	-8.7	-0.64	-6.19	3.37	60.6	**1.2**	9.4	21.2	**7.7**
9.5	0.20	na	0.00	**4.0**	0.1	0.97	4.99	3.39	72.1	**3.1**	34.1	13.9	**7.1**
10.0	na	na	na	**9.5**	0.7	25.74	45.47	2.03	75.8	**4.0**	217.8	0.0	**6.2**
10.0	na	na	na	**9.5**	0.8	20.83	38.86	2.03	81.5	**4.0**	173.9	0.0	**6.6**
8.4	0.00	na	0.00	**4.6**	1.0	1.10	8.93	3.44	66.0	**2.8**	16.1	15.1	**7.1**
6.8	0.94	na	-0.02	**3.2**	0.2	0.39	2.84	3.69	83.6	**1.2**	16.5	29.0	**7.1**

Asset Quality Index	Adjusted Non-Performing Loans as a % of Total Loans	Adjusted Non-Performing Loans as a % of Capital	Net Charge-Offs Avg Loans	Profitability Index	Net Income ($Mil)	Return on Assets (R.O.A.)	Return on Equity (R.O.E.)	Net Interest Spread	Overhead Efficiency Ratio	Liquidity Index	Liquidity Ratio	Hot Money Ratio	Stability Index
0.5	1.40	na	0.09	**7.2**	0.7	2.09	25.44	3.94	43.5	**0.6**	12.0	42.7	**5.8**
8.4	0.47	na	-0.03	**4.9**	4.4	0.96	9.73	3.20	66.9	**3.6**	27.6	15.9	**8.7**
8.0	0.37	na	2.61	**5.5**	0.1	1.39	12.49	6.14	58.6	**5.1**	35.9	7.8	**6.5**
7.1	0.33	1.5	0.44	**3.5**	-12.7	-1.05	-8.14	3.54	70.1	**2.6**	8.3	7.6	**9.4**
3.9	0.99	na	0.01	**5.4**	1.5	1.01	7.35	4.09	66.0	**1.4**	9.5	24.2	**9.1**
3.6	3.15	na	0.07	**5.4**	4.7	1.03	7.61	3.25	40.1	**0.8**	14.8	39.7	**9.9**
8.2	0.43	na	-0.03	**6.0**	0.5	1.14	8.55	4.01	66.7	**1.2**	13.8	19.3	**7.7**
5.3	3.01	na	0.01	**8.2**	0.4	1.93	10.58	3.80	52.5	**4.0**	35.3	13.4	**9.2**
7.6	0.00	na	0.00	**3.7**	0.1	0.77	6.07	3.15	76.2	**5.7**	48.8	7.6	**5.6**
5.8	1.23	na	0.09	**6.3**	0.7	1.23	9.09	4.06	64.6	**4.4**	31.6	10.0	**7.9**
7.9	0.35	na	0.74	**3.2**	0.1	0.20	1.80	3.99	81.4	**3.0**	22.0	14.8	**7.0**
8.2	0.66	2.5	1.24	**3.7**	6.9	0.93	7.78	3.19	69.7	**3.9**	12.9	9.5	**8.8**
9.2	0.00	na	0.00	**5.7**	0.5	1.36	11.99	4.07	65.1	**3.7**	32.6	13.8	**7.2**
9.3	0.01	na	0.00	**4.1**	0.1	0.33	2.90	2.49	44.2	**3.8**	66.1	20.5	**7.3**
6.9	0.45	2.1	0.20	**5.9**	19.4	0.80	5.66	3.29	58.9	**3.8**	17.4	10.4	**10.0**
6.0	2.52	na	1.19	**1.6**	-0.2	-1.03	-6.64	3.23	96.5	**1.3**	32.4	42.8	**5.7**
4.8	0.65	na	-0.09	**5.6**	0.1	1.01	8.11	3.92	73.2	**1.2**	28.4	17.8	**7.6**
4.1	1.30	8.6	0.48	**4.1**	3.7	0.27	1.90	4.20	69.6	**1.8**	7.7	13.5	**9.1**
4.0	3.39	na	-0.01	**4.0**	0.5	0.77	7.30	3.11	65.5	**1.6**	23.5	25.2	**7.0**
7.6	0.00	na	0.00	**5.5**	1.1	1.25	9.81	3.96	61.4	**2.3**	31.7	10.2	**6.9**
7.6	0.72	na	0.00	**1.3**	-0.1	-0.42	-3.03	2.69	125.0	**3.9**	50.9	18.5	**5.8**
4.3	2.03	9.0	-0.04	**10.0**	6.9	1.94	16.86	4.85	47.1	**3.5**	22.1	13.5	**10.0**
5.0	1.31	6.9	0.99	**3.7**	-396.6	-8.99	-65.57	3.88	282.1	**3.0**	15.9	10.4	**9.2**
2.4	1.89	na	0.36	**4.1**	0.4	0.87	8.15	4.63	74.1	**0.8**	18.6	50.2	**4.7**
5.0	0.54	na	0.20	**4.3**	0.3	0.75	7.62	4.01	73.0	**1.8**	13.9	20.0	**6.2**
7.8	0.27	na	-0.04	**3.5**	0.7	0.24	2.05	3.73	87.6	**2.5**	15.1	13.5	**8.3**
7.6	0.00	na	0.00	**0.0**	-0.4	-1.80	-12.57	3.41	144.2	**1.9**	34.0	28.3	**6.2**
9.6	0.00	0.0	0.00	**10.0**	0.6	1.84	3.88	5.94	49.8	**3.3**	65.0	32.5	**9.5**
8.3	0.00	na	-0.97	**0.0**	-0.3	-2.54	-8.61	5.00	163.0	**2.0**	42.2	47.5	**6.2**
4.3	6.10	9.1	0.00	**10.0**	0.4	2.11	4.98	4.92	42.4	**3.3**	47.9	16.5	**9.7**
5.8	0.98	na	0.00	**4.1**	0.9	0.91	9.11	3.87	71.1	**2.4**	4.5	13.9	**5.8**
7.2	0.07	0.5	0.00	**3.7**	2.4	0.88	8.52	4.53	66.1	**1.8**	22.1	13.3	**5.8**
7.1	0.68	na	0.03	**7.8**	1.9	1.42	8.72	3.92	49.9	**5.4**	30.3	2.8	**9.6**
5.5	0.76	5.2	0.00	**3.6**	6.7	0.61	6.17	3.07	64.4	**2.3**	12.4	13.2	**8.1**
8.9	0.29	0.8	-0.01	**0.9**	-0.6	-3.15	-26.58	3.26	-721.6	**6.0**	47.1	5.2	**6.4**
8.4	0.09	na	0.05	**5.3**	7.3	1.02	10.05	3.38	63.6	**4.0**	1.7	4.7	**7.5**
8.1	0.32	1.5	0.05	**6.4**	14.3	1.28	10.93	3.20	55.3	**3.8**	8.0	9.6	**9.8**
5.8	4.69	na	0.00	**3.8**	0.1	2.32	16.01	2.97	54.9	**1.4**	41.8	29.8	**4.5**
9.1	0.00	0.2	0.02	**4.1**	0.7	0.89	8.90	3.10	64.9	**4.5**	26.6	7.2	**5.8**
2.9	1.43	na	0.00	**9.2**	0.7	1.89	12.35	4.68	54.0	**1.4**	14.2	13.3	**9.5**
4.5	0.52	6.5	0.00	**4.2**	0.1	1.35	11.40	3.55	65.6	**2.7**	41.1	19.4	**5.2**
4.1	1.33	na	0.26	**6.5**	8.6	1.13	11.48	3.55	61.8	**3.0**	8.0	13.3	**8.5**
10.0	na	na	na	**0.9**	0.0	0.51	0.56	0.68	98.0	**4.0**	na	0.0	**6.4**
6.2	3.30	na	0.00	**3.3**	0.2	0.56	3.65	3.36	78.5	**4.2**	42.6	14.6	**7.7**
5.7	0.87	na	-0.02	**2.6**	0.0	0.07	0.70	3.65	87.7	**4.3**	23.8	7.6	**5.1**
9.0	0.00	na	0.00	**0.0**	-0.2	-0.99	-8.17	2.76	127.1	**5.7**	34.5	2.1	**6.6**
8.5	1.19	3.3	0.02	**3.7**	-10.4	-6.23	-26.64	2.73	71.4	**2.3**	40.2	30.9	**9.8**
7.7	0.55	4.2	0.00	**3.4**	5.2	0.57	5.84	3.11	75.5	**2.4**	9.4	16.7	**7.5**
4.3	0.68	5.3	0.00	**5.4**	1.1	0.96	10.21	4.06	68.8	**1.4**	19.6	27.5	**6.0**
10.0	na	na	na	**9.5**	11.2	22.57	39.26	2.53	80.8	**9.3**	155.9	0.0	**6.7**
9.5	0.00	na	0.00	**6.4**	0.5	2.37	17.88	2.32	41.6	**6.8**	70.1	4.7	**7.4**
7.1	0.40	4.0	0.07	**6.1**	2.8	0.81	9.54	5.16	74.0	**1.8**	17.2	15.6	**7.6**
6.2	1.05	3.4	0.23	**4.2**	4.7	0.58	4.94	3.83	74.4	**5.5**	22.1	1.1	**9.2**
3.9	1.95	na	1.26	**5.3**	0.9	0.87	7.38	5.20	58.0	**0.7**	18.5	52.4	**5.9**
2.5	0.62	9.1	5.18	**3.7**	-838.4	-2.76	-19.17	11.14	47.2	**0.6**	20.9	77.6	**7.6**
4.7	0.92	3.7	1.16	**2.6**	-434.8	-0.53	-4.01	3.73	68.3	**6.0**	45.2	6.4	**7.3**
7.5	0.03	na	-0.01	**5.5**	1.0	0.97	7.86	3.28	62.7	**1.6**	15.3	20.4	**8.1**
9.8	0.12	0.8	0.02	**3.2**	4.2	0.18	1.46	2.18	49.5	**1.4**	6.6	24.7	**9.8**
3.1	3.70	11.1	-0.40	**3.1**	0.1	0.18	1.41	4.24	84.5	**4.6**	24.5	5.6	**7.4**
4.8	2.48	na	0.11	**4.2**	0.3	0.78	7.05	4.57	75.2	**1.9**	13.6	19.6	**6.0**

Name	City	State	Rating	2019 Rating	2018 Rating	Total Assets ($Mil)	One Year Asset Growth	Asset Mix (As a % of Total Assets) Comm-ercial Loans	Cons-umer Loans	Mort-gage Loans	Secur-ities	Capital-ization Index	Lever-age Ratio	Risk-Based Capital Ratio
CapStar Bank	Nashville	TN	**B+**	B+	B-	2071.4	1.81	21.6	1.3	8.7	10.8	**7.6**	10.6	13.0
Captex Bank, N.A.	Trenton	TX	**D**	D	D	190.5	6.26	4.9	9.8	11.9	13.2	**10.0**	11.8	15.2
Carmine State Bank	Carmine	TX	**B**	B	B	84.4	6.55	2.1	6.6	11.7	34.8	**9.8**	12.7	0.0
Carolina Bank & Trust Co.	Florence	SC	**A-**	A-	B+	510.8	8.11	8.9	1.4	18.0	12.7	**10.0**	12.9	20.7
Carroll Bank and Trust	Huntingdon	TN	**B**	B	B-	309.4	7.99	6.4	5.4	28.8	11.6	**8.1**	9.9	0.0
Carroll Community Bank	Eldersburg	MD	**C-**	C-	C-	186.5	-3.76	2.7	0.1	23.6	7.6	**7.9**	9.6	13.5
Carroll County Trust Co.	Carrollton	MO	**C**	C	C	159.6	0.90	3.5	1.9	5.5	42.9	**6.2**	10.7	11.9
Carrollton Bank	Carrollton	IL	**B-**	B-	B-	2064.6	19.39	24.3	0.4	13.7	10.3	**5.4**	8.0	11.3
Carrollton Federal Bank	Carrollton	KY	**C+**	C+	C+	33.5	5.19	0.2	3.5	47.9	6.0	**9.8**	16.3	0.0
Carson Bank	Mulvane	KS	**C+**	C+	C+	123.3	3.57	8.9	1.6	16.7	16.4	**6.0**	8.0	12.5
Carson Community Bank	Stilwell	OK	**B+**	B+	B+	127.8	160.80	13.4	4.0	7.7	21.8	**9.8**	12.3	0.0
Carter Bank & Trust	Martinsville	VA	**C**	C	D+	4001.9	-2.35	6.6	1.8	13.4	18.2	**9.2**	10.5	14.3
Carthage Federal S&L Assn.	Carthage	NY	**B**	B	B	251.0	7.59	0.0	2.4	55.7	11.5	**10.0**	11.8	27.8
Carver Federal Savings Bank	New York	NY	**D**	D	D	581.7	2.80	1.8	0.6	20.4	13.1	**10.0**	11.3	16.5
Carver State Bank	Savannah	GA	**C**	C	C-	46.1	8.02	16.1	4.5	22.5	6.6	**9.1**	10.5	0.0
▲ Casey County Bank, Inc.	Liberty	KY	**A-**	B+	B-	216.2	11.75	5.3	5.9	22.1	18.2	**10.0**	12.1	19.1
Casey State Bank	Casey	IL	**B-**	B-	B	333.7	6.69	17.8	6.3	9.6	16.9	**9.1**	10.6	14.3
Cashmere Valley Bank	Cashmere	WA	**A**	A	A-	1677.2	8.62	4.0	12.5	7.2	39.4	**9.8**	11.3	0.0
Cass Commercial Bank	Saint Louis	MO	**A**	A	B+	926.5	11.31	35.0	0.0	0.0	0.0	**10.0**	17.0	18.7
Castle Rock Bank	Castle Rock	MN	**A-**	A-	B+	202.0	2.73	11.1	4.0	12.0	45.6	**10.0**	15.6	29.8
Castroville State Bank	Castroville	TX	**B**	B	B-	184.4	11.39	4.7	4.8	28.2	24.4	**7.0**	9.2	0.0
Cathay Bank	Los Angeles	CA	**A-**	A-	A-	18264.9	6.86	15.0	0.0	27.8	7.4	**8.6**	11.3	13.9
Catlin Bank	Catlin	IL	**B-**	B-	C+	62.2	6.89	8.7	1.7	30.5	17.6	**9.3**	10.5	19.4
Catskill Hudson Bank	Kingston	NY	**C**	C	C	512.1	7.71	6.0	0.2	6.7	19.1	**5.6**	7.6	12.0
Cattaraugus County Bank	Little Valley	NY	**B-**	B-	C+	257.1	1.96	10.4	1.0	16.6	11.7	**6.9**	8.9	12.6
Cattle Bank & Trust	Seward	NE	**A-**	A-	B+	290.9	4.95	4.3	0.8	19.6	19.6	**9.8**	12.8	0.0
Cayuga Lake National Bank	Union Springs	NY	**B-**	B-	B	157.2	3.30	7.1	2.9	33.6	36.9	**7.0**	9.0	19.7
CB&S Bank, Inc.	Russellville	AL	**B**	B	B	1938.0	16.01	6.0	1.5	9.9	40.1	**9.8**	11.0	0.0
▼ CBank	Cincinnati	OH	**B-**	B	B-	206.0	5.43	18.1	1.4	9.9	4.4	**9.2**	11.5	14.3
▲ CBBC Bank	Maryville	TN	**B+**	B	B	360.5	1.13	3.3	0.5	7.4	28.8	**10.0**	16.5	24.2
CBC Bank	Bowling Green	MO	**C**	C	C-	38.2	3.40	3.5	1.6	8.2	39.3	**6.8**	8.8	30.6
CBI Bank & Trust	Muscatine	IA	**B+**	B+	B-	539.3	0.20	11.1	1.6	13.8	19.0	**8.9**	10.5	14.1
CBW Bank	Weir	KS	**A**	A	A-	102.6	80.50	1.8	1.8	0.5	4.5	**10.0**	18.2	245.8
CCB Community Bank	Andalusia	AL	**A-**	A-	A-	532.6	4.11	7.2	1.2	15.5	5.5	**9.8**	11.1	0.0
Cecil Bank	Elkton	MD	**E-**	E-	E-	184.8	-4.25	12.4	0.1	12.7	17.1	**3.8**	5.8	13.3
Cecilian Bank	Cecilia	KY	**B+**	B+	B-	1081.9	19.76	5.4	4.2	20.3	21.9	**8.4**	10.1	0.0
Cedar Hill National Bank	Charlotte	NC	**U**	U	U	13.1	5.57	0.0	0.0	0.0	82.8	**10.0**	83.9	137.1
Cedar Rapids Bank and Trust Co.	Cedar Rapids	IA	**B+**	B+	B+	1723.1	18.90	22.8	0.5	5.3	12.6	**6.6**	10.5	12.2
Cedar Rapids State Bank	Cedar Rapids	NE	**C-**	C-	C-	53.0	7.73	12.2	2.4	17.9	5.3	**6.2**	8.8	11.9
Cedar Security Bank	Fordyce	NE	**B-**	B-	C+	48.3	2.57	9.0	2.4	11.4	3.7	**9.8**	15.5	0.0
Cedar Valley Bank & Trust	La Porte City	IA	**C+**	C+	C	71.6	2.87	7.1	4.8	25.9	16.2	**6.9**	8.9	12.6
CedarStone Bank	Lebanon	TN	**B**	B	B	220.8	7.91	6.3	2.7	28.9	18.7	**8.6**	10.1	15.5
Celtic Bank	Salt Lake City	UT	**B+**	B+	B-	1189.4	39.99	32.1	2.4	0.4	0.5	**9.8**	19.5	0.0
CenBank	Buffalo Lake	MN	**B**	B	B-	65.7	-4.94	7.8	6.1	1.9	19.4	**5.2**	8.1	11.1
Cendera Bank, N.A.	Bells	TX	**B+**	B+	B	112.4	13.93	5.9	1.1	36.7	2.4	**10.0**	11.7	17.8
Cenlar FSB	Ewing	NJ	**A-**	A-	A-	1157.3	2.35	0.0	0.0	39.8	48.2	**7.1**	9.1	23.8
Centennial Bank	Conway	AR	**A-**	A-	B+	15500.3	2.18	11.4	5.5	9.9	13.5	**9.6**	12.0	14.7
Centennial Bank	Trezevant	TN	**B-**	B-	C+	589.7	27.55	10.6	4.9	16.0	8.2	**8.9**	10.5	14.1
Centennial Bank	Lubbock	TX	**B**	B	B+	794.6	-0.26	6.5	0.9	13.3	11.5	**9.8**	10.9	15.2
Center National Bank	Litchfield	MN	**A-**	A-	A-	187.3	-3.47	9.1	6.0	7.7	33.5	**10.0**	12.0	17.1
Center Point Bank and Trust Co.	Center Point	IA	**B**	B	B-	34.2	-2.44	4.8	3.2	25.0	25.3	**6.0**	8.0	12.4
Centera Bank	Sublette	KS	**B-**	B-	B	273.8	-4.17	4.5	1.0	6.1	49.4	**6.9**	8.9	17.6
CenterBank	Milford	OH	**B**	B	B-	237.1	26.18	19.9	0.1	20.0	5.1	**7.2**	9.8	12.7
CenterState Bank, N.A.	Winter Haven	FL	**B+**	B+	B+	18590.8	47.75	6.5	1.3	11.1	12.6	**6.0**	10.2	11.8
▲ Centier Bank	Merrillville	IN	**A-**	B+	B+	4902.3	8.75	5.1	7.5	12.1	9.2	**7.3**	10.5	12.8
Centinel Bank of Taos	Taos	NM	**A-**	A-	B+	290.7	14.04	2.8	1.0	16.0	50.2	**7.0**	9.0	24.2
Central Bank	Little Rock	AR	**B**	B	B+	273.0	23.50	8.6	0.2	19.9	16.4	**7.4**	9.7	12.9
Central Bank	Tampa	FL	**C+**	C+	B-	201.1	15.05	8.4	0.1	21.9	3.9	**6.1**	8.9	11.8
Central Bank	Storm Lake	IA	**B**	B	C+	1282.7	49.13	16.3	2.8	10.8	4.5	**9.8**	11.4	0.0
Central Bank	Savannah	TN	**B**	B	C+	101.0	5.28	4.0	4.6	42.1	12.2	**10.0**	12.0	22.2

Asset Quality Index	Adjusted Non-Performing Loans as a % of Total Loans	Adjusted Non-Performing Loans as a % of Capital	Net Charge-Offs Avg Loans	Profitability Index	Net Income ($Mil)	Return on Assets (R.O.A.)	Return on Equity (R.O.E.)	Net Interest Spread	Overhead Efficiency Ratio	Liquidity Index	Liquidity Ratio	Hot Money Ratio	Stability Index
7.7	0.32	na	0.01	**3.3**	1.5	0.29	2.29	3.49	62.2	**2.6**	13.7	12.7	**8.8**
7.4	0.36	na	0.01	**0.0**	-0.5	-0.94	-6.89	3.93	125.4	**2.8**	19.1	15.5	**6.1**
9.4	0.00	na	-0.21	**3.9**	0.2	0.94	7.45	2.76	61.8	**3.2**	82.6	43.3	**7.1**
6.3	1.42	na	0.06	**6.3**	1.5	1.20	9.33	3.83	59.0	**4.2**	20.5	7.8	**7.6**
5.2	1.33	na	0.10	**4.3**	0.5	0.68	6.72	4.18	78.2	**1.5**	11.5	23.0	**6.0**
5.7	0.47	na	0.04	**1.2**	-0.1	-0.13	-1.40	3.30	104.3	**1.0**	10.0	29.3	**5.3**
4.3	2.34	na	4.43	**2.8**	0.2	0.50	4.59	2.91	78.6	**3.2**	36.5	13.4	**6.0**
8.4	0.10	0.8	0.01	**4.9**	6.5	1.27	15.88	3.06	64.3	**3.0**	21.5	15.8	**7.9**
5.0	4.94	na	-0.05	**3.1**	0.1	0.59	3.67	4.11	80.5	**3.0**	20.6	14.5	**6.7**
8.6	0.05	0.4	0.00	**3.9**	0.3	0.92	11.05	4.00	80.0	**1.8**	16.6	20.5	**4.8**
5.5	0.32	na	0.49	**7.7**	0.3	0.99	7.58	5.53	62.8	**1.7**	16.9	21.7	**8.0**
4.8	1.36	7.8	0.08	**2.4**	4.4	0.44	3.73	2.98	74.8	**1.9**	19.0	21.7	**8.0**
9.5	0.45	na	0.00	**3.8**	0.4	0.63	5.52	2.59	70.5	**1.2**	22.2	31.9	**6.8**
4.0	2.10	11.8	-0.33	**0.2**	-1.6	-1.12	-9.77	3.26	131.9	**0.9**	20.5	27.6	**5.4**
4.2	2.64	na	-0.33	**2.6**	0.0	0.05	0.44	4.73	99.0	**1.3**	31.0	22.8	**4.1**
6.1	1.66	na	-0.03	**6.2**	0.6	1.21	9.97	4.09	61.3	**3.1**	20.9	13.9	**7.3**
2.6	2.62	18.3	0.03	**5.7**	1.3	1.51	14.49	3.83	55.6	**1.6**	15.2	22.7	**7.0**
7.3	1.44	na	0.13	**6.3**	5.5	1.33	10.57	3.09	57.8	**5.8**	45.5	10.0	**10.0**
7.1	0.00	na	0.00	**9.5**	3.7	1.69	10.22	3.63	44.1	**1.4**	18.5	8.7	**10.0**
7.7	1.38	na	-0.13	**5.1**	0.6	1.21	7.77	2.91	49.3	**3.5**	52.0	20.7	**8.1**
6.8	0.37	na	0.06	**5.3**	0.5	1.11	12.18	3.48	59.8	**1.5**	17.1	25.3	**5.6**
7.1	0.57	2.9	0.00	**7.1**	51.7	1.15	8.69	3.35	43.5	**0.7**	11.5	36.1	**10.0**
7.8	0.70	na	0.00	**5.0**	0.2	1.18	11.35	4.03	66.5	**2.7**	20.1	16.1	**5.2**
5.6	0.68	na	-0.01	**2.9**	0.8	0.60	7.89	2.90	86.3	**2.0**	14.6	19.1	**4.2**
5.0	1.64	na	0.05	**3.5**	0.3	0.41	4.56	3.94	85.3	**4.3**	10.6	6.1	**5.7**
6.0	1.05	na	0.00	**5.8**	1.0	1.35	10.53	3.46	61.3	**1.6**	17.0	23.7	**8.8**
9.4	0.08	na	0.01	**3.8**	0.3	0.65	7.20	3.21	78.4	**3.0**	27.8	15.9	**5.0**
5.6	2.14	na	-0.02	**4.5**	4.6	0.95	7.61	3.66	70.9	**4.7**	35.1	12.6	**8.9**
8.2	0.00	na	0.04	**3.7**	0.4	0.85	6.99	3.48	74.7	**0.9**	17.7	34.5	**7.1**
7.9	0.57	na	0.47	**6.4**	2.7	2.95	18.21	3.49	39.7	**2.9**	38.7	19.9	**8.3**
9.9	0.00	na	0.09	**2.5**	0.1	0.51	5.40	2.36	97.1	**7.0**	64.1	1.8	**3.9**
5.9	0.64	na	0.03	**5.2**	1.4	1.07	9.78	3.43	66.6	**2.1**	22.6	19.2	**8.0**
7.4	27.84	na	0.00	**9.5**	0.5	2.28	12.50	1.88	74.7	**8.6**	110.9	0.5	**8.9**
6.3	0.48	na	0.07	**7.0**	1.9	1.52	13.54	4.32	60.8	**1.5**	17.3	23.5	**8.2**
5.9	1.85	7.3	0.00	**0.0**	-0.5	-1.05	-17.37	2.42	165.8	**4.1**	42.7	14.8	**0.3**
7.7	0.48	na	-0.07	**5.6**	2.9	1.07	10.44	3.67	67.0	**2.3**	14.5	17.8	**8.7**
10.0	na	na	na	**9.5**	0.1	3.03	3.62	3.07	79.1	**10.0**	444.7	0.0	**7.0**
7.7	0.37	2.8	0.00	**8.4**	6.5	1.60	14.06	3.17	47.3	**2.4**	27.5	14.1	**8.7**
8.1	0.00	na	0.24	**3.9**	0.1	0.91	10.40	3.53	73.3	**0.6**	7.3	33.4	**4.4**
5.5	1.09	na	-0.04	**5.9**	0.1	1.01	6.58	4.14	68.2	**3.6**	38.5	15.9	**6.7**
7.8	0.05	na	0.09	**5.6**	0.4	2.06	23.65	4.22	61.2	**3.8**	1.3	7.9	**5.0**
8.0	0.23	na	-0.02	**4.2**	0.5	0.83	8.27	3.45	68.5	**1.2**	19.4	29.6	**6.4**
5.1	1.46	na	0.61	**10.0**	8.1	3.18	16.37	6.50	45.9	**1.9**	33.7	0.8	**9.0**
7.2	0.61	na	0.00	**4.3**	0.2	1.10	13.45	4.01	71.9	**3.2**	7.8	12.2	**5.4**
6.7	1.95	na	0.17	**3.9**	0.2	0.56	4.71	4.69	83.2	**0.8**	17.5	30.1	**7.0**
10.0	0.43	1.5	0.00	**8.6**	9.5	3.09	35.19	2.54	92.1	**7.6**	52.8	0.0	**9.0**
6.0	0.56	2.2	0.13	**7.0**	11.6	0.31	1.72	4.56	42.9	**2.1**	13.5	13.0	**10.0**
4.2	1.17	na	0.76	**5.3**	1.1	0.73	6.10	4.53	66.0	**1.6**	20.6	20.8	**6.7**
3.9	0.75	na	0.17	**4.5**	1.6	0.82	7.60	4.12	70.0	**2.9**	9.3	14.2	**8.1**
8.3	0.04	na	0.02	**5.8**	0.7	1.36	11.22	3.82	66.3	**3.1**	11.6	13.2	**8.1**
8.1	0.00	na	0.00	**4.1**	0.1	0.89	11.11	3.33	72.3	**3.5**	35.7	16.0	**4.8**
7.4	0.55	na	0.01	**4.5**	0.8	1.18	11.73	3.25	66.1	**2.3**	30.5	21.2	**5.8**
7.2	0.01	na	0.00	**6.8**	0.7	1.25	12.89	3.99	62.5	**0.7**	10.2	29.3	**6.5**
5.9	0.68	2.3	0.05	**6.0**	36.8	0.85	4.96	4.10	57.7	**2.7**	17.8	8.9	**10.0**
7.2	0.32	2.3	0.08	**7.6**	17.0	1.45	13.71	3.56	54.7	**3.6**	10.4	9.4	**9.3**
8.7	0.27	na	-0.01	**8.4**	1.5	2.06	21.42	3.52	46.1	**5.8**	54.3	9.5	**7.2**
7.5	1.28	na	-0.08	**4.7**	0.8	1.26	12.67	3.09	47.8	**0.8**	24.8	59.1	**6.2**
4.8	0.36	na	0.00	**2.2**	0.1	0.20	2.13	3.42	87.2	**0.7**	13.9	44.0	**5.3**
5.5	0.07	na	0.00	**5.2**	1.9	0.73	6.77	3.74	71.6	**1.7**	10.9	20.9	**7.8**
7.2	4.45	na	-0.10	**3.4**	0.1	0.46	3.63	4.38	88.3	**2.1**	22.5	19.5	**7.3**

Name	City	State	Rating	2019 Rating	2018 Rating	Total Assets ($Mil)	One Year Asset Growth	Asset Mix (As a % of Total Assets) Comm-ercial Loans	Cons-umer Loans	Mort-gage Loans	Secur-ities	Capital-ization Index	Lever-age Ratio	Risk-Based Capital Ratio
Central Bank	Houston	TX	**B+**	B+	B+	803.5	6.71	11.9	0.3	29.2	14.7	**8.0**	9.6	13.7
Central Bank	Provo	UT	**A**	A	B+	1245.8	12.72	5.0	1.1	4.8	26.8	**9.8**	16.7	0.0
Central Bank & Trust Co.	Lexington	KY	**A-**	A-	B	2733.5	4.90	9.0	4.0	15.9	16.6	**10.0**	11.7	15.2
Central Bank and Trust	Lander	WY	**B**	B	B-	155.1	2.26	10.1	1.8	17.4	30.1	**8.2**	9.8	17.9
Central Bank Illinois	Geneseo	IL	**B+**	B+	B	909.5	2.05	6.0	0.7	7.9	33.0	**8.8**	10.4	0.0
Central Bank of Audrain County	Mexico	MO	**B**	B	B	193.3	10.83	5.2	3.4	10.4	38.1	**5.0**	7.0	14.2
Central Bank of Boone County	Columbia	MO	**B+**	B+	B+	2004.0	0.53	6.9	5.4	11.7	25.2	**6.7**	8.7	13.0
Central Bank of Branson	Branson	MO	**B+**	B+	B	343.4	2.49	8.4	6.2	16.4	27.2	**8.7**	10.1	15.1
Central Bank of Kansas City	Kansas City	MO	**A**	A	A	231.2	40.54	28.5	0.0	0.9	0.0	**10.0**	14.6	16.4
Central Bank of Lake of the Ozarks	Osage Beach	MO	**B+**	B+	B+	774.0	1.66	4.6	5.0	18.0	34.4	**6.8**	8.8	14.6
Central Bank of Moberly	Moberly	MO	**B**	B	B	201.9	0.34	4.8	11.8	6.1	38.3	**6.4**	8.4	14.6
Central Bank of Oklahoma	Tulsa	OK	**B**	B	B	704.9	1.96	10.1	0.3	13.5	4.6	**7.9**	12.0	13.2
Central Bank of Sedalia	Sedalia	MO	**B+**	B+	B+	423.6	3.51	7.4	16.0	7.7	24.6	**6.4**	8.4	12.7
Central Bank of St. Louis	Clayton	MO	**B+**	B+	B+	2067.3	1.26	12.2	0.8	10.0	13.8	**6.8**	10.0	12.4
Central Bank of the Midwest	Lee's Summit	MO	**B+**	B+	B+	2506.9	39.22	10.8	7.2	4.7	15.7	**6.1**	9.1	11.8
Central Bank of the Ozarks	Springfield	MO	**B+**	B+	B+	1493.1	5.44	9.1	11.2	11.2	18.3	**6.9**	9.4	12.5
Central Bank of Warrensburg	Warrensburg	MO	**B**	B	B	257.4	1.06	4.1	2.0	8.4	30.4	**8.3**	9.9	18.8
Central Federal S&L Assn.	Cicero	IL	**C-**	C-	C	190.2	6.53	0.0	0.0	56.9	10.8	**8.4**	10.1	0.0
Central National Bank	Junction City	KS	**B**	B	B	974.7	1.94	6.3	1.9	5.7	29.1	**9.8**	11.4	0.0
Central National Bank	Waco	TX	**A-**	A-	B+	962.5	5.64	15.0	0.9	30.9	6.6	**7.6**	9.4	13.4
Central National Bank of Poteau	Poteau	OK	**B+**	B+	B+	258.6	4.22	11.8	3.1	14.4	33.8	**9.2**	10.6	0.0
Central Pacific Bank	Honolulu	HI	**A-**	A-	A-	6102.9	4.63	9.0	9.2	26.8	19.4	**7.5**	9.3	13.2
▼ Central Savings Bank	Sault Sainte Marie	MI	**C+**	B-	B-	264.4	5.43	8.3	5.8	20.2	25.9	**9.8**	12.7	0.0
▼ Central Savings, F.S.B.	Chicago	IL	**B-**	B	B-	110.7	1.14	0.0	0.0	30.6	3.2	**10.0**	24.5	33.4
Central State Bank	Calera	AL	**A-**	A-	A-	339.0	5.28	6.0	2.3	17.0	15.7	**9.8**	11.1	0.0
Central State Bank	Elkader	IA	**B**	B	B	340.7	7.91	11.4	1.9	17.0	14.2	**6.4**	8.7	12.0
▲ Central State Bank	State Center	IA	**C+**	C	C+	318.3	3.12	14.7	1.2	3.4	27.7	**7.9**	12.5	13.2
▼ Central State Bank	Clayton	IL	**C-**	C	C+	152.2	8.23	9.7	7.3	24.6	2.1	**9.8**	15.4	0.0
Central Trust Bank	Jefferson City	MO	**B+**	B+	B+	2925.2	14.56	5.8	6.7	8.0	49.8	**5.3**	7.3	14.0
Central Valley Community Bank	Fresno	CA	**A**	A	A	1618.5	3.48	6.2	2.6	2.2	32.3	**9.8**	10.9	15.2
CentreBank	Veedersburg	IN	**A-**	A-	A-	77.7	-1.46	13.8	3.2	23.7	0.3	**9.8**	13.8	0.0
Centreville Bank	West Warwick	RI	**C+**	C+	D+	1327.4	6.78	0.5	0.1	30.6	21.0	**9.8**	21.7	0.0
Centric Bank	Harrisburg	PA	**B+**	B+	B+	842.0	14.88	22.9	0.1	9.0	3.9	**8.7**	11.5	13.9
CenTrust Bank, N.A.	Northbrook	IL	**C+**	C+	C-	142.2	9.64	27.1	0.1	7.3	9.6	**7.5**	9.7	12.9
▲ Century Bank	Lucedale	MS	**B**	B-	B-	348.4	7.85	6.3	10.8	12.6	22.1	**9.4**	10.8	0.0
Century Bank	Santa Fe	NM	**B+**	B+	B	915.6	4.33	17.3	2.1	4.1	25.6	**7.6**	9.9	13.0
Century Bank and Trust	Milledgeville	GA	**B-**	B-	B-	273.9	5.13	4.0	1.1	11.3	23.3	**9.8**	11.8	0.0
▲ Century Bank and Trust	Coldwater	MI	**B+**	B	B	323.9	1.58	8.6	2.2	16.3	18.7	**10.0**	13.0	17.3
Century Bank and Trust Co.	Medford	MA	**C+**	C+	C+	5545.9	4.86	5.0	0.1	7.6	47.7	**5.0**	7.0	13.6
Century Bank of Florida	Tampa	FL	**C+**	C+	C	86.4	1.34	11.0	2.0	23.6	11.0	**6.9**	8.9	14.1
Century Bank of Georgia	Cartersville	GA	**A-**	A-	A-	212.6	9.15	6.8	1.5	11.6	18.5	**8.8**	10.2	19.3
▲ Century Bank of Kentucky, Inc.	Lawrenceburg	KY	**B-**	C+	C	142.6	-0.37	2.9	1.3	36.5	11.6	**9.8**	11.1	0.0
Century Bank of the Ozarks	Gainesville	MO	**A-**	A-	B	184.7	1.89	8.8	2.9	17.5	2.1	**7.7**	9.7	0.0
▼ Century Next Bank	Ruston	LA	**B-**	B	B	494.0	4.01	11.1	3.4	28.4	0.1	**9.3**	10.7	0.0
▼ Century S&L Assn.	Trinidad	CO	**C**	C+	C	94.2	1.32	0.0	0.4	17.6	56.2	**9.8**	15.3	0.0
▼ Century Savings Bank	Vineland	NJ	**C**	C+	C+	451.2	3.77	0.9	0.0	21.6	36.1	**9.8**	15.0	0.0
CerescoBank	Ceresco	NE	**B**	B	B	50.3	1.28	11.2	5.0	14.4	10.3	**9.8**	16.7	0.0
CFBank, N.A.	Worthington	OH	**B**	B	C+	942.9	31.03	19.3	0.0	24.3	1.2	**7.9**	10.7	13.2
▲ CFG Community Bank	Baltimore	MD	**B-**	C+	C-	1289.7	39.33	25.8	0.1	1.5	3.2	**9.2**	13.2	14.4
cfsbank	Charleroi	PA	**C+**	C+	C	476.4	-3.35	1.0	1.2	51.6	20.1	**10.0**	16.0	31.5
Chain Bridge Bank, N.A.	McLean	VA	**C+**	C+	C+	930.4	51.30	1.4	0.4	18.7	65.7	**5.1**	7.1	22.3
Chambers Bank	Danville	AR	**B-**	B-	C+	989.2	17.18	8.9	0.7	16.6	3.6	**6.0**	9.5	11.8
Chambers State Bank	Chambers	NE	**B+**	B+	B+	64.8	7.96	10.2	3.8	2.0	0.3	**9.8**	29.2	0.0
Champion Bank	Parker	CO	**A-**	A-	B-	64.0	-5.88	0.0	0.0	6.9	0.0	**10.0**	23.1	69.5
Champlain National Bank	Willsboro	NY	**B-**	B-	C+	372.1	2.51	6.7	9.1	19.3	21.2	**7.4**	9.2	14.5
Chappell Hill Bank	Chappell Hill	TX	**C+**	C+	C	36.2	11.64	5.2	2.5	25.6	3.0	**8.0**	9.7	16.6
▼ Charis Bank	Justin	TX	**C**	C+	B	130.2	34.18	27.1	0.9	10.9	0.0	**10.0**	24.3	34.8
Charles River Bank	Medway	MA	**C-**	C-	C-	249.2	1.75	3.5	2.7	37.9	16.1	**6.1**	8.1	13.8
Charles Schwab Bank, SSB	Westlake	TX	**B+**	B+	B+	270245.0	21.67	0.4	1.3	4.9	71.8	**4.9**	6.9	19.8
Charles Schwab Premier Bank, SSB	Westlake	TX	**U**	U	U	22375.0	55.08	0.0	0.0	0.0	86.3	**4.6**	6.6	25.5

Arrows denote recent upgrades ▲ or downgrades ▼

Asset Quality Index	Adjusted Non-Performing Loans as a % of Total Loans	Adjusted Non-Performing Loans as a % of Capital	Net Charge-Offs Avg Loans	Profitability Index	Net Income ($Mil)	Return on Assets (R.O.A.)	Return on Equity (R.O.E.)	Net Interest Spread	Overhead Efficiency Ratio	Liquidity Index	Liquidity Ratio	Hot Money Ratio	Stability Index
7.7	0.36	2.7	-0.11	**5.5**	2.4	1.22	12.16	5.20	74.2	**0.9**	11.4	28.8	**7.4**
7.7	0.08	na	0.01	**10.0**	5.8	1.94	11.63	4.87	53.5	**4.7**	34.7	12.8	**10.0**
7.6	0.69	3.4	0.07	**4.8**	6.0	0.88	7.48	3.72	77.9	**2.6**	17.5	16.5	**9.4**
8.1	0.14	na	-0.23	**7.3**	0.7	1.91	19.16	4.18	57.0	**4.4**	15.6	6.1	**6.7**
5.6	0.81	na	0.00	**7.7**	3.8	1.66	14.30	3.82	52.4	**4.4**	25.8	7.7	**8.5**
6.0	0.68	3.5	0.01	**6.6**	0.6	1.27	17.14	2.84	50.9	**4.9**	24.0	3.6	**6.3**
8.2	0.25	1.0	0.16	**8.1**	7.5	1.46	15.69	3.15	53.5	**4.9**	22.2	5.7	**8.0**
3.8	2.29	12.0	-0.19	**7.6**	1.2	1.36	13.31	3.68	61.2	**3.8**	11.3	8.3	**7.4**
6.8	0.00	0.0	-0.03	**9.8**	2.6	4.38	29.41	4.41	55.9	**0.9**	10.3	11.5	**9.5**
6.4	0.65	3.0	0.03	**9.5**	3.4	1.72	18.70	3.70	54.6	**3.4**	17.8	12.1	**7.6**
7.8	0.13	0.7	-0.34	**5.8**	0.6	1.26	14.79	2.97	57.1	**4.8**	18.6	3.3	**6.6**
3.3	0.68	2.5	0.00	**8.0**	2.5	1.40	7.33	3.89	50.0	**1.0**	7.7	21.0	**8.6**
5.5	0.28	1.9	0.22	**9.6**	1.9	1.73	19.09	3.77	50.1	**3.7**	14.2	9.5	**7.8**
6.5	0.63	3.8	0.02	**7.9**	8.0	1.56	13.85	3.49	53.4	**3.9**	7.6	7.3	**8.6**
4.5	1.05	3.4	0.37	**6.8**	7.7	1.26	8.66	4.01	58.5	**4.9**	16.4	3.4	**8.4**
7.7	0.04	0.3	0.12	**6.8**	4.5	1.26	13.07	3.51	62.1	**4.5**	19.2	6.3	**7.7**
2.7	2.59	8.3	0.02	**5.6**	0.7	1.12	7.82	3.14	61.7	**4.1**	27.7	9.6	**8.4**
6.9	3.61	na	0.00	**2.0**	0.1	0.27	2.70	2.69	91.5	**2.5**	35.1	23.1	**5.4**
7.5	1.16	2.7	-0.08	**5.3**	3.6	1.46	12.80	3.56	67.0	**4.2**	19.2	8.1	**8.0**
8.7	0.00	na	0.01	**8.5**	4.5	1.92	20.45	3.80	48.2	**1.6**	17.7	17.0	**8.3**
5.8	0.86	na	0.18	**7.8**	1.1	1.68	15.78	4.15	60.1	**2.8**	22.1	15.5	**8.1**
8.1	0.21	1.3	0.11	**4.2**	8.2	0.55	5.75	3.45	64.7	**2.6**	11.9	16.2	**8.6**
2.4	4.99	na	-0.02	**5.2**	0.6	0.94	7.33	3.81	63.4	**3.4**	34.1	16.0	**7.4**
5.0	1.63	na	-0.01	**3.2**	0.1	0.40	1.59	3.53	84.1	**0.6**	16.7	37.5	**7.8**
8.8	0.13	na	0.08	**7.1**	1.3	1.55	13.75	4.17	60.7	**1.4**	19.9	27.7	**7.9**
6.9	0.10	0.7	0.01	**4.6**	1.0	1.15	11.36	3.55	58.7	**1.6**	19.3	13.1	**6.5**
3.5	3.22	na	0.11	**5.4**	1.1	1.42	11.69	2.62	53.0	**1.4**	33.6	53.6	**8.8**
0.3	7.49	na	0.12	**8.7**	0.6	1.72	11.29	3.45	58.0	**1.3**	19.1	28.5	**9.4**
7.7	0.55	2.6	0.10	**4.7**	8.1	1.19	15.11	2.69	66.3	**4.6**	14.3	4.8	**6.9**
6.5	1.73	3.7	-0.02	**6.5**	6.7	1.68	11.81	4.46	65.1	**6.0**	34.2	4.4	**10.0**
6.1	0.37	na	0.01	**9.1**	0.4	1.84	13.59	4.76	59.0	**3.8**	26.6	11.3	**7.4**
8.8	1.18	3.3	0.00	**2.8**	-22.5	-6.74	-30.22	2.73	76.4	**4.1**	38.6	16.6	**10.0**
4.7	1.13	6.6	0.00	**5.1**	1.8	0.88	7.62	3.80	63.2	**0.9**	13.7	26.9	**7.1**
4.3	1.77	na	0.07	**3.8**	0.2	0.57	4.44	3.96	78.4	**0.6**	16.2	60.2	**6.2**
5.6	1.54	na	0.50	**5.3**	0.9	1.08	10.20	4.19	72.7	**3.6**	23.1	11.6	**6.9**
8.4	0.17	na	0.08	**5.5**	2.6	1.16	10.87	4.70	72.4	**4.2**	26.4	9.6	**7.7**
6.0	2.00	na	0.01	**7.1**	0.9	1.42	12.42	3.89	60.3	**4.0**	30.6	10.8	**7.5**
6.9	1.02	na	0.00	**7.0**	1.2	1.49	11.67	3.88	64.5	**5.0**	22.5	2.7	**7.7**
9.5	0.16	0.7	-0.02	**3.6**	10.0	0.73	11.15	2.13	60.6	**2.9**	7.9	11.2	**4.6**
4.1	0.98	na	-0.12	**3.0**	0.1	0.63	7.07	3.83	89.9	**2.6**	29.5	18.4	**5.0**
8.7	0.42	na	-0.05	**7.1**	0.9	1.66	16.16	3.97	61.6	**5.0**	35.5	8.2	**7.1**
4.3	3.74	na	-0.01	**6.9**	0.6	1.70	15.47	3.76	57.6	**1.7**	16.9	18.5	**8.3**
7.8	0.19	na	-0.01	**9.4**	0.7	1.58	15.85	5.10	58.5	**3.7**	8.2	9.8	**8.1**
3.5	0.86	na	0.02	**5.2**	1.1	0.86	7.63	4.44	69.7	**1.4**	12.8	10.7	**6.5**
7.2	3.07	na	0.00	**2.1**	0.1	0.23	1.50	2.65	88.8	**2.6**	61.1	41.5	**7.1**
5.8	2.24	na	0.21	**2.6**	0.4	0.35	2.44	3.00	88.7	**5.9**	45.3	5.9	**7.1**
7.7	0.24	na	-0.04	**4.8**	0.2	1.26	7.56	3.58	56.3	**3.3**	27.3	14.4	**7.3**
7.3	0.44	na	0.03	**5.4**	2.4	1.08	10.46	2.94	69.3	**0.6**	9.3	28.4	**7.3**
4.6	0.77	na	0.45	**7.4**	4.3	1.37	10.23	3.98	55.0	**1.4**	24.4	36.3	**10.0**
8.3	1.08	na	-0.02	**2.2**	0.6	0.49	3.06	2.71	75.3	**2.4**	30.5	20.1	**7.1**
10.0	0.00	0.0	0.00	**4.0**	2.1	0.92	12.56	2.45	57.4	**7.4**	74.8	3.0	**4.7**
6.1	0.53	na	-0.01	**4.6**	2.0	0.79	7.77	4.00	65.9	**1.0**	12.8	31.5	**7.5**
6.2	0.79	na	0.00	**8.3**	0.3	1.79	6.18	3.92	47.2	**1.1**	27.6	29.5	**8.1**
9.6	0.91	1.2	0.00	**9.4**	0.3	1.72	7.40	2.10	68.9	**3.7**	82.4	28.4	**9.0**
4.9	1.13	na	-0.01	**4.7**	0.9	1.02	11.65	3.86	67.3	**1.3**	11.0	20.4	**5.4**
6.2	0.00	na	1.35	**4.7**	0.1	1.49	15.70	4.18	76.2	**1.9**	30.1	26.5	**5.9**
7.5	0.75	na	0.00	**0.0**	-0.6	-1.84	-6.61	3.42	125.4	**6.0**	43.2	4.7	**6.8**
6.4	0.38	na	0.00	**2.4**	0.3	0.39	4.70	3.19	84.4	**1.9**	23.3	21.4	**4.4**
10.0	0.13	0.1	0.00	**7.1**	687.0	1.24	16.31	2.21	24.1	**7.8**	85.7	0.0	**6.3**
10.0	na	0.0	na	**8.5**	56.0	1.39	18.05	2.33	20.7	**8.2**	76.0	0.0	**8.1**

Name	City	State	Rating	2019 Rating	2018 Rating	Total Assets ($Mil)	One Year Asset Growth	Asset Mix (As a % of Total Assets) Commercial Loans	Consumer Loans	Mortgage Loans	Securities	Capitalization Index	Leverage Ratio	Risk-Based Capital Ratio
Charlevoix State Bank	Charlevoix	MI	**B+**	B+	B	195.8	4.53	6.6	3.0	19.3	18.5	**7.1**	9.3	0.0
Charlotte State Bank & Trust	Port Charlotte	FL	**A-**	A-	A-	407.4	10.52	0.3	0.3	20.0	25.2	**8.7**	10.3	0.0
Charter Bank	Johnston	IA	**B+**	B+	B+	168.8	3.91	7.1	2.4	19.8	31.1	**10.0**	11.6	18.4
▲ Charter Bank	Corpus Christi	TX	**B+**	B	B	283.8	2.28	17.5	0.2	6.1	35.6	**7.8**	9.6	15.6
Charter Bank	Eau Claire	WI	**A**	A	A	947.3	4.45	12.4	0.6	14.0	16.6	**10.0**	12.7	16.8
▲ Charter West Bank	West Point	NE	**B+**	B	B	301.4	14.25	11.5	2.2	13.7	8.5	**8.1**	9.9	0.0
Chasewood Bank	Houston	TX	**C-**	C-	C	91.3	-3.52	5.5	0.2	8.1	22.1	**9.7**	10.8	15.6
Cheaha Bank	Oxford	AL	**A**	A	A	210.9	1.73	7.1	4.0	19.5	31.0	**9.8**	12.5	0.0
▼ Chelsea Groton Bank	Norwich	CT	**B+**	A-	B	1160.9	2.25	5.4	0.5	48.2	12.7	**10.0**	16.3	21.1
Chelsea Savings Bank	Belle Plaine	IA	**A-**	A-	A-	119.0	2.28	12.4	1.5	12.3	46.6	**9.8**	15.4	0.0
▼ Chelsea State Bank	Chelsea	MI	**A-**	A	A-	354.6	13.03	10.2	0.3	4.9	18.2	**9.8**	11.5	0.0
Chemung Canal Trust Co.	Elmira	NY	**B-**	B-	B-	1836.7	4.03	12.1	7.7	14.0	16.3	**7.0**	9.0	13.1
Cherokee State Bank	Cherokee	IA	**B**	B	B+	223.4	-3.59	4.0	0.8	5.7	27.6	**10.0**	12.5	17.3
Chesapeake Bank	Kilmarnock	VA	**B+**	B+	A-	948.4	6.59	12.7	0.9	10.8	32.6	**9.8**	10.9	15.5
Chesapeake Bank & Trust Co.	Chestertown	MD	**B+**	B+	B	98.7	-1.25	3.0	0.9	43.0	12.3	**8.8**	10.4	0.0
Chesapeake Bank of Maryland	Baltimore	MD	**B-**	B-	B-	228.4	5.19	3.1	0.2	32.6	14.3	**10.0**	18.9	28.5
Chester National Bank	Chester	IL	**B-**	B-	B-	60.5	-16.11	2.3	2.5	57.0	12.0	**10.0**	13.1	24.0
▲ Chesterfield State Bank	Chesterfield	IL	**C**	C-	D+	17.2	-2.82	12.1	5.7	29.7	0.0	**10.0**	11.1	21.5
Cheyenne State Bank	Cheyenne	WY	**B-**	B-	C+	39.4	-0.78	3.6	0.7	23.5	3.1	**10.0**	17.1	23.8
Chicago Trust Co., N.A.	Lake Forest	IL	**U**	U	U	112.5	2.50	0.0	0.0	0.0	1.7	**10.0**	99.2	467.4
▼ Chickasaw Community Bank	Oklahoma City	OK	**B-**	B	B+	199.7	9.56	10.2	2.4	29.1	8.4	**8.5**	10.0	15.8
Chillicothe State Bank	Chillicothe	MO	**B**	B	B	123.8	-2.18	3.4	5.0	25.8	27.7	**6.7**	8.7	18.2
▲ Chino Commercial Bank, N.A.	Chino	CA	**A-**	B+	B	233.0	11.24	1.9	0.1	8.7	18.9	**9.6**	10.9	0.0
Chippewa Valley Bank	Hayward	WI	**B-**	B-	B-	476.8	7.50	7.8	0.4	19.0	7.6	**6.2**	8.2	12.5
▲ Chisholm Trail State Bank	Park City	KS	**C**	C-	C	106.4	27.96	5.5	1.8	20.3	15.5	**10.0**	12.3	15.8
Choice Financial Group	Fargo	ND	**B+**	B+	B+	2429.4	13.31	23.1	0.5	6.1	3.6	**7.7**	9.6	0.0
ChoiceOne Bank	Sparta	MI	**B+**	B+	B	696.2	4.45	12.3	3.3	12.0	23.6	**7.6**	9.9	13.0
▼ CIBC Bank USA	Chicago	IL	**B-**	B	B+	35548.5	17.79	25.5	0.6	4.1	13.9	**7.2**	11.2	12.6
CIBC National Trust Co.	Atlanta	GA	**U**	U	U	267.8	8.80	0.0	0.0	0.0	0.0	**10.0**	23.9	114.1
CIBM Bank	Champaign	IL	**C**	C	C+	697.5	0.03	6.5	0.1	27.8	16.9	**9.5**	10.7	14.9
▲ Ciera Bank	Graham	TX	**B**	B-	B	735.7	25.48	10.8	0.6	8.8	7.7	**7.4**	11.0	12.8
Cincinnati Federal	Cincinnati	OH	**C+**	C+	B-	227.6	10.82	0.2	0.3	50.4	2.7	**10.0**	13.6	20.1
▼ Cincinnatus S&L Co.	Cincinnati	OH	**C+**	B-	B-	97.0	4.69	0.6	1.9	42.2	3.3	**9.8**	22.4	0.0
CIT Bank, N.A.	Pasadena	CA	**B+**	B+	B+	52993.2	19.58	23.2	0.1	14.6	11.0	**6.7**	9.0	12.3
Citibank, N.A.	Sioux Falls	SD	**B+**	B+	B	1632405.0	14.14	11.7	10.7	5.1	22.2	**7.1**	9.1	15.2
Citicorp Trust Delaware, N.A.	Greenville	DE	**U**	U	U	23.5	-6.10	0.0	0.0	0.0	0.9	**10.0**	95.6	485.3
Citizens & Northern Bank	Wellsboro	PA	**A-**	A-	A-	1613.4	26.55	8.2	1.0	33.2	20.3	**10.0**	12.4	19.0
Citizens 1st Bank	Tyler	TX	**A+**	A+	A+	706.5	0.25	1.6	0.7	8.5	57.3	**10.0**	20.5	48.8
Citizens Alliance Bank	Clara City	MN	**B-**	B-	B-	861.6	8.69	12.0	1.3	7.4	18.1	**4.7**	8.5	10.8
Citizens and Farmers Bank	Toano	VA	**A-**	A-	A-	1849.1	19.64	4.1	17.4	22.2	12.7	**8.4**	10.0	13.8
Citizens B&T Co. of Grainger County	Rutledge	TN	**A-**	A-	B+	212.0	-0.38	3.1	1.7	11.0	61.4	**9.8**	17.0	0.0
Citizens Bank	Enterprise	AL	**B**	B	C+	148.7	-4.11	10.4	1.1	19.2	10.4	**9.0**	10.5	0.0
Citizens Bank	Greensboro	AL	**A-**	A-	A-	94.5	0.13	5.2	4.9	6.8	43.4	**10.0**	14.5	27.9
Citizens Bank	Batesville	AR	**B-**	B-	B-	921.4	6.92	8.8	2.4	18.2	11.8	**5.0**	8.3	11.0
▼ Citizens Bank	Sac City	IA	**C-**	C	C	54.9	1.95	13.1	2.5	8.6	26.5	**6.8**	8.8	15.6
Citizens Bank	Mooresville	IN	**B**	B	C+	511.7	4.90	2.1	39.7	4.8	20.4	**9.9**	10.9	14.9
Citizens Bank	Hickman	KY	**B**	B	B+	144.3	4.82	6.4	2.7	14.5	19.4	**10.0**	12.8	20.3
Citizens Bank	Morehead	KY	**B-**	B-	B-	149.1	7.08	2.6	4.6	35.2	11.2	**6.2**	8.2	14.1
▲ Citizens Bank	Mount Vernon	KY	**B-**	C+	C-	148.9	4.31	4.6	4.8	40.7	6.4	**9.5**	10.7	15.6
▲ Citizens Bank	Butler	MO	**B**	B-	C+	160.8	39.24	8.5	2.3	25.9	1.2	**6.1**	8.1	11.9
▼ Citizens Bank	New Haven	MO	**C**	C+	B-	227.8	-2.60	6.7	1.4	19.2	7.3	**7.5**	12.0	13.0
Citizens Bank	Byhalia	MS	**B+**	B+	B	78.6	2.26	3.5	6.5	19.6	24.3	**10.0**	12.4	28.3
Citizens Bank	Columbia	MS	**B-**	B-	B-	440.4	2.39	8.6	4.1	21.7	9.0	**9.0**	10.4	16.1
Citizens Bank	Farmington	NM	**A-**	A-	B+	714.0	2.03	7.7	0.7	11.3	53.0	**8.6**	10.1	22.5
▼ Citizens Bank	Corvallis	OR	**A-**	A	A-	799.5	3.22	6.3	0.4	4.2	30.2	**10.0**	11.4	19.8
Citizens Bank	Olanta	SC	**B**	B	B-	596.2	7.26	7.0	4.0	21.5	11.9	**8.3**	9.9	15.6
Citizens Bank	Carthage	TN	**A**	A	A	634.1	5.79	4.5	2.9	11.1	52.1	**10.0**	17.2	25.7
Citizens Bank	Elizabethton	TN	**A**	A	A-	905.4	2.37	9.9	2.1	6.4	22.5	**10.0**	12.8	16.6
Citizens Bank	Hartsville	TN	**A-**	A-	B	265.9	20.78	4.4	2.8	18.5	13.8	**9.2**	10.4	15.6
Citizens Bank	Amarillo	TX	**A-**	A-	B	190.8	18.99	3.2	0.2	2.9	6.7	**8.1**	9.9	13.4

Asset Quality Index	Adjusted Non-Performing Loans as a % of Total Loans	Adjusted Non-Performing Loans as a % of Capital	Net Charge-Offs Avg Loans	Profitability Index	Net Income ($Mil)	Return on Assets (R.O.A.)	Return on Equity (R.O.E.)	Net Interest Spread	Overhead Efficiency Ratio	Liquidity Index	Liquidity Ratio	Hot Money Ratio	Stability Index
6.0	1.23	na	-0.01	**7.5**	0.8	1.69	18.09	4.10	62.9	**6.0**	39.2	2.8	**7.5**
7.9	1.09	2.4	-0.01	**9.7**	2.3	2.38	23.05	3.60	59.7	**6.9**	53.1	1.4	**8.4**
8.9	0.02	na	0.00	**4.7**	0.4	1.06	9.16	2.92	65.1	**3.6**	43.5	18.1	**7.1**
6.3	0.43	na	0.02	**10.0**	2.2	3.22	28.19	6.95	50.3	**4.0**	43.5	16.1	**8.5**
6.4	1.06	5.2	0.00	**7.6**	3.9	1.64	12.60	3.50	50.8	**2.4**	22.2	14.0	**10.0**
8.3	0.06	na	-0.01	**5.3**	0.7	1.00	10.01	3.45	87.0	**0.9**	18.0	27.8	**7.3**
5.7	0.51	na	0.00	**2.3**	0.0	0.06	0.58	3.50	98.6	**1.4**	32.4	44.3	**4.6**
8.6	0.00	na	0.05	**7.0**	0.7	1.23	9.88	4.23	63.4	**1.4**	30.7	35.5	**8.9**
7.1	1.66	6.2	0.01	**3.2**	-3.0	-1.03	-6.33	3.63	73.2	**4.5**	22.3	8.0	**10.0**
6.1	1.69	na	-0.05	**6.2**	0.4	1.34	8.64	3.54	56.3	**5.6**	60.5	12.1	**9.3**
7.4	1.37	na	-0.02	**5.8**	1.0	1.20	9.88	3.63	66.6	**6.6**	51.9	3.5	**8.5**
4.3	1.41	8.8	0.09	**3.8**	2.2	0.49	4.94	3.53	69.8	**4.6**	14.8	5.0	**7.9**
4.8	2.23	na	0.00	**6.1**	0.8	1.35	10.70	3.34	56.7	**2.1**	26.8	14.0	**8.1**
8.1	0.60	1.7	0.01	**5.8**	3.3	1.40	12.47	4.00	75.8	**3.3**	28.2	12.5	**8.0**
6.5	0.53	na	0.00	**4.9**	0.3	1.07	10.25	3.82	64.2	**3.4**	13.8	11.7	**7.4**
9.0	0.18	na	0.01	**2.6**	0.2	0.28	1.45	3.54	82.3	**1.4**	28.9	33.3	**7.1**
9.5	0.00	na	0.00	**2.8**	0.1	0.30	2.25	3.38	89.5	**2.4**	19.3	17.3	**6.1**
8.0	0.04	na	-0.03	**2.6**	0.0	0.39	3.55	3.72	89.1	**2.6**	34.6	18.2	**4.4**
7.7	0.00	na	0.00	**3.8**	0.1	0.57	3.31	5.32	79.7	**2.8**	18.7	15.6	**6.8**
9.0	na	0.0	na	**9.5**	0.7	2.55	2.58	2.27	73.8	**4.0**	na	0.0	**6.3**
3.6	2.15	8.6	-0.06	**4.4**	0.3	0.50	4.66	5.12	89.3	**0.6**	8.1	27.2	**7.0**
5.2	1.27	na	0.07	**5.1**	0.4	1.27	14.13	3.42	64.7	**5.6**	38.4	5.3	**6.1**
7.1	0.93	na	-0.22	**6.7**	0.7	1.15	10.59	3.91	61.2	**4.5**	26.1	4.4	**7.0**
4.8	0.73	na	0.01	**5.3**	1.1	0.91	10.94	3.59	67.9	**3.3**	14.5	7.9	**6.2**
7.1	0.59	3.4	0.00	**2.6**	0.2	0.58	5.21	4.14	81.9	**3.8**	19.0	7.4	**5.5**
4.6	0.70	6.0	0.00	**8.7**	9.6	1.59	13.15	3.94	50.6	**1.9**	12.6	12.8	**10.0**
4.4	1.13	4.9	0.04	**4.8**	1.5	0.89	7.31	3.64	70.8	**2.4**	30.2	17.5	**8.8**
4.3	1.33	4.1	0.05	**3.0**	-17.5	-0.21	-1.10	3.08	50.7	**3.3**	10.7	6.7	**10.0**
6.5	na	0.0	na	**9.5**	5.5	5.88	11.49	1.44	69.4	**3.7**	111.8	100.0	**5.0**
5.2	1.18	6.0	0.08	**3.1**	0.9	0.55	4.43	3.03	81.1	**1.2**	15.1	20.4	**7.7**
5.9	1.03	na	-0.01	**7.7**	3.1	1.91	16.02	4.40	57.6	**1.7**	24.5	24.2	**9.5**
8.4	0.81	2.6	0.00	**1.5**	-0.2	-0.30	-2.52	2.65	108.8	**1.5**	11.9	23.2	**6.8**
6.2	2.77	na	-0.02	**3.0**	0.1	0.38	1.71	3.51	87.5	**1.9**	21.5	20.4	**7.4**
5.7	1.16	6.8	1.02	**2.6**	-553.2	-4.23	-43.64	2.82	133.4	**1.6**	14.1	17.0	**9.2**
6.5	0.96	4.3	1.10	**4.2**	1909.0	0.51	5.14	2.99	49.3	**3.8**	42.7	6.5	**7.8**
10.0	na	0.0	na	**9.5**	0.7	12.15	12.91	2.29	67.1	**4.0**	na	0.0	**5.7**
6.0	1.07	na	0.01	**6.5**	4.3	1.06	7.42	3.82	65.8	**2.5**	9.5	15.2	**10.0**
9.5	0.54	na	0.01	**6.5**	2.8	1.62	7.61	2.88	41.3	**2.9**	45.9	26.5	**10.0**
4.1	1.16	9.2	0.96	**5.1**	1.6	0.79	8.47	3.92	55.7	**1.2**	18.9	18.3	**7.3**
7.0	0.45	na	0.67	**5.8**	4.1	0.91	8.72	4.95	73.0	**2.0**	16.0	19.1	**8.7**
5.8	4.94	na	0.20	**4.4**	0.5	0.90	5.09	3.46	70.3	**4.9**	58.0	15.1	**8.4**
6.8	2.28	na	-0.25	**3.7**	0.3	0.70	6.74	3.86	78.0	**2.6**	18.4	14.8	**6.1**
7.6	0.37	2.2	0.09	**6.1**	0.3	1.44	9.90	3.14	49.2	**3.1**	50.8	23.3	**7.9**
5.0	0.84	na	0.10	**4.5**	2.0	0.88	9.27	3.86	68.4	**1.7**	12.2	17.5	**6.7**
4.6	1.67	na	2.57	**2.4**	-0.1	-0.45	-4.89	3.50	72.6	**2.6**	34.5	20.2	**4.9**
6.6	0.19	na	0.04	**5.2**	1.3	1.01	8.79	3.51	69.2	**3.9**	14.0	9.0	**7.1**
6.1	0.36	na	0.15	**3.5**	0.5	1.30	10.18	3.51	71.8	**1.5**	12.1	23.8	**7.0**
4.5	1.21	na	0.08	**3.2**	0.2	0.53	5.76	4.09	86.9	**4.0**	17.7	9.2	**5.5**
4.8	1.08	na	-0.09	**4.3**	0.4	0.99	9.03	4.27	75.5	**1.3**	11.3	26.5	**6.5**
5.2	0.60	na	-0.01	**7.9**	0.7	1.75	20.29	4.87	60.3	**3.6**	18.2	11.1	**6.0**
1.4	3.33	19.9	0.07	**4.3**	0.5	0.85	7.10	3.85	65.4	**1.7**	8.7	12.4	**7.9**
8.6	0.14	na	0.15	**4.5**	0.1	0.70	5.57	4.62	77.5	**5.0**	49.6	11.4	**6.7**
4.5	1.82	na	0.07	**6.2**	1.5	1.43	14.71	3.96	68.1	**1.6**	15.9	22.5	**7.1**
5.7	3.06	na	0.02	**6.4**	2.8	1.58	14.98	3.38	54.5	**5.1**	55.7	13.5	**7.7**
8.9	0.37	na	0.00	**4.6**	0.2	0.09	0.74	3.95	59.9	**6.5**	45.2	1.5	**7.8**
6.6	0.57	na	0.02	**5.2**	1.5	1.01	9.46	3.77	70.6	**4.2**	27.2	9.6	**7.2**
9.0	0.00	na	0.00	**9.8**	3.2	2.05	11.03	3.77	29.1	**3.1**	60.1	33.4	**10.0**
6.0	0.72	na	0.20	**6.4**	1.0	0.65	4.88	4.23	71.4	**2.1**	14.3	18.4	**9.6**
5.2	2.02	na	-0.01	**6.4**	0.7	0.99	9.64	3.67	64.4	**1.7**	35.7	36.5	**6.9**
6.0	0.00	na	0.00	**8.6**	0.8	1.76	17.89	3.67	50.5	**2.8**	31.2	18.1	**7.7**

Name	City	State	Rating	2019 Rating	2018 Rating	Total Assets ($Mil)	One Year Asset Growth	Asset Mix (As a % of Total Assets) Comm-ercial Loans	Cons-umer Loans	Mort-gage Loans	Secur-ities	Capital-ization Index	Lever-age Ratio	Risk-Based Capital Ratio
Citizens Bank	Kilgore	TX	B	B	B	427.6	0.88	18.9	0.8	7.1	6.7	10.0	13.9	19.2
▲ Citizens Bank	Mukwonago	WI	A-	B+	B	809.9	5.40	8.1	0.1	7.2	18.3	9.8	13.2	0.0
Citizens Bank & Trust	Guntersville	AL	B	B	B-	599.5	16.46	9.6	1.9	12.4	22.0	7.7	9.5	14.7
Citizens Bank & Trust	Rock Port	MO	B	B	B	97.8	6.42	10.4	2.6	7.1	39.5	10.0	11.3	23.8
Citizens Bank & Trust Co.	Van Buren	AR	A-	A-	A	420.4	2.27	5.6	4.5	15.5	30.8	9.8	13.2	0.0
Citizens Bank & Trust Co.	Eastman	GA	B-	B-	C	174.9	17.80	12.3	2.0	18.3	12.7	7.3	9.2	15.3
Citizens Bank & Trust Co.	Campbellsville	KY	B	B	B	242.3	15.39	16.0	2.8	18.4	34.2	9.8	15.6	0.0
Citizens Bank & Trust Co.	Covington	LA	B	B	C	125.1	4.12	6.1	0.5	20.1	9.4	9.6	10.9	0.0
Citizens Bank & Trust Co.	Plaquemine	LA	B	B	B-	336.8	7.47	5.3	0.8	16.9	8.3	10.0	11.5	16.2
Citizens Bank & Trust Co.	Vivian	LA	B-	B-	B-	137.7	-3.17	4.3	2.5	24.0	28.1	9.8	13.1	0.0
▲ Citizens Bank & Trust Co.	Hutchinson	MN	B	B-	C+	223.2	7.88	13.2	1.6	20.3	27.8	6.9	9.1	0.0
▼ Citizens Bank & Trust Co.	Marks	MS	D-	D	D+	141.9	-0.81	6.3	2.6	12.7	25.9	5.6	7.6	12.8
Citizens Bank & Trust Co.	Big Timber	MT	C+	C+	C+	114.2	0.45	5.2	2.2	7.9	13.9	8.3	9.9	17.4
Citizens Bank & Trust Co.	Saint Paul	NE	D+	D+	C	194.5	-1.90	9.9	2.2	6.4	14.8	9.8	12.4	0.0
Citizens Bank & Trust Co.	Atwood	TN	C-	C-	C-	25.5	-0.94	0.9	11.4	21.3	43.2	8.8	10.2	27.5
Citizens Bank & Trust Co. of Ardmore	Ardmore	OK	B	B	B	233.7	3.08	5.1	2.6	30.3	21.5	7.4	9.4	0.0
Citizens Bank & Trust Co. of Jackson	Jackson	KY	C	C	D+	152.2	5.00	7.3	6.1	29.4	6.7	6.1	8.1	12.8
Citizens Bank & Trust, Inc.	Trenton	GA	A-	A-	B+	104.5	1.44	4.1	7.9	34.8	26.3	10.0	11.2	21.6
Citizens Bank and Trust	Lake Wales	FL	B-	B-	C+	738.8	13.28	7.2	6.9	10.0	38.9	5.6	7.6	12.4
▼ Citizens Bank and Trust Co.	Kansas City	MO	B-	B	B-	941.4	10.57	11.5	0.7	13.2	16.2	8.9	10.9	14.1
Citizens Bank and Trust Co.	Blackstone	VA	A-	A-	A-	423.0	5.55	3.7	2.6	24.3	25.4	9.8	13.6	0.0
Citizens Bank Co.	Beverly	OH	A-	A-	A-	230.7	3.16	7.1	2.0	33.0	18.6	9.8	13.2	0.0
Citizens Bank Minnesota	New Ulm	MN	B	B	B	435.9	6.19	6.3	0.8	20.8	21.2	6.2	10.1	11.9
Citizens Bank of Ada	Ada	OK	B	B	B-	197.2	-3.85	13.8	3.0	19.4	19.5	9.2	10.7	0.0
Citizens Bank of Americus	Americus	GA	B+	B+	B	338.7	4.27	10.9	1.6	8.9	23.0	7.7	9.5	17.4
▼ Citizens Bank of Cape Vincent	Cape Vincent	NY	C	C+	C+	68.0	-8.75	0.8	2.6	41.4	38.9	7.3	9.2	25.4
Citizens Bank of Charleston	Charleston	MO	A-	A-	B+	145.6	7.20	8.1	5.0	7.8	5.5	9.8	17.4	0.0
Citizens Bank of Chatsworth	Chatsworth	IL	D	D	E+	33.1	5.88	9.5	1.6	2.7	26.5	10.0	11.1	17.1
Citizens Bank of Clovis	Clovis	NM	A-	A-	B+	355.1	3.30	4.5	0.5	2.8	36.3	9.8	12.7	0.0
Citizens Bank of Cochran	Cochran	GA	B-	B-	B-	108.2	18.48	9.3	4.2	26.8	7.7	8.7	10.1	15.2
Citizens Bank of Cumberland County	Burkesville	KY	B	B	B-	73.7	-2.39	3.7	12.3	25.8	8.7	9.8	13.5	0.0
▲ Citizens Bank of Edina	Edina	MO	A-	B+	B+	71.3	2.44	7.9	3.1	6.2	4.9	10.0	12.7	17.1
▼ Citizens Bank of Edinburg	Edinburg	IL	C-	C	C-	24.7	1.33	1.4	2.0	11.9	20.7	7.7	9.6	0.0
Citizens Bank of Edmond	Edmond	OK	B-	B-	C+	292.0	1.79	8.0	0.6	21.4	6.3	8.5	10.1	0.0
▼ Citizens Bank of Eldon	Eldon	MO	B+	A-	A-	158.6	6.72	7.6	8.8	24.1	4.3	9.8	13.4	0.0
Citizens Bank of Fayette	Fayette	AL	B+	B+	B+	188.8	0.81	5.3	3.4	3.5	69.1	9.8	20.7	0.0
▲ Citizens Bank of Florida	Oviedo	FL	B-	C+	C	355.7	11.79	5.0	0.6	9.3	17.9	6.6	8.6	12.7
▲ Citizens Bank of Georgia	Cumming	GA	B+	B	B	346.0	7.58	5.3	1.2	9.2	29.2	9.7	10.8	17.0
Citizens Bank of Kansas	Kingman	KS	B-	B-	B-	393.1	1.60	4.6	1.2	16.2	27.8	8.4	9.9	15.0
Citizens Bank of Kentucky	Paintsville	KY	B	B	B	658.6	8.33	7.6	2.7	17.3	22.5	10.0	11.2	17.9
Citizens Bank of Lafayette	Lafayette	TN	B+	B+	B+	947.8	2.37	4.9	4.8	13.9	27.1	10.0	11.8	18.8
Citizens Bank of Las Cruces	Las Cruces	NM	A-	A-	B+	641.4	11.68	12.0	0.5	7.9	20.2	8.6	10.5	13.9
Citizens Bank of Morgantown, Inc.	Morgantown	WV	B-	B-	B-	38.4	0.59	1.4	1.7	47.1	29.4	10.0	19.8	35.9
▼ Citizens Bank of Newburg	Rolla	MO	C-	C	C	151.7	-0.70	9.1	1.9	23.3	8.4	8.1	9.9	0.0
▼ Citizens Bank of Philadelphia, Mississippi	Philadelphia	MS	C+	B-	B-	1216.0	15.03	5.6	1.2	8.0	39.7	6.1	8.1	14.2
Citizens Bank of Rogersville	Rogersville	MO	B-	B-	B-	95.6	0.69	11.8	4.7	28.3	7.2	8.3	10.0	0.0
Citizens Bank of Swainsboro	Swainsboro	GA	B+	B+	B	224.5	6.82	14.5	5.6	26.7	7.8	10.0	11.0	16.5
Citizens Bank of The South	Sandersville	GA	B+	B+	B	263.9	8.43	8.6	3.6	29.7	10.4	10.0	11.6	17.9
Citizens Bank of West Virginia, Inc.	Elkins	WV	B-	B-	C+	295.2	5.53	4.7	18.6	34.5	5.1	10.0	11.1	17.0
▲ Citizens Bank of Weston, Inc.	Weston	WV	A-	B+	B-	198.2	-3.48	24.6	3.6	21.4	23.1	10.0	11.8	17.7
Citizens Bank of Winfield	Winfield	AL	A	A	A	252.6	4.39	2.7	6.8	4.8	69.4	9.8	21.5	0.0
Citizens Bank, N.A.	Providence	RI	B-	B-	B-	176632.6	9.44	24.9	15.9	12.6	14.5	6.6	9.6	12.2
Citizens Bank, N.A.	Abilene	TX	A-	A-	B	105.0	-1.60	9.6	6.3	17.6	18.8	8.2	10.0	0.0
Citizens Building and Loan, SSB	Greer	SC	B+	B+	A-	148.7	9.30	0.0	0.2	51.9	13.5	9.8	20.2	0.0
Citizens Business Bank	Ontario	CA	A-	A-	A	11603.0	2.64	7.3	0.1	3.5	20.1	10.0	11.4	15.3
▲ Citizens Commerce Bank	Versailles	KY	C	C-	C-	269.3	6.28	4.4	0.9	29.1	15.1	8.5	10.2	0.0
Citizens Community Bank	Hahira	GA	A-	A-	B+	144.8	4.69	4.9	3.7	20.8	25.4	10.0	12.6	20.5
Citizens Community Bank	Mascoutah	IL	B+	B+	B+	404.9	2.43	5.5	1.1	9.9	34.5	9.8	11.9	0.0
Citizens Community Bank	Pilot Grove	MO	B	B	B-	110.8	7.55	4.6	2.2	15.2	10.6	9.8	11.9	0.0
▲ Citizens Community Bank	Winchester	TN	A-	B+	B-	239.4	3.38	11.8	3.4	17.8	16.5	10.0	13.3	19.4

Arrows denote recent upgrades ▲ or downgrades ▼

Asset Quality Index	Adjusted Non-Performing Loans as a % of Total Loans	Adjusted Non-Performing Loans as a % of Capital	Net Charge-Offs / Avg Loans	Profitability Index	Net Income ($Mil)	Return on Assets (R.O.A.)	Return on Equity (R.O.E.)	Net Interest Spread	Overhead Efficiency Ratio	Liquidity Index	Liquidity Ratio	Hot Money Ratio	Stability Index
4.7	3.18	na	0.00	4.0	0.6	0.60	4.28	4.06	75.2	4.5	38.1	11.8	7.2
7.1	0.55	1.5	0.01	6.1	2.3	1.13	8.71	3.50	60.7	3.7	16.9	10.7	8.1
7.4	0.23	na	0.03	4.6	1.5	1.05	11.00	3.67	68.4	2.3	20.3	17.8	6.0
8.3	1.10	na	-0.13	4.1	0.2	0.91	7.66	3.09	72.9	3.4	27.5	13.6	7.4
5.0	1.74	6.4	0.08	9.2	1.7	1.65	12.29	4.05	51.7	2.2	16.9	18.4	9.2
8.7	0.06	na	0.05	4.1	0.4	0.82	8.74	4.22	78.8	3.5	28.0	13.3	5.2
7.8	1.41	na	-0.01	4.8	0.6	0.98	6.19	3.43	67.2	4.3	37.5	12.4	7.3
6.1	0.37	na	0.00	4.2	0.2	0.76	7.06	4.11	71.5	1.9	18.2	19.6	6.5
2.6	3.42	na	-0.01	5.0	0.8	0.93	8.65	3.73	64.7	2.1	16.6	18.7	7.2
4.8	2.81	na	0.07	3.6	0.3	0.99	7.30	3.94	83.5	4.5	37.5	11.6	6.9
5.2	2.46	na	0.00	7.0	1.3	2.28	25.76	3.92	53.6	4.1	21.2	9.1	7.0
0.3	9.69	na	5.87	0.7	-0.5	-1.44	-18.46	2.84	8.4	1.9	26.5	23.5	2.6
3.9	2.42	na	-0.02	6.4	0.4	1.49	12.68	4.23	50.6	3.8	31.6	13.5	7.3
0.0	2.20	na	-0.01	6.0	0.5	1.11	9.00	4.15	61.6	1.4	12.0	20.3	8.0
7.6	0.21	1.8	0.00	3.0	0.0	0.41	3.94	2.98	84.4	1.4	27.6	31.3	4.8
8.9	0.00	na	0.00	4.9	0.7	1.21	12.83	3.71	71.6	3.1	21.1	13.9	6.5
3.5	0.68	na	-0.05	3.4	0.3	0.71	7.50	3.98	81.2	1.3	17.7	27.3	4.1
7.9	0.88	na	0.06	6.1	0.3	0.97	8.64	4.84	72.5	3.7	28.8	12.7	6.9
7.1	0.48	na	0.04	4.7	2.0	1.15	13.50	3.66	74.3	5.8	35.1	2.3	5.6
5.5	1.79	5.6	0.08	3.3	1.4	0.65	5.79	3.30	80.6	2.8	16.8	15.4	6.8
8.2	0.72	1.9	-0.03	6.8	1.6	1.49	11.11	3.70	57.4	3.8	35.9	14.5	8.3
8.8	0.04	na	-0.03	5.0	0.5	0.82	6.13	4.27	68.1	2.7	9.9	14.8	8.4
8.7	0.12	0.4	0.00	4.0	0.7	0.67	6.32	3.09	73.3	3.0	19.6	14.3	6.4
4.7	0.25	na	0.17	4.1	0.4	0.85	7.90	4.81	82.2	4.3	17.5	7.3	5.7
6.3	1.07	na	0.34	6.6	1.0	1.18	12.42	3.50	57.1	4.4	30.1	9.4	6.9
5.9	1.41	na	0.48	2.5	0.1	0.39	4.15	3.40	84.1	4.7	18.1	4.7	4.3
7.0	0.67	na	-0.03	8.8	0.6	1.61	9.36	3.64	47.6	3.4	39.1	17.8	9.2
3.7	4.08	na	0.00	0.0	-0.3	-2.89	-23.59	3.24	168.3	4.2	28.6	10.4	2.4
8.4	0.39	na	0.00	6.4	1.3	1.47	11.36	3.24	54.4	2.1	33.5	24.2	8.6
8.5	0.10	na	-0.01	4.0	0.2	0.91	9.11	4.42	73.4	1.1	18.4	32.1	5.8
4.3	2.47	na	0.25	7.6	0.3	1.54	11.35	5.04	68.1	2.6	26.0	17.5	8.6
6.9	0.10	na	0.27	10.0	0.5	2.55	20.28	4.59	34.0	2.3	13.1	17.1	8.2
5.3	0.00	na	0.00	5.2	0.1	0.94	9.74	3.74	61.7	5.4	36.4	3.0	3.7
7.3	0.77	na	0.36	3.8	0.5	0.70	8.27	3.98	83.3	3.3	10.1	12.1	6.0
4.1	1.90	10.7	0.19	6.7	0.5	1.36	10.23	4.40	58.9	2.9	18.6	14.7	7.9
7.0	5.74	na	1.31	4.4	0.5	1.05	5.10	2.93	57.8	4.0	78.2	26.7	8.0
6.7	0.70	na	0.25	4.0	0.8	0.94	10.85	3.59	75.7	3.0	30.1	16.7	5.2
8.6	0.58	na	0.00	7.1	1.1	1.31	11.92	3.85	55.3	3.7	37.8	15.8	7.4
6.5	0.51	na	0.01	3.7	0.6	0.58	4.28	3.86	84.8	4.8	26.8	5.5	7.4
5.8	1.64	na	0.13	3.8	1.2	0.75	5.44	3.34	77.5	1.6	24.9	24.8	8.3
4.7	2.30	10.2	0.15	6.4	2.8	1.19	9.50	3.76	62.3	1.7	27.6	27.8	8.3
7.4	0.35	na	-0.01	9.7	3.5	2.26	20.70	4.38	56.4	4.5	17.0	5.4	9.0
8.6	1.38	na	0.00	3.5	0.1	0.59	3.15	4.48	83.0	3.2	36.6	17.8	7.4
5.3	0.82	na	0.35	2.0	0.3	0.88	8.92	3.55	70.4	0.7	14.4	21.4	4.1
4.9	2.08	na	0.18	2.9	1.2	0.41	4.30	2.70	82.2	2.8	13.2	15.1	6.5
6.3	0.32	na	0.24	4.5	0.2	0.90	8.04	4.18	75.1	1.9	11.5	16.2	7.2
6.2	0.69	na	0.02	6.5	0.7	1.19	10.77	4.82	67.9	2.0	15.1	19.1	7.1
6.6	1.01	na	0.30	5.0	0.6	0.95	8.22	4.38	68.2	2.1	16.6	18.8	6.7
3.9	1.67	na	0.21	5.7	0.8	1.12	10.99	4.26	66.2	2.1	15.1	18.2	6.6
5.5	3.04	na	0.01	8.9	0.8	1.58	13.94	3.92	49.8	4.5	27.7	7.6	7.7
8.7	2.25	na	0.46	8.4	1.4	2.18	10.09	3.78	42.8	2.2	44.2	42.2	8.5
4.6	1.08	4.5	0.44	3.5	35.7	0.09	0.65	3.09	60.4	3.4	17.5	6.8	10.0
7.2	0.00	na	0.00	8.3	0.6	2.43	17.89	4.56	58.7	1.5	10.0	23.4	9.7
9.9	0.07	na	0.00	3.3	0.2	0.40	1.96	2.92	81.2	0.9	26.2	56.7	8.1
5.9	0.12	0.3	-0.01	9.0	39.4	1.39	7.97	4.08	41.0	4.8	14.8	3.4	10.0
8.9	0.18	0.9	-0.05	4.1	0.5	0.78	7.31	3.50	74.3	1.2	7.2	27.4	6.0
6.0	1.11	na	1.38	5.3	0.4	1.11	8.77	4.09	71.4	3.5	37.5	16.7	8.4
5.0	3.16	na	0.00	5.2	1.0	1.00	8.37	2.96	52.6	1.6	14.4	23.1	6.8
7.5	0.45	na	-0.01	4.2	0.2	0.69	5.73	3.52	75.8	2.6	23.0	16.9	7.2
5.3	1.44	na	-0.41	9.9	1.0	1.74	13.19	4.69	44.3	3.0	18.1	14.2	8.6

Name	City	State	Rating	2019 Rating	2018 Rating	Total Assets ($Mil)	One Year Asset Growth	Asset Mix (As a % of Total Assets) Commercial Loans	Consumer Loans	Mortgage Loans	Securities	Capitalization Index	Leverage Ratio	Risk-Based Capital Ratio
Citizens Community Federal N.A.	Altoona	WI	**B-**	B-	B-	1505.0	13.46	6.9	3.6	14.9	11.6	**8.3**	10.3	13.6
Citizens Deposit Bank & Trust	Vanceburg	KY	**B**	B	B-	555.9	20.95	2.4	2.3	17.1	37.9	**6.4**	8.4	14.6
Citizens Deposit Bank of Arlington, Inc.	Arlington	KY	**A-**	A-	B+	240.4	11.63	13.1	5.4	15.6	25.4	**9.8**	15.5	0.0
▼ Citizens Federal S&L Assn.	Covington	KY	**B-**	B	B+	40.6	8.93	0.0	0.0	47.8	17.7	**10.0**	27.8	67.1
Citizens Federal S&L Assn.	Bellefontaine	OH	**C**	C	C	144.6	7.94	0.0	0.1	58.5	12.6	**10.0**	12.7	25.7
▼ Citizens Federal Savings Bank	Leavenworth	KS	**C-**	C	C	182.0	1.83	0.6	1.1	50.2	34.6	**9.8**	21.9	0.0
Citizens First Bank	The Villages	FL	**A+**	A+	A	2533.8	6.90	8.4	0.1	7.2	63.2	**10.0**	12.1	18.9
Citizens First Bank	Clinton	IA	**B-**	B-	C+	228.5	10.06	26.0	2.5	12.2	3.1	**8.1**	9.9	0.0
▲ Citizens First Bank	Viroqua	WI	**B**	B-	C+	224.2	3.03	5.2	2.4	8.1	16.8	**9.8**	11.2	0.0
Citizens First National Bank	Storm Lake	IA	**A**	A	A-	209.3	-2.07	11.6	4.3	3.8	28.0	**10.0**	11.9	18.8
Citizens First State Bank of Walnut	Walnut	IL	**C+**	C+	D+	48.6	4.47	4.9	4.1	22.8	26.2	**7.3**	9.2	17.5
Citizens Guaranty Bank	Irvine	KY	**D+**	D+	C-	211.0	6.07	10.6	7.5	37.6	8.4	**3.3**	6.6	10.1
Citizens Independent Bank	Saint Louis Park	MN	**B-**	B-	C+	294.0	7.59	10.7	6.7	12.6	24.2	**10.0**	12.1	18.1
Citizens National Bank	Greenleaf	KS	**B-**	B-	B-	179.5	3.52	2.9	2.3	10.4	60.0	**9.1**	10.6	0.0
Citizens National Bank	Sevierville	TN	**A**	A	A	1111.0	0.81	6.0	0.5	13.6	12.8	**10.0**	11.5	15.6
Citizens National Bank	Cameron	TX	**B**	B	B	415.8	2.03	5.0	0.7	7.2	28.1	**10.0**	11.4	16.6
Citizens National Bank	Crockett	TX	**B**	B	B-	86.0	-3.22	8.9	6.5	6.7	17.3	**10.0**	11.9	25.2
▲ Citizens National Bank at Brownwood	Brownwood	TX	**A**	A-	B+	218.2	3.06	8.3	6.6	14.1	44.1	**10.0**	12.7	24.7
Citizens National Bank of Albion	Albion	IL	**B**	B	B+	316.1	-1.91	7.4	3.8	14.8	22.8	**10.0**	17.4	26.1
Citizens National Bank of Bluffton	Bluffton	OH	**B-**	B-	C	876.5	3.98	9.4	0.3	8.3	16.8	**9.2**	10.6	0.0
Citizens National Bank of Cheboygan	Cheboygan	MI	**C+**	C+	C	318.5	7.51	3.6	2.0	19.1	34.6	**6.4**	8.4	16.0
Citizens National Bank of Crosbyton	Crosbyton	TX	**B+**	B+	B	52.5	2.67	2.2	2.4	2.1	14.4	**10.0**	16.9	56.7
▲ Citizens National Bank of Greater St. Louis	Maplewood	MO	**B-**	C+	C+	519.5	1.80	16.9	0.7	14.5	16.2	**8.1**	10.7	13.4
Citizens National Bank of Hammond	Hammond	NY	**C-**	C-	D	23.3	-2.67	5.0	12.0	46.7	22.6	**7.5**	9.5	0.0
Citizens National Bank of Hillsboro	Hillsboro	TX	**B+**	B+	B	176.5	4.39	5.7	3.1	7.4	61.2	**10.0**	14.1	33.5
Citizens National Bank of Lebanon	Lebanon	KY	**B**	B	B	129.0	-2.61	2.3	3.8	12.2	48.3	**10.0**	11.4	29.0
▼ Citizens National Bank of McConnelsville	McConnelsville	OH	**B-**	B	B	100.7	4.11	2.0	5.9	43.8	20.6	**9.8**	11.7	0.0
Citizens National Bank of Meridian	Meridian	MS	**A-**	A-	B+	1437.9	-1.11	9.8	1.7	15.9	19.9	**8.9**	11.6	14.1
Citizens National Bank of Park Rapids	Park Rapids	MN	**A-**	A-	B-	268.2	6.03	6.6	8.6	25.1	7.3	**9.8**	11.6	0.0
Citizens National Bank of Quitman	Quitman	GA	**B+**	B+	B	104.5	2.87	2.2	13.7	14.2	12.4	**10.0**	13.2	20.9
Citizens National Bank of Somerset	Somerset	KY	**B+**	B+	B+	462.3	10.65	2.9	4.0	21.8	35.9	**8.3**	10.1	0.0
Citizens National Bank of Texas	Waxahachie	TX	**B-**	B-	C+	1196.9	9.58	6.9	0.7	11.3	0.8	**8.2**	10.8	13.5
Citizens National Bank of Woodsfield	Woodsfield	OH	**C+**	C+	C	136.5	0.41	3.7	1.3	28.3	40.8	**5.2**	7.2	22.5
Citizens National Bank, N.A.	Bossier City	LA	**B+**	B+	B	1102.4	12.20	7.1	0.5	11.6	16.6	**9.4**	10.6	16.0
▼ Citizens Progressive Bank	Winnsboro	LA	**C-**	C	D+	171.7	4.67	8.5	3.5	19.5	6.3	**7.1**	9.5	12.6
Citizens Savings Bank	Anamosa	IA	**A-**	A-	B+	135.7	11.71	4.6	0.8	7.8	32.3	**9.1**	10.4	15.7
▼ Citizens Savings Bank	Hawkeye	IA	**B+**	A-	B+	29.1	1.67	1.1	1.1	9.2	52.5	**9.8**	14.9	0.0
Citizens Savings Bank	Marshalltown	IA	**C+**	C+	C+	64.8	6.08	7.1	1.6	17.6	0.3	**6.2**	8.4	11.9
▼ Citizens Savings Bank	Spillville	IA	**B+**	A-	B+	109.4	-2.63	1.7	0.4	4.2	34.1	**9.8**	18.1	0.0
Citizens Savings Bank	Bogalusa	LA	**B-**	B-	C+	236.5	2.26	2.0	4.7	41.4	7.5	**9.8**	14.7	0.0
Citizens Savings Bank	Clarks Summit	PA	**B-**	B-	B-	317.5	-5.24	0.0	0.1	78.1	8.2	**10.0**	15.9	32.0
Citizens Savings Bank and Trust Co.	Nashville	TN	**E+**	E+	E+	97.1	-6.08	4.6	2.1	9.3	6.7	**3.0**	6.7	10.0
Citizens State Bank	Vernon	AL	**B**	B	B-	71.6	2.82	8.3	5.0	11.1	49.9	**10.0**	14.7	37.6
▼ Citizens State Bank	Monticello	IA	**B+**	A-	A-	421.6	2.72	5.9	0.9	3.1	40.1	**9.8**	11.8	0.0
Citizens State Bank	Sheldon	IA	**A-**	A-	B+	134.5	11.87	7.4	5.8	14.2	11.4	**9.8**	13.0	0.0
▲ Citizens State Bank	Wyoming	IA	**B+**	B	B+	99.0	1.97	7.4	2.4	3.7	30.3	**10.0**	23.1	36.8
Citizens State Bank	Lena	IL	**B**	B	B	286.8	10.82	7.9	5.4	10.5	15.5	**10.0**	11.2	16.5
Citizens State Bank	Gridley	KS	**B+**	B+	B-	204.0	-0.26	9.0	2.6	14.4	20.2	**8.1**	9.9	0.0
▼ Citizens State Bank	Hugoton	KS	**C+**	B-	B-	126.5	3.98	7.1	0.8	4.3	18.3	**9.8**	12.7	0.0
Citizens State Bank	Marysville	KS	**A-**	A-	B+	361.8	5.10	8.0	1.0	8.0	14.6	**7.5**	9.9	12.9
Citizens State Bank	Moundridge	KS	**B+**	B+	B	442.0	3.12	4.5	1.0	6.1	38.0	**9.7**	11.0	0.0
Citizens State Bank	Carleton	NE	**D+**	D+	D	23.3	10.74	10.5	4.5	1.7	0.0	**8.0**	9.8	0.0
Citizens State Bank	Wisner	NE	**C**	C	B-	394.3	14.04	8.4	1.1	7.6	5.7	**8.0**	10.9	13.3
Citizens State Bank	Anton	TX	**C-**	C-	D	33.7	0.31	8.0	1.6	0.0	3.2	**7.8**	9.5	18.4
Citizens State Bank	Buffalo	TX	**B+**	B+	B+	1133.2	17.72	4.7	1.5	4.0	76.8	**9.2**	10.6	0.0
Citizens State Bank	Corrigan	TX	**A-**	A-	B+	135.7	4.93	12.7	12.0	15.1	26.7	**9.8**	12.2	0.0
Citizens State Bank	Ganado	TX	**D**	D	D-	56.9	2.95	0.4	1.8	6.2	67.0	**6.1**	8.1	27.2
Citizens State Bank	Miles	TX	**A-**	A-	A-	158.2	6.61	9.2	2.6	28.4	0.2	**8.1**	9.8	15.4
Citizens State Bank	Roma	TX	**B-**	B-	B-	89.0	5.27	4.4	12.8	18.8	32.8	**7.2**	9.1	18.4
Citizens State Bank	Sealy	TX	**A-**	A-	A-	302.7	7.11	3.5	2.6	27.6	44.5	**9.8**	11.3	0.0

Asset Quality Index	Adjusted Non-Performing Loans as a % of Total Loans	Adjusted Non-Performing Loans as a % of Capital	Net Charge-Offs Avg Loans	Profitability Index	Net Income ($Mil)	Return on Assets (R.O.A.)	Return on Equity (R.O.E.)	Net Interest Spread	Overhead Efficiency Ratio	Liquidity Index	Liquidity Ratio	Hot Money Ratio	Stability Index
4.0	1.70	na	0.17	**4.4**	3.2	0.85	6.84	3.80	60.4	**2.6**	16.2	12.9	**8.9**
6.2	0.64	3.5	0.09	**6.0**	1.6	1.15	11.87	3.38	60.9	**1.7**	18.6	22.3	**6.7**
7.2	0.19	na	0.01	**6.7**	0.9	1.46	9.50	3.68	56.8	**0.7**	22.0	46.3	**9.4**
10.0	0.00	na	0.00	**3.4**	0.1	0.74	2.60	2.50	82.0	**3.4**	58.9	23.0	**8.1**
9.0	0.59	2.5	0.00	**1.8**	0.0	0.05	0.41	2.55	99.4	**0.9**	20.2	35.5	**6.2**
10.0	0.09	na	0.00	**1.0**	0.0	-0.01	-0.04	2.57	106.1	**3.2**	43.2	19.7	**7.2**
9.6	0.09	0.2	-0.12	**8.2**	11.8	1.93	14.93	2.81	46.6	**6.8**	63.7	7.3	**10.0**
5.2	0.27	na	0.00	**4.5**	0.5	0.94	9.59	3.71	70.4	**0.9**	14.6	31.7	**6.0**
4.7	1.21	na	0.10	**5.7**	0.8	1.41	11.86	3.95	64.9	**1.2**	24.1	20.1	**7.9**
7.1	0.00	na	0.00	**9.7**	1.1	2.14	18.47	3.73	48.8	**4.7**	41.2	11.7	**8.7**
8.6	0.25	na	-0.02	**3.9**	0.1	0.79	8.59	3.93	88.3	**6.2**	48.4	4.1	**4.5**
3.7	1.18	na	0.03	**3.5**	0.4	0.71	10.59	4.17	81.0	**1.0**	11.4	31.7	**3.9**
6.8	1.04	3.9	-0.16	**3.6**	0.4	0.53	4.34	3.65	82.7	**5.6**	33.4	3.1	**6.5**
9.3	0.04	na	0.02	**3.8**	0.3	0.75	6.89	3.12	75.9	**5.2**	48.2	11.0	**6.3**
7.6	0.20	1.1	0.05	**8.1**	5.1	1.83	15.48	3.91	54.5	**3.2**	14.0	13.3	**10.0**
8.8	0.00	0.0	0.01	**4.6**	1.0	0.96	8.42	3.35	63.2	**2.8**	28.9	17.5	**7.3**
8.6	0.00	na	0.44	**3.9**	0.2	0.74	6.10	4.16	76.0	**5.7**	46.7	6.7	**7.0**
8.6	0.29	na	-0.01	**7.6**	1.1	2.01	15.62	4.03	54.9	**5.2**	42.7	9.6	**8.7**
4.6	2.87	na	0.11	**5.1**	0.8	1.02	5.78	3.18	58.7	**2.0**	27.3	20.8	**8.3**
7.2	0.92	na	0.00	**8.7**	4.7	2.18	20.37	3.98	52.7	**2.0**	10.2	8.6	**9.2**
7.3	1.50	na	-0.03	**2.9**	0.6	0.69	8.02	3.63	80.3	**6.0**	49.3	6.3	**5.1**
9.4	0.00	na	0.00	**5.0**	0.2	1.14	6.80	2.30	54.4	**3.3**	73.8	32.6	**8.5**
5.4	1.03	na	0.00	**4.6**	1.6	1.19	11.15	3.56	63.8	**2.2**	5.3	16.7	**6.9**
4.9	0.96	na	0.25	**3.5**	0.0	0.53	5.42	4.32	82.9	**5.0**	14.8	1.5	**3.0**
9.4	0.21	0.5	0.03	**4.9**	0.6	1.42	9.24	2.82	66.3	**6.8**	63.6	5.5	**8.2**
9.3	0.32	na	0.08	**3.9**	0.3	0.86	8.09	3.05	76.3	**5.1**	37.0	8.2	**6.7**
4.6	1.48	na	0.45	**3.4**	0.1	0.36	3.09	3.86	79.6	**3.9**	12.4	9.1	**7.2**
7.1	0.60	3.6	-0.02	**7.6**	6.6	1.82	15.83	3.46	59.6	**2.6**	19.4	16.9	**10.0**
5.8	0.42	na	0.16	**6.7**	1.1	1.59	13.69	4.01	58.7	**1.7**	10.6	20.3	**8.0**
7.3	1.54	na	-0.11	**5.8**	0.3	1.13	8.61	3.87	63.9	**1.7**	26.9	26.0	**7.8**
6.3	0.90	na	0.00	**5.8**	1.6	1.36	13.36	3.51	66.9	**2.8**	26.3	16.4	**6.5**
6.3	0.81	na	-0.03	**9.8**	5.9	1.98	17.98	4.84	52.7	**4.8**	14.2	3.5	**10.0**
9.8	0.00	na	0.00	**3.7**	0.2	0.68	8.97	2.88	70.1	**7.2**	57.0	1.1	**3.6**
6.5	0.91	na	0.58	**5.9**	3.3	1.21	11.04	3.58	64.3	**3.6**	22.6	13.5	**8.6**
1.4	0.56	na	0.11	**4.1**	0.3	0.76	6.43	4.37	76.9	**0.7**	15.2	46.2	**5.7**
8.3	0.33	na	0.00	**6.7**	0.5	1.51	13.90	3.59	54.8	**5.2**	35.8	6.7	**7.3**
9.6	0.00	0.0	-0.31	**4.3**	0.1	1.04	7.00	2.67	62.1	**5.8**	73.8	11.2	**6.7**
8.5	0.00	na	0.00	**4.9**	0.2	1.21	14.52	3.64	65.9	**3.7**	22.9	11.4	**4.8**
4.9	0.08	na	0.00	**6.7**	0.4	1.48	7.99	3.60	46.3	**2.9**	43.5	13.0	**9.2**
4.0	1.21	na	0.08	**4.2**	0.4	0.75	5.12	4.61	78.2	**1.6**	18.9	24.8	**7.6**
9.2	0.86	3.4	0.08	**2.6**	0.2	0.23	1.42	3.09	84.6	**2.6**	7.6	15.4	**7.4**
1.6	3.28	na	0.14	**1.9**	0.0	0.13	1.93	4.22	95.9	**0.7**	18.3	55.6	**0.3**
9.1	0.00	na	-0.02	**4.1**	0.2	0.90	6.04	2.13	59.0	**2.2**	46.6	38.0	**6.5**
3.9	5.64	9.9	0.00	**7.6**	2.1	2.03	14.97	4.00	44.7	**2.6**	35.3	20.6	**9.3**
7.9	0.00	na	0.00	**6.1**	0.5	1.37	9.83	3.45	59.4	**4.9**	29.1	6.1	**8.8**
8.3	0.42	na	0.81	**5.3**	0.3	1.42	5.98	3.79	60.4	**4.5**	54.5	15.0	**7.7**
3.8	1.91	na	0.99	**3.9**	0.5	0.63	5.37	3.32	62.3	**2.5**	20.0	16.8	**6.5**
7.1	0.40	na	0.01	**6.1**	0.6	1.21	12.34	3.96	62.7	**4.3**	23.6	8.1	**6.0**
3.0	4.63	na	-0.01	**4.9**	0.3	0.81	6.16	3.67	71.6	**1.1**	23.1	32.4	**8.2**
6.6	0.27	na	-0.02	**9.6**	1.9	2.13	20.14	3.60	37.8	**1.0**	10.7	29.9	**8.7**
5.9	0.90	na	-0.01	**6.6**	1.5	1.40	11.27	3.85	57.0	**4.2**	27.9	9.8	**8.1**
6.7	0.00	na	0.00	**4.2**	0.1	0.81	8.32	3.81	75.0	**0.7**	17.0	36.5	**3.7**
2.7	1.63	10.7	0.01	**5.0**	1.0	1.02	8.82	3.53	71.8	**1.3**	12.6	24.6	**7.8**
6.7	0.80	na	-0.13	**0.6**	0.0	-0.19	-1.95	2.82	106.6	**2.9**	60.2	31.2	**2.8**
9.3	1.18	1.6	0.06	**4.4**	5.1	1.87	14.77	2.49	69.5	**3.2**	57.9	36.9	**8.0**
6.2	0.01	na	0.08	**8.4**	0.7	1.91	16.01	4.13	57.2	**1.6**	21.6	24.9	**8.6**
9.9	0.00	na	0.00	**0.4**	0.0	-0.21	-2.39	2.44	111.1	**5.2**	86.4	16.1	**2.1**
8.6	0.09	na	-0.11	**9.6**	0.9	2.17	22.34	3.97	46.1	**1.1**	27.7	46.0	**7.7**
5.2	1.94	6.7	0.71	**3.2**	0.1	0.38	4.07	4.67	90.0	**1.9**	39.4	46.3	**4.6**
9.3	0.00	na	0.02	**6.0**	1.1	1.46	12.96	3.07	51.2	**3.4**	51.4	23.0	**7.4**

	Name	City	State	Rating	2019 Rating	2018 Rating	Total Assets ($Mil)	One Year Asset Growth	Commercial Loans	Consumer Loans	Mortgage Loans	Securities	Capitalization Index	Leverage Ratio	Risk-Based Capital Ratio
	Citizens State Bank	Somerville	TX	B+	B+	B	664.8	6.45	9.7	3.1	21.1	22.0	10.0	11.2	17.7
	Citizens State Bank	Waco	TX	C+	C+	C+	152.3	1.69	3.9	2.8	42.0	20.6	7.8	9.6	16.9
	Citizens State Bank	Cadott	WI	B-	B-	B-	117.7	4.08	5.9	3.3	16.7	17.5	10.0	11.5	17.5
	Citizens State Bank	Hudson	WI	B-	B-	B-	238.5	16.09	6.0	0.9	26.8	10.8	5.4	8.0	11.3
	Citizens State Bank and Trust Co.	Council Grove	KS	D+	D+	D+	50.6	4.72	15.9	2.1	9.8	1.8	4.7	9.1	10.8
	Citizens State Bank and Trust Co.	Ellsworth	KS	B	B	B-	208.4	9.19	2.0	2.2	15.7	40.3	6.5	8.5	16.6
	Citizens State Bank and Trust Co.	Hiawatha	KS	A-	A-	A-	88.7	1.33	3.8	2.5	13.5	26.0	10.0	16.9	27.6
	Citizens State Bank at Mohall	Mohall	ND	B-	B-	C	60.9	1.89	10.1	3.2	13.2	24.1	10.0	12.3	16.9
▼	Citizens State Bank Norwood Young Ameri	Norwood Young Ame	MN	C-	C	C	87.2	5.75	13.9	1.8	7.6	0.0	9.6	10.7	15.5
	Citizens State Bank of Arlington	Arlington	SD	B	B	B-	112.5	5.92	2.9	1.0	3.4	29.4	9.8	12.2	0.0
	Citizens State Bank of Cheney, Kansas	Cheney	KS	B	B	C+	66.7	9.14	8.5	9.1	10.1	25.5	9.1	10.4	16.0
	Citizens State Bank of Finley	Finley	ND	A-	A-	B-	126.7	-0.94	5.0	1.4	0.8	27.2	9.8	14.2	0.0
	Citizens State Bank of Hayfield	Hayfield	MN	D+	D+	D+	104.2	11.79	14.0	3.1	9.3	18.5	5.6	7.6	11.9
	Citizens State Bank of La Crosse	La Crosse	WI	B	B	B	345.0	18.67	13.7	0.7	19.4	1.1	4.3	8.6	10.7
	Citizens State Bank of Lankin	Lankin	ND	C+	C+	C+	47.2	3.13	7.5	5.6	2.5	30.3	8.1	10.7	13.4
	Citizens State Bank of Loyal	Loyal	WI	B+	B+	B+	207.6	0.06	2.9	0.2	7.7	22.8	10.0	13.5	18.5
	Citizens State Bank of Luling	Luling	TX	B	B	B	69.4	1.86	4.6	1.4	9.6	5.0	9.8	14.7	0.0
	Citizens State Bank of Milford	Milford	IL	C-	C-	C-	43.5	1.49	6.1	1.8	0.6	15.1	7.4	9.3	14.4
	Citizens State Bank of New Castle, Indiana	New Castle	IN	B	B	B	582.1	6.73	7.0	11.3	19.2	14.8	8.5	10.0	17.1
	Citizens State Bank of Ontonagon	Ontonagon	MI	C	C	C+	55.4	-1.05	2.0	6.3	14.0	27.1	9.8	13.3	0.0
▼	Citizens State Bank of Ouray	Ouray	CO	C-	C	C-	119.6	17.58	1.4	0.7	21.5	22.8	8.1	9.7	16.0
	Citizens State Bank of Roseau	Roseau	MN	B+	B+	B	224.0	4.83	7.1	5.9	6.3	38.3	9.8	13.2	0.0
	Citizens State Bank of Tyler, Inc.	Tyler	MN	C-	C-	D+	22.6	2.49	5.5	4.0	3.2	22.9	8.4	9.9	42.5
	Citizens State Bank of Waverly	Waverly	MN	B+	B+	B+	82.3	10.08	4.7	1.5	18.3	17.0	6.4	8.4	13.3
▲	Citizens Tri-County Bank	Dunlap	TN	B-	C+	C+	951.1	7.44	2.2	9.2	20.7	21.1	7.3	9.4	0.0
	Citizens Trust Bank	Atlanta	GA	B+	B+	B+	444.3	10.00	9.5	1.6	14.5	18.8	9.9	11.0	16.2
	Citizens Union Bank of Shelbyville	Shelbyville	KY	B	B	B	880.2	12.46	8.4	0.5	15.4	6.6	9.8	11.4	0.0
	Citizens' Bank, Inc.	Robertsdale	AL	B	B	B	114.2	4.33	6.9	1.5	19.5	17.7	9.8	12.0	0.0
	Citizens-Farmers Bank of Cole Camp	Cole Camp	MO	B+	B+	B+	137.4	3.29	3.7	7.2	27.9	23.9	9.8	15.8	0.0
	City Bank	Lubbock	TX	B+	B+	B	3214.8	17.16	11.0	9.1	13.1	22.9	9.8	10.9	14.9
	City Bank & Trust Co.	Natchitoches	LA	B	B	B	241.7	-2.50	3.2	2.8	12.1	54.9	8.5	10.0	18.0
▼	City Bank & Trust Co.	Lincoln	NE	B-	B	B	205.0	39.62	10.3	2.1	11.3	12.6	9.8	11.7	0.0
▼	City First Bank of D.C., N.A.	Washington	DC	C	C+	C+	360.4	-9.05	11.6	0.0	2.4	27.7	6.9	8.9	19.1
	City National B&T Co. of Lawton, Oklahom	Lawton	OK	A	A	A-	360.5	-0.27	3.0	2.9	20.4	21.0	10.0	14.5	23.5
	City National Bank	Los Angeles	CA	B+	B+	B	65954.9	27.21	13.6	1.1	19.7	23.5	5.8	7.8	12.0
	City National Bank	Corsicana	TX	B-	B-	B-	53.7	10.65	12.2	4.5	37.4	3.8	9.2	10.5	18.4
	City National Bank of Colorado City	Colorado City	TX	B-	B-	B	149.2	13.14	4.4	6.8	29.7	19.0	6.3	8.3	13.5
	City National Bank of Florida	Miami	FL	B	B	B	16241.2	9.86	13.7	0.4	11.2	20.8	9.0	10.8	14.2
	City National Bank of Metropolis	Metropolis	IL	B	B	B	395.8	3.63	3.7	4.1	19.9	45.7	10.0	13.8	30.4
	City National Bank of San Saba	San Saba	TX	C+	C+	C+	74.7	17.95	2.1	3.3	0.3	58.6	9.8	12.6	0.0
	City National Bank of Sulphur Springs	Sulphur Springs	TX	A-	A-	B	783.9	5.90	6.2	5.6	28.4	19.4	9.2	10.6	0.0
	City National Bank of Taylor	Taylor	TX	A-	A-	B+	194.0	-4.15	2.6	0.7	37.1	23.8	9.8	11.8	0.0
▲	City National Bank of West Virginia	Charleston	WV	A-	B+	B+	5028.6	3.59	5.7	1.1	32.5	17.8	8.5	10.0	14.8
	City State Bank	Norwalk	IA	B	B	B	490.8	19.19	8.0	1.1	11.2	8.0	6.7	8.9	12.3
	City State Bank	Fort Scott	KS	C+	C+	C+	41.5	0.95	3.5	3.9	25.7	14.6	7.8	9.7	0.0
	Citywide Banks	Denver	CO	B+	B+	B+	2275.9	2.79	13.6	0.6	8.1	25.1	9.2	10.6	14.3
	Civis Bank	Rogersville	TN	E-	E-	E-	89.0	-2.17	4.9	1.5	25.0	12.9	0.0	2.8	5.7
	Civista Bank	Sandusky	OH	A-	A-	A-	2571.3	13.20	7.5	0.6	13.3	14.2	7.9	9.6	13.9
	Clackamas County Bank	Sandy	OR	A	A	A	230.3	2.34	0.6	0.4	14.3	20.8	10.0	12.8	23.9
	Clare Bank, N.A.	Platteville	WI	B+	B+	B+	281.0	3.17	2.5	1.0	22.6	31.9	9.8	12.1	0.0
▼	Claremont Savings Bank	Claremont	NH	C	B-	C+	456.9	8.59	2.7	1.1	58.9	8.6	9.8	12.9	0.0
▼	Clarion County Community Bank	Clarion	PA	C+	B-	B-	186.5	14.76	8.5	2.0	31.4	14.5	7.7	9.6	0.0
	Clarkson Bank	Clarkson	NE	B+	B+	B	59.1	5.91	7.0	1.3	0.1	34.4	9.8	13.9	0.0
	Classic Bank, N.A.	Cameron	TX	B-	B-	C+	415.8	12.37	3.2	1.8	20.6	14.3	7.3	9.2	13.6
▲	Claxton Bank	Claxton	GA	C+	C	C+	121.2	-1.62	3.2	1.3	9.1	23.3	9.8	11.1	0.0
	Clay City Banking Co.	Clay City	IL	C	C	C+	158.7	11.05	7.9	2.2	23.8	14.7	7.7	9.5	13.5
	Clay County Bank, Inc.	Clay	WV	A-	A-	A-	96.8	-0.33	1.2	12.9	40.3	17.4	9.8	15.2	0.0
▼	Clay County Savings Bank	Liberty	MO	C	C+	C+	126.2	6.47	2.3	0.4	22.9	3.1	7.4	9.4	0.0
	Clay County State Bank	Louisville	IL	B	B	C+	79.9	4.38	9.9	7.9	17.8	20.3	9.8	15.2	0.0
	CLB The Community Bank	Jonesville	LA	C+	C+	C	187.1	2.56	24.4	4.9	8.5	26.4	9.4	10.8	0.0

Asset Quality Index	Adjusted Non-Performing Loans as a % of Total Loans	Adjusted Non-Performing Loans as a % of Capital	Net Charge-Offs / Avg Loans	Profitability Index	Net Income ($Mil)	Return on Assets (R.O.A.)	Return on Equity (R.O.E.)	Net Interest Spread	Overhead Efficiency Ratio	Liquidity Index	Liquidity Ratio	Hot Money Ratio	Stability Index
5.1	1.87	na	0.08	**8.5**	2.9	1.76	15.54	4.50	51.8	**2.8**	16.5	15.1	**8.1**
2.7	3.26	na	1.15	**2.7**	0.1	0.34	3.64	4.15	95.8	**4.0**	15.4	8.5	**5.2**
5.3	1.76	na	-0.16	**3.8**	0.2	0.73	6.38	3.84	77.7	**4.3**	20.7	7.7	**6.4**
7.9	0.20	na	0.00	**4.4**	0.4	0.73	9.09	3.64	67.5	**2.8**	16.8	15.1	**5.0**
3.6	0.67	na	0.00	**6.6**	0.2	1.61	17.13	5.00	62.2	**0.9**	6.9	30.9	**5.5**
6.0	0.81	na	0.04	**4.7**	0.6	1.18	12.03	3.16	66.2	**3.8**	19.8	10.6	**6.3**
7.8	1.35	4.3	0.00	**6.5**	0.3	1.49	8.72	3.84	63.9	**5.5**	30.3	2.1	**8.7**
5.4	0.94	na	0.00	**4.3**	0.1	0.87	7.08	3.79	77.3	**2.2**	8.2	17.1	**6.1**
0.1	6.70	na	0.79	**6.0**	0.3	1.17	8.25	4.20	63.6	**4.8**	34.9	9.1	**6.7**
6.4	0.44	na	-0.02	**4.7**	0.3	1.12	8.78	3.38	63.1	**2.4**	35.2	21.4	**7.7**
7.8	0.30	na	0.01	**6.6**	0.3	1.59	14.35	3.67	57.2	**3.2**	35.8	17.6	**7.5**
6.4	0.00	na	0.12	**5.0**	0.3	0.79	5.50	3.93	81.1	**2.0**	13.5	14.1	**9.0**
1.4	5.48	41.7	0.35	**2.7**	0.0	0.13	1.66	3.84	76.1	**4.9**	29.6	5.9	**3.1**
4.3	0.29	na	0.00	**9.8**	2.5	2.98	35.12	4.23	42.0	**0.6**	8.5	27.1	**6.6**
5.5	1.15	3.7	0.00	**4.9**	0.1	1.00	9.01	4.79	81.7	**4.4**	13.7	5.9	**6.4**
8.3	1.00	na	0.00	**4.8**	0.5	1.04	7.54	3.63	68.7	**4.7**	20.9	4.9	**8.1**
7.3	0.08	na	0.01	**4.9**	0.2	0.99	6.75	4.42	73.4	**3.3**	19.6	12.9	**7.6**
7.3	0.00	na	0.00	**2.6**	0.0	0.24	2.57	3.81	94.2	**5.1**	32.1	6.0	**3.8**
7.9	0.17	1.1	0.08	**5.1**	1.4	1.00	10.04	3.72	66.5	**5.6**	37.3	5.0	**6.5**
6.8	3.35	na	0.24	**2.8**	0.1	0.71	5.05	3.31	77.6	**7.3**	80.0	3.1	**5.1**
6.9	0.39	na	-0.01	**1.4**	-0.1	-0.48	-4.77	3.40	92.2	**4.3**	30.2	10.3	**5.7**
4.9	1.90	na	0.00	**5.5**	0.8	1.38	10.46	3.21	59.3	**1.4**	15.6	25.5	**8.0**
6.3	2.54	na	0.00	**3.4**	0.0	0.63	6.19	3.60	69.5	**6.9**	65.5	1.1	**3.6**
3.6	1.97	8.9	0.12	**6.5**	0.3	1.52	12.57	4.23	58.7	**4.3**	18.8	6.3	**6.9**
4.1	1.45	na	0.08	**7.2**	3.6	1.52	15.38	3.87	62.6	**1.8**	23.1	22.0	**8.2**
5.0	1.95	8.2	0.04	**4.5**	0.7	0.66	5.92	3.65	80.2	**1.8**	20.9	21.2	**6.9**
4.9	1.23	6.7	0.00	**5.4**	2.2	0.99	8.54	3.71	68.8	**3.8**	17.3	10.2	**9.0**
4.9	1.54	na	-0.07	**3.9**	0.2	0.69	5.70	4.54	83.4	**3.6**	26.9	12.8	**6.9**
3.4	4.33	na	0.00	**6.1**	0.5	1.37	8.82	3.55	47.6	**2.7**	22.8	16.0	**8.1**
7.7	0.35	1.8	0.25	**4.7**	8.0	1.00	8.39	4.18	70.7	**3.9**	21.6	9.5	**9.2**
8.4	0.56	na	0.02	**4.8**	0.8	1.31	13.47	3.25	66.0	**6.9**	59.2	4.1	**5.9**
8.5	0.24	na	0.00	**2.8**	0.1	0.28	2.35	3.07	89.1	**2.9**	26.3	15.7	**7.2**
5.9	1.39	5.6	0.00	**1.7**	-0.2	-0.14	-1.52	2.48	102.9	**1.8**	39.9	36.4	**5.3**
7.3	1.04	4.6	0.87	**7.5**	1.3	1.50	10.84	4.19	83.7	**5.7**	35.3	3.4	**9.0**
7.2	0.46	3.4	0.04	**4.6**	97.9	0.63	7.24	2.93	66.2	**5.6**	26.9	2.8	**7.7**
8.6	0.13	na	0.01	**3.6**	0.1	0.62	5.89	4.02	86.1	**1.5**	23.2	26.7	**6.0**
4.8	0.74	na	0.32	**6.2**	0.9	2.61	32.24	4.47	61.8	**1.9**	11.4	18.9	**4.9**
7.7	0.43	2.2	0.12	**4.3**	32.9	0.83	6.85	2.85	54.2	**3.2**	25.0	10.7	**9.1**
6.4	1.97	6.0	0.08	**3.3**	0.8	0.86	6.22	2.58	76.5	**2.2**	46.0	30.8	**6.9**
9.8	0.00	na	0.13	**3.3**	0.1	0.68	5.30	2.71	73.5	**7.0**	75.0	4.4	**6.8**
6.8	0.22	na	0.26	**7.6**	3.1	1.60	13.09	4.65	62.8	**3.2**	26.8	14.4	**9.3**
7.0	0.55	na	0.52	**6.1**	0.8	1.57	13.56	4.20	71.0	**5.9**	37.0	2.5	**7.8**
6.1	1.19	4.2	0.10	**9.5**	31.0	2.49	20.51	3.54	38.2	**2.5**	9.0	15.9	**10.0**
8.5	0.06	na	0.00	**5.0**	1.3	1.12	12.40	3.05	70.7	**3.3**	27.0	13.8	**5.8**
8.8	0.00	0.0	0.00	**5.0**	0.1	1.14	11.74	3.98	71.4	**2.8**	32.3	18.6	**5.7**
6.0	0.76	2.9	0.02	**5.6**	5.5	0.97	6.12	4.19	48.9	**5.6**	28.1	5.0	**8.3**
2.9	5.52	na	1.50	**0.3**	-0.1	-0.26	-10.97	3.93	110.2	**3.7**	21.8	11.1	**0.4**
7.1	0.49	2.1	-0.01	**6.5**	8.2	1.27	10.08	4.11	60.5	**4.6**	21.7	6.9	**10.0**
9.1	0.00	0.0	-0.01	**5.9**	0.7	1.17	8.89	4.17	74.4	**4.8**	28.8	6.1	**9.1**
7.2	2.02	na	0.02	**5.1**	1.0	1.51	11.83	2.71	57.6	**5.4**	39.1	7.2	**7.8**
6.2	1.09	na	0.05	**1.4**	-4.6	-4.12	-30.15	3.09	85.0	**1.4**	16.0	24.5	**7.5**
6.9	0.38	na	0.03	**3.1**	0.2	0.48	4.95	3.47	80.2	**0.8**	16.5	37.5	**5.0**
6.6	0.42	na	0.01	**7.3**	0.3	1.82	13.33	3.61	48.7	**2.4**	30.6	19.7	**8.7**
5.1	0.82	na	0.03	**4.5**	1.4	1.32	14.51	3.62	72.3	**1.6**	8.9	21.0	**5.8**
4.0	2.88	na	0.45	**5.0**	0.4	1.33	11.73	4.41	72.8	**3.3**	29.1	15.0	**6.2**
3.0	2.40	na	0.08	**3.5**	0.2	0.51	5.26	3.61	82.6	**3.7**	16.5	10.7	**5.1**
6.4	0.18	na	0.05	**7.5**	0.4	1.46	9.57	4.07	58.3	**3.4**	35.3	16.7	**8.6**
9.0	0.00	na	0.00	**2.6**	0.1	0.27	2.79	3.39	90.7	**5.2**	31.9	5.2	**5.8**
3.7	0.87	na	-0.01	**4.9**	0.2	1.13	7.46	3.25	66.7	**3.9**	20.0	9.8	**8.0**
1.5	3.39	23.7	0.33	**3.4**	0.3	0.57	5.20	3.88	81.0	**3.7**	26.9	12.3	**6.2**

Name	City	State	Rating	2019 Rating	2018 Rating	Total Assets ($Mil)	One Year Asset Growth	Asset Mix (As a % of Total Assets) Commercial Loans	Consumer Loans	Mortgage Loans	Securities	Capitalization Index	Leverage Ratio	Risk-Based Capital Ratio
Clear Lake Bank and Trust Co.	Clear Lake	IA	B+	B+	B+	447.3	4.12	11.8	3.8	17.7	7.0	6.4	8.6	12.1
Clear Mountain Bank	Bruceton Mills	WV	A-	A-	B+	667.4	6.46	8.3	4.5	32.2	17.7	9.8	12.5	0.0
ClearPoint Federal Bank & Trust	Batesville	IN	U	U	U	112.4	15.28	0.0	0.0	0.0	94.9	9.8	15.2	0.0
▲ Cleo State Bank	Cleo Springs	OK	B-	C+	B-	88.1	-1.95	16.0	3.8	0.1	47.2	9.8	19.5	0.0
▼ Cleveland State Bank	Cleveland	MS	B+	A-	B+	239.2	-0.51	9.0	4.5	16.9	31.1	9.8	11.3	0.0
Cleveland State Bank	Cleveland	WI	B	B	B	134.3	5.96	8.4	4.5	25.0	24.9	9.7	11.0	0.0
Clinton Bank	Clinton	KY	B-	B-	B-	61.1	-7.52	5.0	1.8	11.3	28.8	10.0	18.7	28.0
▼ Clinton National Bank	Clinton	IA	C+	B-	B-	411.3	1.44	7.7	1.5	8.1	36.2	9.8	13.2	0.0
Clinton Savings Bank	Clinton	MA	B	B	C+	584.4	1.43	3.3	1.8	36.0	17.7	10.0	11.4	17.3
CNB Bank	Carlsbad	NM	B+	B+	B+	462.6	12.45	10.2	7.8	12.7	37.3	6.7	8.7	14.8
CNB Bank	Clearfield	PA	B	B	B	3753.5	14.85	13.9	2.1	18.7	15.2	6.1	8.6	11.9
CNB Bank & Trust, N.A.	Carlinville	IL	C+	C+	C-	1338.4	1.74	10.1	1.9	8.7	19.3	6.7	8.7	13.0
▼ CNB Bank, Inc.	Berkeley Springs	WV	C+	B-	B-	420.1	5.86	4.3	1.1	43.6	14.2	7.8	9.5	15.0
Coastal Bank & Trust	Jacksonville	NC	B-	B-	B-	117.5	0.45	6.5	0.8	16.0	14.8	9.8	16.2	0.0
Coastal Carolina National Bank	Myrtle Beach	SC	B-	B-	B-	477.4	20.73	7.3	3.1	19.5	6.5	6.2	9.4	11.9
Coastal Community Bank	Everett	WA	A-	A-	B+	1183.3	6.04	8.8	0.3	8.9	1.7	8.6	11.7	13.8
Coastal Heritage Bank	Weymouth	MA	C	C	C	847.7	161.24	4.8	1.9	51.6	7.1	8.2	10.0	0.0
Coastal States Bank	Hilton Head Island	SC	C-	C-	D	776.5	26.44	26.7	5.2	8.2	9.8	5.6	9.9	11.5
▼ Coatesville Savings Bank	Coatesville	PA	C-	C	C-	234.0	5.82	6.3	0.1	43.7	9.0	8.6	10.1	15.3
Coffee County Bank	Manchester	TN	B	B	B-	202.7	3.57	8.8	6.5	28.6	6.8	9.5	11.8	14.6
Cogent Bank	Orange City	FL	D-	D-	E	338.1	69.39	25.8	0.5	11.0	19.4	8.8	12.3	14.0
Colchester State Bank	Colchester	IL	B	B	B	73.0	9.31	3.4	3.6	6.5	53.9	9.8	15.2	0.0
▲ Coleman County State Bank	Coleman	TX	A-	B+	B-	128.1	10.30	9.2	2.0	12.6	7.7	8.2	9.8	15.2
Colfax Banking Co.	Colfax	LA	B	B	B	116.1	1.59	1.6	2.8	22.8	34.2	8.3	10.0	0.0
Collins State Bank	Collins	WI	B-	B-	B-	93.1	4.73	8.2	3.9	24.0	15.8	7.0	9.0	13.7
▼ Collinsville Bank	Collinsville	CT	C	C+	C	183.4	10.95	8.6	2.3	39.6	6.2	6.8	8.8	12.4
Collinsville Building and Loan Assn.	Collinsville	IL	C	C	C	123.4	4.19	0.0	0.0	75.9	16.5	9.8	27.3	0.0
Colonial Federal Savings Bank	Quincy	MA	B	B	B	319.2	5.99	0.0	0.5	47.8	30.7	10.0	14.7	29.6
▼ Colonial Savings, F.A.	Fort Worth	TX	C-	C	C	1052.4	0.98	0.9	0.2	43.9	19.7	7.9	9.6	21.9
▼ Colony Bank	Fitzgerald	GA	B-	B	B	1506.2	17.95	4.9	1.5	12.6	22.1	7.7	9.4	14.0
▲ Colorado Bank and Trust Co. of La Junta	La Junta	CO	A-	B+	B	150.5	9.78	11.2	2.7	13.2	23.8	8.6	10.3	0.0
Colorado Federal Savings Bank	Greenwood Village	CO	B	B	B-	2075.4	19.20	0.7	0.0	13.7	21.7	10.0	11.4	18.6
▼ Columbia Bank	Fair Lawn	NJ	B-	B	B	8307.3	21.97	6.0	0.0	29.1	16.9	8.2	9.8	14.4
Columbia S&L Assn.	Milwaukee	WI	E-	E-	E-	22.8	-0.32	0.0	2.1	45.9	0.1	6.8	8.8	14.0
Columbia State Bank	Tacoma	WA	B+	B+	B+	14030.1	7.47	16.2	0.3	2.8	25.3	8.1	10.1	13.4
▲ Columbus Bank and Trust Co.	Columbus	NE	B	B-	C+	141.9	5.75	12.8	1.4	5.2	11.6	7.2	9.3	0.0
▲ Columbus State Bank	Columbus	TX	B	B-	B-	108.3	17.56	0.4	0.2	0.6	65.6	10.0	12.6	26.0
Comenity Bank	Wilmington	DE	D+	D+	D+	12143.6	-7.80	0.0	83.5	0.0	1.1	10.0	13.3	18.1
Comenity Capital Bank	Draper	UT	C-	C-	C-	8796.8	-2.76	0.1	84.2	0.0	1.1	10.0	12.2	16.2
Comerica Bank	Dallas	TX	A-	A-	A-	76262.0	8.02	35.9	0.8	2.6	17.1	6.7	9.9	12.3
Comerica Bank & Trust, N.A.	Ann Arbor	MI	U	U	U	60.4	3.55	0.0	0.0	0.0	0.0	10.0	101.	251.5
Commencement Bank	Tacoma	WA	A-	A-	B	395.4	11.53	19.5	0.5	4.2	3.6	10.0	12.2	16.2
▼ Commerce Bank	Edina	MN	C+	B-	B+	211.1	0.73	8.0	0.1	8.3	5.5	10.0	12.9	15.8
Commerce Bank	Kansas City	MO	A	A	A-	26700.0	7.10	13.4	9.0	10.2	32.5	7.8	9.5	13.2
Commerce Bank	Corinth	MS	A-	A-	B+	131.7	10.79	14.3	5.8	28.7	18.1	9.8	11.5	0.0
Commerce Bank	Laredo	TX	A	A	A	532.4	-11.44	4.1	1.0	18.5	52.8	10.0	17.1	34.2
▲ Commerce Bank of Arizona, Inc.	Tucson	AZ	C-	D+	D	243.8	8.05	15.1	0.1	6.8	12.0	9.8	11.1	14.9
▼ Commerce Bank Texas	Stockdale	TX	B-	B	B	53.3	2.22	13.7	0.3	14.9	20.9	9.8	14.2	0.0
Commerce Community Bank	Oak Grove	LA	B	B	B-	60.2	0.24	16.5	1.6	11.5	21.0	9.0	10.3	14.5
Commerce National Bank & Trust	Winter Park	FL	A-	A-	B	121.6	6.33	2.9	1.1	17.6	9.2	10.0	11.8	17.6
Commerce State Bank	West Bend	WI	B-	B-	C+	729.5	6.68	23.9	0.0	14.4	4.4	5.9	10.0	11.7
CommerceWest Bank	Irvine	CA	B+	B+	B+	637.2	11.35	14.5	0.7	0.3	11.0	7.5	9.8	12.9
Commercial & Savings Bank of Millersburg	Millersburg	OH	B+	B+	B-	809.9	10.23	13.3	2.2	17.4	14.8	8.6	10.1	15.6
Commercial Bank	Crawford	GA	A	A	A-	253.4	37.57	5.1	1.9	19.1	14.9	7.2	9.3	0.0
Commercial Bank	Parsons	KS	B+	B+	B+	334.7	0.39	10.1	6.7	10.8	48.1	7.1	9.2	0.0
Commercial Bank	West Liberty	KY	B-	B-	B	157.6	13.12	4.7	5.9	29.8	19.4	10.0	12.5	20.3
Commercial Bank	Alma	MI	B-	B-	C	510.8	-3.09	5.4	1.8	31.5	5.9	7.6	9.4	14.2
Commercial Bank	Saint Louis	MO	C	C	C	217.7	9.19	18.4	2.1	12.7	27.3	6.0	8.1	11.8
Commercial Bank	De Kalb	MS	B	B	B	173.9	9.61	9.7	12.5	11.7	33.4	7.9	9.8	0.0
Commercial Bank	Nelson	NE	B	B	B	51.5	7.65	25.7	4.0	1.2	26.9	10.0	12.4	16.1

Asset Quality Index	Adjusted Non-Performing Loans as a % of Total Loans	Adjusted Non-Performing Loans as a % of Capital	Net Charge-Offs Avg Loans	Profitability Index	Net Income ($Mil)	Return on Assets (R.O.A.)	Return on Equity (R.O.E.)	Net Interest Spread	Overhead Efficiency Ratio	Liquidity Index	Liquidity Ratio	Hot Money Ratio	Stability Index
7.5	0.13	na	0.01	6.2	1.4	1.26	14.17	3.65	69.0	3.1	15.0	13.4	7.2
6.3	0.85	na	0.15	6.6	1.9	1.18	9.60	4.13	64.3	2.0	24.1	19.9	8.3
10.0	na	na	na	3.4	0.1	0.48	2.77	2.26	94.7	8.6	116.4	0.8	4.4
3.9	14.75	na	-0.04	4.9	0.3	1.32	7.04	3.49	61.8	4.3	58.4	16.7	6.5
8.4	0.56	na	0.29	5.1	0.5	0.87	8.28	3.94	71.7	5.2	37.2	7.4	6.2
4.3	1.66	na	-0.04	6.1	0.4	1.34	12.08	3.71	63.9	4.3	31.4	7.1	7.1
5.2	3.45	na	0.01	3.1	0.1	0.87	4.58	3.29	82.8	2.7	19.4	15.8	7.1
7.5	0.72	1.8	-0.01	2.5	0.3	0.31	2.12	2.81	90.0	5.0	41.7	10.3	7.3
6.3	1.61	7.8	0.00	2.2	-0.4	-0.30	-2.60	3.19	79.5	1.7	24.5	19.4	7.6
7.6	0.07	na	0.00	8.4	2.7	2.41	27.19	4.26	48.2	5.9	37.7	2.7	6.5
5.3	1.35	8.7	0.02	5.2	9.1	0.98	10.24	3.59	60.1	4.0	8.5	7.8	8.3
3.6	2.38	na	0.22	5.5	3.5	1.05	9.96	3.62	61.0	1.8	18.3	20.4	8.1
6.6	0.97	na	0.04	3.2	0.6	0.61	6.98	3.37	81.0	2.6	14.3	16.1	5.3
8.5	0.78	na	0.00	3.0	0.2	0.56	3.37	4.19	90.4	3.0	27.7	15.8	7.6
5.7	0.69	na	0.00	3.9	0.8	0.69	6.79	3.62	72.5	1.7	15.2	22.1	5.6
7.3	0.08	0.2	0.05	5.8	2.9	1.02	9.10	4.32	62.9	4.0	12.9	6.7	9.0
5.4	1.01	na	-0.01	2.9	1.0	0.45	4.27	3.59	76.3	2.7	12.4	15.4	5.9
4.2	0.82	5.3	0.02	2.5	1.0	0.51	4.47	3.85	80.2	1.4	12.7	18.6	5.1
4.5	2.13	na	-0.01	1.8	0.0	0.02	0.16	3.15	81.3	1.8	16.7	19.7	5.4
4.4	2.21	na	0.16	9.8	1.2	2.34	19.53	4.39	48.9	1.1	16.4	31.3	8.9
6.9	0.41	na	-0.02	0.7	0.0	-0.02	-0.17	3.89	99.6	1.6	22.5	24.6	5.2
5.3	3.46	na	0.13	4.4	0.2	1.28	8.20	3.00	67.4	3.9	51.5	17.4	6.6
8.0	0.02	na	0.04	9.3	0.7	2.08	21.22	4.96	63.2	3.6	25.0	12.1	7.1
8.7	0.05	na	0.01	4.7	0.3	1.16	11.20	3.82	74.0	1.4	19.3	26.7	6.2
8.2	0.36	na	-0.12	4.4	0.2	0.77	8.51	3.99	81.8	3.6	23.5	11.7	5.7
4.8	0.90	na	0.00	1.9	0.0	-0.02	-0.18	3.17	98.1	1.4	16.3	17.6	4.5
10.0	0.00	na	0.00	2.9	0.2	0.47	1.73	2.36	73.6	1.6	27.4	28.1	7.4
10.0	0.00	na	0.00	3.3	0.4	0.53	3.61	2.63	74.3	2.4	38.6	27.0	7.9
2.2	16.13	7.5	0.60	0.9	-24.9	-9.40	-41.37	4.53	-1741.0	5.6	28.0	4.6	8.6
5.6	1.58	na	0.18	3.8	1.9	0.50	4.57	3.75	76.6	3.7	23.1	12.9	8.2
6.5	0.34	4.9	0.24	9.8	0.7	1.87	17.95	4.85	59.1	4.8	27.6	5.8	7.1
8.8	0.90	1.9	0.00	2.5	-0.6	-0.13	-1.06	2.29	98.6	5.0	50.6	12.8	8.7
8.3	0.64	2.8	0.01	3.1	7.1	0.34	3.57	2.60	66.3	1.9	7.9	18.9	7.7
1.7	5.71	na	0.00	0.8	0.0	-0.59	-6.37	4.51	113.5	0.7	15.2	39.6	0.3
6.2	0.62	2.1	0.23	5.2	15.5	0.45	2.82	4.04	58.1	5.9	27.0	1.9	10.0
6.3	0.15	na	-0.06	5.7	0.5	1.27	11.39	4.01	62.2	1.4	5.6	22.6	7.7
10.0	0.00	na	0.00	3.8	0.2	0.73	5.75	2.30	64.0	6.9	105.4	10.9	6.4
1.0	1.68	17.9	7.21	8.4	46.1	1.42	11.01	22.42	40.2	0.6	20.4	71.0	9.5
1.4	1.27	16.4	6.43	3.7	-39.1	-1.74	-14.53	16.60	45.5	0.9	21.4	9.6	9.3
7.0	0.52	3.5	0.68	3.7	-69.0	-0.38	-3.49	3.05	62.4	4.8	18.1	3.1	10.0
9.7	na	0.0	na	9.5	6.3	44.28	46.37	1.95	56.1	4.0	na	0.0	5.0
5.0	0.87	na	-0.16	6.1	1.0	0.97	7.84	3.67	67.4	1.5	19.4	25.5	7.2
2.3	3.55	na	0.00	3.8	0.3	0.56	4.26	3.04	80.8	0.7	15.3	17.8	7.6
7.7	0.57	2.1	0.30	6.7	59.0	0.91	8.54	3.32	64.5	5.4	27.5	5.5	10.0
5.8	0.46	na	0.38	6.2	0.4	1.21	10.51	3.92	68.7	2.1	28.9	21.8	8.4
8.9	0.56	1.2	0.28	7.3	1.6	1.27	6.56	3.11	47.7	3.2	66.7	37.2	9.2
2.3	3.52	na	-0.66	3.4	0.4	0.72	6.56	4.20	98.6	3.4	30.2	14.9	6.8
7.4	0.00	0.0	0.00	4.0	0.1	0.63	3.47	4.20	79.9	2.5	25.2	17.4	8.2
7.7	0.06	na	0.00	6.0	0.2	1.24	12.08	4.24	64.5	1.9	32.2	28.8	5.9
7.7	0.09	na	0.00	5.8	0.3	0.87	7.34	3.58	77.2	1.5	25.9	27.9	9.0
5.9	0.74	na	0.60	4.5	1.1	0.60	5.99	3.49	52.7	0.7	13.2	25.6	5.9
7.4	0.01	0.1	0.40	5.2	1.1	0.76	6.99	3.91	49.6	4.0	19.3	7.5	6.5
5.8	1.17	na	0.05	6.7	2.6	1.27	12.07	3.65	59.2	4.1	17.7	8.5	7.6
8.8	0.13	na	0.01	9.3	1.2	1.91	20.95	3.97	53.3	3.3	28.9	14.9	7.1
8.3	0.27	na	-0.01	5.0	1.0	1.23	12.59	3.25	64.8	3.1	35.4	18.1	6.6
7.3	0.86	na	0.09	3.4	0.2	0.61	4.18	3.83	83.7	1.8	24.8	23.4	7.6
4.6	3.11	na	0.00	3.9	0.9	0.74	7.30	3.28	63.3	1.6	17.4	5.4	6.9
4.7	1.09	na	-0.05	2.9	0.2	0.46	5.44	3.33	86.5	3.6	32.9	14.7	4.6
5.2	0.58	4.5	0.38	4.7	0.3	0.80	8.17	3.85	71.7	2.2	30.7	22.2	5.8
7.7	0.52	na	0.00	6.2	0.2	1.33	11.22	4.23	62.4	1.4	9.1	24.5	7.6

Name	City	State	Rating	2019 Rating	2018 Rating	Total Assets ($Mil)	One Year Asset Growth	Asset Mix (As a % of Total Assets) Comm-ercial Loans	Cons-umer Loans	Mort-gage Loans	Secur-ities	Capital-ization Index	Lever-age Ratio	Risk-Based Capital Ratio
▼ Commercial Bank	Honea Path	SC	**B+**	A-	B+	198.0	4.77	2.6	3.1	13.3	41.8	**10.0**	14.6	46.9
Commercial Bank	Harrogate	TN	**B+**	B+	B	1496.2	18.14	8.2	1.8	23.7	9.5	**7.3**	9.2	12.9
Commercial Bank	Mason	TX	**B-**	B-	C+	57.1	6.17	3.8	2.4	23.1	38.4	**7.2**	9.2	17.1
Commercial Bank & Trust Co.	Monticello	AR	**B**	B	B-	211.6	0.60	13.4	7.1	14.0	29.5	**8.9**	10.4	0.0
Commercial Bank & Trust Co.	Paris	TN	**A-**	A-	B+	799.0	3.95	9.6	3.8	17.4	25.9	**9.4**	10.6	16.9
▲ Commercial Bank & Trust of PA	Latrobe	PA	**A-**	B+	B+	416.3	-1.23	2.9	0.3	26.5	35.0	**10.0**	13.7	21.8
Commercial Bank of California	Irvine	CA	**B**	B	C+	1048.7	8.62	10.7	3.1	1.2	8.4	**7.9**	9.8	0.0
Commercial Bank of Grayson	Grayson	KY	**B**	B	B	178.8	0.12	7.5	7.5	15.8	40.4	**10.0**	14.8	25.8
Commercial Bank of Mott	Mott	ND	**A-**	A-	B+	110.6	7.57	3.9	1.6	2.3	11.4	**9.8**	13.3	0.0
Commercial Bank of Oak Grove	Oak Grove	MO	**B+**	B+	B+	81.5	6.96	5.8	0.8	27.4	18.8	**9.8**	14.7	0.0
Commercial Bank of Ozark	Ozark	AL	**C**	C	C-	94.9	3.49	2.4	5.1	17.1	29.8	**6.5**	8.5	19.3
▲ Commercial Bank of Texas, N.A.	Nacogdoches	TX	**B+**	B	B-	790.8	7.06	12.9	4.4	16.6	21.6	**9.4**	10.6	15.3
Commercial Banking Co.	Valdosta	GA	**A-**	A-	B+	234.8	1.55	5.6	1.7	30.5	8.7	**10.0**	15.3	23.3
▼ Commercial Capital Bank	Delhi	LA	**C+**	B-	B-	174.0	14.03	5.5	1.9	15.9	5.0	**9.5**	10.7	16.3
Commercial National Bank of Brady	Brady	TX	**A**	A	A-	149.3	-6.65	4.6	2.7	18.6	33.6	**10.0**	12.9	24.3
Commercial National Bank of Texarkana	Texarkana	TX	**B+**	B+	B+	222.5	4.72	13.2	2.9	16.2	29.9	**7.5**	9.3	15.7
Commercial Savings Bank	Carroll	IA	**B**	B	B-	200.2	3.85	8.1	2.5	28.8	6.7	**6.6**	8.6	12.3
Commercial State Bank	Republican City	NE	**B+**	B+	A-	58.5	-0.98	3.1	0.6	0.0	51.1	**10.0**	30.8	39.4
Commercial State Bank	Wausa	NE	**B-**	B-	B-	140.1	9.80	20.9	5.7	2.8	3.7	**6.3**	9.8	11.9
▲ Commercial State Bank	Palmer	TX	**B-**	C+	C	81.6	-0.26	10.9	3.5	9.5	26.4	**7.1**	9.1	20.9
Commercial State Bank of Wagner	Wagner	SD	**B-**	B-	C+	177.6	-4.82	7.6	2.5	8.0	24.5	**9.8**	11.0	0.0
Commercial Trust Co. of Fayette	Fayette	MO	**B+**	B+	B	132.4	5.37	2.6	6.0	43.8	7.2	**7.6**	9.6	0.0
Commodore Bank	Somerset	OH	**D+**	D+	D+	75.6	-8.32	5.2	5.9	35.6	22.1	**6.7**	8.7	15.8
Commonwealth Bank and Trust Co.	Louisville	KY	**B-**	B-	B-	1165.8	13.55	8.0	3.8	12.5	16.7	**7.6**	9.4	13.0
Commonwealth Business Bank	Los Angeles	CA	**A-**	A-	A-	1202.1	2.08	10.8	0.4	1.5	7.7	**10.0**	13.1	16.0
▼ Commonwealth Community Bank, Inc.	Hartford	KY	**C+**	B-	B	146.1	1.62	0.2	2.6	16.5	56.3	**10.0**	16.1	36.8
Commonwealth Cooperative Bank	Hyde Park	MA	**B**	B	B	192.5	6.48	1.1	0.1	53.5	11.1	**9.8**	15.3	0.0
▼ Commonwealth National Bank	Mobile	AL	**D**	D+	D-	47.6	-1.95	2.1	1.1	7.7	33.8	**9.1**	10.4	16.7
Community 1st Bank Las Vegas	Las Vegas	NM	**C+**	C+	C-	142.9	0.64	2.5	1.0	10.5	37.8	**8.6**	10.1	22.3
Community Bank	Dunlap	IA	**B**	B	B	96.2	7.33	2.5	3.0	15.6	7.6	**10.0**	12.4	17.1
Community Bank	Winslow	IL	**A-**	A-	B+	224.7	5.67	7.0	1.5	21.1	29.7	**10.0**	14.7	25.1
▲ Community Bank	Liberal	KS	**B**	B-	C+	132.4	8.24	8.4	14.4	0.0	30.0	**10.0**	11.6	17.9
Community Bank	Topeka	KS	**B+**	B+	B	109.3	17.50	9.0	1.1	23.3	6.0	**6.3**	10.1	11.9
Community Bank	Zanesville	OH	**B-**	B-	C+	458.0	-1.41	6.7	5.6	38.6	13.2	**9.7**	11.0	0.0
▼ Community Bank	Alva	OK	**B+**	A-	A-	106.9	-1.98	5.8	1.9	5.7	53.9	**10.0**	11.8	19.0
▼ Community Bank	Bristow	OK	**B+**	A-	B+	89.5	1.90	5.7	3.7	30.9	12.4	**6.8**	8.8	15.2
Community Bank	Joseph	OR	**B+**	B+	B	410.3	-3.66	2.4	0.3	2.7	50.9	**8.5**	10.0	22.2
Community Bank	Carmichaels	PA	**B-**	B-	B-	1309.9	0.68	5.4	9.3	25.2	12.9	**6.2**	8.2	12.9
▼ Community Bank	Avon	SD	**C+**	B-	B	52.8	-1.58	10.7	6.2	7.0	30.1	**9.8**	15.5	0.0
Community Bank	Lexington	TN	**B**	B	B	160.5	-0.69	8.3	4.7	29.9	8.1	**8.2**	9.8	13.9
Community Bank	Bridgeport	TX	**B-**	B-	C+	105.1	9.80	13.5	2.0	19.0	10.5	**8.8**	10.4	0.0
Community Bank	Longview	TX	**A**	A	A	216.0	-1.71	11.8	2.9	35.4	2.3	**9.8**	11.9	0.0
Community Bank & Trust - Alabama	Union Springs	AL	**D**	D	D-	48.7	3.06	7.9	5.0	12.1	41.3	**6.1**	8.1	20.9
Community Bank & Trust - West Georgia	LaGrange	GA	**E+**	E+	D-	74.0	-8.66	6.2	1.5	18.7	11.2	**0.1**	3.2	6.3
Community Bank & Trust, Waco, Texas	Waco	TX	**A-**	A-	B+	468.2	4.37	23.7	2.4	24.1	25.3	**10.0**	15.7	22.9
Community Bank and Trust	Neosho	MO	**B-**	B-	B-	322.9	0.94	6.7	1.6	15.1	12.3	**6.8**	8.8	18.6
Community Bank and Trust Co.	Muscatine	IA	**D+**	D+	C	241.9	4.48	7.9	3.6	11.6	20.0	**6.9**	8.9	14.0
Community Bank Delaware	Lewes	DE	**B-**	B-	B	232.6	14.47	2.4	0.3	35.3	3.9	**9.0**	10.3	14.3
▲ Community Bank Mankato	Vernon Center	MN	**C+**	C	C	333.0	8.99	6.7	2.4	15.5	0.2	**5.8**	8.4	11.6
Community Bank of Cameron	Cameron	WI	**B**	B	B-	126.0	7.00	3.8	2.9	32.5	7.4	**7.2**	9.1	14.2
Community Bank of Easton	Easton	IL	**A-**	A-	B+	36.8	5.53	24.9	10.1	3.1	1.4	**9.8**	22.0	0.0
Community Bank of El Dorado Springs	El Dorado Springs	MO	**A**	A	B+	107.0	2.88	1.8	2.1	10.5	34.2	**9.8**	16.7	0.0
Community Bank of Elmhurst	Elmhurst	IL	**B-**	B-	B-	151.5	1.28	8.0	0.1	15.1	33.1	**6.9**	10.2	12.4
▲ Community Bank of Georgia	Baxley	GA	**C+**	C	C+	138.7	38.74	6.7	1.3	9.6	13.6	**7.1**	9.0	13.2
Community Bank of Louisiana	Mansfield	LA	**B**	B	B	528.1	5.46	5.0	1.5	10.9	49.2	**6.8**	9.0	0.0
Community Bank of Marshall	Marshall	MO	**B**	B	B	168.6	9.23	4.8	2.5	11.7	45.5	**9.4**	10.6	21.5
Community Bank of Memphis	Memphis	MO	**B-**	B-	B-	44.5	-4.05	2.8	3.5	16.1	17.5	**9.8**	13.4	0.0
Community Bank of Mississippi	Forest	MS	**B-**	B-	B-	3371.5	1.36	5.7	2.6	23.4	20.1	**6.4**	8.4	14.5
Community Bank of Missouri	Richmond	MO	**B+**	B+	B	56.8	6.27	5.3	1.1	17.4	3.6	**10.0**	14.0	20.6
Community Bank of Oelwein	Oelwein	IA	**B**	B	B	109.9	0.01	8.8	2.8	10.5	28.8	**10.0**	13.0	21.4

Arrows denote recent upgrades ▲ or downgrades ▼

Asset Quality Index	Adjusted Non-Performing Loans as a % of Total Loans	Adjusted Non-Performing Loans as a % of Capital	Net Charge-Offs Avg Loans	Profitability Index	Net Income ($Mil)	Return on Assets (R.O.A.)	Return on Equity (R.O.E.)	Net Interest Spread	Overhead Efficiency Ratio	Liquidity Index	Liquidity Ratio	Hot Money Ratio	Stability Index
7.5	2.99	na	0.05	4.8	0.6	1.13	7.72	2.96	64.4	6.1	70.4	11.0	8.4
5.2	1.28	na	0.05	6.7	4.9	1.30	14.30	3.91	54.2	1.2	9.4	20.2	8.3
5.2	1.80	na	0.01	5.9	0.2	1.65	18.60	3.86	58.9	2.8	37.7	20.1	5.0
5.0	1.32	na	0.20	4.8	0.6	1.08	10.34	3.63	70.0	0.9	18.8	34.6	6.3
6.6	0.99	na	0.10	7.5	3.0	1.52	13.66	3.63	66.1	4.4	33.3	10.5	9.1
9.4	0.14	0.4	-0.49	6.2	1.8	1.78	11.73	4.10	62.1	5.1	37.7	8.6	8.8
7.0	0.30	na	0.02	3.8	1.1	0.43	4.22	4.03	79.4	4.8	18.8	4.1	8.5
6.4	0.94	5.7	0.19	3.4	0.2	0.50	3.31	3.88	85.4	6.1	45.2	4.1	7.8
5.7	1.76	na	0.46	9.6	0.7	2.33	16.44	3.86	36.4	1.5	17.1	23.4	10.0
6.1	0.81	na	0.00	3.4	0.1	0.67	4.55	3.10	72.6	3.6	23.5	11.9	7.1
3.7	2.15	na	0.00	2.7	0.1	0.39	4.38	3.59	88.6	3.9	25.3	10.5	4.1
6.3	0.77	na	0.11	5.9	2.4	1.24	11.10	4.18	61.1	3.9	12.3	8.7	7.4
7.8	1.26	na	0.01	6.2	0.7	1.24	8.18	4.57	66.2	2.4	19.5	17.5	8.2
1.8	3.22	na	0.06	6.7	0.6	1.29	11.63	3.98	64.7	1.5	33.8	40.6	8.1
9.0	0.01	na	0.03	6.6	0.6	1.50	11.27	4.00	65.9	4.5	30.0	9.1	8.9
8.6	0.04	0.9	0.01	6.7	0.8	1.53	16.01	4.17	64.5	3.7	27.8	12.6	6.8
6.4	0.19	na	0.00	4.9	0.6	1.15	13.49	3.31	59.8	1.9	23.3	20.8	6.0
9.3	0.00	na	0.00	5.4	0.2	1.39	4.57	3.08	42.3	4.1	92.5	26.3	7.7
4.3	0.46	na	0.33	5.1	0.4	1.13	11.75	3.92	63.8	1.2	14.4	26.8	6.6
5.3	1.27	na	-0.21	5.8	0.4	2.13	24.40	4.26	69.5	5.2	43.0	9.4	4.1
4.6	3.72	na	0.20	9.6	0.9	2.13	18.38	4.63	50.0	0.9	10.8	32.9	8.7
7.7	0.22	na	0.09	4.7	0.4	1.11	11.44	3.15	68.3	2.9	22.1	15.1	6.9
4.3	1.05	na	-0.02	1.4	0.0	0.04	0.47	3.77	97.0	4.9	25.6	4.2	3.2
8.2	0.23	1.7	-0.08	4.0	2.9	1.03	10.68	3.34	80.3	1.6	17.2	8.6	8.0
5.2	0.85	na	0.11	6.0	1.8	0.63	4.79	3.84	71.9	0.7	15.6	44.5	9.9
9.9	0.30	na	0.00	2.5	0.1	0.36	2.41	2.50	87.1	4.3	77.7	21.9	8.0
7.7	0.56	na	0.00	3.9	0.4	0.85	5.57	3.88	77.8	0.9	23.1	34.5	7.9
3.1	3.23	na	3.36	0.0	-0.2	-1.64	-15.79	3.18	150.6	3.1	35.3	17.7	2.8
8.7	0.49	1.8	-0.04	4.5	0.5	1.36	12.75	3.86	67.9	5.3	44.6	9.8	3.8
7.0	0.23	1.3	-0.18	3.4	0.1	0.46	3.52	3.94	82.7	4.4	25.3	7.5	6.9
7.9	0.32	na	-0.05	5.3	0.8	1.36	9.20	2.87	51.8	2.9	33.8	18.5	8.0
4.4	3.78	na	0.02	5.4	0.4	1.11	9.38	3.79	69.2	2.3	33.1	22.8	7.1
8.7	0.00	0.0	0.00	7.1	0.3	1.30	12.91	4.19	56.1	3.1	17.0	13.5	7.0
4.4	2.43	na	0.50	5.3	1.2	1.05	9.18	4.18	73.6	3.0	13.6	13.8	6.5
8.9	0.08	na	0.12	4.6	0.3	1.00	8.34	3.05	66.3	1.9	39.2	40.0	7.6
8.7	0.09	na	0.00	10.0	0.4	1.90	22.16	4.74	56.4	3.9	32.2	12.9	6.3
8.9	0.16	na	0.01	4.1	0.8	0.76	7.38	3.61	80.6	6.5	59.4	6.2	7.0
6.5	0.54	na	0.02	3.3	1.1	0.34	3.11	3.52	70.3	3.5	8.3	10.9	9.0
2.2	6.02	na	0.08	3.2	0.1	0.69	4.31	3.34	69.3	2.7	42.7	26.1	7.0
8.3	0.06	na	0.00	4.7	0.4	1.11	11.28	4.23	71.7	0.7	11.2	32.9	6.3
8.2	0.04	na	0.03	4.4	0.2	0.93	9.06	4.71	73.9	3.2	25.2	14.3	5.7
8.5	0.00	0.0	0.00	9.8	1.4	2.56	21.99	3.99	40.7	2.2	16.0	17.9	9.0
3.2	2.49	na	0.33	0.8	-0.1	-0.99	-11.93	3.37	128.1	2.8	51.3	28.1	2.3
1.7	2.96	42.3	0.07	0.3	-0.1	-0.25	-8.19	4.46	105.2	5.1	30.6	4.9	0.3
8.6	0.39	1.1	0.00	5.5	1.4	1.20	7.59	3.81	66.7	2.7	34.2	19.8	7.6
8.0	0.54	na	0.04	3.3	0.5	0.60	6.18	3.44	85.5	6.0	36.8	1.6	5.6
5.5	0.79	na	-0.10	1.9	0.4	0.59	5.39	3.46	75.2	4.2	38.2	13.2	4.7
7.9	0.06	na	0.00	3.7	0.3	0.61	6.18	3.23	73.8	0.7	14.6	51.4	5.7
4.1	1.00	na	-0.07	5.4	0.8	0.92	11.02	3.53	64.3	1.8	16.6	20.7	5.1
6.7	0.56	na	0.03	5.8	0.4	1.26	14.06	4.02	67.7	2.4	20.1	14.3	6.9
7.5	0.00	na	0.00	9.8	0.2	2.70	12.45	4.50	23.8	3.6	28.8	13.3	9.3
7.3	1.57	na	0.08	6.2	0.4	1.35	7.88	2.94	56.7	4.2	57.2	18.1	10.0
6.7	0.46	na	0.22	3.5	0.2	0.52	4.74	4.03	74.8	6.2	46.2	3.8	5.2
3.9	1.80	na	-0.01	8.2	0.4	1.17	13.11	3.73	49.0	0.9	14.0	33.7	6.4
6.4	0.79	na	0.07	6.5	2.0	1.53	15.44	3.55	58.5	2.2	25.7	19.0	6.3
9.1	0.00	na	0.06	5.0	0.5	1.14	10.36	2.85	56.4	5.1	39.2	9.2	6.7
8.1	0.20	na	0.00	4.8	0.1	0.88	5.88	3.48	60.3	3.8	40.1	16.2	7.2
6.5	0.64	4.8	0.10	4.6	6.8	0.82	9.00	3.57	70.0	1.9	19.5	21.3	7.1
8.2	0.35	na	-0.08	6.5	0.2	1.45	10.34	5.22	67.0	3.4	21.1	12.7	7.6
8.1	0.08	na	0.11	4.7	0.3	1.08	8.41	2.90	50.7	1.9	43.6	52.9	6.9

Name	City	State	Rating	2019 Rating	2018 Rating	Total Assets ($Mil)	One Year Asset Growth	Comm-ercial Loans	Cons-umer Loans	Mort-gage Loans	Secur-ities	Capital-ization Index	Lever-age Ratio	Risk-Based Capital Ratio
Community Bank of Oklahoma	Verden	OK	B-	B-	B-	42.8	-2.03	16.8	6.3	4.0	9.2	9.8	14.1	0.0
Community Bank of Parkersburg	Parkersburg	WV	B+	B+	B+	257.1	2.73	2.8	6.9	57.7	10.6	9.4	10.8	0.0
▲ Community Bank of Pickens County	Jasper	GA	B-	C+	C-	378.3	7.30	5.4	2.1	14.5	9.0	10.0	11.7	16.8
Community Bank of Pleasant Hill	Pleasant Hill	MO	B+	B+	B+	88.8	20.79	12.2	1.3	2.3	49.7	7.9	9.6	18.9
Community Bank of Raymore	Raymore	MO	B+	B+	B+	290.7	10.09	9.7	0.5	1.8	34.1	5.7	7.7	12.7
Community Bank of Santa Maria	Santa Maria	CA	A-	A-	B+	261.8	6.07	10.5	0.4	0.3	20.2	9.2	10.6	0.0
Community Bank of the Bay	Oakland	CA	B	B	B-	527.4	24.43	16.6	0.1	4.6	3.2	9.8	11.6	0.0
Community Bank of the Chesapeake	Waldorf	MD	B-	B-	B-	1825.1	6.74	5.6	0.1	16.5	11.7	7.1	10.0	12.6
▲ Community Bank of the Midwest	Great Bend	KS	B+	B	B	175.9	3.25	13.0	2.7	7.5	8.6	7.5	11.1	12.9
Community Bank of the South	Merritt Island	FL	A-	A-	C+	161.9	2.86	3.6	0.7	5.1	23.9	9.5	10.6	24.9
Community Bank of Trenton	Trenton	IL	B	B	B-	87.8	5.97	6.6	4.4	28.1	10.7	9.8	11.8	0.0
Community Bank of Wichita, Inc.	Wichita	KS	C+	C+	B-	87.8	9.98	22.7	4.4	19.3	7.1	6.8	9.0	0.0
Community Bank Owatonna	Owatonna	MN	C+	C+	C+	63.4	10.91	8.9	1.3	16.7	17.0	6.9	8.9	12.6
Community Bank, N.A.	De Witt	NY	B+	B+	B+	11614.0	8.47	5.3	10.9	23.4	27.1	6.7	8.7	14.7
▼ Community Bankers' Bank	Midlothian	VA	C	C+	C-	156.0	15.26	6.6	0.9	4.3	14.2	9.8	12.7	0.0
▼ Community Banking Co. of Fitzgerald	Fitzgerald	GA	B+	A-	B+	164.2	-0.69	6.2	9.8	23.8	10.8	9.8	12.3	0.0
Community Banks of Shelby County	Cowden	IL	C+	C+	C+	50.9	2.76	7.8	2.7	9.8	29.1	10.0	11.0	21.8
Community Commerce Bank	Claremont	CA	B+	B+	B+	287.4	7.72	0.0	12.9	6.0	0.1	10.0	18.8	25.0
Community Development Bank, FSB	Ogema	MN	C+	C+	B-	167.5	2.05	9.1	2.4	11.5	20.0	8.4	9.9	15.2
Community Federal Savings Bank	New York	NY	C	C	D	186.3	10.29	4.0	5.2	16.6	5.3	7.1	9.1	17.4
Community Financial Bank	Prentice	WI	C+	C+	C+	45.3	-3.72	5.6	1.8	33.6	0.0	9.9	10.9	18.4
▼ Community Financial Services Bank	Benton	KY	C	C+	C+	1227.5	1.37	14.1	11.1	20.2	9.7	5.3	8.5	11.2
▲ Community First Bank	Kansas City	KS	A-	B+	B	197.6	5.34	16.1	0.7	12.6	2.7	7.7	10.5	13.1
Community First Bank	New Iberia	LA	B	B	B	405.4	0.56	12.5	3.5	22.5	8.8	9.0	10.3	15.0
Community First Bank	Menahga	MN	A-	A-	A-	90.2	3.97	8.7	5.8	15.4	21.0	10.0	15.3	25.8
Community First Bank	Butler	MO	B	B	B	178.5	3.30	11.6	3.5	19.5	4.2	6.9	8.9	12.8
Community First Bank	Maywood	NE	D-	D-	D	118.3	-4.49	5.8	2.6	6.4	16.0	7.5	10.6	12.9
Community First Bank	Walhalla	SC	C	C	C	447.4	14.01	3.8	23.5	10.0	9.6	8.7	10.3	0.0
Community First Bank	Kennewick	WA	B+	B+	B+	368.0	17.26	3.9	1.4	9.9	30.8	8.0	9.7	14.3
Community First Bank	Boscobel	WI	B+	B+	B+	441.7	4.29	8.1	1.3	15.3	20.8	9.7	10.8	15.0
Community First Bank	Rosholt	WI	B	B	B-	89.0	9.00	3.7	1.5	15.3	28.9	7.9	9.8	0.0
Community First Bank of Indiana	Kokomo	IN	B-	B-	B-	322.1	18.41	15.9	0.9	10.2	1.3	9.8	11.0	0.0
Community First Bank of the Heartland	Mount Vernon	IL	B	B	B	205.0	2.12	11.1	0.4	9.2	7.4	7.5	10.0	12.9
▲ Community First Bank, N.A.	Forest	OH	C	C-	C-	54.5	-0.62	6.1	1.6	24.7	9.9	8.5	10.0	21.4
Community First Banking Co.	West Plains	MO	A-	A-	A-	198.9	3.05	7.6	3.6	24.6	20.8	9.8	11.6	0.0
▲ Community First National Bank	Manhattan	KS	B-	C+	C+	303.5	9.32	11.6	1.9	19.1	0.0	5.8	9.7	11.6
Community National B&T of Texas	Corsicana	TX	A-	A-	B-	786.1	8.48	5.5	1.3	11.8	10.4	8.6	10.3	13.8
Community National Bank	Seneca	KS	A-	A-	A-	497.0	5.83	3.0	0.4	6.1	58.4	6.7	8.7	18.1
Community National Bank	Monett	MO	B+	B+	B+	142.0	14.04	4.7	3.1	18.3	7.8	6.8	8.8	16.2
Community National Bank	Dayton	TN	C	C	C+	254.5	2.53	4.6	1.7	17.1	17.3	8.8	10.4	0.0
Community National Bank	Hondo	TX	B+	B+	B	217.5	3.37	6.5	1.8	9.7	26.1	9.6	10.7	16.9
Community National Bank	Midland	TX	B+	B+	B	1419.7	1.82	22.4	0.9	6.0	13.5	7.7	9.4	13.4
Community National Bank	Newport	VT	B-	B-	C+	751.3	6.37	13.2	0.5	22.8	4.3	8.1	9.8	14.3
Community National Bank & Trust	Chanute	KS	B-	B-	B-	1358.4	13.42	8.3	2.6	15.6	18.3	6.6	8.6	12.6
▲ Community National Bank in Monmouth	Monmouth	IL	C-	D+	D+	48.2	27.97	4.2	5.9	13.8	11.4	10.0	13.9	26.3
Community National Bank of Okarche	Okarche	OK	A	A	A	116.9	-0.28	8.2	2.5	5.6	50.8	9.8	14.2	0.0
▼ Community Neighbor Bank	Camden	AL	B+	A-	B+	106.6	-0.43	14.5	7.3	16.7	9.9	9.8	14.7	0.0
Community Partners Savings Bank	Salem	IL	B-	B-	C	205.9	1.27	4.3	17.2	28.3	13.6	10.0	11.5	17.7
Community Point Bank	Russellville	MO	B-	B-	B-	140.7	3.75	5.3	3.1	20.8	12.3	7.6	9.4	14.1
▼ Community Resource Bank	Northfield	MN	B+	A-	A-	317.1	4.16	9.9	0.8	17.2	11.8	9.8	13.3	0.0
Community Savings	Caldwell	OH	D	D	D	51.0	-2.32	0.0	16.4	48.3	8.7	10.0	14.3	32.6
▲ Community Savings Bank	Edgewood	IA	D+	D	C-	440.1	3.55	10.2	2.2	8.7	18.6	7.0	9.1	12.5
▼ Community Savings Bank	Chicago	IL	C-	C	C	403.6	3.31	0.0	0.0	34.6	30.5	9.8	16.2	0.0
Community Savings Bank	Bethel	OH	B-	B-	B	80.1	0.08	10.5	0.8	46.2	11.9	9.8	17.0	0.0
▲ Community Shores Bank	Muskegon	MI	C	C-	D+	215.8	8.08	22.7	0.5	9.9	8.2	6.8	8.8	13.2
Community Spirit Bank	Red Bay	AL	B	B	B	152.0	3.22	11.6	5.0	24.5	15.4	9.6	10.8	16.6
Community State Bank	Bradley	AR	C	C	C-	21.8	16.54	33.5	6.6	9.7	5.2	9.8	11.4	0.0
▲ Community State Bank	Lamar	CO	A	A-	A-	129.9	9.81	13.2	3.1	6.0	8.9	10.0	13.1	16.7
▼ Community State Bank	Starke	FL	C	C+	C	140.5	-1.61	7.4	4.1	14.5	24.9	6.4	8.4	17.1
Community State Bank	Ankeny	IA	B+	B+	B	865.1	10.09	19.0	0.2	7.4	20.0	7.1	10.3	12.6

Asset Mix (As a % of Total Assets): Commercial Loans, Consumer Loans, Mortgage Loans, Securities.

Asset Quality Index	Adjusted Non-Performing Loans as a % of Total Loans	Adjusted Non-Performing Loans as a % of Capital	Net Charge-Offs / Avg Loans	Profitability Index	Net Income ($Mil)	Return on Assets (R.O.A.)	Return on Equity (R.O.E.)	Net Interest Spread	Overhead Efficiency Ratio	Liquidity Index	Liquidity Ratio	Hot Money Ratio	Stability Index
4.6	9.26	na	0.00	6.3	0.2	1.62	11.30	5.26	69.3	1.9	24.4	21.0	7.5
7.8	0.27	na	0.01	4.9	0.7	1.07	9.70	3.98	74.4	3.1	9.1	12.7	7.7
3.8	4.16	na	0.25	7.7	1.3	1.43	12.42	3.55	55.0	0.9	19.9	40.1	6.8
9.0	0.00	na	0.05	5.0	0.2	0.99	9.88	2.77	73.2	7.3	65.8	0.3	5.9
8.8	0.00	na	0.02	8.5	1.8	2.50	29.90	3.26	50.0	5.3	32.2	4.5	6.7
7.4	0.34	na	-0.03	6.6	0.7	0.99	9.34	4.48	69.3	4.8	29.5	6.8	6.6
7.3	0.06	na	-0.01	4.5	0.9	0.72	6.25	4.13	65.0	1.9	24.6	20.1	6.5
4.0	1.14	8.5	-0.01	4.4	3.5	0.78	7.04	3.59	55.3	2.6	11.7	15.1	8.7
8.3	0.08	na	0.00	6.9	0.8	1.79	16.27	3.55	52.4	5.1	38.0	8.4	6.5
9.5	0.00	na	-0.06	5.7	0.5	1.19	11.09	3.53	58.2	6.3	58.2	7.5	6.4
4.3	2.64	12.6	-1.57	4.6	0.3	1.15	9.81	3.38	67.3	1.9	22.8	20.4	6.5
4.3	0.83	na	0.01	4.4	0.2	0.72	8.08	4.44	71.9	0.9	11.6	32.3	5.6
8.3	0.00	0.0	0.57	3.3	0.1	0.61	6.93	3.59	76.9	1.9	30.8	24.4	4.0
6.1	0.32	1.9	0.12	6.4	32.9	1.17	8.20	3.68	59.8	4.9	17.2	3.6	10.0
8.6	0.00	na	-0.05	2.2	0.1	0.27	2.11	2.88	86.7	0.9	24.5	21.1	7.0
4.6	1.14	na	0.09	6.5	0.5	1.19	9.07	4.17	58.2	2.0	20.0	19.3	8.4
7.4	0.97	na	-0.12	2.9	0.1	0.43	3.87	2.82	85.3	4.5	47.6	13.7	6.2
5.9	1.26	3.0	-0.01	4.0	0.4	0.56	2.98	3.45	78.3	0.6	22.9	73.4	8.0
3.9	1.71	7.4	0.02	3.2	0.2	0.55	4.41	3.63	76.6	3.1	26.2	15.0	5.6
4.1	2.10	13.7	0.00	2.7	0.4	0.75	8.17	2.95	84.8	1.6	33.0	34.0	4.5
7.6	0.72	na	0.00	3.3	0.1	0.64	5.84	3.10	80.8	1.5	28.2	29.5	6.2
1.2	4.11	na	0.34	1.9	-5.9	-1.89	-21.15	3.23	74.7	1.1	8.2	23.3	7.1
8.4	0.00	na	0.00	9.9	0.9	1.73	16.79	4.84	52.4	0.4	1.8	48.9	7.5
4.9	0.71	na	0.04	6.2	1.4	1.41	13.46	4.30	66.3	1.7	17.6	22.7	8.2
8.2	0.16	na	-0.04	6.8	0.4	1.87	11.54	4.13	60.7	4.6	43.2	11.0	8.9
4.4	0.93	na	0.01	7.4	0.8	1.82	20.06	4.12	49.8	1.1	14.7	28.0	7.1
0.0	6.38	na	-2.89	2.0	0.0	0.04	0.38	4.14	99.0	1.4	8.9	19.3	5.4
5.6	0.94	na	0.01	2.6	0.4	0.34	3.15	3.77	86.2	1.8	15.2	20.4	5.6
7.5	0.37	1.9	-0.01	5.0	1.1	1.25	11.85	3.53	78.0	6.1	38.1	1.7	6.8
4.5	1.63	7.1	-0.01	5.4	1.3	1.25	10.11	3.90	69.2	2.7	23.3	13.3	7.4
8.3	0.26	na	0.01	4.2	0.2	0.95	9.27	3.85	77.4	6.3	42.5	2.0	6.6
5.9	0.82	na	-0.05	4.4	0.4	0.50	4.58	4.34	84.4	1.2	5.0	18.4	7.1
4.6	1.02	na	0.07	7.0	0.8	1.60	15.66	4.48	63.7	3.1	6.1	12.7	7.5
9.3	0.00	na	0.00	2.7	0.1	0.34	3.39	3.60	87.1	6.3	48.7	3.3	4.9
8.1	0.67	na	-0.01	6.1	0.7	1.46	12.28	3.69	63.9	3.2	18.1	11.7	8.8
7.3	0.44	na	0.00	4.7	0.8	1.05	10.88	3.60	74.0	0.8	11.7	30.8	5.8
6.1	0.57	na	0.01	7.5	2.7	1.46	11.77	4.72	62.2	3.8	19.8	10.6	8.4
5.0	3.82	na	0.03	9.5	2.7	2.18	23.36	3.32	45.8	5.9	44.9	5.8	7.3
8.4	0.08	na	0.29	6.0	0.5	1.52	17.01	3.31	58.6	4.2	35.1	12.2	6.4
1.6	5.85	na	-0.05	3.2	0.0	0.01	0.07	3.89	103.9	2.2	25.1	19.2	7.4
6.7	0.47	na	-0.15	5.6	0.8	1.42	11.95	3.87	68.9	4.4	35.7	11.4	7.6
5.9	1.01	5.0	-0.06	7.8	4.8	1.35	12.29	4.14	52.8	6.0	30.3	3.5	8.8
4.6	0.77	na	0.08	5.9	2.1	1.12	10.03	3.83	64.2	3.7	7.2	9.4	8.0
4.7	1.53	na	0.05	4.3	2.5	0.75	7.84	3.62	76.0	2.9	17.2	15.1	8.1
7.4	0.76	3.0	0.17	1.8	0.1	0.41	2.93	3.92	81.4	4.1	51.8	13.2	4.3
8.9	0.00	na	0.00	7.6	0.6	1.90	13.35	3.39	43.4	0.8	17.1	37.4	9.9
4.9	1.41	na	0.18	5.6	0.2	0.75	5.11	4.83	73.0	2.5	30.1	19.0	8.7
3.7	1.78	na	0.41	3.3	0.3	0.48	4.04	3.93	78.9	2.4	20.3	17.7	5.9
8.4	0.10	na	0.00	4.5	0.4	1.21	12.84	2.89	59.5	1.6	17.3	21.7	6.4
4.2	2.44	na	-0.03	8.0	1.2	1.51	10.59	4.19	57.5	1.6	14.5	20.2	8.6
4.7	2.17	na	0.00	0.6	0.0	-0.07	-0.49	4.08	103.1	4.0	21.7	9.3	6.1
5.7	0.84	na	0.28	2.5	1.0	0.94	9.22	3.31	74.7	1.6	18.9	19.4	4.3
8.1	2.76	na	0.00	1.9	0.2	0.16	0.96	2.59	94.7	3.1	45.5	22.5	7.5
8.8	0.28	na	-0.02	3.3	0.1	0.42	2.47	3.86	83.2	1.8	16.0	20.0	7.7
2.7	3.65	16.9	0.31	3.2	0.3	0.52	5.65	3.34	83.8	2.9	29.7	17.2	5.3
7.5	1.25	na	0.04	4.4	0.4	1.08	9.95	4.48	74.9	1.3	20.7	28.0	6.1
3.8	1.27	na	0.00	5.7	0.1	1.35	10.51	4.53	67.9	1.3	24.8	28.9	5.0
8.0	0.04	0.2	-0.01	8.3	0.6	1.81	13.65	4.21	53.2	0.7	15.6	47.2	9.9
2.6	4.37	na	0.40	2.4	0.2	0.55	6.29	3.82	95.1	4.9	22.9	3.9	4.4
7.8	0.18	na	0.60	4.4	1.1	0.50	4.26	3.89	65.7	3.0	19.4	14.3	7.8

Name	City	State	Rating	2019 Rating	2018 Rating	Total Assets ($Mil)	One Year Asset Growth	Asset Mix (As a % of Total Assets) Commercial Loans	Consumer Loans	Mortgage Loans	Securities	Capitalization Index	Leverage Ratio	Risk-Based Capital Ratio
Community State Bank	Paton	IA	**B**	B	B	44.4	-4.96	3.6	2.1	1.7	45.2	**10.0**	20.0	37.7
Community State Bank	Spencer	IA	**B+**	B+	B+	201.5	-1.57	14.3	1.5	5.1	39.4	**8.1**	9.7	17.5
Community State Bank	Galva	IL	**B-**	B-	C	228.3	-2.01	6.4	1.7	11.4	17.3	**9.3**	10.7	0.0
▲ Community State Bank	Avilla	IN	**A**	A-	B+	283.7	7.30	15.4	1.2	27.6	8.3	**10.0**	11.0	15.8
▼ Community State Bank	Brook	IN	**C+**	B-	C+	71.6	11.14	4.6	1.2	33.8	7.5	**9.8**	12.9	0.0
Community State Bank	Royal Center	IN	**B-**	B-	C+	131.8	8.08	6.5	2.8	15.6	21.5	**9.8**	10.9	17.8
▼ Community State Bank	Coffeyville	KS	**A-**	A	A-	164.0	-0.64	9.5	1.1	6.4	33.1	**9.8**	11.7	0.0
Community State Bank	Shelbina	MO	**B-**	B-	B-	83.2	6.52	5.3	11.1	26.6	22.9	**7.0**	9.2	0.0
Community State Bank	Colon	NE	**D+**	D+	D	36.2	101.09	2.9	1.2	0.8	5.3	**7.1**	9.3	0.0
Community State Bank	Hennessey	OK	**C-**	C-	D	74.6	1.04	9.2	3.0	5.5	47.9	**4.9**	6.9	18.5
Community State Bank	Poteau	OK	**B-**	B-	B-	278.1	0.53	7.4	3.3	20.4	11.8	**7.8**	9.6	14.5
▲ Community State Bank	Union Grove	WI	**B**	B-	C+	414.8	4.45	15.8	0.4	9.0	19.7	**7.8**	9.6	13.9
Community State Bank of Canton	Canton	OK	**B-**	B-	C+	54.4	11.44	11.2	7.7	5.0	22.9	**9.5**	10.8	0.0
Community State Bank of Missouri	Bowling Green	MO	**B+**	B+	B+	241.2	3.28	7.8	0.6	19.4	23.1	**9.8**	12.9	0.0
▼ Community State Bank of Orbisonia	Orbisonia	PA	**B-**	B	B	339.3	2.27	2.2	8.6	58.5	8.6	**9.8**	11.5	0.0
▼ Community State Bank of Rock Falls	Rock Falls	IL	**D+**	C-	C	285.8	7.21	9.9	1.6	26.6	13.5	**8.3**	9.9	17.5
Community State Bank Of Southwestern In	Poseyville	IN	**B**	B	B-	89.6	6.68	11.4	1.9	24.6	2.3	**8.1**	9.7	17.3
Community Trust Bank	Irvington	IL	**B-**	B-	B-	79.7	-0.52	5.1	1.0	9.6	31.8	**10.0**	14.1	25.4
▼ Community Trust Bank, Inc.	Pikeville	KY	**B-**	B	B-	4331.3	0.93	7.3	17.6	19.6	14.3	**9.8**	13.3	0.0
▼ Community Valley Bank	El Centro	CA	**B+**	A-	B+	208.8	6.36	10.2	0.0	4.9	0.7	**9.8**	11.2	0.0
Community West Bank, N.A.	Goleta	CA	**C+**	C+	C-	925.0	5.20	3.5	28.5	3.1	2.6	**7.1**	9.2	0.0
CommunityBank of Texas, N.A.	Beaumont	TX	**A-**	A-	A-	3425.9	4.32	15.8	1.1	7.7	6.8	**10.0**	12.1	15.2
Compass Savings Bank	Wilmerding	PA	**D-**	D-	D+	49.7	-5.03	0.2	0.7	70.9	11.9	**6.8**	8.8	18.2
Computershare Trust Co., N.A.	Canton	MA	**U**	U	U	30.1	9.13	0.0	0.0	0.0	0.0	**10.0**	95.2	267.4
▲ Concorde Bank	Blomkest	MN	**B-**	C+	C+	54.9	-6.71	7.3	2.9	20.1	2.5	**10.0**	11.1	15.0
Concordia Bank	Concordia	MO	**B+**	B+	B	76.3	0.60	3.8	1.3	20.3	5.3	**9.7**	11.0	0.0
▼ Concordia Bank & Trust Co.	Vidalia	LA	**B-**	B	B	552.4	8.86	4.3	2.1	12.6	34.3	**9.8**	11.7	0.0
Congressional Bank	Bethesda	MD	**C**	C	C-	1174.4	9.98	36.7	2.0	9.2	2.7	**9.7**	13.4	14.8
Conneaut Savings Bank	Conneaut	OH	**C**	C	C	76.4	0.24	1.6	0.5	48.6	22.5	**9.8**	14.9	0.0
Connect Bank	Star City	AR	**B+**	B+	A-	97.6	3.14	11.5	1.3	17.5	20.3	**9.8**	15.7	0.0
▼ Connecticut Community Bank, N.A.	Norwalk	CT	**C-**	C	C	465.9	1.99	29.7	0.3	3.7	1.3	**9.7**	10.9	0.0
▲ Connection Bank	Fort Madison	IA	**B**	B-	B-	314.5	4.09	10.7	1.9	31.4	6.2	**6.3**	8.7	12.0
Connections Bank	Kirksville	MO	**B**	B	C+	91.4	4.13	2.4	0.9	38.9	8.1	**9.7**	11.0	0.0
ConnectOne Bank	Englewood Cliffs	NJ	**C+**	C+	C	7275.9	20.30	10.8	0.0	7.8	6.1	**6.7**	10.4	12.3
Consumers National Bank	Minerva	OH	**B**	B	B-	663.2	25.87	8.2	3.3	14.0	21.6	**6.8**	8.8	12.5
Continental Bank	Salt Lake City	UT	**B**	B	B-	158.2	0.07	72.5	0.0	0.0	6.9	**10.0**	16.6	20.6
Converse County Bank	Douglas	WY	**B+**	B+	B	697.0	14.87	6.8	3.8	4.2	64.4	**6.7**	8.8	27.5
Conway Bank	Conway Springs	KS	**D+**	D+	D+	97.8	-5.16	12.7	0.9	16.3	9.6	**5.5**	7.5	14.3
Conway National Bank	Conway	SC	**B+**	B+	B	1269.8	5.60	4.9	3.9	13.2	49.6	**8.5**	10.0	20.3
Cooperative Bank	Roslindale	MA	**C+**	C+	C+	445.6	3.50	2.0	0.9	45.4	9.5	**8.1**	9.8	14.8
Cooperative Bank of Cape Cod	Hyannis	MA	**C+**	C+	C+	959.5	2.39	3.6	0.1	53.8	5.2	**8.9**	10.4	0.0
Copiah Bank	Hazlehurst	MS	**B-**	B-	B-	237.1	2.58	6.9	2.7	19.6	11.2	**8.4**	10.0	14.0
▼ Corder Bank	Corder	MO	**C-**	C	C-	19.8	3.09	10.0	5.3	20.1	5.0	**10.0**	11.2	20.7
Core Bank	Omaha	NE	**C+**	C+	B-	640.0	15.09	19.1	0.4	16.2	6.7	**4.4**	8.4	10.7
COREBANK	Waynoka	OK	**C-**	C-	D	72.7	51.09	13.8	0.4	24.2	6.4	**10.0**	11.2	17.1
CoreFirst Bank & Trust	Topeka	KS	**C+**	C+	C+	973.7	6.09	12.0	4.2	8.5	26.1	**8.0**	9.6	13.9
Corn City State Bank	Deshler	OH	**B+**	B+	B+	72.9	8.35	0.1	2.2	26.1	50.0	**9.8**	14.6	0.0
Corn Growers State Bank	Murdock	NE	**D+**	D+	D-	25.1	-0.51	4.1	8.0	8.9	6.7	**6.4**	8.4	20.0
Cornerstone Bank	Eureka Springs	AR	**B-**	B-	B-	347.8	12.51	5.2	4.0	20.3	9.3	**5.7**	8.0	11.6
▼ Cornerstone Bank	Atlanta	GA	**D-**	D	D+	204.8	-6.56	11.8	0.3	13.0	19.1	**8.6**	10.0	16.8
Cornerstone Bank	Clarinda	IA	**C-**	C-	C-	40.9	1.82	5.6	6.4	34.1	7.0	**10.0**	13.6	27.0
Cornerstone Bank	Overland Park	KS	**B+**	B+	B	239.6	7.17	17.5	0.5	18.5	7.2	**7.4**	9.5	0.0
Cornerstone Bank	Worcester	MA	**C**	C	C	1197.2	3.70	4.0	0.6	41.8	4.6	**8.3**	9.8	14.0
▲ Cornerstone Bank	South West City	MO	**B**	B-	C+	140.1	0.75	11.0	9.4	28.4	10.4	**10.0**	14.5	22.5
▲ Cornerstone Bank	Fargo	ND	**C+**	C	C	1010.5	8.64	10.9	2.1	9.9	17.3	**6.5**	8.5	12.3
Cornerstone Bank	York	NE	**B+**	B+	B+	1688.5	2.79	16.3	1.5	3.2	13.9	**8.5**	10.2	0.0
Cornerstone Bank	Mount Laurel	NJ	**D+**	D+	D	256.5	2.17	8.4	0.0	31.5	10.8	**4.5**	7.0	10.8
Cornerstone Bank	Watonga	OK	**C+**	C+	C	220.2	1.25	5.6	3.8	9.0	44.9	**6.5**	8.5	16.0
▼ CornerStone Bank, N.A.	Lexington	VA	**C**	C+	B	164.9	8.83	9.7	2.5	26.4	5.6	**8.9**	10.4	0.0
Cornerstone Community Bank	Red Bluff	CA	**B**	B	B-	323.4	21.57	12.8	0.8	3.4	4.1	**6.7**	10.1	12.3

Asset Quality Index	Adjusted Non-Performing Loans as a % of Total Loans	Adjusted Non-Performing Loans as a % of Capital	Net Charge-Offs Avg Loans	Profitability Index	Net Income ($Mil)	Return on Assets (R.O.A.)	Return on Equity (R.O.E.)	Net Interest Spread	Overhead Efficiency Ratio	Liquidity Index	Liquidity Ratio	Hot Money Ratio	Stability Index
7.2	0.00	na	-0.07	**4.7**	0.1	1.05	5.14	3.01	58.6	**4.4**	67.0	17.7	**7.2**
7.2	0.38	na	-0.01	**5.4**	0.7	1.36	12.52	3.44	52.4	**2.5**	28.9	9.5	**7.9**
3.4	1.16	na	0.18	**6.3**	0.9	1.46	13.07	4.23	59.8	**0.7**	8.0	26.4	**7.6**
8.6	0.50	na	0.00	**8.0**	1.0	1.46	13.12	4.26	57.1	**4.0**	19.2	9.0	**7.7**
3.3	5.31	na	-0.05	**6.4**	0.2	1.25	10.26	3.91	57.8	**1.1**	25.9	26.6	**5.4**
4.4	2.26	10.4	-0.01	**4.6**	0.4	1.16	10.33	3.83	74.8	**4.4**	22.0	6.9	**6.8**
5.8	3.53	na	-0.02	**8.8**	0.7	1.72	14.12	4.09	46.2	**4.5**	8.5	4.7	**8.3**
6.3	0.43	na	0.12	**7.4**	0.3	1.49	16.56	3.55	45.1	**3.2**	16.8	9.6	**6.0**
7.3	1.01	na	0.00	**1.5**	0.0	0.24	3.44	2.65	88.3	**3.6**	59.3	14.2	**4.1**
4.3	4.99	na	0.05	**5.1**	0.2	1.12	16.39	4.09	69.0	**6.5**	46.5	1.4	**2.9**
4.0	1.72	11.3	0.22	**4.2**	0.8	1.07	11.09	4.50	78.1	**0.9**	20.2	33.9	**6.4**
5.1	1.56	na	-0.56	**5.5**	1.2	1.17	12.03	3.99	72.9	**4.9**	35.1	7.8	**7.3**
6.2	0.25	na	2.44	**5.3**	0.1	0.81	7.46	4.73	71.8	**2.2**	6.9	17.3	**5.8**
8.8	0.19	na	0.00	**4.7**	0.6	1.06	8.00	3.28	69.9	**2.9**	13.0	14.1	**8.4**
4.3	2.10	na	0.28	**3.3**	0.3	0.33	2.90	4.10	81.4	**1.7**	10.1	20.7	**6.6**
1.2	3.62	na	0.01	**3.8**	0.4	0.61	5.89	3.29	65.8	**2.0**	25.6	20.0	**6.0**
8.9	0.00	na	0.00	**4.3**	0.2	0.85	8.78	3.57	77.7	**4.2**	32.1	11.3	**6.3**
6.9	1.86	na	0.00	**3.6**	0.1	0.69	4.87	3.73	76.8	**5.8**	42.4	5.2	**6.1**
3.7	2.28	8.8	0.17	**4.9**	6.0	0.55	3.79	3.64	58.5	**2.0**	8.5	17.5	**10.0**
4.2	0.73	na	-0.03	**6.6**	0.6	1.08	9.46	4.77	66.0	**1.7**	14.1	20.6	**7.0**
4.7	0.63	na	-0.03	**4.7**	1.7	0.77	8.33	3.95	69.9	**0.7**	10.7	24.4	**6.2**
6.6	0.61	1.7	-0.05	**6.2**	8.0	0.92	6.40	4.06	60.1	**3.6**	16.0	7.5	**10.0**
9.8	0.00	na	0.00	**0.2**	-0.1	-0.95	-10.37	1.49	158.7	**0.9**	21.2	40.3	**2.6**
6.5	na	na	na	**9.5**	1.6	21.63	23.06	1.21	63.5	**4.0**	na	0.0	**6.9**
4.3	1.95	na	0.00	**5.9**	0.2	1.32	11.88	4.90	67.6	**2.5**	20.9	17.0	**6.7**
3.4	5.51	na	0.00	**4.6**	0.2	0.90	8.14	4.45	70.3	**4.6**	20.4	5.6	**6.6**
5.0	1.19	na	0.14	**3.4**	0.8	0.57	4.58	3.25	73.3	**1.4**	14.7	25.6	**8.2**
2.4	3.25	na	0.26	**4.7**	0.3	0.09	0.59	4.92	89.0	**1.0**	16.2	16.4	**8.4**
9.3	0.34	na	0.00	**1.6**	0.0	-0.01	-0.03	3.19	101.1	**5.4**	40.8	7.9	**6.9**
4.7	2.59	na	0.06	**6.4**	0.3	1.18	7.54	4.53	73.9	**1.9**	24.3	22.0	**8.7**
4.1	1.86	na	0.03	**2.2**	0.1	0.08	0.74	3.89	97.7	**3.7**	23.3	11.2	**5.6**
6.8	0.14	na	0.12	**5.2**	1.0	1.23	12.14	3.72	69.5	**4.3**	12.4	6.6	**6.2**
7.9	0.27	na	0.00	**5.1**	0.2	0.87	6.88	4.23	68.2	**0.7**	14.8	44.7	**6.9**
3.2	1.35	7.7	0.01	**4.4**	7.5	0.42	3.41	3.48	59.1	**0.7**	9.8	22.4	**9.2**
7.8	0.33	na	0.06	**4.4**	1.4	0.87	9.88	3.76	70.0	**3.0**	17.2	13.3	**5.9**
5.2	4.49	na	1.05	**4.9**	0.0	0.01	0.06	5.51	83.8	**0.4**	18.0	92.0	**7.9**
9.3	0.02	na	0.06	**6.2**	2.6	1.50	16.25	2.35	45.5	**3.3**	54.5	25.9	**6.7**
1.8	3.82	na	0.14	**1.6**	0.0	0.05	0.52	3.70	95.3	**1.7**	23.9	22.6	**3.5**
8.9	0.43	1.7	0.06	**5.6**	3.7	1.19	11.83	3.08	57.2	**5.0**	46.1	14.2	**8.5**
7.3	0.61	na	0.00	**3.0**	0.5	0.41	4.17	3.40	83.5	**1.4**	14.4	21.4	**6.1**
5.6	1.31	7.9	-0.04	**3.6**	1.3	0.56	5.37	3.30	73.6	**2.9**	9.0	12.5	**6.7**
5.1	1.08	na	0.04	**4.7**	0.6	0.97	9.74	4.01	72.3	**2.4**	14.3	16.7	**6.1**
1.9	2.77	na	0.12	**4.2**	0.0	0.84	7.48	3.81	75.3	**4.3**	35.8	9.7	**5.0**
5.6	1.38	na	0.00	**4.0**	0.9	0.60	7.11	4.02	83.5	**3.9**	12.2	9.1	**5.5**
8.7	0.01	na	-0.01	**1.3**	0.0	0.17	1.44	3.18	85.0	**1.0**	28.0	67.2	**5.8**
3.3	2.40	na	0.16	**4.8**	2.7	1.14	11.88	3.65	71.1	**4.7**	12.3	3.9	**6.8**
9.5	0.22	na	-0.01	**4.9**	0.3	1.42	9.40	2.70	51.5	**2.8**	40.8	23.3	**8.2**
5.7	0.78	na	-0.08	**2.1**	0.0	0.09	1.12	3.79	97.6	**5.8**	40.4	4.5	**3.0**
7.0	0.25	na	0.00	**5.8**	1.2	1.36	17.12	4.24	67.2	**1.1**	8.5	22.1	**5.5**
2.0	10.59	na	-0.03	**0.0**	-0.5	-1.08	-10.55	3.08	123.3	**1.5**	28.2	30.9	**2.9**
5.7	1.99	na	0.00	**0.9**	0.0	0.07	0.50	2.71	98.7	**2.2**	36.6	28.0	**5.6**
4.5	1.33	na	-0.13	**5.0**	0.5	0.88	9.19	3.57	50.0	**3.7**	13.2	10.5	**7.3**
7.8	0.61	3.5	0.00	**2.4**	0.7	0.24	2.48	2.99	85.6	**1.5**	11.1	20.1	**7.4**
4.5	2.16	na	0.01	**5.6**	0.5	1.50	10.46	4.92	68.8	**0.9**	20.2	33.2	**8.5**
4.3	3.40	15.4	-0.01	**4.9**	3.0	1.18	13.80	3.51	78.4	**2.7**	17.5	16.3	**6.8**
5.0	0.68	8.9	0.03	**5.7**	5.2	1.22	11.42	3.71	68.4	**1.1**	10.6	24.4	**9.1**
6.5	0.51	3.6	-0.02	**1.3**	0.1	0.08	0.97	2.96	105.1	**2.0**	19.0	19.4	**2.9**
8.8	0.05	1.3	0.01	**4.1**	0.5	0.87	10.71	3.56	75.4	**5.3**	41.3	8.5	**3.8**
3.9	2.60	na	0.05	**2.4**	-0.1	-0.19	-1.80	3.71	85.0	**0.7**	8.7	34.9	**6.4**
7.3	0.00	na	0.00	**4.7**	0.1	0.17	1.71	4.22	56.5	**1.3**	18.4	20.3	**6.3**

Name	City	State	Rating	2019 Rating	2018 Rating	Total Assets ($Mil)	One Year Asset Growth	Asset Mix (As a % of Total Assets) Comm-ercial Loans	Cons-umer Loans	Mort-gage Loans	Secur-ities	Capital-ization Index	Lever-age Ratio	Risk-Based Capital Ratio
Cornerstone Community Bank	Grafton	WI	C+	C+	C+	211.4	4.18	8.0	0.1	10.6	0.1	4.9	9.5	11.0
Cornerstone National Bank & Trust Co.	Palatine	IL	B-	B-	B-	684.5	17.37	21.2	0.4	8.0	14.4	4.8	8.4	10.9
▼ CornerStone State Bank	Montgomery	MN	B+	A-	B+	176.3	3.28	7.1	4.6	22.5	24.7	9.8	11.7	0.0
Cornhusker Bank	Lincoln	NE	B-	B-	B-	632.4	1.17	6.8	0.9	15.6	14.9	7.2	9.1	12.8
Cortland Savings and Banking Co.	Cortland	OH	B	B	C	709.3	3.96	10.1	0.5	11.2	18.4	7.7	9.5	13.7
▼ CorTrust Bank N.A.	Mitchell	SD	C+	B-	B-	1206.6	36.14	10.7	3.3	6.8	26.0	8.0	9.7	14.2
Corydon State Bank	Corydon	IA	B+	B+	B+	102.5	-3.93	9.0	2.3	11.9	20.6	9.8	20.9	0.0
Cottonport Bank	Cottonport	LA	B+	B+	B+	393.1	17.62	5.8	3.0	13.9	12.0	9.8	12.3	0.0
Cottonwood Valley Bank	Cedar Point	KS	C+	C+	C+	34.8	4.17	9.2	1.3	0.5	28.8	10.0	13.4	25.8
Coulee Bank	La Crosse	WI	C+	C+	B-	390.1	-2.36	14.5	2.2	10.1	17.7	7.6	9.6	13.0
▼ Country Bank for Savings	Ware	MA	B-	B	B	1669.1	0.16	1.5	0.5	31.8	19.5	9.8	14.9	0.0
Country Club Bank	Kansas City	MO	A-	A-	A-	1539.3	11.94	18.7	0.6	8.4	25.8	7.7	9.6	0.0
Country Club Trust Co., N.A.	Kansas City	MO	U	U	U	13.6	-36.38	0.0	0.0	0.0	27.5	9.8	100.	0.0
COUNTRY Trust Bank	Bloomington	IL	U	U	U	28.3	-1.02	0.0	0.0	0.0	68.9	10.0	95.8	134.8
▼ Countryside Bank	Unadilla	NE	B-	B	B	83.8	8.84	4.9	5.2	17.4	16.6	9.8	16.6	0.0
County Bank	Rehoboth Beach	DE	B-	B-	C-	383.0	5.31	9.0	7.2	10.3	10.2	10.0	12.8	15.8
County Bank	Sigourney	IA	C	C	C+	176.3	1.69	11.7	2.2	10.8	5.1	6.9	10.2	12.4
County Bank	Brunswick	MO	B-	B-	B-	94.6	-1.07	8.2	4.4	21.8	13.3	5.9	7.9	13.7
County National Bank	Hillsdale	MI	B	B	B-	791.6	14.26	17.8	4.2	19.7	3.1	7.2	9.1	12.7
County Savings Bank	Essington	PA	C	C	C-	84.8	0.46	0.0	0.1	37.5	9.9	5.3	7.3	23.6
Countybank	Greenwood	SC	B-	B-	B-	453.1	7.95	5.2	1.2	24.1	24.5	6.4	8.4	13.0
Covenant Bank	Doylestown	PA	B-	B-	C	522.3	6.86	9.5	0.1	14.0	2.2	7.5	10.2	12.9
Covington County Bank	Collins	MS	C+	C+	C	73.1	-9.61	11.0	4.0	5.9	32.3	7.9	9.6	13.5
Covington S&L Assn.	Covington	OH	B-	B-	B-	69.4	-1.28	0.1	0.4	49.8	22.7	9.8	16.4	0.0
Cowboy Bank of Texas	Maypearl	TX	A-	A-	A-	92.2	3.95	0.6	3.7	26.0	15.3	9.6	10.8	17.3
▲ Cowboy State Bank	Ranchester	WY	D+	D	D-	46.5	-2.58	4.0	4.7	10.5	20.2	6.8	8.8	13.6
▲ Crawford County Trust and Savings Bank	Denison	IA	B-	C+	C+	200.6	3.66	5.9	3.5	9.2	10.6	7.9	9.6	13.4
Credit First N.A.	Brook Park	OH	U	U	U	29.8	18.77	0.0	0.0	0.0	0.0	10.0	97.2	475.6
Credit One Bank, N.A.	Las Vegas	NV	U	U	U	687.6	45.70	0.0	58.0	0.0	4.7	9.8	45.1	0.0
Crescent Bank & Trust	New Orleans	LA	C-	C-	D	983.8	-0.17	2.7	79.3	2.3	8.6	10.0	14.1	16.5
Crest Savings Bank	Wildwood	NJ	C+	C+	C+	470.4	-0.76	0.8	4.2	58.8	1.1	6.7	8.7	13.7
Crews Bank & Trust	Arcadia	FL	A-	A-	A-	177.1	12.78	1.1	2.2	16.6	19.2	9.8	11.4	0.0
Crockett National Bank	San Antonio	TX	A	A	B+	672.3	1.29	3.2	0.1	31.0	5.9	10.0	12.8	17.7
Croghan Colonial Bank	Fremont	OH	B+	B+	B+	880.0	5.85	6.9	10.7	10.6	18.8	8.5	11.6	13.7
Cross County Bank	Wynne	AR	B+	B+	B+	265.4	7.64	8.0	1.1	11.0	3.9	9.8	12.1	0.0
▼ Cross County Savings Bank	Middle Village	NY	B-	B	B	469.2	8.77	0.0	0.0	51.3	3.8	10.0	11.0	18.5
Cross Keys Bank	Saint Joseph	LA	B+	B+	B+	386.4	3.45	7.5	1.0	13.1	28.8	10.0	11.9	16.9
Cross River Bank	Fort Lee	NJ	A-	A-	B	2528.3	68.29	2.8	43.0	3.6	0.4	10.0	11.0	15.4
CrossFirst Bank	Leawood	KS	B-	B-	C	5066.1	18.85	34.1	0.4	6.5	14.5	6.4	10.7	12.1
Crossroads Bank	Effingham	IL	A-	A-	A-	187.6	8.97	16.7	1.1	8.7	24.3	9.8	14.1	0.0
Crossroads Bank	Wabash	IN	B	B	C+	425.4	6.93	6.3	4.3	28.7	19.4	7.7	9.5	14.3
Crossroads Bank	Yoakum	TX	A	A	A-	224.0	10.38	9.9	7.1	21.8	34.8	9.8	11.3	0.0
Crowell State Bank	Crowell	TX	B-	B-	B-	39.5	-2.54	12.6	7.3	8.4	19.7	9.2	10.6	0.0
▼ Crown Bank	Edina	MN	D+	C-	B-	196.0	-0.23	37.3	0.8	2.1	13.7	8.0	10.7	13.4
▲ Crown Bank	Elizabeth	NJ	B-	C+	C-	512.5	-4.38	4.0	0.1	2.5	11.4	10.0	20.8	26.4
Crystal Lake Bank & Trust Co., N.A.	Crystal Lake	IL	B	B	B	1231.4	9.66	34.3	13.8	3.0	12.8	5.6	9.5	11.4
CTBC Bank Corp. (USA)	Los Angeles	CA	A-	A-	A-	3756.7	6.62	7.5	0.0	34.5	9.2	9.8	14.0	0.0
▼ Culbertson Bank	Culbertson	NE	C-	C	C-	14.1	-3.66	7.5	0.7	0.1	32.4	9.8	14.5	0.0
Cullman Savings Bank	Cullman	AL	A-	A-	B+	311.0	4.11	8.4	0.8	40.9	6.5	9.8	16.0	0.0
Cumberland Federal Bank, FSB	Cumberland	WI	B+	B+	A-	168.7	12.31	1.7	1.2	19.2	48.4	9.6	10.7	17.6
Cumberland Security Bank, Inc.	Somerset	KY	A	A	B+	232.3	9.08	7.1	4.8	29.7	10.5	10.0	14.1	19.0
Cumberland Valley National B&T Co.	London	KY	C+	C+	C+	546.7	7.54	7.1	1.8	13.4	13.6	8.8	10.2	15.3
▼ Currie State Bank	Currie	MN	D+	C-	C-	83.8	5.68	6.8	1.5	6.4	0.4	7.2	9.3	0.0
CUSB Bank	Cresco	IA	B+	B+	C+	514.3	8.02	8.0	4.4	7.6	19.7	10.0	13.7	16.2
Custer Federal State Bank	Broken Bow	NE	B-	B-	B	111.8	-7.63	5.5	2.2	16.1	18.4	9.8	11.9	0.0
▼ Customers Bank	Phoenixville	PA	C+	B-	B	12010.3	18.51	14.2	11.3	4.2	5.8	6.6	10.0	12.2
Cypress Bank, SSB	Pittsburg	TX	B-	B-	C+	195.9	2.61	6.1	7.3	32.1	22.9	9.8	11.1	0.0
D.A. Davidson Trust Co.	Great Falls	MT	U	U	U	10.6	23.30	0.0	0.0	0.0	70.4	10.0	75.9	152.0
D.L. Evans Bank	Burley	ID	A-	A-	B+	1800.6	14.75	7.4	1.9	5.8	26.0	7.2	9.3	0.0
Dacotah Bank	Aberdeen	SD	B-	B-	B	2696.6	4.26	11.4	2.9	3.8	9.6	9.7	11.5	14.7

Asset Quality Index	Adjusted Non-Performing Loans as a % of Total Loans	Adjusted Non-Performing Loans as a % of Capital	Net Charge-Offs Avg Loans	Profitability Index	Net Income ($Mil)	Return on Assets (R.O.A.)	Return on Equity (R.O.E.)	Net Interest Spread	Overhead Efficiency Ratio	Liquidity Index	Liquidity Ratio	Hot Money Ratio	Stability Index
4.5	0.55	na	0.00	**5.8**	0.5	1.02	10.84	3.79	63.2	**1.9**	8.3	18.4	**6.3**
5.0	0.75	na	0.00	**5.2**	1.4	0.82	9.88	3.36	72.9	**3.4**	25.0	12.9	**6.4**
3.0	5.49	18.4	0.13	**4.7**	0.5	1.07	8.83	3.45	70.9	**4.3**	23.8	7.6	**7.2**
5.6	0.46	na	0.06	**4.5**	1.6	1.02	11.03	3.69	75.4	**2.6**	18.6	12.6	**7.0**
6.1	1.71	na	-0.02	**5.3**	1.7	0.93	9.39	3.55	64.6	**2.8**	16.1	11.4	**6.5**
5.8	0.89	na	0.69	**3.1**	1.3	0.45	4.20	4.04	86.0	**3.5**	19.1	12.0	**7.3**
0.3	13.71	na	2.33	**4.0**	0.6	2.16	10.14	3.38	34.4	**1.4**	31.6	30.0	**6.6**
5.2	1.21	na	-0.07	**4.4**	0.5	0.50	4.07	3.85	71.1	**3.2**	33.8	17.1	**6.4**
9.4	0.00	na	-0.08	**2.1**	0.1	0.58	4.23	2.44	96.2	**5.2**	64.0	13.1	**6.9**
4.4	0.81	na	0.00	**4.0**	0.7	0.76	7.80	3.39	79.5	**3.2**	11.9	11.9	**5.9**
6.4	1.39	5.2	-0.02	**3.7**	2.5	0.61	4.04	3.31	71.3	**2.3**	22.0	16.1	**9.7**
7.3	0.66	4.3	-0.02	**5.4**	4.0	1.07	10.60	3.77	72.3	**5.6**	27.4	4.5	**9.4**
10.0	na	na	na	**9.5**	0.3	10.40	8.80	1.76	89.1	**4.0**	na	0.0	**7.0**
10.0	na	na	na	**9.5**	0.1	1.63	1.66	3.61	99.0	**4.0**	na	0.0	**7.0**
8.6	0.00	na	0.00	**3.9**	0.2	0.84	4.99	3.12	76.6	**5.3**	45.0	9.3	**7.9**
6.5	3.99	na	-0.09	**7.3**	1.2	1.30	10.29	4.46	61.6	**4.9**	24.5	4.1	**7.7**
3.1	1.17	na	0.03	**6.6**	0.8	1.95	18.44	4.37	61.1	**2.4**	12.2	16.9	**7.2**
4.3	1.11	8.0	0.02	**4.6**	0.3	1.19	13.12	4.31	74.6	**3.0**	16.2	13.8	**5.9**
5.1	1.03	na	-0.03	**6.7**	2.4	1.28	13.74	4.05	64.2	**4.0**	18.3	9.1	**6.9**
10.0	0.30	na	0.00	**2.9**	0.1	0.32	4.42	3.29	86.3	**6.1**	53.4	5.8	**3.4**
5.9	0.68	na	0.02	**4.8**	1.4	1.23	14.45	3.78	82.8	**5.2**	21.1	1.3	**5.5**
6.2	0.59	2.2	0.12	**4.6**	1.3	1.01	9.77	3.51	63.0	**1.2**	14.2	26.9	**5.5**
6.0	1.04	3.8	-0.40	**3.7**	0.2	0.77	8.24	3.38	72.3	**2.6**	43.5	28.5	**4.5**
10.0	0.13	na	0.00	**3.7**	0.1	0.67	4.06	3.04	73.9	**5.9**	38.3	3.3	**8.0**
5.7	0.27	4.7	-0.01	**9.3**	0.5	2.13	19.52	3.70	56.2	**1.4**	20.7	23.7	**8.1**
6.0	1.10	na	0.00	**2.4**	0.1	0.58	7.06	4.86	87.0	**2.7**	30.0	18.1	**3.6**
6.1	0.22	na	0.02	**7.5**	0.8	1.66	17.02	3.77	59.3	**3.0**	13.3	13.7	**7.7**
10.0	na	0.0	na	**9.5**	2.2	29.37	31.41	-0.01	76.1	**4.0**	na	100.0	**6.7**
3.4	0.00	3.8	9.76	**10.0**	67.9	44.20	97.13	18.20	65.4	**2.3**	56.3	99.8	**8.7**
1.0	3.18	20.3	7.74	**2.7**	0.0	0.01	0.06	13.05	54.6	**0.6**	14.5	62.8	**7.0**
8.4	0.26	na	0.00	**2.8**	0.3	0.25	2.94	2.99	86.8	**3.5**	5.9	10.6	**4.8**
5.6	1.84	6.5	0.01	**3.7**	0.3	0.68	5.96	3.51	86.7	**5.3**	49.4	10.7	**7.9**
8.4	0.08	na	0.00	**9.8**	3.7	3.52	26.33	4.16	69.6	**1.3**	9.1	26.0	**10.0**
5.8	0.52	1.7	0.03	**6.4**	2.8	1.26	9.02	4.23	62.3	**4.3**	6.1	5.4	**9.1**
5.3	1.16	na	0.05	**6.5**	0.7	1.07	8.52	4.36	64.6	**1.2**	17.2	27.4	**8.0**
8.9	0.39	na	0.00	**3.1**	0.3	0.28	2.56	3.84	88.6	**2.4**	17.7	17.2	**6.6**
5.7	2.82	na	0.07	**4.3**	0.8	0.86	7.03	3.66	71.5	**2.4**	34.8	22.8	**7.2**
6.0	0.58	3.7	1.72	**3.7**	-2.1	-0.37	-3.37	7.41	49.3	**1.1**	22.4	53.5	**8.9**
5.6	0.95	5.2	1.99	**2.7**	3.9	0.31	2.80	3.26	55.7	**1.4**	19.4	18.0	**7.7**
6.0	0.00	na	0.00	**6.6**	0.6	1.28	8.96	3.06	48.3	**3.2**	31.6	16.4	**8.2**
5.5	1.41	na	0.19	**5.3**	1.1	1.05	10.49	3.73	67.8	**2.2**	20.7	18.4	**7.2**
7.3	0.46	na	0.03	**7.9**	1.2	2.19	19.57	3.92	48.4	**3.6**	46.5	18.9	**7.9**
6.5	0.32	na	-0.02	**8.0**	0.2	1.75	16.73	4.37	63.2	**1.2**	18.2	29.6	**6.3**
7.4	0.37	na	-0.02	**1.6**	0.1	0.28	2.71	3.72	93.4	**0.8**	16.9	27.1	**5.8**
3.8	3.29	9.2	-0.01	**9.3**	3.5	2.74	13.06	4.76	48.0	**0.8**	21.9	40.6	**10.0**
7.2	0.22	1.7	0.03	**6.1**	3.2	1.10	11.02	2.93	43.3	**1.4**	16.2	17.3	**8.0**
8.8	0.30	1.6	1.41	**4.9**	7.0	0.75	5.33	3.13	57.8	**0.9**	15.2	30.8	**10.0**
7.9	0.00	3.6	0.00	**1.9**	0.0	0.56	3.86	3.63	83.6	**4.5**	51.9	12.7	**3.9**
8.1	0.08	na	0.00	**6.0**	0.8	1.09	6.86	3.96	64.1	**0.7**	13.4	32.9	**8.6**
8.5	0.59	2.5	0.00	**5.1**	0.4	1.01	10.49	2.81	54.5	**2.1**	40.3	9.0	**5.8**
8.4	0.17	na	0.00	**10.0**	1.7	3.09	22.30	4.83	46.1	**2.6**	12.5	15.5	**9.7**
4.9	1.33	na	0.23	**3.1**	0.6	0.46	4.56	3.29	81.0	**1.5**	24.7	27.9	**7.0**
0.3	3.19	na	0.26	**8.4**	0.3	1.31	13.39	4.89	59.5	**0.4**	0.7	23.6	**7.6**
3.9	1.21	9.9	0.01	**6.7**	2.2	1.73	11.86	3.77	53.3	**0.9**	19.4	19.1	**8.5**
5.0	1.17	7.7	0.80	**4.0**	0.4	1.23	10.43	2.96	69.8	**1.3**	29.1	33.9	**5.3**
6.3	0.58	4.7	0.78	**2.9**	6.6	0.23	2.34	3.02	64.3	**1.7**	9.3	5.2	**7.5**
4.9	1.10	na	0.09	**4.2**	0.3	0.70	6.24	3.84	80.3	**1.7**	33.0	31.4	**6.6**
10.0	na	na	na	**9.5**	0.3	13.52	18.27	2.36	77.1	**10.0**	250.5	0.0	**5.9**
8.4	0.56	2.2	-0.01	**6.7**	5.4	1.19	12.42	4.15	63.4	**3.9**	22.7	11.8	**8.9**
4.2	2.67	13.3	0.13	**5.8**	6.9	1.03	8.73	3.80	67.2	**2.7**	10.8	15.1	**9.7**

	Name	City	State	Rating	2019 Rating	2018 Rating	Total Assets ($Mil)	One Year Asset Growth	Asset Mix (As a % of Total Assets) Comm-ercial Loans	Cons-umer Loans	Mort-gage Loans	Secur-ities	Capital-ization Index	Lever-age Ratio	Risk-Based Capital Ratio
	Dairy State Bank	Rice Lake	WI	**B**	B	B	540.7	10.59	10.2	0.9	8.1	50.4	**10.0**	12.1	23.5
	Dakota Community Bank & Trust, N.A.	Hebron	ND	**B+**	B+	B	842.1	2.36	9.1	1.5	3.7	28.7	**6.6**	8.6	14.3
	Dakota Heritage Bank	Hunter	ND	**C+**	C+	B+	216.4	10.34	7.7	3.5	3.0	12.0	**9.2**	10.6	0.0
	Dakota Prairie Bank	Fort Pierre	SD	**A-**	A-	B+	96.2	4.60	8.6	2.4	2.6	5.6	**10.0**	12.2	17.4
	Dakota Western Bank	Bowman	ND	**B+**	B+	B	280.7	4.31	7.7	2.7	1.3	22.4	**10.0**	11.2	15.6
	Dalhart Federal S&L Assn., SSB	Dalhart	TX	**C**	C	C+	112.0	-0.59	0.5	2.2	47.5	32.2	**10.0**	12.2	28.4
	Dallas Capital Bank, N.A.	Dallas	TX	**C-**	C-	C	922.6	9.84	10.4	0.0	8.1	11.0	**8.4**	10.1	0.0
	Damariscotta Bank & Trust Co.	Damariscotta	ME	**C+**	C+	C	195.2	0.15	3.6	1.0	36.1	18.5	**7.7**	9.4	17.3
	Danville State Savings Bank	Danville	IA	**B+**	B+	B+	150.4	4.59	4.1	4.4	21.8	36.6	**9.8**	12.8	0.0
	Dart Bank	Mason	MI	**C+**	C+	B-	520.7	5.18	5.5	0.9	27.0	7.8	**7.7**	9.5	13.6
▼	Davis Trust Co.	Elkins	WV	**B-**	B	B-	147.2	2.50	8.8	3.7	17.4	9.4	**9.8**	13.1	0.0
	De Witt Bank & Trust Co.	De Witt	IA	**B**	B	B	179.5	6.35	8.3	2.3	9.4	22.6	**7.3**	10.4	12.7
	Dean Co-operative Bank	Franklin	MA	**C+**	C+	C+	351.7	8.08	4.4	1.0	49.5	15.3	**6.7**	8.7	14.0
▼	Dearborn Federal Savings Bank	Dearborn	MI	**B-**	B	B+	263.1	-2.32	0.0	0.0	71.2	2.8	**10.0**	30.0	59.6
▲	Decatur County Bank	Decaturville	TN	**C**	C-	D+	142.3	18.04	14.9	4.7	20.9	10.8	**5.3**	8.1	11.2
	Decorah Bank & Trust Co.	Decorah	IA	**A-**	A-	A-	496.2	3.11	14.0	2.3	8.9	19.4	**9.8**	11.0	0.0
▼	Dedham Institution for Savings	Dedham	MA	**B-**	B	B	1567.0	2.01	2.5	0.1	40.7	18.2	**10.0**	12.4	17.0
▲	Dedicated Community Bank	Darlington	SC	**C+**	C	C	69.9	-2.07	16.6	2.9	18.0	14.4	**7.8**	9.5	13.3
	Deerwood Bank	Waite Park	MN	**B**	B	C+	724.8	1.66	17.9	1.3	14.7	6.5	**6.0**	9.0	11.7
▲	Defiance State Bank	Defiance	IA	**C**	C-	D+	35.7	1.62	8.9	7.0	8.0	7.7	**7.3**	9.3	0.0
	Del Norte Bank	Del Norte	CO	**B-**	B-	C+	100.9	2.98	4.9	1.1	26.3	8.6	**7.3**	9.3	0.0
	Delaware National Bank of Delhi	Delhi	NY	**B-**	B-	C+	302.2	-3.24	7.0	1.5	25.1	23.5	**9.2**	10.6	0.0
▲	Delta Bank	Vidalia	LA	**B**	B-	B-	332.6	7.35	4.7	2.0	19.1	16.4	**6.6**	8.6	13.2
▼	Delta National Bank and Trust Co.	New York	NY	**C-**	C	C	387.5	16.00	24.9	9.6	0.0	21.7	**9.8**	15.5	0.0
	DeMotte State Bank	Demotte	IN	**B+**	B+	B	442.8	5.98	9.9	0.9	13.5	29.9	**10.0**	12.6	20.5
	Denali State Bank	Fairbanks	AK	**B-**	B-	B-	306.7	6.60	19.0	8.2	7.8	23.8	**8.6**	10.1	14.4
	Denison State Bank	Holton	KS	**A-**	A-	B+	364.6	5.12	10.1	2.0	12.0	31.6	**9.8**	14.6	0.0
	Denmark State Bank	Denmark	WI	**B**	B	B	547.5	9.91	15.2	1.8	8.8	6.9	**8.1**	10.1	13.4
▲	Denver Savings Bank	Denver	IA	**C+**	C	C+	175.3	-2.31	13.6	1.3	16.1	18.2	**7.9**	9.7	0.0
	Department Stores National Bank	Sioux Falls	SD	**B+**	B+	B+	348.0	-7.05	0.0	15.8	0.0	0.0	**10.0**	19.0	50.8
	Depository Trust Co.	New York	NY	**U**	U	U	4009.7	15.21	0.0	0.0	0.0	0.0	**10.0**	20.2	86.9
	Desjardins Bank, N.A.	Hallandale Beach	FL	**B-**	B-	B-	225.0	2.92	2.2	4.2	62.7	9.0	**10.0**	14.7	29.7
	Deutsche Bank National Trust Co.	Los Angeles	CA	**U**	U	U	290.5	4.45	0.0	0.0	0.0	32.1	**9.8**	81.6	0.0
	Deutsche Bank Trust Co. Americas	New York	NY	**A**	A	A-	41537.0	-0.48	6.5	0.5	5.2	0.0	**10.0**	24.3	65.9
	Deutsche Bank Trust Co. Delaware	Wilmington	DE	**A+**	A+	A-	302.3	-1.64	0.0	0.0	0.0	0.7	**9.8**	95.0	0.0
	Deutsche Bank Trust Co., N.A.	New York	NY	**U**	U	U	151.7	3.35	0.0	0.0	0.0	64.0	**9.8**	92.5	0.0
	Devon Bank	Chicago	IL	**C**	C	C-	317.7	7.89	12.0	2.9	14.9	18.0	**5.4**	8.2	11.3
	Dewey Bank	Dewey	IL	**C-**	C-	D+	21.8	1.12	9.0	2.1	8.7	28.1	**6.3**	8.4	13.3
▼	DeWitt Savings Bank	Clinton	IL	**C+**	B-	B	119.0	4.87	0.0	20.8	28.8	31.1	**10.0**	12.5	24.7
	Diamond Bank	Glenwood	AR	**B**	B	B-	647.1	2.15	6.1	2.1	18.9	20.6	**8.6**	10.1	15.7
	Dickinson County Bank	Enterprise	KS	**E+**	E+	D+	16.9	5.02	11.5	7.2	33.4	3.1	**6.3**	8.3	14.0
	Dieterich Bank	Effingham	IL	**B-**	B-	C+	801.4	19.92	8.9	1.8	9.8	28.5	**7.5**	9.4	13.4
	Dilley State Bank	Dilley	TX	**B+**	B+	B+	140.3	7.37	1.4	0.6	0.1	42.3	**9.8**	17.0	0.0
	Dime Bank	Norwich	CT	**B-**	B-	C+	918.5	7.98	5.9	0.1	34.1	15.6	**10.0**	12.3	18.5
▲	Dime Bank	Honesdale	PA	**B**	B-	C+	758.0	10.45	12.6	1.5	13.3	19.2	**9.4**	11.4	14.5
	Dime Community Bank	Brooklyn	NY	**B-**	B-	B+	6339.6	-1.97	5.2	0.0	2.8	8.8	**8.2**	9.9	13.5
	Discover Bank	Greenwood	DE	**D+**	D+	C-	111140.1	1.91	0.2	82.1	1.4	9.7	**8.0**	9.7	14.0
▼	Dixon Bank	Dixon	KY	**B-**	B	B	82.9	-12.88	2.8	2.7	4.0	40.4	**9.8**	25.1	0.0
	DMB Community Bank	De Forest	WI	**A-**	A-	B+	514.6	2.43	1.0	0.5	21.4	11.5	**10.0**	12.7	18.8
	DNB National Bank	Clear Lake	SD	**C+**	C+	C+	82.6	8.03	5.8	1.0	6.7	54.4	**8.0**	9.7	24.3
	Dogwood State Bank	Raleigh	NC	**D+**	D+	C	394.9	27.47	17.5	0.5	11.1	11.5	**10.0**	21.3	25.0
	Dollar Bank, Federal Savings Bank	Pittsburgh	PA	**B**	B	B	9284.1	8.06	8.3	3.0	51.5	11.6	**10.0**	12.0	18.7
	Dolores State Bank	Dolores	CO	**A-**	A-	B+	264.2	0.65	11.8	5.7	29.6	25.7	**10.0**	14.5	23.6
	Dominion Bank	Dallas	TX	**C**	C	C+	191.3	471.08	33.8	1.1	5.6	2.2	**10.0**	27.9	36.4
▼	Donley County State Bank	Clarendon	TX	**C**	C+	C	39.9	-4.63	4.8	1.6	0.1	31.2	**10.0**	19.2	58.0
	Douglas National Bank	Douglas	GA	**A**	A	A-	188.9	1.23	9.9	2.7	19.9	3.5	**10.0**	11.9	15.7
	DR Bank	Darien	CT	**D-**	D-	D-	362.3	-23.52	0.6	13.6	21.8	18.5	**7.8**	10.0	13.2
	Drake Bank	Saint Paul	MN	**C+**	C+	B-	120.7	-3.47	32.4	1.0	18.9	2.5	**8.3**	10.1	0.0
	Drummond Community Bank	Chiefland	FL	**A-**	A-	A-	686.7	10.85	5.0	2.3	14.7	35.1	**9.8**	11.6	0.0
	DSRM National Bank	Albuquerque	NM	**U**	U	U	3.9	1.73	0.0	0.0	0.0	54.9	**9.8**	84.7	0.0

Asset Quality Index	Adjusted Non-Performing Loans as a % of Total Loans	Adjusted Non-Performing Loans as a % of Capital	Net Charge-Offs Avg Loans	Profitability Index	Net Income ($Mil)	Return on Assets (R.O.A.)	Return on Equity (R.O.E.)	Net Interest Spread	Overhead Efficiency Ratio	Liquidity Index	Liquidity Ratio	Hot Money Ratio	Stability Index
8.8	1.53	na	-0.05	**3.8**	0.8	0.62	4.82	2.69	72.2	**5.1**	46.3	11.2	**7.8**
7.4	0.29	na	0.08	**7.1**	3.9	1.88	21.78	3.59	59.1	**4.5**	32.5	8.1	**8.1**
3.6	0.01	na	0.01	**7.2**	0.8	1.47	12.72	4.48	64.3	**2.2**	12.3	17.6	**8.4**
7.0	0.25	na	0.00	**6.2**	0.3	1.23	10.16	4.59	70.5	**1.8**	19.2	21.2	**8.2**
4.5	1.28	na	0.00	**8.5**	1.4	1.90	17.03	4.04	48.9	**1.7**	13.5	20.0	**8.7**
9.1	0.30	na	0.08	**2.2**	0.1	0.29	2.41	3.70	91.6	**2.1**	43.2	39.8	**6.0**
7.6	0.13	na	0.00	**3.2**	1.5	0.73	6.26	2.72	67.0	**0.8**	5.5	27.4	**6.0**
4.4	2.19	na	0.00	**2.8**	0.1	0.27	2.82	3.40	89.5	**3.2**	27.4	15.0	**5.3**
4.8	1.39	na	0.57	**5.4**	0.5	1.29	9.30	2.26	64.1	**5.0**	61.1	15.0	**8.0**
4.1	2.24	11.7	0.11	**4.0**	0.8	0.63	6.39	3.71	83.1	**3.3**	23.9	13.3	**5.5**
2.0	1.06	na	0.07	**3.9**	0.2	0.55	5.68	4.55	81.9	**4.5**	21.7	6.3	**6.2**
8.4	0.01	na	0.07	**5.1**	0.6	1.38	13.75	3.23	69.9	**3.1**	24.4	14.4	**7.1**
6.6	0.89	4.7	-0.04	**3.6**	0.5	0.61	6.91	3.68	78.1	**3.7**	17.3	10.6	**5.2**
9.3	2.18	na	0.00	**3.1**	0.2	0.36	1.22	2.90	84.7	**4.0**	31.0	12.0	**7.7**
5.9	0.46	na	0.02	**3.8**	0.3	0.82	11.46	4.80	76.7	**1.7**	15.7	20.3	**4.0**
5.2	0.54	3.5	0.00	**6.2**	1.6	1.32	10.64	3.69	62.2	**3.3**	23.2	13.1	**9.3**
9.1	0.29	1.8	0.00	**2.1**	-2.7	-0.70	-6.00	3.19	80.9	**2.9**	23.8	13.5	**9.3**
7.0	1.24	na	0.00	**3.6**	0.1	0.57	5.97	4.19	82.4	**2.8**	15.2	15.0	**5.0**
6.3	0.32	na	0.07	**5.5**	1.1	0.63	5.77	4.39	68.6	**4.8**	11.5	3.1	**8.1**
8.1	0.00	na	-0.37	**4.0**	0.1	1.11	12.04	3.73	71.6	**2.7**	36.6	20.7	**4.1**
6.4	0.41	na	0.00	**4.9**	0.2	0.82	8.69	4.46	73.6	**0.7**	12.2	23.2	**5.8**
6.8	0.63	na	0.03	**4.1**	0.6	0.81	7.55	3.03	68.1	**2.1**	22.8	19.3	**5.8**
5.7	0.56	na	0.08	**6.6**	1.2	1.51	17.38	4.16	67.9	**1.3**	17.5	29.0	**6.9**
8.5	0.00	0.0	0.00	**2.1**	0.1	0.13	0.85	1.94	96.3	**3.3**	51.5	12.7	**6.9**
5.6	2.37	na	0.14	**4.5**	1.0	0.94	7.62	3.72	70.1	**4.9**	38.4	10.1	**7.2**
4.6	1.03	5.7	0.28	**4.4**	0.6	0.75	7.06	4.99	79.6	**4.6**	19.8	5.2	**6.3**
6.8	0.45	na	0.10	**7.9**	1.6	1.74	11.89	3.60	55.5	**2.3**	12.6	17.4	**9.8**
8.2	0.16	1.0	-0.04	**3.8**	0.8	0.61	6.09	3.48	78.0	**3.2**	14.8	12.2	**7.6**
8.3	0.00	na	0.00	**3.7**	0.4	0.84	7.90	3.12	63.5	**0.9**	22.5	40.2	**5.4**
7.9	0.71	2.1	2.63	**5.2**	0.6	0.76	3.94	3.56	74.3	**3.4**	94.1	99.9	**7.6**
10.0	na	0.0	na	**9.5**	21.5	2.38	11.88	1.04	75.0	**4.0**	118.4	0.0	**7.0**
8.7	0.72	na	0.00	**3.1**	0.2	0.38	2.61	4.32	90.2	**4.7**	22.0	4.8	**7.6**
10.0	na	0.0	na	**9.5**	3.8	5.29	6.55	2.24	89.9	**4.0**	399.3	0.0	**7.0**
9.5	0.57	0.7	0.00	**7.9**	229.0	2.27	9.44	1.47	39.3	**8.3**	83.8	0.3	**10.0**
10.0	1.38	0.0	-18.64	**9.5**	1.9	2.44	2.58	1.28	54.0	**4.0**	na	100.0	**9.7**
10.0	na	0.0	na	**8.7**	0.5	1.38	1.57	2.15	96.5	**4.0**	na	0.0	**7.0**
4.5	2.01	na	-0.01	**3.0**	0.4	0.50	5.47	3.76	92.4	**3.3**	20.5	13.1	**5.0**
4.2	1.16	na	-0.15	**0.9**	0.0	-0.12	-1.01	3.81	103.5	**4.3**	23.2	7.4	**4.0**
5.3	1.53	na	0.85	**2.6**	0.1	0.22	1.75	2.97	80.7	**2.6**	38.8	21.6	**6.9**
5.4	1.65	na	0.32	**4.8**	1.7	1.06	10.28	3.64	65.0	**1.2**	12.5	28.8	**7.9**
3.7	2.82	12.4	-0.07	**1.4**	0.0	-0.25	-3.04	3.58	103.0	**1.6**	27.3	25.5	**3.8**
4.6	1.62	9.3	0.04	**4.1**	1.6	0.82	8.70	2.89	65.4	**3.5**	18.2	11.6	**5.8**
10.0	0.10	na	-0.05	**3.6**	0.2	0.68	4.03	1.83	67.0	**7.2**	97.4	8.0	**8.1**
7.0	1.70	na	0.01	**2.6**	0.8	0.34	2.96	2.97	75.9	**2.4**	20.4	16.3	**7.1**
4.8	1.85	na	0.11	**4.9**	1.8	1.00	8.71	3.90	66.9	**1.7**	9.5	19.5	**7.5**
6.7	0.35	2.7	0.00	**3.8**	10.0	0.62	5.91	2.82	55.4	**1.1**	13.4	22.0	**8.2**
1.3	3.28	16.6	3.26	**3.7**	-91.4	-0.33	-3.57	9.00	36.4	**1.1**	21.2	13.4	**10.0**
6.6	5.21	na	-1.11	**3.5**	0.1	0.62	2.45	2.45	72.4	**4.1**	89.6	26.1	**6.7**
7.5	0.00	na	0.00	**5.4**	1.2	0.99	7.82	2.77	58.7	**0.7**	14.9	28.8	**7.7**
9.6	0.00	na	0.00	**3.7**	0.2	0.71	7.28	2.74	79.9	**4.1**	57.8	17.3	**5.4**
7.9	0.11	na	0.01	**0.7**	-0.6	-0.69	-2.96	3.62	118.0	**1.3**	25.8	22.9	**6.2**
8.0	0.67	3.5	0.14	**3.6**	12.6	0.55	4.69	2.80	76.0	**2.9**	10.4	9.2	**9.0**
6.2	1.24	na	0.12	**7.9**	0.9	1.40	9.40	4.10	55.9	**4.6**	29.3	7.8	**9.0**
8.1	0.06	na	0.01	**0.6**	-0.8	-2.10	-7.30	3.18	172.0	**2.4**	43.9	32.6	**5.5**
9.7	0.34	na	0.05	**1.9**	0.0	0.16	0.82	2.29	94.5	**3.0**	60.7	30.5	**7.0**
8.1	1.28	na	-0.01	**9.8**	1.0	2.06	16.70	4.84	54.8	**1.5**	16.1	20.1	**9.2**
6.4	0.41	na	0.42	**0.0**	-0.3	-0.36	-3.57	2.58	105.2	**1.8**	37.3	43.8	**6.7**
8.2	0.27	na	-0.14	**2.7**	0.2	0.54	5.38	3.72	83.0	**1.7**	9.9	19.9	**5.5**
7.0	0.68	2.6	0.08	**6.2**	2.1	1.28	10.13	4.45	68.1	**4.6**	29.0	7.5	**8.4**
10.0	na	na	na	**8.2**	0.0	1.43	1.69	1.33	89.1	**4.0**	na	100.0	**5.3**

Name	City	State	Rating	2019 Rating	2018 Rating	Total Assets ($Mil)	One Year Asset Growth	Comm-ercial Loans	Cons-umer Loans	Mort-gage Loans	Secur-ities	Capital-ization Index	Lever-age Ratio	Risk-Based Capital Ratio
								Asset Mix (As a % of Total Assets)						
Du Quoin State Bank	Du Quoin	IL	**B+**	B+	B+	106.5	0.71	3.7	1.7	15.9	66.7	**7.1**	9.3	0.0
Dubuque Bank and Trust Co.	Dubuque	IA	**B+**	B+	B+	1591.3	2.63	15.7	0.9	5.4	31.1	**7.4**	9.3	13.7
▲ Dundee Bank	Omaha	NE	**B**	B-	C-	309.8	8.22	12.7	0.3	23.5	10.2	**8.3**	10.1	0.0
Durand State Bank	Durand	IL	**B**	B	B-	106.3	2.83	5.2	2.1	11.9	26.2	**10.0**	11.4	19.3
Durden Banking Co., Inc.	Twin City	GA	**A**	A	A-	186.6	3.57	5.0	5.2	28.3	24.2	**10.0**	16.7	28.0
▲ Dysart State Bank	Dysart	IA	**D**	D-	E	13.0	-3.87	1.2	0.9	18.6	5.7	**8.6**	10.1	15.2
E*TRADE Bank	Arlington	VA	**B**	B	B	50294.2	-4.50	0.0	0.4	1.7	94.2	**5.4**	7.4	35.8
E*TRADE Savings Bank	Arlington	VA	**B**	B	B	4536.1	-19.01	0.0	4.3	0.0	64.1	**10.0**	38.5	200.4
▼ Eagle Bank	Everett	MA	**C+**	B-	C	476.8	4.52	10.8	0.0	29.4	15.1	**9.8**	11.9	0.0
Eagle Bank	Glenwood	MN	**A**	A	A	153.7	2.36	8.7	3.8	12.9	15.0	**10.0**	14.4	23.3
Eagle Bank	Polson	MT	**B+**	B+	C+	72.7	8.97	12.9	3.1	11.9	13.2	**9.8**	12.2	0.0
Eagle Bank and Trust Co.	Little Rock	AR	**B**	B	B-	397.0	-0.39	2.3	0.4	24.5	37.9	**9.8**	14.2	0.0
▲ Eagle Community Bank	Maple Grove	MN	**D+**	D	E	27.5	8.36	10.6	1.4	22.5	0.4	**6.7**	8.7	13.5
Eagle Savings Bank	Cincinnati	OH	**B-**	B-	B	144.1	5.55	4.9	0.0	50.1	0.0	**10.0**	15.7	17.2
Eagle State Bank	Eagle	NE	**C-**	C-	D+	45.4	3.22	10.5	1.2	17.3	5.0	**4.5**	8.4	10.7
▼ EagleBank	Bethesda	MD	**A-**	A	A	9984.4	19.09	14.6	0.0	3.4	8.4	**9.8**	13.0	0.0
Eaglemark Savings Bank	Carson City	NV	**A-**	A-	A-	51.7	16.59	0.0	20.4	0.0	38.7	**10.0**	23.6	41.3
Earlham Savings Bank	West Des Moines	IA	**C**	C	C+	320.0	2.85	11.2	1.6	11.5	39.4	**6.3**	8.4	17.1
East Boston Savings Bank	East Boston	MA	**B**	B	B-	6348.3	1.40	1.5	0.2	10.4	0.2	**9.3**	10.7	0.0
East Cambridge Savings Bank	Cambridge	MA	**C+**	C+	C+	1150.6	3.01	2.3	0.9	45.0	10.7	**9.7**	10.8	16.8
East West Bank	Pasadena	CA	**A-**	A-	A-	45939.3	9.19	21.8	0.0	17.1	8.1	**8.1**	10.1	13.4
East Wisconsin Savings Bank	Kaukauna	WI	**D+**	D+	D+	241.6	-2.98	0.1	22.8	47.6	7.4	**7.4**	9.3	15.9
Eastbank, N.A.	New York	NY	**B-**	B-	B	171.3	-11.14	0.8	0.0	11.3	17.6	**10.0**	19.5	28.4
Eastern Bank	Boston	MA	**B+**	B+	B	12341.3	8.91	14.8	2.8	14.5	12.6	**8.2**	11.2	13.5
Eastern Colorado Bank	Cheyenne Wells	CO	**A-**	A-	B+	448.8	11.40	6.7	0.4	9.3	16.5	**9.6**	10.7	15.0
▼ Eastern Connecticut Savings Bank	Norwich	CT	**D**	D+	D	191.1	5.23	5.2	2.7	37.5	0.2	**5.9**	7.9	12.2
▼ Eastern International Bank	Los Angeles	CA	**B-**	B	B	132.0	26.68	0.0	0.0	0.1	3.4	**9.8**	15.9	0.0
Eastern Michigan Bank	Croswell	MI	**B**	B	B-	373.3	3.43	9.1	3.8	8.3	30.6	**8.8**	10.2	18.4
Eastern National Bank	Miami	FL	**D+**	D+	C-	338.2	-12.89	18.4	0.5	24.1	1.3	**6.0**	8.6	11.8
Eastern Savings Bank, FSB	Hunt Valley	MD	**B**	B	B-	315.9	-1.66	0.0	0.0	48.3	0.0	**10.0**	25.6	37.3
Easthampton Savings Bank	Easthampton	MA	**B-**	B-	B-	1486.3	7.86	8.6	0.5	32.2	11.2	**7.2**	9.1	13.2
▼ Eaton Federal Savings Bank	Charlotte	MI	**C+**	B-	C+	382.2	3.20	1.8	1.4	39.4	29.1	**9.8**	15.0	0.0
Eclipse Bank, Inc.	Louisville	KY	**C+**	C+	C+	181.6	15.78	4.9	1.7	13.4	5.0	**8.3**	11.9	13.6
Edgewater Bank	Saint Joseph	MI	**C+**	C+	C-	187.9	10.99	12.8	0.5	29.7	4.2	**7.1**	9.1	13.4
Edison National Bank	Fort Myers	FL	**B-**	B-	B-	356.8	6.59	2.1	1.9	21.3	6.7	**6.0**	8.0	21.0
Edmonton State Bank	Edmonton	KY	**A-**	A-	B+	555.6	2.24	7.6	7.7	17.8	9.7	**9.8**	15.0	0.0
▼ Edon State Bank Co. of Edon, Ohio	Edon	OH	**B-**	B	B	59.6	-1.98	1.5	0.4	6.6	9.0	**10.0**	18.6	68.0
Edward Jones Trust Co.	Saint Louis	MO	**U**	U	U	100.3	12.84	0.0	0.0	0.0	0.1	**10.0**	95.4	362.8
EH National Bank	Beverly Hills	CA	**C**	C	C-	247.2	14.15	6.6	0.0	1.5	5.5	**10.0**	13.0	16.0
El Dorado Savings Bank, F.S.B.	Placerville	CA	**B**	B	B-	2218.3	1.43	0.0	0.0	25.5	54.6	**10.0**	11.3	38.1
▼ Elberfeld State Bank	Elberfeld	IN	**B-**	B	B	82.1	0.05	3.6	0.6	9.8	24.0	**9.8**	12.0	0.0
▼ Elberton Federal S&L Assn.	Elberton	GA	**D+**	C-	D+	24.5	3.39	0.0	1.2	74.0	12.7	**9.8**	20.6	0.0
Elderton State Bank	Elderton	PA	**B+**	B+	B	296.8	4.68	12.3	1.0	12.7	5.4	**9.8**	11.8	0.0
Elgin State Bank	Elgin	IA	**D-**	D-	D-	24.9	-2.51	3.7	2.7	15.4	25.6	**5.5**	7.5	16.9
Elizabethton Federal Savings Bank	Elizabethton	TN	**A**	A	A-	295.0	0.61	0.0	0.7	34.1	35.2	**10.0**	41.2	109.0
Elk State Bank	Clyde	KS	**C+**	C+	C+	96.1	-0.06	5.8	1.3	10.9	33.4	**9.2**	10.5	18.6
Elkhorn Valley Bank & Trust	Norfolk	NE	**B**	B	B	799.9	-1.07	14.3	3.4	5.8	26.8	**10.0**	13.0	17.5
Elkton Bank & Trust Co.	Elkton	KY	**A-**	A-	A-	146.7	4.74	3.8	4.2	15.3	44.1	**10.0**	12.8	27.6
Elmira Savings Bank	Elmira	NY	**C+**	C+	C+	598.2	0.23	4.7	6.4	54.2	2.8	**6.3**	8.3	12.4
Elysian Bank	Elysian	MN	**B+**	B+	B-	50.8	2.91	7.2	7.1	20.1	3.0	**10.0**	11.3	19.5
Embassy Bank for the Lehigh Valley	Bethlehem	PA	**B**	B	B	1194.9	6.38	4.7	0.1	51.0	7.4	**6.5**	8.5	13.0
Embassy National Bank	Lawrenceville	GA	**A**	A	A	120.8	7.02	1.9	0.1	2.0	0.0	**10.0**	16.3	24.4
Emerald Bank	Burden	KS	**D+**	D+	C-	18.4	2.46	5.7	7.7	33.2	8.4	**9.0**	10.3	20.4
Emigrant Bank	New York	NY	**B-**	B-	B-	6305.7	10.71	31.6	0.7	14.1	8.1	**10.0**	18.4	19.1
Emigrant Mercantile Bank	New York	NY	**U**	U	U	3.4	-0.35	0.0	0.0	0.0	0.0	**10.0**	85.3	424.9
▼ Empire National Bank	Islandia	NY	**C**	C+	C+	1001.0	-4.34	9.1	0.4	7.9	24.2	**7.3**	9.2	16.5
▼ Empire State Bank	Newburgh	NY	**C-**	C	D+	429.4	2.95	4.4	0.0	39.8	2.0	**7.2**	9.3	0.0
Emprise Bank	Wichita	KS	**B+**	B+	B+	1864.9	7.92	11.5	2.7	18.4	21.0	**5.6**	7.6	11.4
Encore Bank	Little Rock	AR	**D+**	D+	C-	408.0	147.36	15.5	0.6	17.8	5.9	**9.8**	14.0	0.0
Endeavor Bank	San Diego	CA	**D**	D	D	144.3	62.12	27.3	1.8	11.4	0.0	**10.0**	18.5	20.0

Asset Quality Index	Adjusted Non-Performing Loans as a % of Total Loans	Adjusted Non-Performing Loans as a % of Capital	Net Charge-Offs Avg Loans	Profitability Index	Net Income ($Mil)	Return on Assets (R.O.A.)	Return on Equity (R.O.E.)	Net Interest Spread	Overhead Efficiency Ratio	Liquidity Index	Liquidity Ratio	Hot Money Ratio	Stability Index
8.0	1.02	2.5	0.00	**4.8**	0.3	1.23	10.55	3.89	73.9	**4.3**	54.1	17.0	**6.8**
6.0	2.28	7.5	-0.19	**6.3**	4.1	1.02	10.66	3.11	62.2	**6.2**	34.2	3.3	**8.1**
6.3	0.66	na	0.02	**5.4**	0.9	1.24	12.35	3.88	67.5	**0.8**	13.2	31.0	**5.7**
6.6	2.56	6.1	-0.07	**3.7**	0.2	0.64	5.84	3.34	76.0	**2.8**	24.6	15.9	**6.3**
8.4	0.47	1.9	-0.13	**8.9**	1.0	2.17	13.19	5.26	59.3	**2.8**	23.2	15.6	**9.6**
9.0	0.00	na	0.06	**1.5**	0.0	-0.22	-2.22	3.41	105.6	**5.6**	31.3	0.0	**3.3**
7.5	19.89	6.7	-1.22	**4.7**	96.9	0.83	11.05	2.54	57.1	**3.4**	76.8	0.0	**6.3**
7.7	0.24	0.0	0.00	**3.8**	9.2	0.89	2.11	2.81	72.2	**4.3**	142.8	0.0	**7.6**
8.8	0.12	na	0.00	**1.6**	-0.6	-0.47	-4.15	3.39	80.7	**1.6**	21.4	21.3	**6.9**
8.5	0.02	0.1	0.00	**7.3**	0.7	1.78	12.09	3.87	58.5	**5.6**	33.9	3.4	**9.4**
8.3	0.06	na	0.01	**9.1**	0.4	2.35	19.24	5.18	55.1	**1.2**	22.3	13.7	**6.8**
5.7	2.30	na	0.01	**4.1**	0.8	0.80	5.45	3.87	82.3	**4.0**	31.8	12.2	**7.6**
8.6	0.00	0.0	0.00	**3.8**	0.1	1.85	21.72	5.11	69.8	**2.2**	17.6	18.4	**2.3**
7.5	1.33	na	-0.02	**3.1**	0.2	0.55	3.50	3.22	83.6	**2.1**	15.1	18.4	**7.8**
8.2	1.35	na	0.00	**3.0**	0.1	1.07	13.96	3.16	61.7	**0.9**	7.6	31.7	**2.1**
5.7	0.68	3.6	0.12	**8.0**	27.8	1.18	8.39	3.62	41.9	**0.9**	16.4	7.4	**10.0**
7.7	0.00	0.0	0.00	**10.0**	0.8	7.67	32.78	11.38	81.0	**4.4**	85.6	20.0	**9.2**
8.8	0.00	na	-0.04	**2.5**	0.3	0.37	4.31	3.14	86.7	**5.7**	48.0	8.3	**4.8**
7.1	0.09	0.5	0.01	**4.6**	13.1	0.83	7.56	3.02	54.0	**1.4**	8.5	15.7	**8.7**
8.9	0.34	2.6	0.02	**2.9**	1.0	0.34	3.32	3.00	79.5	**1.5**	18.2	25.4	**7.6**
7.5	0.53	2.8	0.01	**7.1**	148.2	1.33	12.04	3.44	41.8	**1.5**	17.6	20.6	**10.0**
6.4	0.61	na	0.00	**1.3**	0.1	0.09	0.98	2.70	100.4	**1.9**	21.8	19.9	**4.9**
7.9	0.00	0.0	0.00	**1.8**	0.0	-0.04	-0.19	3.06	100.7	**2.1**	42.5	35.5	**7.5**
5.8	0.91	3.5	0.08	**4.2**	8.6	0.29	2.13	3.78	70.6	**5.4**	20.8	1.5	**10.0**
8.3	0.12	na	-0.07	**6.9**	2.0	1.81	15.95	4.14	57.0	**1.6**	13.2	22.4	**8.4**
1.7	4.12	na	0.02	**0.8**	-0.1	-0.16	-1.96	3.31	104.4	**1.4**	11.9	24.5	**4.2**
7.5	0.00	na	0.00	**3.2**	0.2	0.60	3.81	3.31	87.0	**1.3**	31.9	50.8	**7.3**
7.3	0.87	1.3	-0.01	**4.4**	0.8	0.86	8.48	3.23	67.5	**6.4**	44.2	2.1	**6.3**
2.6	3.43	17.9	1.11	**0.0**	-1.3	-1.52	-15.00	3.19	155.4	**0.7**	13.4	44.1	**3.8**
4.6	5.24	na	0.06	**5.7**	0.9	1.16	4.57	6.21	79.0	**3.0**	24.4	15.1	**8.2**
8.7	0.34	na	0.00	**3.4**	1.6	0.44	4.91	2.79	68.2	**1.5**	16.7	26.0	**6.6**
7.9	1.10	na	-0.07	**3.0**	0.6	0.60	3.98	3.38	79.3	**4.4**	37.5	12.0	**7.8**
4.9	1.51	na	-0.05	**3.4**	0.3	0.57	4.81	3.38	77.8	**0.7**	12.4	32.9	**6.9**
3.9	1.30	14.7	-0.01	**3.1**	0.3	0.69	7.00	3.67	76.8	**3.2**	12.9	12.8	**5.7**
9.6	0.00	0.0	-0.25	**3.9**	0.8	0.92	11.69	3.05	71.4	**6.8**	56.5	3.3	**5.2**
6.0	0.53	na	0.03	**8.6**	2.6	1.94	13.12	4.02	58.1	**3.4**	21.7	12.9	**10.0**
9.7	0.00	na	0.00	**3.3**	0.1	0.54	2.91	2.26	77.2	**7.0**	87.0	6.1	**8.3**
10.0	na	na	na	**9.5**	3.1	12.48	13.27	1.61	77.5	**4.0**	na	0.0	**6.7**
4.5	1.79	na	0.15	**1.0**	-0.2	-0.34	-2.14	3.32	114.5	**0.8**	18.5	44.1	**6.0**
9.9	1.14	2.0	0.01	**3.9**	3.9	0.70	6.12	2.27	64.5	**6.3**	77.2	12.0	**8.7**
8.9	2.91	na	0.00	**3.6**	0.1	0.54	4.46	3.27	81.2	**4.9**	43.9	11.4	**6.7**
9.8	0.00	na	0.00	**0.5**	0.0	-0.08	-0.39	3.25	105.8	**1.7**	23.9	23.6	**6.2**
3.7	3.49	na	0.03	**6.8**	1.0	1.36	11.68	3.68	48.3	**1.7**	14.1	21.0	**7.6**
8.9	0.03	na	0.00	**0.9**	0.0	-0.20	-2.63	3.24	105.7	**5.6**	49.5	6.1	**1.5**
10.0	0.00	na	0.00	**6.3**	0.8	1.12	2.72	2.87	41.5	**4.5**	87.4	22.1	**8.7**
6.0	2.47	na	-0.02	**3.3**	0.1	0.41	3.91	3.50	76.8	**1.7**	17.9	17.9	**5.1**
8.2	0.37	na	0.25	**3.6**	1.2	0.61	4.70	3.18	54.2	**4.4**	30.4	9.9	**7.8**
8.7	0.69	na	0.01	**5.3**	0.4	1.01	7.84	3.71	66.8	**3.6**	51.1	19.7	**7.3**
4.2	0.89	na	0.05	**3.6**	1.0	0.68	6.93	3.16	75.3	**1.4**	5.3	23.6	**6.7**
6.4	1.27	na	-0.48	**8.4**	0.2	1.91	16.96	4.56	57.1	**6.1**	36.6	1.2	**7.6**
9.1	0.26	1.2	-0.01	**4.4**	2.5	0.87	10.06	3.14	61.9	**2.4**	4.9	16.3	**7.2**
7.3	0.00	na	0.00	**6.7**	0.1	0.24	1.44	4.12	90.7	**2.3**	36.7	26.7	**10.0**
4.2	3.60	na	0.30	**2.5**	0.0	0.26	2.50	4.13	93.0	**3.9**	40.8	13.1	**4.8**
3.4	3.95	15.0	-0.02	**5.4**	6.2	0.49	2.45	4.52	69.3	**3.4**	14.7	8.9	**10.0**
10.0	na	0.0	na	**0.2**	0.0	-0.35	-0.41	1.05	144.4	**4.0**	na	0.0	**6.8**
5.8	0.74	5.0	0.00	**2.5**	0.7	0.26	2.84	2.60	79.4	**4.9**	7.9	2.1	**6.6**
5.9	0.61	na	0.00	**1.7**	0.0	0.02	0.16	3.12	77.5	**1.3**	11.6	23.0	**4.3**
4.4	1.76	na	0.04	**5.8**	5.0	1.08	12.21	3.64	64.2	**4.3**	20.6	7.3	**9.2**
7.4	0.12	na	0.00	**1.7**	0.3	0.37	2.61	2.97	83.5	**0.6**	13.4	20.0	**4.7**
8.2	0.00	na	0.00	**0.0**	-0.3	-0.96	-6.13	3.97	114.5	**3.0**	21.3	14.7	**1.5**

Name	City	State	Rating	2019 Rating	2018 Rating	Total Assets ($Mil)	One Year Asset Growth	Asset Mix (As a % of Total Assets) Comm-ercial Loans	Cons-umer Loans	Mort-gage Loans	Secur-ities	Capital-ization Index	Lever-age Ratio	Risk-Based Capital Ratio
EnerBank USA	Salt Lake City	UT	**B+**	B+	A-	2670.0	22.27	0.0	95.2	0.0	1.1	**8.7**	10.3	0.0
Englewood Bank & Trust	Englewood	FL	**A-**	A-	A-	332.6	8.22	1.6	0.9	21.2	20.0	**7.9**	9.7	0.0
Ennis State Bank	Ennis	TX	**B+**	B+	B-	250.2	9.26	12.6	0.7	8.8	18.5	**8.1**	9.8	14.5
Enterprise Bank	Omaha	NE	**B-**	B-	C+	356.9	17.51	10.8	0.9	4.8	1.4	**6.4**	9.8	12.0
Enterprise Bank	Allison Park	PA	**D-**	D-	D	315.4	6.19	10.0	0.0	4.0	0.0	**5.0**	9.2	11.0
Enterprise Bank & Trust	Clayton	MO	**B+**	B+	B+	7479.3	8.22	32.5	0.3	3.9	17.9	**6.8**	10.3	12.4
Enterprise Bank and Trust Co.	Lowell	MA	**B**	B	B-	3367.2	9.54	14.1	0.3	12.9	15.0	**5.8**	9.1	11.6
Enterprise Bank of South Carolina	Ehrhardt	SC	**C-**	C-	D	351.9	4.66	6.3	3.1	17.7	24.1	**6.3**	8.3	15.5
▼ Envision Bank	Stoughton	MA	**D+**	C	D	653.1	6.22	1.4	2.4	51.2	8.5	**9.6**	11.5	14.7
▼ Ephrata National Bank	Ephrata	PA	**B-**	B	B-	1177.4	5.93	5.1	0.5	23.3	27.8	**8.2**	9.8	14.2
Equitable Bank	Grand Island	NE	**C+**	C+	C	367.6	13.66	12.8	1.1	19.5	5.2	**5.7**	9.0	11.5
▲ Equitable Bank, S.S.B.	Wauwatosa	WI	**D+**	D	E	297.4	-2.77	0.7	0.1	46.0	7.3	**7.3**	9.3	0.0
Equitable S&L Assn.	Sterling	CO	**B**	B	B	166.0	0.53	0.0	0.8	80.3	2.7	**10.0**	16.1	32.4
▼ Equitable S&L Co.	Cadiz	OH	**D**	D+	D	13.3	2.53	0.0	0.4	53.9	16.0	**10.0**	19.2	43.8
Equity Bank	Andover	KS	**C+**	C+	B-	3939.8	-3.01	13.5	1.5	14.9	23.8	**7.6**	9.4	13.5
Ergo Bank	Markesan	WI	**B-**	B-	C	95.1	12.12	13.7	1.0	10.5	14.6	**10.0**	12.5	17.0
▲ ESB Bank	Caledonia	MN	**B-**	C+	C	115.2	4.53	12.1	3.8	9.8	9.7	**8.5**	10.1	0.0
▼ ESB Financial	Emporia	KS	**C**	C+	B-	247.2	3.53	9.7	2.0	19.5	15.9	**8.7**	10.3	0.0
Escambia County Bank	Flomaton	AL	**C+**	C+	B-	72.9	-2.43	11.5	5.9	16.7	53.6	**9.8**	15.5	0.0
Esquire Bank, N.A.	Jericho	NY	**A**	A	A-	813.6	13.78	35.7	5.8	6.4	17.0	**10.0**	12.4	17.0
ESSA Bank & Trust	Stroudsburg	PA	**C+**	C+	C+	1952.7	6.78	3.7	3.1	34.0	15.7	**8.0**	9.7	14.1
Essex Bank	Richmond	VA	**B+**	B+	B	1453.4	3.94	13.2	0.7	11.4	15.7	**8.7**	10.9	13.9
▼ Essex Savings Bank	Essex	CT	**C+**	B-	B-	422.9	6.37	3.3	0.4	44.0	0.2	**8.6**	10.3	0.0
ETHIC	Boston	MA	**D**	D	D-	240.2	-4.87	1.3	17.1	15.1	0.0	**10.0**	13.1	17.2
Eureka Homestead	Metairie	LA	**C**	C	C	107.1	8.85	0.0	0.2	67.6	4.8	**10.0**	18.0	41.2
Eureka Savings Bank	La Salle	IL	**C+**	C+	C+	346.0	7.86	0.9	0.5	33.4	49.8	**10.0**	23.9	60.1
▲ EvaBank	Cullman	AL	**B**	B-	B-	383.0	2.42	2.3	4.9	31.7	18.3	**10.0**	24.6	33.7
Evangeline Bank and Trust Co.	Ville Platte	LA	**B+**	B+	B	604.6	3.90	6.9	3.3	25.8	18.7	**9.8**	19.0	0.0
Evans Bank, N.A.	Hamburg	NY	**B-**	B-	C+	1508.3	4.69	15.1	0.1	11.7	10.8	**7.6**	9.8	13.0
Evercore Trust Co., N.A.	New York	NY	**U**	U	U	23.4	-0.51	0.0	0.0	0.0	71.5	**10.0**	97.2	369.8
Everence Trust Co.	Goshen	IN	**U**	U	U	10.4	21.64	0.0	0.0	0.0	55.5	**10.0**	96.4	187.8
Everett Co-operative Bank	Everett	MA	**B+**	B+	B+	524.7	3.87	0.4	0.1	38.9	7.8	**10.0**	13.5	19.9
Evergreen Bank Group	Oak Brook	IL	**B+**	B+	B	1203.3	19.26	2.7	51.5	3.5	6.4	**7.7**	11.0	13.1
Evergreen Federal Bank	Grants Pass	OR	**B**	B	B	491.2	5.39	1.5	0.2	26.8	7.6	**9.8**	12.7	0.0
▼ Evergreen National Bank	Evergreen	CO	**C**	C+	C+	116.7	4.01	3.1	0.6	16.0	28.3	**7.6**	9.5	0.0
EverTrust Bank	Pasadena	CA	**B+**	B+	A-	934.5	2.74	11.9	0.0	1.5	12.0	**9.8**	17.1	0.0
Evolve Bank & Trust	Memphis	TN	**B-**	B-	C+	487.0	1.82	18.6	0.7	23.5	2.8	**7.3**	9.2	12.8
Exchange Bank	Santa Rosa	CA	**A**	A	A-	2640.4	0.28	7.2	1.0	11.2	28.7	**9.5**	10.7	16.1
Exchange Bank	Milledgeville	GA	**A-**	A-	A-	269.6	7.33	2.3	1.1	18.6	29.2	**10.0**	13.8	22.3
Exchange Bank	Kearney	NE	**B+**	B+	B+	1006.1	7.63	5.7	0.8	11.6	24.6	**7.7**	9.6	0.0
Exchange Bank	Skiatook	OK	**A-**	A-	B+	110.5	2.54	9.1	1.3	12.4	33.7	**9.8**	11.4	0.0
Exchange Bank & Trust	Atchison	KS	**A-**	A-	B+	429.3	1.37	7.0	15.0	16.4	23.9	**9.5**	10.8	0.0
Exchange Bank and Trust Co.	Natchitoches	LA	**A-**	A-	A-	161.9	2.78	3.6	1.8	21.8	49.9	**8.4**	9.9	22.7
Exchange Bank and Trust Co.	Perry	OK	**B-**	B-	A-	299.0	3.00	6.3	5.0	21.0	27.8	**9.3**	10.5	16.7
Exchange Bank of Alabama	Altoona	AL	**B+**	B+	A-	296.8	4.53	3.5	3.0	15.3	23.3	**10.0**	14.5	22.4
▲ Exchange Bank of Missouri	Fayette	MO	**A-**	B+	B	230.1	11.86	6.2	1.3	10.1	7.3	**8.9**	10.6	14.1
Exchange Bank of Northeast Missouri	Kahoka	MO	**C+**	C+	C	172.0	14.14	5.3	1.2	11.7	14.0	**7.0**	9.0	12.5
Exchange State Bank	Adair	IA	**B**	B	B	38.7	6.74	3.7	1.7	7.9	19.2	**10.0**	12.6	23.1
Exchange State Bank	Collins	IA	**B**	B	B	114.4	1.60	8.6	0.9	13.0	5.9	**8.9**	10.3	15.2
Exchange State Bank	Springville	IA	**B**	B	B-	45.7	1.67	4.9	1.2	18.1	30.2	**7.7**	9.6	0.0
Exchange State Bank	Lanark	IL	**B**	B	B	86.4	2.08	6.7	1.4	10.0	44.9	**9.8**	12.0	0.0
Exchange State Bank	Carsonville	MI	**A-**	A-	B+	171.9	5.62	6.1	2.4	12.2	28.4	**9.8**	12.2	0.0
Exchange State Bank of St. Paul, Kansas	Saint Paul	KS	**B-**	B-	B-	75.1	5.97	10.7	2.4	13.5	21.6	**9.1**	10.6	0.0
Executive National Bank	Miami	FL	**B-**	B-	B-	489.1	8.24	6.2	0.1	16.3	9.5	**9.7**	10.8	17.5
Extraco Banks, N.A.	Temple	TX	**B**	B	B-	1541.0	3.64	2.4	7.2	20.2	21.1	**9.5**	10.6	17.2
▲ F & C Bank	Holden	MO	**B-**	C+	B	238.2	7.09	5.0	2.3	23.0	5.3	**8.9**	10.8	14.1
F & M Bank and Trust Co.	Manchester	GA	**E-**	E-	E-	70.9	8.12	5.0	2.8	13.4	0.6	**0.6**	5.0	7.2
F & M Bank Minnesota	Clarkfield	MN	**B**	B	B-	126.0	0.54	3.8	0.3	1.8	27.4	**6.0**	9.0	11.7
F & M Community Bank, N.A.	Preston	MN	**B**	B	B	139.3	2.45	7.2	1.5	15.0	15.2	**9.8**	11.7	0.0
F&M Bank	Washington	GA	**B+**	B+	B+	268.9	2.26	3.5	2.8	18.7	30.1	**9.8**	17.5	0.0

Asset Quality Index	Adjusted Non-Performing Loans as a % of Total Loans	Adjusted Non-Performing Loans as a % of Capital	Net Charge-Offs Avg Loans	Profitability Index	Net Income ($Mil)	Return on Assets (R.O.A.)	Return on Equity (R.O.E.)	Net Interest Spread	Overhead Efficiency Ratio	Liquidity Index	Liquidity Ratio	Hot Money Ratio	Stability Index
5.2	0.02	2.3	1.41	**10.0**	13.8	2.07	21.27	6.64	36.9	**0.2**	5.9	8.9	**9.0**
7.6	0.49	1.5	0.00	**9.4**	1.7	2.06	21.14	3.84	57.4	**6.3**	43.7	2.5	**8.5**
5.7	0.87	na	0.01	**6.4**	1.0	1.52	15.36	4.36	62.5	**4.2**	19.2	7.8	**7.5**
7.3	0.00	na	0.00	**4.4**	0.7	0.77	7.93	2.69	64.1	**0.8**	21.3	42.1	**6.0**
0.2	7.39	na	0.08	**3.2**	0.3	0.42	4.61	3.49	83.1	**0.6**	11.0	4.3	**5.2**
6.0	0.68	3.3	0.09	**6.2**	14.9	0.81	6.13	3.92	47.9	**2.5**	16.8	6.5	**10.0**
5.1	0.96	5.8	0.00	**4.5**	4.3	0.53	5.48	3.90	65.7	**4.1**	2.6	6.7	**8.4**
2.0	5.00	26.9	-0.02	**4.8**	0.6	0.65	7.46	3.62	85.7	**4.6**	31.1	9.0	**3.8**
5.8	0.96	na	0.01	**0.6**	-0.8	-0.51	-4.44	2.90	100.8	**0.7**	13.2	24.9	**6.9**
8.7	0.51	na	0.00	**3.9**	2.4	0.83	8.46	3.41	75.8	**5.3**	24.4	4.3	**8.5**
5.1	0.84	na	0.00	**3.2**	0.4	0.39	4.09	3.27	80.7	**1.5**	8.8	22.1	**5.7**
6.5	0.49	na	0.07	**1.6**	0.1	0.12	1.40	3.56	95.0	**2.2**	10.3	17.7	**1.6**
9.9	0.00	na	0.00	**3.4**	0.2	0.55	3.40	3.06	79.8	**2.3**	20.9	18.1	**7.9**
10.0	0.56	na	0.00	**0.0**	0.0	-0.88	-4.55	2.61	134.9	**2.1**	29.4	19.7	**6.7**
4.1	1.67	8.0	0.04	**3.5**	2.2	0.22	1.74	3.70	66.3	**2.3**	8.9	17.0	**8.1**
6.8	0.39	na	0.00	**3.6**	0.2	0.64	4.92	4.07	80.1	**1.7**	24.2	17.6	**6.4**
8.1	0.00	na	0.00	**7.4**	0.6	2.12	20.29	3.79	49.4	**2.1**	5.4	17.7	**7.9**
2.4	3.14	na	0.00	**4.1**	0.6	0.97	9.36	3.36	72.0	**4.0**	17.6	9.3	**6.4**
5.3	2.75	na	-0.03	**2.8**	0.1	0.45	2.83	3.47	89.0	**2.9**	59.3	31.0	**7.2**
7.9	0.13	na	0.01	**9.5**	3.0	1.51	11.88	4.70	51.4	**5.4**	28.7	2.6	**8.5**
6.1	1.19	na	0.02	**3.6**	3.5	0.76	7.39	2.73	68.0	**1.6**	15.7	11.3	**7.4**
7.2	0.47	3.7	-0.03	**4.1**	1.6	0.44	3.95	3.70	62.4	**1.2**	15.8	30.4	**9.0**
1.7	3.10	na	0.00	**2.5**	0.1	0.09	0.70	3.22	97.3	**3.7**	21.7	10.9	**7.0**
6.9	0.96	na	0.09	**0.0**	-2.6	-4.67	-34.00	3.78	208.5	**1.3**	25.2	30.7	**5.0**
10.0	0.00	na	0.00	**2.2**	0.1	0.21	1.16	1.83	92.0	**0.9**	27.0	69.9	**7.3**
7.4	3.16	na	0.15	**2.8**	0.5	0.60	2.48	2.57	72.4	**6.3**	75.7	10.7	**6.9**
4.2	3.71	na	0.02	**9.7**	1.6	1.71	6.37	6.28	46.7	**0.9**	23.7	39.1	**8.9**
5.6	1.46	na	-0.04	**4.5**	1.2	0.80	4.23	4.09	75.7	**1.5**	24.2	27.7	**8.7**
4.5	1.52	8.0	0.01	**4.1**	0.9	0.24	2.43	3.57	71.9	**2.8**	6.8	12.2	**8.7**
10.0	na	na	na	**7.2**	0.1	1.07	1.09	1.36	95.2	**4.0**	na	0.0	**6.1**
10.0	na	na	na	**3.7**	-0.3	-12.14	-12.14	4.27	104.5	**5.0**	260.6	100.0	**3.9**
9.1	0.20	1.2	0.00	**4.7**	1.3	1.03	7.75	3.12	58.9	**1.0**	18.7	33.2	**8.3**
5.7	0.15	1.5	0.71	**6.7**	3.2	1.12	10.18	4.54	47.3	**0.8**	16.8	37.1	**8.5**
7.2	0.54	na	0.00	**4.5**	1.1	0.90	7.11	3.87	70.2	**4.1**	17.6	8.4	**7.4**
2.5	2.28	na	0.08	**3.4**	0.1	0.43	4.41	4.04	90.2	**6.6**	43.2	0.2	**5.6**
2.1	2.25	na	0.00	**7.4**	2.6	1.11	5.44	3.56	49.3	**0.7**	18.9	56.0	**9.5**
4.5	1.01	7.8	0.23	**4.8**	0.9	0.75	7.61	4.52	91.8	**1.8**	13.6	17.2	**6.1**
8.0	0.60	4.4	-0.01	**7.8**	8.6	1.31	12.52	3.77	59.8	**5.7**	31.3	5.9	**9.6**
7.2	0.82	na	0.10	**5.6**	0.7	1.02	7.33	4.16	69.9	**3.9**	33.6	13.2	**8.3**
4.8	0.37	12.7	-0.02	**7.0**	4.3	1.77	17.88	3.12	49.3	**1.0**	20.2	36.3	**9.1**
5.5	2.26	na	0.03	**5.4**	0.3	1.08	9.50	4.34	67.5	**2.8**	32.7	18.4	**7.5**
7.7	0.04	na	0.03	**7.1**	1.6	1.52	13.88	3.72	53.7	**4.4**	21.2	6.6	**7.2**
6.9	0.95	3.5	0.01	**7.4**	0.7	1.69	15.37	3.81	53.1	**4.1**	17.3	8.6	**8.5**
3.6	2.31	13.2	-0.01	**5.3**	1.2	1.59	14.84	4.28	66.3	**1.1**	12.5	30.2	**6.1**
8.6	0.31	1.3	0.03	**4.6**	0.6	0.84	5.71	3.74	70.5	**3.0**	21.7	14.5	**8.1**
8.1	0.02	0.7	0.06	**6.7**	0.6	1.13	10.00	3.90	60.3	**2.6**	15.6	15.9	**7.3**
4.3	1.95	na	0.31	**3.3**	0.2	0.58	5.60	3.42	82.5	**2.9**	24.8	15.5	**5.7**
7.9	0.00	na	0.00	**6.6**	0.2	1.80	11.88	3.44	55.5	**4.7**	42.6	12.1	**8.0**
8.3	0.00	na	0.00	**4.3**	0.3	1.10	10.77	3.31	62.8	**1.6**	17.6	24.1	**6.9**
8.7	0.20	na	0.00	**4.5**	0.1	0.84	9.46	3.69	70.0	**5.1**	36.9	7.8	**5.5**
6.8	0.92	na	0.00	**3.8**	0.2	0.85	6.55	2.86	72.4	**2.6**	40.0	23.5	**7.0**
7.2	0.45	na	0.02	**5.8**	0.6	1.37	10.86	3.75	62.3	**4.5**	40.4	12.5	**7.6**
7.7	0.36	na	0.00	**4.1**	0.2	0.83	7.91	3.77	69.7	**2.7**	36.5	21.7	**5.8**
7.4	0.20	na	0.00	**3.2**	0.5	0.40	3.65	3.36	82.5	**3.3**	24.0	13.4	**6.7**
8.3	0.03	0.2	-0.07	**4.1**	3.1	0.83	7.76	3.51	75.5	**4.8**	24.7	5.4	**9.4**
4.5	2.20	na	-0.01	**8.9**	1.2	2.04	19.15	4.93	58.2	**3.3**	8.0	12.0	**8.7**
2.5	5.00	na	0.10	**1.4**	0.0	0.11	2.20	4.21	97.5	**1.5**	22.4	26.1	**0.3**
7.3	0.15	na	0.00	**4.4**	0.2	0.60	5.67	4.27	75.1	**4.0**	9.0	7.6	**7.1**
4.3	1.53	na	0.01	**4.7**	0.4	1.05	9.06	4.20	76.8	**3.5**	7.4	9.1	**7.7**
8.3	0.58	na	0.01	**5.3**	0.7	1.10	6.18	4.18	70.5	**2.0**	25.5	20.8	**8.0**

Name	City	State	Rating	2019 Rating	2018 Rating	Total Assets ($Mil)	One Year Asset Growth	Asset Mix (As a % of Total Assets) Commercial Loans	Consumer Loans	Mortgage Loans	Securities	Capitalization Index	Leverage Ratio	Risk-Based Capital Ratio
F&M Bank	Falls City	NE	B+	B+	B+	109.8	1.92	1.4	2.1	10.2	33.2	9.0	10.5	0.0
F&M Bank	West Point	NE	B+	B+	B	308.8	7.22	5.6	1.1	7.2	9.6	8.3	10.0	0.0
F&M Bank	Edmond	OK	A-	A-	B+	502.8	2.31	7.0	2.0	13.5	24.0	8.7	10.3	0.0
F&M Bank	Clarksville	TN	C+	C+	B-	1181.4	2.74	4.8	1.5	20.9	9.1	5.1	9.1	11.1
F&M Bank and Trust Co.	Hannibal	MO	B-	B-	C+	129.4	-2.51	5.3	2.9	37.8	12.8	7.6	9.5	0.0
▼ Fahey Banking Co.	Marion	OH	B-	B+	B+	283.1	-5.40	1.7	0.5	6.5	15.7	9.8	16.9	0.0
▼ Fairfax State Savings Bank	Fairfax	IA	B-	B	B	174.4	10.14	7.0	2.0	11.7	30.1	9.8	11.6	0.0
▼ Fairfield County Bank	Ridgefield	CT	B-	B	B	1562.2	0.13	9.0	0.1	21.1	18.5	9.8	13.6	0.0
▼ Fairfield Federal S&L Assn. of Lancaster	Lancaster	OH	C	C+	C+	266.4	0.97	0.0	0.4	81.8	2.3	9.8	11.6	0.0
Fairfield National Bank	Fairfield	IL	B+	B+	B+	564.6	-1.18	20.8	2.4	11.9	34.1	9.8	12.6	0.0
Fairmount State Bank	Fairmount	IN	C+	C+	C+	45.5	3.61	1.9	11.5	19.7	16.4	10.0	14.7	22.9
Fairview S&L Assn.	Fairview	OK	B+	B+	B+	46.3	-2.13	3.0	2.1	29.1	1.5	9.8	20.2	0.0
Fairview State Banking Co.	Fairview	IL	C+	C+	C+	27.7	-2.12	3.7	6.6	26.9	10.0	9.8	13.9	0.0
Falcon International Bank	Laredo	TX	A	A	A-	1349.6	12.60	8.8	1.7	8.1	17.4	10.0	12.6	19.1
Falcon National Bank	Foley	MN	B	B	B	575.2	16.55	30.4	0.5	7.8	8.2	7.8	9.7	0.0
Fall River Five Cents Savings Bank	Fall River	MA	C	C	C	1105.3	8.98	11.2	1.4	35.8	13.2	6.7	8.7	12.6
▲ Falls City National Bank	Falls City	TX	B+	B	B-	438.8	6.82	2.0	3.0	9.1	41.4	9.8	12.1	0.0
Family Bank	Pelham	GA	B+	B+	B	112.7	9.16	5.2	7.2	47.9	3.4	10.0	12.6	20.0
Fannin Bank	Bonham	TX	B	B	B	112.7	4.91	10.1	2.9	18.3	27.2	7.2	9.1	15.5
Farm Bureau Bank, FSB	Sparks	NV	C-	C-	D	785.0	0.60	6.5	66.3	0.1	4.9	8.3	10.3	13.6
Farmers & Mechanics Bank	Galesburg	IL	B+	B+	B-	373.1	0.15	10.9	5.1	13.7	22.6	9.2	10.5	15.4
Farmers & Merchants Bank	Piedmont	AL	B+	B+	B	234.5	5.75	7.9	2.5	13.2	30.8	10.0	13.1	20.5
Farmers & Merchants Bank	Waterloo	AL	B+	B+	B+	90.0	3.31	1.3	2.0	0.2	83.6	10.0	20.7	48.2
Farmers & Merchants Bank	Stuttgart	AR	B+	B+	B+	1492.0	42.31	8.1	1.5	16.9	13.4	8.8	10.4	0.0
Farmers & Merchants Bank	Lodi	CA	A-	A-	A-	3720.2	9.56	10.7	0.4	7.5	15.9	7.4	10.2	12.8
Farmers & Merchants Bank	Eatonton	GA	B-	B-	C+	189.5	3.36	9.7	2.2	10.8	34.2	10.0	14.3	24.9
Farmers & Merchants Bank	Lakeland	GA	E-	E-	E-	521.2	5.86	8.6	5.4	18.1	11.0	3.2	6.2	10.1
Farmers & Merchants Bank	Salisbury	NC	A-	A-	B-	668.3	5.68	4.0	0.3	13.2	0.2	10.0	11.7	18.5
▲ Farmers & Merchants Bank	Tolna	ND	B-	C+	C	102.8	-0.03	8.1	3.2	2.5	26.5	8.9	10.2	14.4
Farmers & Merchants Bank	Miamisburg	OH	B+	B+	B+	185.5	15.31	8.1	1.2	15.2	19.2	8.7	10.2	14.9
Farmers & Merchants Bank	Duke	OK	C+	C+	C	19.7	3.23	7.2	1.9	0.0	19.5	9.4	10.6	22.5
Farmers & Merchants Bank	Dyer	TN	C-	C-	D+	104.2	3.13	5.1	3.3	7.7	31.0	7.2	9.3	0.0
Farmers & Merchants Bank	New Castle	VA	A-	A-	B+	60.5	-0.32	0.8	4.9	29.5	37.8	9.8	20.6	0.0
Farmers & Merchants Bank	Timberville	VA	C+	C+	B-	827.4	6.37	3.3	10.7	23.8	0.9	9.4	10.8	14.5
▲ Farmers & Merchants Bank	Berlin	WI	B-	C+	C	331.3	5.70	9.7	2.9	21.7	13.0	9.1	10.6	0.0
Farmers & Merchants Bank & Trust	Burlington	IA	C-	C-	C+	221.5	10.89	6.5	1.5	28.0	19.9	7.6	9.4	15.5
Farmers & Merchants Bank & Trust	Marinette	WI	B-	B-	C+	149.7	7.27	10.3	1.4	18.7	24.4	10.0	11.7	16.4
Farmers & Merchants Bank of Colby	Colby	KS	A-	A-	B+	250.0	11.49	9.2	0.3	0.9	26.0	9.8	13.4	0.0
Farmers & Merchants Bank of Hutsonville	Hutsonville	IL	B	B	B	44.9	-0.30	6.6	8.4	26.3	6.2	9.8	18.5	0.0
▼ Farmers & Merchants Bank of Long Beach	Long Beach	CA	B+	A-	A-	7950.7	7.81	0.8	0.4	7.6	38.1	10.0	14.1	20.9
Farmers & Merchants Savings Bank	Lone Tree	IA	B	B	B	91.1	4.66	7.5	1.4	21.6	17.3	10.0	12.1	16.2
▲ Farmers & Merchants Savings Bank	Manchester	IA	B	B-	C+	585.6	-3.65	34.1	0.6	7.6	5.9	9.8	13.4	14.9
▲ Farmers & Merchants State Bank	Winterset	IA	A-	B+	B+	187.0	-4.36	3.6	3.1	10.2	25.5	8.8	10.2	14.9
Farmers & Merchants State Bank	New York Mills	MN	B	B	B	62.3	3.22	9.0	3.7	6.6	36.1	10.0	15.2	27.7
Farmers & Merchants State Bank	Archbold	OH	A-	A-	A-	1631.4	12.70	8.8	3.0	8.3	11.4	7.2	10.1	12.7
▲ Farmers & Merchants State Bank	Waterloo	WI	B	B-	C+	185.1	3.91	1.5	1.0	16.2	8.0	9.8	11.4	0.0
▲ Farmers & Merchants Union Bank	Columbus	WI	B-	C+	B-	393.3	-2.64	9.3	0.6	7.8	7.7	10.0	12.1	15.3
Farmers & Stockmens Bank	Clayton	NM	B	B	B	228.3	9.52	4.8	0.8	7.3	1.3	10.0	13.8	16.9
Farmers & Traders Bank of Campton	Campton	KY	B-	B-	B-	49.4	3.19	1.9	4.2	24.8	40.8	9.3	10.6	14.8
Farmers & Traders Savings Bank	Bancroft	IA	B-	B-	B-	58.9	2.35	2.7	1.6	4.0	30.4	9.2	10.4	17.6
▼ Farmers and Drovers Bank	Council Grove	KS	B+	A-	B+	186.1	4.72	2.7	8.3	14.9	35.9	9.8	26.8	0.0
▼ Farmers and Mechanics FSB	Bloomfield	IN	D+	C-	C-	71.4	-3.22	4.6	0.1	33.5	46.5	9.8	17.4	0.0
Farmers and Merchants Bank	LaFayette	AL	A-	A-	B+	173.3	5.92	9.9	5.7	10.1	47.1	10.0	13.6	22.9
Farmers and Merchants Bank	Sylvania	GA	B	B	B	121.3	2.31	1.8	2.6	10.5	35.9	9.8	15.2	0.0
▼ Farmers and Merchants Bank	Boswell	IN	B-	B	B	134.4	6.64	4.4	0.7	16.8	17.2	9.8	11.3	0.0
Farmers and Merchants Bank	Laotto	IN	A-	A-	B+	165.3	5.43	11.1	2.7	27.7	15.6	10.0	11.3	17.5
Farmers and Merchants Bank	Mound City	KS	D+	D+	D	39.7	2.14	13.9	5.4	33.0	11.7	5.9	7.9	13.5
Farmers and Merchants Bank	Upperco	MD	B-	B-	C	460.2	7.27	5.5	0.1	8.9	12.9	8.9	11.0	14.1
Farmers and Merchants Bank	Baldwyn	MS	A-	A-	B+	362.9	4.39	5.1	7.7	16.9	30.0	9.8	14.4	0.0
Farmers and Merchants Bank	Axtell	NE	D+	D+	D+	7.8	-3.02	5.8	3.7	0.3	49.9	8.8	10.2	35.2

Arrows denote recent upgrades ▲ or downgrades ▼

Asset Quality Index	Adjusted Non-Performing Loans as a % of Total Loans	Adjusted Non-Performing Loans as a % of Capital	Net Charge-Offs Avg Loans	Profitability Index	Net Income ($Mil)	Return on Assets (R.O.A.)	Return on Equity (R.O.E.)	Net Interest Spread	Overhead Efficiency Ratio	Liquidity Index	Liquidity Ratio	Hot Money Ratio	Stability Index
8.5	0.15	na	0.00	**5.2**	0.4	1.44	14.20	3.41	54.6	**3.0**	30.8	10.8	**6.4**
8.3	0.03	na	0.00	**6.9**	1.3	1.68	17.32	3.59	59.0	**3.1**	17.9	13.9	**7.2**
8.5	0.17	na	0.00	**7.3**	2.2	1.74	16.71	3.95	61.9	**2.4**	16.8	17.4	**7.7**
7.8	0.25	1.8	0.02	**3.7**	1.6	0.54	4.74	3.09	85.1	**1.3**	18.5	26.6	**8.6**
4.8	1.33	na	-0.08	**4.7**	0.3	0.92	9.11	3.61	69.5	**3.8**	12.8	9.8	**5.8**
7.5	0.08	na	0.04	**1.5**	-0.2	-0.25	-1.49	3.45	66.2	**0.6**	9.3	38.1	**8.0**
9.0	0.02	na	-0.06	**3.6**	0.3	0.66	5.45	2.93	73.1	**3.6**	50.5	19.5	**6.9**
7.5	0.63	na	0.23	**4.0**	2.6	0.68	4.79	3.60	79.2	**4.4**	23.3	7.0	**9.0**
6.5	0.36	na	0.05	**2.5**	0.2	0.23	1.98	3.18	90.9	**1.5**	7.6	22.7	**6.1**
3.1	2.37	10.3	0.04	**5.0**	1.4	1.06	7.78	2.84	54.1	**1.2**	21.6	28.3	**8.4**
5.1	2.13	na	0.66	**3.0**	0.0	0.20	1.50	4.22	78.0	**4.2**	20.4	8.3	**5.5**
8.8	0.00	na	0.00	**6.8**	0.2	1.46	7.29	4.09	56.1	**3.1**	28.2	15.8	**8.1**
3.1	4.78	17.0	0.36	**3.5**	0.1	0.94	6.78	4.07	68.3	**2.0**	26.8	22.1	**6.1**
7.9	0.93	2.6	0.04	**8.2**	4.7	1.42	11.35	3.82	60.9	**2.0**	25.1	27.0	**10.0**
7.2	0.31	na	0.17	**4.8**	1.2	0.85	8.66	4.61	65.7	**1.4**	12.1	20.6	**6.8**
8.3	0.35	2.2	0.00	**2.7**	0.9	0.34	3.90	2.79	87.3	**1.6**	16.4	22.0	**6.6**
6.0	2.98	na	-0.03	**9.5**	2.1	1.98	16.77	3.38	23.2	**6.1**	59.7	9.4	**7.7**
5.1	1.62	10.5	-0.08	**5.3**	0.3	1.18	9.42	5.00	70.9	**1.4**	17.0	26.7	**6.9**
4.0	1.08	15.1	0.19	**4.7**	0.3	1.05	11.79	4.52	76.7	**2.1**	27.8	16.2	**5.9**
2.6	0.87	na	0.77	**1.9**	-0.2	-0.12	-1.18	4.23	78.6	**0.5**	16.1	33.7	**5.5**
5.7	0.93	na	0.16	**5.4**	1.0	1.06	8.27	3.55	66.9	**4.1**	19.5	8.8	**8.0**
8.7	0.43	na	0.07	**4.7**	0.6	0.98	7.56	4.16	70.2	**3.6**	25.6	12.3	**7.7**
10.0	3.51	na	6.49	**3.9**	0.3	1.14	5.59	2.16	50.3	**3.6**	85.9	32.8	**7.2**
7.0	0.40	na	0.05	**4.2**	2.6	0.69	4.97	4.11	77.3	**3.3**	13.3	12.6	**9.5**
8.4	0.47	1.4	0.03	**8.7**	14.5	1.57	14.85	4.10	50.3	**3.4**	14.9	12.4	**10.0**
5.6	5.56	na	-0.37	**3.1**	0.2	0.48	3.41	3.43	81.3	**4.0**	31.8	12.0	**6.6**
0.3	4.71	na	0.76	**2.5**	0.4	0.29	4.52	3.61	77.0	**0.8**	16.4	38.2	**1.3**
6.6	1.69	na	-0.03	**8.6**	2.9	1.76	15.16	4.16	59.9	**5.3**	33.9	5.4	**8.3**
4.8	1.71	na	-0.01	**4.2**	0.2	0.94	7.84	3.69	73.9	**3.0**	32.5	16.8	**6.9**
6.3	0.86	3.1	0.03	**6.4**	0.6	1.30	12.66	4.34	62.9	**3.6**	10.4	10.4	**6.9**
8.8	0.00	na	0.00	**3.4**	0.0	0.65	6.22	3.09	78.8	**4.7**	63.4	13.7	**4.9**
6.6	2.57	na	-0.04	**2.2**	0.3	0.96	10.35	2.82	96.9	**5.7**	46.6	7.4	**3.7**
9.6	0.00	na	0.04	**6.2**	0.2	1.20	5.85	4.13	62.0	**5.1**	42.1	9.8	**7.9**
4.9	0.59	4.3	0.28	**3.9**	1.2	0.61	5.66	3.90	71.6	**4.2**	13.2	7.0	**6.9**
4.0	1.85	na	0.56	**4.9**	0.8	1.06	9.83	4.16	56.6	**0.7**	13.1	24.8	**6.0**
3.3	2.49	na	0.09	**3.1**	0.7	1.35	15.30	3.29	70.9	**4.7**	25.0	5.3	**3.5**
6.5	0.99	na	-0.01	**3.8**	0.3	0.79	6.65	3.81	71.6	**4.0**	38.2	14.4	**6.1**
7.9	0.34	na	0.00	**9.3**	1.1	1.79	13.01	3.65	30.7	**0.7**	17.2	33.8	**9.2**
8.4	0.00	na	0.00	**6.1**	0.2	1.84	10.09	3.24	42.6	**2.0**	32.9	27.4	**8.0**
9.3	0.90	1.9	-0.02	**4.8**	18.0	0.92	6.58	3.28	65.9	**4.5**	27.0	10.8	**10.0**
8.1	0.00	na	0.00	**3.9**	0.2	0.80	5.91	3.37	67.2	**2.0**	13.2	15.2	**7.0**
5.1	0.76	na	0.00	**7.5**	2.2	1.55	11.70	3.91	57.5	**1.9**	17.2	19.8	**9.9**
8.5	0.39	na	-0.01	**6.1**	0.6	1.28	12.48	3.54	56.3	**3.8**	27.7	11.9	**7.0**
8.7	0.00	na	0.00	**3.4**	0.1	0.58	3.53	3.47	80.6	**4.3**	41.4	13.7	**7.3**
7.0	0.42	2.0	0.04	**5.4**	3.9	0.97	7.39	3.80	63.9	**3.2**	13.2	12.4	**9.7**
7.6	0.00	na	0.00	**5.7**	0.5	1.03	9.15	3.28	64.1	**3.9**	20.0	10.1	**7.6**
5.7	1.59	5.7	-0.02	**6.2**	1.3	1.29	10.65	3.65	46.0	**0.8**	19.5	38.9	**7.6**
6.9	0.13	na	-0.03	**6.8**	0.5	0.87	6.16	4.75	85.7	**4.4**	23.5	7.3	**9.6**
8.2	0.52	1.2	-0.02	**3.9**	0.1	0.77	6.42	3.86	79.9	**2.2**	31.1	22.6	**5.6**
7.4	0.08	na	-0.02	**3.7**	0.1	0.85	7.90	2.99	69.7	**2.4**	32.2	21.9	**6.3**
8.4	0.46	na	0.00	**5.0**	0.5	1.04	3.88	3.32	58.7	**2.2**	26.1	19.2	**8.3**
10.0	0.00	na	0.00	**0.0**	-0.1	-0.42	-2.35	2.04	148.1	**4.5**	69.1	17.6	**7.4**
6.5	1.80	5.7	0.06	**5.9**	0.6	1.34	9.71	3.73	58.9	**2.8**	37.0	20.4	**7.7**
6.7	2.96	na	0.15	**4.2**	0.3	0.84	5.64	3.40	71.8	**3.9**	48.7	17.5	**7.4**
8.3	0.31	1.5	-0.01	**3.4**	0.2	0.45	4.01	3.45	84.1	**2.3**	24.8	18.4	**6.9**
8.8	0.04	na	0.01	**6.2**	0.7	1.60	14.36	3.96	61.2	**5.5**	32.4	3.2	**7.4**
3.8	4.99	na	0.00	**5.6**	0.1	1.28	16.11	4.28	67.4	**1.6**	17.7	23.3	**3.7**
7.0	0.57	na	-0.02	**3.6**	0.6	0.50	4.60	3.55	79.5	**1.4**	17.7	19.7	**6.7**
5.9	0.94	na	0.04	**8.1**	1.4	1.49	10.32	4.69	66.8	**1.9**	25.6	22.9	**9.0**
9.4	0.00	0.0	0.00	**1.7**	0.0	0.31	2.96	3.46	90.6	**5.6**	58.8	4.2	**4.0**

Name	City	State	Rating	2019 Rating	2018 Rating	Total Assets ($Mil)	One Year Asset Growth	Asset Mix (As a % of Total Assets) Commercial Loans	Consumer Loans	Mortgage Loans	Securities	Capitalization Index	Leverage Ratio	Risk-Based Capital Ratio
Farmers and Merchants Bank	Milford	NE	**B**	B	B	801.8	23.26	1.5	3.2	3.6	50.9	**6.0**	10.5	11.7
Farmers and Merchants Bank	Milligan	NE	**B**	B	B-	120.2	3.65	9.8	1.0	2.9	0.0	**10.0**	11.6	15.1
Farmers and Merchants Bank	Caldwell	OH	**B-**	B-	C+	112.5	0.51	6.8	6.2	43.6	16.6	**9.8**	14.6	0.0
Farmers and Merchants Bank	Arnett	OK	**B**	B	B	54.6	-3.57	3.5	7.6	1.1	41.7	**9.8**	14.2	0.0
Farmers and Merchants Bank	Maysville	OK	**B-**	B-	C+	20.6	4.93	49.0	9.9	0.2	5.4	**6.3**	8.3	12.0
Farmers and Merchants Bank	Holly Hill	SC	**B+**	B+	B	341.7	-3.00	1.5	2.0	7.9	25.1	**10.0**	11.5	49.0
Farmers and Merchants Bank	De Leon	TX	**C+**	C+	C	96.2	8.01	4.8	4.7	22.1	17.8	**7.8**	9.7	0.0
Farmers and Merchants Bank of Ashland	Ashland	NE	**B**	B	B	82.7	7.62	4.0	1.2	21.2	10.5	**9.6**	10.9	0.0
Farmers and Merchants Bank of Kendall	Kendall	WI	**C+**	C+	B-	73.8	1.09	3.9	1.8	8.6	0.0	**9.8**	15.9	0.0
Farmers and Merchants Bank of St. Clair	Saint Clair	MO	**A-**	A-	B+	216.2	9.15	7.5	1.6	24.8	14.8	**10.0**	13.0	20.4
Farmers and Merchants National Bank	Nashville	IL	**A-**	A-	A-	189.7	5.32	3.3	1.0	14.6	23.8	**9.8**	12.2	0.0
Farmers and Merchants National Bank	Fairview	OK	**A**	A	A	114.8	-4.53	3.2	2.4	9.4	52.7	**10.0**	12.8	26.1
Farmers and Merchants State Bank	Bushnell	IL	**B-**	B-	C+	74.6	2.17	4.3	5.3	10.5	15.6	**6.8**	8.8	17.8
Farmers and Merchants State Bank	Alpha	MN	**C-**	C-	C-	40.5	-2.18	4.6	2.8	10.3	1.3	**10.0**	11.1	18.8
Farmers and Merchants State Bank	Appleton	MN	**B-**	B-	C+	50.7	16.24	5.1	2.0	2.7	9.1	**10.0**	13.7	16.9
Farmers and Merchants State Bank	Blooming Prairie	MN	**C+**	C+	C	88.6	6.15	8.1	2.0	12.5	0.2	**6.2**	8.3	12.9
▲ Farmers and Merchants State Bank	Pierz	MN	**B**	B-	B-	226.3	2.39	9.5	2.1	11.9	19.0	**8.5**	10.2	0.0
Farmers and Merchants State Bank	Springfield	MN	**C+**	C+	C+	122.2	2.44	5.1	1.5	5.2	14.3	**6.4**	8.4	13.0
Farmers and Merchants State Bank	Langdon	ND	**B**	B	B+	111.9	4.75	5.4	2.1	1.1	27.4	**9.8**	14.8	0.0
▲ Farmers and Merchants State Bank	Bloomfield	NE	**B+**	B	B-	133.0	1.06	5.7	5.3	0.1	22.4	**9.7**	14.2	14.8
Farmers and Merchants State Bank	Plankinton	SD	**C**	C	B-	111.7	-1.33	8.2	4.2	7.2	5.9	**8.1**	11.2	13.4
Farmers and Merchants State Bank	Scotland	SD	**C+**	C+	B-	30.1	2.84	5.7	10.0	1.8	39.1	**9.5**	10.8	0.0
Farmers and Merchants Trust Co.	Chambersburg	PA	**B+**	B+	C+	1262.3	4.00	6.2	0.5	12.2	16.5	**8.1**	9.7	15.8
▼ Farmers and Miners Bank	Pennington Gap	VA	**B+**	A-	B+	135.5	-1.72	3.0	6.9	20.5	19.0	**9.8**	14.5	0.0
Farmers Bank	Greenwood	AR	**B+**	B+	B+	222.8	4.83	6.2	5.6	28.2	27.4	**9.8**	17.3	0.0
Farmers Bank	Ault	CO	**A**	A	A	258.8	9.31	6.1	0.5	4.4	12.8	**9.8**	13.1	0.0
Farmers Bank	Greensboro	GA	**B-**	B-	B-	109.9	5.84	7.8	0.8	14.5	46.7	**10.0**	13.5	27.6
Farmers Bank	Buhl	ID	**A**	A	A-	477.3	3.79	11.8	2.0	5.5	31.7	**10.0**	15.2	24.0
Farmers Bank	Nicholasville	KY	**B**	B	B	163.4	9.72	1.8	1.0	27.4	20.4	**10.0**	11.1	20.7
Farmers Bank	Carnegie	OK	**D-**	D-	C-	86.6	-28.48	6.4	2.3	25.5	3.5	**1.0**	4.4	8.0
Farmers Bank	Parsons	TN	**C+**	C+	C+	40.2	9.49	5.3	10.4	16.1	11.2	**9.8**	12.4	0.0
Farmers Bank	Portland	TN	**A-**	A-	A-	680.1	-1.03	5.3	1.4	16.9	22.9	**10.0**	12.5	16.2
Farmers Bank	Windsor	VA	**B+**	B+	B	487.7	5.72	12.6	2.0	7.7	33.7	**9.0**	10.3	14.7
Farmers Bank & Trust	Atwood	KS	**B-**	B-	C+	108.7	11.01	4.8	1.0	2.9	35.3	**6.5**	8.5	17.4
Farmers Bank & Trust	Great Bend	KS	**A**	A	A	853.2	0.27	2.1	0.2	5.9	55.2	**9.8**	18.9	0.0
Farmers Bank & Trust Co.	Magnolia	AR	**B**	B	B-	1709.1	4.91	12.0	1.6	18.2	13.7	**7.1**	9.5	12.6
Farmers Bank and Savings Co.	Pomeroy	OH	**B**	B	B-	337.6	3.32	4.7	5.4	36.3	13.8	**8.9**	10.4	0.0
Farmers Bank and Trust Co.	Blytheville	AR	**B**	B	B	302.3	11.98	11.8	2.8	16.7	4.7	**6.6**	8.6	13.7
Farmers Bank and Trust Co.	Marion	KY	**B+**	B+	B+	377.9	83.42	4.6	3.2	31.4	9.5	**8.6**	10.1	14.3
Farmers Bank and Trust Co.	Princeton	KY	**A**	A	A	138.9	5.16	5.2	1.4	15.3	12.9	**10.0**	13.9	20.3
Farmers Bank of Appomattox	Appomattox	VA	**B+**	B+	B	239.6	2.25	6.1	16.3	24.0	21.8	**10.0**	14.6	21.1
Farmers Bank of Green City	Green City	MO	**C**	C	C-	58.0	5.32	18.0	4.5	13.8	13.9	**7.4**	9.2	13.0
Farmers Bank of Lincoln	Lincoln	MO	**A-**	A-	A-	132.0	4.60	3.0	3.1	36.2	7.4	**10.0**	11.1	20.1
Farmers Bank of Lohman	Jefferson City	MO	**B-**	B-	B-	67.5	3.23	5.7	3.0	14.2	48.4	**9.8**	15.8	0.0
Farmers Bank of Milton	Milton	KY	**B**	B	B	256.6	3.66	4.6	2.7	29.5	30.7	**10.0**	14.3	22.5
Farmers Bank of Mt. Pulaski	Mount Pulaski	IL	**C**	C	C	53.6	13.85	2.9	3.0	22.3	31.9	**9.8**	12.4	0.0
Farmers Bank of Northern Missouri	Unionville	MO	**B+**	B+	B+	378.2	2.75	3.5	1.9	9.6	32.4	**9.8**	12.3	0.0
Farmers Bank of Willards	Willards	MD	**B**	B	C	397.0	3.64	8.3	2.0	35.9	6.3	**10.0**	11.2	16.6
▲ Farmers Bank, Frankfort, Indiana, Inc.	Frankfort	IN	**B**	B-	C+	619.0	9.38	8.8	2.4	6.6	22.6	**8.7**	11.1	13.9
Farmers Building and Savings Bank	Rochester	PA	**B**	B	B+	103.9	8.85	0.2	0.0	41.5	25.9	**10.0**	20.2	54.3
Farmers National Bank	Prophetstown	IL	**A**	A	A	745.0	9.11	3.2	0.7	3.9	39.2	**10.0**	13.7	19.0
Farmers National Bank	Phillipsburg	KS	**A-**	A-	B+	144.2	7.87	17.9	2.9	7.3	20.3	**10.0**	16.4	22.1
Farmers National Bank of Canfield	Canfield	OH	**B+**	B+	B	2652.9	13.57	9.1	8.0	15.9	16.7	**6.7**	9.3	12.3
Farmers National Bank of Danville	Danville	KY	**B+**	B+	B+	661.0	18.69	5.5	1.8	24.3	18.0	**7.7**	9.5	14.2
Farmers National Bank of Emlenton	Emlenton	PA	**B-**	B-	C+	938.8	6.17	4.4	2.0	43.7	12.2	**6.1**	8.1	13.0
▼ Farmers National Bank of Griggsville	Griggsville	IL	**C-**	C	C	99.2	10.96	5.0	5.8	15.0	3.7	**9.8**	11.0	0.0
Farmers National Bank of Lebanon	Lebanon	KY	**B**	B	C+	98.6	-5.02	6.2	2.5	8.4	34.4	**10.0**	12.5	19.3
Farmers Savings Bank	Colesburg	IA	**B**	B	B+	218.4	2.87	6.8	2.4	5.1	31.9	**10.0**	12.4	17.2
▼ Farmers Savings Bank	Fostoria	IA	**B-**	B	B	134.6	4.63	8.7	2.3	21.5	15.3	**9.8**	14.4	0.0
Farmers Savings Bank	Frederika	IA	**B**	B	B	46.4	0.96	4.5	3.1	10.9	18.0	**9.8**	18.9	0.0

Asset Quality Index	Adjusted Non-Performing Loans as a % of Total Loans	Adjusted Non-Performing Loans as a % of Capital	Net Charge-Offs Avg Loans	Profitability Index	Net Income ($Mil)	Return on Assets (R.O.A.)	Return on Equity (R.O.E.)	Net Interest Spread	Overhead Efficiency Ratio	Liquidity Index	Liquidity Ratio	Hot Money Ratio	Stability Index
7.9	0.51	na	0.01	**4.1**	2.5	1.35	15.26	1.89	64.5	**2.7**	56.6	10.0	**5.8**
4.6	0.00	na	0.01	**7.9**	0.5	1.81	14.32	4.44	50.8	**0.7**	16.0	24.8	**8.7**
3.4	2.93	na	0.07	**5.4**	0.3	0.94	6.48	4.69	68.5	**3.2**	19.6	13.5	**8.1**
8.5	0.01	na	-0.04	**4.6**	0.2	1.10	7.66	2.58	60.6	**3.9**	43.6	16.3	**7.6**
7.6	0.00	na	0.13	**9.0**	0.1	2.72	32.82	5.43	53.4	**4.4**	35.7	9.2	**5.3**
7.2	5.42	na	-0.02	**4.2**	0.8	0.76	6.70	2.50	65.4	**6.3**	64.8	8.9	**7.0**
6.5	0.59	na	-0.03	**3.4**	0.2	0.66	6.73	4.12	81.9	**5.2**	32.1	5.2	**5.7**
8.7	0.00	0.0	0.00	**4.4**	0.2	0.98	8.99	4.32	72.5	**4.2**	13.9	7.3	**6.6**
2.9	5.92	na	0.03	**10.0**	0.5	2.43	15.49	4.77	50.0	**1.7**	14.8	21.5	**9.0**
8.8	0.37	na	0.17	**5.0**	0.5	0.93	7.06	2.31	60.9	**3.3**	25.0	13.3	**7.2**
7.2	0.55	na	0.00	**5.6**	0.6	1.26	10.49	3.75	66.4	**4.4**	17.9	6.2	**8.2**
9.3	0.00	na	0.02	**7.7**	0.6	2.02	15.41	3.82	51.7	**3.6**	36.6	15.8	**9.2**
8.7	0.04	na	0.00	**4.4**	0.2	0.83	9.18	3.27	73.6	**5.8**	38.8	4.0	**4.7**
3.1	2.77	na	0.00	**2.6**	0.0	0.33	2.94	3.16	86.9	**2.2**	41.4	23.7	**1.0**
4.0	1.91	na	0.01	**7.2**	0.2	1.60	11.18	4.34	52.1	**3.9**	30.7	7.7	**8.5**
5.5	0.71	4.9	0.00	**8.6**	0.5	2.06	24.78	4.65	55.1	**4.6**	21.8	5.4	**5.0**
5.7	4.02	na	0.40	**8.6**	1.1	1.96	18.36	4.32	56.2	**4.0**	24.0	9.9	**8.6**
4.3	0.82	na	0.00	**4.4**	0.3	0.95	11.00	3.49	66.9	**2.7**	9.4	12.9	**5.1**
3.9	3.54	na	0.01	**8.7**	0.6	2.17	14.36	3.94	41.6	**2.2**	27.2	19.6	**9.9**
5.2	0.34	na	0.02	**8.5**	0.5	1.61	11.33	4.09	54.3	**4.4**	7.8	4.9	**8.5**
1.1	2.15	na	0.13	**9.0**	0.6	2.07	18.57	4.65	42.9	**0.7**	11.4	17.4	**8.1**
8.0	0.14	na	0.00	**3.5**	0.0	0.50	4.31	3.66	77.4	**4.3**	32.6	11.0	**5.9**
7.0	1.33	na	0.10	**4.0**	2.1	0.67	6.67	3.74	65.8	**5.0**	15.3	2.9	**8.8**
6.4	1.51	na	0.24	**4.7**	0.3	0.89	6.19	4.48	77.2	**3.9**	52.3	18.5	**8.1**
6.4	0.33	3.2	0.03	**4.7**	0.7	1.33	7.45	4.16	75.7	**3.5**	15.1	11.7	**8.0**
8.5	0.10	na	0.00	**9.4**	1.2	1.94	14.76	4.20	51.1	**1.7**	19.2	23.2	**9.7**
7.6	0.00	na	-0.06	**2.4**	0.2	0.71	5.29	2.47	88.8	**3.4**	14.8	11.8	**6.7**
7.2	1.59	na	-0.01	**7.5**	1.7	1.48	9.65	3.92	54.6	**5.3**	49.7	10.9	**9.0**
9.1	0.43	na	0.00	**4.4**	0.3	0.84	7.56	3.39	68.2	**1.8**	22.0	22.7	**6.9**
0.3	8.96	na	0.05	**0.0**	-0.3	-1.44	-47.14	2.04	163.1	**1.1**	30.3	66.2	**0.7**
4.2	2.34	na	0.00	**4.7**	0.1	1.16	9.16	3.91	56.1	**3.3**	52.8	21.7	**6.4**
8.1	1.11	na	0.03	**7.1**	2.4	1.38	11.21	4.41	62.7	**1.3**	15.4	27.4	**8.4**
7.4	0.41	na	0.18	**4.7**	1.1	1.00	7.68	3.52	76.3	**2.3**	25.1	18.5	**7.6**
5.3	4.27	na	-0.01	**3.7**	0.2	0.76	8.60	3.03	66.9	**6.1**	44.1	4.4	**5.7**
9.0	1.58	na	0.04	**8.1**	4.2	2.01	9.90	3.45	44.5	**2.1**	46.0	37.9	**10.0**
5.0	1.30	na	0.12	**6.1**	5.1	1.23	12.21	3.78	53.1	**1.1**	9.4	29.8	**8.5**
5.1	1.43	na	0.16	**4.4**	0.7	0.81	7.65	3.95	73.7	**1.7**	13.6	21.0	**6.6**
5.0	1.14	na	0.17	**7.5**	1.2	1.57	18.25	3.26	55.0	**1.1**	27.9	38.4	**7.3**
6.1	0.35	na	-0.04	**4.6**	1.1	1.20	10.82	4.41	69.4	**1.6**	10.5	22.1	**6.8**
8.7	0.05	na	0.10	**7.2**	0.6	1.67	11.95	4.17	63.4	**3.9**	19.8	10.1	**9.7**
6.7	1.01	na	0.07	**5.0**	0.6	1.08	7.74	3.96	69.7	**3.3**	26.8	13.9	**7.6**
4.0	1.33	na	-0.01	**2.8**	0.0	0.14	1.53	3.59	85.6	**0.6**	12.3	42.4	**5.0**
8.6	0.08	na	0.00	**6.4**	0.5	1.50	13.71	3.65	60.8	**3.1**	24.6	14.7	**8.3**
9.6	0.00	na	0.00	**3.4**	0.1	0.58	3.59	2.52	73.7	**6.1**	76.0	10.5	**7.4**
5.0	3.19	na	-0.01	**4.7**	0.6	0.94	6.54	3.65	69.6	**1.7**	22.1	23.4	**7.9**
9.5	0.10	0.9	-0.11	**2.5**	0.1	0.51	4.09	2.45	82.6	**4.4**	62.5	17.0	**6.4**
7.9	0.32	1.3	0.07	**5.8**	1.2	1.28	9.27	3.88	56.3	**4.2**	27.2	9.4	**7.9**
4.9	1.71	na	0.22	**4.8**	0.8	0.82	7.35	4.32	66.3	**1.7**	14.6	20.9	**6.3**
6.4	0.51	na	-0.03	**5.5**	1.3	0.85	7.60	3.82	63.8	**4.0**	22.7	9.6	**8.1**
7.6	3.45	na	0.00	**3.6**	0.2	0.73	3.64	2.47	58.8	**7.7**	66.4	0.0	**7.8**
5.8	1.09	9.6	-0.02	**7.0**	3.0	1.64	11.45	3.26	42.2	**1.5**	33.0	37.7	**9.9**
6.2	0.91	na	0.02	**6.5**	0.4	1.24	6.91	3.79	59.1	**2.5**	20.1	16.4	**8.6**
6.3	0.60	4.0	0.13	**6.4**	8.6	1.31	12.54	3.71	59.6	**1.5**	8.8	13.5	**9.0**
5.3	1.21	na	0.03	**4.5**	1.3	0.83	8.50	3.85	78.6	**4.8**	23.8	4.7	**6.6**
6.0	0.35	na	0.07	**3.1**	1.4	0.58	6.41	3.16	69.2	**2.5**	11.0	16.1	**6.3**
1.8	2.33	na	-0.05	**6.2**	0.3	1.34	12.23	4.11	61.0	**1.0**	15.5	27.9	**7.7**
8.8	0.00	na	0.08	**3.7**	0.2	0.95	7.95	3.75	71.7	**4.1**	33.8	12.5	**5.4**
4.9	2.37	na	0.57	**5.5**	0.8	1.60	12.43	4.27	48.4	**1.6**	34.4	39.3	**8.0**
2.8	1.21	na	0.35	**4.6**	0.3	0.85	5.89	3.47	63.1	**2.4**	20.7	17.7	**8.1**
7.9	0.32	na	-0.09	**5.1**	0.1	1.20	6.37	3.01	47.9	**5.0**	44.0	10.4	**7.3**

Name	City	State	Rating	2019 Rating	2018 Rating	Total Assets ($Mil)	One Year Asset Growth	Asset Mix (As a % of Total Assets) Comm-ercial Loans	Cons-umer Loans	Mort-gage Loans	Secur-ities	Capital-ization Index	Lever-age Ratio	Risk-Based Capital Ratio
Farmers Savings Bank	Marshalltown	IA	**A-**	A-	B+	116.3	5.63	5.2	1.5	11.9	20.2	**9.8**	14.8	0.0
Farmers Savings Bank	Wever	IA	**C**	C	C+	111.4	-6.46	14.7	1.5	29.5	11.2	**10.0**	15.6	23.4
Farmers Savings Bank	Spencer	OH	**A-**	A-	B+	293.3	4.50	1.5	0.5	18.2	65.2	**10.0**	26.3	67.0
Farmers Savings Bank	Mineral Point	WI	**B**	B	B	327.7	9.69	7.2	6.6	11.1	36.6	**6.9**	8.9	15.7
Farmers Savings Bank & Trust	Traer	IA	**A-**	A-	B+	170.8	0.17	3.6	1.3	9.5	27.3	**9.3**	10.7	0.0
Farmers Security Bank	Washburn	ND	**B-**	B-	C-	61.0	1.82	6.1	2.2	1.3	19.6	**9.2**	10.6	0.0
Farmers State Bank	Dublin	GA	**A-**	A-	B+	123.2	-1.98	7.9	7.4	18.9	17.0	**10.0**	15.7	21.0
Farmers State Bank	Lincolnton	GA	**A**	A	A-	135.5	8.30	3.5	6.6	22.2	18.5	**10.0**	16.4	25.5
Farmers State Bank	Algona	IA	**A-**	A-	B+	107.5	-1.40	10.5	1.4	16.6	11.0	**9.8**	12.3	0.0
▼ Farmers State Bank	Lake View	IA	**B-**	B	B-	37.2	8.55	6.3	4.9	12.7	22.5	**10.0**	11.2	33.8
Farmers State Bank	Marcus	IA	**B+**	B+	B+	65.9	2.99	5.9	3.1	6.1	26.5	**9.8**	13.6	0.0
▼ Farmers State Bank	Marion	IA	**A-**	A	A	852.3	6.57	8.1	1.2	7.9	12.2	**9.8**	14.1	0.0
Farmers State Bank	Mason City	IA	**A-**	A-	B+	198.3	3.37	4.9	2.0	16.8	40.2	**10.0**	12.3	21.6
▲ Farmers State Bank	Waterloo	IA	**B+**	B	B	1163.9	8.25	9.1	8.2	20.1	10.2	**7.7**	9.7	13.1
Farmers State Bank	Yale	IA	**B**	B	B-	51.9	3.07	5.6	2.1	13.3	37.0	**9.8**	11.1	0.0
Farmers State Bank	Elmwood	IL	**C-**	C-	C-	54.8	0.83	3.1	1.3	23.7	34.4	**6.9**	8.9	16.8
Farmers State Bank	Pittsfield	IL	**A-**	A-	B+	259.6	2.52	1.9	1.1	4.1	15.6	**10.0**	13.8	17.3
Farmers State Bank	Lagrange	IN	**B+**	B+	B	816.9	7.40	4.0	1.9	33.4	12.6	**7.0**	9.0	15.4
Farmers State Bank	Dwight	KS	**C-**	C-	C-	15.4	-2.89	4.1	1.0	8.2	0.0	**9.8**	12.5	0.0
▲ Farmers State Bank	Fairview	KS	**C-**	D+	D	19.5	-9.45	1.7	4.7	9.5	5.1	**9.3**	10.5	15.5
Farmers State Bank	Holton	KS	**B+**	B+	B	57.6	0.77	4.4	1.1	24.4	23.8	**10.0**	13.3	22.9
Farmers State Bank	McPherson	KS	**A-**	A-	A-	124.5	5.82	8.4	4.3	17.7	35.1	**8.3**	9.9	15.6
▼ Farmers State Bank	Phillipsburg	KS	**C-**	C	C-	35.7	-0.60	7.0	10.5	11.4	24.7	**9.7**	11.0	0.0
Farmers State Bank	Wathena	KS	**B**	B	B	65.0	4.17	7.3	4.9	16.1	50.8	**10.0**	16.3	34.8
Farmers State Bank	Westmoreland	KS	**B+**	B+	B+	190.8	5.63	9.2	2.2	12.8	15.9	**9.8**	14.4	0.0
Farmers State Bank	Booneville	KY	**B-**	B-	B-	52.3	5.66	4.0	5.3	17.5	47.3	**10.0**	12.6	18.4
Farmers State Bank	Cameron	MO	**B-**	B-	B-	250.6	5.64	2.6	3.0	40.8	12.7	**7.3**	9.2	13.1
▼ Farmers State Bank	Victor	MT	**B-**	B	C+	448.2	12.74	5.6	2.8	13.6	25.6	**8.1**	9.8	14.3
Farmers State Bank	Dodge	NE	**C+**	C+	C+	277.9	9.90	13.5	1.0	2.6	4.9	**6.1**	8.7	11.8
Farmers State Bank	New Madison	OH	**B**	B	B	185.5	0.70	4.0	4.0	26.2	15.7	**10.0**	12.6	18.7
Farmers State Bank	West Salem	OH	**C+**	C+	C+	133.6	8.66	8.4	1.5	23.0	10.1	**7.1**	9.2	0.0
Farmers State Bank	Quinton	OK	**B-**	B-	C+	115.3	4.34	8.4	10.1	17.5	26.8	**6.5**	8.5	13.7
Farmers State Bank	Hosmer	SD	**B-**	B-	B-	19.3	-0.60	34.3	6.0	0.0	7.9	**10.0**	15.6	16.3
Farmers State Bank	Parkston	SD	**B**	B	B	221.8	1.42	5.2	2.9	0.0	35.9	**7.6**	9.6	0.0
▼ Farmers State Bank	Mountain City	TN	**B-**	B	B	150.7	2.80	5.8	4.7	28.2	26.8	**9.8**	15.8	0.0
Farmers State Bank	Center	TX	**B-**	B-	B-	349.0	5.74	18.3	2.2	7.2	20.8	**10.0**	13.3	18.8
Farmers State Bank	Groesbeck	TX	**B+**	B+	B+	133.5	0.79	2.7	6.0	17.4	21.1	**8.5**	10.1	0.0
Farmers State Bank	Winthrop	WA	**B-**	B-	C+	41.5	0.74	3.3	1.0	0.9	51.6	**8.5**	10.2	0.0
Farmers State Bank	Pine Bluffs	WY	**C-**	C-	C+	30.0	2.75	4.8	1.6	6.7	1.2	**5.3**	7.3	15.6
Farmers State Bank & Trust Co.	Mount Sterling	IL	**B-**	B-	C+	95.7	3.08	12.9	3.6	17.4	17.3	**7.2**	9.1	13.4
▲ Farmers State Bank & Trust Co.	Church Point	LA	**B**	B-	B-	121.1	9.95	9.8	2.4	10.4	25.5	**9.4**	10.6	16.7
Farmers State Bank and Trust Co.	Jacksonville	IL	**B-**	B-	C	209.6	4.65	5.8	6.5	11.1	35.2	**9.8**	12.4	0.0
Farmers State Bank Hillsboro	Hillsboro	WI	**A**	A	A-	176.6	1.84	2.0	1.8	8.9	40.1	**9.8**	19.6	0.0
Farmers State Bank of Aliceville, Kansas	Westphalia	KS	**A-**	A-	B+	153.2	2.88	5.3	6.4	17.0	18.2	**9.8**	15.6	0.0
Farmers State Bank of Alto Pass, Ill.	Harrisburg	IL	**C-**	C-	C+	240.0	2.63	16.7	1.9	15.1	8.7	**4.8**	8.6	10.9
Farmers State Bank of Blue Mound	Blue Mound	KS	**B-**	B-	B-	44.5	-1.89	7.5	3.2	1.2	5.1	**9.8**	18.9	0.0
Farmers State Bank of Brush	Brush	CO	**A-**	A-	B+	108.9	3.15	3.2	1.3	3.3	29.3	**9.8**	19.4	0.0
Farmers State Bank of Bucklin, Kansas	Bucklin	KS	**C+**	C+	C-	44.6	2.08	7.3	1.0	1.4	25.0	**7.6**	9.4	21.2
Farmers State Bank of Calhan	Calhan	CO	**B**	B	B-	295.0	7.10	6.2	2.5	11.8	46.6	**9.5**	10.7	19.9
Farmers State Bank of Canton	Canton	SD	**B-**	B-	B-	47.3	0.83	2.3	4.5	24.5	13.4	**10.0**	12.2	18.6
Farmers State Bank of Emden	Emden	IL	**B-**	B-	B-	33.9	-1.78	3.9	1.5	1.8	53.4	**10.0**	28.0	57.5
Farmers State Bank of Hamel	Hamel	MN	**B**	B	B-	134.4	1.30	3.3	0.4	12.0	35.9	**10.0**	11.0	26.2
▲ Farmers State Bank of Hartland	Hartland	MN	**A-**	B+	B-	170.5	9.53	10.2	0.9	2.9	17.3	**9.8**	11.2	0.0
▼ Farmers State Bank of Hoffman	Hoffman	IL	**B-**	B	B	153.1	3.58	3.6	1.3	12.1	42.9	**9.8**	15.6	0.0
Farmers State Bank of Hoffman	Hoffman	MN	**B**	B	B-	30.2	5.68	5.7	3.8	9.3	32.2	**9.8**	12.8	0.0
▼ Farmers State Bank of Medora	Medora	IL	**C-**	C	C	20.0	2.65	9.5	6.4	3.2	52.1	**10.0**	15.0	29.7
▲ Farmers State Bank of Munith	Munith	MI	**B**	B-	B-	84.3	1.09	2.9	5.1	27.5	15.7	**9.1**	10.4	22.0
Farmers State Bank of Newcastle	Newcastle	TX	**B-**	B-	B-	48.7	6.38	6.2	2.7	7.3	31.0	**8.4**	10.0	19.3
Farmers State Bank of Oakley, Kansas	Oakley	KS	**A-**	A-	B+	154.4	6.41	3.8	0.5	0.9	25.2	**9.8**	16.1	0.0
Farmers State Bank of Trimont	Trimont	MN	**B**	B	B-	62.1	0.03	7.6	2.3	4.1	31.4	**10.0**	16.6	25.4

Asset Quality Index	Adjusted Non-Performing Loans as a % of Total Loans	Adjusted Non-Performing Loans as a % of Capital	Net Charge-Offs Avg Loans	Profitability Index	Net Income ($Mil)	Return on Assets (R.O.A.)	Return on Equity (R.O.E.)	Net Interest Spread	Overhead Efficiency Ratio	Liquidity Index	Liquidity Ratio	Hot Money Ratio	Stability Index
7.5	0.33	na	0.16	**5.8**	0.4	1.24	8.27	3.63	61.8	**2.4**	34.3	15.9	**8.4**
2.1	6.30	na	0.05	**4.5**	0.2	0.88	5.62	3.80	74.8	**3.9**	27.2	11.4	**7.7**
7.1	5.89	na	-1.26	**6.8**	1.2	1.75	6.17	3.39	46.7	**4.3**	87.9	25.4	**9.8**
8.1	0.18	na	0.00	**4.1**	0.7	0.85	9.14	3.06	62.5	**5.7**	37.2	3.9	**6.4**
8.9	0.00	0.0	0.00	**5.6**	0.5	1.26	11.93	3.49	64.6	**5.4**	41.0	7.7	**6.6**
6.8	2.54	na	0.00	**4.2**	0.2	0.97	9.06	3.71	63.3	**4.7**	32.5	8.7	**5.5**
7.2	2.21	na	0.01	**5.7**	0.4	1.33	8.49	4.45	70.8	**3.0**	28.6	16.4	**8.6**
8.6	0.22	1.0	0.34	**7.6**	0.6	1.81	10.95	5.38	66.4	**3.3**	26.3	14.0	**9.2**
6.3	0.37	na	0.00	**6.3**	0.5	1.74	14.08	3.68	63.2	**4.1**	24.3	9.4	**8.1**
7.0	2.27	na	0.06	**3.1**	0.0	0.45	4.06	3.16	78.7	**6.9**	70.0	3.8	**6.1**
8.3	0.14	na	0.16	**5.8**	0.3	1.48	10.45	3.61	55.8	**5.0**	37.3	8.8	**7.2**
7.8	0.15	na	0.00	**6.3**	3.0	1.42	10.05	3.39	60.3	**3.5**	19.7	12.0	**9.9**
8.1	0.69	na	0.02	**5.3**	0.5	1.02	7.74	3.51	65.3	**2.5**	42.2	28.9	**7.8**
7.9	0.00	na	0.04	**5.8**	4.3	1.52	15.76	3.36	52.0	**0.9**	11.2	20.6	**8.5**
8.1	0.00	na	0.00	**4.5**	0.1	0.95	8.14	3.34	65.5	**3.2**	47.5	20.1	**6.4**
6.1	1.91	na	0.29	**3.0**	0.1	0.86	9.75	3.54	75.8	**3.2**	32.9	16.8	**3.7**
6.8	0.34	na	0.00	**6.2**	1.0	1.56	11.51	3.82	63.8	**3.9**	17.6	9.9	**8.6**
8.4	0.26	na	-0.02	**7.0**	3.0	1.47	15.34	3.94	57.0	**3.6**	24.6	11.1	**7.5**
8.6	0.00	na	0.00	**2.4**	0.0	0.82	6.63	3.51	75.8	**5.0**	53.2	10.6	**5.1**
6.2	0.34	na	-0.03	**3.2**	0.0	0.56	5.32	3.95	85.6	**4.4**	27.7	7.0	**3.8**
9.0	0.43	na	-0.03	**6.0**	0.2	1.08	8.01	4.10	69.7	**1.9**	23.0	20.6	**7.3**
8.8	0.10	na	0.01	**6.1**	0.5	1.54	15.30	3.97	60.4	**3.7**	43.2	17.4	**7.0**
1.4	7.02	na	0.03	**3.9**	0.1	0.79	7.21	4.01	76.6	**1.2**	22.2	29.2	**5.0**
8.9	0.11	na	-0.33	**3.2**	0.1	0.44	2.55	3.65	87.9	**5.9**	58.0	8.1	**7.6**
4.5	3.01	na	-0.03	**4.2**	0.5	0.96	6.53	3.26	62.0	**1.9**	24.0	20.9	**7.6**
6.5	1.94	6.1	0.09	**4.9**	0.1	1.08	8.31	4.01	78.7	**2.8**	35.8	19.4	**6.6**
7.1	0.27	2.0	0.01	**4.4**	0.5	0.75	7.35	4.02	77.5	**3.2**	21.5	13.8	**6.2**
6.3	0.78	na	0.04	**3.4**	0.6	0.57	5.46	4.34	79.7	**3.5**	26.4	12.9	**6.7**
4.4	0.32	na	0.94	**4.2**	0.5	0.76	8.03	3.59	75.0	**0.8**	15.3	35.9	**5.6**
8.5	0.08	1.4	-0.01	**4.6**	0.4	0.92	7.96	3.57	71.6	**1.3**	11.4	26.3	**7.2**
7.0	0.19	na	-0.01	**3.2**	0.1	0.42	4.58	4.34	90.8	**5.2**	23.8	1.8	**5.0**
6.9	0.78	na	0.29	**4.8**	0.5	1.61	20.88	5.25	75.1	**5.0**	32.2	6.7	**4.5**
7.7	0.32	na	-0.03	**6.6**	0.1	1.39	8.60	5.28	71.4	**1.5**	21.6	25.1	**5.7**
8.5	0.03	na	0.00	**5.0**	0.6	1.07	11.03	3.45	61.2	**4.5**	39.6	12.4	**5.5**
7.0	3.60	na	-0.04	**3.4**	0.2	0.46	2.91	4.17	84.7	**2.9**	16.5	14.5	**7.6**
5.2	2.19	na	0.82	**3.3**	0.6	0.66	4.83	3.59	82.6	**4.3**	41.8	13.8	**6.2**
8.3	0.54	na	0.01	**5.8**	0.4	1.20	11.44	4.06	73.0	**4.7**	33.0	9.1	**7.0**
9.0	0.04	na	0.17	**3.6**	0.1	0.70	6.89	2.51	64.5	**8.1**	93.0	0.0	**5.3**
8.8	0.00	na	0.00	**0.9**	0.0	-0.03	-0.37	3.69	153.2	**6.1**	53.3	5.8	**2.9**
7.9	0.20	na	0.00	**6.3**	0.3	1.24	13.55	3.76	55.5	**1.7**	22.1	23.9	**5.6**
4.8	2.03	na	0.04	**6.4**	0.4	1.40	12.42	4.67	72.5	**2.6**	26.9	17.8	**8.1**
4.8	2.46	na	0.06	**3.3**	0.3	0.62	5.02	3.64	75.7	**6.0**	41.3	3.5	**6.4**
9.1	0.28	na	0.00	**8.0**	0.7	1.63	8.37	3.32	43.3	**5.5**	54.7	11.1	**9.5**
8.1	0.00	na	0.00	**7.4**	0.7	1.72	10.92	3.25	29.9	**1.2**	11.0	27.5	**8.8**
1.9	2.69	23.2	0.14	**4.3**	0.5	0.85	9.93	4.68	80.5	**3.2**	11.8	12.5	**4.9**
5.8	1.23	na	0.06	**5.3**	0.1	1.14	6.07	4.98	75.0	**3.0**	21.3	14.4	**7.7**
7.7	0.00	na	0.00	**8.9**	0.5	1.68	8.64	4.24	54.3	**2.1**	25.8	19.7	**8.9**
8.7	0.00	na	0.00	**3.4**	0.1	1.03	9.09	3.40	80.5	**5.2**	47.0	10.4	**6.3**
8.2	0.51	na	0.04	**5.1**	0.9	1.30	11.59	3.77	66.0	**3.4**	33.3	15.9	**6.9**
6.0	0.00	na	0.54	**2.6**	0.0	0.18	1.46	3.69	95.3	**4.4**	21.7	6.9	**5.8**
9.2	0.00	na	0.00	**3.8**	0.1	0.66	2.37	2.65	67.9	**3.2**	51.1	23.2	**7.0**
9.8	0.00	na	0.00	**4.2**	0.4	1.16	10.21	2.95	62.7	**5.6**	56.4	10.9	**6.8**
7.0	1.24	na	0.00	**7.5**	0.7	1.71	14.14	4.13	58.1	**3.8**	29.0	6.1	**8.7**
8.5	0.93	na	-0.02	**3.9**	0.3	0.64	4.05	3.16	72.8	**5.2**	46.1	10.7	**8.0**
8.7	0.00	na	0.00	**3.9**	0.1	0.77	5.66	3.45	73.4	**3.4**	52.2	19.9	**7.0**
4.2	0.00	na	0.25	**1.7**	0.0	-0.04	-0.25	3.54	101.4	**5.5**	78.0	12.3	**5.1**
4.7	1.95	na	-0.06	**4.6**	0.2	0.92	8.79	4.12	74.9	**6.1**	44.6	3.7	**6.2**
7.7	0.29	na	-0.18	**5.0**	0.1	0.89	9.20	3.70	71.8	**6.9**	52.2	0.0	**5.7**
7.4	0.00	na	0.02	**7.6**	0.5	1.45	9.13	3.68	48.2	**1.3**	18.0	28.8	**9.1**
8.0	0.82	na	-0.14	**4.9**	0.2	0.95	5.62	3.46	66.2	**2.0**	36.0	20.4	**7.1**

Name	City	State	Rating	2019 Rating	2018 Rating	Total Assets ($Mil)	One Year Asset Growth	Asset Mix (As a % of Total Assets) Commercial Loans	Consumer Loans	Mortgage Loans	Securities	Capitalization Index	Leverage Ratio	Risk-Based Capital Ratio
Farmers State Bank of Turton	Turton	SD	**B**	B	B	29.9	-3.12	2.9	2.8	0.0	16.9	**10.0**	12.4	24.7
Farmers State Bank of Underwood	Underwood	MN	**B-**	B-	C+	72.9	3.79	14.7	4.1	14.8	6.6	**7.7**	9.6	0.0
Farmers State Bank of Waupaca	Waupaca	WI	**A-**	A-	A-	201.7	4.13	7.7	4.0	23.4	24.3	**9.8**	12.8	0.0
▼ Farmers State Bank of Western Illinois	Alpha	IL	**B+**	A-	B+	139.6	4.05	4.2	2.3	6.3	25.5	**10.0**	12.8	20.8
▼ Farmers State Bank, Allen, Oklahoma	Allen	OK	**B-**	B	B-	41.4	-6.09	17.4	13.3	15.5	8.2	**9.8**	13.5	0.0
▼ Farmers State Bank, S/B	Bolivar	MO	**C-**	C	C+	69.1	0.36	1.0	2.5	28.3	5.2	**7.1**	9.2	0.0
Farmers Trust & Savings Bank	Earling	IA	**B+**	B+	B	98.3	6.78	9.4	1.5	7.7	0.8	**7.7**	9.5	14.7
Farmers Trust & Savings Bank	Williamsburg	IA	**A**	A	A-	155.4	15.05	6.7	3.4	13.3	39.1	**9.8**	23.9	0.0
Farmers Trust and Savings Bank	Buffalo Center	IA	**A-**	A-	B+	261.2	0.57	13.6	1.1	5.6	1.0	**9.8**	12.7	0.0
▲ Farmers Trust and Savings Bank	Spencer	IA	**B-**	C+	C+	460.5	3.10	10.5	0.8	7.9	13.7	**5.5**	9.1	11.3
Farmers-Merchants Bank & Trust Co.	Breaux Bridge	LA	**D+**	D+	D	334.9	3.40	4.6	4.8	15.0	9.9	**10.0**	13.1	18.6
▲ Farmers-Merchants Bank of Illinois	Joy	IL	**B+**	B	C+	220.2	26.93	2.0	1.2	7.8	7.2	**9.4**	10.8	0.0
Farmington State Bank	Farmington	WA	**C**	C	C-	10.3	8.09	10.1	1.4	0.4	0.9	**10.0**	18.1	49.8
Fauquier Bank	Warrenton	VA	**B**	B	B-	726.6	3.79	5.0	2.0	31.1	11.2	**8.1**	9.8	13.4
Fayette County National Bank of Fayettevill	Fayetteville	WV	**B+**	B+	B	102.1	14.22	0.6	3.6	44.6	25.1	**9.8**	12.7	0.0
Fayette Savings Bank, SSB	La Grange	TX	**B**	B	B	219.6	22.16	1.6	2.1	49.2	11.0	**7.5**	9.3	14.3
Fayetteville Bank	Fayetteville	TX	**B**	B	B+	581.8	14.66	3.7	0.8	3.9	80.5	**9.4**	10.7	0.0
FBT Bank & Mortgage	Fordyce	AR	**B+**	B+	B	175.2	4.68	10.7	6.9	20.1	26.8	**9.8**	11.8	0.0
FCB Banks	Collinsville	IL	**B**	B	B	1779.1	8.91	3.4	4.3	35.5	9.2	**6.5**	8.6	14.7
FCN Bank, N.A.	Brookville	IN	**B+**	B+	B+	477.4	6.86	8.8	1.6	16.0	32.7	**9.6**	10.8	18.0
FDS Bank	Mason	OH	**A+**	A+	A+	140.3	4.15	0.8	0.2	0.0	73.2	**10.0**	30.9	45.1
Federal Savings Bank	Chicago	IL	**A**	A	A	759.4	63.65	0.0	1.5	84.9	0.1	**10.0**	18.8	27.2
Federated Bank	Onarga	IL	**C**	C	C+	93.6	9.83	5.6	2.6	12.7	37.7	**6.9**	8.9	18.3
▲ Federation Bank	Washington	IA	**B-**	C+	C+	139.0	6.83	9.5	3.8	13.4	15.3	**6.9**	9.1	0.0
Feliciana Bank & Trust Co.	Clinton	LA	**B+**	B+	B-	129.7	-1.19	9.2	2.0	32.4	12.6	**9.8**	11.3	0.0
Fidelity Bank	West Memphis	AR	**A-**	A-	B+	449.9	16.85	3.2	0.7	3.9	50.7	**9.8**	11.2	0.0
Fidelity Bank	West Des Moines	IA	**B-**	B-	C+	83.1	1.94	0.1	0.1	44.3	4.1	**9.2**	10.5	14.8
▼ Fidelity Bank	New Orleans	LA	**B-**	B	B	797.0	-1.93	4.1	0.7	31.3	13.9	**10.0**	18.8	25.9
Fidelity Bank	Edina	MN	**A-**	A-	A	605.5	27.75	23.6	0.6	0.0	6.6	**6.5**	12.4	12.1
Fidelity Bank	Fuquay-Varina	NC	**A-**	A-	B+	2150.5	7.49	6.0	0.5	3.5	27.7	**8.7**	10.1	15.4
Fidelity Bank & Trust	Dubuque	IA	**B**	B	B+	1360.7	65.73	10.4	1.6	10.1	15.5	**6.3**	9.2	12.0
Fidelity Bank of Texas	Waco	TX	**B+**	B+	B+	91.4	2.19	0.9	1.3	21.8	1.1	**9.8**	18.4	0.0
▼ Fidelity Bank, N.A.	Wichita	KS	**C+**	B-	B-	2572.9	10.41	9.9	5.1	15.5	7.9	**5.9**	9.8	11.6
▼ Fidelity Co-operative Bank	Leominster	MA	**C**	C+	C+	1170.2	19.94	9.8	0.3	30.9	11.9	**6.3**	8.3	12.3
Fidelity Deposit and Discount Bank	Dunmore	PA	**A-**	A-	B+	1065.4	10.39	7.7	10.1	22.8	19.2	**8.9**	10.3	15.7
Fidelity Federal S&L Assn. of Delaware	Delaware	OH	**C-**	C-	C-	106.4	2.30	0.0	1.0	34.0	38.3	**10.0**	21.0	49.2
Fidelity Personal Trust Co., FSB	Boston	MA	**U**	U	U	100.0	4.85	0.0	0.0	0.0	0.0	**9.8**	99.6	0.0
Fidelity State Bank and Trust Co.	Dodge City	KS	**A-**	A-	B+	181.6	3.89	3.4	0.4	1.3	29.2	**10.0**	18.8	76.8
Fidelity State Bank and Trust Co.	Topeka	KS	**C+**	C+	C	128.3	-3.49	10.9	19.9	8.6	26.7	**7.7**	9.7	0.0
▲ Field & Main Bank	Henderson	KY	**B-**	C+	C	488.6	8.47	11.3	0.8	20.6	7.5	**6.9**	9.2	12.4
▼ Fieldpoint Private Bank & Trust	Greenwich	CT	**B-**	B	B	920.4	1.24	3.2	9.5	34.0	11.6	**10.0**	12.0	17.4
Fifth District Savings Bank	New Orleans	LA	**B-**	B-	B-	438.1	1.13	0.0	0.3	70.3	14.8	**10.0**	17.8	37.1
Fifth Third Bank, N.A.	Cincinnati	OH	**B**	B	B	183723.7	24.64	28.9	9.5	10.0	20.7	**7.8**	10.2	13.2
▼ Finance Factors, Ltd.	Honolulu	HI	**B-**	B	B-	596.5	2.90	0.0	0.9	28.8	20.5	**10.0**	11.4	17.6
Financial Federal Bank	Memphis	TN	**A-**	A-	B+	657.5	8.96	15.1	2.5	24.3	0.0	**9.8**	12.8	0.0
Financial Security Bank	Kerkhoven	MN	**C+**	C+	C	107.7	9.12	9.5	0.6	9.4	4.7	**4.4**	8.8	10.7
FineMark National Bank & Trust	Fort Myers	FL	**B-**	B-	B-	2460.3	27.79	5.1	3.6	36.3	23.5	**7.8**	9.5	16.4
▼ Finwise Bank	Murray	UT	**B+**	A-	B+	177.3	35.74	5.7	18.7	7.6	1.2	**9.8**	16.2	0.0
First & Farmers National Bank, Inc.	Somerset	KY	**B-**	B-	B+	529.3	2.47	3.8	3.0	28.5	32.7	**10.0**	11.0	15.7
▼ First & Peoples Bank and Trust Co.	Russell	KY	**B-**	B	B	204.8	2.52	11.8	17.3	10.0	41.0	**9.8**	19.7	0.0
▼ First American Bank	Elk Grove Village	IL	**C**	C+	B-	5600.0	0.56	8.1	2.0	5.8	56.8	**4.8**	6.8	13.5
First American Bank	Artesia	NM	**A**	A	A	1263.7	8.12	9.4	0.2	7.6	37.8	**8.3**	9.9	17.8
First American Bank	Stonewall	OK	**B**	B	B	33.0	3.86	13.6	11.1	20.6	6.4	**9.8**	11.5	0.0
First American Bank and Trust	Vacherie	LA	**A**	A	A-	945.7	2.66	3.6	1.5	27.4	20.8	**10.0**	15.0	22.8
First American Bank and Trust Co.	Athens	GA	**A-**	A-	A-	578.9	6.22	2.6	0.4	16.9	10.9	**10.0**	11.4	18.6
First American Bank, N.A.	Hudson	WI	**B-**	B-	B	127.3	-2.97	9.9	1.3	10.2	11.1	**4.6**	8.7	10.8
▼ First American National Bank	Iuka	MS	**C+**	B-	B-	282.5	2.84	4.1	5.6	24.2	29.5	**9.8**	11.2	0.0
First American State Bank	Greenwood Village	CO	**B-**	B-	B-	260.4	5.07	2.4	0.1	37.7	14.4	**6.8**	8.8	15.3
First American Trust, F.S.B.	Santa Ana	CA	**U**	U	U	4056.6	-5.38	0.0	0.0	0.0	83.5	**6.4**	8.4	36.3
▼ First Arkansas Bank and Trust	Jacksonville	AR	**C+**	B-	B-	779.4	1.59	16.2	9.1	9.6	23.5	**9.8**	14.5	0.0

Asset Quality Index	Adjusted Non-Performing Loans as a % of Total Loans	Adjusted Non-Performing Loans as a % of Capital	Net Charge-Offs Avg Loans	Profitability Index	Net Income ($Mil)	Return on Assets (R.O.A.)	Return on Equity (R.O.E.)	Net Interest Spread	Overhead Efficiency Ratio	Liquidity Index	Liquidity Ratio	Hot Money Ratio	Stability Index
6.3	0.00	na	0.00	**5.7**	0.1	1.02	8.05	3.83	63.2	**2.9**	38.8	20.9	**8.1**
4.3	1.10	na	0.02	**6.4**	0.3	1.38	13.88	4.78	70.4	**1.3**	18.3	28.9	**7.2**
8.3	0.29	na	-0.03	**6.7**	0.8	1.59	12.45	4.33	57.2	**3.5**	31.9	14.8	**7.8**
7.6	0.34	na	0.01	**4.6**	0.3	0.90	6.90	4.00	71.6	**5.1**	36.9	8.0	**7.6**
2.4	0.37	17.8	0.03	**5.2**	0.1	1.03	7.64	4.98	74.7	**1.7**	18.4	23.2	**7.7**
5.2	0.51	na	0.00	**2.3**	0.0	-0.05	-0.42	5.45	92.1	**1.6**	15.6	23.1	**7.1**
7.4	0.00	na	-0.02	**7.5**	0.4	1.65	17.44	4.02	58.0	**3.9**	26.3	11.2	**7.0**
8.4	0.90	na	0.05	**9.3**	0.8	2.17	8.97	3.80	44.3	**6.1**	53.5	6.8	**9.6**
6.1	0.11	na	0.02	**7.1**	1.0	1.54	11.82	3.89	53.7	**3.8**	10.7	9.7	**9.1**
7.0	0.95	na	0.01	**5.2**	1.4	1.23	13.29	3.42	53.8	**1.5**	7.1	10.3	**6.7**
4.0	4.76	na	0.15	**5.0**	0.9	1.13	8.51	4.16	72.7	**2.9**	27.6	16.5	**8.3**
4.3	0.41	3.8	0.00	**5.3**	0.6	1.11	7.51	3.17	55.5	**0.6**	2.9	22.7	**8.1**
8.9	0.00	na	0.00	**1.6**	0.0	0.21	1.18	3.18	93.3	**7.2**	70.8	0.0	**6.7**
8.9	0.18	na	-0.01	**4.6**	1.6	0.88	8.79	3.78	72.0	**4.4**	14.9	6.0	**6.2**
5.5	1.68	na	-0.02	**5.8**	0.3	1.33	10.43	4.11	64.1	**4.0**	24.1	9.9	**7.2**
6.3	0.63	5.5	0.00	**4.7**	0.6	1.03	11.21	3.23	64.4	**0.5**	3.5	37.8	**5.6**
10.0	0.00	0.0	-0.02	**4.5**	3.5	2.47	20.78	2.15	59.0	**2.9**	59.0	43.4	**7.4**
4.7	6.41	na	0.12	**6.8**	1.3	2.94	26.98	4.04	55.0	**2.8**	37.5	20.9	**5.9**
5.9	0.86	8.0	0.01	**5.3**	4.2	0.96	11.03	2.68	60.0	**3.1**	16.7	14.3	**7.6**
6.1	0.93	5.6	-0.13	**4.5**	1.0	0.87	7.42	3.46	70.1	**4.1**	36.6	13.4	**6.9**
10.0	0.00	na	0.00	**9.5**	129.7	270.74	662.85	1.64	19.8	**9.1**	138.2	0.0	**9.0**
8.1	0.57	3.5	0.03	**9.5**	11.7	8.00	43.27	2.09	79.5	**0.3**	5.5	29.9	**9.0**
8.0	0.00	na	0.02	**2.8**	0.1	0.48	3.99	3.46	85.9	**5.5**	45.3	7.9	**6.6**
4.6	0.56	na	-0.05	**4.5**	0.3	0.99	10.14	4.05	70.6	**3.3**	20.6	12.5	**6.4**
3.5	2.42	na	0.08	**5.3**	0.4	1.15	10.16	3.86	70.8	**0.7**	12.7	41.4	**7.9**
9.1	0.01	na	-0.01	**5.8**	1.6	1.41	11.92	3.07	56.6	**1.4**	22.4	27.7	**7.6**
5.5	0.45	na	0.00	**3.7**	0.3	1.29	10.23	2.52	92.4	**0.7**	12.9	37.2	**7.7**
8.4	0.74	na	0.27	**2.9**	0.7	0.35	1.79	4.98	93.6	**3.7**	14.7	9.2	**8.4**
6.8	0.02	na	0.04	**8.3**	2.2	1.71	9.39	5.48	61.4	**2.8**	1.3	0.9	**10.0**
7.8	1.39	na	0.02	**6.5**	6.2	1.19	10.52	3.61	61.9	**6.4**	37.9	3.2	**9.4**
5.7	0.82	4.1	0.10	**5.4**	4.3	1.26	10.06	3.23	60.4	**3.5**	23.9	14.4	**9.9**
6.2	2.05	na	0.00	**3.7**	0.1	0.34	1.88	3.44	86.3	**6.0**	63.7	8.4	**8.0**
5.5	1.93	na	0.08	**3.1**	3.6	0.58	6.01	3.45	80.6	**3.2**	5.9	11.1	**7.5**
5.9	1.68	8.5	0.01	**2.5**	1.3	0.46	5.67	3.37	67.2	**2.7**	14.7	11.1	**5.7**
7.1	0.59	na	0.02	**6.2**	3.2	1.25	11.61	3.63	61.4	**4.2**	10.8	7.4	**8.9**
9.8	0.00	0.1	-0.01	**1.3**	0.0	-0.04	-0.20	3.01	105.1	**6.2**	59.1	8.4	**7.4**
10.0	na	na	na	**9.5**	10.9	44.04	46.82	2.87	43.8	**4.0**	na	100.0	**7.0**
9.8	0.59	0.6	-0.01	**5.5**	0.5	1.22	6.38	2.92	52.6	**7.5**	79.7	3.1	**8.4**
6.4	0.28	na	0.01	**3.9**	0.4	1.23	12.24	3.31	70.5	**4.6**	25.1	5.8	**5.8**
4.4	0.77	na	0.45	**4.9**	1.6	1.37	12.49	3.76	75.1	**1.3**	12.9	26.5	**6.2**
4.8	1.46	9.1	0.00	**2.6**	0.3	0.14	1.19	2.54	85.9	**1.3**	7.7	25.7	**7.3**
10.0	0.33	1.2	0.00	**3.1**	0.4	0.39	2.17	2.70	81.7	**1.6**	24.5	25.6	**7.9**
4.7	1.25	4.6	0.43	**6.0**	119.5	0.28	2.05	3.44	60.5	**5.3**	25.9	2.0	**10.0**
7.0	0.11	7.4	-0.21	**1.9**	-2.0	-1.37	-11.58	3.34	280.3	**1.1**	23.3	32.5	**8.0**
6.3	0.27	na	0.00	**6.9**	2.9	1.81	14.39	2.96	48.8	**0.3**	5.2	68.9	**10.0**
6.1	0.48	na	0.00	**4.1**	0.2	0.64	7.19	3.61	83.2	**1.5**	15.3	24.1	**5.4**
9.0	0.08	0.6	0.00	**4.0**	5.7	1.03	11.13	2.46	67.7	**4.7**	19.0	4.9	**7.1**
4.8	1.05	na	3.75	**10.0**	2.1	4.59	27.52	17.08	43.0	**2.1**	43.1	32.5	**8.2**
7.0	0.59	na	0.00	**4.0**	1.0	0.72	5.49	3.73	78.8	**2.3**	30.4	20.5	**8.2**
5.8	1.00	na	0.23	**3.2**	0.2	0.31	1.64	3.80	86.5	**4.6**	32.1	9.3	**7.6**
5.7	2.10	10.3	-0.07	**1.1**	7.1	0.53	7.63	2.56	147.5	**4.2**	10.9	6.7	**5.7**
8.8	0.48	na	0.01	**8.9**	6.4	2.01	19.27	3.95	53.0	**5.7**	31.4	5.8	**10.0**
3.9	2.28	11.5	-0.14	**7.1**	0.1	1.72	14.97	4.61	62.4	**1.9**	27.3	23.5	**7.2**
7.3	1.71	na	0.00	**7.2**	3.2	1.38	9.20	4.12	62.3	**3.4**	23.4	13.0	**9.8**
8.4	0.72	2.7	-0.01	**6.9**	2.3	1.61	14.34	3.46	59.6	**4.6**	23.3	5.7	**8.1**
3.7	0.99	na	-0.05	**4.3**	0.4	1.15	7.96	3.91	49.6	**0.9**	21.7	36.9	**7.4**
5.4	1.25	na	0.12	**3.1**	0.3	0.40	3.37	4.42	92.1	**4.4**	35.7	11.4	**6.3**
9.1	0.00	na	0.00	**3.6**	0.5	0.72	8.21	3.11	75.0	**0.8**	20.5	47.7	**4.5**
10.0	na	0.0	na	**7.4**	10.8	1.08	11.63	1.67	34.4	**8.7**	108.2	0.1	**7.0**
2.5	3.15	na	0.42	**6.2**	2.7	1.38	7.69	4.63	68.8	**4.2**	20.6	8.3	**8.7**

Name	City	State	Rating	2019 Rating	2018 Rating	Total Assets ($Mil)	One Year Asset Growth	Asset Mix (As a % of Total Assets) Commercial Loans	Consumer Loans	Mortgage Loans	Securities	Capitalization Index	Leverage Ratio	Risk-Based Capital Ratio
▼ First Bank	Ketchikan	AK	**C+**	B-	C+	582.9	5.81	3.8	1.4	5.8	54.4	**8.0**	9.6	20.4
First Bank	Wadley	AL	**B+**	B+	B+	92.7	4.93	3.6	1.8	4.9	53.2	**7.0**	9.0	13.6
First Bank	Clewiston	FL	**B**	B	B-	433.5	13.11	5.6	1.9	13.3	8.5	**7.7**	9.5	14.4
▼ First Bank	Dalton	GA	**C+**	B-	B-	418.9	9.17	10.0	1.5	14.5	15.8	**7.4**	9.5	0.0
First Bank	Sterling	KS	**B+**	B+	B+	145.0	0.21	4.6	0.6	12.0	29.3	**9.8**	14.2	0.0
First Bank	Creve Coeur	MO	**B+**	B+	B	6260.7	0.41	10.7	0.3	11.7	32.9	**8.4**	9.9	14.9
▼ First Bank	McComb	MS	**B-**	B	B	611.0	6.20	9.0	1.3	23.1	6.2	**8.6**	10.1	15.0
▲ First Bank	Southern Pines	NC	**A-**	B+	B	6377.2	5.38	5.5	0.9	17.8	13.6	**9.3**	11.0	14.4
First Bank	Hamilton	NJ	**B**	B	B	2092.4	17.73	11.8	0.2	6.1	4.6	**7.2**	10.2	12.7
First Bank	Erick	OK	**A-**	A-	B+	76.7	2.09	17.1	4.3	9.2	3.5	**10.0**	11.8	18.3
First Bank	Burkburnett	TX	**B-**	B-	B-	487.7	16.12	11.8	1.0	29.2	0.8	**10.0**	11.3	15.0
First Bank	Strasburg	VA	**A-**	A-	B+	815.5	5.24	6.7	1.2	24.2	17.9	**8.6**	10.1	15.0
First Bank & Trust	Brookings	SD	**B+**	B+	B+	2069.1	6.05	11.7	2.2	6.2	16.6	**8.2**	10.0	0.0
First Bank & Trust	Sioux Falls	SD	**B+**	B+	B+	1069.5	9.83	20.8	1.1	5.6	15.4	**9.6**	10.9	0.0
First Bank & Trust	Lubbock	TX	**B+**	B+	B	1163.2	5.77	12.9	1.1	10.7	31.1	**8.6**	10.0	14.5
First Bank & Trust	Seymour	TX	**B-**	B-	C	123.0	-26.05	8.9	0.9	0.1	56.8	**10.0**	14.1	34.6
First Bank & Trust Co.	Duncan	OK	**B+**	B+	A-	577.4	-3.79	5.9	2.4	25.7	6.4	**9.8**	16.1	0.0
▼ First Bank & Trust Co.	Perry	OK	**B+**	A-	A	209.5	38.01	4.1	6.1	15.3	33.1	**9.8**	11.4	0.0
First Bank and Trust	New Orleans	LA	**B-**	B-	B-	1007.8	8.30	8.3	1.1	21.0	4.7	**6.4**	10.1	12.1
First Bank and Trust Co.	Minden	NE	**C+**	C+	C+	71.4	5.13	7.3	2.7	13.7	33.1	**9.6**	10.7	19.7
▼ First Bank and Trust Co.	Clinton	OK	**B-**	B	B-	54.3	-5.33	2.1	10.4	17.3	33.3	**9.8**	13.7	0.0
First Bank and Trust Co.	Lebanon	VA	**A**	A	A	2007.2	7.87	7.6	2.6	15.5	1.5	**10.0**	11.8	16.5
First Bank and Trust Co. of Illinois	Palatine	IL	**C-**	C-	C	184.5	1.74	19.6	0.0	1.5	1.1	**8.0**	9.7	14.9
▲ First Bank and Trust Co. of Murphysboro	Murphysboro	IL	**D+**	D	D+	77.6	-3.90	10.3	5.3	20.6	17.8	**7.0**	9.0	12.6
First Bank and Trust of Childress	Childress	TX	**C+**	C+	C+	124.1	9.19	15.2	3.3	8.5	45.1	**6.7**	8.7	20.8
First Bank and Trust of Fullerton	Fullerton	NE	**B+**	B+	B	90.6	0.37	3.9	1.1	0.3	14.9	**9.8**	14.6	0.0
First Bank and Trust of Memphis	Memphis	TX	**B+**	B+	B	57.8	-9.38	7.9	0.4	12.8	0.0	**10.0**	13.1	24.0
First Bank Blue Earth	Blue Earth	MN	**A-**	A-	B+	245.0	9.29	7.5	1.5	4.5	29.9	**8.5**	10.2	0.0
▼ First Bank Elk River	Elk River	MN	**C**	C+	C	285.2	5.80	18.3	0.7	6.3	31.7	**7.9**	9.8	0.0
First Bank Hampton	Hampton	IA	**A-**	A-	B+	179.9	10.26	14.9	3.9	12.7	14.3	**9.8**	12.4	0.0
First Bank Kansas	Salina	KS	**B+**	B+	B	449.3	2.76	5.9	3.4	17.4	36.5	**7.3**	9.2	16.5
First Bank of Alabama	Talladega	AL	**A-**	A-	A-	587.7	7.11	9.9	1.7	12.7	22.4	**10.0**	12.2	18.9
First Bank of Baldwin	Baldwin	WI	**B-**	B-	C	192.0	4.47	5.2	1.2	9.6	34.9	**7.7**	9.5	16.5
First Bank of Bancroft	Bancroft	NE	**B-**	B-	B-	23.2	5.86	5.8	1.6	3.9	20.1	**9.8**	16.6	0.0
First Bank of Beloit	Beloit	KS	**B-**	B-	C+	79.2	3.98	7.5	1.6	14.6	22.8	**10.0**	13.3	22.0
▲ First Bank of Berne	Berne	IN	**A-**	B+	B	740.7	6.50	5.0	0.9	18.2	15.9	**9.4**	10.6	14.6
First Bank of Boaz	Boaz	AL	**A+**	A+	A+	226.3	-1.95	5.4	2.2	5.8	69.1	**10.0**	18.4	33.8
First Bank of Celeste	Celeste	TX	**C+**	C+	C	53.4	2.03	7.7	7.0	4.2	38.5	**6.1**	8.1	18.7
First Bank of Coastal Georgia	Pembroke	GA	**B-**	B-	B	125.9	7.48	2.4	0.6	9.4	63.7	**10.0**	13.8	32.8
▼ First Bank of Greenwich	Cos Cob	CT	**C+**	B-	B-	427.8	19.11	8.4	0.2	33.4	3.4	**7.5**	9.4	13.1
First Bank of Highland Park	Highland Park	IL	**C+**	C+	C+	1922.6	9.56	41.8	0.1	2.7	14.0	**7.9**	9.7	0.0
First Bank of Linden	Linden	AL	**B**	B	B+	77.2	-0.14	8.8	6.7	4.2	47.7	**10.0**	14.9	30.0
▼ First Bank of Manhattan	Manhattan	IL	**C+**	B-	B	175.6	9.58	1.2	2.1	19.1	24.0	**8.2**	9.8	22.9
First Bank of Muleshoe	Muleshoe	TX	**B-**	B-	B-	88.4	-8.29	4.2	1.2	0.2	76.7	**10.0**	15.2	63.6
First Bank of Ohio	Tiffin	OH	**B+**	B+	B+	209.7	13.36	0.0	69.9	0.0	21.2	**9.8**	35.2	0.0
First Bank of Okarche	Okarche	OK	**A**	A	A-	113.6	7.12	7.3	1.7	1.2	38.4	**9.8**	11.6	0.0
First Bank of Owasso	Owasso	OK	**A-**	A-	A-	442.7	2.46	2.2	0.4	10.6	2.5	**8.4**	11.3	13.7
▲ First Bank of Pike	Molena	GA	**C**	C-	C-	53.1	4.07	5.3	10.2	24.1	20.3	**6.8**	8.8	15.6
▲ First Bank of the Lake	Osage Beach	MO	**C+**	C	C	119.7	31.56	15.4	0.6	5.1	18.2	**6.1**	8.1	21.5
First Bank of Thomas	Thomas	OK	**B+**	B+	B+	46.5	-3.93	5.5	0.7	10.0	17.9	**10.0**	15.5	27.8
First Bank of Utica	Utica	NE	**C+**	C+	C+	71.2	6.86	9.5	5.1	10.5	2.2	**10.0**	11.8	15.8
First Bank Richmond	Richmond	IN	**B-**	B-	C+	1005.7	14.46	7.0	1.3	13.1	25.1	**10.0**	14.3	19.1
▲ First Bank, Upper Michigan	Gladstone	MI	**C-**	D+	D	467.6	0.19	13.9	9.7	17.2	12.5	**9.9**	11.3	14.9
First Bankers Trust Co., N.A.	Quincy	IL	**B-**	B-	C+	918.7	1.15	7.1	4.6	6.8	39.3	**8.3**	9.9	16.6
First Bethany Bank & Trust	Bethany	OK	**B**	B	B	226.7	3.34	5.5	0.5	11.6	37.5	**8.4**	10.1	0.0
First Business Bank	Madison	WI	**B-**	B-	C+	2183.4	9.56	24.1	0.3	1.8	9.7	**5.5**	10.1	11.4
First Cahawba Bank	Selma	AL	**B**	B	B	132.1	9.43	17.1	4.2	16.6	11.2	**10.0**	11.3	16.1
▼ First Capital Bank	Laurinburg	NC	**D+**	C-	C+	182.2	82.72	2.1	1.1	21.5	6.6	**10.0**	14.8	20.0
▲ First Capital Bank	Germantown	TN	**B**	B-	B-	355.5	11.94	17.2	0.5	9.2	1.0	**8.9**	10.4	0.0
First Capital Bank	Quanah	TX	**C**	C	C-	65.2	5.77	17.2	7.2	15.2	0.0	**6.3**	8.5	12.0

Asset Quality Index	Adjusted Non-Performing Loans as a % of Total Loans	Adjusted Non-Performing Loans as a % of Capital	Net Charge-Offs Avg Loans	Profitability Index	Net Income ($Mil)	Return on Assets (R.O.A.)	Return on Equity (R.O.E.)	Net Interest Spread	Overhead Efficiency Ratio	Liquidity Index	Liquidity Ratio	Hot Money Ratio	Stability Index
7.1	1.46	na	-0.01	3.2	0.8	0.58	5.75	3.20	86.2	4.4	55.4	17.1	6.7
8.8	0.31	na	-0.04	5.4	0.3	1.19	11.97	4.00	68.4	5.5	59.5	10.5	6.4
8.6	0.02	0.2	0.00	5.1	1.0	0.98	10.46	3.95	66.6	4.7	28.3	7.0	5.6
2.4	2.03	na	0.16	7.5	1.5	1.40	14.95	4.30	61.4	2.0	22.4	19.6	6.4
7.6	0.05	na	0.00	5.7	0.7	1.88	13.34	3.41	54.8	2.2	30.5	20.2	8.4
8.3	0.60	3.1	0.26	4.9	11.7	0.76	7.18	3.19	67.6	5.3	32.0	7.9	9.7
4.2	0.13	na	0.02	3.2	0.7	0.50	4.98	3.14	77.5	2.1	26.8	15.3	7.5
6.3	0.74	2.9	0.22	7.1	18.9	1.22	8.32	4.00	58.2	3.4	18.1	10.9	10.0
4.1	0.78	5.7	0.16	4.2	3.2	0.63	5.71	3.28	58.1	1.3	11.3	22.5	7.9
8.1	0.05	na	-0.16	9.5	0.4	2.06	17.17	5.09	59.6	4.7	34.6	8.6	8.0
4.6	1.34	na	0.05	8.3	1.9	1.61	14.40	4.41	72.2	2.5	19.9	17.0	8.3
8.0	0.26	na	0.17	5.8	2.0	1.00	9.70	3.85	64.2	4.3	18.2	7.4	6.9
4.9	1.00	7.5	0.00	6.4	5.7	1.13	9.83	3.65	64.4	2.1	10.4	15.7	8.5
4.7	1.00	6.2	0.07	7.4	3.4	1.28	10.42	4.48	65.5	2.9	15.2	11.2	8.5
6.6	0.45	1.0	0.07	4.2	1.8	0.61	3.06	3.93	73.8	2.4	21.8	19.2	8.5
8.1	0.12	na	0.00	3.5	0.2	0.51	2.96	2.60	81.9	6.7	61.7	5.5	6.4
2.2	4.57	na	-0.03	8.6	2.9	2.03	12.64	4.46	60.2	3.4	15.0	12.0	10.0
4.2	5.48	na	0.08	7.7	1.0	2.16	19.09	4.44	65.1	2.6	22.7	16.7	7.6
3.7	1.29	na	-0.02	6.8	3.7	1.49	14.88	4.44	69.1	0.8	9.0	34.3	9.4
7.1	4.40	na	-0.01	3.5	0.2	0.99	8.85	3.27	75.5	3.7	33.9	14.5	6.0
7.5	0.00	na	0.17	3.2	0.1	0.48	3.36	3.79	88.8	2.9	28.0	16.5	6.2
8.0	0.24	2.7	0.06	7.7	6.9	1.41	12.04	3.95	57.1	3.7	14.4	10.8	10.0
7.4	0.00	na	0.00	1.6	0.4	0.78	8.13	4.32	81.6	1.0	24.3	37.8	5.0
1.5	3.03	na	-0.01	2.2	0.1	0.30	3.39	3.76	83.4	2.8	15.9	15.1	3.5
7.8	0.87	na	0.01	3.5	0.2	0.71	8.23	2.34	72.3	0.7	16.7	52.3	4.9
7.4	0.00	na	-0.01	4.2	0.2	0.73	5.01	3.11	70.8	1.8	23.1	18.7	8.2
8.9	0.00	na	0.00	3.6	0.1	0.46	3.51	2.91	85.0	2.3	48.0	34.7	8.1
7.6	0.30	1.6	0.01	6.5	1.0	1.57	15.05	3.33	53.9	2.5	14.9	16.3	8.5
7.6	0.43	na	-0.01	2.6	0.3	0.38	3.72	3.12	89.1	3.3	23.3	11.3	5.8
7.5	0.87	na	-0.01	7.3	0.7	1.61	12.95	3.71	52.4	3.3	21.5	13.4	8.3
6.7	0.07	2.5	0.07	7.6	2.0	1.81	18.46	3.68	66.2	4.6	33.9	10.1	7.5
6.5	1.19	na	0.30	6.6	1.7	1.14	8.80	4.16	56.9	1.3	16.4	27.5	9.7
4.8	2.08	na	0.00	3.7	0.3	0.57	5.29	3.68	70.2	5.7	34.0	2.6	6.7
7.2	3.68	na	-0.07	5.1	0.1	0.95	5.85	3.56	63.9	5.5	51.3	6.9	7.2
8.5	0.15	na	0.00	2.8	0.1	0.25	1.88	3.81	75.0	4.2	14.9	7.7	7.3
6.0	0.56	na	0.04	9.0	5.2	2.91	27.54	3.95	43.5	4.8	18.0	3.5	8.7
9.5	0.13	0.2	0.00	7.9	1.0	1.78	9.42	3.76	43.5	4.0	67.3	23.1	9.5
8.7	0.00	na	0.04	4.1	0.1	0.94	11.64	3.49	74.9	5.4	58.7	11.3	4.7
9.7	0.14	na	0.00	3.3	0.3	0.81	6.05	3.02	80.8	4.8	27.0	5.8	6.9
5.8	0.89	na	0.00	2.8	0.2	0.15	1.60	2.94	75.7	0.7	14.5	33.1	4.7
6.8	3.34	na	-0.13	2.9	1.5	0.32	3.34	2.24	78.0	0.7	13.0	28.8	7.4
8.3	0.00	na	0.29	3.7	0.1	0.57	3.79	3.51	82.6	2.7	62.1	35.1	7.3
7.5	1.38	na	0.00	2.9	0.2	0.36	3.52	3.29	89.3	5.2	36.8	6.9	7.0
9.8	0.09	0.2	0.00	3.4	0.1	0.55	3.74	2.62	77.2	7.5	90.2	3.4	6.9
5.6	0.12	na	0.82	7.1	0.7	1.39	3.97	4.93	39.8	1.3	36.3	60.5	7.4
8.1	0.53	na	-1.37	8.3	0.5	1.86	16.25	3.31	44.0	5.0	65.3	15.5	9.0
7.3	0.00	0.0	0.04	9.4	2.4	2.19	19.57	4.00	46.6	1.1	10.8	18.1	9.1
6.7	0.13	na	0.10	3.6	0.1	0.66	7.53	5.31	83.2	3.5	34.5	15.8	3.6
7.3	1.17	na	0.33	3.7	-0.7	-2.53	-25.52	2.73	152.5	2.6	55.5	56.2	5.6
7.4	1.39	4.7	0.00	6.6	0.2	1.58	9.78	3.56	57.0	3.8	43.5	16.4	8.5
4.0	1.55	8.1	0.02	3.7	0.1	0.53	4.41	3.67	77.5	1.2	16.8	29.0	6.6
8.3	0.17	na	0.00	2.7	2.5	1.02	6.97	3.41	62.4	1.6	15.0	17.3	6.5
2.7	3.21	na	0.12	7.9	2.3	1.95	14.07	4.59	60.7	2.0	19.4	18.6	8.7
4.8	1.79	7.4	0.21	4.2	2.2	0.98	9.06	3.11	60.8	2.0	8.9	14.0	6.5
7.8	0.45	na	0.00	5.0	1.4	2.54	25.68	3.17	67.9	2.8	26.4	15.4	6.5
4.4	1.60	7.7	-0.01	4.6	4.2	0.79	7.50	3.61	64.6	2.7	11.9	7.8	9.1
8.4	0.21	na	0.20	3.4	0.2	0.49	4.29	4.22	80.6	3.8	21.5	10.8	6.9
8.3	0.88	na	0.02	0.5	0.2	0.47	3.17	3.14	97.1	1.1	26.4	35.6	5.8
7.3	0.01	na	0.00	4.6	0.8	0.85	8.18	2.73	53.7	0.6	15.2	58.2	5.9
4.4	1.14	na	0.50	4.0	0.1	0.48	5.70	4.66	81.0	0.8	16.0	35.1	4.7

Name	City	State	Rating	2019 Rating	2018 Rating	Total Assets ($Mil)	One Year Asset Growth	Asset Mix (As a % of Total Assets) Comm-ercial Loans	Cons-umer Loans	Mort-gage Loans	Secur-ities	Capital-ization Index	Lever-age Ratio	Risk-Based Capital Ratio
First Carolina Bank	Rocky Mount	NC	**B**	B	C+	808.0	55.09	6.9	0.1	7.5	27.7	**10.0**	12.5	15.8
First Central Bank	Cambridge	NE	**C-**	C-	C	110.4	0.29	14.9	3.7	3.0	9.6	**8.9**	10.4	0.0
▼ First Central Bank McCook	McCook	NE	**D+**	C-	C-	121.2	-0.52	18.9	2.4	3.4	8.0	**9.4**	10.8	0.0
▼ First Central National Bank of Saint Paris	Saint Paris	OH	**B-**	B	B	96.8	1.08	3.1	2.2	13.5	15.5	**10.0**	17.7	26.0
First Central Savings Bank	Glen Cove	NY	**D+**	D+	D+	632.5	3.44	12.5	0.0	18.8	2.3	**5.7**	8.4	11.5
First Central State Bank	De Witt	IA	**A-**	A-	A-	576.0	2.47	10.1	2.0	11.9	21.1	**9.8**	11.9	0.0
First Century Bank	Tazewell	TN	**B+**	B+	B+	421.9	4.40	7.1	1.4	28.4	1.5	**7.9**	9.6	13.7
▲ First Century Bank, N.A.	Gainesville	GA	**B+**	B	B	409.3	164.95	0.7	5.5	1.9	25.9	**5.8**	7.8	29.1
▲ First Chatham Bank	Savannah	GA	**C**	C-	D-	377.2	4.81	7.0	0.6	8.0	6.9	**6.9**	8.9	12.9
First Choice Bank	Cerritos	CA	**B+**	B+	B+	1775.6	7.52	16.1	0.0	11.2	2.3	**9.8**	11.7	0.0
First Choice Bank	Pontotoc	MS	**A-**	A-	B+	325.9	3.35	8.2	5.8	23.4	24.6	**9.8**	12.8	0.0
First Citizens Bank	Luverne	AL	**A-**	A-	A-	255.4	2.74	8.2	5.1	13.5	29.1	**10.0**	14.0	21.1
First Citizens Bank	Mason City	IA	**A-**	A-	A-	1316.9	3.00	12.8	1.0	9.4	23.8	**10.0**	12.5	15.5
First Citizens Bank of Butte	Butte	MT	**B-**	B-	B-	71.3	5.76	9.8	5.1	19.5	13.9	**9.6**	10.9	0.0
First Citizens Community Bank	Mansfield	PA	**B**	B	B	1463.7	1.14	4.1	0.7	19.4	17.6	**7.4**	9.5	0.0
First Citizens National Bank	Dyersburg	TN	**B+**	B+	B+	1833.3	5.25	4.3	1.5	10.4	36.5	**8.4**	10.1	0.0
First Citizens National Bank of Upper Sand	Upper Sandusky	OH	**B-**	B-	B-	288.6	-0.91	6.1	1.1	18.3	19.4	**9.8**	14.5	0.0
First Citizens State Bank	Whitewater	WI	**A-**	A-	A-	323.2	4.63	5.3	0.8	21.7	23.8	**9.8**	19.3	0.0
First Citrus Bank	Tampa	FL	**B-**	B-	C+	436.7	10.47	7.4	0.1	8.1	0.0	**8.0**	9.8	0.0
First City Bank	Columbus	OH	**C+**	C+	C+	65.4	-0.15	2.1	0.1	21.6	2.1	**9.8**	11.5	0.0
First City Bank of Florida	Fort Walton Beach	FL	**E-**	E-	E-	138.3	-11.08	5.1	0.7	14.0	5.9	**0.0**	2.2	4.5
▲ First Colony Bank of Florida	Maitland	FL	**B+**	B	B-	222.8	1.05	13.9	0.3	1.0	13.7	**8.0**	10.1	13.3
▼ First Colorado National Bank	Paonia	CO	**B-**	B	C+	73.0	6.89	0.9	0.3	1.8	0.0	**10.0**	21.0	164.9
First Columbia Bank & Trust Co.	Bloomsburg	PA	**A-**	A-	B+	734.3	1.74	3.0	0.7	31.3	25.5	**9.8**	12.1	0.0
First Command Bank	Fort Worth	TX	**A-**	A-	B+	812.7	0.92	10.9	24.4	0.0	48.2	**5.6**	7.6	13.3
First Commerce Bank	Marysville	KS	**B+**	B+	B-	99.3	-2.90	10.3	5.1	30.7	6.8	**9.2**	10.7	0.0
▲ First Commerce Bank	Lakewood	NJ	**B-**	C+	C-	1011.3	3.34	5.4	0.0	22.5	9.8	**10.0**	14.4	19.2
First Commerce Bank	Lewisburg	TN	**B**	B	B	453.5	4.56	7.7	2.8	14.9	11.2	**7.0**	9.0	13.3
First Commercial Bank	Jackson	MS	**B**	B	B	410.5	3.15	20.0	1.3	8.7	4.9	**10.0**	13.1	15.2
First Commercial Bank (USA)	Alhambra	CA	**A-**	A-	B+	720.1	25.44	8.4	0.0	11.6	4.6	**10.0**	19.8	25.3
First Commercial Bank, N.A.	Seguin	TX	**B**	B	B	382.5	15.59	4.4	1.6	12.0	13.7	**7.4**	9.3	15.8
First Commonwealth Bank	Indiana	PA	**B+**	B+	B+	8492.0	6.76	13.2	8.8	13.2	15.3	**7.7**	9.5	13.7
First Community Bank	Batesville	AR	**B-**	B-	B-	1545.4	2.96	12.9	3.7	19.0	13.8	**6.2**	9.3	11.9
First Community Bank	Newell	IA	**B**	B	B-	100.3	1.33	5.6	2.3	5.6	12.5	**7.3**	9.4	0.0
First Community Bank	Harbor Springs	MI	**B+**	B+	B	325.1	5.78	11.5	0.6	8.9	7.8	**6.1**	9.4	11.9
First Community Bank	Lester Prairie	MN	**B-**	B-	B-	62.7	3.21	4.1	1.6	10.2	25.5	**8.9**	10.4	0.0
First Community Bank	Glasgow	MT	**B**	B	B-	302.0	4.03	4.6	1.4	8.8	21.7	**10.0**	11.3	17.0
First Community Bank	Beemer	NE	**B-**	B-	C+	146.1	-1.23	7.5	1.6	7.2	9.6	**9.2**	10.5	14.8
First Community Bank	Lexington	SC	**B+**	B+	B+	1185.2	8.06	3.7	0.9	9.6	24.4	**8.4**	9.9	14.3
First Community Bank	Corpus Christi	TX	**A-**	A-	B+	444.9	8.09	11.7	2.6	16.4	14.8	**10.0**	12.2	17.6
First Community Bank	San Benito	TX	**B**	B	B	505.1	14.33	11.7	1.0	8.9	21.5	**6.7**	8.7	13.3
First Community Bank	Bluefield	VA	**B**	B	B	2738.3	22.27	4.5	4.1	29.0	3.9	**8.7**	10.1	14.0
First Community Bank	Milton	WI	**A-**	A-	B+	110.7	7.78	4.0	1.1	15.9	28.0	**6.2**	9.7	11.9
First Community Bank and Trust	Beecher	IL	**A-**	A-	B+	147.8	3.67	11.8	2.0	7.8	21.8	**10.0**	12.6	20.1
First Community Bank of Central Alabama	Wetumpka	AL	**B+**	B+	B+	399.5	5.42	7.7	5.2	16.1	24.2	**5.7**	8.0	11.5
First Community Bank of Cullman	Cullman	AL	**C+**	C+	C	132.7	9.41	4.1	2.3	35.1	2.9	**6.2**	8.2	12.7
▲ First Community Bank of East Tennessee	Rogersville	TN	**B+**	B	B-	182.1	-2.05	6.0	2.1	20.2	10.1	**9.8**	13.1	0.0
First Community Bank of Hillsboro	Hillsboro	IL	**B**	B	C+	101.2	-4.58	8.9	3.3	17.6	25.8	**8.6**	10.2	0.0
First Community Bank of Moultrie County	Sullivan	IL	**B**	B	C+	89.9	3.94	4.3	5.3	25.8	11.5	**8.4**	10.1	0.0
First Community Bank of Tennessee	Shelbyville	TN	**B+**	B+	B+	632.1	25.79	4.3	0.9	40.2	10.7	**8.6**	12.0	13.8
First Community Bank of the Heartland, Inc	Clinton	KY	**B-**	B-	C+	267.8	16.53	4.0	3.3	13.3	19.4	**5.5**	7.8	11.4
First Community Bank of the Ozarks	Branson	MO	**B+**	B+	B+	113.7	5.72	3.7	1.8	24.5	13.0	**9.2**	10.6	0.0
First Community Bank, Xenia-Flora	Xenia	IL	**B**	B	B-	43.3	2.22	3.7	5.9	22.7	26.3	**9.8**	12.0	0.0
First Community National Bank	Cuba	MO	**C-**	C-	D-	130.1	-2.19	2.6	1.7	20.8	16.4	**7.8**	9.5	15.8
First Community Trust, N.A.	Dubuque	IA	**U**	U	U	12.0	81.09	0.0	0.0	0.0	40.8	**9.8**	84.8	0.0
▼ First County Bank	Stamford	CT	**C**	C+	C+	1771.2	4.35	4.0	1.0	49.0	12.9	**7.6**	9.4	15.4
First Credit Bank	Los Angeles	CA	**B-**	B-	C	427.4	-2.12	1.3	0.0	13.6	4.8	**10.0**	44.6	53.6
First Dakota National Bank	Yankton	SD	**B**	B	B	1764.9	5.57	9.4	1.9	6.9	11.6	**6.6**	10.1	12.2
First Eagle Bank	Chicago	IL	**A**	A	A	544.5	7.55	1.9	0.0	19.2	26.4	**9.8**	17.3	0.0
First Electronic Bank	Salt Lake City	UT	**A-**	A-	B	39.4	2.63	11.0	7.1	0.0	0.1	**10.0**	31.1	172.3

Asset Quality Index	Adjusted Non-Performing Loans as a % of Total Loans	Adjusted Non-Performing Loans as a % of Capital	Net Charge-Offs Avg Loans	Profitability Index	Net Income ($Mil)	Return on Assets (R.O.A.)	Return on Equity (R.O.E.)	Net Interest Spread	Overhead Efficiency Ratio	Liquidity Index	Liquidity Ratio	Hot Money Ratio	Stability Index
7.3	0.00	0.0	0.00	**4.5**	2.0	1.09	8.60	2.99	49.3	**1.3**	31.3	33.8	**7.3**
0.0	7.96	na	0.13	**5.9**	0.3	1.04	10.00	3.68	67.0	**0.8**	16.5	32.0	**5.4**
0.0	20.06	na	-0.22	**7.3**	0.4	1.34	12.49	3.90	56.6	**0.5**	13.9	47.1	**5.5**
9.0	0.11	0.3	0.00	**3.3**	0.1	0.52	2.93	2.84	79.6	**4.7**	48.9	13.0	**7.7**
3.0	2.72	12.6	0.17	**1.8**	0.7	0.44	4.83	3.17	79.3	**0.7**	12.2	37.8	**4.8**
6.5	0.77	na	0.01	**5.7**	1.5	1.08	8.68	3.19	60.1	**3.1**	25.8	14.1	**8.0**
8.1	0.29	1.8	0.02	**8.1**	2.0	1.90	20.28	4.11	46.8	**2.3**	12.2	13.5	**6.5**
9.6	0.36	na	5.17	**8.9**	4.6	3.28	42.27	9.22	25.6	**6.5**	76.8	9.8	**5.8**
4.4	1.92	na	0.17	**3.0**	0.2	0.23	2.21	4.19	89.9	**3.8**	22.7	10.5	**4.6**
4.7	0.66	na	0.00	**7.6**	4.8	1.11	7.07	4.79	54.3	**2.3**	14.3	8.5	**10.0**
7.7	0.38	na	0.05	**5.7**	0.9	1.14	8.96	3.87	62.4	**1.7**	23.0	23.3	**7.5**
6.5	1.15	6.2	0.03	**7.3**	1.0	1.63	11.42	4.37	54.9	**1.9**	23.1	21.6	**8.5**
8.0	0.50	na	0.09	**6.6**	4.9	1.54	11.99	3.40	53.9	**2.5**	14.4	16.5	**10.0**
6.9	2.28	na	0.00	**4.1**	0.2	1.02	9.11	3.95	75.4	**4.8**	32.3	7.9	**6.7**
5.0	1.71	7.8	0.00	**6.6**	5.0	1.38	12.79	3.85	57.6	**3.3**	8.1	11.4	**9.6**
8.4	0.27	na	0.05	**5.1**	5.4	1.22	9.98	3.44	66.5	**2.3**	25.4	24.0	**9.8**
7.1	0.50	na	-0.03	**3.8**	0.5	0.66	4.55	4.00	80.1	**4.1**	19.8	8.9	**7.4**
9.3	0.00	na	0.04	**5.8**	1.0	1.17	6.09	3.37	60.4	**3.9**	41.1	15.8	**8.8**
4.9	0.92	na	0.01	**5.0**	0.9	0.86	8.85	3.78	69.6	**2.8**	21.0	11.8	**5.6**
7.5	0.00	0.0	0.00	**3.1**	0.1	0.62	5.32	3.67	86.5	**1.8**	13.1	20.1	**6.5**
0.3	11.63	na	-0.20	**0.0**	-0.4	-1.06	-43.90	3.89	130.3	**5.1**	24.2	2.9	**0.7**
6.7	0.09	na	-0.05	**8.8**	1.0	1.84	18.54	3.98	47.8	**2.2**	30.0	22.3	**7.8**
9.5	0.00	na	-0.73	**2.2**	-0.4	-1.90	-8.02	1.39	216.8	**6.9**	114.0	10.9	**8.7**
6.3	0.97	na	-0.02	**5.5**	2.4	1.28	9.80	3.24	60.6	**3.5**	13.1	11.2	**8.7**
7.2	0.26	0.9	0.20	**8.5**	3.5	1.77	23.96	3.42	62.8	**7.1**	56.9	1.8	**6.1**
5.5	0.81	na	0.00	**6.8**	0.4	1.56	12.80	3.82	60.9	**2.8**	22.4	16.0	**8.0**
4.9	1.17	na	-0.03	**5.6**	2.4	0.95	6.64	3.53	61.9	**1.3**	21.9	33.9	**9.7**
8.2	0.08	na	0.01	**6.8**	1.4	1.27	14.45	3.62	53.0	**0.9**	16.6	33.9	**6.4**
7.1	0.09	na	-0.10	**4.3**	0.9	0.89	6.66	3.53	75.7	**0.7**	11.4	26.3	**7.8**
7.2	0.00	na	0.00	**7.4**	2.1	1.20	6.13	2.98	51.7	**0.7**	14.3	48.7	**8.7**
6.5	0.39	na	-0.59	**5.8**	1.4	1.50	15.38	4.11	67.6	**6.0**	40.9	3.6	**6.2**
5.1	0.92	4.8	0.23	**5.0**	6.3	0.30	2.32	3.67	56.1	**4.4**	5.6	5.3	**10.0**
5.5	1.49	na	0.31	**5.0**	3.7	0.96	10.37	3.66	69.0	**0.9**	14.6	34.9	**7.4**
7.2	0.00	na	0.00	**4.5**	0.3	1.06	8.70	3.41	67.4	**3.6**	30.7	14.0	**7.6**
7.3	0.04	na	0.12	**6.1**	1.1	1.37	14.08	4.67	69.1	**4.2**	2.5	5.8	**7.2**
8.9	0.00	na	0.00	**4.3**	0.2	0.97	8.71	3.82	74.3	**4.2**	37.5	12.9	**5.9**
5.0	2.66	na	0.01	**4.0**	0.5	0.68	5.74	3.66	80.0	**3.5**	24.4	8.4	**7.2**
6.7	0.54	na	0.00	**4.1**	0.3	0.68	6.08	3.98	78.0	**0.9**	18.2	29.5	**7.1**
6.9	0.44	2.2	0.00	**4.4**	2.0	0.69	6.01	3.61	71.2	**4.2**	17.0	8.5	**9.2**
7.7	0.62	3.1	0.31	**5.7**	1.4	1.30	10.57	5.52	76.3	**3.2**	25.2	14.3	**7.7**
7.8	0.12	na	0.04	**7.0**	2.0	1.57	18.07	4.44	64.5	**2.5**	19.4	17.1	**6.0**
4.5	1.41	na	0.15	**7.8**	8.1	1.19	8.16	4.69	61.6	**4.2**	13.7	7.8	**10.0**
8.8	0.08	na	0.02	**6.7**	0.5	1.60	16.70	3.14	59.1	**3.5**	38.0	16.7	**7.7**
5.8	1.71	na	-0.67	**7.9**	0.7	1.93	14.76	4.51	51.2	**5.3**	29.3	3.5	**7.1**
6.7	0.51	2.7	0.13	**9.7**	2.4	2.43	30.60	3.96	48.3	**2.7**	27.3	17.1	**7.0**
5.9	0.55	4.6	0.05	**3.5**	0.2	0.67	8.28	3.23	68.6	**0.7**	14.3	44.8	**4.8**
6.4	0.98	na	-2.49	**6.3**	0.9	2.05	15.35	4.32	77.6	**4.2**	22.5	8.1	**7.4**
8.1	0.48	na	0.00	**5.3**	0.4	1.44	14.16	3.28	57.7	**4.1**	15.5	7.8	**6.6**
7.5	0.36	na	0.04	**4.5**	0.2	1.00	9.51	3.57	71.6	**5.4**	37.5	6.6	**6.6**
8.3	0.15	0.8	0.02	**6.7**	3.6	2.56	21.42	3.04	75.0	**0.5**	8.6	40.8	**8.4**
5.9	1.14	na	0.00	**4.0**	0.7	1.04	10.66	4.09	79.5	**1.4**	13.3	20.8	**5.9**
5.2	1.91	na	0.00	**3.9**	0.2	0.72	6.81	3.36	81.4	**2.3**	17.9	18.0	**7.0**
7.7	0.34	na	0.51	**6.4**	0.2	1.62	13.22	3.66	56.5	**5.2**	41.1	9.1	**7.8**
5.5	2.31	na	-0.11	**1.1**	0.1	0.27	2.79	3.79	107.8	**4.6**	41.0	12.3	**3.6**
10.0	na	na	na	**9.5**	0.2	7.17	8.07	1.18	77.1	**4.0**	na	0.0	**6.1**
5.8	1.67	10.0	0.10	**2.4**	1.1	0.26	2.91	2.88	78.9	**1.4**	14.5	20.9	**6.8**
3.6	5.06	na	2.20	**10.0**	2.7	2.41	5.40	5.74	21.2	**2.1**	45.8	46.6	**9.4**
5.2	0.96	8.7	0.02	**4.9**	4.3	0.98	9.28	4.15	64.0	**3.8**	8.4	9.7	**8.6**
8.9	0.00	na	-0.01	**9.6**	3.0	2.18	12.28	3.57	45.9	**1.5**	22.9	23.8	**10.0**
8.4	0.00	na	0.00	**8.9**	0.1	0.89	2.87	9.91	92.6	**4.8**	133.0	17.5	**8.0**

Name	City	State	Rating	2019 Rating	2018 Rating	Total Assets ($Mil)	One Year Asset Growth	Asset Mix (As a % of Total Assets)				Capital-ization Index	Lever-age Ratio	Risk-Based Capital Ratio
								Comm-ercial Loans	Cons-umer Loans	Mort-gage Loans	Secur-ities			
First Enterprise Bank	Oklahoma City	OK	B-	B-	C-	168.6	4.83	11.6	0.6	16.1	0.0	9.8	12.7	0.0
First Exchange Bank	White Hall	WV	C-	C-	C-	300.3	8.13	8.4	3.8	41.4	7.1	7.3	9.3	0.0
▲ First FarmBank	Greeley	CO	B-	C+	C-	262.7	7.48	7.6	0.3	9.8	19.0	6.8	8.8	12.9
First Farmers & Merchants Bank	Cannon Falls	MN	B+	B+	A-	335.0	7.08	10.8	2.3	9.1	11.4	10.0	13.7	17.5
First Farmers & Merchants National Bank	Fairmont	MN	B	B	B+	110.3	2.96	18.1	3.5	17.2	7.5	10.0	14.2	16.2
First Farmers & Merchants National Bank	Luverne	MN	B	B	B+	190.3	6.12	13.4	1.5	2.5	3.7	10.0	16.0	17.5
First Farmers & Merchants State Bank	Brownsdale	MN	B	B	B+	78.4	4.89	7.5	0.4	4.2	15.9	10.0	17.9	23.1
First Farmers & Merchants State Bank	Grand Meadow	MN	B	B	B+	70.8	3.69	6.9	0.3	4.6	7.1	8.8	10.7	14.0
First Farmers and Commercial Bank	Pikeville	TN	B-	B-	C+	147.6	23.27	9.1	3.4	16.0	14.1	9.2	10.5	14.5
First Farmers and Merchants Bank	Columbia	TN	B+	B+	B	1435.9	6.64	9.2	0.9	22.1	23.5	8.0	9.7	14.8
First Farmers Bank & Trust Co.	Converse	IN	B-	B-	B-	1974.7	9.45	14.9	0.6	4.3	19.6	8.4	10.2	13.7
First Farmers National Bank of Waurika	Waurika	OK	B	B	B	46.2	-1.55	1.5	3.6	0.7	44.5	10.0	20.2	40.4
First Farmers State Bank	Minier	IL	A-	A-	A-	186.3	8.25	4.4	0.3	7.1	17.8	10.0	12.0	21.8
First Federal Bank	Lake City	FL	A-	A-	A-	2459.3	28.86	2.0	2.7	23.6	29.9	9.6	10.7	15.9
First Federal Bank	Dunn	NC	C+	C+	C	187.1	0.69	6.6	0.5	35.3	15.9	10.0	11.5	19.3
First Federal Bank	Dickson	TN	A-	A-	A-	760.1	6.95	2.8	2.1	20.3	31.9	9.8	11.2	0.0
First Federal Bank & Trust	Sheridan	WY	B	B	C+	342.5	1.77	9.0	1.1	25.7	22.7	10.0	15.9	19.3
▼ First Federal Bank Littlefield, Texas	Littlefield	TX	B-	B	B	49.8	4.52	10.6	10.3	17.0	0.0	9.8	19.6	0.0
First Federal Bank Of Kansas City	Kansas City	MO	D+	D+	C-	774.0	-6.41	0.0	2.8	66.2	8.9	9.8	15.0	0.0
First Federal Bank of Louisiana	Lake Charles	LA	C+	C+	C+	936.8	5.41	2.8	1.8	28.0	16.0	10.0	12.4	21.5
First Federal Bank of Ohio	Galion	OH	C+	C+	C	235.7	-1.81	0.6	1.1	28.3	27.0	10.0	15.2	32.6
▼ First Federal Bank of the Midwest	Defiance	OH	B-	B	B	6519.3	104.45	12.8	2.0	21.4	8.2	6.2	11.3	11.9
First Federal Bank of Wisconsin	Waukesha	WI	B-	B-	C+	278.0	7.09	5.2	0.2	20.5	19.5	10.0	26.1	36.0
First Federal Bank, A FSB	Tuscaloosa	AL	C	C	C-	145.9	18.47	0.1	0.3	72.3	0.6	9.9	10.9	16.8
First Federal Community Bank of Bucyrus	Bucyrus	OH	C+	C+	C+	194.5	19.16	5.6	4.6	46.9	6.7	6.6	8.6	13.2
First Federal Community Bank, N.A.	Dover	OH	B	B	B	455.7	11.98	9.1	2.5	26.9	3.7	7.0	9.0	13.1
First Federal Community Bank, SSB	Paris	TX	B	B	B	450.6	2.07	10.0	2.6	40.8	3.1	10.0	11.8	17.2
▼ First Federal S&L Assn.	Hazard	KY	C	C+	C	83.8	4.02	0.0	1.3	76.0	0.2	9.8	21.9	0.0
First Federal S&L Assn.	Morehead	KY	C+	C+	C+	33.2	-4.23	2.3	1.6	56.0	0.0	10.0	29.8	52.6
▼ First Federal S&L Assn.	Aberdeen	MS	C	C+	B-	44.0	6.94	0.0	1.8	61.4	11.9	9.8	16.7	0.0
First Federal S&L Assn. of Bath	Bath	ME	B	B	B	137.8	2.58	0.9	1.3	71.0	2.3	10.0	17.3	31.3
First Federal S&L Assn. of Centerburg	Centerburg	OH	C+	C+	C+	22.3	-7.24	0.0	0.3	63.7	2.6	9.8	21.7	0.0
First Federal S&L Assn. of Central Illinois,	Shelbyville	IL	B+	B+	B+	134.2	6.30	7.3	5.0	30.2	16.2	10.0	11.3	16.3
First Federal S&L Assn. of Delta	Delta	OH	C+	C+	C-	164.6	1.59	0.4	0.3	48.7	17.5	10.0	12.9	33.2
First Federal S&L Assn. of Greene County	Waynesburg	PA	B-	B-	C+	959.6	2.11	0.0	0.4	63.0	17.3	10.0	14.4	32.6
First Federal S&L Assn. of Greensburg	Greensburg	IN	C+	C+	C	146.0	3.14	0.7	2.3	46.0	20.1	9.4	10.6	22.3
First Federal S&L Assn. of Lakewood	Lakewood	OH	C-	C-	C-	2049.1	4.17	2.0	3.7	60.8	4.2	9.4	10.8	0.0
▼ First Federal S&L Assn. of Lorain	Lorain	OH	C-	C	C	444.1	-0.08	0.0	0.2	55.0	9.4	10.0	15.1	33.4
First Federal S&L Assn. of McMinnville	McMinnville	OR	B	B	B	474.0	8.60	0.6	0.2	40.0	26.4	10.0	14.8	30.0
First Federal S&L Assn. of Newark	Newark	OH	C	C	C	220.0	-1.09	0.0	0.3	48.7	7.3	10.0	16.1	26.6
First Federal S&L Assn. of Pascagoula-Mo	Pascagoula	MS	C	C	C	323.9	4.42	0.0	0.3	76.8	8.9	7.6	9.4	20.2
First Federal S&L Assn. of Port Angeles	Port Angeles	WA	B-	B-	C+	1384.4	9.68	1.0	8.6	24.0	22.1	10.0	11.8	18.1
First Federal S&L Assn. of Ravenswood	Ravenswood	WV	D+	D+	D	24.1	1.13	0.0	0.5	74.3	0.1	5.6	7.6	16.0
First Federal S&L Assn. of San Rafael	San Rafael	CA	B-	B-	B-	204.8	3.19	0.0	0.0	1.3	0.0	10.0	20.3	25.9
▼ First Federal S&L Assn. of Valdosta	Valdosta	GA	C+	B-	C+	194.9	5.68	0.0	2.5	68.6	1.3	10.0	15.2	25.5
First Federal S&L Assn. of Van Wert	Van Wert	OH	C+	C+	C+	115.6	4.40	0.0	0.2	44.7	31.6	9.8	20.4	0.0
▼ First Federal S&L Bank	Olathe	KS	B-	B	B	96.9	2.27	0.4	0.0	75.0	0.0	10.0	11.7	23.8
▼ First Federal Savings Bank	Ottawa	IL	C-	C	C	378.6	2.07	0.3	0.9	52.2	4.8	9.8	11.4	0.0
First Federal Savings Bank	Evansville	IN	C	C	C	426.4	-2.36	14.9	0.8	23.0	13.7	6.6	8.7	12.8
First Federal Savings Bank	Huntington	IN	B-	B-	B	357.8	4.09	15.0	3.3	13.2	18.0	10.0	11.4	16.2
▲ First Federal Savings Bank	Rochester	IN	B	B-	C	443.6	3.23	1.2	0.1	66.9	0.0	9.2	10.5	18.8
First Federal Savings Bank of Angola	Angola	IN	B	B	B	128.5	0.00	0.4	3.4	63.9	0.0	9.8	21.6	0.0
First Federal Savings Bank of Kentucky	Frankfort	KY	C	C	C	247.6	3.56	0.5	0.4	62.4	0.4	9.8	12.7	0.0
First Federal Savings of Middletown	Middletown	NY	C+	C+	C-	152.0	2.60	0.0	0.0	0.5	27.3	10.0	36.5	61.0
First Fidelity Bank	Fort Payne	AL	C+	C+	C+	102.1	1.79	8.5	2.3	25.5	35.3	8.0	9.6	20.0
First Fidelity Bank	Oklahoma City	OK	B	B	B	1868.1	12.46	8.0	14.1	6.8	21.3	7.0	9.2	0.0
First Fidelity Bank	Burke	SD	B+	B+	B	382.8	6.18	4.2	2.4	1.6	30.3	8.1	9.8	14.1
First Financial Bank	Bessemer	AL	C+	C+	B-	175.9	4.20	6.8	1.6	11.4	29.8	7.4	9.3	15.4
First Financial Bank	El Dorado	AR	B+	B+	B+	1429.3	34.76	7.6	1.8	5.3	4.5	8.6	10.2	0.0
First Financial Bank	Cincinnati	OH	B+	B+	B+	14986.6	7.07	15.0	0.6	9.2	20.4	7.4	9.8	12.8

Asset Quality Index	Adjusted Non-Performing Loans as a % of Total Loans	Adjusted Non-Performing Loans as a % of Capital	Net Charge-Offs / Avg Loans	Profitability Index	Net Income ($Mil)	Return on Assets (R.O.A.)	Return on Equity (R.O.E.)	Net Interest Spread	Overhead Efficiency Ratio	Liquidity Index	Liquidity Ratio	Hot Money Ratio	Stability Index
4.0	0.63	na	0.00	**8.6**	0.8	1.86	14.65	5.33	67.3	**0.8**	19.0	34.4	**9.3**
2.5	3.15	19.4	0.17	**4.3**	0.6	0.78	8.22	4.00	65.9	**1.6**	9.9	21.5	**7.1**
7.2	0.00	na	0.15	**4.4**	0.5	0.75	8.50	3.85	73.0	**1.4**	15.4	26.2	**5.2**
4.3	3.18	15.0	0.14	**7.3**	1.3	1.51	10.50	4.38	55.6	**4.3**	21.5	7.3	**8.2**
4.1	3.86	16.7	0.28	**3.9**	0.1	0.45	3.16	3.96	68.9	**0.9**	6.0	30.5	**7.4**
3.1	3.31	14.8	0.07	**7.9**	0.8	1.59	9.96	4.33	57.3	**1.9**	14.0	19.5	**8.2**
5.5	2.37	8.3	0.04	**4.5**	0.1	0.51	2.80	4.01	72.8	**4.6**	26.8	6.6	**7.8**
0.0	16.58	82.3	0.75	**3.9**	0.0	0.19	1.72	3.63	75.5	**2.8**	17.8	15.3	**6.6**
5.1	1.65	na	0.05	**4.3**	0.3	0.85	8.17	3.88	64.4	**0.8**	15.1	34.8	**4.9**
8.7	0.21	1.0	0.00	**4.4**	3.3	0.94	9.00	3.40	71.5	**3.8**	12.9	7.1	**8.8**
3.1	3.71	19.3	-0.01	**7.3**	6.7	1.41	13.02	3.80	55.8	**3.2**	17.5	10.4	**9.8**
8.1	0.00	na	-0.10	**6.0**	0.2	1.73	8.30	4.16	55.2	**1.8**	24.3	22.9	**7.7**
7.4	0.04	0.3	-0.01	**5.8**	0.6	1.35	11.34	3.35	61.5	**2.0**	16.8	19.1	**8.3**
5.6	0.96	4.0	0.02	**6.5**	7.4	1.34	11.18	3.69	66.3	**2.1**	21.9	10.3	**10.0**
6.1	1.60	na	0.00	**2.8**	0.3	0.52	4.69	3.69	96.0	**1.8**	20.9	22.0	**6.4**
7.1	0.86	na	0.01	**6.7**	2.7	1.50	11.80	3.56	55.6	**3.7**	35.1	14.8	**9.0**
5.3	2.00	na	-0.16	**3.5**	0.5	0.62	3.87	3.38	83.3	**3.4**	20.3	12.5	**7.6**
6.4	0.00	4.4	0.36	**3.3**	0.0	0.12	0.60	4.33	80.2	**1.0**	25.3	38.2	**6.5**
8.5	0.30	na	0.04	**1.6**	1.3	0.67	5.02	2.47	75.6	**1.3**	16.8	28.7	**6.8**
8.5	0.85	na	0.00	**2.9**	1.1	0.48	3.80	2.97	85.0	**3.2**	21.2	13.6	**7.4**
9.4	1.28	na	0.82	**2.5**	0.2	0.32	2.17	2.91	97.0	**6.2**	58.6	8.3	**7.2**
5.3	0.77	3.6	-0.07	**3.7**	-24.9	-1.87	-15.13	3.63	76.3	**3.3**	6.2	11.7	**10.0**
8.5	0.95	na	-0.01	**3.9**	0.5	0.69	3.03	3.57	72.4	**2.9**	33.7	18.6	**7.5**
6.7	1.59	na	-0.01	**6.1**	1.0	3.18	28.69	3.12	73.8	**0.5**	5.7	54.0	**5.2**
5.4	2.17	na	0.04	**3.9**	0.3	0.66	7.73	3.83	81.3	**1.7**	12.9	21.2	**4.5**
6.9	0.38	2.7	0.04	**7.3**	1.6	1.43	15.81	3.66	54.4	**2.6**	14.3	14.4	**6.5**
6.2	0.78	na	0.01	**4.0**	0.7	0.64	5.49	3.66	75.9	**1.2**	10.7	28.0	**6.7**
3.5	3.08	na	0.01	**3.2**	0.1	0.60	2.73	3.03	74.1	**1.0**	5.5	28.5	**5.9**
5.7	3.37	na	0.00	**3.2**	0.0	0.53	1.77	3.60	82.1	**1.6**	22.6	25.5	**6.5**
9.3	0.00	na	0.00	**2.7**	0.0	0.34	2.03	1.68	82.4	**1.7**	37.0	49.4	**6.9**
5.3	4.73	na	-0.02	**4.8**	0.3	0.82	4.91	4.72	75.9	**3.4**	15.5	12.2	**8.1**
9.9	0.00	na	0.00	**3.6**	0.0	0.53	2.47	3.51	79.2	**3.0**	24.5	14.7	**7.4**
6.1	0.96	na	0.21	**4.5**	0.3	0.81	6.81	3.75	73.1	**1.8**	18.9	21.6	**6.3**
9.7	0.37	na	0.00	**2.0**	0.1	0.16	1.23	3.24	94.8	**6.3**	46.5	3.3	**6.7**
9.8	0.54	na	0.02	**3.0**	0.8	0.35	2.41	2.39	80.0	**2.3**	35.4	25.4	**8.1**
6.0	1.08	na	0.00	**2.7**	0.1	0.35	3.30	3.14	85.5	**5.9**	35.0	2.0	**6.3**
8.5	0.39	na	0.01	**2.8**	4.4	0.92	8.47	2.33	70.0	**2.3**	13.2	14.1	**7.1**
5.7	5.68	na	-0.10	**1.2**	0.3	0.28	1.91	2.55	110.7	**3.3**	35.0	16.8	**7.2**
9.7	0.50	na	0.00	**4.1**	0.9	0.77	5.19	3.30	72.6	**5.3**	45.1	10.0	**8.0**
7.5	2.34	na	0.00	**2.5**	0.3	0.45	2.78	3.34	78.4	**1.3**	15.7	28.2	**7.3**
7.2	0.78	na	0.22	**2.4**	0.3	0.35	3.80	2.88	83.5	**0.7**	16.9	52.4	**4.7**
8.2	0.46	na	0.03	**2.5**	1.0	0.30	2.66	3.12	83.2	**1.7**	24.8	22.5	**8.2**
9.7	0.00	na	0.00	**3.2**	0.0	0.53	6.23	2.95	76.7	**0.7**	13.0	35.9	**3.0**
7.1	0.00	na	0.00	**2.7**	0.1	0.27	1.35	3.31	88.6	**0.6**	4.5	36.1	**7.6**
5.2	3.31	na	-0.02	**2.5**	0.2	0.35	2.28	3.98	87.0	**1.7**	9.8	19.8	**7.2**
10.0	0.00	na	0.00	**3.4**	0.2	0.79	3.83	3.33	72.6	**4.7**	43.8	12.4	**7.8**
2.9	5.25	na	-0.01	**9.8**	0.6	2.34	20.13	3.71	34.9	**0.5**	21.8	42.0	**9.1**
7.3	2.04	na	-0.01	**1.7**	0.0	0.04	0.39	2.24	99.1	**2.7**	35.9	20.6	**6.4**
6.0	0.53	3.1	-0.02	**2.5**	0.3	0.25	2.48	3.05	93.1	**2.4**	18.4	9.8	**5.4**
3.9	2.95	na	-0.05	**5.9**	1.1	1.21	10.29	3.45	60.2	**1.1**	21.3	18.7	**8.0**
4.7	4.99	na	0.02	**4.7**	1.4	1.23	11.90	3.70	74.5	**1.5**	11.1	23.9	**6.6**
9.0	0.15	na	0.01	**4.1**	0.3	0.97	4.50	3.26	62.9	**4.1**	36.1	13.0	**7.6**
2.9	1.84	na	0.00	**2.2**	0.2	0.28	1.57	3.02	88.1	**0.8**	8.7	33.6	**6.3**
9.8	0.00	na	0.00	**2.7**	0.1	0.38	1.03	3.08	75.5	**5.3**	84.6	16.5	**7.4**
6.2	0.94	na	0.00	**3.3**	0.2	0.56	5.98	3.06	77.5	**3.7**	48.6	18.7	**5.5**
6.0	0.97	4.1	-0.10	**4.9**	5.7	1.23	12.78	3.37	66.0	**5.1**	21.5	3.4	**8.9**
6.2	0.08	na	0.03	**7.7**	1.5	1.55	16.12	4.08	60.1	**4.2**	25.3	8.5	**7.3**
6.8	0.85	na	0.19	**3.6**	0.6	1.28	15.23	3.81	78.4	**5.3**	30.9	4.1	**3.4**
4.8	4.11	na	0.29	**8.5**	5.8	1.65	13.94	3.99	66.6	**1.1**	19.9	29.0	**10.0**
5.6	0.75	2.5	-0.04	**6.1**	32.9	0.92	5.90	3.84	57.8	**2.8**	17.0	6.6	**9.9**

Name	City	State	Rating	2019 Rating	2018 Rating	Total Assets ($Mil)	One Year Asset Growth	Asset Mix (As a % of Total Assets): Commercial Loans	Consumer Loans	Mortgage Loans	Securities	Capitalization Index	Leverage Ratio	Risk-Based Capital Ratio
First Financial Bank in Winnebago	Winnebago	MN	**B**	B	B	50.1	7.48	14.4	2.3	6.8	18.1	**10.0**	14.9	18.4
First Financial Bank, N.A.	Terre Haute	IN	**A-**	A-	A-	3946.8	34.35	15.5	7.5	10.9	23.5	**10.0**	12.1	16.5
First Financial Bank, N.A.	Abilene	TX	**A**	A	A	9664.7	22.09	7.1	4.4	12.9	42.1	**10.0**	11.1	18.4
▼ First Financial Northwest Bank	Renton	WA	**B**	B+	A-	1331.0	3.44	1.4	1.8	27.0	10.1	**8.9**	10.3	14.7
First Financial Trust & Asset Mgmt Co.	Abilene	TX	**U**	U	U	34.3	30.19	0.0	0.0	0.0	79.8	**10.0**	101.	335.4
First Financial Trust, N.A.	Wellesley	MA	**U**	U	U	10.3	7.44	0.0	0.0	0.0	23.3	**9.8**	97.6	0.0
First Florida Integrity Bank	Naples	FL	**B**	B	B-	1646.6	10.77	9.8	0.3	9.8	16.6	**6.6**	8.8	12.2
First Foundation Bank	Irvine	CA	**B-**	B-	B-	6498.7	8.62	7.6	0.2	13.0	14.8	**5.1**	8.4	11.1
First Freedom Bank	Lebanon	TN	**B-**	B-	C+	505.3	5.45	17.6	3.4	10.7	0.0	**8.5**	10.1	0.0
▼ First FSB of Champaign-Urbana	Champaign	IL	**C+**	B-	C+	178.8	2.83	5.4	1.3	23.2	0.1	**8.4**	10.1	0.0
▼ First FSB of Lincolnton	Lincolnton	NC	**B+**	A-	B+	394.5	-0.44	0.5	0.6	60.6	5.4	**10.0**	16.8	32.0
▲ First FSB of Mascoutah	Mascoutah	IL	**C+**	C	C	115.7	8.79	3.3	1.1	42.5	29.0	**10.0**	12.6	23.5
First FSB of Twin Falls	Twin Falls	ID	**A-**	A-	B+	734.5	10.29	5.7	5.1	32.7	3.9	**10.0**	12.1	16.3
First FSB of Washington	Washington	IN	**C-**	C-	C-	77.4	2.37	5.6	2.2	51.6	3.5	**10.0**	11.9	22.2
▲ First General Bank	Rowland Heights	CA	**A**	A-	B+	977.9	2.46	5.5	0.0	3.3	0.7	**9.8**	15.1	0.0
First Guaranty Bank	Hammond	LA	**B**	B	B	2247.9	18.17	13.3	1.4	12.6	19.3	**6.3**	9.7	11.9
First Harrison Bank	Corydon	IN	**B+**	B+	B-	827.0	2.13	5.4	6.9	13.5	30.6	**8.9**	10.5	0.0
First Hawaiian Bank	Honolulu	HI	**B+**	B+	B	20756.2	1.54	12.9	7.1	17.2	19.6	**6.5**	8.5	12.8
First Heritage Bank	Shenandoah	IA	**B-**	B-	B-	42.9	11.69	13.1	4.2	20.7	17.4	**9.8**	11.2	0.0
▲ First Heritage Bank	Centralia	KS	**B+**	B	B	177.4	2.49	21.8	0.9	7.5	26.9	**7.5**	9.5	0.0
▼ First Home Bank	Saint Petersburg	FL	**B-**	B+	A-	562.5	37.46	33.9	0.2	23.6	0.0	**8.0**	9.6	16.3
First Hope Bank, A National Banking Assn.	Hope	NJ	**C**	C	C	531.7	6.03	5.2	0.3	12.1	21.3	**7.6**	9.4	13.7
First Horizon Bank	Memphis	TN	**B-**	B-	B-	47026.2	14.93	18.9	0.7	10.8	9.6	**3.7**	9.0	10.4
First IC Bank	Doraville	GA	**B+**	B+	A	684.1	21.50	7.2	0.0	8.2	7.1	**10.0**	11.2	15.2
First Independence Bank	Detroit	MI	**B-**	B-	B-	265.4	-2.44	13.0	0.0	17.8	2.5	**6.8**	9.1	0.0
First Independent Bank	Russell	MN	**C**	C	C	286.7	5.56	7.2	3.0	6.2	26.9	**10.0**	11.6	15.8
First Independent Bank	Aurora	MO	**B**	B	B	94.7	0.95	8.0	3.9	23.0	30.1	**9.8**	12.3	0.0
First International Bank & Trust	Watford City	ND	**B**	B	B	3594.6	21.49	13.6	2.8	10.0	12.2	**6.3**	8.6	12.0
First Internet Bank of Indiana	Fishers	IN	**B-**	B-	B-	4165.5	13.56	10.3	7.3	5.7	16.3	**6.5**	8.5	12.5
First Interstate Bank	Billings	MT	**B+**	B+	B-	14351.9	6.80	8.8	7.1	8.6	21.4	**7.1**	9.1	12.6
First Iowa State Bank	Albia	IA	**B+**	B+	B+	142.4	1.23	6.5	1.4	12.3	23.3	**9.8**	13.1	0.0
▼ First Iowa State Bank	Keosauqua	IA	**B**	B+	B+	131.6	-1.50	16.5	3.2	16.5	17.2	**9.5**	10.9	0.0
First Jackson Bank, Inc.	Stevenson	AL	**A-**	A-	B+	294.9	11.79	6.7	3.7	17.1	19.2	**9.8**	12.2	0.0
First Kansas Bank	Hoisington	KS	**B+**	B+	B	189.7	2.75	3.8	1.1	11.1	62.1	**6.6**	8.6	23.9
First Kentucky Bank, Inc.	Mayfield	KY	**B**	B	B	462.5	4.15	5.3	5.1	24.1	23.5	**7.2**	9.1	13.9
First Keystone Community Bank	Berwick	PA	**B**	B	B	1025.8	3.69	6.4	0.6	20.9	27.7	**7.8**	9.5	14.3
First Liberty Bank	Oklahoma City	OK	**B-**	B-	B-	459.8	8.48	27.7	0.2	16.6	2.3	**6.5**	9.5	12.1
▼ First Liberty National Bank	Liberty	TX	**B+**	A-	B+	354.1	13.87	6.7	4.6	18.7	26.3	**10.0**	11.1	19.5
First Merchants Bank	Muncie	IN	**A-**	A-	A-	12670.4	24.27	17.4	1.0	9.2	21.6	**7.9**	10.2	13.2
First Metro Bank	Muscle Shoals	AL	**A**	A	A	717.9	8.52	8.5	2.3	17.5	23.3	**9.8**	11.2	0.0
First Mid Bank & Trust, N.A.	Mattoon	IL	**B+**	B+	B+	3834.7	10.44	14.8	2.1	7.3	16.8	**9.0**	10.3	14.5
First Midwest Bank	Chicago	IL	**B**	B	B	18739.3	19.14	21.5	2.6	12.0	18.2	**4.9**	8.6	11.0
First Midwest Bank of Dexter	Dexter	MO	**B-**	B-	B-	377.4	10.05	22.3	1.8	12.9	2.8	**9.1**	11.1	14.3
▲ First Midwest Bank of Poplar Bluff	Poplar Bluff	MO	**B**	B-	B-	467.1	10.32	22.2	3.3	23.5	5.2	**7.5**	9.7	12.9
First Midwest Bank of the Ozarks	Piedmont	MO	**B-**	B-	B-	127.9	3.29	13.4	5.3	14.5	9.2	**9.0**	10.8	14.2
First Minnetonka City Bank	Minnetonka	MN	**A-**	A-	B+	230.0	4.39	10.8	1.4	14.3	28.3	**10.0**	11.3	19.7
▼ First Missouri Bank	Brookfield	MO	**C+**	B-	B-	337.8	19.24	7.9	1.0	12.1	4.4	**7.4**	9.3	13.0
First Missouri Bank of SEMO	Kennett	MO	**B+**	B+	A-	182.4	-0.08	9.9	1.8	23.8	2.1	**8.6**	10.1	14.3
First Missouri State Bank	Poplar Bluff	MO	**B+**	B+	B+	182.4	5.92	6.6	4.2	34.7	1.0	**7.6**	9.4	14.0
First Missouri State Bank of Cape County	Cape Girardeau	MO	**B-**	B-	B-	178.2	5.97	8.8	1.7	18.6	6.6	**6.1**	8.8	11.8
First Montana Bank, Inc.	Missoula	MT	**C+**	C+	B-	323.9	4.70	13.5	5.0	8.7	13.0	**8.2**	10.8	13.5
First Mutual Bank, FSB	Belpre	OH	**C-**	C-	C-	89.8	-1.29	0.2	1.1	41.3	26.3	**6.7**	8.7	16.3
First National B&T Co. of Ardmore	Ardmore	OK	**B**	B	B	561.8	7.38	11.3	3.5	8.8	27.7	**8.3**	10.1	0.0
First National B&T Co. of Bottineau	Bottineau	ND	**B-**	B-	B-	147.9	-0.27	2.3	2.5	6.6	35.1	**9.8**	12.1	0.0
▲ First National B&T Co. of Broken Arrow	Broken Arrow	OK	**B+**	B	C+	190.9	2.38	13.0	2.4	21.3	3.4	**10.0**	11.6	16.7
First National B&T Co. of Iron Mountain	Iron Mountain	MI	**C+**	C+	C+	322.0	-0.19	13.3	2.5	13.5	30.8	**7.7**	9.7	0.0
First National B&T Co. of McAlester	McAlester	OK	**B**	B	C+	476.0	2.49	4.1	2.0	9.9	30.6	**10.0**	11.3	18.2
First National B&T Co. of Miami	Miami	OK	**B**	B	C+	132.9	-3.58	4.3	3.4	15.4	19.3	**8.9**	10.5	0.0
First National B&T Co. of Newtown	Newtown	PA	**B+**	B+	B-	984.3	4.68	0.7	0.2	13.3	45.8	**8.8**	10.3	0.0
First National B&T Co. of Okmulgee	Okmulgee	OK	**B**	B	B+	260.3	-3.96	9.5	2.7	16.9	32.1	**10.0**	11.8	16.2

Asset Quality Index	Adjusted Non-Performing Loans as a % of Total Loans	Adjusted Non-Performing Loans as a % of Capital	Net Charge-Offs Avg Loans	Profitability Index	Net Income ($Mil)	Return on Assets (R.O.A.)	Return on Equity (R.O.E.)	Net Interest Spread	Overhead Efficiency Ratio	Liquidity Index	Liquidity Ratio	Hot Money Ratio	Stability Index
8.2	0.71	na	0.00	**5.4**	0.2	1.52	10.18	3.96	68.8	**3.0**	21.2	14.6	**8.0**
7.1	0.52	na	0.16	**6.6**	11.7	1.19	8.54	3.99	61.9	**4.1**	11.6	7.6	**10.0**
7.0	0.84	2.7	0.16	**8.8**	35.0	1.55	11.30	4.00	50.4	**5.1**	21.0	3.7	**10.0**
7.5	0.39	na	0.00	**4.3**	2.0	0.59	5.86	3.16	74.3	**0.8**	12.0	35.9	**9.4**
10.0	na	0.0	na	**9.5**	3.8	51.89	51.14	2.75	39.1	**4.0**	na	0.0	**7.0**
6.5	na	na	na	**9.5**	0.2	6.88	7.05	1.80	69.2	**4.0**	na	0.0	**3.7**
8.6	0.01	0.1	0.14	**4.6**	4.7	1.16	12.76	3.36	58.5	**3.7**	14.2	10.9	**7.6**
6.7	0.23	1.9	0.01	**4.7**	13.6	0.86	8.82	3.05	53.0	**0.8**	14.6	15.7	**7.2**
4.7	0.87	na	0.26	**5.4**	1.3	1.05	10.16	3.69	62.6	**0.8**	10.0	32.8	**6.5**
3.0	3.72	na	0.03	**4.1**	0.3	0.73	7.26	3.23	80.3	**6.5**	48.2	3.0	**6.0**
8.1	1.30	na	0.00	**4.6**	0.7	0.73	4.35	3.45	61.4	**1.0**	21.9	34.4	**8.6**
9.6	0.00	na	0.00	**2.8**	0.1	0.39	3.10	2.57	79.7	**1.8**	26.5	24.2	**6.6**
8.3	0.23	na	0.02	**5.8**	1.9	1.05	8.71	4.90	74.8	**4.3**	18.2	6.8	**7.7**
5.8	1.41	na	0.04	**1.1**	0.0	-0.11	-0.93	2.98	103.6	**1.5**	24.9	26.8	**6.4**
7.0	0.19	na	0.00	**9.8**	5.0	2.08	13.97	3.97	30.5	**0.5**	6.3	48.3	**10.0**
5.2	1.12	10.1	0.05	**4.6**	4.5	0.84	7.89	3.58	68.7	**1.3**	18.5	27.5	**7.8**
7.0	0.62	na	0.09	**5.7**	2.3	1.13	9.80	3.83	64.9	**5.8**	36.2	3.3	**6.9**
7.1	0.19	1.0	0.19	**5.9**	40.4	0.80	6.14	3.11	50.5	**3.4**	17.1	12.9	**10.0**
8.4	0.01	na	0.00	**4.9**	0.1	1.33	11.92	4.21	67.8	**3.7**	22.7	11.3	**5.9**
8.2	0.05	na	0.01	**5.6**	0.7	1.51	15.32	3.63	61.3	**1.3**	23.9	16.4	**7.1**
4.5	1.01	na	1.15	**1.8**	-0.4	-0.28	-2.58	3.44	98.9	**1.8**	18.5	21.2	**7.6**
5.5	0.97	5.9	0.10	**3.2**	0.6	0.48	5.19	3.38	83.7	**4.6**	22.5	5.4	**5.6**
4.9	1.02	5.0	0.09	**4.9**	31.4	0.29	2.36	3.18	60.8	**2.5**	11.1	5.2	**10.0**
4.8	2.00	na	-0.01	**7.0**	1.3	0.71	6.41	3.42	59.7	**0.9**	20.7	38.8	**10.0**
4.7	1.76	na	-0.03	**5.8**	0.4	1.14	13.90	4.25	89.4	**1.3**	11.0	17.2	**5.3**
4.3	2.68	na	0.64	**6.1**	1.0	1.43	11.79	4.03	58.2	**3.2**	30.5	15.8	**7.7**
5.3	1.75	na	0.05	**4.5**	0.2	0.90	7.25	3.57	70.5	**3.7**	44.8	17.3	**6.5**
5.4	1.51	7.5	0.02	**5.6**	11.4	1.30	14.08	4.05	71.7	**3.3**	13.5	12.6	**8.3**
7.8	0.26	na	0.06	**3.8**	7.6	0.75	9.16	1.79	56.0	**0.7**	13.4	41.8	**6.5**
5.4	0.62	3.2	0.14	**6.3**	31.0	0.86	6.55	3.91	57.6	**4.5**	18.0	6.2	**10.0**
3.9	0.19	na	-0.07	**8.1**	0.7	1.90	13.80	4.53	54.3	**3.4**	29.9	14.7	**8.2**
4.4	1.54	na	0.02	**5.3**	0.4	1.27	11.20	5.16	71.2	**3.3**	17.9	12.8	**6.8**
8.4	0.22	na	0.02	**7.7**	1.1	1.49	12.49	3.80	44.0	**0.9**	22.2	43.1	**7.0**
9.7	0.00	0.0	0.00	**5.2**	0.6	1.31	13.55	3.05	55.0	**4.8**	31.8	7.5	**6.7**
8.5	0.11	0.8	0.02	**4.4**	1.3	1.09	11.55	3.42	69.1	**1.8**	22.2	17.6	**6.4**
5.4	2.04	na	0.01	**4.2**	2.5	0.99	8.49	3.25	66.8	**3.8**	12.0	10.1	**9.0**
7.9	0.15	na	0.00	**3.9**	0.6	0.53	5.64	3.72	71.6	**0.7**	14.7	36.4	**6.4**
6.7	0.52	na	0.41	**5.0**	1.0	1.14	10.09	4.31	71.7	**4.3**	26.1	8.3	**7.1**
7.3	0.18	0.8	0.03	**6.5**	36.3	1.16	7.99	3.52	54.1	**3.7**	21.9	7.0	**10.0**
8.8	0.13	na	0.06	**7.8**	2.3	1.33	11.72	3.31	51.6	**2.0**	26.0	21.5	**8.5**
5.2	0.89	4.1	0.18	**5.1**	7.7	0.81	6.20	3.56	58.6	**3.3**	7.3	11.2	**9.4**
4.3	1.09	5.8	0.38	**5.3**	28.3	0.63	4.89	3.61	59.0	**3.4**	14.4	9.5	**9.7**
4.2	1.44	na	0.04	**5.7**	0.6	0.71	6.44	3.86	63.9	**1.3**	16.5	28.6	**6.1**
4.6	0.75	na	0.08	**6.6**	1.9	1.65	16.97	3.95	58.1	**1.3**	11.1	23.3	**6.5**
2.3	2.63	na	0.09	**5.3**	0.2	0.52	4.68	3.80	68.8	**1.1**	15.0	26.6	**6.1**
9.2	0.00	na	0.01	**5.2**	0.7	1.23	10.58	3.47	65.7	**5.6**	45.0	7.4	**7.2**
2.4	2.69	na	-0.03	**6.0**	1.0	1.28	13.93	3.39	63.2	**3.5**	25.2	12.6	**6.7**
7.0	0.12	0.7	0.11	**5.8**	0.6	1.34	13.34	3.91	61.6	**2.4**	11.8	16.7	**7.1**
5.0	0.76	7.4	0.01	**7.1**	0.9	2.04	21.97	3.74	51.7	**0.8**	10.4	31.4	**7.3**
4.9	0.78	7.1	-0.02	**4.0**	0.4	0.85	9.67	3.15	74.7	**0.8**	16.6	31.2	**5.7**
3.3	1.17	na	0.05	**5.3**	0.8	1.01	9.15	4.47	73.8	**4.4**	6.6	4.6	**6.7**
3.8	2.01	na	0.00	**1.1**	0.0	0.18	1.32	3.75	106.7	**5.4**	48.3	9.4	**5.8**
4.4	1.72	na	0.04	**4.7**	1.4	0.99	10.08	3.66	73.4	**2.3**	14.3	17.6	**7.3**
4.6	3.84	na	0.00	**3.7**	0.2	0.56	4.71	2.89	74.2	**3.5**	26.0	13.1	**7.1**
7.3	0.95	na	-0.03	**6.3**	0.5	1.04	9.05	4.90	65.1	**4.2**	22.2	8.0	**7.1**
5.2	2.56	na	0.10	**3.6**	0.4	0.50	4.88	3.91	77.6	**5.2**	42.1	9.3	**5.0**
4.3	3.66	na	1.30	**5.5**	1.4	1.16	9.35	3.40	60.5	**3.3**	27.5	14.5	**8.6**
6.2	0.43	na	0.03	**5.5**	0.4	1.04	10.86	4.71	70.4	**4.7**	10.4	3.3	**5.9**
8.4	0.41	na	0.00	**5.0**	2.8	1.20	11.84	3.11	58.8	**6.5**	48.3	2.5	**6.1**
4.5	2.98	na	-0.22	**6.0**	0.9	1.34	10.57	3.79	63.5	**1.9**	24.8	21.6	**8.5**

	Name	City	State	Rating	2019 Rating	2018 Rating	Total Assets ($Mil)	One Year Asset Growth	Asset Mix (As a % of Total Assets) Comm-ercial Loans	Cons-umer Loans	Mort-gage Loans	Secur-ities	Capital-ization Index	Lever-age Ratio	Risk-Based Capital Ratio
▼	First National B&T Co. of Vinita	Vinita	OK	**C-**	C+	C	385.6	-16.80	17.4	4.3	7.0	23.7	**5.2**	7.7	11.1
	First National B&T Co. of Weatherford	Weatherford	OK	**B+**	B+	B+	260.9	2.85	12.3	1.9	7.2	2.5	**10.0**	12.6	15.8
	First National Bank	Hamilton	AL	**A**	A	A-	300.2	3.84	5.9	8.1	10.8	37.7	**9.8**	17.9	0.0
▼	First National Bank	Paragould	AR	**B+**	A-	A-	1639.6	-0.98	6.7	2.4	27.0	9.1	**9.2**	10.6	14.3
	First National Bank	Waverly	IA	**B+**	B+	A-	535.8	28.22	13.2	1.2	10.4	6.1	**10.0**	11.3	15.4
	First National Bank	Mattoon	IL	**C-**	C-	C-	89.4	-3.53	10.9	3.6	11.1	23.3	**6.8**	9.1	0.0
	First National Bank	Cloverdale	IN	**C+**	C+	C+	308.0	5.13	4.1	1.4	18.0	20.4	**8.6**	10.1	21.6
	First National Bank	Arcadia	LA	**B-**	B-	C-	259.2	2.30	7.0	1.2	19.3	1.3	**7.7**	9.6	0.0
	First National Bank	Damariscotta	ME	**B**	B	B	2102.8	7.31	9.5	1.4	23.9	31.5	**6.7**	8.7	15.0
▲	First National Bank	Alamogordo	NM	**A**	A-	B+	371.5	6.59	3.2	0.8	4.5	50.9	**10.0**	11.7	22.5
	First National Bank	Heavener	OK	**B+**	B+	B+	85.5	3.21	3.7	3.5	16.8	11.0	**6.9**	8.9	15.2
	First National Bank	Fort Pierre	SD	**A-**	A-	A	1359.6	33.98	7.7	13.0	7.7	8.6	**10.0**	19.0	24.7
	First National Bank	Oldham	SD	**A-**	A-	A-	325.0	6.16	5.9	14.2	7.9	15.3	**10.0**	13.9	19.6
▲	First National Bank	Rotan	TX	**B-**	C+	C	73.6	7.82	6.7	3.3	0.4	56.0	**10.0**	11.5	23.7
	First National Bank	Spearman	TX	**A-**	A-	B+	229.6	9.71	11.0	2.6	6.7	22.0	**10.0**	13.9	20.1
	First National Bank	Wichita Falls	TX	**B**	B	C+	581.5	20.74	6.3	0.8	29.9	3.3	**6.3**	9.8	12.0
	First National Bank	Altavista	VA	**B-**	B-	B-	501.6	2.91	10.6	19.4	13.2	8.4	**7.7**	9.6	0.0
	First National Bank & Trust of Elk City	Elk City	OK	**A-**	A-	B+	301.7	-2.82	8.0	0.6	13.1	36.6	**9.8**	11.6	0.0
	First National Bank Alaska	Anchorage	AK	**A**	A	A	3859.3	4.12	9.3	0.4	2.5	38.9	**10.0**	14.1	21.7
	First National Bank and Trust	Atmore	AL	**B-**	B-	B-	165.8	7.73	9.2	3.2	14.3	25.7	**9.8**	11.3	0.0
	First National Bank and Trust	Phillipsburg	KS	**B**	B	B-	222.8	0.12	9.5	4.7	10.9	23.7	**9.8**	15.4	0.0
	First National Bank and Trust Co.	Clinton	IL	**C+**	C+	B-	183.9	-1.57	1.5	0.3	5.1	78.2	**8.0**	9.7	18.1
	First National Bank and Trust Co.	Chickasha	OK	**B+**	B+	B-	676.8	6.72	10.1	1.1	6.9	31.3	**9.8**	12.3	0.0
	First National Bank and Trust Co.	Shawnee	OK	**C+**	C+	C	238.6	-4.69	8.1	0.8	6.7	42.7	**10.0**	15.6	31.4
	First National Bank and Trust Co.	Beloit	WI	**B-**	B-	B-	1160.9	2.15	9.1	1.0	18.5	11.6	**7.8**	9.7	0.0
	First National Bank at Darlington	Darlington	WI	**B+**	B+	B+	154.1	1.39	5.3	2.6	7.0	8.2	**10.0**	15.3	21.6
	First National Bank at Paris	Paris	AR	**B+**	B+	B	187.6	6.66	4.9	9.2	19.6	10.1	**10.0**	11.9	16.5
	First National Bank at Saint James	Saint James	MN	**D+**	D+	D	29.7	-2.20	4.3	4.2	21.8	4.0	**6.9**	8.9	14.3
▲	First National Bank Baird	Baird	TX	**B-**	C+	C+	456.8	6.88	17.4	1.5	12.7	3.1	**7.5**	9.8	12.9
▼	First National Bank in Amboy	Amboy	IL	**B-**	B	B	209.7	4.58	7.0	2.6	10.2	40.3	**9.7**	11.0	0.0
	First National Bank in Carlyle	Carlyle	IL	**B**	B	B	202.1	6.04	5.3	1.6	7.5	28.9	**9.8**	11.3	0.0
	First National Bank in Cimarron	Cimarron	KS	**B**	B	B-	105.6	6.54	13.1	2.6	6.4	48.0	**5.9**	7.9	13.6
	First National Bank in Cooper	Cooper	TX	**B**	B	B-	42.8	-8.03	3.9	6.2	23.3	15.0	**9.8**	15.3	0.0
	First National Bank in Creston	Creston	IA	**B+**	B+	B+	253.0	2.97	7.5	2.5	10.6	19.5	**9.7**	10.8	15.9
	First National Bank in DeRidder	DeRidder	LA	**B**	B	B+	308.0	14.30	6.9	2.6	24.1	17.0	**7.2**	9.3	0.0
	First National Bank in Fairfield	Fairfield	IA	**C+**	C+	C	142.5	-10.13	10.0	0.9	13.5	6.5	**8.9**	10.3	15.0
	First National Bank in Falfurrias	Falfurrias	TX	**C+**	C+	C+	80.8	0.28	7.7	3.5	1.4	54.7	**7.9**	9.8	0.0
	First National Bank in Frankfort	Frankfort	KS	**B**	B	B-	48.2	1.67	6.7	3.2	9.7	44.6	**9.0**	10.5	0.0
	First National Bank in Fredonia	Fredonia	KS	**A-**	A-	B+	92.3	1.82	6.5	7.1	10.7	58.8	**9.8**	17.4	0.0
▲	First National Bank in Howell	Howell	MI	**B+**	B	B-	430.0	4.92	7.7	11.4	11.3	7.5	**9.3**	12.5	14.4
	First National Bank in Marlow	Marlow	OK	**C+**	C+	C+	58.4	-1.29	7.6	9.4	15.6	16.7	**7.8**	9.7	0.0
	First National Bank in New Bremen	New Bremen	OH	**B+**	B+	B+	308.8	6.77	5.8	0.7	9.7	28.9	**9.1**	10.4	23.3
▲	First National Bank in Okeene	Okeene	OK	**C+**	C	C+	84.4	-0.29	5.1	0.3	0.0	33.7	**10.0**	16.0	25.5
	First National Bank in Olney	Olney	IL	**B+**	B+	B+	346.1	3.16	5.6	2.6	15.8	26.6	**9.8**	11.9	0.0
	First National Bank in Ord	Ord	NE	**B**	B	C+	131.2	0.69	3.7	2.0	11.3	36.1	**7.3**	9.2	18.3
	First National Bank in Philip	Philip	SD	**A-**	A-	B+	276.8	6.96	5.5	0.6	0.1	15.2	**10.0**	13.4	17.4
	First National Bank in Pinckneyville	Pinckneyville	IL	**A-**	A-	A-	102.3	0.76	2.3	4.4	24.0	48.9	**10.0**	15.5	33.9
	First National Bank in Port Lavaca	Port Lavaca	TX	**B**	B	B	339.0	5.71	3.2	1.7	31.4	38.3	**8.7**	10.2	23.3
▼	First National Bank in Sioux Falls	Sioux Falls	SD	**B+**	A-	B	1270.8	5.70	11.5	0.8	20.3	22.8	**10.0**	12.8	17.8
	First National Bank in Taylorville	Taylorville	IL	**A-**	A-	A	195.8	1.42	8.0	2.6	9.2	47.0	**9.8**	18.0	0.0
▼	First National Bank in Tigerton	Tigerton	WI	**C**	C+	C+	24.2	-6.40	0.1	2.1	27.3	24.9	**9.8**	14.0	0.0
▼	First National Bank in Tremont	Tremont	IL	**B-**	B	B	120.8	1.44	7.2	1.8	22.8	26.7	**9.8**	12.3	0.0
▼	First National Bank in Trinidad	Trinidad	CO	**C+**	B-	C+	210.5	0.54	0.9	0.8	31.0	36.9	**9.8**	12.4	0.0
▲	First National Bank Minnesota	Saint Peter	MN	**B-**	C+	C+	223.7	4.60	12.3	2.6	7.7	8.3	**6.4**	9.6	12.1
	First National Bank North	Walker	MN	**A**	A	A-	566.8	4.46	5.3	7.5	23.0	16.6	**9.8**	11.3	0.0
	First National Bank Northwest Florida	Panama City	FL	**B+**	B+	B+	177.1	2.26	0.9	0.0	8.7	4.8	**9.8**	10.9	38.4
	First National Bank of Absecon	Absecon	NJ	**C+**	C+	C	147.1	-0.27	4.9	0.2	30.1	31.3	**10.0**	11.4	22.9
	First National Bank of Albany	Albany	TX	**A-**	A-	B+	548.0	-7.08	21.6	2.4	10.4	24.3	**9.8**	11.6	0.0
	First National Bank of Allendale	Allendale	IL	**B**	B	B-	255.1	8.77	9.5	6.3	18.5	21.8	**9.2**	10.6	0.0
	First National Bank of Alvin	Alvin	TX	**B+**	B+	B+	154.7	8.51	0.4	0.2	1.1	75.3	**9.8**	11.7	0.0

Asset Quality Index	Adjusted Non-Performing Loans as a % of Total Loans	Adjusted Non-Performing Loans as a % of Capital	Net Charge-Offs Avg Loans	Profitability Index	Net Income ($Mil)	Return on Assets (R.O.A.)	Return on Equity (R.O.E.)	Net Interest Spread	Overhead Efficiency Ratio	Liquidity Index	Liquidity Ratio	Hot Money Ratio	Stability Index
1.1	4.84	na	-0.34	0.6	-1.4	-1.40	-17.14	3.40	76.4	1.5	14.3	15.5	3.0
5.6	1.12	na	0.07	6.8	1.0	1.45	10.98	4.41	62.7	1.4	15.4	26.7	8.5
8.6	0.15	na	0.31	7.1	1.2	1.59	8.67	3.82	57.6	6.1	57.1	8.3	8.9
7.8	0.35	2.3	0.56	5.3	4.3	1.05	9.55	3.31	61.3	0.9	9.2	33.2	9.0
5.6	1.14	5.5	0.00	5.8	1.6	1.20	9.71	3.47	54.4	2.9	18.2	15.0	7.8
4.3	1.54	na	0.02	2.9	0.1	0.58	6.22	3.15	84.9	1.8	25.2	22.6	4.8
7.9	0.79	na	-0.02	2.8	0.3	0.38	3.78	2.98	86.1	6.2	52.5	5.9	6.1
3.9	1.11	na	0.01	6.9	0.9	1.36	14.00	5.70	75.1	0.6	7.6	14.2	7.7
6.0	0.80	7.2	0.05	5.8	6.6	1.27	14.28	3.28	58.9	1.4	24.9	26.5	8.2
8.1	1.89	na	0.08	6.9	1.8	1.96	15.48	3.86	58.5	6.1	45.9	4.4	8.6
8.5	0.14	na	0.56	7.2	0.3	1.22	13.99	5.26	73.6	3.1	23.3	14.5	5.9
5.4	1.20	4.0	4.08	10.0	6.5	1.94	9.25	8.27	40.0	3.2	17.6	13.9	9.3
6.0	0.99	3.4	5.02	6.6	0.7	0.86	6.15	8.61	52.6	3.4	16.4	12.3	6.4
4.7	4.23	na	0.09	3.9	0.2	1.28	12.09	3.72	82.3	4.3	28.9	9.8	5.4
5.7	1.56	na	0.00	6.2	1.4	2.42	17.08	4.06	65.3	1.2	21.0	29.9	8.9
6.6	0.29	na	-0.02	5.2	1.6	1.23	12.61	4.09	72.7	1.0	5.3	28.8	7.1
5.4	0.44	na	0.16	4.2	0.9	0.74	8.15	3.64	77.7	4.2	16.8	7.6	5.6
5.6	2.12	na	0.15	8.0	1.9	2.44	20.38	3.64	51.3	2.3	34.3	24.9	8.8
7.9	1.42	3.3	-0.01	8.0	14.2	1.49	10.07	3.77	53.4	4.9	15.7	3.1	10.0
4.4	2.25	na	-0.45	3.5	0.4	0.92	8.12	3.73	81.9	3.1	31.2	16.3	6.7
3.8	2.71	na	0.06	5.2	0.7	1.20	7.75	4.01	68.9	1.9	13.0	19.3	8.3
9.9	0.37	na	0.03	1.7	0.3	0.58	6.83	2.38	125.3	1.7	38.6	34.3	5.0
5.3	1.45	na	0.06	9.7	3.0	1.79	13.56	4.58	50.2	3.0	26.0	11.6	9.3
7.5	1.05	na	0.10	2.2	0.1	0.17	1.02	3.27	93.6	5.6	42.7	7.0	7.2
7.7	0.38	na	0.04	3.4	1.6	0.55	4.67	3.33	81.6	4.6	24.2	9.0	9.2
7.3	0.22	1.0	0.00	5.0	0.4	0.95	6.16	3.40	65.5	2.4	33.7	23.1	8.1
4.7	1.05	na	0.05	8.6	0.9	1.98	14.10	4.64	60.4	1.1	9.8	28.9	8.8
3.5	1.21	na	0.00	2.2	0.0	0.07	0.76	4.21	96.6	2.1	26.7	20.4	4.2
3.7	1.90	na	0.06	4.6	0.8	0.79	8.01	4.89	77.3	2.1	19.5	19.0	5.1
8.7	0.25	na	-0.13	3.6	0.4	0.74	6.65	3.29	75.7	5.1	35.8	7.2	6.8
8.5	0.12	na	0.00	4.5	0.5	0.91	8.23	3.09	63.4	3.9	24.8	9.8	6.8
8.7	0.07	0.4	0.00	6.0	0.5	1.67	21.78	3.77	59.1	2.7	20.8	16.1	5.0
6.3	0.00	4.6	0.04	4.2	0.1	0.76	5.01	3.13	70.4	4.8	47.9	12.1	6.6
7.8	0.51	na	0.10	6.4	0.8	1.19	10.95	3.77	73.6	3.4	24.5	12.8	8.1
7.0	0.55	na	0.03	4.3	0.6	0.80	9.08	3.66	76.4	4.4	31.4	9.9	5.5
1.4	4.85	na	-0.01	1.8	0.1	0.34	3.28	3.41	88.1	2.7	15.9	10.4	4.8
7.0	1.80	na	0.00	2.7	0.1	0.40	3.93	2.38	86.0	4.7	36.8	10.3	5.1
5.9	2.22	na	-0.07	4.6	0.1	0.84	8.02	3.22	72.1	4.5	41.4	12.5	6.4
6.5	1.54	na	-0.13	5.5	0.3	1.26	6.97	3.36	65.9	3.5	58.3	21.1	8.4
5.7	0.46	na	0.01	6.5	1.4	1.31	10.63	4.44	68.0	4.2	10.7	6.9	8.3
8.2	0.00	na	-0.02	3.2	0.1	0.42	4.27	4.19	90.8	2.3	22.0	18.4	5.0
9.0	0.33	na	-0.02	5.4	1.0	1.30	12.27	2.82	54.7	5.9	52.4	8.5	7.2
8.5	0.66	na	-0.04	4.9	0.2	1.03	6.58	3.27	56.3	1.9	33.1	28.0	7.0
5.4	1.63	na	0.06	6.2	1.4	1.57	12.41	3.51	58.8	3.5	24.9	12.6	7.8
8.9	0.15	0.7	-0.01	4.6	0.4	1.28	13.86	3.09	59.6	3.9	23.4	8.6	5.6
7.2	0.06	na	-0.08	7.8	1.1	1.60	11.71	3.54	51.0	1.8	18.0	8.0	9.6
8.8	0.92	na	-0.02	5.6	0.3	1.31	7.74	4.09	63.7	5.3	31.1	3.9	8.6
7.6	0.51	na	0.00	5.2	0.9	1.10	10.39	3.12	52.6	3.9	29.4	11.9	6.8
4.8	2.94	na	-0.18	5.2	2.9	0.90	6.78	3.66	75.3	4.3	4.8	5.6	10.0
9.0	0.10	na	-0.02	6.1	0.8	1.62	8.88	3.21	49.9	5.1	57.0	13.5	7.9
9.8	0.00	na	0.00	1.7	0.0	-0.15	-1.08	3.34	99.5	5.1	46.4	8.1	6.1
6.7	0.62	na	-0.03	3.6	0.2	0.52	4.07	3.62	83.2	3.2	29.4	15.6	6.8
5.2	4.78	na	0.01	2.7	0.1	0.27	2.03	3.67	92.0	4.8	29.8	6.5	7.1
4.4	1.44	na	0.03	5.9	0.7	1.25	12.80	4.41	69.3	3.8	12.5	10.0	7.0
6.7	1.44	4.5	0.28	8.6	2.8	2.01	17.10	4.01	53.2	1.9	26.8	23.2	9.4
9.6	0.30	na	0.00	4.8	0.5	1.09	9.99	2.96	63.8	6.0	69.5	11.4	7.6
8.8	0.74	na	0.00	3.1	0.2	0.42	3.69	3.62	81.2	6.7	49.6	2.1	6.0
5.6	0.92	na	-0.05	8.4	3.1	2.20	17.68	4.53	39.7	0.9	22.1	21.4	8.7
4.7	1.01	na	0.03	5.1	0.6	0.94	8.69	3.75	61.1	1.9	17.5	19.7	6.4
10.0	0.00	na	0.00	4.4	0.4	0.97	7.55	2.19	60.7	4.3	80.4	23.0	7.2

Name	City	State	Rating	2019 Rating	2018 Rating	Total Assets ($Mil)	One Year Asset Growth	Asset Mix (As a % of Total Assets): Comm-ercial Loans	Cons-umer Loans	Mort-gage Loans	Secur-ities	Capital-ization Index	Lever-age Ratio	Risk-Based Capital Ratio
First National Bank of America	East Lansing	MI	**B-**	B-	C	2651.2	35.42	0.2	0.2	83.9	1.8	**7.6**	9.4	17.8
First National Bank of Anderson	Anderson	TX	**B**	B	B	186.7	7.57	10.2	4.0	12.3	10.2	**10.0**	11.0	18.1
▲ First National Bank of Anson	Anson	TX	**B**	B-	C+	67.2	2.32	10.4	9.6	19.6	21.4	**6.8**	8.9	17.3
First National Bank of Arenzville	Arenzville	IL	**B-**	B-	B-	91.1	6.93	9.8	4.3	13.0	15.9	**7.5**	9.5	0.0
First National Bank of Aspermont	Aspermont	TX	**B+**	B+	B+	58.9	-10.18	2.7	3.0	7.1	63.3	**9.8**	17.6	0.0
First National Bank of Assumption	Assumption	IL	**C**	C	C-	20.1	-6.22	1.4	4.0	10.2	27.6	**9.2**	10.6	0.0
First National Bank of Ava	Ava	IL	**B**	B	B	65.7	4.30	4.3	3.6	18.4	44.7	**10.0**	12.6	21.4
First National Bank of Bagley	Bagley	MN	**C+**	C+	C+	86.3	-0.26	8.8	9.2	24.9	15.8	**6.4**	8.4	13.6
First National Bank of Ballinger	Ballinger	TX	**B-**	B-	B-	190.5	7.69	11.1	1.1	10.0	12.7	**8.6**	10.0	16.3
First National Bank of Bangor	Bangor	WI	**A**	A	B+	226.3	3.12	3.6	1.5	19.6	12.6	**9.8**	31.6	0.0
First National Bank of Bastrop	Bastrop	TX	**A-**	A-	B+	634.9	6.13	2.2	1.8	16.6	32.0	**9.6**	10.8	18.1
▼ First National Bank of Beardstown	Beardstown	IL	**B+**	A-	B+	133.6	5.91	3.7	5.4	10.9	12.3	**9.8**	11.7	0.0
First National Bank of Bellevue	Bellevue	OH	**C+**	C+	C+	246.8	4.05	14.7	1.3	6.4	10.9	**8.9**	10.4	0.0
First National Bank of Bellville	Bellville	TX	**B+**	B+	A-	765.4	6.70	2.3	1.6	9.7	68.7	**9.8**	11.2	0.0
▼ First National Bank of Bemidji	Bemidji	MN	**A-**	A	A	734.2	9.99	10.5	10.1	11.3	43.7	**9.8**	14.0	0.0
▼ First National Bank of Benton	Benton	LA	**B+**	A-	B+	63.9	5.63	2.1	1.8	38.1	13.2	**10.0**	17.9	40.9
First National Bank of Blanchester	Blanchester	OH	**B+**	B+	B+	64.1	0.59	1.8	4.3	43.8	13.2	**10.0**	12.3	23.5
First National Bank of Bosque County	Valley Mills	TX	**B+**	B+	B-	123.3	2.43	13.4	5.7	30.5	3.6	**10.0**	11.4	16.5
▼ First National Bank of Brookfield	Brookfield	IL	**B+**	A-	B	230.9	24.50	0.3	6.4	15.2	5.7	**9.1**	10.4	15.3
First National Bank of Brooksville	Brooksville	KY	**B-**	B-	B-	64.9	6.22	1.3	2.2	32.1	39.5	**9.8**	11.2	0.0
First National Bank of Brownstown	Brownstown	IL	**C+**	C+	C	43.7	14.85	3.6	6.2	13.8	25.9	**8.7**	10.3	0.0
First National Bank of Brundidge	Brundidge	AL	**B-**	B-	B-	86.0	1.61	4.7	3.7	13.8	13.2	**10.0**	17.2	29.8
First National Bank of Buhl	Mountain Iron	MN	**D**	D	D-	26.0	1.84	7.1	10.1	44.1	0.0	**6.1**	8.1	15.2
First National Bank of Burleson	Burleson	TX	**A-**	A-	B+	197.4	0.54	7.1	2.6	1.9	42.1	**9.1**	10.5	0.0
First National Bank of Carmi	Carmi	IL	**B**	B	B-	426.8	1.12	9.8	0.8	4.7	17.1	**7.4**	9.3	14.6
First National Bank of Central Texas	Waco	TX	**B+**	B+	B+	889.0	3.31	16.0	1.0	14.5	4.5	**6.7**	10.1	12.3
First National Bank of Chadron	Chadron	NE	**A-**	A-	B	128.8	3.74	3.7	1.1	0.2	30.0	**10.0**	14.1	20.8
First National Bank of Chisholm	Chisholm	MN	**C-**	C-	D+	73.0	0.81	8.1	5.1	5.0	60.2	**7.0**	9.2	0.0
First National Bank of Clarksdale	Clarksdale	MS	**B+**	B+	A-	369.6	-0.67	5.2	2.8	7.3	30.7	**9.8**	12.6	0.0
First National Bank of Coffee County	Douglas	GA	**B+**	B+	B+	245.2	16.82	4.0	0.7	12.5	2.6	**8.6**	10.1	18.0
First National Bank of Cokato	Cokato	MN	**B**	B	C+	68.7	10.38	13.8	2.7	15.0	15.6	**7.3**	9.2	15.4
First National Bank of Coleraine	Coleraine	MN	**C+**	C+	C	84.3	-1.39	3.8	3.2	15.9	42.8	**6.7**	8.7	20.0
First National Bank of Decatur County	Bainbridge	GA	**B-**	B-	B-	180.4	0.26	12.0	3.1	22.7	11.2	**7.3**	9.2	14.3
▼ First National Bank of Dennison	Dennison	OH	**B-**	B	B-	232.0	0.49	3.6	19.2	14.9	26.9	**9.1**	10.6	0.0
First National Bank of Dighton	Dighton	KS	**B-**	B-	B	59.2	3.05	6.6	2.2	2.2	27.3	**9.8**	19.6	0.0
▼ First National Bank of Dozier	Dozier	AL	**C+**	B-	B-	34.7	4.92	6.3	2.5	6.2	55.8	**9.8**	14.9	0.0
First National Bank of Dryden	Dryden	NY	**B+**	B+	B+	190.4	4.16	3.6	5.4	15.3	35.1	**9.0**	10.5	0.0
First National Bank of Dublin	Dublin	TX	**B+**	B+	B	95.3	5.55	13.2	9.4	4.2	1.8	**8.5**	11.1	13.8
First National Bank of Eagle Lake	Eagle Lake	TX	**B**	B	B+	119.1	4.99	10.5	0.4	3.2	14.1	**9.7**	10.8	16.0
First National Bank of Eastern Arkansas	Forrest City	AR	**B+**	B+	B+	454.7	10.12	5.6	1.8	6.7	26.0	**8.2**	10.0	0.0
First National Bank of Eldorado	Eldorado	TX	**A-**	A-	A-	61.6	0.25	15.8	2.9	16.7	25.4	**10.0**	16.7	28.0
▲ First National Bank of Elmer	Elmer	NJ	**C+**	C	D+	286.1	0.60	6.0	0.2	29.5	3.9	**7.9**	9.6	13.2
First National Bank of Ely	Ely	NV	**B+**	B+	B	103.4	0.70	4.2	0.2	1.3	86.5	**9.7**	11.0	0.0
First National Bank of Evant	Evant	TX	**B+**	B+	B-	104.4	1.28	7.9	6.2	33.4	9.8	**8.5**	10.0	18.8
First National Bank of Fairfax	Fairfax	MN	**B+**	B+	B	30.8	1.61	10.5	0.5	0.7	21.5	**9.8**	37.7	0.0
First National Bank of Fleming	Fleming	CO	**C**	C	C-	23.7	5.01	4.8	2.0	3.6	8.9	**10.0**	13.1	26.2
First National Bank of Fletcher	Fletcher	OK	**B+**	B+	B+	18.8	0.46	10.7	5.6	3.5	55.1	**9.8**	11.6	0.0
First National Bank of Floydada	Floydada	TX	**A-**	A-	B+	108.2	-0.64	4.2	2.2	0.2	21.4	**9.4**	10.6	21.3
First National Bank of Fort Smith	Fort Smith	AR	**A-**	A-	A-	1467.2	10.73	13.3	0.9	11.4	11.2	**9.8**	11.4	0.0
First National Bank of Fort Stockton	Fort Stockton	TX	**B**	B	B-	131.6	0.73	14.0	1.5	4.7	36.5	**8.9**	10.4	0.0
First National Bank of Frederick	Frederick	SD	**C+**	C+	C+	19.9	1.07	3.2	0.2	0.0	28.4	**9.8**	14.8	0.0
First National Bank of Germantown	Germantown	OH	**C**	C	C-	66.0	3.75	8.4	4.6	32.6	21.6	**6.7**	8.7	16.5
First National Bank of Giddings	Giddings	TX	**B**	B	B-	230.7	10.26	4.0	1.9	20.4	31.6	**9.8**	11.2	0.0
First National Bank of Gilbert	Gilbert	MN	**D+**	D+	C-	48.6	12.61	4.3	5.6	50.4	3.5	**5.1**	7.1	14.0
First National Bank of Gillette	Gillette	WY	**B**	B	B-	559.7	3.40	6.8	1.6	2.2	71.0	**10.0**	12.2	35.8
First National Bank of Gilmer	Gilmer	TX	**B-**	B-	C+	458.1	15.49	9.5	5.1	18.7	18.3	**7.5**	9.5	0.0
▲ First National Bank of Gordon	Gordon	NE	**A-**	B+	B	213.7	10.71	5.0	2.4	0.1	39.2	**10.0**	14.0	23.5
First National Bank of Granbury	Granbury	TX	**A-**	A-	A-	634.5	2.29	4.0	2.8	21.3	35.7	**9.8**	11.9	0.0
First National Bank of Grayson	Grayson	KY	**A-**	A-	B	261.2	3.86	4.3	12.6	23.5	21.6	**9.8**	12.1	0.0
First National Bank of Griffin	Griffin	GA	**C**	C	C	291.8	3.99	2.8	1.3	6.3	36.9	**5.1**	7.1	14.3

Asset Quality Index	Adjusted Non-Performing Loans as a % of Total Loans	Adjusted Non-Performing Loans as a % of Capital	Net Charge-Offs / Avg Loans	Profitability Index	Net Income ($Mil)	Return on Assets (R.O.A.)	Return on Equity (R.O.E.)	Net Interest Spread	Overhead Efficiency Ratio	Liquidity Index	Liquidity Ratio	Hot Money Ratio	Stability Index
3.7	2.42	20.1	0.00	**10.0**	16.2	2.53	27.70	5.26	34.8	**0.4**	7.2	35.7	**9.2**
8.4	0.24	na	0.05	**4.5**	0.4	0.82	7.48	3.60	68.6	**1.7**	28.5	28.7	**6.4**
7.4	0.00	na	0.08	**9.2**	0.4	2.19	25.20	4.93	57.6	**5.0**	27.3	4.3	**6.3**
6.9	1.15	na	-0.02	**4.6**	0.3	1.12	11.32	3.65	66.9	**2.9**	22.0	15.2	**6.5**
9.4	0.00	na	0.00	**5.2**	0.2	1.27	7.02	3.17	58.1	**3.2**	49.1	21.9	**7.8**
8.7	0.00	na	0.00	**3.7**	0.1	0.98	9.23	3.20	70.4	**6.0**	57.6	5.3	**4.7**
5.1	4.37	13.3	-0.09	**5.3**	0.2	1.08	8.42	3.97	68.3	**4.6**	39.1	11.7	**7.8**
6.2	0.49	na	-0.01	**4.5**	0.3	1.21	13.98	4.09	70.9	**3.7**	14.6	10.5	**5.2**
3.6	3.64	na	0.01	**6.3**	0.7	1.41	13.22	4.48	60.0	**1.6**	24.1	26.0	**7.1**
7.6	2.10	na	0.00	**9.8**	1.4	2.41	7.68	4.12	24.1	**4.9**	23.5	4.0	**9.5**
7.5	0.40	na	0.12	**7.9**	2.9	1.85	17.28	4.11	57.4	**2.5**	24.7	17.2	**9.1**
8.3	0.12	na	0.00	**5.2**	0.4	1.27	10.77	3.82	67.8	**4.3**	28.2	9.2	**7.4**
4.3	2.27	na	0.00	**5.9**	0.7	1.20	11.42	4.26	65.5	**1.4**	13.9	10.4	**6.9**
8.6	0.04	0.1	0.03	**5.3**	4.6	2.50	16.85	2.56	57.6	**2.5**	51.3	39.2	**8.6**
5.6	1.49	3.7	0.06	**7.2**	2.9	1.71	11.37	3.37	53.0	**2.7**	36.7	20.5	**10.0**
6.2	7.63	na	0.32	**3.7**	-0.3	-1.82	-9.85	3.73	65.0	**1.3**	27.7	20.0	**8.4**
7.0	1.01	na	0.21	**4.9**	0.2	1.00	8.25	4.10	69.0	**5.0**	30.5	5.8	**6.4**
4.8	1.27	na	0.01	**5.8**	0.4	1.37	12.07	4.15	68.4	**3.8**	22.3	10.7	**7.4**
7.2	0.00	na	-0.41	**5.0**	0.9	1.70	16.18	3.45	68.5	**2.0**	26.5	20.9	**6.8**
6.7	1.32	na	0.29	**3.9**	0.1	0.80	6.89	3.58	75.5	**4.4**	23.7	7.0	**6.4**
5.4	0.76	na	-0.31	**3.7**	0.1	0.81	7.84	3.10	68.3	**4.9**	51.1	12.3	**4.9**
8.4	0.62	na	0.23	**3.3**	0.1	0.46	2.70	3.74	79.9	**1.4**	25.8	29.4	**7.6**
2.2	2.43	na	0.02	**2.7**	0.0	0.66	6.99	4.30	84.9	**2.3**	24.2	18.5	**4.4**
9.2	0.12	na	0.00	**5.4**	0.7	1.37	12.80	3.58	56.0	**7.1**	66.1	4.0	**7.1**
6.5	0.65	5.4	-0.05	**4.0**	0.8	0.74	7.59	3.34	75.3	**4.9**	32.0	7.2	**5.8**
3.2	1.17	na	0.01	**7.9**	5.1	2.34	23.41	4.27	47.8	**2.1**	7.2	17.5	**7.2**
8.0	0.26	na	-0.01	**6.1**	0.4	1.25	7.90	3.94	63.1	**3.8**	34.5	13.9	**8.1**
7.8	0.12	1.9	-0.02	**1.9**	0.0	0.04	0.44	3.69	97.1	**5.9**	45.1	5.0	**4.2**
7.9	0.70	na	0.01	**4.5**	1.0	1.06	8.21	3.32	59.9	**2.8**	28.6	17.3	**6.9**
8.8	0.36	na	0.09	**5.3**	0.7	1.13	12.34	4.77	69.5	**5.3**	37.7	7.0	**6.8**
8.4	0.12	na	0.24	**6.0**	0.2	1.27	13.59	4.11	62.3	**5.0**	24.1	3.3	**5.5**
9.2	0.00	na	0.00	**3.5**	0.2	0.74	8.25	3.11	69.9	**4.6**	38.1	11.3	**4.3**
5.5	0.71	na	0.08	**4.0**	0.3	0.59	6.35	3.72	74.6	**1.7**	18.9	22.6	**5.2**
6.9	0.13	na	0.31	**3.2**	0.0	0.01	0.05	3.93	98.2	**5.0**	36.0	8.3	**6.0**
6.3	1.18	na	0.04	**2.5**	0.1	0.66	3.35	3.36	66.0	**6.0**	44.3	4.5	**5.0**
9.6	0.00	na	0.00	**3.1**	0.1	0.70	4.68	2.77	72.9	**4.1**	78.9	22.0	**7.1**
6.3	1.34	na	0.01	**5.4**	0.7	1.51	14.32	3.54	50.9	**6.5**	44.7	1.8	**5.9**
7.3	0.18	na	0.13	**6.8**	0.3	1.45	13.13	5.13	69.6	**4.2**	21.8	8.2	**7.5**
5.3	0.94	5.2	0.09	**4.0**	0.2	0.79	7.33	4.21	76.4	**4.8**	26.3	5.5	**6.6**
7.0	0.34	na	1.38	**4.9**	1.2	1.09	10.47	3.17	64.8	**4.0**	41.9	15.6	**7.0**
8.7	0.19	1.3	0.00	**10.0**	0.4	2.33	14.24	5.68	55.0	**5.4**	24.5	0.6	**9.5**
4.2	1.62	na	0.05	**4.1**	0.5	0.68	7.21	4.04	74.9	**3.5**	6.5	10.9	**5.7**
9.2	4.10	na	0.00	**4.5**	0.3	1.12	9.59	2.57	56.0	**7.9**	74.8	0.0	**5.7**
8.1	0.19	na	0.04	**7.8**	0.4	1.76	17.36	4.99	67.1	**3.9**	26.9	11.1	**7.7**
8.8	0.39	na	-0.02	**5.1**	0.1	1.18	3.14	3.64	67.3	**6.9**	70.9	4.4	**7.1**
8.2	8.50	na	0.28	**4.3**	0.0	0.77	5.93	3.63	74.2	**0.8**	21.6	40.7	**5.8**
8.7	0.39	na	0.00	**3.1**	0.0	0.55	4.46	4.26	89.9	**5.7**	59.1	7.6	**5.8**
8.8	0.00	na	-0.01	**5.1**	0.3	0.97	9.04	2.53	61.5	**3.5**	53.1	21.9	**8.5**
7.2	0.57	3.0	-0.21	**9.7**	6.0	1.73	13.95	4.16	53.5	**4.0**	16.9	9.5	**9.6**
8.3	0.00	1.4	0.01	**5.1**	0.5	1.37	13.14	4.22	71.4	**3.1**	27.5	15.1	**6.4**
9.0	0.00	na	0.00	**2.9**	0.0	0.28	1.83	3.96	89.8	**4.8**	52.0	11.1	**7.7**
6.1	0.80	na	0.02	**4.2**	0.1	0.86	9.65	3.80	71.1	**4.5**	23.6	6.2	**4.5**
6.3	1.05	na	0.44	**4.3**	0.6	1.00	8.89	3.09	64.6	**2.9**	21.5	15.0	**6.3**
5.3	0.77	na	0.00	**2.1**	0.0	-0.01	-0.11	3.72	77.8	**2.6**	21.9	16.8	**3.0**
6.6	5.94	na	-0.13	**4.2**	1.4	0.98	7.50	2.40	58.2	**4.3**	72.2	20.6	**7.1**
4.2	1.02	na	0.58	**5.1**	1.1	0.96	9.11	3.59	65.5	**2.4**	30.9	20.4	**7.8**
6.2	1.32	na	1.06	**7.7**	1.1	2.25	15.90	4.72	41.4	**2.4**	20.3	16.5	**7.4**
6.7	0.98	4.2	-0.05	**5.8**	2.3	1.47	12.50	3.86	62.0	**4.9**	44.3	11.3	**7.9**
5.3	0.95	na	0.09	**8.5**	1.1	1.74	14.39	4.32	55.7	**4.0**	26.6	10.6	**7.8**
7.1	0.48	2.1	0.03	**3.1**	0.4	0.51	6.28	3.42	86.1	**6.5**	54.7	5.0	**3.2**

Name	City	State	Rating	2019 Rating	2018 Rating	Total Assets ($Mil)	One Year Asset Growth	Asset Mix (As a % of Total Assets) Comm-ercial Loans	Cons-umer Loans	Mort-gage Loans	Secur-ities	Capital-ization Index	Lever-age Ratio	Risk-Based Capital Ratio
First National Bank of Groton	Groton	NY	**A-**	A-	B+	192.4	1.94	6.5	8.3	23.9	37.5	**9.8**	14.7	0.0
First National Bank of Hartford	Hartford	AL	**B**	B	B	122.9	2.18	5.5	5.2	24.6	26.0	**10.0**	14.7	23.7
First National Bank of Harveyville	Harveyville	KS	**C-**	C-	D+	14.6	-3.14	9.1	5.8	24.8	0.0	**8.0**	9.8	0.0
First National Bank of Hebbronville	Hebbronville	TX	**A-**	A-	A-	90.4	-3.46	0.9	12.2	10.6	48.9	**10.0**	17.9	48.5
First National Bank of Henning	Ottertail	MN	**A-**	A-	B+	219.7	7.06	6.0	5.6	20.3	26.6	**10.0**	12.2	19.0
First National Bank of Hereford	Hereford	TX	**B**	B	C+	170.5	6.51	19.4	1.2	8.2	11.0	**8.3**	9.9	13.6
First National Bank of Hooker	Hooker	OK	**B**	B	B+	76.4	-0.47	6.1	2.9	13.7	27.3	**10.0**	14.6	22.9
First National Bank of Hope	Hope	KS	**D-**	D-	D+	88.3	6.48	4.8	1.5	2.2	20.6	**10.0**	11.3	15.3
▲ First National Bank of Hughes Springs	Hughes Springs	TX	**B+**	B	B+	274.6	-1.69	10.7	5.1	19.2	9.2	**10.0**	12.2	19.5
First National Bank of Hugo	Hugo	CO	**A-**	A-	A-	124.0	3.71	1.1	1.7	4.3	23.6	**9.8**	11.5	0.0
First National Bank of Huntsville	Huntsville	TX	**B+**	B+	B	483.5	2.53	5.7	5.3	18.2	35.0	**9.8**	11.9	0.0
First National Bank of Hutchinson	Hutchinson	KS	**A-**	A-	B	748.8	3.41	12.4	1.5	8.2	18.0	**10.0**	12.5	16.9
First National Bank of Izard County	Calico Rock	AR	**A**	A	A	170.9	2.31	2.2	5.4	17.6	26.5	**9.8**	34.9	0.0
First National Bank of Jasper	Jasper	TX	**B**	B	B	251.6	-3.75	3.7	4.2	7.9	63.1	**10.0**	14.0	46.8
First National Bank of Jeanerette	Jeanerette	LA	**B**	B	C+	280.8	6.69	7.3	2.7	25.2	6.3	**10.0**	11.0	15.8
First National Bank of Johnson	Johnson	NE	**C+**	C+	C+	71.7	2.99	1.4	2.6	4.7	25.9	**9.8**	20.6	0.0
First National Bank of Kansas	Burlington	KS	**C+**	C+	C+	90.5	4.20	5.2	2.0	8.6	66.7	**6.3**	8.3	22.8
First National Bank of Kemp	Kemp	TX	**B-**	B-	C+	99.4	7.43	14.5	1.4	17.3	16.6	**7.7**	9.6	0.0
First National Bank of Kentucky	Carrollton	KY	**B+**	B+	B+	122.5	-1.67	2.1	2.4	38.8	15.3	**10.0**	11.5	19.0
First National Bank of Lacon	Lacon	IL	**C+**	C+	C	58.4	2.70	9.3	7.8	15.1	7.7	**7.7**	9.6	0.0
First National Bank of Lake Jackson	Lake Jackson	TX	**B**	B	B	264.9	-1.93	1.8	0.5	0.1	82.2	**7.8**	9.5	38.9
First National Bank of Las Animas	Las Animas	CO	**A**	A	A	395.8	6.02	4.6	1.2	10.6	22.6	**9.8**	12.3	0.0
First National Bank of Lawrence County	Walnut Ridge	AR	**B+**	B+	B+	236.1	11.18	8.5	2.0	15.1	24.9	**9.8**	11.0	0.0
First National Bank of Le Center	Le Center	MN	**A-**	A-	A-	138.2	4.04	4.4	4.0	10.4	22.4	**9.0**	10.5	0.0
First National Bank of Lindsay	Lindsay	OK	**B+**	B+	B	68.8	10.12	26.2	3.4	14.4	14.5	**9.8**	12.0	0.0
First National Bank of Lipan	Lipan	TX	**C-**	C-	D+	23.0	-2.64	3.6	12.3	9.8	7.7	**7.2**	9.1	27.7
▲ First National Bank of Litchfield	Litchfield	IL	**A-**	B+	B+	102.5	-0.82	9.3	3.2	10.1	8.4	**10.0**	12.7	16.0
First National Bank of Livingston	Livingston	TX	**B+**	B+	B+	378.8	1.24	2.4	3.6	17.8	36.6	**9.8**	14.7	0.0
First National Bank of Long Island	Glen Head	NY	**B**	B	B	4092.9	-3.06	3.1	0.1	38.1	16.6	**7.3**	9.4	0.0
First National Bank of Louisburg	Louisburg	KS	**A-**	A-	B+	130.6	15.58	3.1	0.6	27.7	42.8	**9.8**	13.3	0.0
First National Bank of Louisiana	Crowley	LA	**A**	A	A-	417.0	4.06	13.4	0.9	13.1	7.9	**10.0**	12.5	18.1
▼ First National Bank of Manchester	Manchester	KY	**B-**	B	B	146.0	4.80	4.6	3.1	13.5	26.5	**9.8**	14.3	0.0
First National Bank of Manchester	Manchester	TN	**A-**	A-	B+	304.0	2.76	6.5	4.4	22.6	18.0	**9.8**	13.0	0.0
First National Bank of Manning	Manning	IA	**B+**	B+	B	65.2	2.43	5.9	1.5	7.9	14.4	**10.0**	18.6	30.8
First National Bank of McConnelsville	McConnelsville	OH	**C+**	C+	C+	157.7	-0.44	1.0	4.3	33.0	18.9	**5.3**	7.3	16.9
First National Bank of McGregor	McGregor	TX	**B+**	B+	C+	533.9	14.79	10.1	3.2	31.1	0.0	**9.9**	11.5	14.9
First National Bank of McIntosh	McIntosh	MN	**B**	B	B-	27.0	2.44	4.0	3.8	11.1	29.6	**10.0**	25.5	74.0
First National Bank of Mertzon	Mertzon	TX	**B-**	B-	C	500.2	8.12	3.5	0.6	1.2	51.2	**5.5**	7.5	42.2
First National Bank of Michigan	Kalamazoo	MI	**B-**	B-	B-	634.5	14.20	15.8	0.3	3.7	5.3	**6.4**	9.7	12.1
▼ First National Bank of Middle Tennessee	McMinnville	TN	**B+**	A-	B+	548.0	6.44	5.7	0.4	27.4	17.0	**10.0**	12.4	20.1
First National Bank of Milaca	Milaca	MN	**A-**	A-	B	215.5	2.79	14.8	5.0	17.6	19.7	**10.0**	11.7	20.7
▼ First National Bank of Monterey	Monterey	IN	**B-**	B	B	328.1	0.76	3.6	1.3	12.2	27.7	**9.8**	13.1	0.0
First National Bank of Moody	Moody	TX	**B-**	B-	B-	47.3	1.06	3.7	3.1	19.9	38.5	**9.8**	21.5	0.0
First National Bank of Moose Lake	Moose Lake	MN	**A-**	A-	B+	113.5	6.85	5.7	3.5	21.5	13.4	**9.8**	13.0	0.0
First National Bank of Mount Dora	Mount Dora	FL	**A-**	A-	B+	251.4	6.57	2.9	1.7	12.7	47.0	**10.0**	15.5	24.8
First National Bank of Muscatine	Muscatine	IA	**B-**	B-	B	311.4	-3.84	13.2	2.3	29.1	2.6	**10.0**	11.8	17.5
First National Bank of Nevada	Nevada	MO	**B**	B	B	99.9	3.99	4.4	1.5	12.7	35.5	**10.0**	15.8	26.6
First National Bank of Nokomis	Nokomis	IL	**B**	B	B	155.4	3.53	2.8	2.3	12.6	28.1	**10.0**	11.5	18.8
First National Bank of North Arkansas	Berryville	AR	**B**	B	C+	214.2	7.31	9.0	10.2	29.1	1.0	**9.8**	11.7	0.0
First National Bank of Okawville	Okawville	IL	**B**	B	B	68.1	0.71	1.2	1.3	6.8	36.0	**10.0**	11.6	20.2
First National Bank of Oklahoma	Oklahoma City	OK	**B-**	B-	B+	579.7	10.64	8.4	1.8	18.5	4.6	**6.4**	8.7	12.1
First National Bank of Omaha	Omaha	NE	**B-**	B-	B-	22265.2	2.81	8.6	30.9	4.6	18.0	**7.6**	10.2	13.0
First National Bank of Oneida	Oneida	TN	**A-**	A-	B+	230.8	4.39	3.4	2.6	26.2	19.5	**10.0**	11.5	19.2
First National Bank of Orwell	Orwell	VT	**C-**	C-	D+	76.7	6.24	4.5	2.5	57.7	0.0	**7.1**	9.2	0.0
First National Bank of Osakis	Osakis	MN	**B-**	B-	B	70.9	4.95	7.3	2.3	24.3	19.2	**6.9**	8.9	12.6
▼ First National Bank of Ottawa	Ottawa	IL	**B-**	B	B-	565.1	89.72	21.6	0.4	13.7	5.8	**8.2**	10.0	0.0
▼ First National Bank of Pana	Pana	IL	**B+**	A-	B+	194.1	5.91	6.8	1.5	17.2	13.9	**9.8**	11.9	0.0
First National Bank of Pandora	Pandora	OH	**C+**	C+	C+	194.3	9.44	8.2	2.6	19.0	22.0	**6.7**	8.7	12.4
First National Bank of Pasco	Dade City	FL	**C+**	C+	C	191.6	5.10	12.5	3.3	11.2	17.0	**9.8**	12.5	0.0
First National Bank of Pennsylvania	Pittsburgh	PA	**B-**	B-	B-	35014.8	4.08	14.9	5.8	15.4	18.4	**5.2**	8.9	11.2

Asset Quality Index	Adjusted Non-Performing Loans as a % of Total Loans	Adjusted Non-Performing Loans as a % of Capital	Net Charge-Offs Avg Loans	Profitability Index	Net Income ($Mil)	Return on Assets (R.O.A.)	Return on Equity (R.O.E.)	Net Interest Spread	Overhead Efficiency Ratio	Liquidity Index	Liquidity Ratio	Hot Money Ratio	Stability Index
5.7	1.13	na	0.41	**6.4**	0.6	1.20	8.04	4.43	57.6	**4.0**	19.8	9.3	**7.8**
6.2	2.30	na	0.21	**3.5**	0.2	0.65	4.35	4.05	83.9	**1.8**	24.2	22.0	**7.7**
7.6	0.00	na	0.00	**2.9**	0.0	0.52	5.29	3.81	85.0	**2.1**	35.6	23.2	**4.6**
8.4	1.12	na	0.26	**5.8**	0.3	1.42	7.92	3.43	65.0	**2.1**	45.2	38.3	**8.6**
6.4	0.39	na	0.00	**6.6**	0.9	1.63	12.89	3.76	59.9	**2.4**	21.6	17.4	**7.8**
5.5	0.56	na	-0.16	**5.9**	0.6	1.36	13.63	4.10	67.0	**2.2**	19.8	18.5	**5.5**
6.9	0.41	na	-0.02	**5.7**	0.2	1.16	7.87	4.51	64.6	**3.2**	28.4	15.3	**7.4**
0.0	9.88	na	1.99	**2.5**	0.1	0.41	3.58	3.48	74.9	**3.5**	30.2	14.4	**5.9**
5.0	3.66	na	-0.40	**7.5**	1.1	1.65	13.40	5.15	69.5	**4.1**	22.7	8.7	**8.8**
6.0	0.58	3.4	0.04	**6.1**	0.4	1.41	11.47	4.26	65.1	**5.1**	28.1	4.1	**8.5**
8.4	0.08	na	0.00	**4.7**	1.2	0.97	7.49	3.32	67.9	**4.4**	34.4	11.1	**7.9**
8.5	0.05	na	0.00	**4.7**	1.8	0.95	7.49	3.44	71.6	**4.1**	17.0	8.5	**8.6**
8.0	1.60	2.0	0.01	**6.4**	0.6	1.46	4.19	4.16	58.0	**4.4**	62.4	18.6	**8.6**
9.3	0.12	0.2	-0.01	**4.4**	0.6	1.02	7.27	3.24	64.5	**4.9**	36.1	9.0	**7.3**
4.7	1.19	na	0.01	**5.8**	0.8	1.20	10.94	4.74	68.2	**3.0**	24.4	14.7	**7.9**
8.5	0.96	na	0.35	**3.0**	0.1	0.38	1.82	2.59	81.2	**6.7**	67.4	4.6	**6.6**
8.3	1.18	na	-0.02	**3.1**	0.1	0.41	4.48	2.57	85.3	**2.1**	30.2	23.9	**4.9**
8.4	0.00	na	0.05	**4.2**	0.2	0.86	7.56	4.14	75.2	**5.3**	37.1	6.7	**6.4**
9.0	0.37	na	0.00	**4.5**	0.3	1.00	8.59	3.80	73.2	**1.6**	15.7	23.9	**7.8**
6.2	0.00	na	0.04	**5.1**	0.2	1.57	16.48	4.34	63.2	**3.1**	14.7	13.3	**5.5**
10.0	0.00	na	0.00	**4.1**	0.6	0.93	8.83	1.99	53.8	**3.2**	28.6	15.3	**6.3**
8.6	0.11	0.2	-0.02	**10.0**	2.3	2.39	17.95	4.58	49.7	**3.3**	21.0	12.7	**9.6**
7.9	0.42	na	0.05	**5.3**	0.6	1.09	9.94	3.81	72.7	**1.6**	28.7	29.1	**6.7**
5.5	1.08	6.5	-0.08	**5.9**	0.5	1.56	14.95	3.11	52.1	**4.1**	23.3	9.1	**7.4**
6.7	0.45	na	0.00	**8.1**	0.4	2.27	19.40	4.80	44.6	**1.3**	13.2	26.6	**6.8**
8.4	0.00	0.0	0.00	**2.7**	0.0	0.54	6.01	3.42	81.7	**6.5**	72.5	5.1	**3.4**
7.1	0.03	na	0.07	**5.5**	0.3	1.32	10.41	3.83	66.2	**1.7**	13.3	20.6	**8.2**
9.0	0.40	na	0.29	**5.4**	1.3	1.35	8.76	3.04	70.8	**6.8**	61.3	4.9	**8.6**
9.1	0.18	1.3	0.05	**4.8**	9.4	0.93	9.91	2.62	51.6	**3.2**	10.3	7.9	**8.2**
9.8	0.03	na	-0.01	**5.4**	0.4	1.34	9.92	3.17	60.8	**4.4**	45.9	14.5	**8.5**
8.5	0.00	na	0.01	**8.1**	2.0	1.93	15.50	3.95	54.7	**4.6**	23.0	6.0	**9.5**
5.3	3.22	na	-0.03	**3.5**	0.2	0.66	4.50	3.25	81.1	**2.5**	40.1	27.4	**8.1**
6.4	0.56	na	0.02	**8.2**	1.0	1.40	10.89	4.02	52.5	**1.5**	15.0	24.0	**8.1**
8.6	0.00	0.0	0.00	**4.8**	0.2	1.03	5.54	3.37	60.0	**5.1**	45.2	10.4	**7.8**
4.7	0.41	3.1	0.02	**3.4**	0.2	0.57	5.09	3.20	81.4	**4.7**	25.8	5.8	**6.7**
6.5	0.10	na	0.06	**5.6**	1.3	0.98	8.63	4.96	68.5	**0.3**	7.2	47.3	**6.9**
9.1	0.00	na	0.00	**3.2**	0.0	0.40	1.54	2.52	85.4	**5.4**	69.5	13.1	**7.3**
10.0	0.12	0.2	-0.15	**4.8**	1.2	0.99	13.49	1.98	38.4	**7.2**	81.1	5.5	**4.2**
7.3	0.03	na	-0.16	**4.2**	1.0	0.67	7.02	3.52	63.0	**1.2**	20.4	25.6	**6.9**
9.0	0.09	na	-0.04	**4.4**	1.0	0.76	6.07	3.22	86.9	**0.8**	12.8	30.8	**8.5**
5.4	1.89	na	-0.43	**5.2**	0.5	1.01	8.32	4.05	66.7	**5.3**	32.3	4.3	**8.1**
8.0	0.69	na	0.01	**4.0**	0.7	0.88	6.85	3.22	68.4	**3.3**	30.3	13.4	**7.5**
4.4	5.38	na	-0.16	**4.1**	0.1	0.78	3.51	3.88	79.2	**5.6**	46.2	7.5	**7.8**
5.7	1.20	na	-0.01	**6.1**	0.4	1.27	9.81	4.01	66.1	**1.2**	25.9	21.3	**9.3**
6.2	4.79	na	0.00	**6.2**	0.8	1.23	7.90	3.72	76.2	**6.8**	57.6	4.0	**8.5**
4.3	2.22	na	-0.05	**4.7**	0.7	0.87	7.37	3.13	65.5	**3.5**	20.0	11.8	**6.6**
5.6	2.43	na	0.01	**3.6**	0.2	0.80	5.09	3.48	76.2	**5.4**	53.5	10.1	**7.8**
7.8	1.08	na	0.00	**4.9**	0.3	0.85	6.92	3.52	70.3	**4.5**	40.2	12.5	**6.9**
4.0	1.66	na	0.08	**6.2**	0.7	1.41	12.08	5.50	76.9	**3.6**	20.1	11.6	**7.5**
9.6	0.00	0.0	0.00	**3.3**	0.1	0.51	4.30	2.77	79.0	**6.7**	70.5	5.7	**6.3**
4.7	0.79	9.8	0.38	**6.1**	1.9	1.33	15.51	3.73	55.3	**0.8**	14.3	37.3	**7.3**
4.7	1.16	5.1	1.76	**5.6**	26.2	0.47	4.38	6.30	57.0	**3.6**	10.6	5.0	**9.3**
8.0	0.57	na	-0.03	**6.2**	0.9	1.53	12.98	3.94	59.2	**1.7**	19.6	22.8	**7.7**
3.0	3.00	na	0.11	**4.4**	0.1	0.69	7.60	3.79	71.8	**0.8**	17.0	31.6	**5.5**
3.0	0.22	na	0.00	**3.8**	0.1	0.79	6.63	3.99	74.6	**3.7**	20.4	10.8	**6.8**
6.0	0.82	na	0.27	**3.8**	0.5	0.39	3.97	3.69	75.6	**1.5**	15.6	20.6	**5.6**
4.8	1.65	na	0.02	**7.0**	0.8	1.74	14.69	4.00	55.3	**3.0**	21.9	14.8	**8.2**
7.0	0.94	na	0.01	**4.0**	0.4	0.91	10.21	3.82	73.3	**2.2**	11.7	17.7	**5.3**
5.3	1.02	na	-0.02	**3.4**	0.3	0.54	4.41	4.38	85.3	**3.6**	21.3	11.7	**6.8**
5.3	0.77	2.8	0.10	**4.4**	52.5	0.62	4.33	3.21	61.1	**3.5**	8.5	9.4	**10.0**

Name	City	State	Rating	2019 Rating	2018 Rating	Total Assets ($Mil)	One Year Asset Growth	Asset Mix (As a % of Total Assets) Comm-ercial Loans	Cons-umer Loans	Mort-gage Loans	Secur-ities	Capital-ization Index	Lever-age Ratio	Risk-Based Capital Ratio
First National Bank of Peterstown	Peterstown	WV	**B**	B	B	70.2	7.25	3.5	4.0	38.5	18.9	**10.0**	12.2	22.9
First National Bank of Picayune	Picayune	MS	**B**	B	B	208.3	-1.90	4.9	6.0	27.3	20.3	**10.0**	15.2	24.4
First National Bank of Primghar	Primghar	IA	**B-**	B-	B-	32.1	-3.97	6.8	1.8	1.4	18.5	**10.0**	18.5	22.7
First National Bank of Proctor	Proctor	MN	**C-**	C-	C-	25.3	6.89	1.4	4.3	35.9	7.5	**8.1**	9.7	19.3
First National Bank of Pulaski	Pulaski	TN	**A-**	A-	B+	919.1	6.71	4.8	2.5	12.4	23.9	**9.5**	10.8	0.0
First National Bank of Quitaque	Quitaque	TX	**B**	B	C	73.6	16.64	3.3	4.0	0.0	6.8	**9.8**	13.1	0.0
▲ First National Bank of Raymond	Raymond	IL	**B-**	C+	B	149.4	1.04	5.0	2.0	7.9	39.8	**10.0**	11.1	17.8
First National Bank of River Falls	River Falls	WI	**A-**	A-	B+	286.2	4.62	5.3	1.4	12.1	34.9	**10.0**	11.2	20.4
First National Bank of Russell Springs	Russell Springs	KY	**B**	B	B	235.1	5.82	4.4	1.8	9.1	31.0	**9.8**	12.2	0.0
First National Bank of Sandoval	Sandoval	IL	**B**	B	B-	57.3	13.25	6.2	8.5	35.9	17.5	**10.0**	11.6	18.6
First National Bank of Scotia	Scotia	NY	**C+**	C+	C+	492.2	1.81	10.7	25.6	20.2	6.7	**6.7**	8.7	12.4
First National Bank of Scott City	Scott City	KS	**B**	B	C	125.1	6.05	8.8	5.4	6.0	27.9	**9.8**	12.3	0.0
▼ First National Bank of Sedan	Sedan	KS	**D+**	C-	D	53.8	-7.91	8.4	2.2	11.7	21.3	**10.0**	12.4	22.0
First National Bank of Shiner	Shiner	TX	**B+**	B+	B+	884.8	14.38	2.4	0.7	4.0	79.1	**9.5**	10.8	0.0
First National Bank of Sonora	Sonora	TX	**B**	B	B-	456.6	8.54	5.9	3.8	19.4	2.1	**8.4**	9.9	17.0
First National Bank of South Carolina	Holly Hill	SC	**B**	B	B	207.0	5.75	2.1	1.4	10.0	19.5	**10.0**	12.9	27.4
▼ First National Bank of South Miami	South Miami	FL	**C+**	B-	B-	807.4	4.01	3.4	0.1	12.2	9.2	**7.8**	9.5	15.7
First National Bank of South Padre Island	South Padre Island	TX	**B**	B	B	58.0	-1.36	2.1	0.4	32.8	5.7	**9.8**	11.6	0.0
First National Bank of Sparta	Sparta	IL	**A-**	A-	B+	81.2	1.47	9.5	9.1	22.6	34.8	**10.0**	13.4	28.3
First National Bank of Spearville	Spearville	KS	**B**	B	B	40.4	6.99	6.6	3.8	0.0	7.9	**9.8**	14.7	0.0
First National Bank of St. Ignace	Saint Ignace	MI	**C-**	C-	C-	263.1	2.65	3.6	1.6	9.0	51.9	**5.5**	7.5	15.6
First National Bank of Stanton	Stanton	TX	**B+**	B+	B-	250.5	12.52	4.4	1.1	1.8	57.5	**7.8**	9.5	25.8
First National Bank of Steeleville	Steeleville	IL	**B+**	B+	B+	216.0	8.67	5.6	3.8	19.4	41.9	**10.0**	14.7	29.1
First National Bank of Sterling City	Sterling City	TX	**C**	C	C-	201.2	2.12	1.2	2.2	4.5	67.2	**6.3**	8.3	32.7
▲ First National Bank of Stigler	Stigler	OK	**B+**	B	B	116.5	2.15	5.6	2.2	5.8	48.9	**6.5**	8.5	19.1
First National Bank of Sycamore	Sycamore	OH	**C**	C	C	155.0	2.62	5.6	1.5	22.7	35.7	**9.7**	10.8	18.0
First National Bank of Syracuse	Syracuse	KS	**B**	B	B	383.4	10.86	12.2	1.2	6.1	12.9	**8.4**	10.0	13.7
First National Bank of Tahoka	Tahoka	TX	**C+**	C+	B-	52.3	-5.52	1.3	2.7	1.6	33.3	**8.5**	10.1	0.0
▼ First National Bank of Tennessee	Livingston	TN	**B+**	A-	B+	891.0	5.11	8.5	2.8	14.6	20.6	**9.8**	12.9	0.0
First National Bank of Tom Bean	Tom Bean	TX	**D+**	D+	D+	114.7	-0.68	16.6	12.4	28.6	8.9	**7.9**	9.6	14.8
First National Bank of Trinity	Trinity	TX	**B**	B	B-	59.1	3.02	4.7	14.9	13.2	37.8	**9.4**	10.8	0.0
First National Bank of Wakefield	Wakefield	MI	**C+**	C+	C	50.0	2.01	2.2	8.9	18.3	22.9	**8.1**	9.9	0.0
▲ First National Bank of Waseca	Waseca	MN	**B+**	B	B-	138.1	2.12	7.9	2.3	33.1	7.3	**7.8**	9.7	0.0
First National Bank of Waterloo	Waterloo	IL	**C+**	C+	C+	490.8	2.34	3.8	0.6	16.6	31.5	**8.4**	9.9	14.7
▼ First National Bank of Wauchula	Wauchula	FL	**C**	C+	C	76.2	7.11	6.7	2.9	30.9	9.6	**9.8**	11.2	0.0
First National Bank of Waverly	Waverly	OH	**C**	C	C	163.9	4.15	3.5	3.1	18.6	18.7	**7.2**	9.1	19.5
First National Bank of Waynesboro	Waynesboro	GA	**A**	A	A	150.9	9.34	6.6	8.6	27.8	8.9	**10.0**	17.2	30.9
First National Bank of Weatherford	Weatherford	TX	**B-**	B-	C+	291.4	15.08	14.0	1.8	9.1	5.2	**7.4**	9.6	12.8
▼ First National Bank of Williamson	Williamson	WV	**B-**	B	B-	89.4	10.65	6.0	6.6	37.3	11.1	**8.7**	10.1	18.2
First National Bank of Winnsboro	Winnsboro	TX	**B+**	B+	B	134.5	-1.89	6.7	2.1	16.4	14.0	**9.8**	21.0	0.0
First National Bank Texas	Killeen	TX	**B+**	B+	B+	2318.7	9.33	0.3	12.8	11.3	28.4	**6.6**	8.6	23.3
▼ First National Bank USA	Boutte	LA	**B+**	A-	B+	136.1	4.04	3.4	0.9	22.1	2.1	**10.0**	12.4	22.1
First National Bank, Ames, Iowa	Ames	IA	**A-**	A-	A-	952.0	13.12	3.1	0.6	10.7	28.2	**6.8**	9.1	0.0
First National Bank, Cortez	Cortez	CO	**B**	B	B-	105.6	-0.71	5.7	3.6	10.5	18.7	**10.0**	11.4	17.1
First National Bankers Bank	Baton Rouge	LA	**B-**	B-	C+	875.6	-2.27	4.8	0.0	1.5	4.5	**9.8**	15.3	0.0
First National Community Bank	Chatsworth	GA	**B**	B	B	277.6	70.62	5.0	0.9	16.8	5.9	**9.8**	11.7	0.0
▲ First National Community Bank	New Richmond	WI	**C**	C-	C+	213.6	3.88	6.6	3.3	17.5	23.1	**7.5**	9.3	14.5
First National Trust Co.	Pittsburgh	PA	**U**	U	U	35.5	25.01	0.0	0.0	0.0	0.0	**10.0**	84.2	140.7
First Nations Bank	Chicago	IL	**A-**	A-	B+	376.8	7.11	2.9	0.6	6.8	2.4	**10.0**	13.1	17.6
First NaturalState Bank	McGehee	AR	**B-**	B-	C+	65.0	9.28	16.2	6.0	16.1	17.7	**8.6**	10.1	15.9
First Nebraska Bank	Valley	NE	**B+**	B+	B	291.7	3.13	8.4	1.2	10.5	18.7	**8.7**	10.3	0.0
First Neighbor Bank, N.A.	Toledo	IL	**B-**	B-	C+	474.2	12.54	17.0	4.5	11.5	6.3	**7.6**	10.7	13.0
First Neighborhood Bank	Spencer	WV	**C+**	C+	B-	147.3	9.27	6.7	2.3	28.4	23.9	**9.4**	10.8	0.0
First New Mexico Bank	Deming	NM	**A**	A	A	207.9	0.66	14.8	1.8	9.0	31.7	**9.8**	14.2	0.0
First New Mexico Bank of Silver City	Silver City	NM	**A**	A	A	117.9	3.74	1.5	0.8	9.0	31.9	**10.0**	12.4	20.1
First New Mexico Bank, Las Cruces	Las Cruces	NM	**A**	A	A	122.3	4.19	3.8	2.0	16.1	17.4	**10.0**	14.8	24.7
▼ First Northeast Bank of Nebraska	Lyons	NE	**B+**	A-	B	296.4	-2.88	5.0	1.3	1.9	32.5	**9.8**	13.9	0.0
First Northern Bank and Trust Co.	Palmerton	PA	**B**	B	B-	729.4	4.32	5.3	0.5	30.0	18.6	**9.8**	14.3	0.0
▼ First Northern Bank of Dixon	Dixon	CA	**B+**	A-	B+	1341.2	10.03	7.9	0.1	5.4	26.5	**8.6**	10.1	16.2
First Northern Bank of Wyoming	Buffalo	WY	**B-**	B-	C+	390.9	11.69	9.2	3.9	14.1	20.4	**6.9**	9.0	12.4

Asset Quality Index	Adjusted Non-Performing Loans as a % of Total Loans	Adjusted Non-Performing Loans as a % of Capital	Net Charge-Offs Avg Loans	Profitability Index	Net Income ($Mil)	Return on Assets (R.O.A.)	Return on Equity (R.O.E.)	Net Interest Spread	Overhead Efficiency Ratio	Liquidity Index	Liquidity Ratio	Hot Money Ratio	Stability Index
5.5	1.86	na	-0.05	**4.1**	0.2	1.07	8.89	3.61	67.7	**3.5**	33.8	15.6	**6.3**
4.8	2.02	na	0.06	**9.8**	1.4	2.70	17.43	4.26	49.7	**2.3**	27.7	19.7	**9.8**
7.3	0.00	0.0	0.00	**4.6**	0.1	0.99	5.36	4.01	69.3	**1.8**	26.1	24.1	**7.3**
7.1	0.57	na	0.00	**2.0**	0.0	0.24	2.43	3.41	91.1	**5.6**	44.9	7.4	**4.7**
7.6	0.42	2.3	0.08	**5.7**	2.6	1.15	10.66	3.54	62.6	**1.9**	26.3	22.9	**7.8**
6.3	4.92	na	-0.06	**4.4**	0.1	0.75	5.72	3.05	72.5	**3.3**	60.7	25.2	**7.3**
7.5	0.77	na	-0.02	**3.8**	0.3	0.83	7.74	3.57	72.9	**3.9**	44.1	16.8	**5.2**
8.9	0.09	na	-0.01	**5.2**	1.0	1.41	12.57	3.52	66.1	**5.6**	35.3	4.0	**7.3**
7.9	1.29	na	0.00	**4.2**	0.5	0.79	6.37	3.55	72.4	**1.9**	22.7	20.8	**6.5**
6.1	0.34	na	0.02	**6.2**	0.2	1.48	12.55	4.65	58.3	**2.4**	16.4	17.2	**6.7**
5.3	0.19	3.0	0.07	**3.9**	0.8	0.64	8.03	3.86	77.1	**4.8**	11.7	3.2	**4.5**
4.6	1.83	na	0.58	**4.4**	0.3	0.96	7.75	4.22	66.5	**5.2**	37.3	7.5	**6.3**
8.7	0.19	na	0.00	**0.0**	-0.1	-0.90	-7.25	3.28	106.4	**3.7**	26.2	11.7	**3.8**
9.9	0.23	0.3	0.10	**5.0**	5.2	2.44	19.57	2.51	48.1	**3.1**	63.6	35.9	**7.2**
5.5	1.33	5.2	0.05	**4.6**	1.2	1.04	10.25	4.07	69.4	**2.0**	27.7	22.9	**6.9**
8.2	1.13	na	0.14	**3.5**	0.3	0.53	4.15	3.37	81.6	**6.8**	59.5	4.6	**7.3**
4.1	1.20	na	0.00	**3.0**	0.4	0.21	2.21	2.85	78.6	**3.8**	24.7	10.8	**6.8**
9.0	0.25	na	-0.07	**4.4**	0.1	1.01	8.80	3.86	74.5	**5.9**	51.2	6.5	**7.0**
8.1	0.71	na	0.07	**7.7**	0.4	2.02	15.15	4.54	60.5	**5.2**	30.5	4.5	**8.0**
6.3	0.00	4.1	-0.04	**7.2**	0.2	1.50	9.01	3.21	52.3	**3.7**	56.2	16.2	**8.2**
3.2	4.73	na	0.29	**2.5**	0.3	0.40	4.47	2.72	89.1	**5.0**	65.2	15.5	**4.6**
9.7	0.08	na	1.88	**5.6**	0.7	1.06	10.88	3.09	53.0	**7.1**	65.3	3.3	**5.8**
8.7	1.27	na	0.09	**4.7**	0.7	1.39	9.46	3.16	71.2	**4.7**	43.1	12.1	**8.9**
9.7	0.49	na	-0.03	**4.0**	0.5	0.92	12.48	2.43	63.8	**5.9**	62.5	10.8	**3.3**
7.7	0.79	4.6	-0.01	**7.6**	0.9	2.96	34.35	3.42	45.8	**5.5**	48.2	9.2	**5.8**
5.1	0.30	7.3	0.00	**3.3**	0.3	0.68	5.91	3.34	78.3	**3.0**	28.6	16.2	**6.8**
4.2	1.20	na	0.00	**7.1**	1.2	1.25	11.73	4.42	53.5	**0.7**	14.8	45.5	**7.6**
7.5	2.25	na	0.00	**2.0**	-0.1	-0.36	-3.40	2.71	115.3	**4.2**	78.1	20.0	**5.3**
6.8	1.62	na	0.10	**4.8**	1.1	0.51	3.93	3.42	59.3	**4.4**	42.4	13.7	**8.9**
1.7	1.47	na	0.62	**3.7**	0.1	0.35	3.57	4.98	90.5	**0.8**	5.0	31.5	**4.6**
6.8	0.43	na	0.17	**5.1**	0.2	1.27	12.55	4.30	74.8	**4.0**	30.9	11.9	**5.4**
7.0	1.22	na	-0.02	**3.2**	0.1	0.65	6.46	3.85	84.1	**4.9**	62.2	14.4	**4.7**
7.3	0.43	na	0.00	**6.6**	0.5	1.57	15.15	4.32	66.2	**3.9**	11.2	9.2	**7.8**
5.8	1.37	na	0.02	**3.5**	0.8	0.63	5.75	3.17	76.8	**4.2**	19.2	8.1	**6.7**
4.2	2.26	na	0.00	**2.7**	0.1	0.26	2.46	4.74	100.2	**1.4**	19.0	26.5	**6.3**
4.2	2.95	na	0.02	**2.8**	0.2	0.51	5.56	3.26	84.0	**4.6**	26.4	6.5	**4.4**
8.1	0.43	2.1	0.02	**8.9**	0.6	1.56	9.18	4.52	58.7	**3.6**	30.3	13.7	**9.0**
5.5	0.32	na	0.07	**5.9**	0.7	0.99	10.50	4.64	70.9	**1.7**	23.2	23.3	**6.1**
6.3	0.27	2.7	0.01	**3.6**	0.2	0.66	6.44	4.07	80.1	**0.9**	16.6	33.4	**5.8**
6.1	4.31	na	0.08	**6.0**	0.3	0.81	3.79	4.82	72.3	**1.8**	20.5	21.4	**8.6**
8.3	0.14	na	1.53	**6.5**	8.3	1.52	16.54	3.41	86.0	**7.2**	47.3	0.9	**7.2**
6.1	1.13	6.1	-0.13	**4.5**	0.3	0.91	7.31	4.07	77.4	**2.4**	27.7	19.0	**8.6**
5.8	1.60	9.4	0.00	**4.5**	1.9	0.83	8.55	2.92	59.5	**4.8**	32.9	8.5	**6.9**
5.8	1.35	na	0.01	**4.8**	0.3	0.97	8.35	4.18	73.3	**3.7**	15.2	10.5	**6.4**
3.5	2.55	na	-0.01	**3.1**	1.2	0.51	3.28	2.91	78.9	**6.2**	35.9	0.0	**8.1**
4.0	1.50	na	-0.05	**6.0**	0.9	1.28	10.30	4.74	65.7	**4.0**	14.5	8.7	**8.0**
3.3	4.23	na	0.33	**3.9**	0.4	0.79	8.61	3.83	77.6	**4.5**	16.0	5.3	**5.6**
6.5	na	0.0	na	**9.5**	2.6	30.94	39.69	1.48	74.1	**4.0**	201.3	0.0	**5.7**
7.3	0.00	na	-0.01	**5.5**	0.7	0.77	5.88	2.86	63.3	**0.8**	17.4	45.0	**8.4**
4.5	2.76	na	0.00	**3.8**	0.1	0.65	6.53	3.61	76.4	**3.1**	17.2	13.5	**5.3**
6.3	0.65	na	0.15	**5.0**	0.8	1.15	10.93	3.97	73.1	**4.3**	15.6	6.8	**7.0**
3.7	1.79	na	0.13	**5.6**	1.2	1.00	9.18	3.88	64.5	**1.3**	13.4	22.8	**6.8**
9.0	0.05	na	-0.48	**2.9**	0.2	0.52	4.78	3.22	85.6	**4.2**	36.7	13.0	**6.0**
6.8	1.12	na	-0.03	**7.7**	0.8	1.52	10.66	4.22	53.5	**6.6**	46.8	1.7	**8.7**
9.5	0.06	na	0.00	**7.6**	0.4	1.47	11.89	4.27	67.5	**7.3**	63.4	1.9	**8.3**
9.0	0.16	na	-0.02	**8.8**	0.5	1.64	11.18	4.71	62.1	**5.2**	48.1	10.8	**9.0**
8.4	0.00	na	0.03	**4.7**	0.7	0.90	6.54	3.20	63.9	**3.0**	28.8	12.2	**7.9**
6.3	0.88	na	-0.02	**4.0**	1.5	0.82	5.59	3.72	69.2	**3.7**	13.9	10.5	**8.1**
8.8	0.52	na	0.07	**5.1**	2.7	0.83	8.16	3.63	66.3	**6.6**	40.2	2.7	**8.1**
4.5	1.27	na	0.02	**5.8**	1.4	1.46	16.30	4.15	69.3	**1.2**	13.9	19.4	**6.0**

Name	City	State	Rating	2019 Rating	2018 Rating	Total Assets ($Mil)	One Year Asset Growth	Asset Mix (As a % of Total Assets) Comm-ercial Loans	Cons-umer Loans	Mort-gage Loans	Secur-ities	Capital-ization Index	Lever-age Ratio	Risk-Based Capital Ratio
First Oklahoma Bank	Jenks	OK	**C**	C	C-	747.6	9.00	19.8	0.4	15.5	0.2	**7.2**	9.3	0.0
First Option Bank	Osawatomie	KS	**B**	B	B	417.3	29.38	3.5	2.4	21.9	41.1	**6.5**	8.5	19.1
▲ First Palmetto Bank	Camden	SC	**A-**	B+	B	718.3	0.70	2.7	0.8	15.3	17.3	**10.0**	11.1	17.8
▼ First Peoples Bank	Pine Mountain	GA	**B+**	A-	B+	190.5	21.47	3.7	1.4	16.6	18.7	**7.6**	9.4	16.6
First Peoples Bank of Tennessee	Jefferson City	TN	**B-**	B-	C+	157.0	6.45	10.7	1.5	11.5	15.4	**7.1**	9.1	12.6
First Piedmont Federal S&L Assn. of Gaffn	Gaffney	SC	**A**	A	A	429.8	2.70	2.2	0.9	41.6	0.8	**10.0**	26.2	42.7
First Pioneer National Bank	Wray	CO	**A-**	A-	B+	189.9	7.69	2.1	2.7	3.2	21.3	**10.0**	14.2	22.0
First Port City Bank	Bainbridge	GA	**B+**	B+	B+	258.2	19.16	9.1	1.2	16.1	12.9	**5.7**	7.7	12.2
▼ First Premier Bank	Sioux Falls	SD	**A-**	A	A	2128.6	15.75	5.5	36.8	2.5	11.2	**10.0**	14.3	22.5
First Progressive Bank	Brewton	AL	**C**	C	C+	30.1	0.29	7.6	3.9	14.0	56.5	**9.8**	27.9	0.0
First Pryority Bank	Pryor	OK	**B**	B	B	217.0	20.03	29.6	6.2	5.7	3.6	**9.4**	10.8	0.0
First Reliance Bank	Florence	SC	**C+**	C+	C+	658.8	9.35	9.2	11.3	20.0	6.8	**6.9**	10.3	12.5
First Republic Bank	San Francisco	CA	**B**	B	B	123914.9	21.67	8.6	4.0	39.8	15.8	**6.5**	8.5	12.6
First Resource Bank	Lino Lakes	MN	**B-**	B-	B-	229.6	20.59	12.6	0.1	22.5	3.1	**7.3**	9.2	12.9
First Resource Bank	Exton	PA	**C+**	C+	C-	340.8	11.62	8.3	0.3	21.9	4.8	**6.6**	8.6	13.3
▼ First Robinson Savings Bank, N.A.	Robinson	IL	**C+**	B-	B-	344.2	2.38	5.4	4.1	20.6	29.2	**7.3**	9.2	16.9
First S&L Assn.	Mebane	NC	**C+**	C+	C+	56.4	2.20	0.0	0.0	59.1	19.0	**10.0**	22.4	53.2
First Savanna Savings Bank	Savanna	IL	**D-**	D-	D	11.7	-3.50	0.0	10.1	55.3	7.2	**5.5**	7.5	15.0
▲ First Savings Bank	Danville	IL	**C+**	C	B-	36.9	5.45	0.0	0.9	27.6	55.8	**10.0**	25.5	89.9
First Savings Bank	Jeffersonville	IN	**B+**	B+	B-	1364.3	21.11	5.9	1.1	24.5	13.7	**5.9**	8.9	11.7
First Savings Bank	Beresford	SD	**A-**	A-	A-	878.7	11.53	2.0	15.4	8.4	15.1	**10.0**	15.8	22.1
▼ First Savings Bank of Hegewisch	Chicago	IL	**B-**	B	B	687.4	2.77	0.0	0.1	47.6	29.2	**10.0**	15.9	45.9
First Seacoast Bank	Dover	NH	**C**	C	C	412.6	4.51	5.7	0.5	52.8	10.5	**10.0**	11.5	18.3
First Secure Bank and Trust Co.	Palos Hills	IL	**B-**	B-	C	201.1	33.92	6.1	1.1	14.8	9.1	**7.5**	9.3	13.0
First Secure Community Bank	Sugar Grove	IL	**C+**	C+	C	379.2	21.92	17.1	2.9	3.9	19.0	**5.1**	9.3	11.0
First Security Bank	Searcy	AR	**A+**	A+	A+	5775.8	7.01	5.9	0.8	5.8	41.8	**10.0**	18.3	23.7
First Security Bank	Mapleton	IA	**A-**	A-	B+	71.0	3.24	3.3	3.1	3.6	20.6	**10.0**	12.4	18.1
▲ First Security Bank	Mackinaw	IL	**C-**	D+	D	83.0	8.81	6.0	0.5	16.1	3.9	**7.8**	9.5	13.8
First Security Bank	Overbrook	KS	**C+**	C+	C+	65.0	5.04	7.7	1.5	24.0	5.1	**5.4**	8.2	11.3
First Security Bank	Byron	MN	**C+**	C+	C	70.9	0.70	6.4	3.0	19.6	21.2	**7.0**	9.0	13.4
First Security Bank	Union Star	MO	**C**	C	C-	34.3	4.75	3.3	9.2	32.5	28.1	**6.3**	8.3	16.3
▼ First Security Bank	Batesville	MS	**B+**	A-	B+	652.2	8.82	5.5	3.3	16.6	21.7	**8.5**	10.0	16.7
▼ First Security Bank	Beaver	OK	**D**	D+	C-	117.9	0.69	10.2	1.7	7.8	5.3	**7.9**	10.0	13.2
▲ First Security Bank & Trust Co.	Charles City	IA	**C+**	C	C-	520.0	5.66	5.0	1.2	12.8	26.2	**7.9**	9.6	15.2
▲ First Security Bank - Canby	Canby	MN	**A-**	B+	B+	67.0	-0.87	21.5	1.7	1.4	12.5	**10.0**	13.1	19.1
First Security Bank - West	Beulah	ND	**A-**	A-	B+	67.6	0.76	17.5	1.5	0.8	22.5	**10.0**	12.4	18.8
▼ First Security Bank and Trust Co.	Oklahoma City	OK	**D+**	C-	C	57.5	8.30	14.2	3.6	37.8	3.2	**6.1**	8.6	11.8
First Security Bank of Deer Lodge	Deer Lodge	MT	**B+**	B+	B+	42.3	7.76	11.7	6.1	29.5	0.0	**9.6**	10.8	17.6
First Security Bank of Nevada	Las Vegas	NV	**A**	A	A	244.6	8.16	4.9	0.0	0.8	2.3	**9.8**	19.6	0.0
First Security Bank of Roundup	Roundup	MT	**B**	B	B-	67.1	6.94	8.3	4.1	4.2	34.2	**10.0**	11.5	21.4
First Security Bank-Hendricks	Hendricks	MN	**B+**	B+	B+	33.2	5.60	14.9	2.6	6.3	25.1	**10.0**	12.0	25.5
▲ First Security Bank-Sleepy Eye	Sleepy Eye	MN	**A-**	B+	B+	190.0	4.83	9.4	1.7	7.5	24.2	**10.0**	13.0	20.1
▲ First Security State Bank	Evansdale	IA	**B-**	C+	C	97.4	-5.79	33.7	30.7	5.8	2.3	**10.0**	12.0	15.1
First Security State Bank	Cranfills Gap	TX	**B**	B	B-	123.2	4.11	2.8	3.5	21.6	44.1	**5.6**	7.6	16.4
First Security Trust and Savings Bank	Elmwood Park	IL	**B-**	B-	C	294.1	-7.66	11.6	4.3	4.7	13.5	**7.0**	9.0	17.7
First Sentinel Bank	Richlands	VA	**B-**	B-	C+	297.0	11.26	6.0	36.5	19.8	0.4	**6.8**	8.9	12.4
First Service Bank	Greenbrier	AR	**C+**	C+	B-	370.5	19.54	9.6	0.9	21.5	3.4	**5.9**	8.9	11.6
First Shore Federal S&L Assn.	Salisbury	MD	**B**	B	B	318.3	3.32	2.4	9.1	52.0	4.0	**10.0**	15.5	26.8
First Sound Bank	Seattle	WA	**C-**	C-	C-	107.6	-0.92	27.7	1.8	4.0	2.9	**9.8**	12.5	0.0
▲ First Southeast Bank	Harmony	MN	**C-**	D+	D	101.8	2.08	10.8	2.8	9.6	1.2	**7.4**	9.4	0.0
First Southern Bank	Florence	AL	**B**	B	B-	278.2	17.32	13.1	1.7	23.1	7.2	**8.1**	9.9	0.0
First Southern Bank	Patterson	GA	**E**	E	E-	141.3	14.80	7.5	2.2	10.2	12.6	**9.8**	12.9	0.0
First Southern Bank	Marion	IL	**A-**	A-	A-	699.8	2.84	7.3	7.2	13.7	21.5	**9.8**	12.3	0.0
First Southern Bank	Columbia	MS	**B+**	B+	B	199.9	2.40	8.1	5.8	16.7	17.6	**9.8**	11.4	0.0
First Southern National Bank	Lancaster	KY	**B**	B	C+	907.6	5.38	5.9	2.1	25.0	14.8	**7.6**	9.4	15.6
First Southern State Bank	Stevenson	AL	**B+**	B+	B+	561.2	42.19	5.9	5.5	19.7	28.1	**8.2**	10.0	0.0
▲ First Southwest Bank	Alamosa	CO	**B**	B-	C+	331.4	9.33	10.5	1.2	7.6	15.0	**6.9**	8.9	15.5
First State B&T Co. of Larned	Larned	KS	**A-**	A-	A-	167.0	10.61	7.9	0.7	1.6	26.3	**9.8**	13.6	0.0
▼ First State Bank	Lonoke	AR	**C-**	C	C	245.9	-5.46	2.1	0.5	12.9	34.2	**8.4**	10.1	0.0
First State Bank	Russellville	AR	**A-**	A-	A-	312.8	5.91	11.0	0.9	17.9	10.3	**9.5**	10.7	15.7

Asset Quality Index	Adjusted Non-Performing Loans as a % of Total Loans	Adjusted Non-Performing Loans as a % of Capital	Net Charge-Offs / Avg Loans	Profitability Index	Net Income ($Mil)	Return on Assets (R.O.A.)	Return on Equity (R.O.E.)	Net Interest Spread	Overhead Efficiency Ratio	Liquidity Index	Liquidity Ratio	Hot Money Ratio	Stability Index
5.9	0.74	na	0.17	**2.6**	0.6	0.31	3.27	3.31	79.1	**0.6**	12.5	58.2	**5.3**
8.5	0.87	na	-0.52	**4.6**	1.1	1.02	11.70	3.18	72.9	**3.0**	24.4	14.7	**5.6**
7.0	0.62	na	-0.15	**5.6**	2.1	1.20	10.65	3.33	59.1	**1.9**	29.4	25.5	**8.3**
6.5	1.06	na	0.00	**4.9**	0.4	0.81	8.55	4.39	68.8	**4.8**	30.9	7.5	**6.2**
7.5	0.04	na	-0.01	**4.3**	0.3	0.84	9.21	4.41	73.7	**4.4**	13.2	6.1	**5.4**
9.3	0.49	na	0.00	**9.1**	1.7	1.55	5.59	4.26	58.0	**5.1**	34.5	7.2	**9.4**
8.5	0.00	na	0.01	**6.7**	0.6	1.35	9.28	3.62	53.6	**1.9**	23.7	20.4	**8.6**
8.5	0.26	na	0.00	**3.9**	0.2	0.35	4.54	3.32	85.9	**1.8**	25.6	24.2	**5.5**
6.7	0.58	2.2	2.82	**5.3**	1.9	0.37	2.55	3.47	59.6	**3.9**	32.1	2.6	**10.0**
8.3	2.26	na	0.00	**2.4**	0.0	0.28	1.00	3.05	89.9	**5.1**	95.3	17.7	**6.7**
5.6	0.89	na	0.41	**7.5**	1.0	1.84	17.47	3.86	46.2	**0.9**	22.1	42.3	**7.1**
5.6	1.01	na	0.04	**4.0**	1.1	0.70	6.34	4.22	77.7	**2.3**	12.8	17.4	**7.3**
8.8	0.15	1.2	0.00	**4.1**	218.7	0.74	8.66	2.78	65.2	**3.3**	16.0	10.0	**7.7**
6.0	0.43	na	0.01	**4.0**	0.3	0.54	5.40	3.52	74.3	**1.5**	12.8	16.7	**7.1**
4.6	0.86	na	0.18	**4.2**	0.6	0.77	9.02	3.68	70.6	**1.1**	11.3	27.9	**4.6**
3.2	3.24	na	0.03	**3.9**	0.6	0.68	7.13	3.39	74.3	**4.6**	26.5	6.6	**5.4**
7.2	0.00	na	0.00	**2.3**	0.1	0.33	1.46	3.22	80.5	**2.0**	43.2	53.8	**7.5**
2.3	3.55	23.5	-0.05	**0.0**	-0.1	-3.82	-45.30	3.65	211.5	**1.3**	24.8	28.5	**2.5**
9.9	0.60	na	0.00	**4.0**	0.2	2.41	9.47	2.24	58.2	**4.3**	93.2	24.4	**6.4**
5.6	1.87	na	0.22	**3.7**	-0.6	-0.34	-3.37	3.83	99.7	**1.4**	16.4	8.6	**8.6**
5.6	1.30	3.9	5.06	**10.0**	4.4	2.01	12.38	8.70	43.5	**3.6**	19.5	11.2	**8.8**
10.0	0.13	na	0.05	**2.6**	0.4	0.25	1.57	2.16	81.0	**3.5**	55.7	24.0	**8.3**
9.0	0.30	na	-0.02	**1.9**	0.3	0.25	2.18	3.27	91.9	**3.6**	13.8	10.9	**5.9**
4.3	0.77	5.5	0.00	**3.7**	0.2	0.45	4.50	3.09	79.7	**1.0**	26.5	42.6	**5.4**
4.7	1.84	na	0.00	**2.9**	0.3	0.30	3.21	3.00	80.6	**1.5**	31.8	32.5	**5.0**
9.0	0.19	0.4	0.20	**8.7**	26.3	1.86	9.44	3.86	45.5	**4.8**	25.7	8.3	**10.0**
6.0	0.00	na	0.00	**6.6**	0.3	1.61	9.61	3.69	56.5	**3.7**	37.4	15.6	**8.3**
2.3	1.89	na	0.18	**3.0**	0.2	0.83	8.22	3.55	76.6	**1.8**	15.6	20.0	**5.4**
8.3	0.00	0.0	-0.01	**4.0**	0.1	0.77	8.38	4.09	79.5	**1.6**	12.9	23.0	**5.4**
7.4	0.34	na	-0.01	**4.8**	0.2	1.30	14.94	3.71	69.0	**2.9**	28.6	16.7	**4.8**
8.4	0.00	na	0.09	**4.6**	0.1	0.81	9.45	4.10	72.3	**4.0**	23.9	9.6	**4.2**
5.2	1.53	na	0.07	**6.6**	2.0	1.32	12.34	4.00	64.3	**4.7**	29.3	7.3	**7.5**
0.5	3.32	na	0.78	**7.9**	0.5	1.85	18.49	4.20	45.4	**0.7**	15.9	45.1	**7.3**
3.7	4.06	na	-0.01	**3.7**	1.1	0.84	7.47	3.23	76.1	**4.6**	32.0	8.2	**6.0**
6.2	0.14	na	0.02	**7.5**	0.3	1.86	11.95	4.13	54.7	**5.1**	28.6	4.3	**8.8**
8.5	0.00	na	0.00	**7.0**	0.3	1.92	14.86	4.04	50.2	**5.8**	31.2	1.1	**8.3**
1.6	2.75	na	0.02	**3.2**	0.1	0.61	7.23	5.71	86.0	**0.6**	8.8	43.1	**3.6**
8.2	0.00	na	0.00	**9.8**	0.3	2.82	27.08	4.88	45.0	**4.1**	20.0	8.4	**7.6**
6.8	0.01	0.0	-0.02	**8.8**	0.8	1.35	6.22	4.31	51.2	**5.7**	37.3	4.4	**10.0**
4.6	3.89	na	-0.31	**8.7**	0.3	1.94	16.02	4.75	54.3	**5.4**	38.9	6.8	**8.4**
8.9	0.00	na	-0.26	**7.6**	0.2	1.98	15.98	3.67	48.7	**5.4**	51.3	10.0	**8.1**
8.2	0.03	na	0.00	**6.0**	0.7	1.51	10.28	3.90	61.1	**5.2**	30.7	4.7	**8.3**
4.4	0.95	na	0.25	**6.3**	0.3	1.37	11.49	3.79	57.7	**0.9**	15.6	28.1	**7.6**
8.9	0.03	na	0.02	**5.1**	0.4	1.20	14.78	3.64	71.0	**6.0**	55.4	8.6	**5.1**
5.0	1.83	na	-0.05	**3.9**	0.8	0.99	10.95	2.36	69.1	**6.5**	53.3	4.5	**5.1**
4.2	0.55	na	0.40	**5.5**	0.6	0.84	9.46	4.70	62.3	**0.8**	13.6	33.9	**4.9**
6.9	1.23	na	0.14	**4.3**	0.7	0.77	8.73	4.40	76.6	**0.6**	5.7	18.2	**5.1**
6.3	1.13	na	-0.04	**3.7**	0.5	0.62	4.00	3.33	71.9	**1.5**	18.4	25.3	**7.7**
3.6	1.99	na	0.34	**1.0**	-0.1	-0.28	-2.24	3.36	107.5	**4.2**	13.5	7.3	**6.2**
2.9	1.88	na	0.02	**4.8**	0.3	1.13	12.23	4.20	70.8	**1.4**	9.8	17.6	**6.0**
8.2	0.35	na	-0.01	**5.4**	0.7	1.05	10.62	3.82	62.6	**2.5**	14.7	16.5	**5.6**
5.5	2.60	na	0.00	**0.3**	-0.3	-0.88	-6.70	3.96	132.5	**3.7**	25.3	11.4	**1.7**
3.8	1.36	na	0.07	**7.0**	2.3	1.33	9.51	3.94	53.1	**2.7**	19.5	16.1	**9.0**
8.3	0.08	na	-0.20	**5.2**	0.6	1.23	10.62	4.54	74.5	**2.6**	15.0	16.0	**7.1**
4.7	1.11	na	0.04	**6.0**	2.7	1.22	10.94	4.28	65.8	**4.0**	19.4	9.1	**7.9**
7.5	0.27	1.4	-0.03	**5.2**	1.2	0.85	7.62	3.69	71.6	**2.3**	28.9	20.1	**6.8**
7.2	0.93	na	0.07	**4.7**	0.7	0.84	8.42	3.94	72.6	**3.1**	24.9	14.7	**6.6**
5.3	1.53	na	0.01	**6.8**	0.6	1.54	11.49	3.48	56.6	**4.0**	32.9	10.5	**9.0**
8.9	0.00	na	0.47	**2.2**	0.3	0.48	4.35	3.00	77.1	**1.4**	27.7	31.7	**5.5**
8.7	0.07	na	0.01	**6.7**	0.9	1.19	11.33	3.69	60.6	**1.9**	22.9	19.4	**7.7**

	Name	City	State	Rating	2019 Rating	2018 Rating	Total Assets ($Mil)	One Year Asset Growth	Asset Mix (As a % of Total Assets) Commercial Loans	Consumer Loans	Mortgage Loans	Securities	Capitalization Index	Leverage Ratio	Risk-Based Capital Ratio
	First State Bank	Wrens	GA	B	B	B-	165.2	7.73	12.4	2.6	30.0	10.7	6.9	8.9	12.5
	First State Bank	Belmond	IA	B	B	B	96.7	-1.90	9.7	3.2	10.8	40.5	9.8	12.2	0.0
	First State Bank	Britt	IA	A	A	A	112.5	2.66	3.3	1.3	10.2	32.9	10.0	14.0	25.2
	First State Bank	Ida Grove	IA	B	B	B	167.7	1.02	8.1	4.0	9.0	15.8	9.8	11.8	0.0
	First State Bank	Lynnville	IA	A-	A-	B	197.2	6.98	8.2	2.0	12.4	10.8	10.0	13.4	16.7
	First State Bank	Nashua	IA	B+	B+	B+	55.6	5.33	8.8	2.9	22.7	7.6	9.8	11.1	0.0
	First State Bank	Stuart	IA	B-	B-	B-	107.0	1.67	8.8	2.1	8.3	41.5	8.9	10.3	21.0
	First State Bank	Sumner	IA	C+	C+	C	100.3	-4.81	8.1	2.7	12.7	30.2	10.0	13.5	20.3
	First State Bank	Webster City	IA	A-	A-	A-	498.7	10.35	11.0	0.6	8.9	8.1	9.8	13.8	0.0
▲	First State Bank	Mendota	IL	B	B-	B-	1220.7	9.47	8.7	1.0	23.1	8.3	7.4	10.0	12.8
	First State Bank	Monticello	IL	B-	B-	C+	268.6	0.85	3.5	1.3	9.4	33.0	6.3	8.3	14.6
	First State Bank	Ness City	KS	B+	B+	B+	64.2	4.77	5.6	2.2	0.0	50.8	9.8	18.1	0.0
	First State Bank	Norton	KS	B-	B-	B-	452.4	4.50	9.2	2.2	2.0	42.2	9.2	10.6	0.0
	First State Bank	Irvington	KY	B+	B+	A-	202.8	-1.80	2.2	4.8	34.3	16.2	10.0	12.0	15.8
	First State Bank	Saint Clair Shores	MI	B	B	B	828.5	8.37	9.3	0.5	11.2	19.5	9.0	10.5	0.0
	First State Bank	Holly Springs	MS	C	C	C+	127.3	-0.01	8.8	1.6	13.5	36.2	9.7	11.0	0.0
	First State Bank	Waynesboro	MS	B+	B+	B+	822.1	0.21	4.0	2.0	22.2	23.3	9.8	12.1	0.0
▲	First State Bank	Buxton	ND	B+	B	B+	256.7	33.86	15.7	1.0	10.1	6.6	9.4	10.8	0.0
	First State Bank	Farnam	NE	A-	A-	B+	147.2	7.07	8.5	2.3	4.7	20.8	9.8	12.5	0.0
▼	First State Bank	Gothenburg	NE	C-	C	C	602.9	19.63	5.7	0.8	2.1	21.9	9.8	11.7	0.0
	First State Bank	Hordville	NE	B-	B-	C+	39.7	-6.26	12.1	0.7	5.0	0.6	9.8	12.1	0.0
▲	First State Bank	Loomis	NE	B	B-	C+	146.4	2.72	8.5	3.1	5.3	9.1	9.3	12.1	14.4
	First State Bank	Randolph	NE	B+	B+	B+	60.8	-6.18	2.5	1.4	1.7	4.4	9.8	14.0	0.0
	First State Bank	Scottsbluff	NE	A-	A-	A-	300.1	38.24	11.3	1.5	8.0	19.0	7.5	9.9	12.9
	First State Bank	Socorro	NM	B	B	B	163.3	11.64	0.4	0.6	3.0	81.3	8.2	9.8	46.4
	First State Bank	Winchester	OH	B	B	B-	528.7	12.70	2.2	9.2	18.5	26.2	8.6	10.0	15.7
	First State Bank	Anadarko	OK	B	B	A-	94.3	-5.43	0.8	2.5	2.8	50.6	10.0	14.8	33.0
▲	First State Bank	Boise City	OK	B-	C+	C	83.8	5.89	8.3	5.8	2.0	13.2	9.0	10.5	0.0
▲	First State Bank	Elmore City	OK	B-	C+	C-	16.3	26.24	17.0	2.2	40.1	0.0	10.0	13.5	23.9
	First State Bank	Noble	OK	C+	C+	C+	44.9	-5.64	2.2	4.8	18.8	28.3	9.8	11.6	0.0
	First State Bank	Oklahoma City	OK	C+	C+	C	358.3	7.15	16.8	0.6	15.1	2.2	5.7	9.3	11.5
▼	First State Bank	Tahlequah	OK	D+	C-	C+	62.3	-1.79	10.9	2.2	15.2	20.2	9.8	12.2	0.0
▲	First State Bank	Valliant	OK	C	C-	D	68.5	2.77	7.9	4.6	25.7	10.2	7.4	9.3	13.5
	First State Bank	Watonga	OK	B+	B+	B+	76.2	-7.24	12.9	3.0	2.2	31.3	9.8	11.3	0.0
	First State Bank	Abernathy	TX	C+	C+	C+	41.0	-0.01	5.7	9.8	0.3	10.3	9.1	10.4	16.8
▼	First State Bank	Abilene	TX	C-	C	D+	46.2	22.79	5.1	1.1	2.4	7.6	5.1	7.1	25.1
	First State Bank	Athens	TX	A-	A-	A-	485.9	0.98	5.6	2.9	29.0	24.1	10.0	11.7	21.9
▲	First State Bank	Clute	TX	B	B-	B	211.5	11.69	12.5	8.0	16.8	20.6	7.6	9.6	0.0
▼	First State Bank	Columbus	TX	C+	B-	B-	151.8	4.49	1.8	3.5	4.5	52.1	10.0	14.0	32.3
	First State Bank	Gainesville	TX	B+	B+	B+	1173.9	4.10	7.5	1.4	10.8	35.6	7.8	9.5	14.6
	First State Bank	Graham	TX	B+	B+	B+	156.8	3.73	16.3	1.7	12.9	15.4	7.4	9.2	15.7
	First State Bank	Junction	TX	C+	C+	C-	59.1	15.85	4.8	2.6	10.3	27.6	6.4	8.4	14.9
	First State Bank	Louise	TX	A-	A-	B+	518.8	7.43	10.5	0.8	8.8	16.8	7.0	9.2	0.0
	First State Bank	Rice	TX	B-	B-	B-	158.0	3.35	14.1	2.7	9.5	24.3	9.8	11.9	0.0
	First State Bank	Shallowater	TX	B-	B-	B+	96.6	-9.96	8.1	1.5	3.3	13.7	10.0	17.9	27.0
	First State Bank	Spearman	TX	B	B	B-	145.4	-1.97	6.4	0.8	5.3	8.9	8.3	10.1	0.0
	First State Bank	Stratford	TX	A-	A-	A-	240.9	1.41	8.8	1.0	5.8	33.7	9.8	12.1	0.0
	First State Bank	New London	WI	B-	B-	B-	447.7	47.73	5.2	3.3	11.9	24.6	8.5	10.1	0.0
	First State Bank & Trust	Williston	ND	A-	A-	B	471.4	2.33	5.1	1.0	2.8	56.6	9.8	13.4	0.0
	First State Bank & Trust Co.	Fremont	NE	B+	B+	B-	255.9	3.00	18.8	2.1	21.9	8.7	7.2	9.3	0.0
	First State Bank and Trust	Tonganoxie	KS	B-	B-	C+	318.1	8.38	6.3	2.1	15.5	21.6	6.3	8.3	12.7
	First State Bank and Trust	Bayport	MN	B	B	B-	276.6	7.13	6.2	5.5	31.3	19.2	6.6	8.6	14.8
	First State Bank and Trust Co.	Carthage	TX	A-	A-	A-	503.4	-1.86	2.0	4.9	18.5	57.4	9.8	16.1	0.0
	First State Bank and Trust Co., Inc.	Caruthersville	MO	A-	A-	A-	375.5	4.65	7.1	3.5	15.2	20.6	9.8	13.0	0.0
	First State Bank in Temple	Temple	OK	C+	C+	C+	25.4	-2.76	3.6	3.6	2.7	30.1	10.0	20.0	28.4
▼	First State Bank Minnesota	Le Roy	MN	B-	B	B-	70.3	8.19	7.7	1.6	5.0	4.9	9.8	11.1	0.0
	First State Bank Nebraska	Lincoln	NE	B	B	B-	590.2	1.09	10.6	1.1	12.9	9.8	7.2	9.1	13.0
	First State Bank of Bedias	Bedias	TX	A	A	A	164.0	4.17	11.3	4.6	10.7	21.2	9.8	17.1	0.0
	First State Bank of Beecher City	Beecher City	IL	B+	B+	B	73.0	-2.31	8.6	11.9	20.2	5.5	10.0	14.6	19.7
	First State Bank of Ben Wheeler, Texas	Ben Wheeler	TX	A-	A-	A-	158.2	7.73	6.9	3.5	19.8	46.1	9.8	14.1	0.0

Asset Quality Index	Adjusted Non-Performing Loans as a % of Total Loans	Adjusted Non-Performing Loans as a % of Capital	Net Charge-Offs Avg Loans	Profitability Index	Net Income ($Mil)	Return on Assets (R.O.A.)	Return on Equity (R.O.E.)	Net Interest Spread	Overhead Efficiency Ratio	Liquidity Index	Liquidity Ratio	Hot Money Ratio	Stability Index
5.0	0.66	na	0.00	**8.3**	0.7	1.64	18.85	5.58	59.6	**1.0**	13.0	30.1	**6.0**
8.6	0.40	na	0.05	**4.5**	0.3	1.04	8.34	2.83	55.1	**4.3**	57.0	16.3	**6.8**
9.0	0.00	0.0	0.02	**7.1**	0.4	1.41	9.94	2.82	41.1	**3.9**	45.1	16.6	**8.9**
5.4	0.54	na	1.10	**7.1**	0.9	2.15	18.04	3.88	42.3	**1.1**	21.7	32.4	**7.7**
6.6	0.36	na	0.02	**8.6**	0.9	1.87	13.50	4.31	52.4	**2.4**	15.3	13.5	**9.4**
8.5	0.00	0.0	-0.01	**7.3**	0.2	1.45	13.15	3.28	46.8	**1.3**	27.3	33.5	**7.0**
8.8	0.00	na	-0.02	**3.6**	0.2	0.63	5.92	3.08	75.3	**5.9**	50.3	7.6	**6.3**
3.7	1.55	na	0.28	**0.9**	0.0	-0.14	-0.95	3.29	74.1	**5.0**	47.7	11.8	**5.7**
7.9	0.15	na	0.00	**5.7**	1.3	1.06	7.60	3.23	67.7	**1.2**	13.3	24.5	**8.3**
6.1	0.55	na	0.15	**4.8**	3.5	1.23	11.53	3.30	65.4	**1.4**	8.7	23.9	**8.4**
5.5	1.51	na	-0.01	**5.6**	0.9	1.36	14.81	3.38	67.1	**3.7**	31.8	13.7	**6.3**
6.8	0.00	na	0.12	**5.1**	0.2	0.99	5.28	3.33	68.0	**4.8**	48.9	12.4	**8.8**
4.0	1.91	11.3	0.12	**5.1**	1.3	1.15	9.71	3.71	63.2	**1.2**	22.4	21.4	**7.3**
5.2	2.88	11.1	0.03	**7.6**	1.0	1.86	15.84	4.38	48.1	**3.9**	8.9	6.1	**7.8**
6.5	0.95	3.3	-0.14	**5.0**	2.2	1.12	10.39	3.43	68.6	**2.9**	32.4	17.9	**7.7**
5.6	2.13	na	-0.03	**2.6**	0.2	0.47	4.14	3.17	93.0	**2.8**	18.9	15.5	**6.7**
4.4	2.18	na	0.25	**4.4**	1.6	0.79	5.97	3.40	65.8	**1.8**	17.2	21.3	**8.8**
6.4	0.35	2.4	0.00	**6.3**	1.0	1.55	13.74	3.68	60.4	**1.3**	4.8	19.0	**7.7**
5.5	0.68	na	-0.01	**6.7**	0.6	1.66	12.39	3.61	60.5	**1.2**	16.0	28.9	**8.9**
2.1	3.38	na	-0.03	**8.3**	3.4	2.37	19.40	3.96	38.2	**1.4**	13.5	19.8	**8.8**
7.1	0.00	na	0.00	**3.8**	0.1	0.63	5.22	3.30	74.9	**4.0**	24.8	9.9	**6.3**
6.2	0.00	na	0.00	**8.6**	0.6	1.65	11.57	4.46	53.0	**1.0**	8.3	21.2	**9.1**
4.5	0.00	na	0.58	**7.3**	0.3	1.62	11.45	3.64	52.5	**1.7**	19.6	18.8	**9.0**
7.1	0.54	na	-0.26	**9.4**	1.4	1.94	19.73	4.31	54.4	**2.7**	31.6	18.7	**8.4**
10.0	1.99	na	0.47	**2.8**	0.0	0.10	1.01	3.12	70.8	**7.0**	63.4	3.6	**5.2**
5.2	0.88	na	0.07	**4.9**	1.4	1.08	10.18	3.56	69.1	**3.0**	17.1	12.6	**6.2**
9.0	0.00	na	-0.07	**4.7**	0.9	3.72	26.23	3.32	52.7	**5.4**	46.8	9.1	**5.0**
4.1	0.60	na	0.07	**7.7**	0.5	2.30	27.34	4.32	47.3	**0.2**	3.6	46.4	**5.9**
8.2	0.52	na	0.00	**8.1**	0.1	2.48	18.09	2.97	91.1	**5.1**	29.2	2.5	**6.3**
5.9	1.86	na	-0.10	**2.9**	0.0	0.31	2.66	4.45	93.3	**5.9**	41.1	4.5	**4.9**
7.1	0.05	na	0.00	**4.4**	0.7	0.80	8.36	3.40	69.0	**0.6**	9.4	42.2	**5.5**
5.0	4.32	na	0.03	**1.5**	0.0	-0.14	-1.14	3.43	102.3	**2.0**	28.1	23.8	**6.2**
5.3	0.58	na	0.53	**3.7**	0.1	0.77	8.28	4.80	83.2	**1.5**	13.8	24.2	**4.9**
8.2	0.86	na	0.00	**7.1**	0.3	1.48	12.51	4.41	60.7	**4.8**	44.9	12.0	**7.7**
4.1	0.85	na	-0.23	**5.9**	0.2	1.70	14.68	6.88	76.3	**3.5**	22.1	12.1	**6.8**
8.8	0.00	na	0.00	**2.7**	0.0	0.38	4.52	2.73	84.7	**6.4**	71.7	7.5	**2.6**
5.7	1.80	na	-0.08	**6.2**	1.5	1.26	10.79	3.94	62.2	**3.9**	17.7	9.6	**7.3**
4.9	0.68	na	0.09	**7.6**	0.9	1.80	18.42	4.41	62.4	**4.3**	28.4	9.4	**6.3**
8.4	0.02	na	0.01	**1.5**	-0.3	-0.68	-4.79	2.59	71.0	**2.9**	57.0	33.6	**7.2**
6.5	0.76	4.6	0.04	**4.3**	2.7	0.92	9.50	4.00	79.2	**5.5**	31.3	6.8	**8.7**
8.7	0.04	na	0.04	**6.0**	0.5	1.35	13.77	4.09	69.4	**3.0**	41.5	21.2	**7.3**
5.6	1.24	na	-0.04	**5.2**	0.2	1.28	15.13	3.62	65.3	**3.8**	31.1	13.0	**5.0**
8.4	0.02	na	0.12	**10.0**	3.1	2.38	25.21	5.37	54.5	**4.5**	23.9	6.8	**8.3**
7.3	0.49	na	0.08	**3.4**	0.2	0.49	3.79	3.90	87.3	**3.4**	24.4	12.9	**7.1**
3.4	3.42	10.1	1.43	**8.1**	0.3	1.37	6.77	4.53	70.0	**2.4**	21.5	17.8	**9.2**
8.6	0.06	na	0.27	**5.1**	0.3	0.93	10.64	3.90	67.9	**1.3**	23.1	29.6	**5.8**
8.5	0.00	na	0.00	**7.1**	1.0	1.63	12.99	3.52	57.8	**2.7**	35.6	20.0	**8.4**
4.9	3.73	na	-0.02	**4.6**	0.9	0.81	8.51	4.65	72.5	**3.9**	25.6	9.5	**7.0**
5.4	2.80	na	0.00	**5.6**	1.0	0.85	5.79	3.30	51.2	**5.7**	53.0	9.5	**8.8**
8.0	0.10	na	-0.01	**7.0**	1.0	1.59	17.29	4.45	63.1	**3.6**	16.2	11.3	**7.0**
7.8	0.28	1.1	0.02	**4.0**	0.5	0.69	8.06	3.84	83.4	**4.1**	17.3	8.3	**5.2**
8.6	0.15	na	0.01	**5.0**	0.8	1.12	12.82	3.74	75.9	**4.0**	25.3	10.1	**6.1**
6.7	1.45	na	0.05	**5.4**	1.5	1.19	7.26	3.20	56.7	**1.5**	33.5	39.9	**8.4**
7.9	0.26	na	0.07	**7.0**	1.7	1.77	13.42	4.14	62.8	**2.8**	13.6	14.7	**8.7**
7.1	0.06	na	0.00	**4.6**	0.1	1.31	6.55	4.62	61.4	**1.3**	10.1	25.8	**6.9**
3.2	3.68	na	0.00	**5.6**	0.2	1.20	10.68	3.75	65.7	**5.3**	29.9	3.4	**7.4**
7.6	0.21	na	0.00	**5.6**	2.0	1.35	13.11	3.54	59.2	**1.7**	9.6	19.8	**8.2**
7.4	0.45	1.8	-0.81	**8.9**	1.0	2.43	14.38	4.64	45.7	**2.7**	46.3	29.1	**9.7**
5.0	1.29	6.4	-0.03	**9.7**	0.4	2.28	15.59	4.46	52.6	**3.2**	18.0	13.4	**9.0**
9.2	0.05	na	-0.15	**6.8**	0.8	2.14	15.52	3.35	49.6	**2.0**	34.7	30.4	**8.7**

Name	City	State	Rating	2019 Rating	2018 Rating	Total Assets ($Mil)	One Year Asset Growth	Asset Mix (As a % of Total Assets) Commercial Loans	Consumer Loans	Mortgage Loans	Securities	Capitalization Index	Leverage Ratio	Risk-Based Capital Ratio
▼ First State Bank of Bigfork	Bigfork	MN	D	D+	D	85.0	4.79	10.0	10.9	36.8	1.0	9.8	10.9	15.3
First State Bank of Blakely	Blakely	GA	A-	A-	B+	494.9	3.91	7.9	2.6	13.6	12.3	9.8	15.8	0.0
▲ First State Bank of Bloomington	Bloomington	IL	B-	C+	C+	125.8	7.61	7.7	2.0	23.9	20.9	7.0	9.0	15.4
First State Bank of Brownsboro	Brownsboro	TX	B-	B-	C+	108.4	5.23	6.1	8.0	19.5	43.6	8.5	10.0	18.7
▼ First State Bank of Burnet	Burnet	TX	B+	A-	A-	244.6	-1.28	4.2	1.6	8.8	56.7	9.8	14.0	0.0
▲ First State Bank of Campbell Hill	Campbell Hill	IL	A-	B+	B	117.2	2.99	6.1	3.9	27.9	16.4	10.0	12.2	20.5
First State Bank of Cando	Cando	ND	C+	C+	C+	61.5	0.39	4.0	5.8	4.1	35.9	7.6	9.4	17.3
First State Bank of Claremont	Groton	SD	B-	B-	B-	59.9	1.59	6.7	0.9	0.0	18.1	10.0	11.9	24.5
▼ First State Bank of Decatur	Decatur	MI	B-	B	B	52.4	-2.83	12.6	3.4	40.4	28.4	9.8	21.4	0.0
First State Bank of DeKalb County	Fort Payne	AL	B-	B-	C+	198.8	6.52	8.2	6.4	19.7	16.2	9.9	10.9	16.2
▼ First State Bank of DeQueen	De Queen	AR	B	B+	B+	290.8	13.97	8.9	3.6	14.2	15.0	7.4	9.5	0.0
First State Bank of Dongola	Dongola	IL	C+	C+	C	25.9	4.96	5.5	11.4	27.2	8.9	10.0	11.2	19.7
First State Bank of Forrest	Forrest	IL	C-	C-	C-	230.1	5.78	14.7	4.9	31.5	8.1	6.3	8.3	12.6
First State Bank of Forsyth	Forsyth	MT	B	B	B-	121.7	0.37	4.5	3.8	9.9	37.6	9.8	12.5	0.0
First State Bank of Fountain	Fountain	MN	D	D	D+	32.7	-0.71	4.8	1.3	9.3	37.6	8.2	10.0	0.0
First State Bank of Golva	Golva	ND	A-	A-	B+	81.4	3.54	3.6	2.5	4.0	42.1	8.5	10.0	18.5
First State Bank of Grove City	Grove City	MN	B-	B-	B	33.7	36.80	7.3	2.8	17.9	0.7	9.7	11.0	0.0
▼ First State Bank of Harvey	Harvey	ND	B-	B	B-	83.2	-2.58	2.0	3.3	5.1	52.4	9.2	10.6	0.0
First State Bank of Healy	Healy	KS	B-	B-	C	77.3	3.26	10.1	0.9	1.3	33.7	9.8	21.0	0.0
▲ First State Bank of Kiester	Kiester	MN	C-	D+	D	22.3	19.45	14.7	2.7	10.4	1.1	7.9	9.6	17.4
First State Bank of Le Center	Le Center	MN	B+	B+	B	83.6	-0.67	10.8	7.0	20.0	14.8	9.5	10.7	17.0
First State Bank of Livingston	Livingston	TX	B	B	B	369.2	5.26	1.7	2.6	4.2	46.3	9.8	14.7	0.0
▼ First State Bank of Malta	Malta	MT	D-	D	D+	135.0	-1.40	2.8	1.7	0.0	26.6	9.8	15.5	0.0
First State Bank of Middlebury	Middlebury	IN	B+	B+	B-	598.8	5.60	13.9	2.1	23.0	17.0	10.0	11.6	16.6
First State Bank of Newcastle	Newcastle	WY	B	B	B	151.1	4.26	6.1	2.4	7.7	55.2	10.0	13.4	38.3
First State Bank of Odem	Odem	TX	A	A	A-	143.5	4.50	11.7	1.7	5.6	28.2	10.0	12.9	24.2
▲ First State Bank of Olmsted	Olmsted	IL	B	B-	B-	55.9	11.41	14.4	3.6	28.2	19.9	10.0	12.6	21.4
First State Bank of Paint Rock	Paint Rock	TX	A-	A-	B	114.7	8.94	6.9	3.7	3.5	32.3	9.8	12.1	0.0
First State Bank of Porter	Porter	IN	B+	B+	A-	143.7	2.55	1.3	0.3	21.7	31.9	9.8	16.5	0.0
First State Bank of Purdy	Monett	MO	B-	B-	C	167.4	-2.92	14.5	0.9	9.0	9.6	6.3	9.1	12.0
First State Bank of Randolph County	Cuthbert	GA	D+	D+	C-	80.9	-0.64	8.7	3.5	4.3	47.1	7.5	9.5	0.0
First State Bank of Ransom	Ransom	KS	B	B	B	42.0	-1.22	6.5	1.4	1.0	52.4	10.0	23.2	47.9
▼ First State Bank of Red Wing	Red Wing	MN	D	D+	D+	84.4	7.88	3.9	12.4	10.6	43.4	6.5	8.6	20.6
First State Bank of Roscoe	Roscoe	SD	A-	A-	B+	115.4	9.12	6.6	0.5	0.2	4.6	10.0	11.9	17.1
▲ First State Bank of Rosemount	Rosemount	MN	D	D-	D-	74.3	5.47	5.9	9.6	17.2	18.9	5.0	7.0	11.3
First State Bank of San Diego	San Diego	TX	C+	C+	C+	69.2	8.86	13.3	3.5	2.9	37.4	6.6	8.6	22.9
First State Bank of Sauk Centre	Sauk Centre	MN	A-	A-	B+	114.0	5.57	8.1	4.4	18.1	13.0	10.0	13.1	21.7
▼ First State Bank of Shelby	Shelby	MT	A-	A	A	127.1	1.19	3.6	0.6	0.0	78.6	10.0	23.1	70.7
First State Bank of St. Charles, Missouri	Saint Charles	MO	A-	A-	A-	402.4	8.10	10.1	0.1	48.9	12.2	10.0	13.8	15.8
First State Bank of St. Peter	Saint Peter	IL	B+	B+	B+	29.6	5.76	0.9	3.8	3.8	53.4	10.0	17.1	38.2
First State Bank of Swanville	Swanville	MN	C+	C+	C+	23.4	-6.66	17.8	3.6	16.6	1.9	10.0	17.0	24.3
First State Bank of Texas	Orange	TX	B-	B-	B-	184.8	7.37	20.6	9.4	13.8	9.4	9.8	11.1	0.0
First State Bank of the Florida Keys	Key West	FL	B	B	B-	1018.3	5.46	5.6	0.7	17.6	30.4	6.9	8.9	16.1
First State Bank of the South, Inc.	Sulligent	AL	B+	B+	B+	106.4	2.76	4.1	7.8	14.9	40.3	10.0	15.5	26.5
First State Bank of the Southeast, Inc.	Middlesboro	KY	C+	C+	B-	335.4	-6.04	11.1	3.0	29.3	9.3	7.4	9.3	13.1
First State Bank of Uvalde	Uvalde	TX	B+	B+	B	1792.7	0.02	3.2	0.5	5.9	52.0	7.9	9.6	28.4
First State Bank of Van Orin	Van Orin	IL	C	C	C-	40.4	-1.88	3.4	1.5	2.1	36.5	8.1	9.7	24.3
▼ First State Bank of Warren	Warren	AR	C+	B-	C+	106.0	-1.72	13.2	2.1	5.3	50.7	10.0	11.4	21.8
▼ First State Bank of Wyoming	Wyoming	MN	B+	A-	B+	183.1	0.53	4.3	1.8	14.5	49.2	9.8	18.1	0.0
First State Bank Shannon-Polo	Shannon	IL	C+	C+	C+	174.3	9.17	8.8	2.6	9.1	33.0	7.0	9.2	0.0
First State Bank Southwest	Worthington	MN	A	A	A-	266.7	2.65	8.3	2.9	4.3	33.0	10.0	11.5	19.9
First State Bank, Pond Creek, Oklahoma	Pond Creek	OK	B	B	B-	46.9	-1.66	17.1	3.4	19.6	14.5	9.8	12.2	0.0
▲ First State Community Bank	Farmington	MO	A-	B+	B	2674.2	6.16	6.5	2.0	21.0	11.3	7.3	10.5	12.8
First Summit Bank	Ryan	OK	C	C	C+	27.0	-0.90	10.9	2.9	7.2	0.0	9.8	13.1	0.0
First Texas Bank	Georgetown	TX	B+	B+	B-	675.9	4.51	2.6	1.1	2.6	55.9	6.8	8.8	18.3
First Texas Bank	Killeen	TX	B	B	B-	314.8	1.06	1.2	0.4	10.6	44.6	9.5	10.8	0.0
First Texas Bank	Lampasas	TX	A-	A-	B-	148.1	10.21	2.6	1.2	15.1	38.8	9.8	11.4	0.0
▼ First Texoma National Bank	Durant	OK	B+	A-	B+	187.8	5.59	6.2	5.3	27.4	10.3	9.8	10.8	15.7
First Tri-County Bank	Swanton	NE	C	C	C	54.8	5.96	9.1	5.1	18.8	2.7	8.1	10.5	13.4
▼ First Trust and Savings Bank	Coralville	IA	D+	C-	C+	49.2	-4.83	5.5	1.6	3.5	68.1	10.0	12.8	27.6

Arrows denote recent upgrades ▲ or downgrades ▼

Asset Quality Index	Adjusted Non-Performing Loans as a % of Total Loans	Adjusted Non-Performing Loans as a % of Capital	Net Charge-Offs Avg Loans	Profitability Index	Net Income ($Mil)	Return on Assets (R.O.A.)	Return on Equity (R.O.E.)	Net Interest Spread	Overhead Efficiency Ratio	Liquidity Index	Liquidity Ratio	Hot Money Ratio	Stability Index
0.3	4.42	35.9	-0.04	**4.6**	0.2	0.87	8.00	4.37	69.4	**1.6**	16.9	20.1	**6.3**
4.3	2.70	na	0.27	**7.0**	1.6	1.25	7.89	4.11	59.9	**1.1**	17.8	30.1	**9.3**
4.7	1.09	na	0.00	**5.3**	0.4	1.34	14.28	3.74	71.7	**3.8**	26.9	11.5	**6.3**
6.2	1.03	na	0.04	**4.5**	0.3	1.12	11.31	3.86	72.1	**3.4**	27.0	13.8	**6.2**
9.4	0.30	na	-0.21	**4.9**	0.8	1.30	9.03	3.31	61.6	**5.7**	65.7	12.1	**8.5**
5.7	1.47	9.2	0.01	**6.4**	0.4	1.31	10.77	3.88	58.2	**4.6**	27.7	7.0	**7.0**
7.0	0.16	na	0.99	**3.6**	0.1	0.85	8.71	3.21	77.4	**3.1**	33.3	17.5	**5.6**
6.0	3.73	8.3	-0.02	**3.6**	0.1	0.74	6.09	3.40	12.9	**5.6**	51.8	9.0	**5.1**
8.8	0.73	na	0.00	**3.6**	0.1	0.66	3.06	3.79	79.9	**4.5**	48.8	14.2	**7.5**
4.1	0.74	na	0.83	**5.2**	0.5	0.97	8.07	4.87	58.6	**2.8**	28.3	17.3	**6.7**
5.0	1.17	na	0.15	**5.6**	1.0	1.42	15.23	3.87	61.8	**0.7**	12.7	19.5	**6.2**
7.5	1.57	na	-0.36	**4.7**	0.1	1.23	11.30	4.37	74.8	**5.3**	41.3	8.0	**5.8**
2.6	1.70	na	0.26	**3.0**	0.3	0.57	6.81	2.89	74.8	**1.4**	16.5	25.4	**4.6**
4.0	4.22	na	-0.05	**7.2**	0.5	1.56	11.78	3.95	44.1	**4.6**	45.1	13.5	**7.9**
9.2	0.00	na	0.00	**0.9**	0.0	-0.02	-0.24	3.29	107.1	**4.4**	51.8	15.0	**4.5**
8.0	0.00	na	0.00	**8.5**	0.4	1.77	16.59	3.89	50.7	**5.3**	35.4	5.9	**8.0**
6.3	0.32	na	-0.11	**4.8**	0.1	0.79	4.59	2.78	62.1	**5.6**	54.5	9.2	**7.3**
7.6	0.00	2.1	0.04	**3.9**	0.2	0.86	7.57	3.12	76.0	**6.3**	66.1	6.9	**6.9**
4.7	2.91	na	-0.09	**5.7**	0.3	1.44	6.71	3.58	56.7	**2.0**	31.3	25.0	**7.0**
8.5	0.00	na	0.32	**2.5**	0.0	0.49	4.50	3.90	69.4	**5.1**	38.3	5.8	**2.8**
5.0	0.75	na	0.18	**7.1**	0.3	1.39	12.50	4.54	58.7	**4.0**	16.8	8.6	**8.3**
7.8	0.60	na	-0.11	**5.2**	1.2	1.36	8.90	3.50	64.7	**4.9**	37.3	9.7	**8.2**
0.0	29.39	na	3.19	**1.1**	-0.8	-2.27	-14.01	3.10	60.9	**3.1**	27.1	15.4	**6.0**
4.8	1.72	na	-0.01	**6.5**	2.1	1.41	12.07	4.20	67.1	**2.0**	19.9	18.9	**8.4**
9.4	1.54	na	-0.02	**3.3**	0.3	0.66	4.68	2.64	76.1	**3.7**	59.5	24.8	**7.9**
8.7	0.00	na	-0.28	**6.7**	0.4	1.23	9.52	4.98	66.8	**5.5**	35.7	4.8	**7.9**
6.3	0.06	na	0.00	**5.0**	0.2	1.09	8.88	3.91	63.6	**2.6**	19.0	16.4	**6.5**
4.8	4.54	na	-0.06	**7.3**	0.5	1.66	13.87	3.81	52.8	**4.4**	48.6	15.3	**8.3**
8.5	1.28	na	0.14	**4.7**	0.3	0.93	5.45	3.78	72.7	**2.6**	39.9	25.3	**8.5**
4.2	1.93	na	0.03	**4.8**	0.4	1.07	11.99	4.22	77.9	**3.3**	27.0	8.1	**5.5**
2.0	6.93	na	0.00	**2.9**	0.2	0.75	8.10	2.82	87.0	**5.1**	42.5	9.7	**4.8**
8.9	1.25	2.3	0.00	**5.0**	0.1	1.11	4.76	3.14	59.7	**5.7**	72.3	11.8	**7.1**
7.5	0.02	na	0.00	**0.7**	0.0	-0.21	-2.22	2.05	114.4	**3.9**	52.5	17.9	**4.2**
7.4	0.00	na	0.04	**5.9**	0.4	1.22	10.16	3.61	60.1	**2.3**	24.9	18.3	**8.8**
4.2	1.86	na	-0.02	**3.2**	0.1	0.65	8.95	3.91	77.9	**4.7**	25.1	5.3	**1.8**
7.2	0.69	2.0	0.00	**4.1**	0.2	0.96	10.52	3.13	72.2	**4.8**	46.2	11.8	**5.1**
8.0	0.00	na	-0.02	**7.0**	0.4	1.44	10.04	3.64	54.6	**2.8**	22.5	16.0	**8.4**
10.0	1.17	na	1.97	**4.3**	0.1	0.42	1.81	2.26	74.7	**6.8**	109.3	11.7	**8.7**
7.3	0.82	4.3	0.05	**6.5**	1.0	1.03	7.42	3.53	85.6	**2.0**	12.4	18.7	**8.4**
9.1	0.00	na	-0.05	**6.7**	0.1	1.32	7.72	3.54	54.6	**6.6**	78.6	7.2	**8.3**
7.7	1.85	na	0.00	**2.9**	0.0	0.26	1.52	4.93	90.0	**3.9**	28.4	10.3	**5.9**
5.4	0.85	na	-0.03	**3.6**	0.3	0.74	5.48	4.46	83.9	**1.9**	16.3	19.9	**7.3**
7.8	1.36	na	0.00	**4.6**	2.7	1.11	12.33	3.21	71.6	**5.2**	25.1	5.2	**8.0**
8.4	0.07	na	0.08	**3.9**	0.2	0.76	4.90	3.89	75.1	**3.2**	50.5	25.0	**7.9**
2.1	2.67	21.2	0.00	**2.9**	0.5	0.59	6.37	3.76	80.7	**1.4**	13.1	22.6	**3.8**
9.7	0.27	na	0.04	**5.6**	5.4	1.21	11.71	2.16	35.2	**3.1**	58.0	50.5	**7.7**
6.6	1.35	na	0.00	**2.7**	0.1	0.71	6.88	2.61	78.7	**5.0**	65.4	14.3	**4.6**
8.1	1.48	na	0.00	**2.6**	0.1	0.33	3.12	2.89	88.0	**3.9**	44.8	16.7	**5.9**
7.1	2.97	na	-0.01	**4.7**	0.4	0.94	5.04	3.09	64.8	**6.4**	66.2	8.2	**8.3**
5.7	0.55	na	0.89	**3.2**	0.3	0.76	7.48	3.16	69.3	**3.4**	28.1	13.9	**4.7**
8.5	0.17	na	0.02	**7.7**	1.1	1.71	14.04	3.81	62.0	**3.8**	25.6	11.2	**8.9**
6.7	0.24	3.7	0.00	**6.2**	0.2	1.69	13.88	4.87	66.1	**3.0**	23.5	14.8	**5.6**
7.3	0.39	2.2	0.03	**7.7**	10.6	1.62	13.15	3.85	59.2	**2.8**	7.5	12.8	**10.0**
5.6	0.57	4.7	-0.11	**1.5**	0.0	-0.44	-3.33	4.53	110.3	**1.6**	24.8	25.4	**6.3**
9.8	1.62	na	0.02	**5.7**	2.0	1.17	13.31	3.00	52.5	**6.9**	67.9	5.0	**6.8**
9.3	1.14	na	0.00	**4.2**	0.7	0.88	8.04	3.43	65.6	**7.2**	60.1	2.3	**7.3**
9.6	0.21	na	-0.05	**6.8**	0.5	1.36	11.76	3.88	54.8	**6.7**	55.7	3.8	**7.7**
6.8	0.51	na	0.04	**4.5**	0.3	0.54	4.83	4.62	79.3	**2.3**	16.8	17.8	**7.4**
6.8	0.00	na	0.00	**3.2**	0.1	0.63	5.60	3.87	79.0	**4.2**	12.6	7.1	**5.7**
6.8	3.66	na	0.00	**0.5**	-0.1	-0.75	-5.77	2.30	137.1	**2.2**	33.6	25.2	**5.2**

	Name	City	State	Rating	2019 Rating	2018 Rating	Total Assets ($Mil)	One Year Asset Growth	Comm-ercial Loans	Cons-umer Loans	Mort-gage Loans	Secur-ities	Capital-ization Index	Lever-age Ratio	Risk-Based Capital Ratio
									Asset Mix (As a % of Total Assets)						
	First Trust and Savings Bank	Wheatland	IA	**B-**	B-	B-	202.8	9.06	13.7	3.1	4.8	3.9	**8.9**	10.4	0.0
▼	First Trust and Savings Bank of Watseka	Watseka	IL	**A-**	A	A	250.7	1.60	8.7	1.2	6.1	28.9	**9.8**	16.1	0.0
▼	First Trust Bank of Illinois	Kankakee	IL	**B-**	B	B	302.7	26.94	11.6	1.0	7.4	43.2	**7.0**	9.0	15.0
▲	First United Bank	Park River	ND	**B-**	C+	C-	263.3	4.84	5.2	2.1	3.9	20.1	**9.1**	10.5	14.3
	First United Bank	Dimmitt	TX	**A-**	A-	A-	1407.3	4.49	12.7	0.4	7.0	24.0	**9.5**	10.7	14.6
▼	First United Bank & Trust	Oakland	MD	**B-**	B	B-	1444.7	3.40	8.1	2.5	25.5	15.1	**9.7**	10.8	15.3
	First United Bank and Trust Co.	Madisonville	KY	**A-**	A-	A-	340.3	5.36	9.5	2.6	26.6	13.9	**9.8**	12.3	0.0
	First United Bank and Trust Co.	Durant	OK	**B**	B	B	8135.9	13.08	7.6	2.0	22.6	12.4	**5.3**	9.1	11.3
	First United National Bank	Fryburg	PA	**B**	B	B	264.3	0.36	4.3	6.4	44.2	19.6	**7.8**	9.7	0.0
	First US Bank	Birmingham	AL	**B-**	B-	C+	788.2	-0.85	6.1	17.5	10.6	14.0	**7.7**	9.5	14.3
	First Utah Bank	Salt Lake City	UT	**B-**	B-	C	446.8	11.41	15.6	0.8	2.2	7.0	**8.8**	11.5	14.0
	First Vision Bank of Tennessee	Tullahoma	TN	**B+**	B+	B+	289.6	7.46	5.1	2.6	19.5	6.3	**8.8**	10.2	15.1
	First Volunteer Bank	Chattanooga	TN	**A-**	A-	B+	1035.4	3.65	7.1	2.2	13.7	2.7	**10.0**	12.8	16.9
	First Western Bank	Booneville	AR	**B-**	B-	C+	466.1	7.76	3.0	1.0	34.3	5.7	**6.5**	8.5	12.6
	First Western Bank & Trust	Minot	ND	**B-**	B-	B+	1158.4	3.42	18.3	3.0	4.1	21.5	**7.5**	9.5	0.0
	First Western Federal Savings Bank	Rapid City	SD	**A-**	A-	A-	60.9	5.50	0.1	0.1	85.2	0.0	**10.0**	14.6	29.2
	First Western Trust Bank	Denver	CO	**C+**	C+	C+	1344.5	18.72	15.6	6.2	29.6	3.9	**5.3**	8.3	11.2
	First Westroads Bank, Inc.	Omaha	NE	**A**	A	A	289.3	8.50	9.1	0.2	8.6	11.3	**10.0**	13.7	18.4
	First Whitney Bank and Trust	Atlantic	IA	**B+**	B+	B+	241.2	6.38	17.0	1.2	5.3	25.1	**3.2**	9.4	10.1
	First, A National Banking Assn.	Hattiesburg	MS	**B+**	B+	A-	4053.8	14.90	8.0	1.0	14.9	18.8	**10.0**	11.4	16.2
	First-Citizens Bank & Trust Co.	Raleigh	NC	**B+**	B+	B+	41377.0	15.49	9.0	4.3	13.5	20.6	**7.8**	9.7	13.2
	First-Lockhart National Bank	Lockhart	TX	**B**	B	B	294.6	9.42	1.9	0.7	20.6	19.3	**7.9**	9.6	16.5
	Firstar Bank	Sallisaw	OK	**B-**	B-	C+	714.4	18.86	18.9	2.7	19.8	5.0	**4.4**	8.3	10.7
	FirstBank	Lakewood	CO	**A-**	A-	A-	20199.3	6.09	1.0	0.4	31.7	33.1	**6.4**	8.4	16.6
	FirstBank	Antlers	OK	**B**	B	B-	481.2	43.14	6.8	12.2	28.2	7.1	**6.4**	8.4	13.0
	FirstBank	Nashville	TN	**B+**	B+	B+	6651.4	24.74	15.3	3.2	16.1	11.5	**7.2**	10.4	12.7
	FirstBank of Nebraska	Wahoo	NE	**B+**	B+	B-	288.8	7.60	4.5	1.2	7.6	38.2	**7.4**	9.4	0.0
▲	FirstBank Puerto Rico	San Juan	PR	**C**	C-	D+	13034.3	5.39	8.8	14.3	21.9	15.7	**10.0**	17.1	24.9
	FirstBank Southwest	Amarillo	TX	**B+**	B+	B	1036.3	2.49	17.2	3.4	8.8	28.9	**7.6**	9.4	14.7
	FirstCapital Bank of Texas, N.A.	Midland	TX	**B-**	B-	C+	1729.2	57.81	17.0	0.8	14.8	5.9	**8.9**	10.4	0.0
	FirsTier Bank	Kimball	NE	**A-**	A-	B+	449.0	25.15	38.2	1.7	2.9	5.2	**9.8**	13.0	0.0
	FirstOak Bank	Independence	KS	**A-**	A-	B+	186.8	1.67	10.2	1.3	14.4	7.4	**8.2**	10.0	0.0
	Firstrust Savings Bank	Conshohocken	PA	**B+**	B+	B+	3797.4	12.85	23.7	5.3	13.3	6.9	**7.3**	10.9	12.8
▼	FirstState Bank	Lineville	AL	**B+**	A-	B+	257.0	10.06	2.8	4.4	10.3	39.0	**9.8**	11.9	0.0
	Fisher National Bank	Fisher	IL	**A-**	A-	B+	134.6	6.57	4.0	2.2	38.0	16.6	**10.0**	13.4	22.1
	Five Points Bank	Grand Island	NE	**A-**	A-	A	1297.1	14.43	17.2	1.4	6.0	26.8	**9.1**	10.5	0.0
	Five Points Bank of Hastings	Hastings	NE	**A-**	A-	A	352.8	10.52	9.4	0.4	4.7	23.5	**9.8**	11.2	0.0
	Five Star Bank	Rancho Cordova	CA	**B+**	B+	B	1559.9	13.21	8.3	0.5	1.8	5.2	**4.5**	9.0	10.8
▼	Five Star Bank	Warsaw	NY	**B-**	B	B	4435.7	3.94	11.0	19.4	13.9	18.0	**6.5**	9.3	12.1
	Flagler Bank	West Palm Beach	FL	**B+**	B+	B-	339.3	9.62	17.1	0.0	11.0	12.4	**8.4**	9.9	14.2
▼	Flagship Bank	Clearwater	FL	**B-**	B	B-	163.6	34.09	12.1	0.8	4.8	4.7	**9.8**	15.4	0.0
	Flagship Bank Minnesota	Wayzata	MN	**B**	B	C+	257.8	16.07	8.7	0.3	23.7	3.9	**8.2**	10.1	13.5
	Flagstar Bank, FSB	Troy	MI	**B+**	B+	B+	26767.7	38.13	4.6	3.2	30.3	11.3	**5.4**	8.2	11.3
▼	Flanagan State Bank	Flanagan	IL	**C+**	B-	C+	197.0	4.24	4.0	2.2	26.7	24.8	**8.1**	9.9	0.0
	Flatirons Bank	Boulder	CO	**B**	B	B+	192.7	4.81	11.4	0.2	33.4	31.1	**8.2**	9.9	0.0
	Flatwater Bank	Gothenburg	NE	**C**	C	B+	216.7	4.80	12.6	2.0	4.4	17.4	**8.6**	10.2	0.0
	Fleetwood Bank	Fleetwood	PA	**C+**	C+	C+	263.7	-1.19	2.5	0.2	40.3	16.4	**7.8**	9.7	0.0
	Flint Community Bank	Albany	GA	**C**	C	C	251.8	10.30	8.2	1.4	29.0	1.6	**5.5**	8.2	11.4
	Flint Hills Bank	Eskridge	KS	**A-**	A-	B+	132.8	3.60	4.8	3.2	13.7	38.2	**10.0**	12.8	24.8
	Flora Bank & Trust	Flora	IL	**B-**	B-	B-	74.9	7.91	7.5	11.0	19.9	12.8	**10.0**	11.8	19.1
	Florence Bank	Florence	MA	**B**	B	B	1484.0	8.98	2.7	0.0	42.6	20.5	**9.8**	11.3	0.0
	Florida Business Bank	Melbourne	FL	**A-**	A-	B+	159.1	15.70	6.6	0.1	1.4	13.9	**9.8**	11.7	14.9
	Florida Capital Bank, N.A.	Jacksonville	FL	**C**	C	C-	522.3	20.55	6.8	0.0	27.5	3.8	**6.4**	8.4	13.5
	Flushing Bank	Uniondale	NY	**B**	B	B+	7245.8	5.51	10.2	0.0	10.5	10.5	**7.6**	9.5	13.0
	FMB Bank	Wright City	MO	**D+**	D+	D+	41.1	-3.65	7.6	3.3	15.2	35.2	**5.7**	7.7	13.9
	FMS Bank	Fort Morgan	CO	**C+**	C+	B-	203.6	12.08	13.3	14.7	10.0	12.8	**5.5**	10.5	11.4
	FNB Bank	Scottsboro	AL	**B-**	B-	C+	702.8	5.67	8.2	2.3	15.2	16.2	**9.8**	10.8	15.4
	FNB Bank	Fontanelle	IA	**B+**	B+	B+	211.4	2.68	4.5	0.9	7.9	10.5	**9.8**	13.2	0.0
	FNB Bank	Goodland	KS	**B+**	B+	B+	192.9	7.37	3.8	1.0	1.6	24.3	**10.0**	13.5	20.1
	FNB Bank, Inc.	Mayfield	KY	**B-**	B-	C+	511.2	-0.17	8.3	11.6	19.9	18.4	**6.6**	8.7	12.2

Arrows denote recent upgrades ▲ or downgrades ▼

Asset Quality Index	Adjusted Non-Performing Loans as a % of Total Loans	Adjusted Non-Performing Loans as a % of Capital	Net Charge-Offs Avg Loans	Profitability Index	Net Income ($Mil)	Return on Assets (R.O.A.)	Return on Equity (R.O.E.)	Net Interest Spread	Overhead Efficiency Ratio	Liquidity Index	Liquidity Ratio	Hot Money Ratio	Stability Index
6.7	10.29	na	0.00	**2.6**	0.0	0.49	4.94	3.47	80.0	**6.3**	57.1	3.3	**4.0**
9.0	0.98	na	0.57	**4.3**	2.0	0.97	8.10	2.93	67.3	**6.8**	67.5	6.2	**7.1**
7.7	0.12	0.8	0.12	**5.7**	2.2	0.33	3.53	2.80	30.3	**0.7**	10.7	37.7	**8.3**
4.5	0.89	5.5	0.10	**7.3**	9.7	1.17	8.96	3.61	51.6	**1.8**	21.0	14.2	**8.4**
8.4	0.08	0.8	0.03	**6.4**	0.6	1.50	14.76	3.57	64.1	**1.5**	13.9	24.5	**7.5**
8.3	0.75	na	0.00	**9.8**	5.2	4.01	30.77	4.19	37.6	**3.3**	18.8	12.8	**10.0**
7.8	0.29	na	0.04	**4.9**	0.6	0.90	8.26	3.52	70.2	**4.1**	24.7	9.5	**6.7**
5.1	2.54	na	1.45	**10.0**	0.5	2.46	13.04	4.97	43.5	**2.2**	34.5	26.6	**8.8**
4.9	1.62	na	0.33	**3.6**	0.4	0.84	8.08	3.73	71.8	**2.1**	16.9	18.8	**5.2**
5.8	2.30	7.3	0.02	**6.5**	0.1	0.96	5.67	4.48	71.5	**2.6**	35.7	21.5	**8.7**
5.5	5.63	na	0.23	**3.4**	0.2	0.69	5.32	3.28	76.6	**3.6**	35.5	15.3	**6.9**
8.6	0.03	na	0.06	**5.8**	0.4	1.43	19.10	3.69	68.8	**1.6**	14.6	22.4	**5.6**
7.5	0.00	na	0.00	**9.6**	0.8	1.82	13.34	4.61	59.1	**0.5**	8.9	52.5	**10.0**
7.5	0.67	na	-0.15	**3.3**	0.5	0.58	4.51	3.49	83.7	**4.8**	38.6	10.5	**7.2**
4.1	1.61	8.3	0.06	**4.8**	2.0	0.35	2.56	4.22	65.4	**3.4**	8.2	11.5	**10.0**
6.3	0.90	na	0.00	**3.2**	0.2	0.79	7.46	3.50	84.6	**4.0**	49.8	16.5	**5.4**
9.2	0.00	na	0.00	**5.5**	0.5	1.24	10.38	2.53	48.2	**2.2**	45.7	12.4	**9.6**
5.4	2.08	na	0.04	**4.5**	1.1	0.91	8.19	3.31	67.6	**1.4**	25.1	25.2	**7.0**
8.6	0.70	na	-0.04	**4.3**	0.8	0.78	6.65	3.62	76.1	**1.6**	18.0	24.1	**7.1**
6.2	1.64	na	0.00	**0.0**	-0.3	-2.37	-20.04	3.05	189.7	**0.9**	28.0	72.3	**6.1**
9.6	0.31	na	-0.10	**3.0**	2.1	0.38	2.06	2.30	81.3	**4.4**	52.8	18.5	**9.2**
6.1	1.45	na	0.01	**1.6**	-0.1	-0.56	-4.34	3.50	112.6	**0.6**	14.3	56.3	**5.9**
6.6	0.82	na	-0.01	**2.6**	0.2	0.30	2.46	3.55	90.2	**4.3**	20.8	7.6	**7.0**
6.6	0.81	na	0.00	**2.4**	0.1	0.39	3.08	2.52	71.4	**0.7**	15.3	46.3	**6.7**
6.1	0.32	na	-0.01	**5.2**	1.5	0.78	7.10	3.67	71.1	**4.1**	15.9	8.3	**8.3**
1.6	4.42	na	0.64	**3.5**	0.2	0.24	2.55	4.30	76.5	**0.5**	10.0	52.5	**6.1**
4.4	2.31	na	0.34	**8.6**	0.8	1.45	12.19	4.32	53.1	**1.9**	8.1	17.8	**8.6**
4.4	10.57	na	0.00	**4.9**	0.3	0.94	11.13	4.02	71.6	**4.6**	19.0	5.3	**4.6**
1.7	5.63	26.8	0.27	**4.4**	0.2	0.87	6.91	4.79	76.2	**1.5**	12.2	24.2	**7.3**
4.6	2.88	11.4	0.05	**3.8**	0.2	0.55	5.49	3.53	77.5	**2.9**	13.6	14.2	**6.0**
6.9	1.74	na	0.19	**2.2**	0.1	0.37	1.83	2.58	91.6	**2.7**	37.9	22.7	**7.0**
8.0	1.03	na	0.03	**3.5**	0.2	0.61	2.24	2.83	74.7	**2.0**	43.6	34.9	**7.4**
8.8	0.07	na	0.00	**3.8**	0.1	0.65	3.15	3.55	75.4	**1.7**	28.1	24.7	**7.8**
7.8	0.29	na	0.00	**7.0**	0.3	1.04	7.37	3.58	62.9	**0.7**	22.8	54.6	**8.2**
6.9	0.55	na	0.00	**2.3**	0.2	0.52	5.63	3.02	80.6	**1.3**	19.8	21.5	**4.3**
9.9	0.00	na	0.00	**2.6**	0.0	0.37	2.65	2.84	87.5	**3.5**	22.4	12.2	**7.3**
3.1	5.62	na	0.00	**0.0**	-0.1	-0.95	-6.70	2.16	139.0	**2.6**	52.0	31.7	**5.8**
4.5	1.25	na	0.03	**5.6**	0.8	1.16	13.58	3.72	67.9	**1.9**	20.1	13.4	**6.8**
7.4	0.09	na	0.00	**7.2**	0.2	1.87	5.97	3.93	50.6	**4.9**	42.7	10.8	**7.0**
8.7	0.13	0.7	-0.08	**4.5**	0.4	1.02	8.90	3.91	78.7	**4.1**	21.3	8.7	**7.5**
7.1	1.39	na	0.11	**4.3**	1.5	0.94	7.32	3.97	78.6	**3.9**	26.5	10.8	**7.8**
5.0	0.18	na	0.03	**5.5**	0.9	1.49	13.50	2.74	41.9	**3.4**	32.7	15.6	**6.9**
6.2	0.33	na	0.09	**4.8**	1.1	1.05	10.78	4.07	74.9	**3.5**	12.9	11.2	**6.5**
4.4	1.72	na	0.00	**0.7**	0.0	-0.18	-1.69	3.96	102.6	**0.8**	19.3	46.6	**4.5**
8.6	0.00	na	0.01	**8.8**	1.0	1.85	17.02	4.44	55.3	**1.9**	26.0	21.3	**7.9**
3.9	2.20	na	0.04	**4.0**	0.3	0.79	8.64	3.44	73.9	**1.9**	26.0	21.9	**5.6**
4.2	1.35	na	0.17	**5.8**	1.2	1.40	14.06	4.09	67.3	**0.6**	11.8	46.3	**6.5**
5.1	1.19	8.9	1.24	**0.0**	-0.3	-1.17	-14.28	4.04	125.4	**1.2**	19.0	30.3	**2.9**
5.1	0.85	na	0.00	**8.1**	1.1	1.60	9.79	4.11	56.3	**4.4**	22.5	7.2	**9.0**
3.9	1.50	na	0.01	**1.7**	0.0	-0.07	-0.99	3.85	101.1	**4.9**	27.6	5.0	**2.7**
5.3	1.19	4.7	0.00	**3.4**	8.3	0.49	4.50	3.08	70.3	**2.5**	15.5	13.2	**8.2**
5.6	1.60	na	0.01	**3.8**	1.7	0.66	5.70	3.45	74.7	**2.3**	18.9	18.4	**7.3**
5.8	0.62	na	0.05	**6.4**	1.0	1.14	9.91	4.02	67.2	**4.4**	26.6	7.8	**8.0**
2.8	2.17	na	0.00	**2.8**	0.2	0.40	5.01	3.37	88.4	**0.9**	15.1	32.8	**3.7**
7.7	0.42	na	-0.12	**8.1**	1.6	1.31	9.69	4.04	60.4	**4.3**	15.7	6.5	**8.5**
7.6	0.52	na	0.08	**8.5**	1.8	1.79	12.60	4.29	60.0	**1.7**	15.2	21.1	**8.6**
6.7	0.47	na	0.00	**4.3**	0.4	0.81	8.93	4.08	78.0	**3.3**	24.7	13.6	**5.7**
6.0	0.85	4.7	0.00	**3.3**	0.3	0.45	5.40	3.01	81.1	**1.8**	24.2	22.4	**5.0**
8.7	0.25	na	0.00	**7.1**	2.2	1.38	10.93	3.77	57.5	**2.1**	29.1	22.0	**8.4**
6.5	0.00	na	-0.07	**4.1**	0.1	0.91	8.34	3.56	69.1	**1.6**	17.4	24.2	**4.9**

Name	City	State	Rating	2019 Rating	2018 Rating	Total Assets ($Mil)	One Year Asset Growth	Asset Mix (As a % of Total Assets) Comm-ercial Loans	Cons-umer Loans	Mort-gage Loans	Secur-ities	Capital-ization Index	Lever-age Ratio	Risk-Based Capital Ratio
Hometown National Bank	LaSalle	IL	**B+**	B+	B+	242.0	5.69	14.7	0.4	6.1	24.7	**10.0**	11.1	15.2
HomeTrust Bank	Asheville	NC	**B-**	B-	B-	3547.4	2.68	12.6	4.2	14.2	12.4	**6.3**	10.4	11.9
Homewood Federal Savings Bank	Baltimore	MD	**B-**	B-	B-	61.0	0.38	0.5	2.5	57.2	1.0	**10.0**	27.2	53.0
Hondo National Bank	Hondo	TX	**B+**	B+	B+	282.0	7.76	10.6	2.4	14.6	26.3	**7.6**	9.4	14.9
Honesdale National Bank	Honesdale	PA	**A-**	A-	A-	701.2	4.61	10.7	3.7	24.3	15.5	**10.0**	15.0	19.9
Honor Bank	Honor	MI	**B-**	B-	C+	244.4	2.28	12.1	2.2	13.1	8.2	**6.8**	9.7	12.4
▼ Hoosier Heartland State Bank	Crawfordsville	IN	**C+**	B-	B-	212.1	3.55	3.3	4.5	10.8	27.8	**6.9**	8.9	13.6
▲ Hopeton State Bank	Hopeton	OK	**C-**	D+	C	26.1	-4.85	15.5	3.8	0.0	37.5	**9.4**	10.6	14.7
▼ Horatio State Bank	Horatio	AR	**B-**	B	B-	230.1	7.86	6.1	18.9	27.9	8.0	**9.8**	11.7	0.0
Horicon Bank	Horicon	WI	**C-**	C-	C+	885.0	17.49	11.9	0.8	14.1	2.8	**6.0**	10.2	11.8
Horizon Bank	Michigan City	IN	**B+**	B+	B+	5340.4	5.85	7.5	7.5	15.2	20.7	**7.3**	9.4	12.7
Horizon Bank	Waverly	NE	**A-**	A-	B+	382.2	20.94	7.3	0.1	9.7	6.5	**9.5**	13.6	14.6
Horizon Bank, SSB	Austin	TX	**B+**	B+	B+	1230.5	15.03	20.7	0.1	9.2	11.2	**5.1**	8.1	11.1
Horizon Community Bank	Lake Havasu City	AZ	**B-**	B-	B-	355.1	15.24	16.2	0.3	7.3	8.0	**6.8**	8.8	12.8
Horizon Financial Bank	Munich	ND	**B+**	B+	B+	149.5	9.16	3.9	1.6	4.4	9.2	**9.8**	12.2	0.0
▲ Houghton State Bank	Red Oak	IA	**B+**	B	B-	173.9	-3.20	6.4	0.7	5.8	10.9	**10.0**	11.9	16.2
Howard Bank	Baltimore	MD	**C+**	C+	C+	2507.8	11.45	15.2	1.8	17.4	11.3	**7.7**	10.3	13.1
Howard State Bank	Howard	KS	**B+**	B+	B-	53.7	-0.74	3.0	2.4	4.5	34.0	**9.8**	11.9	0.0
▼ Hoyne Savings Bank	Chicago	IL	**D+**	C-	D+	443.4	-0.36	0.0	0.0	30.7	39.8	**9.8**	16.8	0.0
▼ HSBC Bank USA, N.A.	McLean	VA	**C-**	C	C	201885.7	13.74	18.5	0.8	9.0	26.9	**10.0**	11.0	18.1
HSBC Trust Co. (Delaware), N.A.	Wilmington	DE	**U**	U	U	54.8	-3.02	0.0	0.0	0.0	0.0	**9.8**	96.1	0.0
Huntingdon Savings Bank	Huntingdon	PA	**C**	C	C+	16.3	-1.47	0.0	0.0	78.5	0.0	**10.0**	21.9	47.3
Huntingdon Valley Bank	Doylestown	PA	**C-**	C-	C-	353.4	17.37	4.8	1.7	68.1	5.7	**6.7**	8.7	13.8
▼ Huntington Federal Savings Bank	Huntington	WV	**C**	C+	B-	542.0	1.13	0.0	0.3	34.7	53.8	**9.8**	16.7	0.0
Huntington National Bank	Columbus	OH	**B-**	B-	B-	113764.1	5.29	21.5	15.9	11.7	22.1	**8.3**	10.0	13.6
Huron Community Bank	East Tawas	MI	**B**	B	B	229.5	7.53	9.7	1.2	10.8	17.6	**9.8**	11.8	0.0
Huron National Bank	Rogers City	MI	**B-**	B-	C	62.3	-0.70	2.0	4.3	36.0	5.8	**10.0**	15.6	25.0
Huron Valley State Bank	Milford	MI	**B**	B	B	162.9	5.49	10.0	0.5	5.9	1.1	**7.8**	10.9	13.2
Hustisford State Bank	Hustisford	WI	**B+**	B+	B+	55.1	7.04	4.3	1.8	50.3	6.5	**9.8**	18.9	0.0
Hyden Citizens Bank	Hyden	KY	**B-**	B-	B-	124.2	-3.11	11.5	3.5	23.0	32.0	**8.3**	9.9	14.6
Hyperion Bank	Philadelphia	PA	**D+**	D+	D	200.9	12.19	8.1	0.2	34.7	1.0	**10.0**	11.4	15.4
IBERIABANK	Lafayette	LA	**B**	B	B-	32147.5	3.13	16.9	1.7	18.0	12.8	**6.3**	9.8	11.9
Idabel National Bank	Idabel	OK	**B+**	B+	B+	132.0	3.58	4.0	6.3	18.9	37.5	**7.9**	9.8	0.0
Idaho First Bank	McCall	ID	**C+**	C+	C-	236.7	11.39	14.9	2.8	11.2	8.7	**10.0**	11.5	15.0
Idaho Trust Bank	Boise	ID	**C**	C	C	165.3	32.64	13.8	1.6	0.9	0.3	**7.1**	9.2	12.6
Illini State Bank	Oglesby	IL	**B**	B	B-	118.4	-3.40	7.2	1.1	12.8	26.1	**9.8**	13.7	0.0
Illinois Bank & Trust	Rockford	IL	**B+**	B+	B+	1296.0	59.93	19.3	1.2	8.8	25.5	**6.1**	8.7	11.9
Impact Bank	Wellington	KS	**B-**	B-	B-	137.9	1.15	11.9	2.2	3.4	24.7	**5.7**	10.6	11.6
INB, N.A.	Springfield	IL	**B-**	B-	C+	1183.3	18.09	10.7	0.1	10.4	8.0	**6.7**	9.0	12.2
▼ InBank	Raton	NM	**C**	C+	B	420.7	11.41	9.3	1.6	7.7	29.5	**7.6**	12.4	13.0
Incommons Bank, N.A.	Mexia	TX	**B-**	B-	B-	178.5	3.84	9.3	4.4	25.1	18.9	**7.3**	9.2	14.7
IncredibleBank	Wausau	WI	**B-**	B-	B-	1461.3	5.85	23.6	5.0	7.6	14.3	**4.1**	8.1	10.5
▲ Independence Bank	Havre	MT	**A**	A-	B+	807.0	6.69	5.3	2.1	7.0	7.4	**10.0**	13.3	16.2
Independence Bank	Independence	OH	**B**	B	B	169.4	-14.56	26.3	0.6	5.0	17.4	**9.8**	14.4	0.0
▼ Independence Bank	East Greenwich	RI	**B-**	B	B	67.6	2.65	77.7	0.3	2.8	0.0	**9.8**	27.1	0.0
Independence Bank of Kentucky	Owensboro	KY	**B+**	B+	B+	2667.2	7.29	4.1	0.4	12.6	42.6	**6.1**	8.1	12.9
▲ Independence State Bank	Independence	WI	**D+**	D	D	70.9	4.12	10.6	1.1	9.5	12.0	**6.2**	8.3	11.9
Independent Bank	Grand Rapids	MI	**B-**	B-	B-	3631.6	7.37	8.7	12.6	25.6	16.4	**7.5**	9.3	13.0
Independent Bank	Memphis	TN	**B-**	B-	C+	1111.4	8.74	8.9	44.1	1.3	0.6	**6.1**	11.1	11.8
Independent Bank	McKinney	TX	**B+**	B+	B+	15568.7	10.12	9.2	0.3	9.6	7.0	**6.5**	10.9	12.1
▲ Independent Farmers Bank	Maysville	MO	**B+**	B	B	123.9	2.95	6.5	3.5	10.6	43.4	**7.9**	9.6	17.5
▼ Industrial & Commerc. Bank of China (USA	New York	NY	**B-**	B	B	2853.4	-3.90	30.1	0.0	9.2	0.5	**10.0**	13.8	16.0
Industrial Bank	Washington	DC	**C-**	C-	D+	559.7	29.39	6.3	0.2	17.7	16.5	**5.3**	7.3	12.0
Industry State Bank	Industry	TX	**B+**	B+	A-	922.1	12.97	4.7	1.1	4.2	72.3	**9.1**	10.6	0.0
Inez Deposit Bank	Inez	KY	**C+**	C+	C	140.7	-1.93	1.9	2.8	24.0	34.8	**9.8**	13.7	0.0
Infinity Bank	Santa Ana	CA	**D**	D	D	110.2	31.51	41.9	1.6	1.6	5.9	**10.0**	22.2	28.4
▼ InFirst Bank	Indiana	PA	**C+**	B-	B-	431.6	5.48	6.2	0.8	51.9	9.5	**8.3**	9.9	14.3
▼ Inland Bank and Trust	Oak Brook	IL	**B-**	B	B	1139.7	4.25	8.4	0.1	13.4	18.4	**10.0**	12.7	15.1
InsBank	Nashville	TN	**B**	B	B-	561.1	7.48	22.7	1.5	6.2	4.5	**8.1**	11.5	13.5
INSOUTH Bank	Brownsville	TN	**B**	B	B-	355.3	10.93	16.0	2.6	15.8	10.7	**8.5**	10.1	0.0

Asset Quality Index	Adjusted Non-Performing Loans as a % of Total Loans	Adjusted Non-Performing Loans as a % of Capital	Net Charge-Offs Avg Loans	Profitability Index	Net Income ($Mil)	Return on Assets (R.O.A.)	Return on Equity (R.O.E.)	Net Interest Spread	Overhead Efficiency Ratio	Liquidity Index	Liquidity Ratio	Hot Money Ratio	Stability Index
5.4	2.16	na	-0.14	5.2	0.5	0.92	7.96	3.47	71.0	4.2	30.6	9.9	7.5
5.8	1.13	5.6	0.09	2.9	1.4	0.16	1.36	3.15	78.1	2.0	15.8	13.5	9.2
9.4	1.13	na	0.00	2.6	0.0	0.14	0.51	2.69	88.2	1.6	36.8	52.5	7.2
1.9	5.48	na	0.03	3.0	0.1	0.14	1.47	3.72	74.0	2.3	26.5	19.1	5.5
7.9	0.43	na	0.11	6.1	2.1	1.22	8.16	4.02	62.8	2.8	16.8	15.2	9.2
5.0	0.46	na	-0.03	4.1	0.4	0.71	7.39	4.16	74.3	4.2	14.2	7.4	6.0
5.5	1.71	na	-0.01	3.2	0.2	0.42	4.45	4.18	91.4	4.6	27.5	7.0	5.7
7.6	0.00	2.5	-0.03	2.9	0.1	1.74	14.63	3.91	99.2	2.0	41.2	41.3	5.5
3.8	1.02	na	0.46	9.1	1.0	1.70	14.72	4.45	40.2	0.6	13.5	46.5	7.9
2.7	3.60	na	-0.01	4.9	2.2	1.01	9.68	3.94	66.7	3.4	9.4	8.3	7.9
5.8	0.63	3.3	0.04	5.4	12.3	0.94	7.49	3.64	58.2	2.9	17.6	15.0	9.6
7.4	0.00	na	0.00	9.7	1.7	1.90	16.93	4.04	39.4	1.4	11.6	24.8	8.0
8.4	0.03	na	0.09	8.4	4.8	1.60	19.05	4.39	57.5	4.3	22.3	6.5	8.8
6.6	1.00	na	0.06	4.6	0.7	0.80	8.95	4.27	76.4	2.8	24.9	16.1	5.7
4.8	0.78	na	-0.01	4.5	0.3	0.84	6.79	3.57	69.9	2.3	22.7	18.3	7.4
5.8	0.17	na	-0.03	6.3	0.5	1.25	8.70	4.06	58.1	2.8	12.3	15.0	8.4
5.0	0.97	na	0.10	2.3	3.7	0.63	4.43	3.42	67.2	1.1	21.6	24.0	8.8
8.8	0.24	na	0.10	5.0	0.2	1.13	9.41	3.73	66.0	6.0	42.6	3.6	6.6
8.9	0.82	na	-0.34	1.6	0.0	0.00	0.01	2.33	100.7	3.5	59.2	26.7	6.2
7.4	1.44	4.2	0.28	0.9	-1213.8	-2.62	-22.41	1.27	191.4	3.2	54.7	19.8	8.6
10.0	na	0.0	na	7.7	0.2	1.17	1.20	1.40	56.1	4.0	na	0.0	2.3
6.8	1.91	na	0.00	3.2	0.0	0.39	1.80	3.14	81.0	1.0	17.9	31.9	8.0
5.1	1.30	na	0.00	2.2	0.2	0.18	2.10	2.55	93.5	2.7	10.8	9.8	3.7
8.9	0.86	na	-0.73	2.4	0.4	0.31	1.90	2.01	83.6	3.5	68.9	30.8	8.0
4.4	1.55	6.5	0.61	4.9	103.4	0.39	3.40	3.26	52.1	4.4	13.7	2.1	10.0
6.4	0.97	na	0.29	4.0	0.4	0.64	5.43	3.78	78.4	4.3	25.9	8.4	6.8
5.6	4.08	na	-0.86	3.8	0.1	0.66	4.24	3.71	76.8	4.5	47.0	13.7	6.4
3.9	1.00	6.0	0.00	5.4	0.4	1.00	9.29	3.96	68.0	1.7	14.0	17.5	6.9
7.1	4.22	na	0.00	5.8	0.2	1.06	5.64	4.26	66.3	2.7	15.6	10.6	8.1
6.6	0.59	3.5	0.04	4.3	0.3	1.05	10.25	3.91	77.3	1.8	17.2	21.2	5.9
6.0	1.58	na	-0.01	0.6	-0.1	-0.17	-1.49	3.61	92.7	0.7	16.5	48.2	4.7
5.1	0.92	4.5	0.16	4.5	39.9	0.50	3.74	3.16	59.3	3.1	10.3	9.6	10.0
6.3	0.57	na	0.69	8.0	0.6	1.88	18.91	3.95	53.9	1.0	23.7	35.2	7.6
8.3	0.32	na	0.00	2.1	0.0	0.02	0.13	3.53	95.9	1.8	21.7	19.6	5.7
8.6	0.12	na	-0.01	3.2	0.2	0.56	4.41	3.35	92.2	5.0	32.8	7.0	6.8
7.2	0.34	na	0.00	4.7	0.4	1.34	8.09	3.40	55.6	2.6	17.0	5.9	8.4
7.4	0.39	2.0	0.16	4.8	2.6	0.79	8.05	3.57	68.8	4.6	23.0	8.2	7.1
3.4	3.60	na	-0.01	3.4	0.5	1.27	12.03	3.32	79.2	2.8	24.8	16.2	6.9
5.1	0.73	na	0.00	4.1	2.5	0.84	9.39	3.35	70.9	3.2	16.2	3.6	7.6
5.8	2.25	na	-0.01	0.9	0.0	0.00	0.03	4.37	100.6	1.8	4.9	19.0	6.3
6.6	0.43	na	0.04	4.4	0.4	0.92	9.65	4.75	78.3	3.7	12.4	10.3	5.7
4.5	1.38	7.3	0.09	6.3	5.0	1.42	14.84	4.02	67.4	1.6	20.5	9.4	8.9
7.6	1.09	na	0.00	9.8	4.3	2.15	15.86	4.46	42.6	0.7	11.5	18.8	10.0
6.7	0.54	na	-0.01	4.2	0.4	0.93	6.47	3.21	66.2	0.7	16.9	47.6	7.1
3.7	4.01	5.5	6.39	9.2	0.2	1.44	5.00	6.33	59.7	1.5	35.4	55.1	8.2
9.7	0.31	1.7	0.00	5.0	8.7	1.32	16.13	3.42	62.9	2.7	11.2	6.0	7.5
3.9	3.07	na	0.01	2.6	0.0	0.25	2.71	3.47	87.9	2.5	22.1	17.4	4.7
4.2	2.32	10.2	0.05	5.1	4.9	0.55	5.39	3.69	69.3	3.7	19.9	6.7	9.5
5.1	0.36	na	0.27	6.6	3.3	1.18	9.60	4.51	66.1	1.2	2.8	15.1	9.2
5.6	0.37	1.4	0.05	7.2	48.7	1.30	7.49	3.86	50.5	2.0	10.3	11.7	10.0
6.9	0.64	na	0.71	6.4	0.4	1.28	12.34	4.38	61.1	3.2	26.2	14.6	6.1
3.8	2.13	9.0	0.00	2.9	-1.1	-0.15	-0.99	2.75	68.8	0.6	8.5	38.8	9.3
3.2	2.02	na	0.09	2.3	-0.4	-0.27	-3.54	3.91	107.3	2.9	24.7	15.3	4.6
9.3	0.51	0.9	0.19	6.4	5.9	2.68	21.71	2.50	54.9	2.9	59.3	40.4	8.4
5.4	1.88	na	0.01	2.8	0.2	0.47	3.34	2.94	85.7	4.2	52.1	16.9	6.7
8.2	0.00	0.0	0.00	0.0	-0.2	-0.63	-2.83	4.21	112.7	6.4	37.9	0.0	1.5
5.2	1.33	na	0.32	2.7	0.2	0.22	2.15	3.48	81.0	1.3	11.1	24.5	6.2
4.8	2.34	8.7	-0.25	3.1	1.0	0.36	2.78	3.14	84.9	2.5	15.9	17.0	8.6
4.4	0.69	4.7	0.00	4.3	1.0	0.71	6.17	3.00	62.3	0.6	13.3	53.7	7.0
4.7	0.88	na	0.15	5.6	0.8	0.93	9.16	4.64	80.8	2.1	9.8	17.9	6.3

Name	City	State	Rating	2019 Rating	2018 Rating	Total Assets ($Mil)	One Year Asset Growth	Asset Mix (As a % of Total Assets) Commercial Loans	Consumer Loans	Mortgage Loans	Securities	Capitalization Index	Leverage Ratio	Risk-Based Capital Ratio
▼ Institution for Savings	Newburyport	MA	**B**	A-	C+	3717.8	6.20	0.3	0.3	60.2	5.8	**7.2**	9.1	12.8
Integrity Bank & Trust	Monument	CO	**B**	B	B-	217.8	6.30	3.8	0.7	15.6	6.0	**7.0**	9.0	13.4
Integrity Bank Plus	Wabasso	MN	**C+**	C+	C+	66.2	12.04	5.2	1.3	9.1	19.2	**10.0**	11.2	17.3
▲ Interamerican Bank, A FSB	Miami	FL	**C+**	C	C-	200.2	-0.95	0.3	0.3	27.9	0.0	**10.0**	14.2	19.7
Interaudi Bank	New York	NY	**B+**	B+	B	2079.9	5.22	6.2	0.2	17.7	23.2	**6.2**	8.2	21.9
InterBank	Oklahoma City	OK	**C-**	C-	C+	3358.9	-5.52	18.0	0.6	6.2	0.0	**9.1**	10.6	0.0
Intercity State Bank	Schofield	WI	**A**	A	B+	186.9	1.19	11.1	1.2	21.7	10.2	**10.0**	22.2	32.0
▼ Intercredit Bank, N.A.	Miami	FL	**D**	D+	C	367.5	-0.07	10.5	2.5	26.8	12.2	**9.1**	10.4	14.4
International Bank of Amherst	Amherst	WI	**A-**	A-	A-	75.4	2.96	5.8	0.9	11.2	25.6	**10.0**	14.1	30.2
▼ International Bank of Chicago	Chicago	IL	**C+**	B-	C	674.2	8.40	5.7	0.0	20.2	25.3	**10.0**	11.3	19.8
International Bank of Commerce	Brownsville	TX	**A**	A	A	1079.8	3.08	14.4	0.5	3.0	26.8	**10.0**	15.9	23.6
International Bank of Commerce	Laredo	TX	**A**	A	A	8988.8	5.46	9.8	0.7	9.6	27.0	**10.0**	14.3	18.2
International Bank of Commerce	Zapata	TX	**A**	A	A	397.3	-5.15	4.2	1.5	20.1	50.2	**10.0**	18.1	36.4
International Bank of Commerce Oklahoma	Oklahoma City	OK	**A-**	A-	A-	1503.2	0.04	20.3	0.1	1.2	26.8	**10.0**	14.6	17.1
International City Bank	Long Beach	CA	**B+**	B+	A-	381.9	32.27	1.4	0.0	2.4	56.4	**6.2**	8.2	20.4
International Finance Bank	Miami	FL	**C+**	C+	C+	774.3	12.63	32.4	1.6	20.7	5.2	**4.8**	6.8	10.9
Interstate Bank	Perryton	TX	**B**	B	C+	192.8	-3.17	17.8	1.7	11.2	28.6	**8.9**	10.4	0.0
Interstate Federal S&L Assn. of McGregor	McGregor	IA	**C-**	C-	C	8.5	7.00	0.0	0.4	69.6	0.0	**10.0**	20.3	42.3
Intracoastal Bank	Palm Coast	FL	**B**	B	B	360.5	6.77	8.6	0.2	1.7	22.0	**5.4**	8.7	11.3
▼ INTRUST Bank, N.A.	Wichita	KS	**B-**	B	B	5875.9	13.68	23.0	4.1	3.5	25.6	**4.8**	8.2	10.9
▼ Investar Bank, N.A.	Baton Rouge	LA	**B-**	B	B	2197.5	11.93	14.1	1.3	13.7	13.2	**7.4**	10.5	12.9
▼ Investment Savings Bank	Altoona	PA	**C**	C+	C+	101.9	-1.99	0.6	0.7	39.0	39.7	**9.8**	21.6	0.0
Investors Bank	Short Hills	NJ	**B**	B	B+	26670.1	0.39	3.3	1.4	19.7	14.0	**6.5**	8.5	12.7
▼ Investors Community Bank	Chillicothe	MO	**B**	B+	B+	69.7	-0.76	1.6	4.2	21.2	55.5	**10.0**	13.2	31.9
Investors Community Bank	Manitowoc	WI	**B-**	B-	B-	1351.0	-8.97	5.3	0.0	1.3	18.2	**10.0**	14.9	18.0
Inwood National Bank	Dallas	TX	**A-**	A-	A-	3032.6	7.45	3.2	0.2	11.0	31.7	**8.3**	10.1	0.0
▼ Ion Bank	Naugatuck	CT	**C+**	B-	C+	1383.9	4.14	10.6	12.7	26.7	5.1	**8.1**	10.2	13.4
▼ Iowa Falls State Bank	Iowa Falls	IA	**C+**	B-	B-	134.7	-2.47	11.3	2.2	13.7	26.5	**9.8**	11.5	0.0
Iowa Prairie Bank	Brunsville	IA	**D**	D	D+	64.1	-1.22	8.5	2.6	0.8	45.8	**5.4**	7.4	13.5
Iowa Savings Bank	Carroll	IA	**B**	B	B	207.5	4.89	12.9	0.6	5.0	12.2	**7.1**	9.2	0.0
Iowa State Bank	Algona	IA	**A-**	A-	A-	318.2	-2.91	9.5	1.5	9.9	23.3	**10.0**	12.2	18.2
Iowa State Bank	Clarksville	IA	**D-**	D-	D+	378.3	3.25	10.8	0.7	2.8	13.5	**6.7**	8.7	12.4
Iowa State Bank	Des Moines	IA	**A**	A	A	388.3	2.52	4.9	0.3	12.7	37.2	**9.8**	17.5	0.0
▼ Iowa State Bank	Hull	IA	**B+**	A-	B+	622.9	1.85	5.7	1.1	4.1	9.6	**9.8**	13.7	0.0
▲ Iowa State Bank	Sac City	IA	**A**	A-	B+	136.4	4.67	9.3	5.2	20.6	5.8	**9.8**	12.6	0.0
Iowa State Bank and Trust Co.	Fairfield	IA	**B**	B	B	135.3	-7.19	9.9	1.7	20.9	7.4	**9.5**	10.7	14.8
▲ Iowa State Savings Bank	Creston	IA	**C+**	C	C-	220.3	4.37	2.7	1.3	11.0	17.2	**8.0**	9.8	0.0
Iowa Trust & Savings Bank	Emmetsburg	IA	**B+**	B+	B+	329.9	39.48	4.0	0.4	8.3	17.2	**7.5**	10.4	12.9
Iowa Trust and Savings Bank	Centerville	IA	**A**	A	B+	178.7	0.24	4.9	1.9	6.2	53.4	**9.8**	11.4	0.0
Ipava State Bank	Ipava	IL	**B+**	B+	B+	167.0	14.44	6.8	2.9	19.7	14.4	**6.1**	8.1	15.0
Ipswich State Bank	Ipswich	SD	**B**	B	B	57.8	4.99	4.6	0.9	0.0	16.6	**10.0**	15.7	23.2
▲ Ireland Bank	Malad City	ID	**A-**	B+	B-	250.8	5.73	14.7	1.1	3.3	23.6	**10.0**	11.0	19.4
▼ Iron Workers Savings Bank	Aston	PA	**C-**	C	C	179.2	2.66	0.6	0.0	45.1	9.7	**8.3**	10.0	0.0
Iroquois Farmers State Bank	Iroquois	IL	**B-**	B-	B-	113.0	1.04	2.2	3.1	12.7	16.2	**7.4**	9.3	14.6
Iroquois Federal S&L Assn.	Watseka	IL	**B-**	B-	B-	684.2	3.27	8.6	1.1	18.9	22.4	**9.8**	11.6	0.0
Isabella Bank	Mount Pleasant	MI	**B-**	B-	B-	1765.5	0.74	8.6	4.0	17.3	23.1	**6.7**	8.7	12.8
▼ Islanders Bank	Friday Harbor	WA	**B+**	A-	B+	293.5	5.43	5.9	1.0	16.5	21.3	**8.6**	10.1	17.0
Israel Discount Bank of New York	New York	NY	**B+**	B+	B+	10998.3	16.28	25.6	0.1	0.8	23.8	**9.3**	10.6	14.8
Itasca Bank & Trust Co.	Itasca	IL	**B+**	B+	B-	567.8	1.52	22.6	0.2	12.8	24.1	**8.3**	10.0	0.0
ITS Bank	Johnston	IA	**U**	U	U	8.3	7.13	0.0	0.0	0.0	37.7	**9.8**	92.7	0.0
▲ Iuka State Bank	Salem	IL	**C+**	C	D+	107.0	11.77	10.3	10.8	11.7	5.7	**7.1**	9.5	12.6
▼ Ixonia Bank	Ixonia	WI	**C+**	B-	C+	396.2	9.89	21.3	0.1	3.9	24.3	**9.6**	10.9	14.7
Jacksboro National Bank	Jacksboro	TX	**B+**	B+	B+	240.6	1.09	6.6	3.2	10.1	49.7	**10.0**	12.8	23.8
Jackson County Bank	Seymour	IN	**B-**	B-	B-	611.8	4.48	5.0	1.0	22.3	14.5	**7.3**	9.5	12.8
Jackson County Bank	McKee	KY	**A**	A	A-	142.8	4.74	1.5	9.6	19.6	36.1	**9.8**	27.6	0.0
Jackson County Bank	Black River Falls	WI	**D-**	D-	C-	205.3	-8.09	0.7	1.0	11.9	40.1	**6.5**	8.5	17.6
Jackson Federal S&L Assn.	Jackson	MN	**C**	C	C	36.7	-4.26	5.5	3.4	28.8	39.5	**10.0**	24.5	40.5
Jackson Parish Bank	Jonesboro	LA	**B-**	B-	B-	68.4	0.13	4.6	4.6	12.4	54.0	**9.8**	14.7	0.0
▼ Jackson Savings Bank, SSB	Sylva	NC	**C+**	B-	C+	34.4	5.92	0.0	0.6	61.0	0.0	**10.0**	22.0	42.4
James Polk Stone Community Bank	Portales	NM	**A-**	A-	B+	235.9	3.94	7.3	4.8	22.8	26.7	**9.8**	11.7	0.0

Asset Quality Index	Adjusted Non-Performing Loans as a % of Total Loans	Adjusted Non-Performing Loans as a % of Capital	Net Charge-Offs Avg Loans	Profitability Index	Net Income ($Mil)	Return on Assets (R.O.A.)	Return on Equity (R.O.E.)	Net Interest Spread	Overhead Efficiency Ratio	Liquidity Index	Liquidity Ratio	Hot Money Ratio	Stability Index
9.5	0.11	0.8	0.00	**2.5**	-57.6	-6.14	-60.73	1.92	64.9	**0.9**	16.9	39.2	**8.8**
6.6	1.05	na	0.00	**5.3**	0.5	0.92	10.29	4.54	73.2	**4.3**	17.4	7.0	**6.1**
3.0	7.36	na	0.00	**5.5**	0.2	1.22	10.21	4.84	72.0	**3.4**	23.8	12.7	**7.9**
3.0	6.32	na	-0.04	**2.9**	0.2	0.37	2.61	4.01	94.7	**2.4**	14.9	17.0	**8.0**
9.6	0.39	2.0	0.01	**5.6**	4.6	0.87	10.61	2.20	56.3	**3.2**	61.6	43.6	**7.1**
0.0	4.24	26.2	-0.07	**8.1**	16.8	1.96	15.43	4.02	47.8	**3.8**	10.0	9.5	**10.0**
5.9	2.58	na	-0.01	**8.9**	0.7	1.46	6.65	3.58	47.8	**3.8**	30.4	12.6	**8.9**
5.0	0.90	6.4	1.07	**0.6**	-0.5	-0.51	-4.97	3.12	94.7	**0.8**	16.1	32.9	**5.8**
9.3	0.01	na	0.00	**6.7**	0.3	1.64	11.58	3.81	57.4	**6.1**	50.5	5.3	**8.8**
2.2	5.65	na	0.06	**4.3**	1.5	0.91	7.66	2.87	71.2	**1.5**	32.7	32.5	**8.7**
8.6	0.09	0.5	0.11	**9.7**	5.0	1.84	10.79	4.18	46.4	**3.1**	35.8	23.4	**9.2**
6.3	0.13	3.6	0.10	**8.2**	28.8	1.31	7.65	3.96	54.0	**3.7**	28.4	15.8	**9.4**
8.9	0.48	1.4	0.67	**5.4**	1.1	1.13	5.64	3.78	63.8	**3.0**	40.2	20.6	**8.2**
7.9	0.11	0.3	0.15	**4.3**	2.0	0.56	3.27	4.02	71.7	**4.3**	13.5	6.9	**7.0**
10.0	0.04	na	0.00	**2.3**	-2.0	-2.13	-17.82	2.34	-692.5	**2.7**	45.6	24.4	**6.6**
6.5	0.61	5.6	0.00	**3.7**	1.2	0.62	8.98	3.13	77.0	**1.1**	19.0	32.3	**5.6**
5.2	2.08	na	0.17	**4.9**	0.4	0.85	7.71	3.69	76.6	**3.7**	43.1	17.3	**7.2**
9.9	0.61	1.1	0.00	**1.1**	0.0	-0.19	-0.92	2.97	105.0	**1.7**	26.0	23.0	**7.0**
6.7	0.77	na	0.00	**7.7**	1.5	1.74	18.96	3.88	50.0	**2.6**	27.0	17.4	**7.6**
5.2	1.16	10.7	0.21	**5.4**	15.0	1.08	13.95	3.44	63.6	**1.7**	13.5	13.3	**7.1**
6.2	0.46	2.9	0.05	**3.5**	2.0	0.37	3.17	3.60	69.2	**1.3**	11.2	26.9	**8.7**
9.7	0.56	na	0.00	**2.6**	0.1	0.33	1.53	2.77	84.7	**4.1**	57.2	18.8	**7.6**
5.9	0.53	4.2	0.15	**3.8**	39.2	0.59	6.93	2.71	56.7	**1.8**	13.5	9.0	**8.4**
9.3	0.15	na	-0.11	**3.8**	0.1	0.76	5.29	3.39	78.4	**5.8**	62.7	9.4	**7.9**
2.8	5.25	16.6	-0.02	**4.1**	0.6	0.16	1.07	3.03	76.1	**1.0**	20.6	27.3	**9.7**
7.7	0.03	0.2	0.00	**8.0**	14.5	1.89	17.42	3.26	42.2	**4.2**	27.8	13.0	**10.0**
4.9	1.59	na	0.03	**1.8**	-1.8	-0.53	-6.04	3.42	82.1	**4.1**	12.2	6.6	**6.9**
4.4	1.22	na	3.22	**3.0**	-0.2	-0.67	-5.81	3.63	64.0	**3.9**	34.3	13.6	**7.2**
6.3	0.76	na	-0.08	**0.5**	0.0	-0.12	-1.58	3.05	103.9	**4.1**	26.2	10.0	**2.4**
7.7	0.54	na	0.00	**5.8**	0.7	1.33	14.18	3.29	62.0	**3.5**	22.1	7.9	**7.2**
5.5	3.68	na	0.00	**5.5**	0.8	1.03	7.67	3.95	61.0	**2.7**	14.1	15.2	**8.2**
0.0	9.35	na	-0.01	**2.5**	0.2	0.22	2.50	2.75	61.1	**1.1**	27.5	33.9	**3.9**
9.2	0.38	na	-0.11	**6.5**	1.4	1.49	8.25	3.24	64.4	**5.8**	50.2	8.2	**10.0**
4.3	0.76	na	0.08	**7.7**	3.0	1.87	13.05	3.77	52.1	**3.3**	14.2	12.6	**9.7**
7.9	0.04	na	0.06	**8.4**	0.6	1.86	14.03	3.54	46.8	**3.0**	16.8	14.2	**9.7**
7.4	0.00	na	0.00	**4.4**	0.3	0.79	7.44	3.58	69.1	**1.6**	18.1	23.7	**6.1**
6.7	0.31	na	0.00	**3.5**	0.3	0.62	5.32	4.35	60.1	**2.9**	21.2	15.0	**6.1**
8.0	0.00	na	-0.01	**7.2**	1.7	2.02	16.96	3.72	58.6	**0.8**	13.2	26.7	**7.0**
9.1	0.00	na	0.00	**6.6**	0.7	1.58	13.79	3.49	55.8	**4.7**	42.6	12.3	**7.9**
8.0	0.01	2.6	-0.56	**6.0**	0.5	1.35	16.81	3.91	68.6	**3.0**	26.9	15.7	**5.6**
7.6	0.00	na	0.01	**5.0**	0.2	1.19	7.33	3.35	62.7	**2.0**	32.1	27.1	**8.2**
7.9	1.21	na	-0.06	**5.6**	0.6	0.98	8.73	4.97	74.6	**5.2**	32.0	4.9	**7.1**
8.6	0.33	na	0.00	**1.8**	0.0	0.06	0.56	2.88	98.0	**1.8**	21.1	21.7	**5.4**
5.6	0.74	na	0.41	**3.9**	0.2	0.77	8.30	3.21	70.1	**3.7**	29.1	12.8	**5.3**
8.4	0.31	na	0.02	**3.3**	0.9	0.51	4.31	2.79	76.2	**1.2**	15.3	26.2	**7.4**
5.0	2.27	9.8	0.01	**3.9**	3.5	0.80	8.72	2.96	70.2	**2.0**	19.4	18.4	**7.7**
5.4	2.23	8.0	-0.01	**8.4**	1.1	1.54	13.91	4.15	55.6	**5.8**	38.0	3.5	**7.9**
8.2	0.25	2.3	0.21	**4.5**	22.4	0.89	8.38	2.55	54.9	**2.1**	32.3	24.4	**8.3**
5.1	1.80	na	0.00	**6.2**	1.7	1.19	11.87	3.83	66.0	**1.7**	23.8	23.6	**7.3**
10.0	na	na	na	**10.0**	0.1	5.42	5.84	6.36	18.0	**4.0**	na	100.0	**5.7**
3.4	1.54	na	0.07	**3.4**	0.2	0.68	7.19	4.35	73.4	**1.6**	19.8	21.5	**5.0**
8.3	0.01	na	0.34	**2.8**	0.5	0.56	4.63	3.24	88.4	**2.7**	35.9	14.9	**6.9**
7.2	1.34	na	0.02	**4.2**	0.6	0.93	7.05	3.84	78.0	**3.6**	35.6	15.5	**7.2**
5.6	1.58	na	0.00	**4.3**	1.5	1.02	10.09	3.32	69.7	**3.6**	21.8	11.5	**6.9**
7.7	1.09	na	0.14	**7.2**	0.5	1.37	4.93	4.09	60.7	**4.4**	49.4	15.5	**8.6**
4.7	13.88	na	12.16	**0.0**	-2.9	-5.72	-58.74	2.44	124.5	**3.0**	51.8	11.9	**3.0**
9.3	0.02	0.2	0.00	**2.2**	0.1	0.49	1.99	3.24	85.5	**3.2**	37.0	17.9	**6.2**
7.3	0.98	na	-0.07	**3.4**	0.1	0.59	3.97	2.94	77.6	**5.7**	45.5	6.8	**6.4**
7.3	0.75	7.0	0.00	**2.3**	0.0	0.14	0.64	3.15	91.7	**1.5**	33.6	41.9	**6.7**
5.6	1.63	na	0.21	**7.4**	1.2	2.11	18.86	5.29	61.2	**6.0**	35.3	1.4	**7.7**

Name	City	State	Rating	2019 Rating	2018 Rating	Total Assets ($Mil)	One Year Asset Growth	Asset Mix (As a % of Total Assets) Comm- ercial Loans	Cons- umer Loans	Mort- gage Loans	Secur- ities	Capital- ization Index	Lever- age Ratio	Risk- Based Capital Ratio
▲ Janesville State Bank	Janesville	MN	**A-**	B+	B+	74.0	9.59	3.1	2.7	19.5	7.4	**9.8**	12.4	0.0
▼ Jarrettsville Federal S&L Assn.	Jarrettsville	MD	**C**	C+	B-	121.3	-2.35	1.1	0.0	59.8	8.4	**9.8**	14.3	0.0
JD Bank	Jennings	LA	**B+**	B+	B	910.4	0.89	8.2	3.7	17.9	18.4	**10.0**	11.1	16.3
Jeff Bank	Jeffersonville	NY	**B+**	B+	B	532.9	3.40	5.5	0.6	20.9	25.2	**9.8**	11.5	0.0
Jefferson Bank	Greenville	MS	**A-**	A-	B+	130.0	2.71	10.8	0.3	2.9	19.5	**10.0**	18.5	21.5
Jefferson Bank	San Antonio	TX	**B+**	B+	B+	1940.8	0.62	6.9	1.4	23.9	17.9	**7.9**	9.6	13.3
Jefferson Bank and Trust Co.	Saint Louis	MO	**B**	B	B	628.1	2.11	12.9	1.3	4.7	21.9	**8.9**	12.2	14.1
Jefferson Bank of Missouri	Jefferson City	MO	**B+**	B+	B+	656.4	7.84	7.8	22.4	19.3	18.0	**7.9**	9.6	13.2
Jefferson Security Bank	Shepherdstown	WV	**B-**	B-	C+	327.4	4.11	1.3	1.2	35.9	26.5	**7.7**	9.5	16.5
Jersey Shore State Bank	Williamsport	PA	**B-**	B-	B-	1226.0	-3.66	2.9	11.9	20.9	10.0	**5.5**	8.3	11.4
▼ Jersey State Bank	Jerseyville	IL	**B**	B+	B+	143.0	-1.91	6.3	0.7	7.9	43.5	**9.8**	14.6	0.0
Jewett City Savings Bank	Jewett City	CT	**B**	B	B-	315.9	11.59	9.8	1.6	36.6	5.6	**10.0**	15.6	23.3
Jim Thorpe Neighborhood Bank	Jim Thorpe	PA	**C+**	C+	C+	191.5	2.73	1.4	0.6	25.1	32.3	**8.7**	10.2	20.7
John Deere Financial, F.S.B.	Madison	WI	**A-**	A-	A-	2971.9	2.33	4.8	14.9	0.0	0.0	**9.8**	22.6	0.0
John Marshall Bank	Reston	VA	**B+**	B+	B+	1622.3	13.82	5.0	0.1	12.3	8.6	**8.6**	11.9	13.9
Johnson Bank	Racine	WI	**A-**	A-	A-	5516.4	11.11	19.0	1.7	17.3	10.6	**10.0**	12.5	16.6
Johnson City Bank	Johnson City	TX	**A-**	A-	A-	119.4	-1.34	8.3	8.4	23.4	9.8	**9.8**	12.6	0.0
Johnson County Bank	Mountain City	TN	**B**	B	B	125.4	5.60	3.6	4.2	32.6	34.8	**9.8**	15.6	0.0
▼ Johnson State Bank	Johnson	KS	**B-**	B	B	78.0	-0.63	4.4	1.9	4.7	42.3	**9.8**	15.7	0.0
▲ Jonah Bank of Wyoming	Casper	WY	**B+**	B	B-	353.5	8.80	18.4	0.4	9.4	7.0	**8.6**	10.2	0.0
Jones Bank	Seward	NE	**B+**	B+	B-	315.7	34.35	9.7	1.3	8.1	32.6	**9.8**	11.4	0.0
▼ Jonesboro State Bank	Jonesboro	LA	**B+**	A-	A	385.5	36.77	1.1	0.9	3.6	84.6	**10.0**	11.3	33.0
Jonesburg State Bank	Jonesburg	MO	**B**	B	B-	102.7	5.61	8.0	2.5	21.4	2.2	**6.6**	8.6	15.5
Jonestown Bank and Trust Co.	Jonestown	PA	**C+**	C+	C	651.9	7.32	3.3	24.8	18.7	5.4	**7.3**	9.4	0.0
JPMorgan Chase Bank, Dearborn	Dearborn	MI	**U**	U	U	61.5	2.77	0.0	0.0	0.0	0.0	**10.0**	99.4	511.2
JPMorgan Chase Bank, N.A.	Columbus	OH	**B+**	B+	B+	2690959.0	17.39	8.3	7.3	8.0	17.6	**6.4**	8.4	14.6
Junction National Bank	Junction	TX	**B**	B	B+	71.8	8.15	3.8	2.5	6.4	58.6	**7.9**	9.6	31.5
Juniata Valley Bank	Mifflintown	PA	**B-**	B-	B-	672.7	7.36	6.8	1.2	20.3	29.8	**7.6**	9.6	0.0
Kahoka State Bank	Kahoka	MO	**B-**	B-	C+	54.8	9.90	3.8	4.4	26.8	27.9	**8.8**	10.2	18.6
Kalamazoo County State Bank	Schoolcraft	MI	**C+**	C+	C	98.7	-0.46	3.6	15.2	12.2	42.9	**10.0**	12.1	22.4
Kansas State Bank	Ottawa	KS	**B+**	B+	B-	146.0	0.37	7.1	1.6	14.2	51.5	**7.3**	9.4	0.0
Kansas State Bank Overbrook Kansas	Overbrook	KS	**B+**	B+	B+	68.1	8.69	7.5	3.0	6.4	48.1	**10.0**	13.3	22.7
KansasLand Bank	Quinter	KS	**C-**	C-	C+	53.5	-0.92	5.2	1.8	10.0	21.3	**6.6**	8.6	14.6
▼ Kanza Bank	Kingman	KS	**C+**	B-	B-	233.3	4.86	9.8	0.8	22.3	15.6	**7.7**	9.6	0.0
Karnes County National Bank	Karnes City	TX	**B**	B	C	416.8	0.74	1.8	0.7	3.0	76.8	**9.7**	10.8	37.4
Katahdin Trust Co.	Patten	ME	**B-**	B-	B-	903.5	12.93	19.4	0.8	17.6	13.4	**7.8**	9.5	13.5
▲ Kaw Valley Bank	Topeka	KS	**B**	B-	C+	310.8	0.07	14.7	2.5	20.0	5.2	**9.8**	11.2	0.0
Kaw Valley State Bank	Eudora	KS	**B-**	B-	C	53.4	5.96	5.7	5.2	18.3	40.0	**8.0**	9.7	18.5
Kaw Valley State Bank and Trust Co.	Wamego	KS	**A-**	A-	A	196.0	10.90	8.0	1.8	14.0	32.3	**9.8**	11.8	0.0
Kearney Trust Co.	Kearney	MO	**A-**	A-	A-	219.6	12.51	5.7	3.3	15.9	21.2	**8.0**	9.6	15.8
Kearny Bank	Fairfield	NJ	**B-**	B-	B-	6751.7	1.68	1.1	0.1	20.6	22.2	**10.0**	11.9	20.7
Kearny County Bank	Lakin	KS	**A-**	A-	B+	214.8	4.72	15.5	1.7	13.0	22.8	**9.8**	16.6	0.0
KEB Hana Bank USA, N.A.	New York	NY	**D**	D	D	237.2	9.66	0.0	0.0	1.4	26.0	**10.0**	14.9	27.7
Kendall State Bank	Valley Falls	KS	**C-**	C-	C	39.7	10.78	5.1	2.0	13.5	0.2	**8.7**	10.1	15.2
▼ Kennebec Federal S&L Assn. of Waterville	Waterville	ME	**C-**	C	C-	94.5	-2.35	0.0	0.1	76.2	3.0	**7.0**	9.0	16.0
Kennebec Savings Bank	Augusta	ME	**A-**	A-	B+	1154.6	6.87	3.8	0.3	57.4	7.3	**9.8**	12.6	0.0
Kennebunk Savings Bank	Kennebunk	ME	**B**	B	B	1327.3	7.54	3.2	0.1	26.9	8.6	**9.8**	12.0	0.0
Kennett Trust Bank	Kennett	MO	**B**	B	C+	102.5	-5.82	9.9	3.2	34.4	22.6	**9.8**	12.1	0.0
Kensington Bank	Kensington	MN	**C-**	C-	C+	282.9	0.31	8.9	1.1	8.3	7.6	**5.7**	9.1	11.5
Kentland Bank	Kentland	IN	**A**	A	A-	306.0	0.09	9.9	1.5	8.3	30.2	**10.0**	14.6	20.0
Kentland Federal S&L Assn.	Kentland	IN	**D**	D	D	4.1	-6.27	0.6	0.0	93.0	1.7	**9.8**	13.6	0.0
Kentucky Bank	Paris	KY	**B+**	B+	B+	1140.2	5.13	4.6	2.0	21.7	21.7	**7.2**	9.3	0.0
Kentucky Farmers Bank Corp.	Ashland	KY	**A**	A	A	205.7	10.15	4.3	5.3	27.4	40.9	**10.0**	21.5	32.3
Kerndt Brothers Savings Bank	Lansing	IA	**B-**	B-	C+	298.5	6.31	10.8	0.8	7.7	20.9	**9.3**	10.7	0.0
Key Community Bank	Inver Grove Heights	MN	**C+**	C+	C+	49.9	3.99	8.2	4.5	8.5	0.5	**9.4**	10.6	19.6
Key National Trust Co. of Delaware	Wilmington	DE	**U**	U	U	4.8	7.41	0.0	0.0	0.0	0.0	**10.0**	97.6	448.1
KeyBank N.A.	Cleveland	OH	**B**	B	B	154993.5	10.81	28.8	6.9	7.4	19.9	**6.5**	9.8	12.1
KeySavings Bank	Wisconsin Rapids	WI	**C-**	C-	C-	81.8	7.65	0.8	1.3	43.0	28.6	**10.0**	13.8	31.1
▼ Keystone Bank, N.A.	Austin	TX	**C-**	C	C	222.8	165.14	5.7	0.8	13.1	9.9	**10.0**	14.7	20.9
Keystone Savings Bank	Keystone	IA	**B-**	B-	B	151.4	4.87	5.8	1.8	18.5	23.6	**7.1**	9.8	12.6

Asset Quality Index	Adjusted Non-Performing Loans as a % of Total Loans	Adjusted Non-Performing Loans as a % of Capital	Net Charge-Offs Avg Loans	Profitability Index	Net Income ($Mil)	Return on Assets (R.O.A.)	Return on Equity (R.O.E.)	Net Interest Spread	Overhead Efficiency Ratio	Liquidity Index	Liquidity Ratio	Hot Money Ratio	Stability Index
7.4	0.00	na	0.00	**7.6**	0.4	2.01	15.63	3.95	50.2	**2.4**	9.7	16.4	**8.8**
8.4	0.62	na	0.00	**2.5**	0.0	0.11	0.76	2.44	90.1	**1.8**	28.7	26.3	**7.6**
4.8	2.42	10.5	0.01	**5.1**	1.9	0.85	7.29	4.59	74.4	**4.3**	28.7	9.7	**7.5**
2.2	4.71	na	0.01	**5.2**	1.2	0.92	8.35	4.04	69.4	**5.2**	30.3	4.6	**7.7**
8.5	0.02	na	0.39	**6.7**	1.3	4.13	22.44	5.21	34.1	**0.8**	25.9	49.8	**7.8**
8.2	0.42	3.3	0.05	**5.2**	5.9	1.24	13.85	3.63	70.9	**2.8**	25.2	18.5	**8.3**
7.3	0.03	0.2	0.00	**4.9**	1.5	0.98	7.98	2.81	57.6	**1.0**	9.6	27.2	**8.1**
4.5	0.58	4.1	0.16	**9.8**	3.0	1.87	19.64	3.98	47.6	**3.6**	19.9	9.9	**7.8**
4.4	2.49	na	0.00	**4.1**	0.6	0.77	8.82	3.46	70.8	**4.3**	15.1	6.9	**5.1**
4.7	1.22	8.9	0.05	**4.5**	2.6	0.86	10.51	3.06	65.2	**1.4**	7.8	17.7	**6.8**
6.7	3.10	na	0.00	**4.2**	0.3	0.85	5.72	3.30	73.2	**5.3**	38.8	7.5	**7.9**
5.8	1.78	6.7	0.15	**2.0**	-0.4	-0.46	-2.86	3.69	87.8	**4.2**	20.8	8.2	**7.0**
8.4	0.47	1.7	0.00	**3.0**	0.3	0.67	6.15	3.04	84.6	**4.4**	29.3	9.1	**5.8**
5.6	0.55	na	0.49	**10.0**	28.7	4.23	18.46	6.43	37.1	**0.0**	0.1	99.2	**10.0**
7.5	0.05	0.2	0.00	**5.6**	4.9	1.23	10.40	3.41	52.5	**0.8**	14.6	29.8	**9.1**
8.1	0.23	1.1	-0.38	**5.2**	11.7	0.89	6.89	3.49	72.4	**4.7**	17.0	4.7	**9.8**
7.5	1.24	na	0.01	**5.4**	0.4	1.32	10.55	3.64	65.4	**2.7**	40.9	25.1	**7.7**
5.3	3.41	na	0.10	**4.1**	0.2	0.78	4.86	3.46	68.6	**2.3**	38.0	28.6	**8.0**
3.2	7.14	na	-1.00	**3.6**	0.1	0.45	2.82	2.92	83.1	**4.0**	41.9	15.3	**8.4**
5.4	0.73	na	0.00	**7.0**	1.1	1.29	12.81	4.29	60.9	**4.4**	17.3	6.2	**7.4**
5.6	0.98	na	-0.52	**6.3**	1.2	1.46	11.78	3.79	59.8	**3.5**	22.2	12.3	**7.5**
9.2	3.15	na	-0.32	**3.6**	1.1	1.31	10.65	2.33	100.4	**2.9**	77.1	63.7	**7.6**
8.1	0.00	na	0.01	**6.6**	0.4	1.69	19.87	4.02	61.0	**3.6**	27.5	12.8	**6.4**
3.6	0.96	6.3	0.19	**3.5**	0.8	0.49	5.25	3.55	74.0	**2.4**	9.8	16.2	**6.4**
10.0	na	0.0	na	**9.1**	0.3	1.92	1.93	2.09	0.0	**4.0**	na	100.0	**5.7**
6.6	1.11	3.7	0.61	**4.3**	1693.0	0.27	2.76	2.60	63.9	**6.8**	55.7	4.4	**8.3**
9.6	0.40	na	-0.03	**4.9**	0.2	1.13	11.85	2.91	59.6	**4.9**	71.7	15.7	**5.7**
5.1	1.33	na	-0.02	**3.4**	1.1	0.69	6.15	3.31	76.8	**4.7**	30.9	8.2	**7.1**
7.8	0.36	na	1.38	**3.4**	0.1	0.57	5.46	3.25	77.4	**1.8**	31.4	29.1	**5.3**
8.0	0.02	na	0.05	**2.4**	0.1	0.37	3.06	3.46	87.2	**6.3**	58.9	5.8	**6.0**
9.3	0.17	na	0.04	**4.6**	0.4	1.14	11.79	3.14	65.0	**3.7**	8.6	10.0	**6.4**
3.7	2.34	na	-0.17	**4.8**	0.1	0.68	4.89	3.59	69.8	**3.2**	50.2	21.8	**8.2**
0.3	23.07	99.7	-0.01	**0.6**	0.0	-0.06	-0.58	3.31	102.9	**1.0**	19.5	33.7	**3.5**
8.3	0.14	na	-0.05	**3.0**	0.2	0.36	3.44	3.89	72.4	**2.4**	11.7	16.8	**6.4**
6.4	4.69	na	-0.15	**4.5**	1.0	0.93	8.51	2.63	59.7	**6.8**	68.9	6.1	**5.7**
5.1	0.81	5.7	-0.01	**4.1**	1.5	0.68	6.81	3.54	69.5	**0.5**	6.0	17.8	**6.7**
5.7	4.04	na	-0.10	**5.5**	0.8	1.07	9.47	4.34	60.3	**1.1**	13.1	30.0	**7.6**
6.3	0.92	na	0.34	**5.5**	0.2	1.40	13.19	3.85	71.5	**5.2**	33.5	5.9	**6.1**
4.8	2.10	na	0.00	**6.2**	0.6	1.32	10.84	3.17	60.2	**3.6**	32.6	14.7	**8.3**
8.5	0.77	na	0.90	**5.7**	0.7	1.34	13.20	3.59	57.8	**4.8**	36.3	9.7	**6.4**
5.5	0.96	3.9	0.00	**2.8**	9.2	0.55	3.75	2.51	67.3	**1.6**	17.4	23.6	**8.9**
6.2	0.09	na	0.00	**9.4**	1.3	2.32	13.68	4.55	49.7	**2.5**	21.5	15.3	**10.0**
7.5	1.12	na	-0.14	**0.0**	-1.1	-1.86	-12.20	2.79	156.5	**6.4**	54.4	5.3	**6.1**
7.3	0.29	1.5	0.00	**0.9**	-0.1	-0.54	-4.30	4.75	107.9	**3.3**	35.0	16.9	**3.8**
6.7	0.48	na	0.29	**2.0**	0.0	0.12	1.36	3.28	93.1	**1.1**	9.9	27.0	**4.7**
8.5	0.52	na	-0.01	**3.5**	-7.4	-2.57	-19.77	3.24	61.6	**2.8**	13.2	6.1	**10.0**
8.1	0.22	2.5	-0.01	**3.8**	1.7	0.53	4.63	3.78	78.1	**5.1**	10.9	1.2	**9.0**
7.8	0.06	na	0.05	**3.5**	0.1	0.49	3.98	3.76	84.1	**1.1**	27.1	30.0	**5.9**
2.5	2.33	na	-0.01	**2.9**	0.4	0.63	5.87	3.80	82.5	**3.4**	20.9	12.8	**5.9**
8.7	0.34	na	0.01	**7.5**	1.0	1.37	9.16	4.40	59.8	**2.3**	29.9	20.1	**9.0**
5.9	1.42	na	0.00	**0.6**	0.0	-0.69	-5.05	3.95	117.5	**1.0**	6.2	28.5	**5.7**
6.9	0.54	3.8	0.09	**3.9**	1.6	0.56	5.45	3.54	75.4	**1.5**	9.9	17.7	**9.0**
6.6	1.27	na	0.12	**6.9**	0.7	1.27	5.87	4.98	69.6	**4.5**	48.3	14.2	**9.1**
5.5	1.35	na	-0.01	**4.1**	0.8	1.06	8.69	3.75	72.9	**3.2**	30.1	15.6	**7.2**
7.1	0.05	na	0.00	**3.4**	0.1	0.65	6.15	3.58	82.8	**5.9**	43.7	4.7	**5.8**
10.0	na	0.0	na	**10.0**	0.1	4.01	4.13	6.25	73.9	**4.0**	na	0.0	**6.3**
5.1	0.85	5.1	0.34	**4.8**	214.6	0.59	4.99	3.07	58.0	**4.8**	21.0	4.5	**9.6**
9.2	0.68	na	0.00	**1.3**	0.0	0.08	0.60	2.48	96.4	**4.3**	47.8	14.7	**6.6**
7.7	0.14	na	0.01	**1.1**	0.1	0.13	0.82	3.88	90.7	**3.1**	43.2	21.6	**6.6**
7.1	0.80	na	-0.18	**4.1**	0.3	0.74	6.86	4.13	77.4	**3.8**	32.2	13.3	**5.7**

	Name	City	State	Rating	2019 Rating	2018 Rating	Total Assets ($Mil)	One Year Asset Growth	Comm-ercial Loans	Cons-umer Loans	Mort-gage Loans	Secur-ities	Capital-ization Index	Lever-age Ratio	Risk-Based Capital Ratio
	Killbuck Savings Bank Co.	Killbuck	OH	**A-**	A-	A-	570.0	6.05	10.6	1.1	20.8	24.8	**9.5**	10.8	0.0
	Kindred State Bank	Kindred	ND	**C**	C	D+	33.2	-1.22	4.4	6.9	4.0	3.7	**6.5**	8.5	16.4
▼	Kingston National Bank	Kingston	OH	**B-**	B	B	384.6	7.39	9.2	2.7	20.9	19.0	**6.5**	8.5	12.6
	Kingstree Federal S&L Assn.	Kingstree	SC	**C+**	C+	C+	36.1	7.54	0.7	0.3	38.4	14.3	**10.0**	16.1	35.3
▲	Kinmundy Bank	Kinmundy	IL	**B+**	B	B-	49.9	4.70	7.3	16.9	27.4	15.4	**10.0**	11.2	18.7
▲	Kirkpatrick Bank	Edmond	OK	**A-**	B+	B-	821.6	0.78	6.7	1.0	6.2	15.6	**10.0**	11.9	16.0
	Kirkwood Bank and Trust Co.	Bismarck	ND	**B**	B	B-	257.4	6.39	11.2	3.5	10.3	12.0	**7.9**	9.8	0.0
	Kirkwood Bank of Nevada	Las Vegas	NV	**B+**	B+	B	130.9	47.69	3.1	0.0	2.3	0.0	**10.0**	14.5	20.4
	Kish Bank	Belleville	PA	**C+**	C+	C+	952.0	9.32	10.5	0.7	23.6	13.6	**6.1**	8.7	11.8
	Kitsap Bank	Port Orchard	WA	**A-**	A-	B	1181.5	2.35	9.0	0.4	8.3	24.1	**7.7**	9.5	13.7
	Kleberg Bank, N.A.	Kingsville	TX	**B-**	B-	C	593.8	11.14	9.7	13.4	12.2	22.3	**7.4**	9.2	14.4
	KodaBank	Drayton	ND	**B**	B	C+	282.3	95.35	12.5	4.5	7.7	13.5	**9.8**	12.9	0.0
	Kress National Bank	Kress	TX	**B**	B	B-	38.7	-17.06	11.8	3.3	0.6	30.6	**10.0**	11.5	29.4
▲	KS Bank, Inc.	Smithfield	NC	**B**	B-	B-	426.0	7.40	3.2	0.4	21.6	15.5	**7.7**	9.7	13.1
▼	KS StateBank	Manhattan	KS	**B+**	A-	A-	2194.6	10.31	12.9	0.4	17.5	15.2	**7.3**	9.4	0.0
	La Monte Community Bank	La Monte	MO	**B+**	B+	B+	32.0	-0.01	3.5	2.2	15.2	23.6	**9.5**	10.8	0.0
	Labette Bank	Altamont	KS	**B+**	B+	B+	414.9	1.40	2.9	2.5	24.5	16.9	**9.8**	12.0	0.0
▼	Ladysmith Federal S&L Assn.	Ladysmith	WI	**C+**	B-	C	57.1	8.91	12.1	5.8	49.1	8.9	**9.3**	10.5	20.5
▲	Lafayette State Bank	Mayo	FL	**D-**	E+	E-	127.6	15.10	7.3	2.3	13.4	7.4	**5.7**	7.7	12.5
	Lake Area Bank	Lindstrom	MN	**B**	B	B	362.7	8.89	7.6	0.1	20.4	18.8	**5.0**	10.5	11.0
▲	Lake Bank	Two Harbors	MN	**B+**	B	C	135.4	-0.09	6.4	1.4	34.7	11.6	**9.3**	10.5	17.1
	Lake Central Bank	Annandale	MN	**A**	A	A-	157.8	5.44	7.0	0.7	15.4	39.3	**10.0**	14.2	18.8
	Lake City Bank	Warsaw	IN	**A-**	A-	A-	5020.9	2.96	28.5	1.9	3.7	12.4	**8.9**	11.7	14.1
▼	Lake City Federal Bank	Lake City	MN	**B-**	B	C	72.2	3.72	0.9	2.9	48.0	16.2	**9.8**	13.1	0.0
	Lake Community Bank	Long Lake	MN	**B+**	B+	B	117.8	-2.04	3.2	0.5	8.1	15.0	**10.0**	12.6	16.7
	Lake Country Community Bank	Morristown	MN	**C**	C	C-	28.1	6.20	9.3	1.3	15.9	37.5	**7.7**	9.5	20.9
	Lake Elmo Bank	Lake Elmo	MN	**A-**	A-	B	387.0	3.41	6.5	2.4	26.2	13.9	**9.2**	10.5	16.1
	Lake Forest Bank & Trust Co., N.A.	Lake Forest	IL	**B+**	B+	B+	4696.1	15.22	43.9	7.4	2.3	10.8	**5.2**	9.1	11.1
	Lake Region Bank	New London	MN	**B-**	B-	B-	119.8	6.28	14.9	3.7	9.1	34.5	**7.9**	9.6	18.7
▼	Lake Shore Savings Bank	Dunkirk	NY	**B-**	B	B	628.6	13.29	3.3	0.2	25.9	11.3	**9.8**	12.9	0.0
	Lake-Osceola State Bank	Baldwin	MI	**C+**	C+	C+	288.7	10.82	5.9	18.7	19.5	6.9	**7.2**	9.2	14.0
	Lakeland Bank	Oak Ridge	NJ	**B+**	B+	B+	7009.6	10.21	6.5	0.1	8.9	13.3	**6.7**	10.1	12.3
	Lakeside Bank	Chicago	IL	**A-**	A-	A-	1930.5	12.54	4.8	0.0	8.1	1.9	**9.0**	11.6	14.2
	Lakeside Bank	Lake Charles	LA	**B-**	B-	B-	211.8	8.30	7.0	2.5	19.7	6.9	**10.0**	12.0	18.2
▼	Lakeside Bank	Rockwall	TX	**C**	C+	C+	112.5	83.62	1.1	1.1	5.9	17.8	**10.0**	22.9	41.5
	Lakeside Bank of Salina	Salina	OK	**B**	B	B	42.5	20.00	5.2	25.7	23.4	11.0	**9.8**	12.5	0.0
	Lakeside State Bank	Oologah	OK	**C**	C	C	69.2	-1.98	7.2	9.3	16.9	30.8	**7.1**	9.2	0.0
	Lakeview Bank	Lakeville	MN	**B**	B	B	109.0	13.34	16.7	0.3	26.4	7.0	**8.0**	9.7	14.0
	Lamar Bank and Trust Co.	Lamar	MO	**A-**	A-	B+	170.0	3.18	8.1	2.9	17.8	8.7	**9.6**	10.9	0.0
▲	Lamar National Bank	Paris	TX	**B-**	C+	C+	195.2	19.15	6.1	2.1	29.3	11.3	**10.0**	11.1	18.3
▼	Lamesa National Bank	Lamesa	TX	**C+**	B-	B	379.8	8.16	1.8	0.2	0.0	51.8	**7.2**	9.1	21.4
	Lamont Bank of St. John	Saint John	WA	**B+**	B+	B	54.3	10.93	6.2	10.7	0.3	40.9	**10.0**	13.0	19.9
	Landmark Bank	Clinton	LA	**C+**	C+	C	141.1	4.80	6.9	2.7	30.2	19.3	**8.6**	10.2	0.0
	Landmark Community Bank	Pittston	PA	**D+**	D+	D+	325.1	-1.77	8.9	8.5	12.6	17.7	**8.7**	10.1	14.2
	Landmark Community Bank	Collierville	TN	**B**	B	B	913.5	-5.95	6.0	0.9	48.5	12.1	**8.2**	9.8	15.3
	Landmark National Bank	Manhattan	KS	**B**	B	B+	985.9	0.82	12.5	0.2	16.0	31.7	**9.7**	10.8	16.9
▼	Laona State Bank	Laona	WI	**C+**	B-	B	210.0	13.42	6.2	3.5	26.3	29.7	**9.8**	11.1	0.0
	LaSalle State Bank	La Salle	IL	**C+**	C+	C+	135.7	-1.19	6.0	1.5	12.3	38.4	**9.1**	10.4	18.9
	Latimer State Bank	Wilburton	OK	**B**	B	B-	71.3	4.64	8.1	3.3	4.9	11.3	**10.0**	20.2	58.9
	Lauderdale County Bank	Halls	TN	**B-**	B-	C+	53.5	9.48	17.5	6.4	14.2	29.8	**9.6**	10.9	0.0
	Laurens State Bank	Laurens	IA	**B+**	B+	B+	70.2	2.11	4.4	1.8	6.9	28.6	**9.8**	11.9	0.0
▼	Lawrenceburg Federal Bank	Lawrenceburg	TN	**B-**	B	B	72.3	9.37	0.0	2.9	75.0	0.0	**9.8**	21.2	0.0
	LCA Bank Corp.	Park City	UT	**A**	A	A	155.5	-10.26	1.4	0.0	0.0	0.8	**9.8**	16.1	0.0
▲	LCNB National Bank	Lebanon	OH	**B+**	B	B	1633.4	0.23	5.2	1.8	17.7	10.4	**7.4**	10.4	12.8
	Lea County State Bank	Hobbs	NM	**A-**	A-	B	393.1	12.96	14.3	3.9	0.7	64.4	**8.9**	10.2	21.6
	Lead Bank	Garden City	MO	**C**	C	C+	411.4	34.53	9.4	21.0	9.0	2.4	**6.6**	8.6	14.3
	Leader Bank, N.A.	Arlington	MA	**A**	A	A	1911.8	38.65	1.0	0.0	37.6	1.6	**10.0**	11.8	16.0
	Leaders Bank	Oak Brook	IL	**C+**	C+	C-	346.8	6.82	14.3	1.0	6.3	6.8	**10.0**	11.7	17.2
	Ledyard National Bank	Norwich	VT	**B+**	B+	B	566.6	13.42	7.9	2.2	21.8	33.8	**8.1**	9.7	15.4
	Lee Bank	Lee	MA	**C+**	C+	C	393.7	-0.85	4.2	0.2	39.7	8.1	**7.0**	9.1	0.0

Asset Mix (As a % of Total Assets): Commercial Loans, Consumer Loans, Mortgage Loans, Securities.

Asset Quality Index	Adjusted Non-Performing Loans as a % of Total Loans	Adjusted Non-Performing Loans as a % of Capital	Net Charge-Offs Avg Loans	Profitability Index	Net Income ($Mil)	Return on Assets (R.O.A.)	Return on Equity (R.O.E.)	Net Interest Spread	Overhead Efficiency Ratio	Liquidity Index	Liquidity Ratio	Hot Money Ratio	Stability Index
8.9	0.15	na	0.00	**6.2**	1.7	1.21	11.03	3.62	64.2	**3.8**	24.1	10.8	**8.2**
6.8	0.27	na	0.00	**3.3**	0.1	0.82	9.45	3.35	76.8	**6.4**	49.5	3.0	**3.5**
8.6	0.09	na	-0.01	**3.8**	0.6	0.67	7.97	3.32	74.9	**1.4**	17.2	26.2	**5.2**
4.9	4.61	na	0.00	**2.6**	0.0	0.22	1.34	2.33	93.2	**1.7**	35.3	37.8	**7.2**
5.6	0.02	na	0.01	**10.0**	0.3	2.05	15.14	4.59	42.4	**4.1**	22.5	9.3	**8.5**
7.5	0.23	na	0.00	**7.2**	4.5	2.25	19.27	3.65	52.4	**3.3**	17.9	12.8	**8.5**
8.4	0.31	na	0.00	**3.9**	0.0	-0.06	-0.56	3.38	74.4	**3.7**	17.7	10.7	**6.2**
6.8	0.00	na	0.00	**4.9**	0.3	0.82	3.85	3.65	70.6	**3.3**	52.2	25.2	**8.0**
8.7	0.18	na	-0.01	**3.8**	1.7	0.72	8.38	3.36	73.3	**2.0**	9.2	18.6	**6.0**
8.2	0.04	0.2	0.00	**5.5**	3.2	1.08	9.56	4.45	71.2	**6.2**	32.3	2.6	**9.8**
4.3	0.85	na	0.24	**4.1**	1.2	0.86	7.10	3.97	76.1	**3.1**	22.5	13.7	**7.5**
4.8	1.78	na	0.00	**9.3**	1.3	1.85	18.31	4.26	58.1	**1.7**	9.7	19.7	**8.6**
8.8	0.59	na	0.00	**3.5**	0.1	0.61	5.18	3.16	87.1	**3.0**	57.8	28.9	**6.1**
5.5	0.99	na	0.00	**5.3**	1.1	1.02	10.47	3.76	67.9	**1.4**	14.7	20.7	**6.6**
7.6	0.38	3.3	-0.02	**4.7**	3.4	0.64	6.64	3.12	65.8	**0.9**	20.5	38.5	**9.1**
8.7	0.00	na	-0.02	**3.4**	0.1	0.58	5.29	3.49	77.9	**3.6**	8.5	10.6	**6.3**
6.9	0.70	na	0.03	**4.9**	0.8	0.78	6.33	3.76	70.2	**2.8**	14.5	15.1	**7.4**
6.3	1.73	na	0.00	**2.7**	0.1	0.32	3.02	3.24	88.7	**1.3**	25.2	31.0	**5.1**
0.3	8.97	58.5	0.51	**2.4**	0.1	0.21	2.60	4.06	95.9	**5.5**	36.3	4.9	**0.9**
4.5	2.65	na	0.14	**7.3**	2.3	2.64	23.11	4.03	68.0	**1.7**	20.7	19.8	**7.6**
8.3	0.88	na	-0.02	**6.5**	0.4	1.06	9.91	3.64	61.6	**1.3**	13.7	24.4	**7.2**
8.2	0.25	1.6	0.00	**9.5**	1.7	4.44	31.51	6.17	43.3	**5.6**	32.6	2.9	**9.3**
7.3	0.48	2.6	0.36	**8.5**	17.6	1.42	11.86	3.35	43.5	**1.7**	15.7	22.6	**10.0**
6.8	0.65	na	-0.01	**3.4**	0.1	0.30	2.24	3.34	88.9	**2.5**	26.1	18.1	**7.1**
7.5	0.06	na	1.18	**6.3**	0.4	1.49	11.31	3.73	63.3	**3.4**	24.2	12.9	**7.6**
6.3	4.07	na	0.00	**2.6**	0.0	0.11	1.14	2.80	94.4	**5.4**	61.5	11.8	**4.7**
6.8	0.72	3.6	-0.01	**7.2**	1.6	1.72	16.51	3.94	60.3	**4.5**	20.0	6.2	**7.4**
6.0	0.74	4.6	0.05	**9.5**	22.6	1.97	19.63	3.32	42.7	**2.1**	18.3	7.0	**8.1**
3.8	4.39	na	0.00	**4.2**	0.3	1.07	11.23	4.33	80.3	**6.8**	54.4	2.5	**5.7**
6.2	0.87	na	0.01	**3.2**	0.8	0.50	3.85	3.48	73.9	**2.4**	18.6	17.5	**8.2**
3.6	1.63	9.0	0.06	**5.1**	0.7	1.00	11.05	3.90	65.1	**2.7**	20.2	13.6	**5.6**
5.1	0.69	4.3	0.03	**4.9**	14.6	0.89	7.24	3.35	54.3	**2.0**	9.5	13.9	**9.4**
6.8	0.41	2.9	0.19	**6.6**	8.2	1.75	15.68	3.78	49.5	**0.9**	15.0	18.2	**10.0**
8.6	0.08	na	0.01	**2.9**	0.2	0.28	2.30	3.56	86.7	**1.9**	26.4	23.5	**7.2**
8.8	0.14	na	0.00	**1.8**	0.0	0.05	0.21	4.69	76.7	**7.6**	95.0	5.3	**5.0**
3.2	3.67	na	-0.08	**7.9**	0.1	1.38	11.19	5.28	60.3	**1.4**	14.6	26.1	**6.7**
6.1	2.63	na	-0.02	**3.2**	0.1	0.30	3.24	3.82	89.1	**3.7**	24.6	11.2	**4.0**
5.1	0.96	7.3	0.00	**5.9**	0.2	0.93	9.53	4.34	69.2	**2.2**	23.6	14.6	**6.3**
6.5	0.43	na	0.06	**7.9**	0.9	1.97	18.30	4.05	53.1	**4.0**	16.9	9.3	**8.5**
4.6	2.55	15.4	0.01	**4.5**	0.5	0.99	8.78	4.37	72.5	**2.8**	29.3	13.8	**6.8**
8.7	0.00	na	-0.55	**3.1**	0.7	0.75	8.18	1.47	67.0	**4.0**	69.1	23.2	**4.4**
7.8	1.36	na	9.17	**3.7**	-0.3	-1.95	-14.56	3.94	38.3	**6.6**	43.2	0.0	**6.4**
4.0	1.65	na	0.02	**3.5**	0.3	0.80	7.97	4.41	78.7	**2.3**	24.4	13.5	**5.5**
6.9	0.30	na	0.03	**1.7**	0.2	0.27	2.67	3.13	89.3	**2.9**	9.0	14.0	**5.2**
6.0	0.87	6.4	0.05	**4.8**	2.5	1.09	11.13	2.88	53.6	**0.8**	13.7	28.9	**6.0**
4.8	1.86	6.1	0.14	**5.1**	3.5	1.42	11.03	3.83	67.4	**3.9**	16.2	9.0	**8.3**
2.9	4.91	na	-0.01	**4.1**	0.6	1.08	9.81	2.87	47.0	**4.0**	44.2	16.1	**6.6**
5.7	1.64	na	-0.03	**4.0**	0.4	1.09	10.53	3.09	74.4	**3.4**	17.2	12.2	**5.8**
7.5	3.48	4.7	0.11	**4.0**	0.2	1.03	5.09	2.59	58.2	**3.6**	89.1	33.6	**7.2**
5.4	1.83	na	-0.02	**3.4**	0.1	0.43	3.85	3.80	84.9	**2.4**	45.2	31.2	**5.3**
9.1	0.00	na	0.07	**5.4**	0.2	1.24	10.11	2.94	59.0	**5.5**	59.4	10.8	**7.4**
5.4	1.40	na	0.00	**3.7**	0.1	0.63	3.00	3.18	77.1	**0.8**	15.5	39.9	**7.6**
7.5	0.60	na	1.46	**7.3**	0.2	0.54	3.38	7.54	57.1	**0.3**	14.8	0.0	**8.2**
5.8	0.54	na	0.07	**5.6**	5.0	1.23	8.90	3.89	63.4	**3.3**	4.9	11.5	**10.0**
8.9	0.12	0.3	0.21	**5.4**	1.8	1.96	17.76	3.27	68.0	**5.7**	60.4	6.9	**6.9**
2.8	0.74	na	-0.04	**6.1**	0.9	0.92	10.86	24.93	92.4	**1.0**	21.0	11.0	**4.5**
8.3	0.54	2.9	0.01	**9.2**	8.9	2.23	19.24	2.95	43.0	**1.5**	22.4	14.9	**9.5**
5.7	2.11	na	0.03	**2.2**	0.2	0.26	2.10	2.71	87.6	**1.0**	26.8	45.5	**7.1**
6.8	0.72	2.9	-0.01	**5.3**	1.7	1.30	12.70	3.32	71.6	**4.4**	20.6	6.4	**6.1**
5.4	1.69	na	0.02	**1.5**	-1.1	-1.10	-12.57	3.44	86.5	**3.3**	12.9	9.2	**5.4**

Asset Quality Index	Adjusted Non-Performing Loans as a % of Total Loans	Adjusted Non-Performing Loans as a % of Capital	Net Charge-Offs Avg Loans	Profitability Index	Net Income ($Mil)	Return on Assets (R.O.A.)	Return on Equity (R.O.E.)	Net Interest Spread	Overhead Efficiency Ratio	Liquidity Index	Liquidity Ratio	Hot Money Ratio	Stability Index
6.8	0.29	na	0.02	**3.3**	0.3	0.46	5.36	3.38	85.4	**1.8**	17.3	21.4	**5.4**
4.4	2.11	na	0.19	**8.9**	4.3	1.75	14.47	4.67	53.6	**2.9**	21.8	15.2	**9.4**
4.3	2.51	13.0	0.09	**5.0**	0.6	2.58	22.87	4.04	61.1	**1.6**	17.1	23.8	**4.5**
4.9	0.88	na	2.46	**10.0**	0.9	3.57	13.82	10.86	30.5	**0.2**	1.6	62.7	**8.8**
5.4	1.00	6.1	0.09	**5.7**	13.3	1.32	12.26	3.05	46.3	**1.7**	15.2	13.6	**10.0**
5.3	4.02	na	0.00	**5.4**	1.1	1.11	9.90	3.09	59.2	**1.8**	22.5	19.7	**7.0**
4.0	2.37	na	0.00	**5.0**	0.4	1.12	9.36	3.96	77.0	**3.2**	42.0	19.7	**7.8**
7.5	0.02	na	0.03	**5.5**	0.4	1.26	8.92	3.24	54.8	**3.8**	32.5	12.0	**8.3**
6.8	0.25	1.8	0.00	**6.5**	2.5	1.06	9.37	3.51	44.3	**0.8**	14.2	34.2	**7.6**
6.1	0.88	na	0.15	**4.6**	0.5	0.75	7.66	3.71	72.4	**1.6**	22.0	23.5	**6.6**
4.5	1.69	na	0.17	**3.7**	0.2	0.55	6.10	4.52	79.6	**1.6**	9.4	19.0	**4.7**
8.7	0.02	na	0.00	**5.4**	0.4	1.13	8.26	4.21	69.5	**4.8**	27.0	5.5	**7.7**
7.2	0.10	na	-0.02	**3.1**	0.2	0.48	5.50	3.37	78.9	**0.7**	13.8	38.8	**4.7**
8.0	0.35	na	0.04	**4.6**	1.9	0.85	6.70	3.64	67.7	**0.8**	16.0	24.6	**7.8**
6.0	1.87	na	-0.06	**0.3**	-0.1	-0.63	-4.65	5.42	106.7	**5.7**	46.8	6.9	**3.6**
8.4	0.00	na	-0.01	**8.0**	1.8	1.58	18.64	3.85	42.0	**2.6**	16.5	15.1	**6.4**
8.3	1.34	na	0.00	**4.8**	1.1	0.96	4.74	3.84	71.7	**5.9**	57.7	10.0	**8.3**
8.4	0.00	na	0.26	**2.9**	0.0	0.67	6.48	3.43	75.3	**4.3**	49.1	13.3	**4.5**
6.7	2.65	na	0.02	**6.6**	0.8	1.89	11.32	3.16	45.0	**5.9**	66.1	11.3	**9.2**
7.0	0.77	na	0.29	**0.6**	-305.4	-0.93	-8.15	2.36	87.9	**4.0**	30.0	10.7	**8.7**
6.2	1.11	na	0.14	**5.1**	1.3	1.05	10.20	3.75	67.1	**1.5**	10.4	22.6	**6.6**
9.0	0.28	na	0.00	**9.6**	2.0	2.54	16.61	3.50	33.4	**3.4**	46.5	15.8	**9.8**
5.7	0.23	3.0	-0.02	**7.9**	1.3	1.74	15.73	4.21	51.8	**0.4**	15.2	74.5	**8.4**
2.8	4.15	na	0.00	**3.9**	0.2	0.58	4.89	3.97	75.4	**3.0**	11.1	9.3	**6.7**
5.9	1.06	na	0.36	**5.1**	1.0	1.20	12.28	3.05	63.8	**1.9**	20.9	20.0	**6.4**
5.0	2.52	na	0.00	**2.6**	0.1	0.47	2.42	3.62	92.1	**1.5**	10.7	22.5	**6.9**
9.8	0.27	na	0.00	**3.0**	0.1	0.47	1.69	3.14	80.9	**0.6**	11.8	50.9	**7.8**
7.0	3.20	na	-0.82	**6.1**	0.6	1.15	3.68	3.56	65.7	**3.2**	45.8	16.8	**8.6**
8.8	0.00	na	0.08	**4.4**	0.5	1.07	10.93	3.72	72.4	**2.7**	27.8	17.5	**5.4**
8.3	0.33	na	0.00	**0.6**	0.0	-0.23	-0.94	3.29	106.2	**0.8**	22.3	43.9	**6.4**
6.2	1.22	na	0.00	**6.3**	1.0	0.42	2.33	3.73	46.2	**0.9**	23.6	39.3	**9.4**
6.7	0.63	3.7	0.46	**5.7**	2.6	0.53	4.95	3.72	84.5	**1.8**	14.2	10.8	**8.7**
7.9	0.07	na	0.00	**2.2**	1.1	0.53	5.21	4.35	76.0	**6.1**	26.4	0.0	**7.4**
4.6	1.53	na	-0.01	**1.1**	0.1	0.16	1.93	3.62	108.2	**2.4**	20.6	17.6	**2.2**
5.8	0.33	na	0.02	**6.4**	0.8	1.08	9.72	4.02	62.6	**2.1**	20.5	19.1	**7.2**
7.0	0.00	na	-0.01	**4.9**	0.1	0.87	6.52	2.97	63.2	**1.3**	11.0	25.8	**7.2**
9.7	0.13	na	0.02	**3.9**	0.3	0.67	4.09	4.14	74.6	**2.0**	13.7	13.6	**7.8**
9.1	na	na	na	**9.5**	0.1	2.70	2.99	1.86	96.3	**4.0**	na	100.0	**6.1**
9.3	0.12	na	-0.35	**3.7**	0.4	0.81	5.82	2.61	68.8	**3.2**	46.1	22.3	**6.4**
4.2	1.11	na	0.00	**4.3**	0.1	0.59	5.16	3.30	62.6	**5.3**	45.1	9.4	**7.4**
1.8	3.68	na	0.12	**8.6**	0.8	1.59	14.68	5.35	65.7	**4.4**	25.1	7.5	**8.0**
8.3	0.65	2.2	0.06	**6.0**	4.0	1.21	8.54	3.18	55.4	**5.3**	26.3	5.3	**10.0**
5.1	0.71	na	0.03	**5.4**	1.8	0.76	5.98	4.27	62.7	**2.1**	10.9	13.2	**9.3**
7.3	0.65	2.5	-0.08	**2.8**	0.3	0.36	4.03	3.28	83.5	**4.8**	16.3	3.7	**4.8**
8.4	0.43	2.2	0.00	**4.8**	4.9	0.86	10.54	2.95	65.9	**5.7**	29.6	4.9	**7.6**
5.2	1.47	na	0.00	**5.4**	0.4	1.02	6.72	3.55	64.6	**3.1**	22.9	13.7	**8.0**
7.4	0.11	0.4	-0.25	**4.1**	0.7	0.75	7.81	3.59	75.7	**4.6**	16.7	4.6	**5.8**
7.5	0.00	na	0.00	**2.1**	-0.1	-0.24	-1.36	2.88	70.7	**0.6**	17.4	56.5	**8.3**
5.7	0.38	na	0.00	**4.6**	0.1	0.54	4.69	3.98	71.3	**0.9**	23.0	40.7	**6.7**
8.3	0.36	na	0.44	**3.1**	0.3	0.41	3.69	3.86	80.3	**2.6**	29.7	18.8	**6.4**
8.6	1.07	na	0.07	**2.3**	0.2	0.18	1.91	3.37	80.1	**3.7**	19.5	11.0	**6.4**
7.4	0.55	3.0	-0.07	**1.9**	-2.4	-0.34	-3.14	3.08	90.6	**4.2**	25.7	9.5	**9.2**
7.9	1.53	na	0.11	**7.3**	5.7	1.09	5.65	3.70	59.6	**5.7**	28.2	3.9	**10.0**
9.3	0.67	na	0.00	**5.0**	0.8	0.96	8.14	3.15	60.7	**3.4**	23.6	12.8	**7.3**
9.8	0.00	na	0.00	**2.9**	0.2	0.46	5.80	3.00	82.9	**3.3**	25.2	13.6	**4.2**
6.0	0.78	na	0.07	**4.9**	1.7	1.06	9.66	4.27	67.9	**4.1**	28.7	10.5	**6.9**
10.0	na	na	na	**7.5**	5.2	11.02	36.13	0.39	89.9	**8.4**	96.2	0.0	**7.9**
3.5	3.22	na	-0.06	**2.3**	0.1	0.20	1.84	4.24	92.5	**0.3**	6.2	63.3	**5.6**
4.5	1.24	8.9	0.01	**3.7**	1.3	0.71	8.34	3.73	77.3	**2.8**	20.3	15.4	**5.9**
6.3	0.68	3.3	0.03	**6.0**	17.4	1.19	10.44	3.84	63.0	**3.7**	8.1	9.8	**9.0**

	Name	City	State	Rating	2019 Rating	2018 Rating	Total Assets ($Mil)	One Year Asset Growth	Asset Mix (As a % of Total Assets) Comm-ercial Loans	Cons-umer Loans	Mort-gage Loans	Secur-ities	Capital-ization Index	Lever-age Ratio	Risk-Based Capital Ratio
▲	NBKC Bank	Kansas City	MO	**A-**	B+	B+	934.0	29.84	2.8	1.8	39.3	16.5	**10.0**	14.6	16.4
	NBT Bank, N.A.	Norwich	NY	**B+**	B+	B	9881.1	4.39	10.4	18.0	16.5	16.6	**7.3**	9.5	12.8
	Nebraska Bank of Commerce	Lincoln	NE	**C**	C	C	156.3	6.55	14.9	0.3	14.5	3.2	**6.0**	9.0	11.8
	Nebraska State Bank	Bristow	NE	**C**	C	C	17.9	2.67	9.5	2.2	1.4	0.0	**9.8**	13.6	0.0
▼	Nebraska State Bank	Lynch	NE	**C-**	C	C-	15.7	7.44	3.8	2.0	2.2	0.0	**9.8**	13.3	0.0
	Nebraska State Bank	Oshkosh	NE	**A-**	A-	B+	51.8	5.23	0.6	0.0	0.0	0.0	**9.8**	16.5	0.0
▲	Nebraska State Bank and Trust Co.	Broken Bow	NE	**B+**	B	B	252.0	5.51	9.9	3.1	9.0	6.4	**8.5**	10.2	0.0
▼	NebraskaLand National Bank	North Platte	NE	**B-**	B	B	751.2	5.16	12.7	0.7	6.4	27.0	**9.8**	12.1	0.0
	Needham Bank	Needham	MA	**B-**	B-	B-	2495.4	12.18	3.5	0.4	41.0	7.3	**9.7**	11.8	14.8
▼	Neffs National Bank	Neffs	PA	**B+**	A-	A-	379.4	2.79	1.7	2.7	22.1	44.0	**9.8**	18.8	0.0
	Neighborhood National Bank	San Diego	CA	**D**	D	D+	72.3	16.64	13.1	0.0	7.7	1.6	**10.0**	16.0	26.4
	Neighborhood National Bank	Mora	MN	**A-**	A-	B+	225.6	2.98	13.8	3.5	17.5	30.8	**10.0**	11.7	17.6
▲	Neighbors Bank	Clarence	MO	**C**	C-	C+	40.6	55.86	1.5	0.7	24.5	7.5	**10.0**	14.1	16.4
	Nekoosa Port Edwards State Bank	Nekoosa	WI	**A-**	A-	B+	216.1	6.35	2.3	2.2	32.1	18.7	**10.0**	13.2	29.3
	Nelsonville Home & Savings Bank	Nelsonville	OH	**B-**	B-	B-	31.2	2.68	0.0	3.4	53.0	4.6	**10.0**	12.4	28.7
	Neuberger Berman Trust Co. of Delaware	Wilmington	DE	**U**	U	U	6.5	-2.80	0.0	0.0	0.0	0.0	**10.0**	92.5	264.8
	Neuberger Berman Trust Co., N.A.	New York	NY	**U**	U	U	22.0	-22.31	0.0	0.0	0.0	0.0	**10.0**	54.1	155.8
▲	Nevada Bank and Trust Co.	Caliente	NV	**B-**	C+	C+	153.8	16.64	4.9	4.3	2.7	51.5	**8.2**	9.8	22.2
	New Albin Savings Bank	New Albin	IA	**A**	A	A	279.8	16.08	1.9	0.9	10.4	71.6	**10.0**	17.3	51.1
	New Buffalo Savings Bank	New Buffalo	MI	**C+**	C+	C-	112.2	-6.31	1.2	0.1	22.2	0.0	**10.0**	14.2	18.3
	New Carlisle Federal Savings Bank	New Carlisle	OH	**C+**	C+	C+	136.9	11.75	8.1	1.5	36.6	1.7	**7.9**	9.7	0.0
	New Century Bank	Belleville	KS	**B**	B	B+	60.1	-1.07	1.9	3.8	34.9	0.0	**8.5**	10.0	14.8
	New Covenant Trust Co., N.A.	Jeffersonville	IN	**U**	U	U	6.9	5.68	0.0	0.0	0.0	21.4	**10.0**	85.0	274.7
	New Era Bank	Fredericktown	MO	**A-**	A-	A-	356.9	-0.15	5.2	1.2	26.2	14.6	**9.2**	10.6	0.0
▼	New Foundation Savings Bank	Cincinnati	OH	**C**	C+	C	20.0	7.84	4.3	0.3	67.9	1.6	**9.8**	11.3	0.0
	New Frontier Bank	Saint Charles	MO	**B-**	B-	C	106.7	22.79	7.7	0.1	7.1	16.7	**5.0**	8.4	11.0
▼	New Haven Bank	New Haven	CT	**C**	C+	C	149.9	8.02	3.8	5.4	39.2	3.7	**8.6**	10.1	15.7
▼	New Horizon Bank, N.A.	Powhatan	VA	**C**	C+	C+	89.7	4.03	8.7	1.5	14.9	7.8	**8.5**	10.6	13.7
	New Market Bank	Elko New Market	MN	**C+**	C+	C+	118.3	4.19	9.2	1.0	12.2	21.1	**6.4**	8.5	12.9
	New Mexico Bank & Trust	Albuquerque	NM	**A-**	A-	A-	1675.1	11.67	12.6	0.4	5.3	28.6	**6.6**	8.6	12.3
	New Millennium Bank	Fort Lee	NJ	**C+**	C+	C	371.7	-15.69	14.6	0.0	14.9	0.8	**7.8**	10.4	13.2
	New OMNI Bank, N.A.	Alhambra	CA	**A-**	A-	A-	488.2	6.68	0.3	0.1	33.5	2.9	**10.0**	15.1	24.9
▼	New Peoples Bank, Inc.	Honaker	VA	**C-**	C	C-	713.7	-0.98	7.5	3.2	32.0	6.7	**7.7**	9.4	15.1
	New Republic Savings Bank	Roanoke Rapids	NC	**C-**	C-	C	65.5	0.16	4.2	0.5	48.5	0.0	**8.5**	10.0	15.1
	New Tripoli Bank	New Tripoli	PA	**B**	B	B+	501.9	3.09	5.5	0.4	46.8	16.0	**9.8**	11.2	0.0
	New Washington State Bank	New Washington	IN	**B+**	B+	B-	356.5	3.26	11.8	10.6	15.3	11.3	**8.5**	10.2	0.0
	New York Community Bank	Hicksville	NY	**B**	B	B+	54237.2	4.05	3.6	0.0	0.7	10.1	**7.4**	9.5	12.8
	NewBank	Flushing	NY	**A-**	A-	B+	440.2	2.50	21.3	0.0	0.2	0.0	**10.0**	11.4	20.6
	Newburyport Five Cents Savings Bank	Newburyport	MA	**C+**	C+	B-	1089.0	21.18	5.7	3.0	29.9	10.5	**10.0**	12.7	16.7
	Newfield National Bank	Newfield	NJ	**C+**	C+	C	695.0	3.91	7.1	0.2	19.5	20.8	**7.5**	9.4	17.1
▲	NewFirst National Bank	El Campo	TX	**B+**	B	B	757.8	8.55	8.9	0.6	8.0	5.1	**9.8**	11.4	0.0
▼	Newport Federal Bank	Newport	TN	**B-**	B	B	217.9	3.71	0.1	1.0	37.7	39.2	**9.8**	11.2	0.0
▼	Newton Federal Bank	Covington	GA	**C**	C+	B-	646.0	108.44	24.0	5.9	17.1	2.9	**4.0**	8.3	10.5
	Newtown Savings Bank	Newtown	CT	**C+**	C+	C+	1448.2	9.32	5.4	1.7	39.7	10.3	**6.4**	8.4	13.4
	NexBank SSB	Dallas	TX	**B+**	B+	A-	9777.4	18.93	4.3	0.1	41.3	13.3	**6.5**	8.5	12.1
	NexTier Bank, N.A.	Butler	PA	**B+**	B+	B	1445.5	11.75	7.7	9.0	24.3	7.3	**7.7**	9.6	0.0
	Nicolet National Bank	Green Bay	WI	**B+**	B+	B+	3722.8	22.56	20.8	0.8	12.3	13.8	**5.2**	9.5	11.2
▼	Ninnescah Valley Bank	Cunningham	KS	**B-**	B	B	33.0	6.35	3.9	1.7	5.1	55.8	**9.8**	12.3	0.0
	Noah Bank	Elkins Park	PA	**C-**	C-	C	383.5	-8.29	9.8	0.0	0.5	1.1	**6.6**	8.6	15.0
	NobleBank & Trust	Anniston	AL	**B-**	B-	B-	261.4	-0.67	12.4	2.0	14.4	20.6	**7.9**	9.8	0.0
	Nodaway Valley Bank	Maryville	MO	**A**	A	A-	958.5	6.58	7.0	0.9	6.2	20.4	**10.0**	12.5	18.1
▼	Nokomis Savings Bank	Nokomis	IL	**C-**	C	C+	30.1	6.68	10.3	3.9	18.3	28.5	**9.8**	16.0	0.0
▲	Normangee State Bank	Normangee	TX	**B**	B-	C+	121.3	1.57	2.8	11.0	27.0	29.1	**10.0**	16.7	31.9
	North Adams State Bank	Ursa	IL	**B-**	B-	B-	37.1	2.39	13.9	5.3	16.8	16.8	**9.8**	15.2	0.0
▲	North Alabama Bank	Hazel Green	AL	**B**	B-	C+	119.4	10.61	4.4	1.7	12.6	8.7	**8.0**	9.9	0.0
	North American Banking Co.	Roseville	MN	**A-**	A-	B+	673.2	25.16	11.8	0.3	5.4	18.4	**6.7**	8.7	13.7
	North American Savings Bank, F.S.B.	Kansas City	MO	**A-**	A-	A-	2619.2	15.10	0.4	0.1	70.2	7.8	**10.0**	11.0	15.0
	North Arundel Savings Bank	Pasadena	MD	**C**	C	C	44.2	2.71	0.0	2.2	60.5	2.6	**10.0**	13.1	28.2
▼	North Brookfield Savings Bank	North Brookfield	MA	**C+**	B-	B-	326.5	3.03	0.6	2.1	49.5	16.3	**9.8**	12.0	0.0
▲	North Cambridge Co-operative Bank	Cambridge	MA	**B-**	C+	C+	91.4	1.46	0.0	0.2	55.2	14.0	**10.0**	22.2	51.7

Asset Quality Index	Adjusted Non-Performing Loans as a % of Total Loans	Adjusted Non-Performing Loans as a % of Capital	Net Charge-Offs Avg Loans	Profitability Index	Net Income ($Mil)	Return on Assets (R.O.A.)	Return on Equity (R.O.E.)	Net Interest Spread	Overhead Efficiency Ratio	Liquidity Index	Liquidity Ratio	Hot Money Ratio	Stability Index
6.7	1.03	na	-0.17	**8.6**	18.6	9.16	66.77	2.54	65.3	**0.9**	24.1	35.3	**9.6**
6.0	0.61	2.7	0.31	**4.5**	9.5	0.39	3.31	3.54	60.8	**4.1**	6.3	4.4	**9.0**
7.3	0.02	na	0.00	**3.1**	0.2	0.53	6.00	2.87	74.0	**0.9**	14.0	32.6	**5.4**
7.5	0.00	na	0.00	**1.4**	0.0	-0.35	-2.55	3.86	71.9	**1.9**	49.0	28.4	**4.3**
6.0	0.00	na	0.00	**2.0**	0.0	-0.10	-0.74	3.50	67.8	**4.5**	57.5	10.1	**4.2**
7.3	0.00	na	0.00	**10.0**	0.5	4.02	22.99	4.74	38.2	**1.9**	18.4	20.1	**7.0**
6.5	0.11	na	0.13	**7.0**	1.0	1.62	15.77	3.87	56.8	**1.4**	12.6	16.8	**7.7**
8.7	0.02	0.0	0.00	**3.7**	1.6	0.84	7.07	3.15	74.1	**1.1**	9.2	21.5	**7.9**
6.7	0.92	5.6	0.00	**3.7**	3.8	0.61	5.20	2.85	66.2	**0.8**	14.2	37.9	**8.7**
8.8	1.15	na	-0.01	**4.7**	0.9	0.96	5.06	3.02	60.5	**4.1**	56.3	18.6	**8.9**
8.7	1.40	na	1.21	**0.0**	-0.7	-3.89	-23.48	3.23	191.1	**2.2**	43.9	34.3	**6.2**
6.7	0.85	4.1	-0.07	**5.1**	0.6	1.14	9.40	3.90	72.9	**3.7**	21.9	11.1	**7.8**
9.3	0.09	na	0.00	**4.8**	0.3	3.43	25.16	2.89	85.2	**6.6**	49.2	1.6	**6.2**
8.7	1.60	na	-0.07	**5.4**	0.8	1.30	9.74	2.61	49.1	**2.7**	46.9	29.5	**8.4**
9.3	0.00	na	0.00	**3.7**	0.0	0.52	4.24	3.26	74.0	**2.2**	29.1	21.1	**6.6**
10.0	na	na	na	**8.8**	0.0	0.00	0.00	55.81	96.3	**4.0**	na	0.0	**5.5**
10.0	na	na	na	**10.0**	0.4	6.07	11.38	46.77	95.3	**4.0**	141.8	0.0	**6.7**
8.7	0.44	na	-0.04	**4.1**	0.3	0.84	8.16	3.52	72.8	**7.4**	61.9	0.9	**6.3**
9.8	0.00	na	0.00	**5.8**	0.9	1.35	7.35	2.29	31.7	**4.0**	69.3	23.4	**9.0**
6.4	2.65	na	-0.01	**2.5**	0.0	0.07	0.50	3.57	92.6	**1.0**	16.9	21.8	**7.3**
6.0	0.66	na	0.06	**3.9**	0.2	0.62	6.47	3.53	80.2	**1.2**	11.7	28.3	**5.4**
4.8	1.07	na	0.20	**6.8**	0.2	1.19	12.15	5.06	77.1	**0.6**	11.5	50.1	**7.5**
10.0	na	na	na	**3.7**	-0.1	-3.26	-3.72	1.79	107.1	**4.0**	na	0.0	**4.3**
8.5	0.02	0.3	0.02	**8.4**	1.8	1.99	17.12	3.38	48.6	**4.0**	20.3	9.3	**8.7**
8.9	0.40	na	0.00	**1.0**	0.0	-1.18	-10.35	3.29	113.5	**1.6**	14.4	21.6	**6.2**
2.8	1.96	na	-0.02	**3.1**	0.2	0.73	8.11	3.64	79.5	**3.5**	21.6	11.9	**5.3**
8.4	0.00	na	0.02	**2.4**	0.1	0.20	1.82	2.91	88.9	**0.6**	12.7	48.1	**6.4**
6.3	0.47	na	0.00	**2.3**	0.0	0.03	0.25	4.13	98.7	**1.0**	17.1	31.6	**6.3**
5.1	2.42	na	-0.01	**3.9**	0.3	1.03	12.02	5.17	86.5	**5.6**	30.0	1.3	**4.9**
8.3	0.32	2.0	0.03	**7.4**	4.0	0.93	10.03	3.83	53.8	**4.6**	11.2	4.6	**7.9**
3.0	1.70	na	-0.04	**5.4**	0.7	0.78	7.37	3.77	68.2	**0.6**	10.0	54.3	**6.1**
9.0	0.22	na	0.00	**5.2**	1.1	0.93	6.19	3.73	68.1	**0.7**	23.6	72.6	**8.3**
4.6	1.54	10.2	0.02	**2.2**	0.2	0.12	1.18	3.84	85.3	**1.8**	16.1	20.0	**6.2**
7.4	0.36	na	0.00	**1.6**	0.0	0.09	0.85	3.90	96.4	**0.4**	7.5	62.1	**4.9**
6.4	1.16	na	0.00	**4.1**	1.0	0.83	7.21	3.24	67.2	**1.5**	14.7	24.5	**8.2**
7.0	0.46	na	0.02	**6.7**	1.4	1.58	15.44	4.43	68.1	**4.8**	22.7	4.2	**7.9**
6.1	0.12	0.7	0.10	**4.3**	109.5	0.82	6.13	2.09	45.2	**0.7**	11.4	25.5	**10.0**
6.1	2.20	na	1.91	**5.7**	1.0	0.94	8.24	2.97	64.6	**2.4**	48.8	40.0	**6.5**
8.5	0.18	na	0.07	**1.3**	0.7	0.28	2.21	3.19	78.2	**2.3**	17.3	16.2	**8.4**
6.4	0.73	3.9	0.08	**3.4**	1.2	0.69	7.29	3.23	74.9	**5.1**	30.0	4.6	**6.0**
5.8	0.47	na	-0.04	**9.6**	3.6	1.92	16.75	4.75	50.6	**5.3**	30.0	3.7	**9.2**
7.7	0.82	na	0.00	**3.8**	0.3	0.56	5.05	2.62	72.1	**1.4**	28.2	32.0	**6.5**
4.3	1.17	na	0.00	**1.1**	-1.1	-0.67	-6.32	3.39	120.5	**1.5**	9.8	23.2	**6.7**
5.5	1.57	9.5	0.30	**2.2**	0.2	0.05	0.67	3.22	81.8	**3.7**	23.1	12.5	**6.3**
8.5	0.29	4.6	0.02	**6.0**	27.0	1.20	18.52	2.36	22.6	**5.0**	12.9	2.3	**6.0**
5.7	0.65	na	0.00	**5.3**	3.1	0.86	8.47	3.59	62.9	**3.1**	4.3	10.7	**9.0**
5.7	0.56	2.8	0.01	**7.4**	10.8	1.22	8.89	4.06	57.3	**3.1**	19.1	8.7	**10.0**
6.9	11.16	na	0.00	**4.0**	0.1	0.81	6.64	3.65	76.6	**3.9**	57.4	18.3	**6.8**
0.6	3.76	na	0.82	**2.0**	2.2	2.33	26.69	2.75	157.9	**0.8**	22.8	55.6	**2.9**
4.6	1.98	na	-0.15	**3.8**	0.6	0.90	9.09	4.05	82.4	**3.4**	25.9	13.2	**5.6**
8.1	0.05	na	0.02	**8.7**	4.8	2.03	14.38	3.98	56.5	**4.5**	29.5	8.5	**10.0**
7.7	0.45	1.7	0.00	**2.3**	0.0	0.21	1.29	2.67	80.6	**2.9**	42.8	22.3	**6.8**
4.6	4.65	na	1.08	**4.5**	0.3	1.00	5.90	4.47	62.5	**2.7**	35.6	20.5	**6.3**
6.5	0.08	na	0.11	**4.5**	0.1	0.74	4.81	4.17	76.0	**2.9**	30.3	17.3	**6.9**
7.1	0.75	na	-0.19	**5.4**	0.3	0.93	8.24	4.88	73.5	**1.0**	20.5	30.1	**7.1**
7.1	0.36	2.3	0.00	**8.6**	3.3	2.01	23.25	3.26	48.3	**3.5**	39.3	13.5	**7.5**
6.6	1.07	6.5	-0.01	**8.7**	9.3	1.47	13.32	3.79	64.6	**0.6**	7.0	33.2	**10.0**
9.5	0.72	2.0	-0.01	**1.0**	-0.1	-0.63	-4.76	3.41	99.4	**1.2**	28.1	37.3	**6.2**
7.2	0.64	3.1	0.00	**2.6**	0.4	0.47	3.93	3.02	90.8	**3.1**	24.2	14.3	**6.6**
9.9	0.70	na	0.00	**3.4**	0.1	0.57	2.45	3.53	77.8	**2.7**	49.6	29.8	**7.6**

Name	City	State	Rating	2019 Rating	2018 Rating	Total Assets ($Mil)	One Year Asset Growth	Asset Mix (As a % of Total Assets) Commercial Loans	Consumer Loans	Mortgage Loans	Securities	Capitalization Index	Leverage Ratio	Risk-Based Capital Ratio
North Central Bank	Hennepin	IL	B	B	B	119.6	-1.21	7.9	4.6	22.3	26.4	9.8	12.7	0.0
North Country Savings Bank	Canton	NY	B-	B-	B-	281.6	9.53	0.1	2.3	71.4	0.6	10.0	15.6	25.7
North County Savings Bank	Red Bud	IL	C+	C+	C+	55.4	3.36	0.0	2.6	39.1	14.9	6.9	8.9	26.7
North Dallas Bank & Trust Co.	Dallas	TX	B	B	B	1285.3	-2.00	3.3	0.6	19.1	38.6	9.8	12.6	0.0
▼ North Easton Savings Bank	South Easton	MA	C-	C	C	1137.4	101.06	4.5	2.9	41.6	12.6	6.6	8.6	13.7
North Georgia National Bank	Calhoun	GA	B-	B-	B-	132.6	0.99	6.3	1.1	16.1	25.6	9.8	11.3	0.0
North Salem State Bank	North Salem	IN	B	B	B-	412.8	16.46	6.5	3.6	16.5	7.0	6.4	8.4	12.4
North Shore Bank of Commerce	Duluth	MN	B	B	B	278.3	2.16	3.1	0.5	34.4	12.1	7.2	9.1	15.8
North Shore Bank, a Co-operative Bank	Peabody	MA	B-	B-	C+	1378.6	59.52	9.5	0.2	26.2	9.5	9.1	10.4	14.7
▼ North Shore Bank, FSB	Brookfield	WI	B-	B	B-	2214.2	10.82	1.5	19.5	14.6	11.1	9.8	11.9	0.0
▼ North Shore Trust and Savings	Waukegan	IL	C-	C	C	236.4	3.15	0.1	0.1	37.1	28.2	9.8	19.1	0.0
North Side Bank and Trust Co.	Cincinnati	OH	A-	A-	B+	770.1	16.50	18.3	0.9	11.6	17.9	8.1	12.0	13.4
▼ North Side Federal S&L Assn. of Chicago	Chicago	IL	D	D+	D	40.2	-1.10	0.0	0.0	42.9	15.5	9.6	10.7	25.1
North Star Bank	Roseville	MN	B+	B+	B	293.8	3.88	17.5	2.0	4.1	23.6	9.3	10.7	0.0
North State Bank	Raleigh	NC	B	B	B-	994.6	5.70	9.1	0.4	21.8	2.9	5.9	8.6	11.7
North Valley Bank	Thornton	CO	A	A	A	177.3	1.02	1.0	0.1	40.0	0.0	10.0	12.2	18.3
North Valley Bank	Zanesville	OH	B-	B-	B-	245.2	12.56	6.9	3.6	18.2	13.9	7.6	9.5	0.0
Northbrook Bank & Trust Co., N.A.	Northbrook	IL	B	B	B	3065.4	15.20	28.9	8.3	3.8	16.9	5.7	9.0	11.6
Northeast Bank	Lewiston	ME	C+	C+		1231.5	0.12	1.1	0.1	6.6	5.4	10.0	13.0	18.0
Northeast Bank	Minneapolis	MN	A-	A-	A-	540.9	12.84	19.8	0.2	7.7	17.3	8.2	10.7	13.5
NorthEast Community Bank	White Plains	NY	B	B	B-	899.9	-2.49	9.4	0.0	0.9	1.0	9.2	14.3	14.3
Northeast Georgia Bank	Lavonia	GA	A-	A-	A-	487.5	2.80	4.9	5.4	6.6	20.6	9.8	11.5	0.0
Northeast Missouri State Bank	Kirksville	MO	A-	A-	A-	114.0	3.65	2.1	3.1	10.9	41.5	9.8	14.0	0.0
Northeast Security Bank	Sumner	IA	A-	A-	A-	290.8	7.12	7.6	0.6	9.6	24.1	10.0	11.8	17.1
▲ Northern Bank & Trust Co.	Woburn	MA	A-	B+	B-	2286.5	1.19	36.1	0.1	11.0	2.1	9.5	12.7	14.5
Northern California National Bank	Chico	CA	B+	B+	B	285.9	9.95	3.9	0.3	5.9	25.4	6.8	9.1	0.0
Northern Interstate Bank, N.A.	Norway	MI	B	B	B-	158.8	0.04	6.4	4.0	25.9	28.0	9.8	11.7	0.0
▲ Northern Sky Bank	Crookston	MN	B	B-	C+	78.8	3.70	10.1	1.9	13.9	14.1	9.1	10.4	17.5
Northern State Bank	Ashland	WI	B+	B+	B-	250.6	7.78	6.1	1.1	27.2	18.6	7.8	9.5	18.1
▼ Northern State Bank of Gonvick	Gonvick	MN	B-	B	B-	39.8	6.26	2.9	4.4	5.7	52.2	9.8	17.3	0.0
Northern State Bank of Thief River Falls	Thief River Falls	MN	B+	B+	B-	340.3	1.95	3.9	4.3	10.9	32.1	8.9	10.2	26.7
Northern State Bank of Virginia	Virginia	MN	B-	B-	C	74.3	3.94	12.9	2.6	31.0	7.0	7.9	9.6	14.6
Northern Trust Co.	Chicago	IL	B+	B+	B	161163.5	32.73	3.9	0.2	3.4	31.6	5.6	7.6	13.6
▼ Northfield Bank	Woodbridge	NJ	B-	B	B	5002.7	9.78	1.3	0.0	6.3	21.4	9.8	12.2	0.0
▼ Northfield Savings Bank	Berlin	VT	C+	B-	B-	1068.0	3.52	7.9	0.2	44.1	14.0	9.8	11.8	0.0
▼ Northmark Bank	North Andover	MA	B+	A-	B+	370.6	2.30	6.4	0.6	40.8	7.3	9.8	13.3	0.0
▲ Northpointe Bank	Grand Rapids	MI	B+	B	B	2592.3	64.54	0.3	0.0	59.7	0.1	7.2	9.3	0.0
Northrim Bank	Anchorage	AK	B	B	B	1677.8	11.69	22.2	0.4	7.0	16.0	7.2	10.3	12.7
Northside Community Bank	Gurnee	IL	B	B	B-	249.1	5.19	5.2	0.1	6.5	0.6	10.0	22.9	25.2
NorthStar Bank	Estherville	IA	A-	A-	B+	195.2	1.85	5.1	1.1	13.1	8.3	10.0	11.1	16.8
▲ Northstar Bank	Bad Axe	MI	B-	C+	C-	670.3	3.16	13.1	1.6	10.6	8.1	7.7	9.6	0.0
Northumberland National Bank	Northumberland	PA	C+	C+	C+	544.0	1.96	12.4	0.9	36.3	22.6	9.3	10.5	17.7
Northview Bank	Sandstone	MN	B	B	C+	331.0	4.08	6.1	3.9	22.3	14.3	9.8	12.1	0.0
▼ Northway Bank	Berlin	NH	C+	B	C+	894.4	-4.03	4.5	1.7	20.4	16.1	9.9	11.0	17.3
Northwest Bank	Spencer	IA	B+	B+	B+	1741.9	7.17	15.6	1.6	14.1	7.7	5.5	9.6	11.4
Northwest Bank	Boise	ID	A-	A-	A-	854.4	20.37	41.3	0.0	0.3	9.5	9.2	10.7	0.0
Northwest Bank	Warren	PA	B	B	B	10784.8	3.64	5.8	11.1	35.5	7.3	9.0	10.6	14.1
Northwest Bank & Trust Co.	Davenport	IA	B-	B-	B-	173.2	5.90	12.2	0.6	10.0	3.7	9.0	10.4	14.1
Northwest Bank of Rockford	Rockford	IL	B	B	B-	296.5	5.05	19.4	3.5	11.6	17.1	7.3	9.4	0.0
▼ Northwest Community Bank	Winsted	CT	C+	B-	B-	418.5	2.67	4.5	2.4	46.6	16.5	9.8	11.5	0.0
Northwestern Bank	Orange City	IA	A-	A-	B+	239.2	8.57	4.4	0.9	8.9	9.1	9.8	14.0	0.0
Northwestern Bank	Chippewa Falls	WI	A	A	A-	447.3	-2.80	22.1	0.7	7.9	15.7	9.7	11.6	14.8
Northwestern Bank, N.A.	Dilworth	MN	C+	C+	C+	149.4	7.02	13.9	3.6	9.9	9.1	8.0	9.9	0.0
Northwestern Mutual Wealth Mgmt Co.	Milwaukee	WI	U	U	U	292.0	7.45	0.0	0.0	0.0	98.2	10.0	46.7	226.4
▲ Northwoods Bank of Minnesota	Park Rapids	MN	B	B-	B-	119.9	2.84	6.2	1.6	19.6	35.0	9.8	11.2	0.0
▼ Norway Savings Bank	Norway	ME	A-	A	B+	1248.8	3.39	5.5	6.1	31.8	5.2	9.8	14.7	0.0
Norwood Co-operative Bank	Norwood	MA	B	B	B	638.8	15.93	2.1	0.0	34.8	8.6	9.8	13.4	0.0
NSB Bank	Mason City	IA	A-	A-	A-	220.4	4.32	19.5	1.2	6.5	11.8	7.9	10.9	13.3
NVE Bank	Englewood	NJ	B	B	B	677.6	3.93	0.1	0.0	35.7	12.2	10.0	16.3	28.0
▲ NXT Bank	Central City	IA	B	B-	B-	260.2	-1.80	10.2	0.4	11.8	9.4	10.0	11.3	15.6

Asset Quality Index	Adjusted Non-Performing Loans as a % of Total Loans	Adjusted Non-Performing Loans as a % of Capital	Net Charge-Offs Avg Loans	Profitability Index	Net Income ($Mil)	Return on Assets (R.O.A.)	Return on Equity (R.O.E.)	Net Interest Spread	Overhead Efficiency Ratio	Liquidity Index	Liquidity Ratio	Hot Money Ratio	Stability Index
5.8	1.66	na	0.02	4.9	0.4	1.17	8.19	3.63	70.0	3.8	30.0	12.8	8.7
8.3	0.73	na	0.08	3.4	0.4	0.63	4.83	3.87	76.9	4.5	12.2	4.8	6.9
9.7	0.00	0.0	0.00	2.8	0.1	0.42	4.67	2.56	80.9	2.9	54.6	28.2	4.3
9.6	0.05	na	-0.03	3.9	2.4	0.74	5.75	2.64	68.8	6.0	52.1	10.2	9.0
7.0	0.61	na	0.15	1.8	0.2	0.06	0.62	3.47	77.3	3.5	18.7	12.3	6.2
8.0	1.49	na	-0.02	3.5	0.2	0.72	6.30	3.89	80.9	3.7	14.9	10.6	6.5
6.4	0.63	na	0.00	6.1	1.2	1.18	14.05	3.86	59.4	2.0	23.4	20.0	5.9
7.3	0.50	3.2	0.00	5.1	0.8	1.11	12.24	4.50	81.5	4.7	18.7	4.3	6.2
7.2	0.66	na	0.00	4.1	2.1	0.62	5.79	3.88	66.1	2.1	14.6	18.6	7.9
6.6	0.47	2.3	0.00	3.6	2.6	0.51	4.05	3.35	82.4	4.3	23.5	10.4	8.4
9.5	1.94	na	-0.01	1.3	-0.1	-0.10	-0.51	2.39	99.7	4.8	63.1	16.6	7.3
8.8	0.18	na	-0.03	5.7	1.6	0.83	6.98	2.87	57.2	2.5	21.0	17.2	8.6
2.8	7.50	na	0.00	0.0	-0.1	-0.47	-4.89	3.38	118.9	5.3	39.6	7.9	5.0
7.9	0.21	na	-0.02	5.3	0.9	1.16	11.01	3.87	66.1	3.9	30.5	12.4	7.1
4.6	0.47	na	0.00	5.8	3.3	1.33	15.57	3.89	73.6	4.7	14.9	3.8	6.9
7.8	0.00	na	0.00	10.0	1.2	2.69	22.20	5.32	48.2	3.4	9.2	11.3	9.4
5.7	0.94	na	-0.05	3.1	0.2	0.36	3.60	3.77	92.6	3.9	19.7	8.6	5.4
5.3	0.99	5.8	0.05	7.0	6.8	0.96	9.63	3.06	38.6	2.3	24.4	10.7	7.9
2.9	3.53	na	0.03	7.6	1.9	0.61	4.65	5.48	59.0	0.6	8.8	47.0	10.0
7.0	0.31	1.4	0.00	7.0	2.3	1.72	15.82	4.23	61.9	4.8	14.5	3.3	9.0
5.2	0.51	na	-0.01	7.6	3.2	1.40	9.69	4.54	61.3	0.6	7.6	38.4	8.8
6.8	0.92	na	0.10	6.0	1.6	1.35	12.07	3.54	63.3	4.6	34.9	10.4	7.9
7.7	0.00	na	0.08	6.5	0.5	1.65	10.24	3.57	52.4	3.7	45.7	18.0	9.1
8.4	0.01	na	0.00	5.3	0.8	1.12	8.59	3.27	59.6	3.2	25.7	14.2	7.5
7.8	0.38	na	-0.04	9.7	10.6	1.95	15.81	4.76	40.7	0.8	9.3	21.6	10.0
9.0	0.00	na	-0.01	5.4	0.8	1.07	11.66	2.99	51.4	4.8	40.3	11.0	5.7
5.8	1.42	na	-0.01	4.3	0.4	1.02	8.58	4.09	74.9	5.5	43.2	7.9	6.6
7.2	0.00	na	0.00	5.4	0.3	1.55	10.04	4.02	43.0	3.9	32.2	12.8	6.8
8.2	0.10	na	0.04	5.6	0.8	1.32	13.57	3.45	62.8	4.8	26.4	5.0	6.5
8.8	1.35	na	0.00	3.4	0.1	0.66	3.75	2.05	69.5	7.3	89.5	4.5	7.2
7.8	0.32	na	-0.03	4.4	0.9	1.02	9.68	2.46	61.5	6.5	55.6	5.0	7.3
8.1	0.00	na	0.00	5.0	0.2	0.95	8.26	4.61	78.2	2.0	13.4	18.8	5.9
9.5	0.33	1.2	0.01	6.1	361.0	1.17	14.84	1.48	67.2	7.3	53.4	1.6	5.4
6.7	0.47	2.6	0.01	3.3	4.6	0.37	2.85	2.52	51.5	1.6	10.5	15.6	9.4
9.1	0.28	na	0.00	2.9	1.2	0.45	3.71	3.15	82.9	1.7	7.7	19.9	8.8
9.0	0.00	na	0.00	4.8	0.7	0.75	5.65	3.73	72.2	1.1	14.5	30.5	7.6
6.4	0.57	3.7	0.01	9.3	10.5	1.79	19.60	2.22	77.3	0.8	10.4	24.9	8.5
5.2	1.63	na	0.05	5.6	2.3	0.57	5.12	4.51	79.5	4.3	21.0	8.7	9.9
7.4	0.00	na	-0.02	6.7	0.5	0.88	3.78	3.79	67.0	1.4	12.6	23.8	8.9
7.2	0.00	na	-0.06	5.8	0.7	1.34	10.24	3.18	60.0	3.4	26.4	13.4	9.0
5.0	3.18	na	0.09	4.9	1.4	0.87	8.51	3.95	70.3	2.7	18.2	13.0	8.2
6.8	0.60	na	-0.04	3.3	0.8	0.61	5.77	3.16	77.5	2.8	15.4	15.1	6.6
4.5	1.09	na	0.00	7.7	1.4	1.69	12.90	4.73	65.4	3.2	19.1	11.6	8.7
6.2	0.78	na	0.01	1.7	-0.7	-0.30	-2.52	3.38	86.1	4.1	11.1	7.3	7.7
7.9	0.32	na	-0.01	4.9	3.0	0.72	7.29	3.50	73.0	2.7	11.0	14.8	9.0
5.4	1.04	4.5	0.00	6.6	1.5	0.70	6.56	4.21	53.8	2.2	28.8	12.5	8.4
4.5	1.12	6.4	0.16	4.1	9.0	0.34	2.72	3.78	68.5	4.5	11.0	5.4	9.4
4.0	2.70	na	0.00	6.3	0.6	1.43	13.75	4.07	78.0	4.4	26.4	8.2	6.0
5.1	0.84	5.7	0.02	3.2	0.4	0.58	6.25	3.51	80.3	1.8	17.1	21.2	6.0
7.3	0.66	na	0.00	2.0	-1.1	-1.07	-8.89	2.87	78.2	2.5	21.1	15.3	6.0
5.5	1.78	na	0.00	9.8	1.0	1.84	12.71	3.72	41.9	3.0	24.0	12.6	9.2
8.2	0.04	na	-0.14	8.7	2.5	2.24	18.32	4.09	46.5	4.5	15.8	5.7	9.3
5.8	0.43	na	0.03	3.8	0.3	0.68	6.35	5.09	84.2	2.4	12.9	9.6	6.6
10.0	na	na	na	9.5	26.3	27.11	49.70	1.81	86.5	5.0	271.8	100.0	6.7
5.4	2.36	na	0.06	5.3	0.5	1.65	14.50	4.07	66.4	4.0	30.2	11.5	6.9
8.2	0.21	na	0.01	3.7	-6.7	-2.16	-13.91	4.18	75.1	4.2	10.2	7.3	10.0
8.9	0.23	0.9	0.00	4.4	1.3	0.84	6.41	3.08	59.7	1.2	20.2	29.1	8.4
7.5	0.24	1.2	0.00	9.2	1.1	2.02	18.19	4.18	47.5	3.4	6.3	11.3	8.5
7.7	1.13	na	0.00	4.1	1.3	0.74	4.51	2.81	68.4	3.7	21.2	11.1	8.6
7.2	0.04	na	0.00	4.1	0.5	0.79	6.71	3.04	67.5	0.8	10.9	29.3	6.8

	Name	City	State	Rating	2019 Rating	2018 Rating	Total Assets ($Mil)	One Year Asset Growth	Comm-ercial Loans	Cons-umer Loans	Mort-gage Loans	Secur-ities	Capital-ization Index	Lever-age Ratio	Risk-Based Capital Ratio
	O'Bannon Banking Co.	Buffalo	MO	**B-**	B-	B-	221.2	0.75	8.5	1.8	23.1	10.6	**6.9**	9.1	0.0
▲	Oak Bank	Fitchburg	WI	**B+**	B	B+	332.2	5.37	13.6	1.1	13.5	11.4	**9.8**	11.5	14.8
	Oak Valley Community Bank	Oakdale	CA	**B+**	B+	B+	1156.5	9.57	5.0	0.1	2.6	21.2	**6.5**	9.5	12.1
▼	Oak View National Bank	Warrenton	VA	**C+**	B-	C+	262.0	7.03	7.7	1.1	35.6	1.0	**7.3**	9.4	0.0
	Oakdale State Bank	Oakdale	IL	**C+**	C+	C+	21.6	2.74	7.0	3.6	24.4	1.9	**10.0**	12.4	19.0
	OakStar Bank	Springfield	MO	**B-**	B-	C+	1050.9	8.96	14.8	1.6	19.9	2.5	**8.6**	10.2	0.0
▲	Oakwood Bank	Dallas	TX	**D+**	D	D+	503.3	66.79	20.0	0.7	8.1	10.4	**7.0**	9.5	12.5
	Oakwood Bank	Pigeon Falls	WI	**C**	C	C+	90.1	4.69	4.8	0.5	10.2	1.2	**4.6**	8.8	10.8
▼	Oakworth Capital Bank	Birmingham	AL	**B+**	A-	A-	744.6	20.20	30.2	1.9	1.8	8.8	**9.8**	11.0	0.0
▼	Ocean Bank	Miami	FL	**B**	B+	B+	4080.7	-1.31	7.6	0.6	4.6	10.9	**9.3**	11.2	14.4
	OceanFirst Bank, N.A.	Toms River	NJ	**B**	B	B	10491.7	29.64	3.8	0.9	28.1	10.3	**6.6**	9.5	12.2
	Oconee Federal S&L Assn.	Seneca	SC	**B+**	B+	B+	503.9	-1.65	0.7	1.4	56.9	16.7	**10.0**	16.1	30.1
▼	Oconee State Bank	Watkinsville	GA	**C**	C+	C+	391.1	12.99	6.2	1.1	9.2	17.7	**6.9**	8.9	12.7
	Odin State Bank	Odin	MN	**D**	D	D	48.6	7.61	7.6	6.5	12.0	9.3	**9.8**	10.9	14.9
	Ohana Pacific Bank	Honolulu	HI	**B**	B	B	181.8	12.50	8.1	0.4	14.8	1.1	**9.8**	10.9	17.3
	Ohio Valley Bank Co.	Gallipolis	OH	**B**	B	C+	1021.7	-0.84	6.3	10.7	29.8	12.2	**9.8**	11.7	0.0
	Ohnward Bank & Trust	Cascade	IA	**A-**	A-	A-	297.5	2.45	12.5	2.3	8.3	14.7	**9.8**	12.9	0.0
	Oklahoma Bank and Trust Co.	Clinton	OK	**A-**	A-	B+	163.3	-0.87	2.8	0.8	8.8	50.2	**10.0**	15.1	36.3
	Oklahoma Capital Bank	Tulsa	OK	**B**	B	B	173.7	-1.82	19.7	1.4	10.6	6.5	**9.8**	16.5	0.0
	Oklahoma Heritage Bank	Stratford	OK	**C+**	C+	C-	85.7	3.62	9.0	5.3	29.4	11.8	**9.2**	10.6	0.0
	Oklahoma State Bank	Buffalo	OK	**B+**	B+	B	55.4	1.18	6.9	11.0	5.2	23.7	**8.9**	10.2	14.6
	Oklahoma State Bank	Guthrie	OK	**D+**	D+	C-	150.4	3.31	24.5	0.8	12.7	0.9	**9.5**	11.0	14.6
	Oklahoma State Bank	Vinita	OK	**A-**	A-	B	158.3	3.07	10.5	2.2	21.9	7.7	**10.0**	11.9	17.7
	Old Dominion National Bank	North Garden	VA	**D**	D	D	447.7	54.78	18.5	0.2	12.5	4.2	**10.0**	18.4	21.0
	Old Exchange National Bank of Okawville	Okawville	IL	**B+**	B+	B-	71.4	9.40	1.1	0.6	7.7	43.9	**10.0**	11.3	25.8
	Old Fort Banking Co.	Old Fort	OH	**B**	B	B	582.8	7.94	9.9	0.5	15.0	28.1	**6.2**	8.2	13.3
	Old Mission Bank	Sault Sainte Marie	MI	**B**	B	B	123.0	5.26	6.8	3.0	9.4	41.6	**10.0**	11.2	20.7
	Old Missouri Bank	Springfield	MO	**C+**	C+	C	550.8	11.55	13.5	1.5	15.1	4.8	**6.0**	9.5	11.7
	Old National Bank	Evansville	IN	**B-**	B-	B-	20647.4	3.34	11.5	5.2	12.7	25.8	**7.4**	9.2	12.9
	Old Plank Trail Community Bank, N.A.	Mokena	IL	**B**	B	B	1685.6	7.87	33.8	14.5	2.2	13.1	**5.2**	9.7	11.2
	Old Point National Bank of Phoebus	Hampton	VA	**C+**	C+	C-	1059.0	3.72	6.3	12.7	12.7	13.8	**7.4**	9.7	12.8
	Old Point Trust & Financial Services, N.A.	Newport News	VA	**U**	U	U	6.8	7.35	0.0	0.0	0.0	83.5	**10.0**	94.0	403.5
	Old Second National Bank	Aurora	IL	**A-**	A-	A-	2658.1	1.82	17.5	0.1	8.2	16.9	**8.9**	11.4	14.1
▼	Olpe State Bank	Olpe	KS	**B-**	B	B-	39.4	-8.04	4.6	2.3	18.4	21.9	**9.8**	15.6	0.0
▼	Olympia Federal S&L Assn.	Olympia	WA	**C+**	B-	B-	750.4	10.98	0.2	0.5	62.9	5.5	**9.8**	14.4	0.0
▲	OmniBank	Bay Springs	MS	**C-**	D+	D-	48.0	4.97	7.6	7.2	22.3	8.9	**7.3**	9.2	15.7
	ONB Bank	Rochester	MN	**B**	B	B	120.9	24.31	10.7	1.1	16.0	4.2	**8.5**	11.0	13.7
	One American Bank	Sioux Falls	SD	**C**	C	C	155.4	70.33	6.8	7.6	23.9	0.9	**8.4**	11.4	13.7
	One Bank of Tennessee	Cookeville	TN	**B**	B	B-	1106.1	30.88	4.4	2.7	22.0	23.6	**6.0**	8.0	14.5
	One Florida Bank	Orlando	FL	**C**	C	B-	496.9	241.14	25.6	0.2	6.2	0.9	**10.0**	22.7	25.7
	One South Bank	Blakely	GA	**C+**	C+	C+	149.6	5.28	4.0	1.1	13.1	0.5	**9.3**	10.5	17.2
	One World Bank	Dallas	TX	**B**	B	C+	107.5	4.83	2.8	0.1	1.5	2.7	**9.8**	13.7	0.0
▼	OneUnited Bank	Boston	MA	**D-**	D	D-	656.3	-2.08	0.0	0.3	4.2	15.1	**3.3**	5.3	11.0
▲	Oostburg State Bank	Oostburg	WI	**A-**	B+	B	248.6	9.83	15.2	0.7	17.0	22.0	**10.0**	12.9	17.6
	Open Bank	Los Angeles	CA	**A-**	A-	B+	1209.2	12.26	8.8	0.3	9.9	4.3	**9.5**	11.4	14.6
▲	Opportunity Bank of Montana	Helena	MT	**B+**	B	B	1148.3	18.34	6.6	1.7	13.7	14.2	**10.0**	11.9	15.5
	OptimumBank	Plantation	FL	**C-**	C-	C	141.2	33.73	3.3	3.6	20.6	7.5	**6.0**	8.2	11.8
	Optum Bank, Inc.	Salt Lake City	UT	**A+**	A+	A	11110.2	9.05	2.5	0.0	0.0	77.8	**10.0**	11.5	23.0
	Optus Bank	Columbia	SC	**C**	C	D	90.8	41.85	20.0	0.6	7.2	14.1	**9.8**	13.0	0.0
	Orange Bank & Trust Co.	Middletown	NY	**B-**	B-	C+	1346.5	19.97	17.6	1.2	7.8	20.4	**7.2**	9.1	13.5
	Oregon Coast Bank	Newport	OR	**A-**	A-	B+	267.3	10.89	4.1	1.4	11.3	38.9	**9.8**	11.6	0.0
	Oregon Community Bank	Oregon	WI	**A**	A	B+	631.3	31.38	5.7	0.3	15.1	4.0	**9.8**	12.7	0.0
	Oregon Pacific Banking Co.	Florence	OR	**B+**	B+	B	385.3	19.35	15.7	0.3	9.4	6.8	**9.8**	11.2	0.0
▼	Oriental Bank	San Juan	PR	**D+**	C-	D+	9203.1	40.66	10.3	21.2	26.8	7.2	**8.0**	9.7	14.1
▼	Origin Bank	Choudrant	LA	**B-**	B	B-	6019.2	24.35	21.5	0.3	9.2	10.5	**7.6**	10.4	13.0
	Ormsby State Bank	Ormsby	MN	**B+**	B+	B+	25.4	-3.33	3.7	7.0	2.1	27.4	**10.0**	15.8	29.7
	Orrstown Bank	Shippensburg	PA	**B-**	B-	B-	2385.8	21.03	8.0	1.5	19.5	20.1	**7.7**	9.4	13.4
	Osgood State Bank	Osgood	OH	**B+**	B+	B	285.8	12.82	28.5	1.7	8.6	17.8	**6.7**	10.3	12.3
▼	Ossian State Bank	Ossian	IN	**B-**	B	C+	116.4	6.40	6.3	1.2	5.9	13.7	**8.0**	9.6	16.6
▼	Ottawa Savings Bank	Ottawa	IL	**B-**	B	B	306.8	6.11	8.3	10.3	43.2	7.5	**10.0**	14.2	21.1

Asset Quality Index	Adjusted Non-Performing Loans as a % of Total Loans	Adjusted Non-Performing Loans as a % of Capital	Net Charge-Offs Avg Loans	Profitability Index	Net Income ($Mil)	Return on Assets (R.O.A.)	Return on Equity (R.O.E.)	Net Interest Spread	Overhead Efficiency Ratio	Liquidity Index	Liquidity Ratio	Hot Money Ratio	Stability Index
5.4	0.49	na	0.50	**5.5**	0.6	1.04	11.35	4.10	64.7	**1.6**	14.9	22.6	**5.8**
5.4	0.76	na	0.00	**7.6**	1.2	1.45	12.67	3.67	51.6	**2.3**	19.9	11.9	**7.8**
7.5	0.13	0.8	0.01	**5.6**	2.9	1.01	10.11	3.93	63.0	**5.3**	21.7	2.5	**8.7**
8.9	0.01	0.1	0.00	**2.9**	0.2	0.29	3.08	3.17	77.6	**1.4**	17.2	26.6	**6.2**
4.7	0.94	na	0.00	**6.9**	0.1	1.19	9.59	4.67	62.3	**3.0**	32.6	15.6	**6.6**
6.1	0.43	na	0.14	**4.4**	2.2	0.86	7.67	3.64	70.6	**1.6**	5.8	15.5	**8.2**
8.0	0.12	na	0.00	**1.3**	0.3	0.22	2.20	3.01	86.7	**3.1**	29.7	15.8	**5.8**
3.8	3.39	na	0.01	**4.1**	0.2	1.02	7.47	3.75	72.0	**0.7**	13.3	36.8	**7.5**
8.3	0.00	na	0.01	**5.0**	1.6	0.92	8.28	3.28	73.0	**2.1**	25.4	19.6	**7.9**
5.9	0.94	3.9	0.11	**4.2**	6.1	0.58	5.06	3.60	74.0	**1.5**	15.4	26.0	**9.4**
6.0	0.58	2.5	0.06	**4.3**	17.7	0.68	5.24	3.57	66.3	**3.5**	9.8	10.5	**9.7**
7.5	1.08	na	0.00	**4.0**	1.0	0.82	4.82	3.31	68.3	**1.8**	23.5	22.3	**9.0**
2.5	2.15	na	-0.46	**2.8**	0.2	0.16	1.71	3.42	91.3	**3.8**	16.4	8.7	**5.6**
0.8	3.03	na	0.14	**3.5**	0.1	0.77	7.03	3.77	62.5	**1.5**	27.2	24.2	**4.9**
8.7	0.05	na	0.00	**3.8**	0.2	0.53	4.89	3.07	75.5	**0.9**	24.1	42.9	**7.0**
4.3	2.10	10.4	0.74	**3.2**	0.3	0.13	1.04	4.20	68.5	**2.3**	11.1	12.7	**8.4**
7.6	0.14	na	-0.01	**5.7**	0.8	1.10	8.30	3.60	61.3	**1.5**	17.9	22.4	**8.3**
8.6	0.56	na	0.01	**5.5**	0.6	1.35	8.72	2.94	55.5	**1.8**	25.0	22.5	**8.9**
4.4	0.21	na	-0.01	**4.4**	0.3	0.73	4.33	3.76	73.2	**0.9**	20.5	39.9	**6.3**
4.9	1.17	7.5	0.10	**3.6**	0.1	0.60	5.67	4.51	84.8	**0.8**	17.6	38.9	**4.6**
4.9	0.00	na	0.34	**10.0**	0.4	2.85	28.28	5.39	50.7	**1.9**	5.4	18.5	**7.1**
3.9	1.32	na	0.02	**0.0**	-0.3	-0.68	-5.39	3.32	97.9	**1.0**	15.8	32.6	**5.8**
8.4	0.65	na	-0.10	**6.3**	0.5	1.38	11.54	4.49	69.0	**0.7**	15.0	37.8	**8.8**
5.0	1.78	na	0.11	**0.4**	0.1	0.08	0.43	3.15	98.2	**2.6**	16.1	15.7	**5.3**
9.3	0.12	na	0.00	**5.6**	0.4	2.01	18.11	3.09	58.0	**4.1**	63.2	18.6	**6.7**
8.7	0.04	na	0.02	**5.6**	1.9	1.33	15.80	3.29	62.6	**4.2**	25.0	8.7	**6.9**
6.2	1.51	na	0.76	**3.8**	0.2	0.68	5.70	3.81	83.1	**4.9**	52.6	13.6	**7.1**
4.5	1.05	na	0.04	**4.8**	1.3	0.93	9.48	3.66	59.5	**0.6**	7.2	41.7	**6.6**
4.4	1.21	4.3	0.21	**4.1**	27.6	0.55	3.74	3.36	79.8	**4.5**	20.3	6.4	**10.0**
6.2	0.44	3.1	0.08	**4.1**	2.0	0.49	4.61	3.08	69.1	**3.0**	11.3	11.4	**8.1**
5.4	0.83	5.5	0.15	**3.2**	1.3	0.50	5.03	3.54	83.3	**3.4**	17.4	12.8	**7.5**
10.0	na	na	na	**9.5**	0.1	7.99	8.59	1.51	87.2	**4.0**	na	0.0	**5.0**
5.9	1.04	6.2	0.22	**6.5**	2.5	0.39	3.04	3.90	63.8	**3.7**	8.7	10.0	**10.0**
7.9	0.00	na	0.00	**4.0**	0.1	0.84	5.36	3.14	72.6	**3.5**	40.4	17.4	**6.8**
7.4	0.65	na	0.00	**2.8**	0.6	0.33	2.29	3.41	85.9	**1.6**	16.6	23.8	**8.2**
3.6	1.14	13.2	-0.10	**2.0**	0.0	0.33	3.33	4.28	127.3	**4.3**	28.4	9.6	**4.8**
8.4	0.00	na	-0.01	**3.9**	0.2	0.61	5.37	4.02	73.6	**1.5**	21.9	26.2	**7.1**
5.2	0.50	2.7	2.52	**5.6**	0.6	1.83	14.86	6.38	86.4	**1.1**	20.8	21.7	**5.8**
8.7	0.08	na	0.07	**4.4**	2.3	0.85	10.07	3.16	74.2	**3.5**	33.8	18.3	**7.0**
8.5	0.16	na	-0.02	**0.8**	-1.5	-1.27	-5.56	2.85	126.2	**4.4**	33.9	10.9	**5.8**
4.8	1.25	na	1.03	**2.9**	0.1	0.30	2.85	4.27	87.1	**1.9**	30.3	26.4	**5.3**
4.9	0.82	na	-0.17	**3.2**	0.1	0.24	1.67	3.03	94.1	**2.0**	41.3	45.1	**8.4**
4.2	0.49	3.1	0.00	**0.0**	-2.2	-1.37	-20.40	2.27	101.2	**0.7**	18.5	51.2	**3.2**
7.9	1.31	na	0.00	**6.1**	0.7	1.10	8.32	3.70	65.0	**3.8**	30.7	10.7	**8.5**
7.2	0.12	na	0.02	**8.0**	3.8	1.28	10.98	3.93	56.5	**0.8**	15.6	31.5	**9.8**
6.1	0.58	na	0.01	**7.0**	4.4	1.65	12.73	4.47	65.1	**2.7**	14.9	14.2	**9.8**
3.8	0.74	6.2	0.00	**2.2**	-0.2	-0.44	-5.44	3.25	96.1	**2.3**	22.2	18.2	**3.9**
8.7	0.01	0.0	0.02	**9.5**	67.9	2.41	17.08	2.76	29.5	**8.5**	96.7	0.0	**10.0**
5.1	2.89	7.9	-0.12	**3.1**	2.4	11.52	103.52	3.31	95.5	**1.5**	35.0	56.7	**3.6**
6.4	1.30	6.6	0.00	**4.1**	2.6	0.81	9.08	3.74	65.9	**4.6**	17.5	5.4	**7.1**
5.9	0.84	na	-0.01	**5.9**	1.0	1.59	13.83	3.90	59.0	**3.9**	37.2	14.4	**7.0**
7.3	0.21	na	0.00	**9.7**	2.8	1.78	14.18	3.77	41.0	**4.0**	12.5	7.8	**9.5**
5.4	0.85	na	0.01	**4.7**	0.7	0.75	6.71	4.55	74.8	**4.9**	17.5	3.2	**6.7**
0.8	4.54	24.5	1.44	**3.7**	1.7	0.07	0.65	5.10	65.1	**2.0**	20.7	18.1	**7.5**
5.9	0.78	5.5	0.11	**3.3**	0.6	0.04	0.40	3.39	64.0	**1.8**	19.0	13.2	**7.6**
8.4	0.44	na	0.00	**4.6**	0.1	1.10	6.59	2.98	64.1	**3.2**	63.6	24.2	**8.1**
6.5	0.52	4.2	-0.05	**4.3**	6.1	1.03	10.26	3.49	67.8	**3.3**	7.4	12.0	**7.6**
8.2	0.99	na	0.01	**4.8**	0.7	1.00	9.55	4.20	67.1	**3.5**	18.4	12.1	**6.3**
6.2	0.90	4.3	0.00	**3.4**	0.2	0.61	6.38	3.39	81.8	**6.3**	49.6	4.7	**6.5**
5.9	1.15	na	0.05	**2.7**	0.1	0.13	0.87	3.41	78.9	**1.3**	15.4	27.7	**7.4**

Name	City	State	Rating	2019 Rating	2018 Rating	Total Assets ($Mil)	One Year Asset Growth	Asset Mix (As a % of Total Assets) Commercial Loans	Consumer Loans	Mortgage Loans	Securities	Capitalization Index	Leverage Ratio	Risk-Based Capital Ratio
Ottoville Bank Co.	Ottoville	OH	A-	A-	A-	82.2	1.41	5.4	0.5	13.1	25.9	9.8	22.5	0.0
Our Community Bank	Spencer	IN	C+	C+	C	73.3	1.12	0.0	0.6	59.0	9.8	9.8	11.5	0.0
Owen County State Bank	Spencer	IN	B	B	B-	250.1	8.33	5.2	3.1	29.4	16.5	7.8	9.5	16.1
Owingsville Banking Co.	Owingsville	KY	C-	C-	D+	70.5	-2.50	1.5	5.2	36.2	18.7	8.2	10.0	0.0
Oxford Bank	Oxford	MI	B	B	C+	513.5	12.71	13.1	0.8	7.2	12.9	7.4	9.3	14.0
▲ Oxford Bank & Trust	Oak Brook	IL	B-	C+	C-	637.3	10.70	2.3	13.3	5.6	28.8	7.8	9.7	0.0
Oxford University Bank	Oxford	MS	B	B	B	171.0	6.00	6.3	4.3	33.7	15.6	8.6	10.2	0.0
Ozark Bank	Ozark	MO	B	B	B-	245.5	2.12	5.5	0.7	24.5	12.9	8.6	10.3	0.0
Ozarks Federal S&L Assn.	Farmington	MO	B-	B-	B-	255.2	3.10	0.0	0.2	66.4	5.3	10.0	14.7	21.8
Ozona National Bank	Ozona	TX	B	B	B	273.1	2.99	5.0	1.0	12.1	31.1	10.0	11.6	24.6
Pacific Alliance Bank	Rosemead	CA	B+	B+	B+	280.7	1.08	11.6	0.0	13.1	9.5	9.8	14.2	0.0
Pacific City Bank	Los Angeles	CA	A	A	A	1799.9	4.78	12.7	1.3	14.0	6.6	10.0	12.4	16.5
Pacific Coast Bankers' Bank	Walnut Creek	CA	A-	A-	B+	1407.0	70.80	1.3	0.0	0.1	7.2	7.4	12.0	12.8
Pacific Crest Savings Bank	Lynnwood	WA	B+	B+	B-	230.5	5.81	0.0	0.0	19.4	8.8	10.0	11.2	17.2
▼ Pacific Enterprise Bank	Irvine	CA	B-	B	B+	509.3	1.43	14.1	0.0	3.4	0.0	10.0	11.0	16.2
▼ Pacific Mercantile Bank	Costa Mesa	CA	C+	B-	B	1598.9	14.23	28.4	5.6	2.3	1.7	8.9	11.1	14.1
▼ Pacific National Bank	Miami	FL	C+	B-	B-	661.4	32.56	7.8	0.2	13.9	24.3	10.0	11.0	15.9
Pacific Premier Bank	Irvine	CA	A-	A-	A-	11975.4	3.42	14.8	0.4	1.9	11.5	9.1	12.5	14.3
Pacific Valley Bank	Salinas	CA	B	B	C+	334.1	8.34	9.9	0.3	4.1	0.0	9.3	10.5	14.8
▼ Pacific West Bank	West Linn	OR	C-	C	C+	145.0	56.75	7.2	0.1	10.0	7.0	9.8	24.5	0.0
▼ Pacific Western Bank	Beverly Hills	CA	B	B+	B	26100.4	-0.59	17.5	1.6	0.4	14.4	5.5	9.7	11.4
Paducah Bank and Trust Co.	Paducah	KY	A-	A-	A	716.5	7.28	10.5	1.3	21.8	15.1	10.0	11.1	15.5
Palmetto State Bank	Hampton	SC	A	A	B+	532.7	-4.60	4.9	3.0	9.1	57.5	10.0	13.4	30.4
Palo Savings Bank	Palo	IA	B	B	B+	40.1	15.93	1.7	2.9	25.9	29.1	10.0	11.8	29.1
▼ Pan American Bank & Trust	Melrose Park	IL	C-	C	C	374.7	1.07	6.9	0.2	19.9	10.6	7.0	9.2	12.5
▲ Panola National Bank	Carthage	TX	B	B-	B-	114.4	1.10	2.9	5.2	30.2	41.5	10.0	11.5	26.0
Paper City Savings Assn.	Wisconsin Rapids	WI	B+	B+	B	180.4	14.18	0.0	2.5	48.7	0.7	10.0	14.0	20.5
Paradise Bank	Boca Raton	FL	A	A	A	324.3	3.61	8.8	0.4	12.2	9.7	9.2	10.5	16.3
Paragon Bank	Memphis	TN	B	B	B-	412.9	0.74	16.2	4.2	17.8	15.5	10.0	11.4	15.3
Paramount Bank	Saint Louis	MO	C-	C-	C-	140.8	205.04	0.9	2.4	65.9	0.0	8.6	10.2	0.0
Park Bank	Holmen	WI	B-	B-	B-	56.9	5.04	5.4	4.1	25.1	25.5	10.0	16.1	27.4
Park Bank	Madison	WI	B-	B-	B-	1076.1	7.15	12.4	0.6	16.5	8.9	6.7	10.4	12.3
Park National Bank	Newark	OH	C+	C+	C+	8685.7	11.34	9.1	16.5	17.6	13.6	5.9	8.6	11.7
Park Ridge Community Bank	Park Ridge	IL	A	A	A-	327.5	4.97	1.6	0.0	13.8	22.3	9.8	14.6	0.0
▲ Park State Bank	Duluth	MN	B+	B	B-	165.5	23.23	25.0	2.0	20.7	10.8	9.0	11.2	14.1
▲ Park State Bank & Trust	Woodland Park	CO	B	B-	C+	104.0	2.89	0.9	1.0	22.9	9.7	10.0	11.1	15.5
Parke Bank	Sewell	NJ	A	A	A-	1817.0	16.64	1.4	0.7	35.3	1.5	9.5	10.8	0.0
Parkside Financial Bank & Trust	Clayton	MO	B+	B+	B	564.5	18.62	38.4	0.1	2.5	5.2	8.1	10.9	13.4
Parkway Bank and Trust Co.	Harwood Heights	IL	B-	B-	B-	2647.4	-0.83	10.5	0.1	1.5	10.1	8.9	11.5	14.1
▼ Partners Bank	Helena	AR	C	C+	C+	242.8	38.24	18.7	1.0	5.1	20.5	9.8	11.7	0.0
Partners Bank	Spencer	WI	B+	B+	B	214.0	-0.16	12.0	1.9	16.4	23.8	9.8	14.1	0.0
▼ Partners Bank of California	Mission Viejo	CA	B-	B	B	319.3	17.38	12.0	0.0	9.0	1.7	8.9	12.1	14.1
Partners Bank of New England	Sanford	ME	B+	B+	B-	642.7	13.10	6.3	0.7	38.3	3.9	10.0	11.7	15.8
Passumpsic Bank	Saint Johnsbury	VT	C	C	C-	648.1	-1.83	4.3	10.1	39.5	6.4	9.9	10.9	16.4
Pataskala Banking Co.	Pataskala	OH	D	D	D	33.7	-0.15	2.7	6.0	25.1	20.2	5.7	7.7	14.2
Pathfinder Bank	Oswego	NY	U	U	U	1102.4	13.40	14.2	6.8	20.0	21.6	6.6	8.6	13.5
Pathway Bank	Cairo	NE	C-	C-	C-	169.8	-3.93	7.3	1.3	5.0	10.0	9.8	11.3	0.0
Patriot Bank	Millington	TN	B	B	B	390.2	15.83	3.1	1.5	11.9	44.0	7.0	9.0	13.0
Patriot Bank, N.A.	Stamford	CT	D+	D+	D+	999.8	4.88	18.3	6.7	19.5	4.5	6.0	9.2	11.8
Patriot Community Bank	Woburn	MA	B+	B+	B+	186.7	5.57	3.6	0.0	17.9	0.0	10.0	14.7	21.9
Patriots Bank	Garnett	KS	B	B	C+	131.5	5.82	5.6	2.2	16.0	15.1	8.6	10.2	0.0
Patterson State Bank	Patterson	LA	B-	B-	B	242.5	4.33	3.7	1.9	39.1	27.6	8.2	9.8	19.8
Pauls Valley National Bank	Pauls Valley	OK	B-	B-	C+	253.0	0.88	16.2	10.1	4.2	26.5	9.5	10.9	0.0
Pavillion Bank	Richardson	TX	B	B	B	73.2	-7.97	7.6	1.0	19.5	11.9	10.0	13.7	20.9
Payne County Bank	Perkins	OK	A	A	A	182.0	6.87	8.9	6.0	23.1	23.9	9.8	18.3	0.0
PBK Bank, Inc.	Stanford	KY	B+	B+	B+	119.7	1.25	3.3	6.0	23.4	6.8	9.8	13.1	0.0
PCSB Bank	Clarinda	IA	C+	C+	B-	264.8	3.53	9.0	3.3	7.7	21.0	9.0	10.5	0.0
PCSB Bank	Yorktown Heights	NY	B-	B-	B-	1695.3	11.31	4.3	0.0	15.8	19.1	10.0	13.1	17.4
Peach State Bank & Trust	Gainesville	GA	B+	B+	B	287.4	24.11	8.9	3.6	13.0	21.4	9.7	10.8	15.4
Peapack-Gladstone Bank	Bedminster	NJ	B+	B+	B+	5826.2	25.07	15.0	0.7	9.8	6.9	8.3	10.3	13.6

Asset Quality Index	Adjusted Non-Performing Loans as a % of Total Loans	Adjusted Non-Performing Loans as a % of Capital	Net Charge-Offs Avg Loans	Profitability Index	Net Income ($Mil)	Return on Assets (R.O.A.)	Return on Equity (R.O.E.)	Net Interest Spread	Overhead Efficiency Ratio	Liquidity Index	Liquidity Ratio	Hot Money Ratio	Stability Index
9.0	0.00	na	-0.01	**5.9**	0.2	1.23	5.49	3.83	57.7	**1.7**	23.5	23.4	**8.4**
6.9	0.52	na	0.04	**2.2**	0.1	0.37	3.23	3.84	92.3	**1.4**	20.1	20.6	**6.1**
7.8	0.45	na	0.01	**3.8**	0.3	0.56	5.74	3.84	81.3	**3.5**	33.7	15.3	**6.0**
5.2	1.14	10.4	0.14	**3.1**	0.1	0.39	6.09	4.35	83.3	**1.5**	20.0	26.7	**2.2**
6.8	1.40	na	-0.01	**5.4**	1.4	1.09	11.77	3.84	68.0	**4.7**	27.3	6.2	**6.8**
4.9	0.75	na	0.08	**5.3**	2.2	1.45	14.21	4.02	64.2	**3.0**	25.8	13.8	**6.5**
6.4	0.27	3.0	0.00	**4.7**	0.4	0.91	8.81	3.61	67.4	**1.1**	21.1	31.9	**6.2**
8.8	0.00	na	0.00	**4.6**	0.7	1.11	10.75	3.66	69.7	**2.3**	7.5	16.8	**6.5**
7.3	1.15	5.7	0.00	**2.8**	0.2	0.27	1.92	2.69	86.7	**1.5**	10.0	23.1	**7.5**
8.1	1.62	na	0.04	**5.0**	0.5	0.75	6.40	4.07	82.5	**6.4**	53.2	5.3	**7.7**
7.4	0.00	na	0.00	**5.2**	0.5	0.75	5.25	3.05	67.5	**0.6**	16.5	68.9	**8.3**
7.2	0.32	1.9	0.17	**6.9**	3.8	0.85	6.74	3.83	55.5	**0.7**	12.0	35.8	**10.0**
9.8	0.00	0.0	-0.01	**7.8**	23.0	9.26	85.20	2.06	26.5	**5.1**	29.9	2.6	**7.0**
5.0	1.35	na	-0.01	**4.6**	0.5	0.88	7.87	2.78	67.4	**1.0**	24.3	30.7	**8.1**
6.0	0.52	na	0.10	**3.2**	-0.2	-0.19	-1.68	5.10	88.8	**0.9**	27.0	55.3	**6.8**
4.4	1.74	na	0.82	**2.0**	-2.1	-0.58	-5.19	3.40	74.3	**3.1**	28.7	18.8	**7.0**
8.8	0.00	0.0	0.00	**1.5**	-0.2	-0.14	-1.42	2.53	98.9	**1.5**	33.1	39.2	**6.3**
5.8	0.26	0.9	0.06	**6.2**	29.2	1.01	5.27	4.42	54.7	**3.9**	18.5	8.0	**10.0**
6.0	0.39	na	0.00	**4.3**	0.6	0.69	6.63	3.86	72.1	**3.3**	20.9	13.2	**6.9**
8.8	0.06	na	0.00	**0.0**	-0.4	-1.33	-5.17	3.50	133.5	**4.6**	43.5	13.1	**6.7**
6.2	0.53	2.1	0.40	**3.7**	-1428.1	-21.23	-128.34	4.42	563.0	**2.4**	8.2	5.9	**10.0**
7.9	0.52	2.7	0.06	**6.0**	2.5	1.38	12.10	3.58	65.8	**1.6**	13.4	10.5	**9.3**
8.6	3.03	na	-0.87	**6.1**	1.6	1.14	8.50	3.39	57.8	**5.7**	57.9	11.2	**9.0**
8.7	0.07	na	0.00	**4.1**	0.1	0.58	4.82	2.77	77.2	**2.9**	54.9	28.0	**6.9**
8.6	0.04	na	0.01	**2.1**	0.5	0.53	5.82	3.48	104.4	**1.0**	21.7	29.4	**5.0**
9.1	0.70	na	0.04	**4.0**	0.3	1.00	8.08	3.54	81.6	**5.1**	48.5	11.5	**6.7**
6.8	1.17	5.2	0.02	**4.1**	0.3	0.67	4.80	2.89	75.6	**1.7**	22.8	23.6	**7.3**
8.7	0.13	0.8	0.00	**7.1**	1.0	1.17	11.34	4.16	73.0	**4.7**	28.1	6.6	**8.5**
8.3	1.68	na	-0.11	**3.6**	0.7	0.69	5.97	3.43	81.5	**1.5**	17.2	9.4	**6.3**
9.2	0.00	na	0.00	**4.6**	0.4	1.60	15.09	2.11	90.1	**0.4**	11.9	55.5	**5.6**
6.5	8.50	na	0.82	**3.7**	0.1	0.74	4.67	4.53	86.4	**4.8**	13.2	3.3	**6.1**
3.7	1.47	na	-0.01	**4.8**	2.1	0.80	7.58	3.32	67.9	**3.9**	9.6	5.3	**9.1**
3.2	1.72	10.6	0.05	**6.6**	25.9	1.20	11.49	3.87	62.3	**4.1**	11.6	7.7	**8.4**
7.5	0.25	na	0.00	**9.7**	1.8	2.22	15.12	4.08	43.1	**3.6**	16.7	11.4	**10.0**
7.5	0.17	na	0.01	**9.2**	0.5	1.39	10.71	4.92	58.1	**2.5**	21.5	17.0	**8.2**
5.1	2.41	11.8	0.00	**5.3**	0.3	1.29	11.95	4.86	78.0	**5.4**	28.1	2.3	**6.2**
6.6	1.52	5.9	0.00	**9.3**	7.4	1.66	15.64	3.44	29.4	**0.9**	18.4	33.6	**10.0**
6.0	0.51	na	-0.01	**6.5**	1.7	1.21	11.18	3.07	62.3	**1.5**	19.9	6.1	**7.3**
3.3	3.21	13.2	-0.01	**5.7**	6.3	1.01	8.39	3.16	53.5	**1.1**	14.8	25.2	**9.3**
8.4	0.20	na	0.00	**2.5**	0.3	0.43	3.70	3.86	96.5	**0.8**	17.3	42.8	**6.9**
4.9	1.32	na	-0.01	**4.8**	0.5	1.01	6.56	3.36	66.4	**2.1**	27.0	18.4	**7.4**
6.9	0.22	na	-0.03	**3.4**	0.2	0.29	2.39	4.15	75.6	**4.0**	22.1	7.2	**6.9**
8.9	0.28	na	0.12	**2.6**	-3.4	-2.21	-19.00	3.65	79.4	**2.0**	15.5	13.8	**7.6**
3.6	1.44	na	0.19	**2.5**	-1.1	-0.67	-5.17	3.61	73.6	**1.7**	6.4	8.2	**8.1**
4.4	2.39	na	0.06	**2.6**	0.0	0.28	3.62	4.31	92.2	**6.0**	38.9	2.9	**2.3**
6.1	0.89	na	0.07	**3.4**	2.1	0.80	9.80	3.14	61.4	**0.8**	16.3	27.8	**6.1**
1.9	1.69	na	-0.13	**6.3**	0.8	1.74	15.07	4.72	56.5	**1.6**	15.0	22.3	**7.4**
5.9	1.59	na	-0.02	**4.7**	1.0	1.03	10.64	3.02	74.1	**0.7**	5.0	33.1	**5.6**
2.2	2.22	na	0.00	**1.1**	-0.7	-0.27	-2.82	2.95	101.2	**0.6**	10.7	26.8	**5.7**
6.0	2.50	8.0	0.00	**5.6**	0.5	1.11	7.66	2.70	50.3	**1.1**	26.9	44.5	**8.3**
6.8	2.57	na	0.00	**4.4**	0.3	0.99	9.74	4.43	79.1	**2.8**	10.3	14.7	**7.0**
5.5	1.50	na	0.01	**3.6**	0.4	0.60	6.06	3.41	79.0	**2.3**	15.7	17.8	**5.5**
4.0	1.40	na	0.12	**4.3**	0.5	0.86	7.71	3.78	74.6	**2.5**	36.5	24.6	**6.4**
6.5	0.42	na	-0.01	**6.5**	0.3	1.40	10.15	5.17	67.0	**2.6**	32.5	19.5	**6.3**
7.9	0.26	1.6	-0.02	**7.9**	1.0	2.30	12.45	4.37	45.8	**2.7**	35.5	20.3	**9.5**
5.0	2.11	na	0.03	**9.3**	0.5	1.56	11.56	5.16	65.2	**4.1**	20.6	8.5	**9.2**
4.8	1.54	8.5	0.09	**4.0**	0.7	1.08	10.38	3.58	63.5	**4.9**	35.1	8.6	**5.7**
7.7	0.44	na	-0.04	**2.8**	1.2	0.29	2.23	2.89	70.4	**1.3**	15.3	22.5	**8.3**
8.5	0.00	na	0.03	**4.6**	0.5	0.77	7.18	4.08	74.3	**4.7**	29.5	7.4	**6.0**
6.1	0.72	4.9	-0.01	**3.7**	2.5	0.19	1.76	2.62	59.3	**2.7**	15.9	11.0	**8.5**

Asset Quality Index	Adjusted Non-Performing Loans as a % of Total Loans	Adjusted Non-Performing Loans as a % of Capital	Net Charge-Offs Avg Loans	Profitability Index	Net Income ($Mil)	Return on Assets (R.O.A.)	Return on Equity (R.O.E.)	Net Interest Spread	Overhead Efficiency Ratio	Liquidity Index	Liquidity Ratio	Hot Money Ratio	Stability Index
6.4	0.00	na	-0.80	9.7	0.8	2.27	13.80	4.22	53.4	2.9	33.2	18.0	8.6
3.2	2.28	na	-0.05	8.1	0.4	1.82	21.07	3.84	76.6	0.6	7.2	42.4	7.4
5.2	0.67	na	0.09	6.5	2.9	1.65	15.55	4.30	66.5	1.8	13.8	18.1	8.7
7.2	na	na	na	9.5	1.0	17.09	18.78	2.05	55.0	4.0	na	0.0	5.9
6.9	0.14	na	-0.01	6.6	0.4	1.49	20.36	3.69	60.0	5.9	42.3	4.4	5.4
8.3	0.15	na	0.00	2.1	0.1	0.01	0.17	2.94	86.2	2.0	16.0	18.6	6.7
8.2	1.75	na	0.00	2.2	0.1	0.18	1.54	3.14	94.6	3.1	31.3	16.5	6.3
5.9	0.65	na	-0.17	4.7	0.8	0.78	6.93	3.66	73.6	2.9	9.0	10.0	6.9
7.8	0.39	1.5	0.02	4.5	2.6	0.84	6.65	3.33	69.2	1.7	11.8	22.1	8.9
8.2	0.20	na	-0.07	3.5	0.7	0.44	4.32	3.65	83.5	2.7	15.3	15.3	7.5
9.2	0.09	na	0.01	3.3	0.1	0.39	4.61	3.59	89.5	2.8	38.7	20.9	4.2
6.8	0.45	na	0.07	7.1	0.5	1.58	14.86	4.69	70.4	4.6	6.2	3.8	8.3
8.9	0.31	na	-0.02	4.5	0.2	0.67	6.93	3.72	76.1	4.7	22.1	4.9	5.1
5.8	3.56	na	0.00	7.8	1.7	1.41	11.77	3.40	59.3	1.3	31.6	46.9	8.8
5.5	0.79	na	-0.02	3.5	1.0	0.73	7.64	2.80	72.2	0.8	18.2	24.4	6.8
6.8	0.30	1.0	0.02	8.0	135.0	1.72	9.03	3.78	41.5	3.7	10.9	10.0	10.0
5.6	1.37	na	0.22	3.2	1.7	0.65	4.20	3.44	76.0	1.0	6.6	23.4	9.5
7.2	0.06	na	0.00	7.6	1.7	1.37	10.51	3.96	44.3	0.8	17.2	37.6	7.6
5.8	0.90	na	-0.03	6.5	2.8	1.08	8.54	4.24	65.4	3.6	22.6	11.6	10.0
6.4	2.79	na	0.02	4.3	0.3	0.67	4.97	4.14	79.0	0.9	20.2	33.3	7.6
4.5	2.33	na	0.10	4.1	1.2	0.39	2.72	4.21	64.2	2.7	4.1	3.5	9.2
4.1	1.02	3.9	0.16	4.4	15.1	0.61	4.48	3.20	60.6	4.0	10.1	5.6	10.0
6.1	1.78	na	-0.01	3.5	1.3	0.48	4.70	3.37	72.7	3.4	8.6	11.7	7.9
6.6	0.38	na	0.10	4.5	1.0	0.86	8.29	3.78	69.8	2.5	10.4	15.8	5.7
5.8	2.33	9.9	0.05	3.4	3.0	0.95	8.97	1.96	71.1	2.4	41.4	30.4	8.6
9.6	na	na	na	9.5	1.5	26.62	29.67	2.46	22.9	4.0	na	100.0	6.6
6.8	0.44	na	-0.02	5.4	1.1	1.05	10.77	3.39	59.9	1.9	25.6	18.0	6.1
8.8	0.42	na	-0.56	4.7	1.1	1.01	8.21	4.12	77.9	5.4	30.0	3.2	7.7
5.3	2.30	13.8	0.00	1.2	0.0	0.29	3.85	3.34	90.9	3.8	14.4	9.9	2.3
8.2	0.06	na	-0.02	6.5	0.5	1.46	12.39	3.80	57.3	0.9	21.5	38.8	7.6
6.1	4.52	na	-0.52	3.5	1.3	0.85	5.58	2.68	58.0	1.7	36.1	40.1	7.5
6.0	6.33	na	0.04	4.6	0.4	1.11	4.87	3.29	61.1	6.0	44.3	5.1	7.1
4.0	0.20	na	-0.01	9.2	0.8	1.51	11.31	3.51	41.2	0.7	15.8	49.3	8.9
6.3	0.67	na	-0.01	2.0	0.4	0.39	3.37	2.88	85.4	2.1	27.3	15.4	5.2
5.3	1.93	na	0.03	4.1	2.3	0.77	8.30	3.16	68.9	4.0	16.6	9.5	7.8
7.3	0.48	3.2	0.35	6.4	5.7	1.31	12.98	3.59	45.7	4.3	28.1	9.9	7.6
4.5	1.93	na	0.15	7.4	3.0	1.74	17.73	3.81	50.6	2.7	29.2	17.9	8.5
6.2	0.12	2.7	0.00	4.0	0.5	0.68	6.50	3.31	77.5	0.6	11.8	45.9	6.1
7.3	0.00	0.0	0.00	10.0	3.2	2.55	22.52	4.88	48.7	2.6	11.6	11.1	9.6
5.4	1.92	na	0.00	3.0	0.1	0.50	3.29	3.31	85.5	1.8	21.9	21.3	6.8
2.4	3.66	23.5	0.22	5.4	2.9	0.94	9.36	3.82	72.1	3.3	13.7	12.5	9.2
6.1	2.09	na	0.08	8.4	1.7	1.37	10.02	3.92	52.9	1.7	18.9	22.3	8.5
8.0	0.51	2.3	0.00	7.8	0.8	1.86	15.85	4.49	50.2	1.4	12.2	23.5	7.4
6.4	0.97	na	0.00	5.1	0.6	0.60	5.78	3.34	82.3	0.9	26.2	46.4	6.5
8.1	0.03	0.2	0.01	3.6	0.8	0.57	4.84	4.01	83.3	0.8	11.6	32.5	7.0
6.7	0.79	na	-0.02	4.6	0.3	0.65	4.99	3.80	78.1	4.9	33.4	7.7	8.2
8.2	0.00	na	0.00	5.4	1.0	1.31	15.41	3.60	63.8	1.6	12.6	22.7	6.1
3.5	1.90	13.3	0.10	2.5	0.3	0.08	0.97	3.05	87.2	1.4	12.0	7.9	6.3
8.2	0.01	na	0.00	7.9	1.1	1.73	12.71	3.75	57.8	3.1	13.0	10.9	9.7
3.9	3.18	na	-0.01	8.2	0.2	1.38	11.54	5.34	62.4	2.9	25.1	15.4	8.3
4.4	2.20	na	0.13	3.6	0.6	0.62	5.87	3.55	78.9	4.4	27.6	8.5	6.0
1.9	6.20	na	0.14	4.7	0.4	0.85	7.59	3.30	61.1	1.6	22.3	25.4	6.8
9.5	0.57	na	0.00	1.4	0.0	0.05	0.50	3.40	98.2	1.6	22.0	25.2	6.0
7.9	0.16	1.1	0.00	5.8	13.5	0.20	2.36	3.05	41.1	6.1	36.1	1.2	8.4
10.0	na	0.0	na	9.5	0.9	9.13	11.39	1.43	91.4	4.0	366.5	0.0	7.0
7.5	0.72	na	0.00	2.0	-0.2	-1.39	-4.68	3.77	74.4	2.7	65.2	56.3	7.5
8.7	0.14	na	0.01	6.9	1.5	1.59	12.05	4.28	63.7	4.4	23.0	7.0	9.2
9.7	0.24	1.0	0.24	5.9	9.2	0.85	8.26	2.67	43.6	7.8	69.8	1.3	7.2
7.7	0.35	1.8	0.02	4.5	8.6	1.09	9.56	3.46	71.0	3.2	14.9	11.8	9.2
9.0	0.11	na	0.00	3.8	1.1	0.75	8.16	3.49	69.4	1.4	21.2	12.5	5.8

	Name	City	State	Rating	2019 Rating	2018 Rating	Total Assets ($Mil)	One Year Asset Growth	Asset Mix (As a % of Total Assets) Comm-ercial Loans	Cons-umer Loans	Mort-gage Loans	Secur-ities	Capital-ization Index	Lever-age Ratio	Risk-Based Capital Ratio
	Readlyn Savings Bank	Readlyn	IA	**A-**	A-	A-	78.3	5.66	8.6	1.4	21.6	18.1	**10.0**	15.6	21.9
	Red River Bank	Alexandria	LA	**A-**	A-	A-	2010.7	4.65	12.0	1.4	20.2	20.0	**10.0**	11.6	16.5
	Red River State Bank	Halstad	MN	**B**	B	B+	93.1	5.20	38.7	11.8	7.5	5.6	**8.6**	10.0	14.5
	Red Rock Bank	Sanborn	MN	**A-**	A-	B	39.3	2.80	7.3	2.6	13.0	5.3	**6.2**	8.2	15.4
▼	Redstone Bank	Centennial	CO	**B+**	A-	B+	172.4	8.10	7.1	0.1	12.9	16.9	**10.0**	13.0	20.7
	Redwood Capital Bank	Eureka	CA	**B+**	B+	B	368.4	3.17	6.9	0.4	7.5	9.2	**8.1**	9.7	14.1
	Regal Bank	Livingston	NJ	**C**	C	C	529.4	0.91	1.1	0.0	2.4	6.0	**8.3**	9.9	16.5
	Regent Bank	Tulsa	OK	**C+**	C+	C+	694.7	15.81	25.6	0.5	13.6	1.9	**4.6**	9.7	10.8
▲	Regional Missouri Bank	Marceline	MO	**C+**	C	C	381.0	57.10	8.6	1.9	16.9	14.9	**9.8**	11.4	0.0
	Regions Bank	Birmingham	AL	**B**	B	B-	132707.0	3.61	21.4	5.5	13.3	18.9	**7.5**	10.4	12.9
	Reliabank Dakota	Estelline	SD	**B-**	B-	B-	472.7	19.85	12.9	1.7	6.6	27.2	**6.5**	9.0	12.1
	Reliance Bank	Faribault	MN	**B-**	B-	B	162.3	11.49	23.3	1.1	13.4	12.0	**8.3**	10.0	0.0
	Reliance Savings Bank	Altoona	PA	**C+**	C+	C+	541.8	0.02	3.8	1.4	25.7	21.2	**9.5**	10.7	15.0
	Reliance State Bank	Story City	IA	**B+**	B+	A-	230.0	2.78	5.8	1.0	10.7	22.9	**8.5**	10.1	0.0
	Reliant Bank	Brentwood	TN	**B**	B	B+	2170.6	23.36	12.5	1.1	15.3	11.8	**7.6**	10.6	13.0
▲	Relyance Bank, N.A.	Pine Bluff	AR	**B+**	B	C+	865.8	3.88	7.5	1.1	10.5	11.6	**10.0**	12.7	15.3
▼	Renasant Bank	Tupelo	MS	**B+**	A-	A-	13874.4	7.98	10.0	2.3	18.4	9.7	**7.6**	10.5	13.0
▲	Republic Bank & Trust Co.	Louisville	KY	**A**	A-	A-	5712.0	6.63	6.6	4.8	21.2	10.5	**10.0**	12.6	15.3
▼	Republic Bank of Arizona	Phoenix	AZ	**B**	B+	B+	115.2	-0.80	7.9	0.1	9.6	21.4	**9.8**	13.9	0.0
	Republic Bank of Chicago	Oak Brook	IL	**B+**	B+	B	2153.9	3.46	19.6	0.0	6.1	10.6	**8.4**	11.0	13.7
	Republic Banking Co.	Republic	OH	**B-**	B-	B-	50.0	3.85	5.9	9.5	40.7	5.3	**10.0**	15.8	23.3
	Republic First Bank	Philadelphia	PA	**D+**	D+	C	3291.3	17.68	5.0	0.1	11.7	34.5	**5.4**	7.4	11.3
▲	Resource Bank	Covington	LA	**B+**	B	C+	784.5	2.99	3.5	0.8	22.1	5.8	**9.8**	12.1	0.0
	Resource Bank, N.A.	DeKalb	IL	**C**	C	C+	544.3	10.00	4.7	0.7	14.2	32.4	**6.9**	8.9	14.0
▼	Reynolds State Bank	Reynolds	IL	**A-**	A	A	98.5	0.36	0.8	0.1	0.8	69.5	**10.0**	19.2	42.8
▲	Rhinebeck Bank	Poughkeepsie	NY	**C+**	C	D+	1007.1	13.81	11.7	34.9	6.4	11.4	**7.4**	10.7	12.8
▲	Richland County Bank	Richland Center	WI	**B+**	B	B-	102.9	2.72	4.3	3.2	10.5	41.8	**9.8**	18.7	0.0
	Richland State Bank	Bruce	SD	**B+**	B+	B+	34.5	-1.14	5.9	7.7	2.3	42.4	**10.0**	11.3	23.6
	Richton Bank & Trust Co.	Richton	MS	**B**	B	B	55.6	-0.87	17.4	3.3	9.1	37.9	**10.0**	16.2	29.9
	Richwood Banking Co., Inc.	Richwood	OH	**B-**	B-	B-	740.2	1.35	4.8	0.5	20.9	18.2	**7.4**	9.6	12.8
	Riddell National Bank	Brazil	IN	**C+**	C+	C	245.6	9.71	10.7	5.4	34.4	10.0	**6.6**	8.8	12.2
▼	Ridgewood Savings Bank	Ridgewood	NY	**B-**	B	C+	5935.0	5.75	0.0	0.1	34.5	21.0	**9.8**	12.9	0.0
	Riley State Bank of Riley, Kansas	Riley	KS	**B**	B	B	92.7	3.42	11.8	4.0	6.8	26.1	**9.7**	10.9	0.0
	Rio Bank	McAllen	TX	**B-**	B-	C+	566.4	3.87	11.6	1.3	7.8	19.8	**8.1**	9.7	14.2
▼	Rio Grande S&L Assn.	Monte Vista	CO	**C**	C+	C+	112.8	4.68	2.2	2.3	54.8	6.0	**9.7**	11.0	0.0
	River Bank	La Crosse	WI	**B**	B	B-	693.3	35.98	5.9	0.5	11.6	7.4	**6.9**	11.6	12.5
	River Bank & Trust	Prattville	AL	**A-**	A-	B+	1417.3	29.99	10.2	2.8	16.7	23.0	**8.5**	10.0	14.0
	River City Bank	Sacramento	CA	**B+**	B+	B+	2586.3	14.01	3.7	0.0	5.4	19.5	**7.5**	9.5	0.0
▼	River City Bank	Rome	GA	**B+**	A-	B	155.5	-3.19	7.3	1.5	14.2	20.7	**10.0**	11.9	17.6
	River City Bank, Inc.	Louisville	KY	**B+**	B+	A-	340.5	6.16	0.4	1.4	27.6	11.7	**10.0**	13.3	19.2
	River Falls State Bank	River Falls	WI	**B+**	B+	B-	99.4	6.66	1.1	2.8	32.9	12.4	**9.8**	14.2	0.0
▼	River Valley Community Bank	Yuba City	CA	**B-**	B	B-	468.7	22.28	6.1	0.0	2.5	37.6	**5.9**	7.9	12.8
▼	RiverBank	Pocahontas	AR	**C+**	B-	C+	100.9	0.49	3.8	1.3	9.6	6.0	**9.6**	10.8	18.6
▼	RiverBank	Spokane	WA	**C**	C+	C	144.8	11.10	8.3	0.2	9.2	1.7	**8.6**	10.2	0.0
	RiverHills Bank	Vicksburg	MS	**B+**	B+	B-	346.1	2.83	6.9	1.5	10.2	38.4	**9.3**	10.7	0.0
▲	RiverHills Bank	Milford	OH	**B**	B-	C+	201.3	22.94	6.9	0.3	7.7	24.0	**6.9**	10.4	12.4
▼	Riverland Bank	Jordan	MN	**C**	C+	C+	153.3	6.20	17.9	1.0	21.4	0.9	**10.0**	12.5	15.4
▲	Rivers Edge Bank	Marion	SD	**C+**	C	C	208.9	4.81	6.0	2.5	6.9	1.9	**6.5**	8.6	12.2
	Riverside Bank	Sparkman	AR	**B**	B	B-	60.4	-3.11	15.4	7.5	52.4	2.0	**6.9**	8.9	12.8
	Riverview Bank	Marysville	PA	**C**	C	C	1117.2	-1.89	6.6	0.7	14.9	6.1	**6.5**	9.1	12.1
	Riverview Community Bank	Vancouver	WA	**A**	A	A-	1180.6	2.17	6.1	0.4	8.3	12.6	**10.0**	11.8	17.0
	Riverwind Bank	Augusta	AR	**B**	B	B-	100.9	-4.49	13.8	2.9	15.8	19.0	**9.8**	11.2	0.0
▲	RiverWood Bank	Baxter	MN	**B-**	C+	C	454.2	7.30	10.4	5.0	13.1	15.3	**6.5**	8.5	12.6
	RNB State Bank	Rawlins	WY	**C+**	C+	C+	179.1	3.50	9.6	1.8	5.1	20.1	**8.7**	10.3	0.0
	Roanoke Rapids Savings Bank, SSB	Roanoke Rapids	NC	**C+**	C+	C-	70.3	-5.20	0.1	1.8	35.3	5.7	**9.8**	25.0	0.0
▼	Robert Lee State Bank	Robert Lee	TX	**C+**	B-	C+	48.4	12.64	4.4	5.1	16.6	45.4	**9.8**	12.7	0.0
	Robertson Banking Co.	Demopolis	AL	**A-**	A-	A-	334.0	4.75	6.8	1.4	18.5	8.2	**8.4**	10.2	13.7
	Rochelle State Bank	Rochelle	GA	**C+**	C+	B-	31.7	15.25	3.9	5.2	0.4	36.0	**10.0**	15.4	34.5
▲	Rochester State Bank	Rochester	IL	**C+**	C	C	96.9	3.26	1.7	1.7	10.3	69.3	**9.1**	10.4	18.9
▲	Rock Canyon Bank	Provo	UT	**A-**	B+	B+	548.0	28.28	10.3	0.2	4.0	0.0	**8.5**	10.1	0.0

Asset Quality Index	Adjusted Non-Performing Loans as a % of Total Loans	Adjusted Non-Performing Loans as a % of Capital	Net Charge-Offs Avg Loans	Profitability Index	Net Income ($Mil)	Return on Assets (R.O.A.)	Return on Equity (R.O.E.)	Net Interest Spread	Overhead Efficiency Ratio	Liquidity Index	Liquidity Ratio	Hot Money Ratio	Stability Index
8.6	0.00	0.3	-0.01	7.5	0.3	1.65	10.49	3.23	42.4	1.4	28.6	32.2	9.6
8.2	0.46	2.4	0.01	6.4	7.0	1.41	12.09	3.45	58.0	3.6	21.4	12.9	9.8
4.1	0.64	8.4	-0.16	6.6	0.4	1.73	16.89	4.39	56.8	0.7	12.8	35.2	6.5
7.2	0.00	na	0.52	4.1	0.1	0.53	4.61	3.45	65.9	4.4	42.2	13.6	6.7
7.8	0.00	na	0.00	4.2	0.3	0.81	5.03	4.62	74.6	2.7	40.8	24.6	7.9
7.5	0.18	na	0.00	6.0	0.8	0.85	8.84	3.98	66.5	3.6	14.3	10.7	6.6
6.9	0.25	na	0.00	2.5	0.3	0.26	2.60	2.80	87.1	1.1	21.5	31.8	6.5
4.6	0.86	na	0.26	4.4	1.5	0.88	8.70	3.97	65.1	0.6	8.4	32.3	6.2
6.3	0.74	na	-0.04	8.2	2.0	2.13	17.98	4.04	50.6	3.2	19.5	11.9	8.3
4.8	1.12	4.7	0.59	5.6	198.0	0.64	4.65	3.51	55.6	5.0	20.1	3.4	10.0
5.3	0.87	na	0.10	5.3	1.1	0.95	10.29	3.68	71.7	2.4	2.6	15.6	6.1
4.4	1.03	na	-0.31	5.1	0.5	1.20	11.91	3.75	65.5	1.7	18.3	20.4	5.9
6.3	2.23	na	0.04	3.4	1.0	0.71	6.41	3.04	73.6	2.2	9.2	15.7	6.8
3.0	2.15	13.7	0.03	5.7	0.6	0.99	8.03	3.15	51.2	4.2	21.9	8.2	8.1
7.6	0.27	1.5	0.09	4.0	4.1	0.59	4.73	3.72	68.3	0.8	13.7	36.5	8.8
6.3	1.11	na	0.07	5.3	2.1	1.01	7.48	3.96	68.7	2.2	10.9	17.8	8.0
5.9	0.50	2.3	0.03	5.0	4.4	0.13	0.77	3.78	78.1	3.4	12.4	12.2	10.0
6.5	0.92	4.0	0.19	8.9	26.6	1.89	14.97	5.59	47.0	2.8	15.6	8.3	10.0
8.2	1.12	na	-0.06	2.8	0.0	0.04	0.31	3.64	98.9	1.8	37.9	38.6	7.7
4.5	2.12	12.6	0.15	6.7	5.8	1.13	10.36	3.94	56.5	1.8	20.0	17.1	9.9
3.3	2.65	na	-0.03	8.2	0.2	1.63	10.38	4.30	46.6	2.2	7.7	17.2	8.1
6.7	1.07	6.7	0.00	1.6	0.1	0.01	0.15	2.77	99.7	4.3	11.3	6.3	4.8
7.0	0.48	na	0.00	6.3	2.5	1.29	10.68	4.47	65.0	2.5	10.9	15.9	8.3
2.8	4.11	na	0.02	4.6	1.5	1.10	11.59	3.88	75.1	4.3	26.3	8.8	6.7
10.0	0.00	na	0.00	5.5	0.3	1.24	6.39	2.14	34.0	7.0	90.4	7.1	8.9
4.1	1.01	na	0.27	3.4	1.3	0.52	4.91	3.60	71.5	2.2	12.6	18.0	6.2
9.0	0.02	na	0.03	6.3	0.8	3.17	16.79	3.84	58.9	6.1	60.4	9.1	8.4
8.1	0.00	na	0.00	7.3	0.3	3.06	24.75	3.50	58.5	4.9	71.6	15.8	8.4
8.3	0.00	na	0.00	3.3	0.1	0.50	2.99	3.53	86.3	5.5	51.3	9.5	7.6
5.0	1.13	na	-0.01	3.5	1.0	0.53	4.86	3.94	66.7	2.0	7.7	18.1	6.8
3.9	1.64	na	0.00	4.2	0.4	0.69	8.67	3.61	78.0	1.3	19.1	27.7	4.3
7.3	0.79	4.0	0.05	1.8	-6.4	-0.44	-3.30	2.16	71.9	2.7	30.4	24.7	9.2
7.1	0.00	na	-0.01	4.1	0.2	0.97	8.83	3.30	66.3	1.7	15.1	21.8	6.8
3.2	0.74	na	0.05	5.6	1.6	1.17	10.30	4.90	70.5	3.8	22.2	10.6	7.2
5.0	1.55	na	0.00	2.4	0.1	0.34	3.16	4.07	88.4	1.5	13.3	23.6	6.3
5.1	1.04	na	0.00	7.2	2.8	1.62	15.23	3.18	46.4	0.7	5.4	30.7	8.7
7.3	0.57	2.3	0.03	5.9	4.0	1.17	9.45	4.09	57.3	3.3	21.5	14.3	9.2
7.5	0.00	0.0	0.00	5.9	7.3	1.14	12.02	2.79	39.5	4.5	11.6	5.1	8.8
8.7	0.86	na	0.00	4.2	0.1	0.27	2.23	4.21	73.7	3.7	24.4	11.6	6.8
7.6	0.96	2.7	-0.02	6.8	1.6	1.93	14.83	4.91	57.6	2.3	28.4	19.7	7.6
8.5	0.10	na	-0.01	5.7	0.5	1.86	12.99	3.70	67.2	5.2	31.5	5.2	8.2
9.2	0.00	na	0.06	3.8	0.8	0.74	8.75	3.06	89.4	5.2	43.9	9.9	4.9
2.0	3.54	na	0.01	6.9	0.1	0.43	3.96	2.92	57.0	0.7	19.1	52.3	7.7
7.3	0.57	na	0.00	2.3	0.1	0.14	1.40	3.84	96.2	1.7	25.2	24.2	6.1
5.6	1.08	na	0.00	5.7	1.2	1.38	12.57	3.14	57.7	2.4	32.0	21.6	7.8
7.5	0.43	na	0.00	6.4	0.6	1.37	17.90	4.52	71.0	1.0	18.7	4.9	6.2
8.3	0.27	na	0.00	1.9	0.1	0.27	2.18	3.50	89.9	0.6	12.9	49.8	6.7
4.1	0.89	na	0.01	4.6	0.5	1.00	9.60	3.80	63.8	3.7	17.8	9.3	7.1
7.4	0.19	1.8	0.00	9.5	0.3	2.03	21.75	3.76	57.6	0.6	6.8	44.7	6.3
6.5	0.23	na	0.49	2.7	0.8	0.28	2.45	3.64	83.4	3.4	9.6	11.8	7.1
6.5	0.60	1.9	0.03	6.8	3.1	1.07	7.60	4.22	62.1	4.1	18.1	9.2	10.0
6.3	0.71	na	0.01	4.0	0.2	0.78	7.17	3.79	64.4	1.7	29.3	28.1	5.9
5.0	0.65	na	0.48	4.6	0.9	0.80	8.86	3.58	69.4	2.3	18.3	15.7	6.1
7.2	0.57	na	0.00	2.3	0.0	0.01	0.07	4.18	86.5	3.7	21.1	8.7	6.1
8.4	0.39	na	0.19	2.8	0.1	0.71	2.73	5.01	78.1	3.2	29.3	15.5	6.6
8.1	0.65	na	0.11	3.1	0.1	0.96	7.48	3.49	80.7	1.8	28.6	27.3	5.8
7.8	0.34	2.4	0.00	5.8	0.9	1.06	10.49	3.84	59.2	1.4	16.4	22.6	7.9
3.8	10.06	18.1	0.09	1.3	0.0	0.36	2.28	2.73	125.3	2.9	59.2	30.6	5.8
8.3	1.53	na	-0.02	3.7	0.3	1.37	13.13	2.80	76.5	7.5	76.3	1.0	5.4
6.5	0.23	2.0	0.00	9.2	2.0	1.51	15.16	5.62	60.8	1.8	22.2	16.0	7.6

	Name	City	State	Rating	2019 Rating	2018 Rating	Total Assets ($Mil)	One Year Asset Growth	Comm-ercial Loans	Cons-umer Loans	Mort-gage Loans	Secur-ities	Capital-ization Index	Lever-age Ratio	Risk-Based Capital Ratio
									Asset Mix (As a % of Total Assets)						
	Rockefeller Trust Co., N.A.	New York	NY	**U**	U	U	15.6	14.33	0.0	0.0	0.0	82.3	**10.0**	85.4	286.4
▼	Rockhold Bank	Bainbridge	OH	**E+**	D-	D	40.5	6.96	5.4	0.8	49.1	0.0	**6.4**	8.4	13.4
▼	Rockland Savings Bank, FSB	Rockland	ME	**C**	C+	D+	83.0	11.61	8.4	1.7	51.7	0.1	**9.1**	10.5	0.0
	Rockland Trust Co.	Rockland	MA	**B+**	B+	B+	11986.7	33.24	11.9	0.2	19.8	10.4	**8.8**	11.1	14.0
	Rockwood Bank	Eureka	MO	**A-**	A-	B	245.1	2.48	4.1	1.0	21.6	0.0	**9.8**	15.7	0.0
	Rocky Mountain Bank	Billings	MT	**B**	B	B	576.3	17.81	12.6	1.9	7.6	32.4	**6.7**	8.7	13.2
	Rocky Mountain Bank	Jackson	WY	**B+**	B+	B+	319.6	6.26	9.4	13.1	21.4	5.1	**10.0**	11.8	16.3
▲	Rocky Mountain Bank & Trust	Florence	CO	**B-**	C+	C-	71.8	3.21	19.7	1.0	16.1	22.8	**9.2**	10.6	0.0
	Rolette State Bank	Rolette	ND	**D-**	D-	D	40.0	1.76	13.7	2.2	2.7	9.5	**7.7**	9.6	0.0
	Rolling Hills Bank & Trust	Atlantic	IA	**D+**	D+	C	319.7	4.30	5.9	0.9	3.6	0.7	**8.2**	10.0	0.0
▼	Rollstone Bank & Trust	Fitchburg	MA	**C**	C+	B-	714.2	3.55	5.4	0.1	20.0	22.9	**9.8**	10.9	16.4
	Rondout Savings Bank	Kingston	NY	**C**	C	C+	395.6	-0.24	6.5	0.3	47.9	10.2	**10.0**	11.0	17.9
	Root River State Bank	Chatfield	MN	**C+**	C+	C+	67.6	-2.43	6.0	1.0	9.5	37.2	**9.8**	12.0	0.0
	Roscoe State Bank	Roscoe	TX	**A-**	A-	B+	173.1	5.38	3.6	1.4	13.5	40.3	**8.6**	10.2	0.0
▼	Rosedale Federal S&L Assn.	Baltimore	MD	**B-**	B	B	979.6	2.51	0.0	0.0	43.6	11.3	**9.8**	25.2	0.0
	Round Top State Bank	Round Top	TX	**A-**	A-	A-	619.9	9.63	2.8	2.1	24.4	26.6	**9.8**	11.8	0.0
▲	Roundbank	Waseca	MN	**B+**	B	B	333.4	4.98	9.6	1.2	23.1	21.0	**10.0**	11.0	15.3
	Rowley Savings Bank	Rowley	IA	**C-**	C-	D	15.9	2.75	7.9	5.0	8.0	0.0	**7.1**	9.2	0.0
	Roxboro Savings Bank, SSB	Roxboro	NC	**B+**	B+	B+	233.6	1.75	0.8	0.4	26.2	38.6	**10.0**	21.9	47.7
	Royal Bank	Elroy	WI	**B+**	B+	B	472.9	7.30	8.2	4.4	16.1	16.5	**8.9**	10.2	15.0
▲	Royal Banks of Missouri	Saint Louis	MO	**B**	B-	C	694.0	-2.37	10.1	0.8	4.7	6.3	**10.0**	15.0	16.5
	Royal Business Bank	Los Angeles	CA	**A**	A	A	3127.3	5.04	4.8	0.1	39.2	4.3	**10.0**	14.4	20.8
	Royal Savings Bank	Chicago	IL	**B+**	B+	B+	392.3	-3.11	1.3	0.3	30.5	10.4	**8.6**	10.1	15.8
▼	RSI Bank	Rahway	NJ	**C+**	B-	B-	553.3	1.89	2.1	0.1	40.5	23.1	**9.8**	15.9	0.0
	RSNB Bank	Rock Springs	WY	**A**	A	A-	365.4	1.95	4.4	0.8	4.3	57.3	**9.8**	12.1	0.0
	Rushford State Bank (Inc.)	Rushford	MN	**C-**	C-	D+	59.4	11.98	3.7	2.9	16.5	5.9	**6.4**	8.5	13.5
	Rushville State Bank	Rushville	IL	**A-**	A-	B+	104.2	0.05	7.1	1.7	3.8	45.6	**9.8**	14.3	0.0
	S&T Bank	Indiana	PA	**B**	B	B+	8991.2	24.68	16.4	0.9	13.0	8.9	**6.8**	9.8	12.4
	Sabal Palm Bank	Sarasota	FL	**B-**	B-	C+	259.9	7.96	5.2	0.6	22.8	4.0	**5.7**	9.3	11.5
	Sabine State Bank and Trust Co.	Many	LA	**B+**	B+	B	983.4	0.27	10.6	1.7	10.2	8.2	**7.4**	10.2	12.8
▼	Saco & Biddeford Savings Institution	Saco	ME	**C+**	B	B	1045.2	3.30	1.3	0.6	53.3	10.4	**9.8**	11.7	0.0
	Sacramento Deposit Bank	Sacramento	KY	**A-**	A-	B+	112.2	5.37	5.1	4.9	20.6	24.7	**10.0**	11.4	17.1
	Safra National Bank of New York	New York	NY	**B+**	B+	B+	9245.0	21.59	9.0	0.0	0.1	43.5	**6.5**	8.5	19.4
	Sage Capital Bank	Gonzales	TX	**B+**	B+	B	423.9	3.52	4.8	0.5	10.7	12.8	**9.0**	10.3	15.5
	Sainte Marie State Bank	Sainte Marie	IL	**D**	D	D+	16.6	-12.72	5.4	1.2	0.8	4.9	**10.0**	22.9	27.0
	Saints Avenue Bank	New London	MO	**C-**	C-	D+	107.1	19.90	16.1	17.9	16.3	8.6	**3.4**	7.6	10.2
	Salem Co-operative Bank	Salem	NH	**C**	C	C+	458.3	2.16	2.6	0.0	60.0	14.5	**10.0**	15.1	26.3
▼	Salem Five Cents Savings Bank	Salem	MA	**B+**	A-	B	5324.0	5.97	10.7	2.2	28.9	18.5	**9.6**	10.7	15.0
	Salisbury Bank and Trust Co.	Lakeville	CT	**B**	B	B-	1145.8	2.40	11.7	0.7	30.9	8.0	**7.6**	9.7	13.0
	Sallie Mae Bank	Salt Lake City	UT	**D+**	D+	D+	31775.3	15.12	0.0	73.6	0.0	1.9	**7.6**	9.4	13.7
	Salyersville National Bank	Salyersville	KY	**B**	B	B+	114.2	4.44	2.8	2.4	16.5	32.2	**10.0**	15.2	28.1
	Samson Banking Co., Inc.	Samson	AL	**A-**	A-	B+	86.6	8.26	4.1	5.3	17.6	51.8	**9.8**	13.8	0.0
	San Luis Valley Federal Bank	Alamosa	CO	**B**	B	B	287.5	5.12	2.4	1.8	41.5	14.3	**10.0**	16.9	24.9
	Sanborn Savings Bank	Sanborn	IA	**C+**	C+	C+	65.4	-0.20	5.5	3.3	15.4	11.4	**7.5**	9.5	0.0
	Sandhills Bank	North Myrtle Beach	SC	**C**	C	C	202.0	14.68	4.3	1.7	35.5	9.1	**7.1**	9.0	14.4
	Sandhills State Bank	Bassett	NE	**C+**	C+	C	291.3	-2.09	8.6	0.8	1.2	15.3	**6.2**	8.7	11.9
	Sandy Spring Bank	Olney	MD	**B-**	B-	B	8917.8	7.24	7.1	0.3	16.7	13.2	**7.9**	10.5	13.2
	Sanger Bank	Sanger	TX	**A**	A	A	141.1	2.56	8.1	2.0	13.7	16.5	**10.0**	15.1	28.2
	Sanibel Captiva Community Bank	Sanibel	FL	**B-**	B-	B-	481.6	5.71	5.6	1.2	43.5	1.6	**5.0**	7.7	11.0
	Santa Anna National Bank	Santa Anna	TX	**B+**	B+	B+	51.5	2.28	19.8	8.7	1.1	37.7	**9.8**	11.1	0.0
	Santa Cruz County Bank	Santa Cruz	CA	**A**	A	A-	1069.5	60.08	8.6	0.2	5.0	5.7	**10.0**	12.3	16.6
	Santander Bank, N.A.	Boston	MA	**C+**	C+	C+	87569.2	11.28	17.6	9.1	9.2	16.1	**10.0**	12.6	16.8
	Saratoga National Bank and Trust Co.	Saratoga Springs	NY	**B+**	B+	B+	687.4	21.88	3.9	20.2	23.7	12.4	**7.5**	9.5	0.0
	Sargent County Bank	Forman	ND	**A-**	A-	A-	191.9	2.67	2.5	1.7	0.5	46.6	**6.8**	9.0	0.0
	Sauk Valley Bank & Trust Co.	Sterling	IL	**B-**	B-	B-	464.4	10.02	15.8	0.4	7.7	23.8	**8.1**	9.7	13.4
	Savanna-Thomson State Bank	Savanna	IL	**B**	B	B	91.7	5.63	10.9	0.5	7.8	23.9	**10.0**	12.0	18.7
▼	Savannah Bank, N.A.	Savannah	NY	**C+**	B-	B-	148.4	-0.19	7.7	0.7	22.0	43.5	**6.8**	8.8	19.1
	Savers Co-operative Bank	Southbridge	MA	**B-**	B-	B-	602.9	4.33	4.6	4.6	36.1	9.2	**9.8**	11.2	0.0
	SaviBank	Burlington	WA	**C+**	C+	C+	334.4	18.93	13.2	7.6	10.1	2.8	**7.6**	9.6	0.0
	Savings Bank	Primghar	IA	**A-**	A-	B	214.9	2.43	13.1	1.9	6.6	13.1	**9.8**	12.6	0.0

Asset Quality Index	Adjusted Non-Performing Loans as a % of Total Loans	Adjusted Non-Performing Loans as a % of Capital	Net Charge-Offs Avg Loans	Profitability Index	Net Income ($Mil)	Return on Assets (R.O.A.)	Return on Equity (R.O.E.)	Net Interest Spread	Overhead Efficiency Ratio	Liquidity Index	Liquidity Ratio	Hot Money Ratio	Stability Index
10.0	na	na	na	9.5	0.3	7.82	9.26	1.17	84.4	4.0	na	0.0	6.4
2.9	2.19	na	-0.02	0.1	-0.1	-0.89	-10.46	3.96	121.7	1.1	11.1	25.8	2.3
6.7	1.39	na	-0.02	1.5	0.0	0.08	0.72	3.38	108.1	0.8	17.9	35.6	5.1
5.8	0.74	3.0	0.02	6.6	27.7	0.97	6.30	3.79	53.7	4.1	13.7	6.6	10.0
6.1	0.37	na	-0.08	8.4	1.2	1.93	12.34	4.40	56.3	4.0	18.8	9.0	8.7
4.5	3.07	9.2	0.03	3.3	0.3	0.19	2.00	4.08	69.2	4.6	33.2	9.5	6.3
6.3	0.53	na	0.84	3.9	0.3	0.39	3.12	4.08	59.6	3.9	15.0	6.4	6.7
8.2	0.30	na	0.13	5.0	0.2	1.05	9.36	4.60	76.9	4.8	30.7	7.0	5.4
0.6	9.96	na	0.03	2.4	0.0	0.16	1.66	4.16	96.3	1.9	15.1	13.8	4.8
1.7	2.22	na	0.00	5.3	0.9	1.08	9.03	3.39	58.9	2.5	18.3	16.0	7.8
7.3	1.01	na	0.59	1.2	-0.5	-0.26	-2.45	2.75	77.8	1.3	29.6	18.7	7.4
6.6	1.41	na	0.00	2.8	0.4	0.36	3.44	3.15	84.8	1.5	9.9	23.0	6.1
9.2	0.00	na	0.00	2.8	0.1	0.28	2.27	4.21	90.3	5.1	39.3	8.7	6.2
9.3	0.14	na	0.06	5.7	0.7	1.55	14.54	3.64	69.3	3.2	41.8	19.4	7.5
4.8	7.49	na	0.06	2.2	-0.2	-0.10	-0.39	2.72	84.3	2.2	31.1	22.9	8.7
8.3	0.37	na	0.00	6.2	2.0	1.34	11.33	3.25	52.9	1.7	30.4	29.7	8.1
5.6	1.52	na	-0.01	7.1	1.8	2.17	18.22	3.85	69.8	1.7	19.0	18.2	8.1
9.3	0.00	na	0.00	3.4	0.0	0.76	8.29	3.05	76.5	7.3	83.2	1.9	4.0
8.8	2.12	na	0.00	5.1	0.8	1.41	6.64	3.22	59.2	3.3	54.4	25.6	8.3
5.6	0.98	na	0.00	6.6	1.5	1.28	11.82	4.21	62.9	3.9	22.7	10.4	7.3
5.1	0.88	na	0.00	5.0	1.8	1.00	6.24	3.23	62.1	0.7	12.5	36.2	8.2
7.9	0.78	1.8	0.10	7.9	8.3	1.09	6.72	3.61	53.4	0.8	16.3	45.3	10.0
5.8	0.92	na	0.81	3.5	-0.4	-0.39	-3.25	3.69	69.8	1.3	18.4	28.4	7.3
6.1	1.97	6.6	0.14	2.6	0.4	0.28	1.76	2.73	81.6	3.6	33.0	14.8	8.3
9.5	0.19	na	-0.18	6.8	2.9	3.12	25.52	3.39	55.0	5.5	45.0	8.4	8.2
4.7	2.66	na	0.36	3.6	0.1	0.88	10.48	4.21	77.2	1.9	22.6	20.5	3.9
5.3	2.30	na	0.01	6.0	0.4	1.47	10.29	3.43	56.3	4.8	40.1	10.9	8.9
4.0	1.22	6.7	0.62	5.4	15.8	0.72	5.30	3.55	56.1	2.6	8.8	10.8	9.7
8.8	0.00	na	-0.08	4.2	0.6	0.86	9.30	3.74	70.0	3.1	23.7	14.5	5.3
7.4	0.28	na	0.06	7.3	3.9	1.62	16.03	4.39	68.9	4.6	16.1	4.8	8.3
6.9	0.87	na	0.24	1.8	-1.2	-0.45	-3.94	2.74	84.2	0.8	12.9	25.3	8.6
7.9	0.53	na	0.05	7.4	0.5	1.66	14.24	4.45	59.1	2.5	35.8	22.7	8.2
9.4	0.00	0.0	0.00	2.7	-15.5	-0.71	-6.58	1.43	136.9	1.9	31.5	8.7	8.2
8.3	0.07	na	-0.02	5.1	1.0	0.94	8.38	3.97	71.1	2.2	18.2	18.2	7.3
7.2	0.00	na	-0.83	0.0	-0.1	-1.15	-4.98	2.70	147.6	1.5	22.9	25.7	4.0
6.2	0.21	na	0.17	2.8	0.1	0.37	4.85	3.88	88.2	2.3	9.2	12.2	3.6
9.4	0.54	na	0.00	2.3	0.4	0.33	2.15	2.70	82.9	1.5	19.2	24.7	7.6
7.5	0.49	3.2	-0.02	4.1	5.1	0.39	3.64	2.87	58.3	2.6	16.6	15.0	9.2
7.3	0.57	na	-0.01	4.1	2.3	0.80	7.37	3.39	61.0	3.0	4.7	12.9	9.0
1.1	5.81	20.3	0.97	10.0	381.2	4.73	56.80	5.13	5.8	1.4	26.2	9.7	9.6
7.9	0.24	na	-0.01	4.4	0.3	0.92	6.13	3.70	71.1	1.4	22.6	29.0	7.3
8.9	0.00	na	0.07	6.4	0.3	1.47	10.21	3.54	60.6	4.6	52.1	14.1	8.1
8.0	1.07	na	0.00	4.4	0.6	0.88	5.22	4.06	75.5	3.9	28.0	11.3	8.0
6.2	1.11	na	0.00	4.2	0.2	1.17	11.97	3.28	61.4	3.4	17.6	12.1	5.9
8.1	0.21	na	0.01	2.8	0.2	0.36	3.66	3.39	87.5	1.2	20.4	30.9	5.0
4.0	0.12	na	-0.01	4.5	0.7	0.87	7.64	3.99	69.9	1.8	12.3	16.9	6.7
4.3	0.79	3.6	0.03	5.1	11.8	0.55	3.79	3.33	56.2	1.6	13.4	17.9	10.0
8.2	1.27	na	0.00	5.5	0.4	1.07	7.12	3.70	67.8	3.0	41.4	20.5	8.7
4.3	1.42	na	0.00	9.4	1.8	1.53	20.04	4.81	56.4	4.3	12.2	6.6	5.7
8.0	0.08	na	0.86	7.9	0.2	1.53	13.96	4.73	60.8	2.4	32.5	21.4	7.0
6.7	0.00	0.0	0.05	9.7	4.4	1.66	11.45	4.51	47.3	3.3	22.4	14.5	10.0
5.5	0.84	2.8	0.57	1.3	-78.8	-0.37	-2.30	2.71	91.1	4.5	23.5	3.6	7.7
7.1	0.18	1.4	0.04	5.9	1.7	1.03	10.81	2.97	47.8	2.2	10.8	17.6	7.2
8.4	0.00	na	0.00	6.7	0.9	1.75	17.06	3.50	43.6	4.4	38.0	12.5	7.4
3.7	2.02	13.7	0.09	4.1	0.9	0.79	8.12	3.44	69.6	1.9	15.5	11.5	5.3
3.8	1.06	na	0.00	3.8	0.2	0.89	6.07	3.44	69.7	5.0	18.7	2.2	7.3
7.4	0.74	3.5	0.12	2.9	0.1	0.34	3.74	2.98	86.9	1.8	18.4	20.9	5.6
6.0	0.83	na	0.08	3.6	1.0	0.66	5.90	3.23	75.1	1.9	15.0	19.6	7.2
5.6	0.60	na	0.01	2.9	0.1	0.14	1.39	4.08	85.3	1.1	12.7	24.1	5.6
7.0	0.00	0.5	0.00	7.6	0.9	1.65	13.15	3.11	43.7	1.6	7.9	20.3	9.0

	Name	City	State	Rating	2019 Rating	2018 Rating	Total Assets ($Mil)	One Year Asset Growth	Comm-ercial Loans	Cons-umer Loans	Mort-gage Loans	Secur-ities	Capital-ization Index	Lever-age Ratio	Risk-Based Capital Ratio
									Asset Mix (As a % of Total Assets)						
	Savings Bank	Wakefield	MA	**B-**	B-	C+	615.6	-0.88	1.3	0.1	54.4	7.4	**9.8**	12.3	0.0
▼	Savings Bank	Circleville	OH	**C+**	B-	B-	364.7	3.82	9.0	3.5	38.6	23.6	**9.8**	10.8	20.5
▼	Savings Bank of Danbury	Danbury	CT	**B+**	A-	B+	1132.8	5.21	5.3	0.1	44.3	7.6	**10.0**	12.5	17.5
	Savings Bank of Mendocino County	Ukiah	CA	**A**	A	A	1124.3	0.82	3.4	0.5	5.3	43.5	**9.8**	17.3	0.0
	Savings Bank of Walpole	Walpole	NH	**B-**	B-	C+	463.0	11.36	7.2	0.3	37.0	17.7	**6.2**	8.2	14.7
▲	Savoy Bank	New York	NY	**C+**	C	D+	397.5	6.93	11.1	0.0	13.2	0.4	**8.9**	10.6	14.1
	Sawyer Savings Bank	Saugerties	NY	**D+**	D+	C-	253.8	3.96	3.7	0.1	45.7	22.5	**8.6**	10.0	17.9
▲	SB One Bank	Paramus	NJ	**B-**	C+	C+	2077.4	12.97	6.4	0.1	16.2	11.5	**6.5**	10.0	12.2
	Schaumburg Bank & Trust Co., N.A.	Schaumburg	IL	**B**	B	B	1276.8	6.07	29.0	13.9	2.8	15.4	**5.3**	9.2	11.3
	Schertz Bank & Trust	Schertz	TX	**A-**	A-	B+	433.9	6.51	5.5	0.4	5.1	4.2	**9.8**	12.8	0.0
	Schuyler Savings Bank	Kearny	NJ	**C**	C	C	119.4	-0.94	0.0	0.1	57.2	10.1	**10.0**	16.2	33.0
	Scott State Bank	Bethany	IL	**B**	B	B-	176.6	8.37	8.3	2.8	12.4	32.7	**9.8**	14.6	0.0
	Scottsburg Building and Loan Assn.	Scottsburg	IN	**C+**	C+	C+	85.1	-5.77	1.3	0.1	46.2	35.5	**10.0**	15.8	34.3
	Scribner Bank	Scribner	NE	**A-**	A-	B+	69.5	8.72	6.7	0.9	2.7	10.6	**10.0**	14.8	21.9
▲	Seacoast Commerce Bank	San Diego	CA	**B**	B-	B	1132.8	5.57	1.9	0.0	1.0	0.0	**6.8**	8.8	14.9
	Seacoast National Bank	Stuart	FL	**B+**	B+	B+	7352.6	8.39	10.1	2.8	17.4	15.9	**10.0**	11.4	15.6
	Seamen's Bank	Provincetown	MA	**C+**	C+	C	383.2	2.05	2.6	0.1	45.5	16.8	**9.8**	11.7	0.0
	Seaside National Bank & Trust	Orlando	FL	**B-**	B-	B-	1846.4	-2.44	35.3	2.0	8.1	20.6	**7.4**	9.2	12.9
	Seattle Bank	Seattle	WA	**B**	B	B-	709.6	16.55	5.3	1.0	8.9	6.0	**7.7**	9.5	16.7
▼	Sebree Deposit Bank	Sebree	KY	**D**	D+	D+	21.8	-1.55	4.0	6.5	32.5	14.6	**10.0**	11.5	21.9
	Second Federal S&L Assn. of Philadelphia	Philadelphia	PA	**D**	D	D	17.9	46.90	0.0	0.0	49.3	11.8	**10.0**	34.6	56.8
	Securian Trust Co., N.A.	Saint Paul	MN	**U**	U	U	15.1	2.29	0.0	0.0	0.0	88.2	**10.0**	92.4	100.2
	Security Bank	Stephens	AR	**B+**	B+	B	69.4	1.66	4.6	5.6	55.3	4.8	**7.9**	9.8	0.0
	Security Bank	Laurel	NE	**A-**	A-	B-	227.1	-1.91	8.9	2.3	3.2	25.8	**10.0**	12.1	16.6
	Security Bank	Tulsa	OK	**B-**	B-	B+	609.8	7.56	25.6	1.0	8.0	3.3	**9.5**	11.5	14.6
	Security Bank	Dyersburg	TN	**B-**	B-	B	216.2	8.17	6.6	1.4	5.2	53.3	**9.1**	10.4	15.3
▼	Security Bank	New Auburn	WI	**B-**	B	C+	115.7	14.11	7.2	1.4	14.3	9.5	**9.8**	13.0	0.0
	Security Bank & Trust Co.	Glencoe	MN	**B+**	B+	B+	589.0	14.50	6.4	0.8	5.3	22.9	**6.7**	8.7	14.3
	Security Bank and Trust Co.	Maysville	KY	**B+**	B+	B+	54.2	-0.27	2.5	1.6	16.6	30.7	**9.8**	20.2	0.0
	Security Bank and Trust Co.	Miami	OK	**B-**	B-	B-	92.5	1.33	6.6	4.4	28.6	19.2	**8.0**	9.8	0.0
	Security Bank and Trust Co.	Paris	TN	**B+**	B+	B+	502.5	13.92	24.5	1.6	14.1	14.1	**4.7**	9.1	10.8
	Security Bank Minnesota	Albert Lea	MN	**B+**	B+	B+	136.3	5.30	54.6	3.2	3.4	7.2	**6.4**	9.6	12.1
	Security Bank of Crawford	Crawford	TX	**C+**	C+	C	76.9	18.43	5.0	3.1	38.5	0.0	**7.2**	9.1	15.9
	Security Bank of Kansas City	Kansas City	KS	**A-**	A-	A-	3136.1	3.63	6.0	0.4	2.0	31.5	**9.8**	15.0	0.0
	Security Bank of Pulaski County	Waynesville	MO	**C+**	C+	C+	108.1	2.35	7.4	4.7	21.3	19.2	**7.0**	9.0	13.6
	Security Bank of Southwest Missouri	Cassville	MO	**B+**	B+	B	81.8	0.70	5.8	5.2	31.4	12.8	**9.8**	12.0	0.0
	Security Bank of the Ozarks	Eminence	MO	**C+**	C+	C	95.8	0.94	7.7	8.3	15.1	10.7	**6.6**	8.6	12.4
	Security Bank USA	Bemidji	MN	**B+**	B+	B-	170.5	7.02	14.3	4.9	17.2	6.8	**6.8**	9.0	0.0
	Security Bank, s.b.	Springfield	IL	**C**	C	C-	163.4	-3.23	6.4	3.6	23.9	12.4	**7.3**	9.2	18.6
▼	Security Federal Bank	Aiken	SC	**C+**	B-	B-	1029.3	9.84	2.2	2.3	9.3	47.5	**9.0**	10.3	19.5
	Security Federal Bank	Elizabethton	TN	**B-**	B-	B-	63.8	-6.50	3.0	1.6	34.1	14.5	**10.0**	16.3	27.6
	Security Federal Savings Bank	Jasper	AL	**C+**	C+	C	35.9	-0.51	0.0	8.9	32.4	15.4	**9.8**	12.7	0.0
	Security Federal Savings Bank	Logansport	IN	**B-**	B-	B-	292.6	9.54	4.2	0.9	29.5	8.1	**10.0**	11.3	17.3
	Security Financial Bank	Durand	WI	**B-**	B-	B	498.8	3.80	14.3	0.2	8.4	15.6	**6.6**	9.8	12.2
	Security First Bank	Lincoln	NE	**C+**	C+	C+	1088.5	3.18	5.5	5.3	8.7	19.8	**6.7**	8.8	12.3
▲	Security First Bank of North Dakota	Center	ND	**A**	A-	B+	186.7	6.05	9.1	2.1	8.8	4.1	**9.8**	14.8	0.0
▼	Security First National Bank of Hugo	Hugo	OK	**B+**	A-	B+	121.3	10.28	2.9	1.9	24.9	8.7	**6.7**	8.7	12.8
	Security FSB of McMinnville	McMinnville	TN	**A-**	A-	B+	232.9	6.78	14.1	5.6	24.0	14.0	**9.5**	10.6	15.1
	Security National Bank	Witt	IL	**B**	B	B-	83.2	3.76	10.1	2.3	19.9	11.9	**9.1**	10.4	16.0
	Security National Bank of Enid	Enid	OK	**B+**	B+	B+	340.2	-1.00	3.3	1.1	19.3	44.7	**6.8**	8.8	15.0
▼	Security National Bank of Omaha	Omaha	NE	**A-**	A	A-	863.5	-10.03	22.3	3.3	6.0	22.2	**10.0**	12.8	15.9
	Security National Bank of Sioux City, Iowa	Sioux City	IA	**A-**	A-	B+	1098.7	6.84	5.5	1.4	13.4	24.6	**9.8**	11.6	0.0
	Security National Bank of South Dakota	Dakota Dunes	SD	**A**	A	A-	223.0	19.00	3.6	1.7	11.4	22.4	**9.2**	10.6	0.0
	Security National Trust Co.	Wheeling	WV	**U**	U	U	5.6	-1.59	0.0	0.0	0.0	71.9	**9.8**	126.	0.0
	Security Savings Bank	Gowrie	IA	**A-**	A-	B+	137.7	7.47	4.1	2.1	12.0	23.0	**10.0**	11.1	16.3
	Security Savings Bank	Monmouth	IL	**B-**	B-	C+	204.9	3.58	2.5	6.2	11.6	14.4	**9.8**	11.2	0.0
	Security Savings Bank	Canton	SD	**C+**	C+	B-	433.6	-4.27	3.8	0.9	5.9	9.8	**8.0**	9.7	13.4
	Security State Bank	McRae	GA	**A-**	A-	B+	45.4	-4.67	12.1	2.5	6.2	29.2	**10.0**	15.9	33.5
	Security State Bank	Algona	IA	**A-**	A-	B+	108.0	4.62	9.8	1.0	2.4	2.0	**10.0**	17.7	21.8
	Security State Bank	Radcliffe	IA	**C-**	C-	C-	102.8	-1.83	6.3	1.5	14.2	10.6	**7.1**	9.0	19.9

Asset Quality Index	Adjusted Non-Performing Loans as a % of Total Loans	Adjusted Non-Performing Loans as a % of Capital	Net Charge-Offs Avg Loans	Profitability Index	Net Income ($Mil)	Return on Assets (R.O.A.)	Return on Equity (R.O.E.)	Net Interest Spread	Overhead Efficiency Ratio	Liquidity Index	Liquidity Ratio	Hot Money Ratio	Stability Index
8.5	0.18	na	0.00	**1.7**	-0.9	-0.62	-4.77	3.22	84.1	**1.6**	17.6	22.3	**8.0**
6.0	1.88	na	0.00	**2.2**	-0.1	-0.07	-0.60	3.32	92.1	**3.2**	18.6	13.5	**6.6**
5.2	2.25	13.2	0.00	**3.8**	1.5	0.54	4.42	3.40	63.1	**1.4**	10.5	23.8	**9.6**
9.1	0.59	na	0.04	**7.4**	3.7	1.32	7.62	3.72	55.4	**6.7**	48.7	4.6	**10.0**
5.8	1.00	6.0	0.00	**3.8**	1.1	0.95	11.46	3.27	68.9	**4.8**	28.4	6.1	**5.6**
3.9	0.96	na	-0.04	**6.8**	1.1	1.13	10.56	4.23	62.2	**0.5**	14.3	60.6	**7.3**
5.9	0.83	na	0.01	**1.7**	0.1	0.18	1.75	2.66	91.8	**1.0**	27.0	33.9	**5.2**
4.4	1.01	7.1	0.07	**5.1**	5.4	1.08	9.89	3.26	58.9	**1.0**	14.7	14.8	**9.0**
5.5	0.90	6.3	0.01	**3.9**	0.6	0.21	1.89	2.80	55.2	**1.6**	18.3	19.5	**7.8**
6.1	0.55	na	0.01	**7.6**	1.5	1.39	10.98	3.92	52.9	**0.7**	10.5	39.9	**7.9**
9.2	0.93	na	0.00	**2.1**	0.1	0.21	1.31	2.66	88.9	**1.3**	29.2	34.9	**7.3**
7.7	0.35	na	-0.02	**3.6**	0.4	0.79	5.46	3.25	77.5	**4.8**	41.7	11.5	**7.8**
10.0	0.25	na	0.00	**2.6**	0.1	0.39	2.50	2.50	82.1	**1.4**	33.2	46.4	**7.2**
8.4	0.24	na	-0.01	**9.1**	0.3	1.57	10.56	3.69	68.5	**5.5**	33.7	4.1	**8.0**
6.1	0.84	na	0.00	**7.8**	3.8	1.34	11.47	5.70	66.7	**5.0**	7.9	1.5	**9.5**
6.4	0.68	2.9	0.08	**4.7**	1.3	0.07	0.52	3.95	61.0	**2.4**	18.5	7.5	**9.9**
3.2	4.60	na	0.00	**3.1**	0.5	0.48	4.08	3.35	80.1	**2.1**	26.3	20.4	**6.5**
7.3	0.38	2.5	0.00	**4.4**	4.1	0.88	9.29	2.65	64.2	**1.4**	19.7	17.3	**7.3**
6.4	2.42	na	0.08	**5.1**	1.9	1.06	10.71	3.66	57.3	**0.8**	21.2	45.9	**7.9**
8.7	0.00	na	0.03	**0.0**	0.0	-0.65	-5.27	3.43	119.3	**1.7**	32.7	27.1	**4.6**
9.8	0.00	na	0.00	**0.0**	-0.1	-1.39	-3.98	3.32	102.4	**1.8**	47.1	46.3	**6.0**
10.0	na	0.0	na	**6.4**	0.0	0.06	0.06	3.33	99.0	**4.0**	na	0.0	**6.0**
8.7	0.12	na	-0.04	**5.3**	0.2	1.36	13.88	4.03	62.0	**0.5**	10.5	51.3	**5.7**
8.2	0.36	na	-0.02	**6.6**	0.8	1.51	11.86	4.40	64.9	**4.4**	26.4	8.0	**8.2**
4.6	1.08	na	0.04	**8.5**	2.7	1.83	15.83	3.63	42.6	**0.9**	22.6	35.3	**9.6**
7.0	1.93	na	0.00	**3.9**	0.4	0.80	6.91	3.13	81.0	**1.7**	23.9	23.5	**7.1**
2.2	3.83	na	0.17	**7.2**	0.4	1.36	10.59	3.62	53.0	**1.2**	18.0	19.8	**6.9**
5.4	1.35	5.6	0.00	**5.9**	2.0	1.38	14.13	3.16	60.2	**3.9**	22.0	10.2	**7.8**
9.3	0.21	na	-0.03	**4.9**	0.1	1.02	5.06	3.64	72.9	**5.0**	41.6	10.2	**8.3**
4.7	0.92	na	0.73	**3.8**	0.2	0.74	7.26	3.95	80.0	**1.0**	17.4	28.8	**5.5**
8.4	0.04	na	0.02	**5.8**	1.3	1.12	11.86	3.71	58.6	**1.4**	10.8	17.3	**6.8**
7.4	0.09	na	0.12	**6.1**	0.5	1.44	13.69	4.46	56.1	**1.5**	10.5	22.7	**8.2**
7.6	0.36	na	-0.24	**2.5**	0.0	0.13	1.37	3.75	89.0	**1.1**	28.8	48.9	**4.5**
6.4	2.02	3.8	0.41	**6.7**	10.1	1.33	7.76	3.38	52.3	**5.5**	37.9	9.5	**10.0**
5.4	1.02	5.8	0.20	**3.6**	0.2	0.67	7.27	4.09	82.9	**1.5**	12.5	19.8	**5.2**
4.2	0.42	na	-0.01	**9.8**	0.5	2.25	18.59	4.51	56.3	**2.9**	25.4	15.6	**8.4**
6.1	0.37	na	-0.01	**5.1**	0.3	1.21	12.75	4.99	72.3	**2.5**	12.2	16.2	**5.1**
5.5	0.58	4.6	-0.02	**6.8**	0.7	1.58	17.17	4.08	64.8	**4.4**	23.4	7.3	**6.9**
3.0	2.80	16.1	0.00	**2.6**	0.1	0.25	2.60	3.15	90.7	**5.8**	40.4	4.6	**5.4**
8.0	0.96	na	0.05	**3.2**	1.4	0.57	5.32	3.26	80.5	**3.6**	32.2	12.9	**8.5**
6.2	2.72	na	0.01	**2.5**	0.0	0.23	1.40	3.30	92.3	**0.8**	20.8	35.1	**6.8**
8.9	0.00	na	-0.28	**2.7**	0.0	0.43	3.46	3.16	87.8	**2.4**	45.2	31.5	**5.5**
7.6	1.07	na	0.07	**3.3**	0.4	0.56	4.91	3.63	80.7	**3.3**	20.0	12.8	**6.4**
4.3	1.18	na	0.01	**6.0**	1.7	1.40	12.38	3.86	61.9	**4.0**	19.3	8.4	**8.6**
5.1	1.34	na	0.32	**4.1**	2.2	0.76	8.01	3.25	70.1	**2.6**	21.9	18.0	**8.0**
7.9	0.45	na	0.04	**7.5**	0.8	1.70	11.63	4.58	67.9	**3.6**	12.8	10.6	**9.5**
3.0	2.36	na	0.00	**10.0**	0.6	2.00	23.72	5.57	54.5	**1.8**	11.3	19.7	**6.4**
8.3	0.06	0.4	0.00	**5.5**	0.6	1.02	9.49	3.73	65.8	**1.5**	10.5	23.0	**6.9**
5.7	1.48	4.3	0.01	**4.0**	0.2	0.71	6.78	3.76	72.9	**3.4**	31.7	15.0	**5.9**
7.0	0.37	2.7	0.09	**6.8**	1.2	1.49	15.19	3.17	52.9	**3.7**	20.1	11.0	**7.3**
8.1	0.46	2.1	0.43	**5.5**	2.2	0.98	7.62	3.86	65.4	**4.8**	20.3	4.2	**8.7**
6.7	1.88	na	0.00	**7.6**	3.6	1.43	12.02	2.90	59.3	**4.8**	29.5	9.4	**9.4**
8.9	0.03	na	0.00	**7.5**	0.7	1.24	11.62	2.22	56.9	**2.9**	39.5	18.9	**8.4**
10.0	na	na	na	**9.5**	0.2	17.75	14.21	2.10	85.2	**4.0**	na	0.0	**5.6**
8.1	0.58	na	0.00	**4.4**	0.3	0.91	8.03	3.20	71.1	**2.8**	24.2	15.8	**7.6**
6.7	0.41	na	0.02	**3.4**	0.3	0.55	4.89	3.00	77.0	**1.9**	22.8	20.4	**6.3**
3.7	0.49	na	0.02	**3.4**	0.8	0.71	6.81	3.08	76.7	**1.7**	16.4	20.8	**6.2**
8.9	0.00	na	0.02	**5.4**	0.1	1.19	7.10	4.49	73.9	**5.6**	54.7	9.0	**7.9**
6.1	0.62	na	0.04	**8.1**	0.4	1.48	8.43	3.75	47.6	**2.6**	26.1	17.5	**9.0**
2.9	2.98	na	0.06	**1.8**	0.0	0.07	0.75	2.51	95.7	**4.7**	50.1	14.0	**4.8**

Name	City	State	Rating	2019 Rating	2018 Rating	Total Assets ($Mil)	One Year Asset Growth	Asset Mix (As a % of Total Assets) Comm-ercial Loans	Cons-umer Loans	Mort-gage Loans	Secur-ities	Capital-ization Index	Lever-age Ratio	Risk-Based Capital Ratio
▲ Security State Bank	Sutherland	IA	**A-**	B+	B-	231.9	60.20	8.2	2.1	4.1	0.3	**9.4**	10.8	0.0
▼ Security State Bank	Waverly	IA	**B+**	A-	B+	93.1	12.28	1.2	2.0	9.9	36.6	**9.8**	11.4	0.0
Security State Bank	Scott City	KS	**A-**	A-	B+	305.0	2.72	11.2	2.2	2.4	14.4	**9.8**	15.5	0.0
▼ Security State Bank	Wellington	KS	**C**	C+	C	48.6	-9.04	3.8	0.8	7.7	50.1	**9.8**	14.6	0.0
Security State Bank	Cheyenne	OK	**A-**	A-	A-	167.0	-3.45	5.6	3.7	20.2	28.6	**10.0**	14.3	21.4
Security State Bank	Alexandria	SD	**B**	B	B-	80.8	4.55	8.5	4.0	2.2	22.9	**9.5**	10.8	0.0
Security State Bank	Emery	SD	**B+**	B+	B	50.4	4.22	17.6	2.8	0.0	0.7	**10.0**	14.2	30.0
Security State Bank	Tyndall	SD	**B**	B	C+	234.0	-0.63	9.7	0.5	1.9	7.1	**8.1**	10.6	13.4
Security State Bank	Farwell	TX	**A-**	A-	A-	160.2	4.40	19.1	0.9	9.7	24.9	**9.8**	12.4	0.0
Security State Bank	Pearsall	TX	**A-**	A-	B	681.3	8.32	3.1	0.8	2.8	29.9	**9.8**	12.5	0.0
Security State Bank	Winters	TX	**B-**	B-	C+	59.1	-7.68	8.3	8.3	8.4	31.3	**8.3**	9.9	18.7
Security State Bank	Centralia	WA	**A**	A	A-	500.3	7.98	5.1	1.2	4.7	2.4	**10.0**	13.0	29.0
Security State Bank	Iron River	WI	**B-**	B-	C	103.7	7.73	18.9	1.4	13.1	17.5	**10.0**	18.6	25.2
Security State Bank	Basin	WY	**B**	B	B+	365.0	4.91	5.0	3.1	8.2	37.8	**10.0**	11.0	19.9
Security State Bank & Trust	Fredericksburg	TX	**A**	A	A	1174.6	11.68	9.2	1.9	10.1	19.6	**10.0**	12.7	16.8
Security State Bank of Aitkin	Aitkin	MN	**A-**	A-	B+	99.7	2.08	18.8	2.2	10.3	21.2	**10.0**	12.8	21.1
Security State Bank of Fergus Falls	Fergus Falls	MN	**B+**	B+	B-	126.1	-1.01	6.8	0.4	6.3	22.1	**7.7**	10.5	13.1
Security State Bank of Hibbing	Hibbing	MN	**B**	B	C+	132.3	-0.51	17.5	1.9	11.9	19.6	**9.3**	10.6	20.3
Security State Bank of Kenyon	Kenyon	MN	**D-**	D-	D-	56.5	1.66	5.7	1.5	15.5	1.6	**9.2**	11.7	14.3
Security State Bank of Marine	Marine On Saint Croi	MN	**A-**	A-	B+	144.4	1.25	4.1	2.0	38.0	3.3	**8.1**	10.6	13.4
▲ Security State Bank of Oklahoma	Wewoka	OK	**C+**	C	C	262.6	3.71	16.5	10.7	16.1	12.2	**10.0**	12.0	15.9
Security State Bank of Oklee	Oklee	MN	**B+**	B+	B	34.1	5.83	3.0	5.3	12.9	29.3	**10.0**	16.6	49.2
Security State Bank of Wanamingo	Wanamingo	MN	**B+**	B+	B	65.7	1.53	7.0	1.2	3.3	20.3	**9.8**	11.8	0.0
Security State Bank of Warroad	Warroad	MN	**D**	D	D+	105.4	7.03	15.2	12.2	2.5	32.0	**9.8**	16.7	0.0
Security State Bank, Wishek, North Dakota	Wishek	ND	**B+**	B+	B	77.8	10.64	4.2	2.6	0.7	39.3	**8.6**	10.1	21.0
Security Trust & Savings Bank	Storm Lake	IA	**B-**	B-	B-	236.7	2.22	3.8	1.1	7.5	38.8	**9.4**	10.6	22.0
SEI Private Trust Co.	Oaks	PA	**U**	U	U	193.3	11.12	0.0	0.0	0.0	52.0	**10.0**	93.3	304.4
Seiling State Bank	Seiling	OK	**B**	B	B-	119.0	1.62	10.5	2.5	10.0	23.9	**6.9**	8.9	14.4
Select Bank	Forest	VA	**B-**	B-	B-	261.4	15.23	29.9	2.1	28.1	0.5	**7.5**	9.3	17.6
Select Bank & Trust Co.	Dunn	NC	**B**	B	B	1262.5	1.71	4.3	0.3	12.3	5.1	**10.0**	13.9	15.9
Senath State Bank	Senath	MO	**A**	A	A-	83.6	0.91	6.2	7.4	27.7	5.0	**9.8**	14.6	0.0
SENB Bank	Moline	IL	**B-**	B-	B-	303.2	33.60	11.0	1.1	18.1	18.0	**6.3**	9.1	12.0
Seneca Savings	Baldwinsville	NY	**C**	C	C	211.8	4.76	7.8	0.5	46.4	13.4	**8.7**	10.2	16.8
▲ Sentry Bank	Saint Joseph	MN	**B**	B-	C+	238.8	5.97	9.4	2.9	15.3	22.6	**6.8**	8.8	14.3
ServisFirst Bank	Birmingham	AL	**A-**	A-	A-	9363.3	12.67	28.3	0.6	5.2	8.8	**6.7**	10.1	12.3
Settlers Bank	Marietta	OH	**A-**	A-	B+	126.8	3.31	5.1	4.1	40.4	4.0	**9.8**	13.4	0.0
Settlers bank	Windsor	WI	**C+**	C+	B-	321.5	18.05	23.8	1.6	12.2	2.8	**6.0**	9.9	11.7
▼ Severn Savings Bank, FSB	Annapolis	MD	**B+**	A-	B+	853.7	-3.14	3.7	0.2	31.4	5.0	**9.8**	14.1	0.0
▲ Sevier County Bank	Sevierville	TN	**E**	E-	E-	333.3	10.63	6.5	0.7	12.5	11.3	**7.5**	9.3	15.3
Sewickley Savings Bank	Sewickley	PA	**B-**	B-	B-	313.4	-1.94	1.7	0.1	5.9	49.7	**10.0**	29.8	67.9
▼ Seymour Bank	Seymour	MO	**B-**	B	B	152.1	6.58	3.4	5.3	20.3	24.4	**9.8**	13.4	0.0
Shamrock Bank, N.A.	Coalgate	OK	**A-**	A-	A-	335.7	6.76	7.7	3.9	15.5	25.4	**9.8**	11.6	0.0
Sharon Bank	Springfield	PA	**D+**	D+	D+	181.3	2.28	3.0	0.2	29.8	20.5	**8.8**	10.3	0.0
▲ Shelby County State Bank	Harlan	IA	**B**	B-	C+	271.4	0.45	2.8	1.4	5.5	15.9	**9.8**	11.1	0.0
▲ Shelby County State Bank	Shelbyville	IL	**A-**	B+	B	249.5	0.14	8.8	2.7	18.6	14.5	**9.1**	10.6	0.0
Shelby Savings Bank, SSB	Center	TX	**A-**	A-	B+	322.2	6.42	12.9	4.4	13.6	9.4	**10.0**	12.7	16.5
Shelby State Bank	Shelby	MI	**B-**	B-	B-	275.8	10.39	4.7	1.3	13.1	24.3	**6.3**	8.3	12.5
Shell Lake State Bank	Shell Lake	WI	**A-**	A-	A	213.5	0.51	3.4	3.4	27.9	36.4	**9.8**	16.6	0.0
Sherburne State Bank	Becker	MN	**B**	B	C+	135.5	11.01	10.1	1.4	14.6	13.3	**4.2**	8.0	10.6
Sherwood Community Bank	Creighton	MO	**C+**	C+	C	51.6	4.30	5.1	1.7	24.0	17.0	**8.1**	9.9	0.0
Sherwood State Bank	Sherwood	OH	**C+**	C+	C	74.1	6.61	7.1	5.6	34.9	15.9	**9.9**	10.9	17.3
▼ Shinhan Bank America	New York	NY	**C-**	C	C+	1662.2	13.11	15.4	0.2	14.6	4.5	**10.0**	12.8	17.8
Shore United Bank	Easton	MD	**B+**	B+	B+	1570.8	6.09	5.8	1.4	22.2	7.2	**8.6**	10.9	13.9
Sibley State Bank	Sibley	IA	**B**	B	C	82.5	-0.40	2.4	1.2	3.4	7.2	**9.8**	12.6	0.0
Sicily Island State Bank	Sicily Island	LA	**B-**	B-	B-	62.9	5.72	8.8	4.1	30.3	5.5	**10.0**	13.2	21.0
Sidney Federal S&L Assn.	Sidney	NE	**E+**	E+	D-	19.6	13.38	8.6	2.1	53.6	11.8	**5.7**	7.7	14.3
Sidney State Bank	Sidney	MI	**C**	C	C	86.3	8.14	4.7	4.2	47.3	6.0	**6.2**	8.2	15.1
Signature Bank	Rosemont	IL	**A-**	A-	B+	968.8	22.15	35.4	0.0	2.3	9.7	**7.5**	10.8	12.9
Signature Bank	New York	NY	**B+**	B+	B+	53074.7	9.30	20.8	0.4	1.0	17.0	**7.3**	9.5	12.8
▼ Signature Bank of Arkansas	Fayetteville	AR	**B-**	B	B	711.5	9.74	10.9	3.1	17.5	9.0	**9.1**	11.3	14.2

Asset Quality Index	Adjusted Non-Performing Loans as a % of Total Loans	Adjusted Non-Performing Loans as a % of Capital	Net Charge-Offs Avg Loans	Profitability Index	Net Income ($Mil)	Return on Assets (R.O.A.)	Return on Equity (R.O.E.)	Net Interest Spread	Overhead Efficiency Ratio	Liquidity Index	Liquidity Ratio	Hot Money Ratio	Stability Index
6.9	0.04	na	-0.08	**9.6**	1.2	2.10	19.62	3.93	43.2	**1.5**	6.8	11.9	**7.9**
8.8	0.00	1.3	0.00	**5.0**	0.3	1.36	11.78	2.95	50.4	**6.1**	54.3	5.7	**6.3**
7.2	0.00	na	-0.01	**7.3**	1.1	1.47	9.54	3.28	49.5	**0.8**	21.7	44.2	**8.8**
5.0	3.58	na	0.48	**2.4**	0.1	0.38	2.58	3.28	88.6	**6.0**	44.3	4.7	**5.4**
6.4	1.82	na	0.44	**8.0**	0.6	1.33	8.97	3.95	53.6	**0.9**	7.9	31.1	**9.4**
6.7	0.23	na	0.00	**4.0**	0.2	0.84	7.71	3.34	72.7	**1.5**	25.1	27.1	**6.8**
8.8	0.00	0.0	0.00	**4.6**	0.1	0.82	5.81	3.03	63.2	**5.0**	68.2	14.6	**7.7**
4.1	1.66	na	-0.01	**7.8**	1.0	1.80	16.81	4.48	55.0	**0.9**	20.5	26.8	**7.2**
8.7	0.00	na	0.00	**8.4**	1.3	3.01	25.14	3.22	32.5	**1.4**	21.0	27.4	**9.2**
8.1	0.89	na	0.00	**5.6**	1.8	1.08	8.48	3.01	55.1	**1.1**	21.0	31.8	**7.8**
6.9	0.59	na	0.80	**4.4**	0.1	0.93	9.50	4.19	63.8	**4.8**	28.3	6.2	**4.9**
8.6	0.79	na	0.02	**7.5**	1.9	1.55	11.59	3.36	58.2	**6.7**	64.1	5.8	**9.7**
4.1	4.02	na	0.00	**5.6**	0.3	1.16	6.25	3.47	63.0	**1.8**	32.4	26.9	**6.6**
5.3	1.88	na	0.03	**3.8**	0.8	0.86	7.70	3.16	70.0	**1.8**	31.1	28.3	**6.3**
6.1	1.58	na	0.02	**6.9**	4.4	1.50	11.80	4.33	61.6	**3.2**	18.7	13.9	**10.0**
8.7	0.20	na	-0.03	**5.8**	0.3	1.27	9.88	4.39	58.5	**4.7**	24.1	5.5	**8.4**
6.8	1.15	na	-0.05	**5.9**	0.4	1.46	12.38	4.29	66.3	**3.7**	6.7	9.1	**7.1**
5.3	3.35	na	0.04	**4.5**	0.3	0.85	8.11	3.81	71.9	**5.1**	38.4	8.4	**5.7**
0.0	8.89	na	-0.02	**2.8**	0.1	0.44	3.74	4.21	88.8	**2.9**	10.7	14.3	**5.9**
8.6	0.49	na	0.00	**8.7**	0.7	2.00	18.34	4.16	50.8	**3.6**	27.4	12.7	**8.0**
4.1	1.51	na	0.07	**9.2**	1.2	1.80	14.94	4.78	48.2	**0.7**	10.2	32.7	**7.3**
8.8	0.08	na	0.00	**4.1**	0.0	0.30	1.80	2.55	88.2	**4.2**	64.3	18.1	**8.2**
8.7	0.00	na	0.00	**5.2**	0.2	1.12	9.11	3.61	68.5	**4.6**	37.7	11.1	**7.9**
4.8	2.14	na	-0.80	**1.4**	0.2	0.62	3.69	3.91	76.8	**4.9**	41.4	10.7	**5.0**
8.9	0.00	0.2	0.02	**4.4**	0.2	0.91	8.83	2.83	67.3	**5.6**	57.9	9.7	**7.4**
8.8	0.07	na	0.00	**3.4**	0.4	0.71	5.93	2.43	69.3	**5.7**	62.3	11.6	**6.5**
10.0	na	na	na	**9.5**	20.7	43.99	47.62	2.61	58.0	**4.0**	na	100.0	**6.7**
8.4	0.11	na	-0.04	**4.5**	0.3	1.03	11.15	4.07	70.2	**0.8**	13.5	34.1	**6.0**
5.4	0.75	na	0.13	**3.7**	0.4	0.64	6.97	3.40	73.2	**0.6**	8.1	43.0	**5.4**
4.6	1.19	5.3	0.00	**4.5**	1.4	0.46	2.89	4.08	68.6	**1.1**	10.4	28.2	**9.9**
3.6	0.00	22.6	0.15	**9.1**	0.4	2.07	13.90	4.52	46.8	**6.2**	43.9	2.9	**9.6**
6.6	0.03	na	0.00	**4.0**	0.7	0.88	8.49	3.99	78.1	**3.1**	15.5	13.4	**5.6**
5.2	1.82	na	0.05	**2.8**	0.2	0.36	3.95	3.21	82.7	**0.7**	12.2	30.4	**4.4**
7.5	0.19	na	-0.02	**6.3**	0.7	1.14	9.58	3.53	55.1	**2.0**	30.9	24.3	**7.3**
7.1	0.38	3.3	0.26	**9.0**	35.5	1.56	15.36	3.70	32.2	**3.8**	13.4	8.8	**9.1**
5.6	1.23	na	-0.01	**6.6**	0.4	1.18	8.81	3.67	58.8	**2.5**	22.2	17.1	**8.4**
3.6	1.48	na	0.00	**3.1**	0.5	0.66	6.74	3.29	70.9	**0.7**	11.9	33.4	**4.9**
5.2	2.21	8.6	-0.02	**4.1**	0.9	0.45	3.14	3.46	79.7	**2.1**	22.4	19.2	**9.1**
8.3	0.56	na	0.01	**0.8**	0.2	0.22	2.35	3.37	81.2	**1.6**	20.1	24.7	**1.8**
10.0	0.06	0.0	0.00	**3.2**	0.4	0.53	1.73	1.66	60.6	**4.2**	106.7	33.3	**8.0**
8.2	0.00	na	0.00	**3.5**	0.3	0.87	6.35	4.07	79.6	**2.4**	31.5	16.4	**7.7**
7.8	0.28	na	0.01	**5.4**	1.0	1.21	10.12	4.28	69.5	**2.6**	33.3	19.8	**8.3**
8.0	0.51	na	-0.01	**0.3**	-0.2	-0.50	-4.94	2.64	115.9	**2.4**	33.4	22.9	**4.6**
5.6	0.65	na	0.07	**6.8**	0.9	1.35	10.81	3.68	54.2	**4.4**	22.6	6.9	**7.7**
8.3	0.00	na	0.00	**6.0**	1.0	1.52	14.58	3.80	61.2	**3.8**	12.8	9.9	**7.2**
6.8	0.37	6.3	0.03	**5.6**	1.0	1.27	10.06	5.54	71.0	**1.4**	21.9	27.5	**7.9**
4.3	2.82	12.0	0.02	**3.9**	0.5	0.69	7.74	3.82	80.9	**4.6**	26.6	6.4	**5.0**
8.1	0.67	na	0.00	**5.5**	0.8	1.41	8.05	3.42	62.4	**4.8**	37.7	10.3	**8.8**
7.4	0.85	na	0.03	**9.1**	0.6	1.87	22.45	4.25	52.2	**3.5**	24.6	12.7	**6.4**
6.3	0.18	na	0.00	**3.4**	0.1	0.63	6.40	3.79	85.2	**5.6**	37.5	4.6	**5.4**
4.3	2.12	na	0.03	**3.2**	0.1	0.48	4.39	4.16	83.2	**3.6**	15.2	10.9	**5.6**
7.3	0.17	1.0	-0.02	**1.5**	-0.1	-0.02	-0.14	2.96	101.1	**1.0**	14.8	33.2	**8.3**
4.5	1.25	na	0.15	**5.0**	3.3	0.86	7.20	3.44	67.6	**3.8**	10.8	9.7	**8.9**
5.3	1.24	na	0.01	**5.1**	0.2	0.91	7.25	3.36	63.3	**1.5**	23.7	26.9	**7.3**
4.2	1.78	na	0.14	**4.0**	0.1	0.71	5.37	3.89	81.7	**0.8**	17.9	47.2	**7.2**
5.7	0.13	na	-0.06	**3.0**	0.2	4.21	57.97	3.37	55.7	**1.7**	14.2	20.1	**1.6**
5.1	1.51	7.7	0.38	**3.9**	0.2	0.74	9.02	4.02	75.9	**3.5**	21.1	11.9	**4.7**
8.2	0.11	na	-0.10	**9.7**	4.0	1.73	15.98	4.40	47.9	**3.4**	25.6	7.7	**7.4**
7.1	0.44	2.4	0.02	**4.8**	99.6	0.78	8.36	2.84	40.2	**4.4**	16.2	5.3	**8.3**
7.2	0.27	1.8	-0.01	**3.7**	0.9	0.52	4.60	3.75	74.7	**0.8**	17.2	27.6	**7.9**

Asset Quality Index	Adjusted Non-Performing Loans as a % of Total Loans	Adjusted Non-Performing Loans as a % of Capital	Net Charge-Offs Avg Loans	Profitability Index	Net Income ($Mil)	Return on Assets (R.O.A.)	Return on Equity (R.O.E.)	Net Interest Spread	Overhead Efficiency Ratio	Liquidity Index	Liquidity Ratio	Hot Money Ratio	Stability Index
8.9	0.10	na	0.06	**2.5**	0.3	0.30	3.34	3.30	84.1	**3.1**	38.9	17.8	**4.8**
5.7	0.69	na	0.02	**2.6**	0.3	0.39	3.95	3.23	87.9	**2.7**	25.7	16.9	**5.3**
10.0	0.08	0.4	0.00	**4.7**	4.6	0.88	8.32	2.87	59.4	**1.6**	11.1	22.8	**9.0**
8.7	0.00	na	0.00	**7.0**	0.9	1.41	10.44	3.22	45.5	**5.0**	35.8	8.4	**8.5**
4.7	0.63	na	-0.01	**3.1**	0.5	0.55	4.56	3.90	79.4	**0.8**	14.0	37.7	**5.3**
7.0	0.22	2.0	0.02	**3.1**	0.3	0.64	7.39	4.23	86.4	**0.6**	8.8	32.9	**4.0**
7.9	0.00	na	0.00	**3.4**	0.2	0.50	4.79	3.61	81.8	**1.2**	27.7	34.3	**5.9**
5.1	0.91	na	0.21	**4.2**	1.1	0.85	8.05	3.89	76.6	**2.0**	27.3	21.7	**6.4**
7.1	0.62	3.3	-0.04	**7.6**	9.7	1.45	11.59	3.59	59.2	**3.2**	19.3	13.9	**10.0**
6.1	0.54	na	0.00	**10.0**	2.7	2.48	24.48	4.86	59.5	**0.7**	14.4	42.9	**7.6**
7.3	0.00	na	-0.01	**5.1**	0.6	0.96	7.92	4.46	69.4	**0.9**	24.1	39.0	**7.2**
5.2	0.87	7.8	0.86	**3.3**	-13.7	-0.15	-1.84	2.76	64.8	**3.2**	30.3	1.7	**7.4**
3.1	1.88	na	0.04	**1.9**	-0.4	-0.49	-3.93	4.53	88.5	**4.2**	19.1	7.6	**6.0**
2.6	2.30	15.1	0.31	**0.8**	-1.2	-0.92	-9.10	4.15	103.7	**1.4**	20.3	17.3	**5.4**
8.7	0.01	0.1	0.06	**6.8**	4.8	1.33	11.46	3.57	58.5	**2.2**	26.5	26.0	**10.0**
8.9	0.00	0.0	0.00	**3.7**	-0.6	-0.21	-1.83	1.84	86.2	**3.1**	66.1	29.5	**9.1**
9.4	0.46	na	0.00	**6.2**	0.4	1.35	12.90	3.25	62.3	**4.4**	43.6	14.0	**7.4**
6.7	1.50	na	-0.02	**7.0**	6.0	1.68	14.68	3.93	61.1	**5.2**	33.4	9.8	**9.8**
8.7	0.14	na	0.09	**5.7**	2.2	1.37	13.00	3.69	66.6	**3.6**	21.0	11.7	**8.0**
6.2	0.42	na	-0.03	**6.3**	0.6	1.55	16.25	4.41	67.7	**2.2**	19.8	18.4	**6.8**
3.6	1.92	na	-0.01	**3.5**	0.2	0.46	4.54	3.87	83.7	**1.4**	18.0	27.5	**6.2**
8.5	0.00	na	0.00	**4.7**	0.4	0.86	9.11	3.93	72.6	**1.3**	23.7	30.6	**5.5**
6.9	0.42	na	-0.07	**6.4**	1.0	1.19	13.44	4.74	70.6	**1.2**	16.9	29.0	**5.7**
9.4	0.00	na	0.45	**3.4**	0.3	0.73	7.26	2.89	75.0	**5.8**	49.8	8.1	**5.6**
4.7	0.84	6.5	0.37	**5.4**	1.4	0.96	9.19	3.81	60.1	**0.6**	11.5	46.9	**7.3**
7.9	0.89	na	0.04	**4.0**	1.8	0.68	6.53	4.00	75.7	**3.3**	29.9	18.2	**8.1**
7.5	0.00	na	0.00	**8.8**	1.2	1.56	13.39	4.66	57.8	**0.9**	11.7	32.3	**7.9**
8.6	0.11	na	0.00	**4.9**	1.2	0.78	7.48	3.17	66.0	**1.5**	34.2	32.0	**7.7**
9.2	0.00	na	0.00	**5.9**	1.0	1.39	11.72	3.30	64.8	**6.2**	47.2	4.4	**8.3**
8.6	0.11	na	0.01	**9.7**	2.8	2.21	16.47	4.40	57.0	**3.7**	29.2	13.1	**9.7**
7.1	1.02	na	0.00	**2.0**	0.0	0.38	4.58	3.54	90.5	**7.0**	66.4	0.0	**1.7**
7.4	0.07	na	0.00	**4.8**	0.8	1.09	9.90	3.81	64.8	**0.9**	18.9	24.5	**7.4**
2.8	4.41	na	0.23	**3.2**	0.1	0.45	3.86	3.41	72.5	**1.9**	22.5	21.0	**5.8**
1.1	9.15	na	0.00	**7.7**	1.4	1.54	11.56	3.57	54.3	**4.6**	34.9	8.1	**9.6**
6.6	0.34	na	0.18	**7.9**	0.9	1.42	12.49	5.25	62.9	**1.7**	24.0	20.8	**6.9**
6.4	0.73	na	0.29	**7.9**	0.4	1.55	15.29	5.25	68.7	**0.9**	18.7	34.3	**7.5**
3.6	2.03	na	0.09	**2.2**	0.1	0.07	0.52	2.82	96.2	**1.2**	20.3	15.7	**6.8**
8.2	0.10	na	0.08	**3.4**	1.2	0.29	1.67	2.98	85.6	**6.4**	37.9	3.2	**9.7**
4.7	1.22	na	0.00	**4.1**	3.3	1.01	11.80	4.45	67.8	**0.9**	12.4	33.3	**6.6**
7.4	1.16	7.6	-0.03	**2.9**	15.4	0.41	4.36	1.74	65.5	**0.6**	6.3	31.6	**7.4**
6.6	1.73	na	0.02	**2.4**	0.9	0.31	3.02	3.21	86.0	**2.5**	26.2	21.3	**8.3**
8.0	0.21	na	0.00	**9.8**	4.9	1.99	20.46	3.75	47.8	**3.0**	9.6	11.6	**9.6**
3.4	1.87	14.6	0.26	**5.6**	0.4	0.83	7.11	5.00	71.3	**2.7**	21.7	15.6	**7.6**
6.5	na	na	na	**0.0**	0.0	-0.21	-0.42	-0.42	100.3	**4.1**	145.2	100.0	**1.5**
5.3	0.89	na	-0.07	**3.9**	0.7	0.97	10.56	3.92	73.8	**2.6**	28.8	18.4	**5.5**
4.9	1.12	8.5	0.08	**1.5**	-454.4	-4.32	-50.33	2.08	256.8	**1.0**	9.7	21.7	**6.9**
8.6	0.17	1.6	0.19	**3.4**	4.4	0.60	6.36	1.77	73.9	**4.5**	45.8	7.8	**7.8**
5.7	2.22	na	-0.03	**6.0**	0.3	1.37	12.66	4.02	67.0	**4.6**	19.3	5.1	**7.4**
6.7	0.66	2.5	0.00	**9.2**	5.1	1.59	11.81	4.27	49.4	**4.6**	24.8	8.8	**10.0**
4.9	1.42	na	-0.03	**3.3**	0.2	0.25	2.73	4.27	87.5	**5.0**	21.5	3.0	**5.0**
7.7	0.00	na	0.00	**2.6**	0.0	0.23	2.10	4.20	89.1	**0.4**	8.0	54.3	**5.5**
8.1	1.07	na	0.03	**5.3**	1.2	1.01	8.19	4.07	68.0	**2.8**	11.1	10.4	**7.7**
6.2	1.06	na	-0.10	**4.7**	0.6	1.60	14.74	3.32	50.5	**1.4**	31.6	39.9	**6.9**
9.0	0.05	0.3	-0.01	**9.0**	1.2	2.57	26.64	4.38	47.6	**5.6**	46.8	2.6	**6.8**
6.5	3.19	na	-0.01	**2.6**	0.2	0.49	4.13	2.98	78.3	**3.5**	45.1	18.7	**5.4**
5.9	0.42	na	0.01	**2.1**	0.0	0.20	1.57	2.94	92.3	**3.0**	41.5	20.9	**7.0**
4.4	1.73	na	0.00	**3.7**	0.4	0.62	6.79	3.85	79.3	**1.5**	14.1	23.5	**5.4**
6.4	0.30	na	0.00	**2.9**	0.5	0.73	8.13	3.62	88.8	**0.8**	18.8	43.2	**5.2**
8.5	0.01	na	0.00	**9.1**	2.8	1.98	21.64	3.06	51.3	**4.7**	22.0	5.2	**8.0**
7.0	0.49	na	0.00	**4.3**	0.3	0.75	5.57	4.03	77.8	**4.1**	13.3	7.6	**7.6**

Name	City	State	Rating	2019 Rating	2018 Rating	Total Assets ($Mil)	One Year Asset Growth	Asset Mix (As a % of Total Assets) Comm-ercial Loans	Cons-umer Loans	Mort-gage Loans	Secur-ities	Capital-ization Index	Lever-age Ratio	Risk-Based Capital Ratio
Tompkins State Bank	Avon	IL	**B-**	B-	B-	226.5	7.31	8.8	1.4	7.7	27.1	**6.9**	9.0	13.4
Tompkins Trust Co.	Ithaca	NY	**B+**	B+	B+	2136.8	2.19	4.7	1.5	25.8	25.4	**6.9**	8.9	14.0
▼ Torrington Savings Bank	Torrington	CT	**B-**	B	B-	825.7	-0.40	0.5	0.1	56.8	17.5	**10.0**	20.0	41.7
Touchmark National Bank	Alpharetta	GA	**B**	B	B-	420.2	-0.59	15.7	0.0	1.9	5.4	**10.0**	11.7	22.3
Touchstone Bank	Prince George	VA	**B-**	B-	C+	473.0	7.65	6.5	0.8	23.3	12.5	**8.0**	9.8	0.0
Towanda State Bank	Towanda	KS	**E+**	E+	E+	10.6	1.58	0.5	7.5	53.5	14.8	**3.8**	5.8	12.3
Tower Community Bank	Jasper	TN	**C+**	C+	C-	214.8	5.65	5.4	3.5	16.0	7.5	**6.9**	9.1	0.0
Town & Country Bank	Salem	MO	**A-**	A-	A-	556.6	8.46	2.4	3.2	32.9	17.3	**10.0**	11.4	18.1
Town & Country Bank	Ravenna	NE	**A-**	A-	A-	158.5	-0.88	3.9	1.6	2.9	28.3	**9.8**	13.6	0.0
Town & Country Bank	Las Vegas	NV	**B+**	B+	B+	192.3	17.99	4.8	0.0	3.3	0.1	**9.8**	12.2	0.0
▼ Town & Country Bank and Trust Co.	Bardstown	KY	**A-**	A	A-	320.4	0.28	4.1	1.0	22.5	16.8	**9.8**	12.6	0.0
Town and Country Bank	Springfield	IL	**B-**	B-	B-	837.7	5.59	9.6	0.6	15.3	15.8	**7.2**	9.6	12.7
Town and Country Bank Midwest	Quincy	IL	**A-**	A-	B+	179.0	-6.64	18.1	1.3	15.4	6.5	**10.0**	12.4	18.7
Town Bank, N.A.	Hartland	WI	**B**	B	B	2630.2	19.84	21.6	19.1	5.5	15.1	**5.5**	9.2	11.4
Town Center Bank	New Lenox	IL	**C+**	C+	C	107.3	5.61	13.6	2.3	1.7	17.2	**6.3**	10.7	12.0
Town-Country National Bank	Camden	AL	**A-**	A-	B	110.5	1.32	16.0	13.4	14.3	25.3	**9.8**	19.2	0.0
▼ TowneBank	Portsmouth	VA	**B+**	A-	A-	12623.8	9.12	10.8	2.5	13.3	10.2	**8.7**	10.1	14.4
Toyota Financial Savings Bank	Henderson	NV	**C**	C	C+	1134.4	10.06	0.0	0.1	79.0	0.7	**10.0**	15.3	29.4
TPNB Bank	Paris	MO	**B+**	B+	B+	83.7	2.39	3.0	1.0	9.3	36.7	**10.0**	14.7	24.9
Traders & Farmers Bank	Haleyville	AL	**B**	B	B	364.2	-1.69	3.9	4.2	18.7	43.0	**10.0**	16.5	32.7
Tradition Capital Bank	Wayzata	MN	**C+**	C+	B-	942.7	17.79	12.5	0.9	12.0	9.8	**5.2**	9.7	11.1
Traditional Bank, Inc.	Mount Sterling	KY	**A-**	A-	A-	1658.1	6.37	5.7	0.4	24.0	22.2	**8.7**	10.2	14.2
Traditions Bank	Cullman	AL	**B+**	B+	B	403.5	9.64	14.9	7.2	29.3	5.6	**9.1**	10.4	15.1
Traditions First Bank	Erin	TN	**B-**	B-	B-	165.4	3.19	2.6	1.6	17.5	20.1	**6.8**	8.8	14.5
TrailWest Bank	Lolo	MT	**B+**	B+	B	687.8	8.69	9.2	2.1	29.1	3.2	**7.6**	9.4	13.8
Transact Bank, N.A.	Denver	CO	**D**	D	D	24.3	-53.10	0.0	0.0	0.0	5.0	**10.0**	23.1	156.0
TransPecos Banks, SSB	Pecos	TX	**C+**	C+	B-	250.8	11.73	23.7	1.4	17.3	19.4	**6.7**	8.7	12.9
Transportation Alliance Bank, Inc.	Ogden	UT	**C**	C	C+	879.9	22.99	65.4	2.4	0.0	8.3	**9.8**	11.2	0.0
▲ Treynor State Bank	Treynor	IA	**D+**	D	D+	384.7	-1.85	5.1	0.8	2.5	54.8	**6.7**	8.7	12.9
▼ Tri City National Bank	Oak Creek	WI	**B+**	A-	B+	1462.7	0.88	2.3	0.3	10.9	26.5	**10.0**	11.8	18.3
Tri Counties Bank	Chico	CA	**A**	A	A-	6469.6	-0.01	4.1	1.3	8.3	21.3	**10.0**	11.1	15.0
▼ Tri Valley Bank	Talmage	NE	**C-**	C	C	51.0	12.36	10.8	1.4	9.0	2.1	**4.2**	7.8	10.6
Tri-County Bank	Brown City	MI	**A-**	A-	A-	342.9	10.24	7.6	1.2	8.6	9.8	**9.8**	12.4	0.0
Tri-County Bank	Stuart	NE	**B-**	B-	C+	142.7	12.92	10.0	2.4	14.7	17.5	**6.8**	9.0	12.4
▼ Tri-County Bank & Trust Co.	Roachdale	IN	**B-**	B	B	205.8	3.15	3.4	4.5	15.1	39.1	**9.8**	12.7	0.0
Tri-County Trust Co.	Glasgow	MO	**B-**	B-	B	58.0	-0.76	7.6	6.2	26.0	23.4	**9.8**	11.7	0.0
Tri-State Bank of Memphis	Memphis	TN	**C-**	C-	C-	90.1	-4.72	6.6	3.5	8.2	24.9	**8.7**	10.1	18.4
Tri-Valley Bank	Randolph	IA	**B-**	B-	C+	61.4	6.02	7.1	1.5	11.4	22.6	**10.0**	12.1	18.2
▲ Triad Bank	Frontenac	MO	**B-**	C+	C	410.8	7.90	14.9	0.3	16.1	5.3	**5.7**	9.7	11.5
▲ Triad Bank, N.A.	Tulsa	OK	**B+**	B	B-	165.8	3.21	13.1	2.9	34.7	0.0	**10.0**	12.5	19.3
TriCentury Bank	De Soto	KS	**A-**	A-	B+	115.4	13.54	9.3	0.9	17.8	0.0	**9.8**	12.1	0.0
▲ Trinity Bank, N.A.	Fort Worth	TX	**A**	A-	A	291.7	13.71	34.4	0.2	5.4	25.1	**10.0**	12.5	20.4
TriStar Bank	Dickson	TN	**C+**	C+	C	320.4	5.34	5.6	9.0	20.8	12.7	**5.7**	8.4	11.5
TriState Capital Bank	Pittsburgh	PA	**B-**	B-	B-	8915.1	42.54	31.2	23.6	0.5	6.6	**5.4**	7.4	11.7
Triumph Bank	Memphis	TN	**C+**	C+	B-	829.2	4.97	18.3	0.7	20.8	19.9	**6.3**	9.1	12.0
Triumph State Bank	Trimont	MN	**C+**	C+	C+	72.4	-3.25	8.5	4.1	1.7	10.8	**8.0**	9.9	0.0
Troy Bank & Trust Co.	Troy	AL	**B+**	B+	B+	914.2	0.16	11.7	2.7	15.6	26.9	**9.8**	11.8	0.0
▲ TruBank	Indianola	IA	**B**	B-	B	320.6	3.23	7.9	0.9	10.9	16.9	**9.3**	10.7	0.0
Truist Bank	Charlotte	NC	**B+**	B+	B+	495079.0	125.25	17.5	10.7	11.6	15.8	**6.7**	9.0	12.2
TruPoint Bank	Grundy	VA	**B-**	B-	C	452.7	1.03	18.3	5.6	16.5	15.9	**8.4**	9.9	15.2
Trust Bank	Lenox	GA	**C**	C	C	36.5	-8.55	4.1	7.0	18.5	5.2	**9.8**	10.9	16.9
Trust Co. of Toledo, N.A.	Holland	OH	**U**	U	U	4.8	3.61	0.0	0.0	0.0	76.9	**10.0**	95.3	303.6
TrustBank	Olney	IL	**B+**	B+	B+	234.1	-25.50	8.1	2.6	16.9	9.3	**9.8**	11.1	0.0
TrustCo Bank	Glenville	NY	**A-**	A-	B+	5259.9	2.06	0.4	0.2	69.3	9.9	**8.6**	10.1	19.7
Trustmark National Bank	Jackson	MS	**B+**	B+	B	14017.8	4.03	10.5	1.2	12.8	18.3	**7.1**	10.1	12.6
▼ TrustTexas Bank, SSB	Cuero	TX	**C+**	B-	B-	341.2	1.16	3.7	1.0	26.3	30.0	**9.8**	12.4	0.0
Truxton Trust Co.	Nashville	TN	**A**	A	A	538.2	9.92	9.3	4.4	15.0	22.7	**9.0**	11.2	14.2
▼ TSB Bank	Lomira	WI	**B+**	A-	B+	140.3	0.70	8.8	1.0	18.1	11.5	**9.8**	12.2	0.0
Tucumcari Federal S&L Assn.	Tucumcari	NM	**C+**	C+	C+	35.3	6.32	0.0	0.7	49.5	20.0	**10.0**	15.2	33.2
▲ Turbotville National Bank	Turbotville	PA	**A-**	B+	B+	151.2	3.40	6.4	1.7	27.6	18.0	**10.0**	17.1	24.6

Arrows denote recent upgrades ▲ or downgrades ▼

Asset Quality Index	Adjusted Non-Performing Loans as a % of Total Loans	Adjusted Non-Performing Loans as a % of Capital	Net Charge-Offs Avg Loans	Profitability Index	Net Income ($Mil)	Return on Assets (R.O.A.)	Return on Equity (R.O.E.)	Net Interest Spread	Overhead Efficiency Ratio	Liquidity Index	Liquidity Ratio	Hot Money Ratio	Stability Index
7.9	0.07	na	0.07	**4.1**	0.5	0.94	9.12	3.38	70.2	**2.7**	16.2	12.8	**6.4**
6.8	0.75	5.5	0.38	**6.5**	4.9	0.95	12.63	3.27	67.4	**4.0**	5.4	6.8	**6.3**
9.9	0.63	na	0.01	**1.8**	-6.3	-3.03	-14.92	2.62	77.4	**3.0**	35.9	18.8	**8.8**
4.9	2.28	na	0.42	**4.8**	0.4	0.36	3.04	2.71	56.4	**0.6**	15.3	58.0	**7.5**
5.9	1.00	na	-0.02	**2.6**	0.4	0.33	3.27	4.36	75.8	**2.7**	21.2	16.2	**5.5**
0.3	6.45	67.7	-0.05	**0.0**	-0.1	-1.81	-30.19	4.17	145.3	**3.6**	14.5	10.8	**0.8**
6.5	0.05	na	-0.01	**3.7**	0.4	0.80	8.55	4.05	81.8	**1.9**	13.1	19.3	**4.6**
7.4	0.62	3.4	0.01	**6.4**	2.1	1.51	12.18	3.93	64.6	**3.2**	12.7	12.7	**9.3**
7.4	0.00	0.0	-0.34	**6.8**	0.5	1.31	9.62	3.94	62.3	**2.8**	25.5	16.2	**8.6**
5.7	4.52	na	0.00	**8.4**	0.8	1.75	14.59	4.05	55.7	**5.0**	35.3	7.8	**8.4**
6.9	0.82	2.8	0.00	**6.2**	0.8	1.04	8.13	4.06	70.4	**4.9**	25.6	4.6	**8.4**
5.9	0.52	3.3	0.05	**3.9**	1.4	0.66	6.46	3.44	73.0	**2.4**	15.7	14.4	**6.6**
5.4	0.91	na	-0.04	**9.4**	3.1	6.65	55.37	4.05	25.3	**2.4**	30.2	19.6	**8.3**
6.3	0.46	2.6	0.02	**4.3**	4.6	0.73	6.26	2.82	59.8	**3.8**	21.0	6.6	**8.4**
2.7	2.86	na	0.06	**2.6**	0.1	0.29	2.20	3.64	88.6	**1.2**	10.9	27.1	**7.9**
4.8	1.22	na	-0.27	**9.6**	0.7	2.47	13.04	5.43	55.4	**1.6**	34.0	35.7	**9.4**
7.2	0.32	1.4	0.03	**4.8**	26.4	0.92	6.70	3.37	76.9	**2.2**	16.8	14.0	**9.8**
9.8	0.49	2.0	-0.01	**1.0**	-0.8	-0.29	-1.87	1.20	85.1	**0.5**	11.1	38.7	**7.9**
5.5	3.34	10.1	0.00	**4.3**	0.2	0.87	6.02	3.03	69.5	**4.2**	35.7	12.6	**8.1**
8.0	0.68	na	0.10	**3.4**	0.9	0.94	5.67	4.05	86.1	**3.1**	47.6	24.5	**7.6**
7.3	0.11	0.5	0.00	**3.8**	1.7	0.75	7.82	3.38	65.6	**1.6**	12.8	15.1	**6.5**
7.7	0.71	na	0.02	**6.3**	6.7	1.61	15.83	3.33	54.3	**1.5**	16.9	17.7	**10.0**
5.9	0.52	3.1	0.71	**6.5**	1.2	1.25	12.09	5.48	65.3	**1.3**	17.7	19.1	**6.0**
8.8	0.00	na	0.00	**4.4**	0.4	1.06	11.56	3.58	74.7	**2.1**	31.4	25.5	**5.7**
7.8	0.23	na	-0.02	**5.7**	2.1	1.23	13.26	3.63	61.4	**2.8**	18.5	13.3	**8.1**
9.9	0.00	na	0.00	**0.0**	-0.6	-10.66	-43.51	2.25	291.8	**7.4**	93.6	2.8	**5.3**
4.8	0.14	5.4	1.69	**2.2**	0.0	0.01	0.13	5.12	76.4	**1.2**	20.2	5.6	**4.2**
3.5	1.67	na	3.19	**2.7**	-0.4	-0.18	-1.44	7.77	71.2	**0.8**	24.0	37.2	**7.4**
6.3	1.87	na	0.04	**1.6**	0.9	0.91	10.21	2.79	89.1	**2.1**	44.2	23.8	**3.6**
5.6	1.83	5.8	-0.05	**5.0**	3.0	0.82	6.98	3.68	78.0	**5.8**	26.0	1.7	**9.5**
6.2	0.53	2.0	-0.04	**6.5**	16.8	1.04	7.19	4.37	58.9	**4.7**	19.5	5.0	**10.0**
8.2	0.00	na	0.02	**4.5**	0.2	1.22	17.02	2.93	61.2	**0.8**	17.1	36.5	**3.7**
5.6	0.89	5.0	0.22	**8.8**	1.4	1.75	14.12	4.72	56.1	**4.2**	24.4	8.7	**7.7**
7.2	0.40	na	0.00	**4.8**	0.3	0.80	8.94	4.53	74.1	**3.4**	20.9	12.6	**5.4**
5.5	1.73	na	-0.12	**3.6**	0.2	0.44	3.44	3.08	76.8	**5.8**	61.3	11.3	**6.9**
5.7	0.48	na	0.02	**4.3**	0.1	0.97	8.18	3.94	72.3	**0.8**	19.7	36.8	**7.5**
3.3	9.77	na	0.01	**2.3**	-0.2	-0.76	-5.92	3.50	110.6	**2.9**	26.4	16.0	**6.0**
8.3	0.22	na	0.45	**3.0**	0.1	0.39	3.20	3.85	82.1	**2.5**	24.7	15.1	**6.0**
6.1	0.00	na	-0.01	**5.6**	1.0	1.05	10.91	3.67	59.0	**1.4**	11.5	6.3	**6.2**
5.4	0.84	na	0.08	**5.9**	0.5	1.22	9.82	4.98	68.0	**4.7**	10.0	3.6	**7.9**
8.7	0.00	0.0	0.00	**5.1**	0.3	0.98	8.09	3.18	61.0	**3.0**	31.1	17.0	**7.0**
8.6	0.23	na	-0.02	**7.6**	1.1	1.55	12.01	3.65	51.3	**4.5**	45.4	14.0	**8.1**
7.3	0.33	na	0.21	**4.2**	0.6	0.77	9.07	4.00	73.1	**1.4**	15.2	26.7	**5.2**
6.8	0.00	0.0	-0.01	**4.0**	13.2	0.67	9.63	1.83	51.9	**1.3**	18.9	13.6	**5.1**
4.3	1.42	10.2	0.04	**3.7**	1.2	0.59	6.26	2.59	74.3	**0.8**	22.1	35.8	**6.3**
5.4	1.41	na	0.00	**4.3**	0.1	0.56	5.33	4.10	75.6	**4.7**	37.1	10.7	**5.4**
4.8	2.30	9.2	-0.01	**5.4**	2.2	0.96	7.94	3.58	67.7	**1.9**	24.0	21.1	**7.7**
7.8	0.15	na	0.23	**4.7**	0.7	0.94	8.11	3.73	63.3	**1.3**	11.7	26.4	**6.6**
6.3	0.46	1.9	0.25	**6.0**	1132.0	0.98	7.07	3.51	59.1	**4.8**	26.0	4.6	**10.0**
7.2	0.23	2.0	0.13	**3.9**	0.9	0.80	7.85	3.48	72.6	**3.1**	7.7	12.8	**5.4**
2.2	3.53	na	-0.20	**5.4**	0.1	1.26	11.76	5.84	84.1	**2.7**	20.2	15.9	**5.3**
10.0	na	0.0	na	**9.5**	0.8	67.83	76.18	2.24	66.0	**4.0**	na	0.0	**5.7**
5.2	0.69	na	-0.01	**6.9**	1.0	1.63	13.73	4.05	70.1	**3.4**	5.3	11.1	**8.3**
8.2	0.77	4.5	0.02	**5.5**	13.3	1.02	10.04	3.05	58.2	**2.9**	17.9	15.2	**8.7**
6.4	0.56	2.8	0.13	**4.0**	23.0	0.67	5.40	3.47	72.5	**4.2**	8.8	6.8	**9.6**
9.4	0.10	na	0.02	**1.9**	0.4	0.49	4.01	3.50	96.7	**4.4**	44.5	14.1	**6.7**
8.5	0.18	0.6	0.00	**8.7**	2.2	1.66	14.99	3.35	58.4	**4.5**	23.3	3.2	**8.9**
4.1	2.09	na	0.00	**4.3**	0.1	0.13	1.10	3.55	67.1	**1.4**	15.5	19.0	**7.6**
6.0	2.24	na	0.04	**1.6**	0.0	0.06	0.39	3.19	98.1	**0.7**	17.6	51.9	**6.4**
5.8	1.80	na	0.00	**7.4**	0.7	1.82	10.66	3.75	45.1	**2.4**	31.9	20.3	**9.0**

Name	City	State	Rating	2019 Rating	2018 Rating	Total Assets ($Mil)	One Year Asset Growth	Asset Mix (As a % of Total Assets) Comm-ercial Loans	Cons-umer Loans	Mort-gage Loans	Secur-ities	Capital-ization Index	Lever-age Ratio	Risk-Based Capital Ratio
Turtle Mountain State Bank	Belcourt	ND	**C**	C	D+	39.5	20.49	23.1	5.5	3.4	7.0	**8.9**	10.4	0.0
▼ Tustin Community Bank	Tustin	CA	**B-**	B	B+	74.2	-7.58	3.2	42.6	5.8	0.0	**9.8**	14.4	0.0
Twin City Bank	Longview	WA	**B-**	B-	C+	56.3	7.28	13.4	0.2	16.0	0.0	**9.4**	10.6	15.6
Twin River Bank	Lewiston	ID	**B+**	B+	B-	102.4	-0.48	15.3	3.5	13.7	2.5	**7.3**	9.2	16.3
Twin Valley Bank	West Alexandria	OH	**C+**	C+	C+	82.3	13.90	9.8	2.4	19.7	18.5	**7.6**	9.5	0.0
Two Rivers Bank	Blair	NE	**B+**	B+	B	141.9	0.03	6.1	1.6	14.9	26.4	**10.0**	13.3	19.8
Two Rivers Bank & Trust	Burlington	IA	**B-**	B-	B-	852.6	2.77	16.8	1.2	17.9	10.1	**6.1**	9.5	11.9
U.S. Bank N.A.	Minneapolis	MN	**B**	B	B-	533129.1	14.08	18.7	10.6	14.5	22.9	**6.8**	8.8	12.6
U.S. Bank Trust Co., N.A.	Portland	OR	**U**	U	U	19.4	5.42	0.0	0.0	0.0	0.0	**10.0**	101.	497.5
U.S. Bank Trust N.A.	Wilmington	DE	**U**	U	U	665.9	3.77	0.0	0.0	0.0	0.0	**10.0**	98.4	492.8
U.S. Bank Trust N.A. SD	Sioux Falls	SD	**U**	U	U	106.6	9.32	0.0	0.0	0.0	0.0	**10.0**	99.7	409.6
▼ U.S. Century Bank	Doral	FL	**C+**	B-	B-	1334.4	12.13	4.5	0.2	19.9	12.4	**7.2**	9.1	13.3
UBank	Jellico	TN	**B**	B	B	66.4	-0.98	6.0	8.7	18.6	13.9	**9.8**	14.1	0.0
UBank	Huntington	TX	**B+**	B+	B-	271.2	13.89	11.9	1.9	18.2	6.6	**9.7**	11.0	0.0
UBS Bank USA	Salt Lake City	UT	**A**	A	A	77464.0	36.09	7.0	28.6	23.3	8.8	**8.5**	10.0	36.8
Uinta Bank	Mountain View	WY	**B-**	B-	B-	233.6	19.05	6.2	0.5	3.8	62.8	**6.0**	8.0	21.5
▲ Ulster Savings Bank	Kingston	NY	**B-**	C+	C-	976.5	9.30	4.5	2.5	44.2	6.8	**10.0**	11.0	15.9
▲ Ultima Bank Minnesota	Winger	MN	**B-**	C+	C	190.1	8.36	11.1	1.4	6.3	0.0	**8.9**	10.4	0.0
UMB Bank & Trust, N.A.	Saint Louis	MO	**U**	U	U	3.0	0.20	0.0	0.0	0.0	0.0	**10.0**	100.	103.0
▼ UMB Bank, N.A.	Kansas City	MO	**C+**	B-	B-	26151.1	12.22	24.4	1.3	3.8	33.6	**6.4**	8.4	12.1
▼ Umpqua Bank	Roseburg	OR	**B**	B+	B+	27511.4	0.69	12.6	1.4	15.3	10.5	**7.4**	9.3	13.0
UNB Bank	Mount Carmel	PA	**C-**	C-	D+	146.9	0.86	2.5	1.1	44.7	23.8	**8.0**	9.9	0.0
UniBank	Lynnwood	WA	**A-**	A-	B+	353.9	11.75	5.2	0.0	0.3	15.3	**10.0**	15.0	19.5
UniBank for Savings	Whitinsville	MA	**B-**	B-	B-	2057.1	15.46	3.6	20.6	22.0	10.7	**6.7**	8.7	12.9
▼ UNICO Bank	Mineral Point	MO	**C-**	C	C+	341.1	10.73	5.5	3.5	30.4	11.0	**6.0**	8.1	11.8
▲ Unified Bank	Martins Ferry	OH	**A-**	B+	B	715.2	15.48	14.9	1.3	13.2	27.6	**9.2**	10.5	14.5
Unified Trust Co., N.A.	Lexington	KY	**U**	U	U	15.1	10.77	0.0	0.0	0.0	4.9	**9.8**	64.0	0.0
Union Bank	Lake Odessa	MI	**C**	C	C	199.6	3.94	10.0	0.9	9.0	7.5	**5.3**	9.1	11.3
Union Bank	Greenville	NC	**B**	B	B	866.8	12.46	6.1	0.4	14.7	20.9	**6.8**	8.8	13.0
Union Bank	Halliday	ND	**C+**	C+	C+	168.8	7.29	4.4	5.3	10.6	17.7	**8.1**	9.9	0.0
Union Bank	Jamestown	TN	**C+**	C+	B-	202.6	0.62	6.5	4.2	19.3	27.1	**10.0**	12.4	23.2
Union Bank	Morrisville	VT	**B**	B	B	882.4	8.58	5.4	0.4	22.1	10.2	**6.2**	8.2	13.2
▲ Union Bank & Trust Co.	Monticello	AR	**B**	B-	C-	221.5	6.70	14.2	4.8	19.3	15.2	**9.3**	10.5	15.2
Union Bank & Trust Co.	Livingston	TN	**B+**	B+	B-	88.8	10.00	8.7	5.5	28.2	19.7	**9.8**	12.3	0.0
Union Bank and Trust Co.	Minneapolis	MN	**B-**	B-	B-	167.9	6.19	7.4	0.1	0.1	20.0	**7.8**	9.6	22.9
Union Bank and Trust Co.	Lincoln	NE	**A-**	A-	B+	4807.5	14.32	15.6	13.2	3.2	14.0	**8.1**	10.8	13.4
Union Bank Co.	Columbus Grove	OH	**B**	B	B-	903.3	6.09	6.1	1.0	16.5	20.8	**7.2**	9.2	12.9
▲ Union Bank of Blair	Blair	WI	**C+**	C	C	105.5	-1.96	15.9	2.3	10.5	7.4	**10.0**	17.4	21.1
▲ Union Bank of Mena	Mena	AR	**A-**	B+	B	273.7	1.31	5.4	12.3	30.3	25.1	**9.7**	10.8	19.5
Union Bank, Inc.	Middlebourne	WV	**B+**	B+	B	271.9	2.91	6.1	2.6	16.8	42.5	**7.8**	9.7	0.0
Union Banking Co.	West Mansfield	OH	**B+**	B+	B+	58.3	3.40	0.3	0.3	5.0	83.7	**10.0**	11.1	41.9
▼ Union County Savings Bank	Elizabeth	NJ	**C**	C+	B-	1799.0	1.88	0.0	0.1	5.3	58.7	**9.8**	13.7	0.0
▼ Union Federal S&L Assn.	Kewanee	IL	**C+**	B-	B-	155.0	2.60	2.9	0.1	47.0	3.5	**9.8**	14.1	0.0
Union National Bank	Elgin	IL	**B+**	B+	A-	320.0	6.32	9.5	0.0	3.3	1.5	**10.0**	11.9	17.6
Union S&L Assn.	Connersville	IN	**B-**	B-	C+	170.2	5.84	1.6	12.2	40.9	0.3	**9.0**	10.5	0.0
Union Savings Bank	Danbury	CT	**B+**	B+	B	2390.9	11.12	3.3	0.2	27.1	12.6	**9.8**	12.3	0.0
▼ UNION Savings BANK	Freeport	IL	**C-**	C	C	160.6	1.67	5.6	2.8	31.8	17.5	**8.7**	10.1	17.4
Union Savings Bank	Cincinnati	OH	**A-**	A-	B+	3168.7	15.56	0.3	0.8	66.2	0.0	**9.6**	10.8	19.1
Union State Bank	Pell City	AL	**D+**	D+	D-	204.8	-5.22	5.1	1.3	6.0	25.8	**5.8**	7.8	13.8
▲ Union State Bank	Greenfield	IA	**C**	C-	C-	82.6	5.44	3.6	1.6	17.8	9.6	**8.6**	10.2	0.0
▲ Union State Bank	Winterset	IA	**B-**	C+	C+	107.5	16.94	4.6	2.0	25.2	16.6	**6.7**	8.7	14.4
Union State Bank	Arkansas City	KS	**B**	B	B	473.4	41.20	7.2	5.3	17.3	17.0	**8.6**	10.2	13.8
Union State Bank	Clay Center	KS	**B-**	B-	B-	144.8	-0.97	3.4	1.0	11.2	45.5	**9.8**	11.4	0.0
Union State Bank	Olsburg	KS	**C+**	C+	B	32.4	-0.77	14.4	3.9	4.3	16.6	**10.0**	13.0	27.6
Union State Bank	Uniontown	KS	**C**	C	D+	49.9	-1.58	7.9	4.2	27.9	12.1	**6.8**	8.8	15.1
Union State Bank of Browns Valley	Browns Valley	MN	**B-**	B-	C+	22.3	3.21	7.7	1.7	0.6	5.5	**9.6**	10.9	0.0
▲ Union State Bank of Everest	Everest	KS	**B**	B-	C+	310.8	-2.14	6.6	2.7	18.4	23.2	**8.9**	10.3	15.2
Union State Bank of Fargo	Fargo	ND	**B-**	B-	B-	127.8	20.00	10.1	4.4	18.6	4.3	**7.9**	9.8	0.0
Union State Bank of Hazen	Hazen	ND	**C**	C	B-	157.7	10.54	4.7	4.9	13.3	29.1	**7.5**	9.5	0.0
▼ Union State Bank of West Salem	West Salem	WI	**C+**	B-	B-	84.2	-2.37	6.8	4.9	25.0	19.7	**9.8**	12.1	0.0

Asset Quality Index	Adjusted Non-Performing Loans as a % of Total Loans	Adjusted Non-Performing Loans as a % of Capital	Net Charge-Offs Avg Loans	Profitability Index	Net Income ($Mil)	Return on Assets (R.O.A.)	Return on Equity (R.O.E.)	Net Interest Spread	Overhead Efficiency Ratio	Liquidity Index	Liquidity Ratio	Hot Money Ratio	Stability Index
5.6	6.65	na	4.23	**3.5**	0.1	0.58	5.57	3.36	83.7	**4.3**	61.7	17.0	**3.2**
6.7	0.07	na	0.96	**4.0**	0.1	0.58	4.02	5.80	76.6	**0.8**	22.5	48.8	**6.3**
7.5	0.93	na	0.00	**4.4**	0.1	0.74	6.94	4.86	83.1	**3.1**	15.5	13.6	**6.0**
8.6	0.00	na	0.00	**7.9**	0.6	2.17	23.95	4.76	54.7	**5.3**	37.9	7.2	**6.1**
7.3	0.31	2.1	0.16	**3.0**	0.1	0.46	4.73	3.96	83.4	**2.7**	10.3	14.9	**4.8**
8.8	0.00	1.3	0.00	**5.2**	0.6	1.75	13.09	3.59	67.3	**2.3**	21.5	12.2	**7.8**
4.9	1.10	na	0.01	**5.4**	2.5	1.17	11.41	3.72	64.7	**4.2**	8.4	6.5	**6.9**
5.1	1.08	4.8	0.52	**6.0**	1123.4	0.94	9.15	2.98	57.0	**5.0**	33.9	3.5	**9.3**
10.0	na	0.0	na	**9.5**	0.2	4.88	4.86	0.00	18.1	**4.0**	na	0.0	**7.0**
9.3	na	0.0	na	**9.5**	5.5	3.32	3.39	1.57	26.3	**4.0**	na	0.0	**7.0**
10.0	na	0.0	na	**9.5**	2.4	9.20	9.34	1.48	19.8	**4.0**	na	0.0	**7.0**
8.6	0.47	1.7	-0.05	**3.2**	1.7	0.52	4.33	3.29	70.9	**1.9**	21.2	23.1	**9.3**
7.2	0.32	na	-0.02	**4.5**	0.1	0.83	5.92	4.67	80.0	**1.0**	15.1	32.0	**7.3**
5.3	1.62	na	-0.04	**5.2**	0.7	1.17	10.85	5.13	74.4	**3.7**	14.4	10.4	**6.6**
6.4	0.46	3.1	0.02	**8.5**	216.6	1.30	12.59	2.35	18.2	**5.2**	39.0	0.0	**9.0**
9.0	0.00	na	0.00	**4.2**	0.5	0.94	10.75	2.38	51.0	**2.0**	41.9	33.0	**4.9**
4.8	2.30	11.6	0.12	**3.8**	1.7	0.73	6.44	3.50	76.1	**2.1**	13.2	16.0	**6.6**
4.8	0.88	na	0.00	**9.7**	1.0	2.06	20.20	4.98	59.2	**0.6**	3.2	31.9	**8.3**
10.0	na	na	na	**2.0**	0.0	0.13	0.13	4.44	99.9	**4.0**	0.0	0.0	**6.2**
7.5	0.70	3.7	0.23	**2.9**	6.4	0.10	1.07	3.10	65.5	**4.8**	21.8	2.9	**7.9**
7.2	0.25	2.9	0.40	**3.7**	-1847.1	-25.62	-202.01	3.52	760.9	**2.8**	15.1	11.4	**10.0**
9.5	0.05	na	0.00	**1.8**	0.1	0.21	2.09	2.52	95.4	**3.3**	27.3	14.1	**5.6**
7.3	0.28	na	-0.02	**8.6**	1.4	1.65	11.04	3.79	56.7	**1.1**	19.7	16.8	**9.0**
4.1	1.26	9.0	-0.02	**3.2**	2.1	0.46	5.25	2.90	78.7	**5.1**	27.0	7.4	**6.1**
2.0	2.66	na	0.38	**3.1**	0.5	0.60	6.93	3.66	77.7	**1.5**	14.4	24.4	**4.4**
7.2	0.41	na	0.08	**6.4**	2.3	1.36	11.81	3.96	55.7	**4.6**	28.5	7.6	**7.3**
10.0	na	na	na	**9.5**	1.4	32.86	54.90	1.62	82.8	**4.0**	80.8	0.0	**6.2**
2.8	4.91	na	-0.03	**2.9**	0.2	0.37	3.65	4.12	89.4	**4.3**	14.1	6.5	**6.2**
7.8	0.12	0.8	0.02	**4.5**	1.7	0.83	8.11	3.66	69.5	**1.8**	23.4	16.4	**6.4**
5.4	0.69	na	0.02	**3.4**	0.2	0.42	4.07	3.75	81.4	**4.7**	26.3	6.2	**5.7**
4.1	8.32	na	0.43	**2.2**	0.0	0.06	0.52	3.29	95.0	**1.8**	35.9	34.5	**5.5**
5.1	0.63	6.2	0.02	**5.2**	2.3	1.08	12.68	3.85	69.5	**3.5**	17.1	9.6	**6.6**
6.4	1.10	na	0.03	**6.3**	0.8	1.50	14.62	4.02	61.7	**1.2**	13.6	25.2	**7.5**
4.5	2.66	na	2.03	**10.0**	0.5	2.25	18.21	4.80	56.8	**3.7**	28.4	12.8	**8.5**
9.4	0.00	na	-0.02	**3.9**	0.3	0.75	7.62	3.08	82.3	**7.8**	74.7	0.7	**5.1**
6.0	0.66	4.7	0.08	**6.2**	10.3	0.89	8.58	3.36	68.6	**1.4**	15.0	15.7	**9.1**
6.4	0.48	1.8	0.00	**4.4**	1.4	0.65	5.01	3.78	78.5	**3.7**	25.0	11.2	**8.5**
2.9	9.27	na	0.03	**6.3**	0.3	1.31	7.28	4.24	55.3	**0.8**	21.0	26.1	**6.6**
6.9	0.52	na	0.02	**9.2**	1.4	2.07	19.11	4.52	56.5	**2.6**	21.7	16.6	**8.3**
6.1	0.90	na	0.04	**6.3**	1.0	1.50	11.47	3.70	58.6	**5.5**	33.8	3.8	**8.4**
10.0	0.51	na	0.00	**4.0**	0.1	0.67	5.07	2.56	68.2	**1.5**	22.9	26.3	**7.6**
10.0	1.17	0.1	0.00	**2.4**	0.9	0.20	1.46	0.53	68.3	**4.0**	107.9	63.7	**8.7**
6.5	1.54	na	0.00	**1.5**	-0.7	-1.90	-13.01	3.19	174.0	**3.3**	23.6	13.3	**7.4**
6.7	0.55	3.3	-0.01	**5.0**	0.8	0.97	7.99	2.94	52.5	**0.6**	12.2	53.7	**7.8**
4.3	0.90	na	0.03	**4.0**	0.3	0.64	6.15	3.60	78.4	**1.3**	11.5	26.2	**6.3**
6.5	1.25	na	0.12	**4.3**	4.9	0.83	6.81	3.18	69.4	**4.2**	10.4	7.4	**9.1**
5.9	0.69	na	0.20	**1.9**	0.0	0.07	0.68	3.13	94.7	**4.6**	30.7	8.9	**5.0**
7.5	0.71	na	-0.01	**8.5**	17.0	2.20	20.63	2.50	49.9	**0.8**	10.6	34.0	**10.0**
4.7	2.12	na	-1.55	**1.9**	0.1	0.22	2.77	3.38	97.1	**5.1**	29.6	4.9	**2.5**
4.6	0.37	na	-0.01	**5.2**	0.3	1.29	8.41	4.21	67.8	**0.9**	21.9	31.5	**8.9**
9.0	0.00	na	0.00	**4.1**	0.2	0.98	10.99	3.80	74.8	**3.5**	26.0	13.0	**4.7**
7.5	0.04	na	0.05	**4.3**	1.1	0.89	8.07	3.70	76.8	**2.8**	20.7	15.7	**7.3**
5.4	4.52	na	-0.03	**3.5**	0.3	0.70	5.75	3.08	68.6	**1.4**	7.0	20.5	**6.7**
1.2	17.99	na	0.00	**2.3**	0.1	0.66	4.88	2.69	73.6	**5.6**	47.5	7.8	**4.9**
7.1	0.07	na	1.11	**4.6**	0.1	0.98	11.17	4.93	78.1	**3.8**	13.6	10.0	**4.3**
8.9	0.00	na	0.20	**5.2**	0.1	1.26	11.25	2.94	55.4	**5.5**	64.4	9.8	**6.0**
4.8	1.50	na	0.05	**5.3**	1.0	1.29	11.33	3.95	69.1	**3.7**	12.5	10.2	**7.6**
5.6	0.62	2.0	0.01	**2.4**	0.1	0.28	2.12	3.86	82.9	**2.7**	22.3	15.7	**6.3**
2.3	3.98	na	0.06	**4.3**	0.4	0.98	9.45	4.10	70.8	**4.0**	23.3	9.6	**5.5**
3.6	2.77	na	-0.02	**3.3**	0.1	0.39	3.13	3.61	82.7	**4.0**	29.5	9.1	**6.3**

Name	City	State	Rating	2019 Rating	2018 Rating	Total Assets ($Mil)	One Year Asset Growth	Asset Mix (As a % of Total Assets) Comm-ercial Loans	Cons-umer Loans	Mort-gage Loans	Secur-ities	Capital-ization Index	Lever-age Ratio	Risk-Based Capital Ratio
▲ Unison Bank	Jamestown	ND	**B+**	B	B+	350.8	14.84	1.6	9.1	18.2	19.7	**8.2**	9.8	14.0
▲ United Bank	Atmore	AL	**B+**	B	B-	723.3	7.84	17.9	2.7	10.4	18.4	**8.1**	9.7	14.9
United Bank	Springdale	AR	**B+**	B+	B+	194.2	0.21	9.0	1.4	33.4	2.1	**10.0**	12.0	15.9
United Bank	Zebulon	GA	**A**	A	A	1512.8	7.02	3.8	2.2	11.6	26.3	**9.1**	10.5	0.0
United Bank	Vienna	VA	**B**	B	B	20352.7	3.63	8.6	5.8	18.4	11.8	**8.4**	11.1	13.7
United Bank & Trust	Marysville	KS	**A-**	A-	A-	675.9	9.15	7.1	1.5	7.4	11.2	**9.8**	11.7	0.0
United Bank & Trust N.A.	Marshalltown	IA	**B+**	B+	A-	102.0	-6.50	4.4	0.8	9.1	33.5	**8.3**	10.0	0.0
▼ United Bank and Trust Co.	Hampton	IA	**A-**	A	A-	171.9	6.92	4.0	3.3	11.5	29.8	**9.8**	15.2	0.0
▲ United Bank of El Paso del Norte	El Paso	TX	**C+**	C	C+	245.1	2.97	17.3	0.5	3.3	7.3	**9.6**	12.3	14.7
United Bank of Iowa	Ida Grove	IA	**A-**	A-	A-	1768.3	9.74	3.5	2.8	6.9	18.6	**8.9**	10.4	0.0
▲ United Bank of Michigan	Grand Rapids	MI	**B-**	C+	C-	700.3	4.82	4.0	1.2	11.0	0.5	**8.7**	10.3	0.0
United Bank of Philadelphia	Philadelphia	PA	**E-**	E-	E-	45.6	-7.78	12.6	1.4	8.9	5.7	**3.4**	5.4	11.1
▲ United Bank of Union	Union	MO	**C+**	C	C-	392.7	4.14	13.4	0.8	16.0	16.3	**8.4**	10.7	13.7
United Bankers' Bank	Bloomington	MN	**B-**	B-	B-	995.7	17.66	6.3	0.5	1.0	2.6	**9.6**	12.1	14.7
▼ United Business Bank	Walnut Creek	CA	**B+**	A-	B+	2167.5	46.28	8.0	0.3	8.6	5.7	**7.8**	10.1	13.1
United Citizens Bank & Trust Co.	Campbellsburg	KY	**B+**	B+	B	115.1	2.98	1.7	1.6	23.3	12.9	**10.0**	12.8	21.7
United Citizens Bank of Southern Kentucky	Columbia	KY	**A-**	A-	B+	173.3	7.62	9.9	5.7	32.2	7.0	**10.0**	11.9	16.6
United Community Bank	Blairsville	GA	**A-**	A-	A-	13058.5	4.64	15.3	1.0	11.1	19.5	**9.2**	10.8	14.3
United Community Bank	Milford	IA	**B**	B	B-	214.0	-3.87	8.2	1.3	11.8	1.5	**6.4**	9.6	12.1
▲ United Community Bank	Chatham	IL	**B**	B-	B	2691.1	30.74	10.8	1.7	9.2	26.1	**7.3**	9.2	14.2
United Community Bank	Raceland	LA	**C+**	C+	C-	543.8	-1.00	19.9	0.6	10.8	3.9	**9.8**	14.7	0.0
United Community Bank	Perham	MN	**B+**	B+	B	260.6	6.68	13.8	3.4	10.0	27.3	**9.8**	11.5	0.0
United Community Bank of North Dakota	Leeds	ND	**B**	B	B-	350.7	-5.78	15.2	1.4	4.3	18.1	**8.8**	10.2	14.4
United Community Bank of W Kentucky	Morganfield	KY	**A**	A	A-	280.7	6.55	10.1	5.6	17.4	25.4	**10.0**	12.9	19.2
United Cumberland Bank	Whitley City	KY	**B-**	B-	C+	310.0	4.29	7.6	10.8	27.0	19.2	**9.8**	13.4	0.0
United Farmers State Bank	Adams	MN	**B**	B	B+	154.2	2.53	6.2	1.0	3.8	3.4	**8.4**	12.0	13.7
United Fidelity Bank, FSB	Evansville	IN	**B+**	B+	B+	1035.3	23.23	0.8	0.1	9.7	60.2	**6.8**	8.8	23.8
United Midwest Savings Bank, N.A.	De Graff	OH	**C-**	C-	D+	292.4	-1.31	23.7	16.7	11.8	0.1	**9.7**	10.8	17.1
▼ United Minnesota Bank	New London	MN	**C-**	C	D+	33.5	9.53	14.4	9.5	27.6	3.9	**5.0**	7.0	11.0
United Mississippi Bank	Natchez	MS	**C+**	C+	C+	354.2	-4.44	10.1	3.4	13.3	17.8	**7.6**	10.7	13.0
▼ United National Bank	Cairo	GA	**B-**	B	B	214.4	-1.40	13.7	4.0	15.4	5.3	**10.0**	15.4	20.1
▼ United Orient Bank	New York	NY	**B-**	B	B	79.6	-11.95	1.4	0.0	21.8	2.5	**9.8**	17.0	0.0
United Pacific Bank	City of Industry	CA	**B**	B	B	156.9	13.34	2.0	0.0	0.3	0.8	**10.0**	16.2	22.1
United Prairie Bank	Mountain Lake	MN	**C+**	C+	C+	650.4	9.79	12.2	0.6	4.9	11.4	**5.2**	9.7	11.1
United Republic Bank	Elkhorn	NE	**D+**	D+	C-	135.0	3.97	10.3	0.3	11.9	12.4	**9.8**	11.1	0.0
United Roosevelt Savings Bank	Carteret	NJ	**C-**	C-	D+	144.0	6.07	9.9	0.1	51.8	6.7	**10.0**	11.2	18.5
United Savings Bank	Philadelphia	PA	**B-**	B-	B-	364.7	3.55	0.2	0.0	28.8	22.1	**9.8**	17.2	0.0
United Security Bank	Fresno	CA	**B+**	B+	B+	977.0	1.30	7.0	6.9	4.8	9.6	**10.0**	12.8	17.2
United Security Bank	Auxvasse	MO	**B+**	B+	B+	61.1	-0.19	7.2	6.7	35.1	24.9	**10.0**	13.8	20.5
United Southern Bank	Umatilla	FL	**B**	B	B-	568.6	7.40	2.5	1.2	12.8	31.5	**8.2**	10.0	0.0
United Southern Bank	Hopkinsville	KY	**B+**	B+	B-	226.1	2.79	6.2	2.7	22.9	14.7	**9.8**	12.1	0.0
United Southwest Bank	Cottonwood	MN	**C**	C	C-	47.8	4.48	2.6	1.8	0.4	29.1	**6.3**	8.3	17.0
United State Bank	Lewistown	MO	**B**	B	B-	180.3	-1.52	5.8	1.4	7.6	7.5	**7.1**	9.9	12.6
United Texas Bank	Dallas	TX	**B-**	B-	B-	667.2	36.92	16.8	0.2	7.9	32.1	**3.9**	8.8	10.5
United Trust Bank	Palos Heights	IL	**E+**	E+	E	27.1	4.75	0.3	0.5	26.8	0.3	**7.1**	9.1	14.7
▲ United Valley Bank	Cavalier	ND	**B**	B-	B-	362.6	0.69	13.5	2.8	7.9	15.0	**7.8**	9.5	13.3
Unity Bank	Clinton	NJ	**A-**	A-	B+	1733.6	9.44	4.9	0.1	28.4	3.3	**8.5**	10.2	0.0
Unity Bank	Augusta	WI	**D+**	D+	C-	526.2	6.82	7.6	2.4	13.2	6.0	**6.8**	8.8	12.4
Unity National Bank of Houston	Houston	TX	**D-**	D-	D-	107.9	12.53	14.7	0.5	14.5	6.6	**6.7**	8.7	12.7
Universal Bank	West Covina	CA	**C+**	C+	B	388.6	-3.29	0.6	0.0	4.2	2.6	**9.8**	15.5	0.0
University Bank	Ann Arbor	MI	**B+**	B+	B+	391.7	46.76	1.1	0.1	52.1	2.7	**9.1**	10.6	0.0
University National Bank of Lawrence	Lawrence	KS	**B**	B	C+	79.9	-2.78	4.8	0.7	44.5	2.6	**8.0**	9.7	15.4
Univest Bank and Trust Co.	Souderton	PA	**B**	B	B	5444.0	8.55	15.2	0.5	15.0	7.9	**6.2**	9.9	11.9
Upper Peninsula State Bank	Escanaba	MI	**A-**	A-	A-	223.1	9.99	5.1	5.0	15.4	15.7	**9.8**	16.5	0.0
Upstate National Bank	Rochester	NY	**C**	C	C+	168.2	22.52	4.0	0.1	30.5	9.4	**7.1**	9.0	13.1
US Metro Bank	Garden Grove	CA	**A-**	A-	B+	588.8	30.62	10.7	0.0	0.7	0.0	**10.0**	11.7	15.9
▲ USAA Federal Savings Bank	San Antonio	TX	**B-**	C+	C+	95337.6	10.07	0.0	43.6	3.2	34.0	**7.6**	9.4	17.0
USAA Savings Bank	Las Vegas	NV	**U**	U	U	1792.9	1.66	0.0	0.0	0.0	16.2	**10.0**	18.8	139.1
USNY Bank	Geneva	NY	**B-**	B-	B-	443.8	4.46	13.9	0.8	10.7	4.8	**7.3**	10.6	12.8
Utah Independent Bank	Salina	UT	**A-**	A-	B+	89.4	7.82	18.0	5.5	12.7	13.6	**9.8**	15.6	0.0

Asset Quality Index	Adjusted Non-Performing Loans as a % of Total Loans	Adjusted Non-Performing Loans as a % of Capital	Net Charge-Offs Avg Loans	Profitability Index	Net Income ($Mil)	Return on Assets (R.O.A.)	Return on Equity (R.O.E.)	Net Interest Spread	Overhead Efficiency Ratio	Liquidity Index	Liquidity Ratio	Hot Money Ratio	Stability Index
7.4	0.57	na	0.00	**6.9**	1.1	1.28	12.07	3.96	58.6	**1.6**	19.7	17.2	**7.8**
6.0	0.77	na	0.00	**6.8**	2.3	1.29	13.31	3.95	61.9	**3.9**	27.4	10.9	**6.9**
6.6	1.33	na	-0.08	**4.3**	0.5	0.95	7.88	3.78	78.0	**0.8**	13.4	29.7	**8.1**
7.1	1.15	na	0.00	**9.6**	8.9	2.40	22.88	3.77	54.2	**6.4**	40.8	4.5	**10.0**
4.6	0.87	3.5	0.19	**5.4**	43.2	0.88	4.93	3.33	55.3	**3.3**	9.7	11.7	**9.8**
8.0	0.12	na	0.00	**6.3**	2.0	1.22	9.78	3.47	54.6	**2.1**	19.8	17.1	**8.8**
5.4	2.89	15.5	-0.01	**4.2**	0.2	0.81	7.95	3.07	67.2	**5.1**	38.1	8.5	**6.8**
8.6	0.32	na	-0.02	**6.1**	0.6	1.43	9.41	3.40	54.2	**4.7**	48.4	13.6	**9.3**
4.1	0.69	na	1.28	**5.8**	0.6	1.03	8.41	5.22	64.3	**2.6**	15.6	14.7	**7.3**
5.3	0.86	4.3	0.10	**6.7**	6.8	1.55	13.95	3.16	55.5	**1.9**	24.2	26.8	**10.0**
6.4	0.74	na	0.01	**4.6**	1.4	0.81	7.92	3.72	73.8	**4.1**	12.8	7.8	**7.0**
0.0	13.28	na	-0.04	**0.0**	-0.2	-2.04	-33.03	4.48	134.7	**4.9**	28.5	5.8	**0.0**
3.6	2.75	na	0.02	**6.1**	1.4	1.45	13.28	3.65	63.0	**2.2**	12.2	17.7	**7.6**
7.8	0.24	0.9	0.08	**3.6**	1.6	0.74	6.11	2.84	72.9	**2.1**	36.9	1.0	**7.0**
6.0	0.56	na	0.00	**4.5**	3.0	0.58	4.65	4.28	73.7	**3.4**	21.7	13.8	**8.9**
5.5	1.44	na	0.03	**5.7**	0.3	1.18	9.29	4.03	66.8	**4.4**	29.5	9.3	**7.9**
7.6	0.58	na	0.31	**7.9**	0.7	1.63	13.54	4.17	54.1	**1.0**	12.4	31.9	**8.1**
6.6	0.90	3.1	0.37	**6.7**	37.1	1.15	8.43	4.13	54.7	**4.2**	22.7	9.0	**10.0**
6.4	1.25	na	0.00	**5.6**	0.6	1.17	10.56	4.26	70.7	**3.3**	7.6	11.9	**8.2**
4.7	1.71	9.1	0.05	**4.9**	6.2	0.93	9.25	3.12	62.7	**4.0**	20.8	7.7	**8.3**
3.0	2.82	12.7	-0.01	**5.7**	2.0	1.46	9.81	4.57	63.4	**3.1**	19.9	14.1	**7.8**
6.1	1.05	na	0.00	**4.1**	0.5	0.81	6.89	3.72	78.6	**3.2**	31.2	16.2	**7.5**
7.0	0.75	2.4	-0.01	**5.5**	1.2	1.38	12.52	4.30	54.2	**3.5**	17.4	12.0	**6.6**
8.3	0.31	na	0.00	**8.0**	1.1	1.54	11.30	3.93	55.3	**2.4**	19.1	13.3	**9.1**
4.0	2.95	na	0.19	**8.2**	1.7	2.19	16.49	4.50	57.2	**1.9**	22.0	20.8	**8.9**
4.2	0.71	na	0.02	**8.3**	0.7	1.90	16.11	3.97	50.5	**3.2**	11.6	11.5	**9.3**
7.8	2.89	4.1	-0.05	**2.7**	-1.0	-0.38	-3.11	2.23	130.3	**5.9**	44.9	8.8	**9.5**
2.3	3.38	na	1.61	**7.2**	0.7	0.89	7.70	4.29	74.7	**1.0**	26.2	47.8	**7.2**
8.0	0.05	na	0.00	**3.5**	0.1	0.59	8.33	4.30	85.5	**4.4**	22.0	6.8	**3.3**
3.9	2.16	na	0.08	**3.9**	0.8	0.88	7.98	4.27	82.5	**2.9**	15.4	14.5	**6.5**
3.3	4.07	na	0.01	**8.2**	0.8	1.46	9.54	4.56	55.8	**1.2**	4.4	23.1	**8.5**
7.7	0.00	0.0	0.00	**2.7**	0.0	-0.06	-0.38	5.51	100.6	**2.4**	20.5	17.6	**7.2**
7.3	0.03	na	0.00	**3.5**	0.2	0.48	2.99	3.20	78.9	**1.4**	31.9	48.2	**7.9**
4.3	1.26	na	0.01	**6.4**	2.8	1.81	16.69	4.50	64.5	**1.5**	11.4	16.3	**8.1**
6.4	0.00	na	0.00	**3.1**	0.2	0.59	4.13	3.40	69.6	**0.7**	16.6	44.5	**2.7**
8.7	0.38	2.8	0.00	**1.5**	0.0	0.11	1.08	2.62	86.5	**2.0**	10.8	18.8	**4.9**
10.0	0.00	na	0.00	**3.6**	0.6	0.63	3.57	2.66	67.2	**3.1**	42.9	20.2	**8.0**
4.5	2.24	na	0.33	**7.1**	1.8	0.77	5.90	4.00	55.3	**4.9**	27.7	5.5	**9.5**
8.5	0.00	na	-0.01	**5.1**	0.2	1.29	9.06	4.07	68.1	**2.8**	21.4	15.6	**8.3**
5.3	1.83	na	0.01	**5.1**	1.3	0.90	8.80	3.93	70.2	**6.4**	43.1	1.7	**7.5**
4.7	1.99	na	0.00	**5.3**	0.6	1.01	8.23	4.08	71.9	**2.6**	23.1	16.9	**7.1**
6.5	0.68	na	0.00	**2.5**	0.0	0.33	3.87	3.17	87.7	**6.5**	56.9	3.5	**3.9**
3.7	0.23	8.9	-0.03	**6.6**	0.7	1.47	14.86	3.95	56.5	**2.1**	15.5	17.2	**7.2**
8.7	0.00	0.0	0.00	**4.1**	1.6	0.97	11.35	2.56	53.4	**1.8**	39.5	52.0	**5.5**
4.2	2.22	na	0.09	**0.0**	-0.3	-4.22	-43.86	4.14	210.0	**1.2**	22.6	31.5	**3.2**
5.3	1.02	na	-0.18	**4.6**	0.7	0.82	7.31	4.05	76.0	**3.3**	10.3	11.9	**7.3**
6.0	0.72	na	0.15	**7.1**	5.5	1.34	13.29	3.98	53.6	**1.4**	14.6	15.2	**8.7**
1.8	2.12	na	0.15	**4.9**	1.8	1.37	15.48	4.00	66.1	**1.1**	10.9	23.2	**6.1**
1.3	2.17	na	0.00	**0.2**	-0.1	-0.27	-2.89	3.67	106.7	**0.6**	14.3	50.0	**4.0**
6.9	0.69	na	-0.07	**2.7**	0.1	0.11	0.73	3.16	96.4	**0.8**	15.0	34.8	**7.9**
5.8	1.15	2.9	-0.08	**3.7**	-0.3	-0.69	-6.72	4.62	101.1	**5.3**	19.6	0.4	**5.9**
6.0	0.76	na	-0.04	**4.3**	0.2	0.92	9.15	4.10	78.6	**3.3**	14.0	12.4	**6.3**
5.0	0.82	5.2	0.04	**4.1**	2.0	0.15	1.20	3.58	63.9	**3.4**	5.0	7.3	**9.7**
6.5	0.72	2.7	-0.01	**6.6**	0.7	1.25	7.95	3.73	54.6	**2.5**	32.9	11.0	**8.9**
7.7	0.00	na	0.00	**2.7**	0.4	0.88	8.16	2.96	70.3	**0.4**	15.3	74.4	**6.7**
7.2	0.22	na	0.00	**5.2**	1.0	0.72	6.49	3.67	68.3	**1.4**	30.9	37.6	**9.3**
4.7	1.86	4.5	1.73	**4.1**	147.9	0.67	6.59	4.87	70.0	**5.4**	55.6	4.3	**7.0**
10.0	na	0.0	0.00	**9.5**	56.3	13.90	73.76	1.22	70.3	**3.8**	104.6	56.7	**7.0**
3.7	2.13	na	0.47	**4.7**	0.3	0.30	2.84	3.66	64.0	**0.6**	10.4	39.3	**6.8**
5.6	0.49	na	0.08	**9.9**	0.5	2.21	14.42	5.47	59.9	**5.1**	32.4	6.0	**9.7**

Name	City	State	Rating	2019 Rating	2018 Rating	Total Assets ($Mil)	One Year Asset Growth	Asset Mix (As a % of Total Assets) Commercial Loans	Consumer Loans	Mortgage Loans	Securities	Capitalization Index	Leverage Ratio	Risk-Based Capital Ratio
▼ Uwharrie Bank	Albemarle	NC	C	C+	C+	670.9	2.78	6.2	1.8	11.3	18.5	6.4	8.4	13.0
Valley Bank of Commerce	Roswell	NM	A	A	A-	197.1	9.69	19.0	0.5	5.3	0.1	7.8	9.5	21.2
Valley Bank of Kalispell	Kalispell	MT	B	B	C+	126.6	5.04	15.9	5.1	19.8	14.7	8.3	10.1	0.0
▲ Valley Bank of Nevada	North Las Vegas	NV	C-	D+	D	154.0	16.24	10.1	0.3	1.1	2.6	6.5	8.5	13.4
Valley Bank of Ronan	Ronan	MT	D+	D+	C+	107.2	3.10	14.8	5.0	12.4	5.6	9.5	10.7	18.6
Valley Central Bank	Liberty Township	OH	C-	C-	C	156.2	36.68	2.8	0.5	51.5	3.0	9.8	23.5	0.0
Valley Exchange Bank	Lennox	SD	B	B	B	61.8	-6.87	4.5	1.3	0.2	9.0	10.0	12.1	33.8
Valley National Bank	Wayne	NJ	C+	C+	B-	39109.2	20.50	11.3	5.7	11.6	10.6	5.7	8.8	11.5
Valley Premier Bank	Hawley	MN	B	B	B	108.7	1.34	13.4	3.6	11.9	32.1	8.7	10.3	0.0
Valley Republic Bank	Bakersfield	CA	B+	B+	B-	955.0	16.39	11.8	0.1	4.0	15.8	8.0	10.6	13.4
Valley State Bank	Russellville	AL	B	B	B	123.9	-1.05	7.6	2.9	21.4	33.0	9.8	17.8	0.0
Valley State Bank	Belle Plaine	KS	B	B	B	139.8	7.32	7.4	10.2	16.9	19.9	9.8	13.3	0.0
Valley State Bank	Syracuse	KS	B-	B-	B-	166.5	8.13	8.4	4.8	13.2	9.5	5.9	9.2	11.7
Valliance Bank	Oklahoma City	OK	C	C	C	455.3	3.08	20.2	0.3	11.8	3.9	8.7	10.3	0.0
▲ Valor Bank	Edmond	OK	B+	B	B	100.8	19.13	2.6	0.1	50.7	0.0	6.9	8.9	12.9
ValueBank Texas	Corpus Christi	TX	A	A	B+	245.6	1.50	4.0	0.5	12.8	15.8	9.8	11.4	0.0
▼ Van Wert Federal Savings Bank	Van Wert	OH	C	C+	C+	116.8	2.67	0.3	0.7	47.4	11.2	9.8	21.1	0.0
Vanguard National Trust Co., N.A.	Malvern	PA	U	U	U	97.0	0.45	0.0	0.0	0.0	0.0	10.0	79.4	193.1
Vantage Bank	Alexandria	MN	C-	C-	D+	32.6	15.15	9.1	6.9	31.8	0.0	4.9	8.5	10.9
Vantage Bank Texas	San Antonio	TX	B	B		2265.2	18.58	11.4	0.4	4.9	5.6	9.5	12.9	14.6
▼ Vast Bank, N.A.	Tulsa	OK	C+	B-	B-	681.2	0.11	22.9	1.6	10.5	2.4	6.5	10.2	12.2
VCC Bank	Richmond	VA	D	D	D	209.3	1.23	13.0	0.0	9.5	11.7	8.9	10.4	0.0
▲ VeraBank, N.A.	Henderson	TX	B+	B	B	2496.0	7.40	7.8	3.5	15.9	28.0	7.0	9.0	14.6
▼ Vergas State Bank	Vergas	MN	C+	B-	B-	50.5	6.51	3.4	2.5	9.8	11.8	9.8	15.1	0.0
Veritex Community Bank	Dallas	TX	B	B	B	8528.4	7.55	19.3	0.2	6.0	13.1	9.5	10.8	0.0
Vermilion Bank & Trust Co.	Kaplan	LA	B-	B-	C+	116.6	3.24	6.6	4.5	19.5	19.7	9.0	10.4	18.6
▲ Vermilion Valley Bank	Piper City	IL	A	A-	B+	136.2	9.35	3.4	1.2	10.1	22.1	10.0	16.3	24.8
Vermillion State Bank	Vermillion	MN	A+	A+	A+	615.0	9.81	14.9	1.4	12.0	39.1	9.8	16.3	0.0
Vermont State Bank	Vermont	IL	D	D	D	29.6	5.31	7.2	20.4	31.8	9.2	10.0	12.0	17.9
Versailles S&L Co.	Versailles	OH	B	B	B-	56.3	2.47	1.7	2.0	56.6	0.1	9.8	21.1	0.0
Verus Bank of Commerce	Fort Collins	CO	A-	A-	B+	272.5	1.53	2.8	0.0	9.4	0.0	9.8	12.5	0.0
Victor State Bank	Victor	IA	A-	A-	A-	33.2	-7.06	9.9	1.9	8.2	53.0	9.8	13.9	0.0
Victory Bank	Limerick	PA	B-	B-	C	290.8	11.26	13.2	3.4	12.3	3.7	5.9	9.5	11.7
▼ Victory State Bank	Staten Island	NY	B-	B	B	364.0	-9.11	5.7	0.1	5.2	38.6	9.3	10.5	20.8
Vidalia Federal Savings Bank	Vidalia	GA	C+	C+	B-	199.8	-3.66	0.0	1.9	27.3	44.6	9.8	16.2	0.0
Viking Bank	Alexandria	MN	B	B	B-	214.6	23.59	12.7	2.2	19.1	3.5	8.4	10.1	0.0
Villa Grove State Bank	Villa Grove	IL	B+	B+	B+	74.5	3.63	7.8	2.6	43.8	12.4	10.0	11.4	22.2
Village Bank	Saint Libory	IL	B	B	B-	90.2	1.96	5.8	6.9	22.5	20.0	7.8	9.7	0.0
Village Bank	Auburndale	MA	B	B	B	1353.5	10.70	3.2	0.3	41.6	12.3	9.3	10.7	0.0
Village Bank	Saint Francis	MN	C+	C+	C	305.9	5.44	13.5	1.0	9.0	18.5	7.5	9.3	14.5
▲ Village Bank	Midlothian	VA	C+	C	C-	567.5	9.14	8.1	6.2	15.1	6.9	7.1	10.1	12.6
Village Bank & Trust, N.A.	Arlington Heights	IL	B	B	B	1937.3	24.14	41.6	11.5	3.3	14.1	5.4	8.9	11.3
Vinings Bank	Smyrna	GA	C+	C+	B-	432.7	31.46	4.6	0.1	0.9	50.9	6.3	8.3	12.2
Vintage Bank Kansas	Leon	KS	B	B	B	151.3	13.42	6.6	2.7	14.1	21.8	8.1	9.9	0.0
Vinton County National Bank	McArthur	OH	B	B	B	1051.4	7.04	3.6	18.0	29.0	14.4	10.0	11.0	16.5
Virginia Bank and Trust Co.	Danville	VA	B	B	B+	217.9	8.22	12.5	8.1	21.9	16.6	10.0	12.0	19.1
Virginia Commonwealth Bank	Richmond	VA	C+	C+	C+	1178.9	7.28	14.8	0.8	25.9	8.0	8.0	10.7	13.3
Virginia National Bank	Charlottesville	VA	A-	A-	B-	717.4	12.96	11.1	9.5	14.1	14.2	8.8	10.5	14.0
Virginia Partners Bank	Fredericksburg	VA	C+	C+	C+	467.9	8.82	11.1	0.7	18.6	10.0	7.1	10.5	12.5
Vision Bank, N.A.	Ada	OK	B-	B-	B-	725.6	7.20	5.9	6.2	23.2	22.5	7.1	9.2	0.0
VisionBank	Topeka	KS	C+	C+	B-	195.9	7.55	23.0	2.3	19.4	1.8	4.3	8.5	10.7
VisionBank	Saint Louis Park	MN	A-	A-	B+	114.3	29.78	21.8	0.5	16.7	0.0	8.0	9.8	13.3
VISIONBank	Fargo	ND	D	D	D	192.8	-0.71	25.0	5.0	20.2	0.0	7.7	10.0	13.1
▼ VisionBank of Iowa	Ames	IA	B-	B	B-	532.4	7.80	5.4	0.1	10.9	1.2	7.4	10.3	12.8
VIST Bank	Wyomissing	PA	B+	B+	B	1704.6	-0.18	7.4	0.2	20.0	15.0	7.1	9.1	12.6
▼ Vista Bank	Dallas	TX	C+	B-	B+	905.1	7.68	16.4	0.6	10.4	2.8	7.0	9.1	12.5
Volunteer Federal Savings Bank	Madisonville	TN	B	B	B-	217.4	3.43	0.6	4.5	44.8	8.1	10.0	13.9	27.8
Volunteer State Bank	Portland	TN	B	B	B	772.1	-0.70	8.0	0.6	11.2	1.4	7.6	10.2	13.0
Wabash Savings Bank	Mount Carmel	IL	D-	D-	D-	8.9	-0.95	1.5	8.1	30.8	9.4	10.0	13.1	28.1
Wadena State Bank	Wadena	MN	B+	B+	A-	175.6	0.47	11.6	3.2	15.5	23.3	8.3	10.0	0.0

Asset Quality Index	Adjusted Non-Performing Loans as a % of Total Loans	Adjusted Non-Performing Loans as a % of Capital	Net Charge-Offs Avg Loans	Profitability Index	Net Income ($Mil)	Return on Assets (R.O.A.)	Return on Equity (R.O.E.)	Net Interest Spread	Overhead Efficiency Ratio	Liquidity Index	Liquidity Ratio	Hot Money Ratio	Stability Index
4.8	2.93	12.6	-0.02	**2.4**	0.4	0.21	2.46	3.29	86.8	**5.1**	32.8	6.0	**5.6**
6.8	0.66	na	0.00	**9.4**	1.1	2.33	23.82	3.93	42.3	**6.5**	59.2	6.6	**7.7**
4.8	1.12	na	1.42	**7.7**	0.5	1.38	13.30	5.18	60.8	**1.5**	17.0	25.0	**7.4**
3.6	3.40	9.6	0.10	**2.3**	0.0	-0.01	-0.11	3.56	93.0	**5.4**	37.9	6.7	**5.6**
1.7	7.43	na	-0.04	**4.5**	0.2	0.65	5.93	4.82	81.2	**5.9**	40.1	4.1	**6.8**
8.9	0.35	na	0.00	**2.7**	0.3	0.82	3.47	3.99	76.9	**1.7**	7.0	7.1	**6.9**
9.1	0.00	na	0.04	**3.5**	0.1	0.40	3.27	2.87	80.5	**6.9**	74.2	4.8	**6.1**
3.4	0.95	5.2	0.06	**4.9**	89.9	0.94	7.83	3.08	50.0	**1.4**	9.1	13.7	**9.6**
6.5	0.36	na	-0.01	**4.0**	0.3	0.95	9.19	3.43	77.7	**5.4**	41.1	7.7	**6.6**
8.6	0.00	na	0.00	**5.6**	2.5	1.08	10.27	3.43	52.0	**4.4**	24.2	7.1	**6.9**
8.9	0.20	na	-0.02	**4.7**	0.5	1.39	7.89	3.25	64.1	**1.9**	35.6	31.8	**8.0**
6.0	0.66	na	0.11	**5.1**	0.3	0.99	7.45	4.20	65.3	**1.7**	19.0	20.7	**7.3**
6.9	0.06	4.4	0.00	**6.0**	0.5	1.15	12.26	3.79	65.4	**0.9**	22.4	40.9	**6.7**
4.5	0.53	na	-0.01	**3.5**	0.7	0.65	6.67	3.98	77.3	**0.6**	11.2	37.6	**5.6**
9.1	0.00	na	0.00	**7.4**	0.3	1.34	15.18	3.63	74.2	**0.5**	7.2	45.0	**6.4**
9.0	0.00	na	0.01	**6.9**	0.8	1.26	11.19	4.35	72.3	**5.4**	40.6	7.9	**7.5**
9.8	0.01	na	0.00	**2.6**	0.1	0.28	1.34	2.56	87.1	**3.2**	42.9	20.0	**7.6**
10.0	na	na	na	**7.5**	0.2	1.02	1.29	1.95	98.6	**4.0**	277.3	0.0	**7.0**
8.0	0.00	na	0.00	**3.8**	0.1	0.79	8.47	3.86	80.3	**1.7**	3.8	19.5	**3.7**
5.0	0.78	na	0.02	**6.3**	6.3	1.19	8.93	4.18	68.3	**1.7**	20.3	25.0	**9.5**
5.5	0.82	5.5	0.01	**3.0**	0.4	0.23	2.29	3.30	77.8	**0.7**	15.6	47.5	**6.5**
0.8	3.98	na	0.00	**1.7**	-0.7	-1.36	-12.24	2.69	71.4	**0.5**	13.5	68.4	**5.8**
6.2	0.76	3.9	0.12	**6.2**	10.3	1.69	15.75	3.91	55.1	**5.5**	28.8	5.9	**8.4**
8.1	0.08	0.2	0.00	**2.5**	0.0	0.27	1.78	2.26	86.0	**3.7**	65.2	22.0	**7.3**
3.9	0.65	7.4	-0.02	**4.8**	6.0	0.29	1.85	3.77	50.5	**1.3**	14.8	21.8	**9.9**
4.6	2.83	na	-0.17	**5.9**	0.4	1.43	13.67	4.03	63.6	**2.3**	27.0	19.3	**6.7**
7.3	0.06	na	0.08	**7.9**	0.6	1.87	11.28	3.29	42.2	**1.8**	17.7	20.6	**10.0**
6.9	0.90	2.5	-0.01	**9.5**	3.5	2.33	14.12	3.34	32.2	**5.7**	52.2	9.7	**10.0**
0.0	8.72	na	0.81	**1.0**	0.0	0.32	2.58	2.82	105.6	**0.6**	17.4	51.1	**3.3**
9.4	0.00	na	0.00	**4.2**	0.1	0.78	3.72	3.40	69.6	**2.7**	26.0	16.7	**7.6**
7.3	0.00	na	0.00	**7.2**	0.5	0.66	5.23	4.24	58.3	**1.1**	10.9	12.4	**9.7**
3.1	2.30	na	0.02	**3.6**	0.1	0.75	3.80	3.24	55.0	**3.9**	67.6	19.2	**7.7**
7.0	0.12	na	0.00	**3.9**	0.3	0.45	4.77	4.24	68.3	**3.5**	12.7	11.1	**5.1**
6.4	0.92	8.2	0.02	**3.9**	0.6	0.67	6.41	3.44	73.9	**4.1**	44.2	15.5	**5.7**
7.5	0.95	na	0.00	**1.5**	0.0	-0.05	-0.34	2.02	102.5	**3.7**	78.2	31.6	**7.4**
4.4	0.20	na	0.00	**6.3**	0.9	1.55	10.38	3.56	53.3	**2.1**	16.1	18.7	**9.1**
9.1	0.09	na	0.03	**5.8**	0.3	1.36	12.07	3.51	61.0	**3.9**	22.4	10.1	**7.6**
6.5	0.18	na	0.00	**5.1**	0.3	1.40	14.73	3.45	60.6	**5.6**	37.3	4.6	**5.6**
8.9	0.40	2.5	0.00	**4.2**	2.6	0.78	7.24	3.16	68.2	**1.1**	19.2	33.7	**8.7**
6.6	1.63	na	-0.52	**6.1**	1.0	1.30	14.15	4.52	74.3	**4.3**	31.9	10.9	**6.7**
4.7	1.93	na	0.13	**4.2**	1.1	0.79	7.81	3.72	73.9	**2.4**	15.8	17.2	**6.9**
4.7	1.00	4.9	0.38	**4.7**	1.6	0.34	3.26	2.89	50.3	**1.5**	20.1	17.1	**7.9**
7.1	0.54	2.3	0.00	**3.0**	0.7	0.70	7.76	3.16	83.8	**5.3**	35.6	6.0	**4.9**
4.8	1.48	na	0.00	**4.9**	0.4	1.07	9.91	4.09	68.8	**3.6**	20.1	10.5	**7.2**
6.6	0.53	na	0.21	**4.5**	2.1	0.82	6.97	3.74	72.8	**2.4**	15.6	17.4	**9.2**
7.7	0.10	na	0.02	**4.8**	0.6	1.09	9.68	3.93	69.2	**5.0**	31.1	5.9	**6.9**
6.4	0.97	na	0.07	**2.9**	0.8	0.27	2.41	3.51	65.7	**1.0**	13.5	28.6	**7.9**
7.4	0.42	na	0.20	**5.1**	1.6	0.88	8.39	3.18	61.2	**3.6**	20.1	11.6	**6.8**
8.3	0.04	na	0.00	**3.1**	0.7	0.63	5.46	3.79	72.0	**0.7**	15.8	38.9	**6.2**
4.3	1.87	12.3	0.20	**4.8**	2.0	1.11	11.58	4.00	72.5	**1.7**	11.8	21.1	**6.5**
4.7	0.57	na	0.00	**4.4**	0.5	1.02	11.70	4.00	65.9	**1.1**	3.0	26.9	**4.1**
8.3	0.11	na	0.00	**7.3**	0.4	1.50	15.48	4.05	52.5	**0.7**	16.7	54.2	**7.0**
1.2	4.37	27.8	0.05	**3.0**	0.2	0.30	2.90	3.85	84.9	**1.6**	9.8	22.1	**5.9**
5.8	0.35	na	-0.08	**3.6**	0.7	0.53	5.15	2.94	67.4	**1.6**	14.5	11.5	**8.1**
6.2	0.69	3.6	-0.02	**2.7**	0.7	0.17	1.45	3.32	67.5	**4.0**	6.6	6.5	**7.7**
6.8	0.41	2.0	0.13	**2.9**	2.0	0.89	9.53	3.98	68.5	**1.6**	20.7	20.9	**5.7**
9.2	0.08	na	0.01	**4.3**	0.4	0.75	5.43	3.74	76.0	**3.8**	28.0	12.1	**7.7**
6.6	0.33	0.6	-0.02	**5.6**	2.4	1.29	7.20	4.46	66.6	**2.0**	24.7	18.6	**8.9**
5.4	0.62	na	0.00	**0.0**	0.0	-1.17	-8.81	2.98	137.9	**2.9**	57.9	25.6	**4.7**
6.3	2.40	na	0.26	**7.3**	0.8	1.74	15.55	4.30	58.3	**4.9**	37.4	9.6	**8.3**

Section II Contents

This section provides a list of Weiss Recommended Banks by State and contains all financial institutions receiving a Safety Rating of A+, A, A-, or B+. Recommended institutions are listed in each state in which they currently operate one or more branches. If a company is not on this list, it should not be automatically assumed that the firm is weak. Indeed, there are many firms that have not achieved a B+ or better rating but are in good condition with adequate resources to weather an average recession. Not being included in this list should not be construed as a recommendation to immediately withdraw deposits or cancel existing financial arrangements.

Institutions are ranked within each state by their Weiss Safety Rating, and then listed alphabetically by name. Institutions with the same rating should be viewed as having the same relative safety regardless of their ranking in this table.

- **State** The state in which the institution currently operates one or more branches. With the adoption of interstate branching laws, some institutions operating in your area may actually be headquartered in another state. Even so, there are no restrictions on your ability to do business with an out-of-state institution.

- **Institution Name** The name under which the institution was chartered. A bank's name can be very similar to, or the same as, the name of other banks which may not be on our Recommended List, so make sure you note the exact name.

- **Telephone** The telephone number for the institution's headquarters, or main office.

- **Safety Rating** Weiss rating assigned to the institution at the time of publication. Our ratings are designed to distinguish levels of insolvency risk and are measured on a scale from A to F based upon a wide range of factors. Highly rated companies are, in our opinion, less likely to experience financial difficulties than lower rated firms. See *About Weiss Safety Ratings* for more information and a description of what each rating means.

Weiss Safety Ratings are not deemed to be a recommendation concerning the purchase or sale of the securities of any bank that is publicly owned.

Alabama

Name	Telephone
Rating: A+	
First Bank of Boaz	(256) 593-8670
Rating: A	
Cheaha Bank	(256) 835-8855
Citizens Bank of Winfield	(205) 487-4277
First Metro Bank	(256) 386-0600
First National Bank	(205) 921-7435
Metro City Bank	(770) 455-4989
Rating: A-	
Armed Forces Bank, N.A.	(913) 682-9090
Bank of Vernon	(205) 695-7141
Bank OZK	(501) 978-2265
CCB Community Bank	(334) 222-2561
Centennial Bank	(501) 328-4663
Central State Bank	(205) 668-0711
Citizens Bank	(334) 624-8888
Citizens Bank & Trust, Inc.	(706) 657-5678
Cullman Savings Bank	(256) 734-1740
Farmers and Merchants Bank	(334) 864-9941
First Bank of Alabama	(256) 362-2334
First Citizens Bank	(334) 335-3346
First Jackson Bank, Inc.	(256) 437-2107
First National Bank of Pulaski	(931) 363-2585
HNB First Bank	(334) 693-3352
HomeTown Bank of Alabama	(205) 625-4434
Metro Bank	(205) 884-2265
Pinnacle Bank	(205) 221-4111
River Bank & Trust	(334) 290-1012
Robertson Banking Co.	(334) 289-3564
Samson Banking Co., Inc.	(334) 898-7107
ServisFirst Bank	(205) 949-0302
Town-Country National Bank	(334) 682-4155
West Alabama Bank & Trust	(205) 375-6261
Rating: B+	
Ameris Bank	(404) 814-8114
AuburnBank	(334) 821-9200
BancorpSouth Bank	(662) 680-2000
BankPlus	(662) 247-1811
BankSouth	(334) 677-2265
Brantley Bank and Trust Co.	(334) 527-3206
Bryant Bank	(205) 464-4646
Cadence Bank, N.A.	(800) 636-7622
Capital City Bank	(850) 402-7700
CenterState Bank, N.A.	(863) 291-3900
Citizens Bank of Fayette	(205) 932-8911
Citizens Trust Bank	(678) 406-4000
Community Neighbor Bank	(334) 682-4215
Exchange Bank of Alabama	(205) 589-6334
Farmers & Merchants Bank	(256) 766-2579
Farmers & Merchants Bank	(256) 447-9041
First Bank	(256) 395-2255
First Community Bank of Central Alabama	(334) 567-0081
First Southern State Bank	(256) 437-2171
First State Bank of the South, Inc.	(205) 698-8116
First, A National Banking Assn.	(601) 268-8998
FirstBank	(615) 313-0080
FirstState Bank	(256) 396-2187
Friend Bank	(334) 886-2367
JPMorgan Chase Bank, N.A.	(614) 248-5800
Merchants Bank of Alabama	(256) 734-8110
MidSouth Bank	(334) 702-7774
Oakworth Capital Bank	(205) 263-4700
Phenix-Girard Bank	(334) 298-0691
Renasant Bank	(800) 680-1601
Southern Independent Bank	(334) 493-2265
Synovus Bank	(706) 649-4900
Traditions Bank	(256) 735-2121
Troy Bank & Trust Co.	(334) 566-4000
Truist Bank	(336) 733-2000
Trustmark National Bank	(601) 208-5111
United Bank	(251) 446-6000
Woodforest National Bank	(832) 375-2505

Alaska

Name	Telephone
Rating: A	
First National Bank Alaska	(907) 777-4362
Rating: B+	
Mt. McKinley Bank	(907) 452-1751

Arizona

Name	Telephone
Rating: A	
Western Bank	(575) 542-3521
Rating: A-	
Academy Bank, N.A.	(816) 472-0081
Alerus Financial, N.A.	(701) 795-3369
Armed Forces Bank, N.A.	(913) 682-9090
Bank of Colorado	(970) 206-1160
BNC National Bank	(602) 508-3760
Comerica Bank	(214) 462-4000
First Savings Bank	(605) 763-2009
FirstBank	(303) 232-2000
Gateway Commercial Bank	(480) 358-1000
Glacier Bank	(406) 756-4200
Johnson Bank	(262) 619-2700
Meadows Bank	(702) 471-2265
Metro Phoenix Bank	(602) 346-1800
Pacific Premier Bank	(949) 864-8000
Stearns Bank N.A.	(320) 253-6607
Washington Federal Bank, N.A.	(206) 204-3446
Western Alliance Bank	(602) 389-3500
Zions BanCorp., N.A.	(801) 844-7637
Rating: B+	
1st Bank Yuma	(928) 783-3334
Arizona Bank & Trust	(602) 381-2090
Bank of America, N.A.	(704) 386-5681
Bell Bank	(701) 298-1500
CIT Bank, N.A.	(855) 462-2652
Enterprise Bank & Trust	(314) 725-5500
First National Bank Texas	(254) 554-4236
First-Citizens Bank & Trust Co.	(919) 716-7050
JPMorgan Chase Bank, N.A.	(614) 248-5800
KS StateBank	(785) 587-4000
Northern Trust Co.	(312) 630-6000
Sunwest Bank	(714) 730-4444
TrustBank	(618) 395-4311
Unison Bank	(701) 253-5600

Arkansas

Name	Telephone
Rating: A+	
First Security Bank	(501) 279-3400
Rating: A	
First National Bank of Izard County	(870) 297-3711
FSNB, N.A.	(580) 357-9880
Peoples Bank	(870) 942-5707
Rating: A-	
Bank of Delight	(870) 379-2293
Bank of Lake Village	(870) 265-2241
Bank OZK	(501) 978-2265
Centennial Bank	(501) 328-4663
Citizens Bank & Trust Co.	(479) 474-1201
Fidelity Bank	(870) 735-8700
First National Bank of Fort Smith	(479) 788-4600
First State Bank	(479) 498-2400
Great Southern Bank	(417) 895-5234
McGehee Bank	(870) 222-3151
Petit Jean State Bank	(501) 354-4988
Premier Bank of Arkansas	(870) 739-7300
Union Bank of Mena	(479) 394-2211
Rating: B+	
Arkansas County Bank	(870) 946-3551
BancorpSouth Bank	(662) 680-2000
Bank of America, N.A.	(704) 386-5681
Bank of Bearden	(870) 687-2233
Bank of England	(501) 842-2555
Bank of Salem	(870) 895-2591
Commercial National Bank of Texarkana	(903) 831-4561
Connect Bank	(870) 628-4286
Cross County Bank	(870) 238-8171
Farmers & Merchants Bank	(870) 673-6911
Farmers Bank	(479) 996-4171
FBT Bank & Mortgage	(870) 352-3107
First Financial Bank	(870) 863-7000
First Missouri Bank of SEMO	(573) 717-7177
First National Bank	(870) 215-4000
First National Bank at Paris	(479) 963-2121
First National Bank of Eastern Arkansas	(870) 633-3112
First National Bank of Lawrence County	(870) 886-5959
First National Bank Texas	(254) 554-4236
Focus Bank	(573) 683-3712
Grand Savings Bank	(918) 786-2203
Logan County Bank	(479) 938-2511
Relyance Bank, N.A.	(870) 535-7222
Security Bank	(870) 786-5416
Simmons Bank	(870) 541-1000
Southern Bank	(573) 778-1800
Truist Bank	(336) 733-2000
United Bank	(479) 756-8811

California

Name	Telephone
Rating: A	
Bank of Hemet	(951) 248-2000
California First National Bank	(800) 735-2465
Central Valley Community Bank	(559) 298-1775
Exchange Bank	(707) 524-3000
First General Bank	(626) 820-1234
Home Bank of California	(858) 270-5881
Pacific City Bank	(213) 210-2000
Poppy Bank	(707) 636-9000
Royal Business Bank	(213) 627-9888
Santa Cruz County Bank	(831) 457-5000
Savings Bank of Mendocino County	(707) 462-6613
Sterling Bank and Trust, FSB	(248) 355-2400
Tri Counties Bank	(530) 898-0300
Rating: A-	
American Continental Bank	(626) 363-8988
American First National Bank	(713) 596-2888
American Plus Bank, N.A.	(626) 821-9188
Armed Forces Bank, N.A.	(913) 682-9090
Axos Bank	(858) 350-6200
Bank of America California, N.A.	(925) 988-4801
Bank of Feather River	(530) 755-3700
Bank of Marin	(415) 763-4520
Bank of San Francisco	(415) 744-6700
Bank of Stockton	(209) 929-1600
Bank of the Sierra	(559) 782-4900
Cathay Bank	(213) 625-4791
Chino Commercial Bank, N.A.	(909) 393-8880
Citizens Business Bank	(909) 980-4030
Comerica Bank	(214) 462-4000
Commonwealth Business Bank	(323) 988-3000
Community Bank of Santa Maria	(805) 922-2900
CTBC Bank Corp. (USA)	(424) 277-4612
East West Bank	(626) 768-6000
Farmers & Merchants Bank	(209) 367-2300
First Commercial Bank (USA)	(626) 300-6000
FirstBank	(303) 232-2000
Fresno First Bank	(559) 439-0200
Golden Bank, N.A.	(713) 777-3838
Heritage Bank of Commerce	(408) 947-6900
Malaga Bank F.S.B.	(310) 375-9000
Mission Bank	(661) 859-2500
Mission Valley Bank	(818) 394-2300
New OMNI Bank, N.A.	(626) 284-5555
Open Bank	(213) 892-9999
Pacific Coast Bankers' Bank	(415) 399-1900
Pacific Premier Bank	(949) 864-8000
Pinnacle Bank	(408) 842-8200
Preferred Bank	(213) 891-1188
Silicon Valley Bank	(408) 654-7400
Silvergate Bank	(858) 362-6300
Summit Bank	(510) 839-8800
US Metro Bank	(714) 620-8888
Western Alliance Bank	(602) 389-3500
Zions BanCorp., N.A.	(801) 844-7637
Rating: B+	
1st Capital Bank	(831) 264-4000
Avidbank	(408) 200-7390
Bank of America, N.A.	(704) 386-5681
Bank of Santa Clarita	(661) 362-6000
Banner Bank	(509) 527-3636
C3bank, N.A.	(760) 759-1130
California Pacific Bank	(415) 399-8000
CIT Bank, N.A.	(855) 462-2652
Citibank, N.A.	(605) 370-6261
City National Bank	(800) 773-7100
CommerceWest Bank	(949) 251-6959
Community Commerce Bank	(909) 450-2050
Community Valley Bank	(760) 352-7777
EverTrust Bank	(626) 993-3800
Farmers & Merchants Bank of Long Beach	(562) 437-0011
First Bank	(314) 995-8700
First Choice Bank	(562) 345-9092
First Northern Bank of Dixon	(707) 678-3041
First-Citizens Bank & Trust Co.	(919) 716-7050
Five Star Bank	(916) 851-5440
Flagstar Bank, FSB	(248) 312-5400
Fremont Bank	(510) 505-5226
Golden Valley Bank	(530) 894-1000
Habib American Bank	(212) 532-4444
Hanmi Bank	(213) 382-2200
International City Bank	(562) 436-9800
Israel Discount Bank of New York	(212) 551-8500
JPMorgan Chase Bank, N.A.	(614) 248-5800
Merchants Bank of Commerce	(800) 421-2575
Metropolitan Bank	(510) 834-1933
Mission National Bank	(415) 826-3627
Murphy Bank	(559) 225-0225
Northern California National Bank	(530) 879-5900
Northern Trust Co.	(312) 630-6000
Oak Valley Community Bank	(209) 844-7500
Pacific Alliance Bank	(626) 773-8888

California

Name	Telephone
Plumas Bank	(530) 283-7305
Premier Valley Bank	(559) 438-2002
Redwood Capital Bank	(707) 444-9800
River City Bank	(916) 567-2600
Signature Bank	(646) 822-1500
Southwestern National Bank	(713) 771-9700
State Bank of India (California)	(213) 225-5700
Suncrest Bank	(916) 830-3597
Sunwest Bank	(714) 730-4444
United Business Bank	(925) 476-1800
United Security Bank	(559) 248-4944
Valley Republic Bank	(661) 371-2000
Wallis Bank	(979) 478-6151
WestAmerica Bank	(415) 257-8057
Woori America Bank	(212) 244-1500

Colorado

Name	Telephone
Rating: A	
Commerce Bank	(816) 234-2000
Community State Bank	(719) 336-3272
Farmers Bank	(970) 834-2121
First National Bank of Las Animas	(719) 456-1512
North Valley Bank	(303) 452-5500
Rating: A-	
Academy Bank, N.A.	(816) 472-0081
Alamosa State Bank	(719) 589-2564
Alpine Bank	(970) 945-2424
AMG National Trust Bank	(303) 694-2190
Armed Forces Bank, N.A.	(913) 682-9090
Bank of Colorado	(970) 206-1160
Bank of Estes Park	(970) 586-4485
Champion Bank	(303) 840-8484
Colorado Bank and Trust Co. of La Junta	(719) 384-8131
Dolores State Bank	(970) 882-7600
Eastern Colorado Bank	(719) 767-5652
Farmers State Bank of Brush	(970) 842-5101
First National Bank	(605) 223-2521
First National Bank of Hugo	(719) 743-2415
First Pioneer National Bank	(970) 332-4824
First State Bank	(308) 632-4158
FirstBank	(303) 232-2000
FirsTier Bank	(308) 235-4633
FirstOak Bank	(620) 331-2265
Frontier Bank	(719) 336-4351
Glacier Bank	(406) 756-4200
Gunnison Bank and Trust Co.	(970) 641-0320
High Country Bank	(719) 539-2516
High Plains Bank	(719) 765-4000
Kirkpatrick Bank	(405) 341-8222
Points West Community Bank	(970) 686-0878
Solera National Bank	(303) 209-8600
Verus Bank of Commerce	(970) 204-1010
Waypoint Bank	(308) 784-2515
Yampa Valley Bank	(970) 879-2993
Zions BanCorp., N.A.	(801) 844-7637
Rating: B+	
5Star Bank	(719) 574-2777
Adams Bank & Trust	(308) 284-4071
ANB Bank	(303) 394-5143
Bank of America, N.A.	(704) 386-5681
Bank of Burlington	(719) 346-5376
Bankers' Bank of the West	(303) 291-3700
Central Trust Bank	(573) 634-1302
CIT Bank, N.A.	(855) 462-2652
Citywide Banks	(303) 365-3800
First-Citizens Bank & Trust Co.	(919) 716-7050
FNB Bank	(785) 890-2000
Fowler State Bank	(719) 263-4276
Golden Belt Bank, FSA	(785) 726-3157
Grand Valley Bank	(435) 654-7400
Independent Bank	(972) 562-9004
JPMorgan Chase Bank, N.A.	(614) 248-5800
Legacy Bank	(719) 829-4811
Northern Trust Co.	(312) 630-6000
Pueblo Bank and Trust Co.	(719) 545-1834
Redstone Bank	(720) 880-5000
State Bank	(719) 384-5901
Stockmens Bank	(719) 955-2800
TCF National Bank	(952) 745-2760
United Business Bank	(925) 476-1800
United Fidelity Bank, FSB	(812) 424-0921

Connecticut

Name	Telephone
Rating: A	
Bessemer Trust Co., N.A.	(212) 708-9100
Rating: B+	
Bank of America, N.A.	(704) 386-5681
Chelsea Groton Bank	(860) 823-4800
Citibank, N.A.	(605) 370-6261
JPMorgan Chase Bank, N.A.	(614) 248-5800
Liberty Bank	(860) 638-2922
Northern Trust Co.	(312) 630-6000
Savings Bank of Danbury	(203) 743-3849
Signature Bank	(646) 822-1500
Stafford Savings Bank	(860) 684-4261
Union Savings Bank	(203) 830-4200
Washington Trust Co. of Westerly	(401) 348-1200

Delaware

Name	Telephone
Rating: A+	
Deutsche Bank Trust Co. Delaware	(302) 636-3301
Rating: A	
Applied Bank	(888) 839-7952
Calvin B. Taylor Banking Co.	(410) 641-1700
FSNB, N.A.	(580) 357-9880
Morgan Stanley Private Bank, N.A.	(212) 762-1803
Rating: A-	
Bank of Ocean City	(410) 213-0173
Wilmington Savings Fund Society, FSB	(302) 792-6000
Rating: B+	
Bank of America, N.A.	(704) 386-5681
Bryn Mawr Trust Co.	(610) 581-4839
Citibank, N.A.	(605) 370-6261
JPMorgan Chase Bank, N.A.	(614) 248-5800
Shore United Bank	(410) 822-1400

District of Columbia

Name	Telephone
Rating: A-	
EagleBank	(240) 497-2075
Hingham Institution for Savings	(781) 749-2200
Rating: B+	
Bank of America, N.A.	(704) 386-5681
Citibank, N.A.	(605) 370-6261
City National Bank	(800) 773-7100
FVCbank	(703) 436-4740
John Marshall Bank	(703) 584-0840
JPMorgan Chase Bank, N.A.	(614) 248-5800
MainStreet Bank	(703) 481-4567
Northern Trust Co.	(312) 630-6000
Truist Bank	(336) 733-2000

Federated States of Micronesia

Name	Telephone
Rating: A-	
Bank of the Federated States of Micronesia	

Florida

Name	Telephone
Rating: A+	
Citizens First Bank	(352) 753-9515
Rating: A	
Amerasia Bank	(718) 463-3600
Esquire Bank, N.A.	(516) 535-2002
Hillsboro Bank	(813) 707-6506
Metro City Bank	(770) 455-4989
Paradise Bank	(561) 392-5444
Republic Bank & Trust Co.	(502) 584-3600
Southeastern Bank	(912) 437-4141
Rating: A-	
1st Source Bank	(574) 235-2000
American National Bank	(954) 491-7788
Armed Forces Bank, N.A.	(913) 682-9090
Bank OZK	(501) 978-2265
Busey Bank	(217) 351-6500
CCB Community Bank	(334) 222-2561
Centennial Bank	(501) 328-4663
Charlotte State Bank & Trust	(941) 624-5400
Comerica Bank	(214) 462-4000
Commerce National Bank & Trust	(407) 622-8181
Community Bank of the South	(321) 452-0420
Crews Bank & Trust	(863) 494-2220
Drummond Community Bank	(352) 493-2277
Englewood Bank & Trust	(941) 475-6771
First Federal Bank	(386) 755-0600
First National Bank of Mount Dora	(352) 383-2111
Florida Business Bank	(321) 253-1555
Heartland National Bank	(863) 386-1300
Peoples Bank of Graceville	(850) 263-3267
Raymond James Bank, N.A.	(727) 567-8000
ServisFirst Bank	(205) 949-0302
Stearns Bank N.A.	(320) 253-6607
Thomasville National Bank	(229) 226-3300
TrustCo Bank	(518) 377-3311
Rating: B+	
American Momentum Bank	(979) 774-1111
Ameris Bank	(404) 814-8114
BAC Florida Bank	(305) 789-7000
BancorpSouth Bank	(662) 680-2000
Bank of America, N.A.	(704) 386-5681
Bank of Central Florida	(863) 701-2685
Bank of Tampa	(813) 872-1216
BankUnited, N.A.	(786) 313-1010
Cadence Bank, N.A.	(800) 636-7622
Capital City Bank	(850) 402-7700
CenterState Bank, N.A.	(863) 291-3900
CIT Bank, N.A.	(855) 462-2652
Citibank, N.A.	(605) 370-6261
City National Bank	(800) 773-7100
First Colony Bank of Florida	(407) 740-0401
First National Bank Northwest Florida	(850) 769-3207
First National Bank of Coffee County	(912) 384-1100
First Port City Bank	(229) 246-6200
First, A National Banking Assn.	(601) 268-8998
First-Citizens Bank & Trust Co.	(919) 716-7050
Flagler Bank	(561) 432-2122
FNBT Bank	(850) 796-2000
Interaudi Bank	(212) 833-1000
Israel Discount Bank of New York	(212) 551-8500
JPMorgan Chase Bank, N.A.	(614) 248-5800
Lake Forest Bank & Trust Co., N.A.	(847) 234-2882
MidSouth Bank	(334) 702-7774
Northern Trust Co.	(312) 630-6000
PrimeSouth Bank	(912) 283-6685
Renasant Bank	(800) 680-1601
Safra National Bank of New York	(212) 704-5500
Seacoast National Bank	(772) 221-2760
Sunrise Bank	(321) 784-8333
Synovus Bank	(706) 649-4900
Truist Bank	(336) 733-2000
Trustmark National Bank	(601) 208-5111
United Bank	(251) 446-6000
United Fidelity Bank, FSB	(812) 424-0921
Wauchula State Bank	(863) 773-4151
Woodforest National Bank	(832) 375-2505

Georgia

Name	Telephone
Rating: A	
Commercial Bank	(706) 743-8184
Douglas National Bank	(912) 384-2233
Durden Banking Co., Inc.	(478) 763-2121
Embassy National Bank	(770) 822-9111
Farmers State Bank	(706) 359-3131
First National Bank of Waynesboro	(706) 554-8100
FNB South	(912) 632-7262
FSNB, N.A.	(580) 357-9880
Metro City Bank	(770) 455-4989
Quantum National Bank	(770) 945-8300
South Georgia Bank	(912) 654-1051
Southeastern Bank	(912) 437-4141
United Bank	(770) 567-7211
West Central Georgia Bank	(706) 647-8951
Rating: A-	
Armed Forces Bank, N.A.	(913) 682-9090
Bank of Dade	(706) 657-6842
Bank of Dawson	(229) 995-2141
Bank of Dudley	(478) 277-1500
Bank of Madison	(706) 342-1953
Bank OZK	(501) 978-2265
BankSouth	(706) 453-2943
Century Bank of Georgia	(770) 387-1922
Citizens Bank & Trust, Inc.	(706) 657-5678
Citizens Community Bank	(229) 794-2111
Commercial Banking Co.	(229) 242-7600
East West Bank	(626) 768-6000
Exchange Bank	(478) 452-4531
Farmers State Bank	(478) 275-3223
First American Bank and Trust Co.	(706) 354-5000
First State Bank of Blakely	(229) 723-3711
First Volunteer Bank	(423) 668-4509
Glennville Bank	(912) 654-3471
Northeast Georgia Bank	(706) 356-4444
Peoples Bank of East Tennessee	(423) 442-7262
PromiseOne Bank	(678) 385-0800
RBC Bank (Georgia), N.A.	(919) 206-1060
Security State Bank	(229) 868-6431
ServisFirst Bank	(205) 949-0302
South Georgia Banking Co.	(229) 382-4211
SunMark Community Bank	(478) 783-4036
Thomasville National Bank	(229) 226-3300
United Community Bank	(706) 745-2151
Rating: B+	
American Pride Bank	(478) 784-1448
Ameris Bank	(404) 814-8114
Atlantic Capital Bank, N.A.	(404) 995-6050
Bank of Alapaha	(229) 532-6115
Bank of America, N.A.	(704) 386-5681
Bank of Camilla	(229) 336-5225
Bank of Hancock County	(706) 444-5781
Bank of Monticello	(706) 468-6418
Cadence Bank, N.A.	(800) 636-7622
Capital City Bank	(850) 402-7700
CenterState Bank, N.A.	(863) 291-3900
Citizens Bank of Americus	(229) 924-4011
Citizens Bank of Georgia	(770) 886-9500
Citizens Bank of Swainsboro	(478) 237-7001
Citizens Bank of The South	(478) 552-5116
Citizens National Bank of Quitman	(229) 263-7575
Citizens Trust Bank	(678) 406-4000
City National Bank	(800) 773-7100
Community Banking Co. of Fitzgerald	(229) 423-4321
F&M Bank	(706) 678-2187
Family Bank	(229) 294-2821
First Century Bank, N.A.	(770) 297-8060
First Community Bank	(803) 951-2265
First IC Bank	(770) 451-7200
First National Bank of Coffee County	(912) 384-1100
First Peoples Bank	(706) 663-2700
First Port City Bank	(229) 246-6200
First, A National Banking Assn.	(601) 268-8998
FirstBank	(615) 313-0080
First-Citizens Bank & Trust Co.	(919) 716-7050
Four County Bank	(478) 962-3221
Greater Community Bank	(706) 295-9300
Guardian Bank	(229) 241-9444
JPMorgan Chase Bank, N.A.	(614) 248-5800
Liberty First Bank	(770) 207-3000
Northern Trust Co.	(312) 630-6000
Oconee Federal S&L Assn.	(864) 882-2765
Peach State Bank & Trust	(770) 536-1100
Piedmont Bank	(770) 246-0011
Pinnacle Bank	(706) 283-2854
Pinnacle Bank	(615) 744-3705
PrimeSouth Bank	(912) 283-6685
Rabun County Bank	(706) 782-4571
Renasant Bank	(800) 680-1601
River City Bank	(706) 236-2123
South State Bank	(803) 771-2265
Southern First Bank	(864) 679-9000

Georgia

Name	Telephone
State Bank of Cochran	(478) 934-4501
Synovus Bank	(706) 649-4900
Truist Bank	(336) 733-2000
Wallis Bank	(979) 478-6151
Waycross Bank & Trust	(912) 283-0001
Wheeler County State Bank	(912) 568-7191
Woodforest National Bank	(832) 375-2505

Guam

Name	Telephone
Rating: B+	
First Hawaiian Bank	(808) 525-6340

Hawaii

Name	Telephone
Rating: A-	
Central Pacific Bank	(808) 544-0500
Rating: B+	
American Savings Bank, F.S.B.	(808) 627-6900
CIT Bank, N.A.	(855) 462-2652
First Hawaiian Bank	(808) 525-6340
Territorial Savings Bank	(808) 946-1400

Idaho

Rating: A

Name	Telephone
Altabank	(801) 756-7681
Bank of Commerce	(208) 525-9108
Farmers Bank	(208) 543-4351

Rating: A-

Name	Telephone
D.L. Evans Bank	(208) 678-8615
First FSB of Twin Falls	(208) 733-4222
Glacier Bank	(406) 756-4200
Ireland Bank	(208) 766-2211
Northwest Bank	(208) 332-0700
Washington Federal Bank, N.A.	(206) 204-3446
Washington Trust Bank	(509) 353-4204
Zions BanCorp., N.A.	(801) 844-7637

Rating: B+

Name	Telephone
Bank of America, N.A.	(704) 386-5681
bankcda	(208) 665-5999
Banner Bank	(509) 527-3636
Bell Bank	(701) 298-1500
Columbia State Bank	(253) 305-1900
First Interstate Bank	(406) 255-5000
JPMorgan Chase Bank, N.A.	(614) 248-5800
Sunwest Bank	(714) 730-4444
Twin River Bank	(208) 746-4848

Illinois

Name	Telephone
Rating: A	
Bank of Advance	(573) 722-3517
Commerce Bank	(816) 234-2000
Farmers National Bank	(815) 537-2348
Federal Savings Bank	(312) 738-8422
First Eagle Bank	(312) 850-2900
Germantown Trust & Savings Bank	(618) 526-4202
Grand Ridge National Bank	(815) 249-6414
Lindell Bank & Trust Co.	(314) 645-7700
Municipal Trust and Savings Bank	(815) 935-8000
Park Ridge Community Bank	(847) 384-9200
Royal Business Bank	(213) 627-9888
Teutopolis State Bank	(217) 857-3166
Vermilion Valley Bank	(815) 686-2258
Rating: A-	
Albany Bank and Trust Co., N.A.	(773) 267-7300
AMG National Trust Bank	(303) 694-2190
Apple River State Bank	(815) 594-2351
Armed Forces Bank, N.A.	(913) 682-9090
Bank of Bourbonnais	(815) 933-0570
Bank of O'Fallon	(618) 632-3595
Bank of Pontiac	(815) 844-6155
Blackhawk Bank & Trust	(309) 787-4451
Bradford National Bank of Greenville	(618) 664-2200
Buena Vista National Bank	(618) 826-2331
Burling Bank	(312) 408-8400
Busey Bank	(217) 351-6500
Cathay Bank	(213) 625-4791
Community Bank	(815) 367-5011
Community Bank of Easton	(309) 562-7420
Crossroads Bank	(217) 347-7751
Farmers and Merchants National Bank	(618) 327-4401
Farmers State Bank	(217) 285-5585
First Community Bank and Trust	(708) 946-2246
First Farmers State Bank	(309) 392-2623
First Financial Bank, N.A.	(812) 238-6000
First Merchants Bank	(765) 747-1500
First National Bank	(605) 482-8293
First National Bank in Pinckneyville	(618) 357-9393
First National Bank in Taylorville	(217) 824-2241
First National Bank of Litchfield	(217) 324-2105
First National Bank of Sparta	(618) 443-2187
First Nations Bank	(773) 594-5900
First Southern Bank	(618) 997-4341
First State Bank of Campbell Hill	(618) 426-3396
First Trust and Savings Bank of Watseka	(815) 432-2494
Fisher National Bank	(217) 897-1136
FNB Community Bank	(618) 283-1141
Frederick Community Bank	(815) 457-2111
Gold Coast Bank	(312) 587-3200
Goodfield State Bank	(309) 965-2221
Heartland Bank and Trust Co.	(309) 662-4444
Lakeside Bank	(312) 435-5100
Milledgeville State Bank	(815) 225-7171
Millennium Bank	(847) 296-9500
Old Second National Bank	(630) 892-0202
Petefish, Skiles & Co.	(217) 452-3041
Prairie State Bank & Trust	(217) 993-6260
Reynolds State Bank	(309) 372-4242
Rushville State Bank	(217) 322-3323
Shelby County State Bank	(217) 774-3911
Signature Bank	(847) 268-1001
State Bank of Cherry	(815) 894-2345
State Bank of Lincoln	(217) 735-5551
Sterling Bank	(573) 778-3333
Town and Country Bank Midwest	(217) 222-0015
Warren-Boynton State Bank	(217) 488-6091
Rating: B+	
American Community Bank & Trust	(815) 338-2300
Anna State Bank	(618) 833-2151
Anna-Jonesboro National Bank	(618) 833-8506
Bank of America, N.A.	(704) 386-5681
Bank of Carbondale	(618) 549-2181
Bank of Hillsboro, N.A.	(217) 532-3991
BankChampaign, N.A.	(217) 351-2870
BankFinancial, N.A.	(800) 894-6900
CBI Bank & Trust	(563) 263-3131
Central Bank Illinois	(309) 944-5601
Central Bank of St. Louis	(314) 862-8300
Citibank, N.A.	(605) 370-6261
Citizens Community Bank	(618) 566-8800
Du Quoin State Bank	(618) 542-2111
Evergreen Bank Group	(630) 413-9580
Fairfield National Bank	(618) 842-2107
Farmers & Mechanics Bank	(309) 343-7141
Farmers State Bank of Western Illinois	(309) 629-4361
Farmers-Merchants Bank of Illinois	(309) 584-4146
First Bank	(314) 995-8700
First Federal S&L Assn. of Central Illinois, S.B.	(217) 774-3322
First Financial Bank	(877) 322-9530
First Mid Bank & Trust, N.A.	(217) 234-7454
First National Bank in Olney	(618) 395-8541

Illinois

Name	Telephone	Name	Telephone
First National Bank of Beardstown	(217) 323-4105		
First National Bank of Brookfield	(708) 485-2770		
First National Bank of Pana	(217) 562-3961		
First National Bank of Steeleville	(618) 965-3441		
First State Bank of Beecher City	(618) 487-5161		
First State Bank of St. Peter	(618) 349-8343		
Forreston State Bank	(815) 938-3121		
Hanmi Bank	(213) 382-2200		
Hometown National Bank	(815) 223-7300		
Illinois Bank & Trust	(815) 637-7000		
Ipava State Bank	(309) 753-8202		
Itasca Bank & Trust Co.	(630) 773-0350		
JPMorgan Chase Bank, N.A.	(614) 248-5800		
Kinmundy Bank	(618) 547-3533		
Lake Forest Bank & Trust Co., N.A.	(847) 234-2882		
Lena State Bank	(815) 369-4901		
Liberty Bank	(217) 645-3434		
Lisle Savings Bank	(630) 852-3710		
Mason City National Bank	(217) 482-3246		
Midland Community Bank	(217) 237-4324		
Morton Community Bank	(309) 266-5337		
Northern Trust Co.	(312) 630-6000		
Old Exchange National Bank of Okawville	(618) 243-5234		
Peoples National Bank of Kewanee	(309) 853-3333		
Peoples State Bank of Colfax	(309) 723-2111		
Philo Exchange Bank	(217) 684-2600		
Poplar Grove State Bank	(815) 765-3333		
Providence Bank & Trust	(708) 333-0700		
Quad City Bank and Trust Co.	(563) 344-0600		
Republic Bank of Chicago	(630) 570-7700		
Royal Savings Bank	(773) 768-4800		
Simmons Bank	(870) 541-1000		
Southern Bank	(573) 778-1800		
Southern Illinois Bank	(618) 983-8433		
Spring Valley City Bank	(815) 663-2211		
State Bank	(815) 297-0900		
State Bank of Davis	(815) 865-5125		
State Bank of Herscher	(815) 426-2156		
State Bank of St. Jacob	(618) 644-5555		
State Bank of Texas	(972) 252-6000		
TCF National Bank	(952) 745-2760		
TrustBank	(618) 395-4311		
Union National Bank	(847) 888-7500		
United Fidelity Bank, FSB	(812) 424-0921		
Villa Grove State Bank	(217) 832-2631		
Woodforest National Bank	(832) 375-2505		

Indiana

Name	Telephone
Rating: A	
Alliance Bank	(219) 567-9151
Community State Bank	(260) 897-3361
Kentland Bank	(219) 474-5155
Republic Bank & Trust Co.	(502) 584-3600
Stock Yards Bank & Trust Co.	(502) 582-2571
Rating: A-	
1st Source Bank	(574) 235-2000
Bank of Wolcott	(219) 279-2185
Busey Bank	(217) 351-6500
Centier Bank	(219) 755-6100
CentreBank	(765) 294-2228
Civista Bank	(419) 625-4121
Farmers & Merchants State Bank	(419) 446-2501
Farmers and Merchants Bank	(260) 637-5546
First Bank of Berne	(260) 589-2151
First Financial Bank, N.A.	(812) 238-6000
First Merchants Bank	(765) 747-1500
Fountain Trust Co.	(765) 793-2237
Fowler State Bank	(765) 884-1200
Freedom Bank	(812) 683-8998
Friendship State Bank	(812) 667-5101
German American Bank	(812) 482-1314
Lake City Bank	(574) 267-6144
Logansport Savings Bank	(574) 722-3855
Merchants Bank of Indiana	(317) 324-4660
Morris Plan Co. of Terre Haute, Inc.	(812) 238-6063
Napoleon State Bank	(812) 852-4002
Union Savings Bank	(513) 247-0300
Rating: B+	
Bank of America, N.A.	(704) 386-5681
Bippus State Bank	(260) 356-8900
DeMotte State Bank	(219) 987-4141
Farmers State Bank	(260) 463-7111
FCN Bank, N.A.	(765) 647-4116
First Financial Bank	(877) 322-9530
First Harrison Bank	(812) 738-2198
First Savings Bank	(812) 283-0724
First State Bank of Middlebury	(574) 825-2166
First State Bank of Porter	(219) 926-2136
Flagstar Bank, FSB	(248) 312-5400
Garrett State Bank	(260) 357-3133
Greenfield Banking Co.	(317) 462-1431
Greenville National Bank	(937) 548-1114
Horizon Bank	(219) 874-9245
JPMorgan Chase Bank, N.A.	(614) 248-5800
New Washington State Bank	(812) 293-3321
Providence Bank & Trust	(708) 333-0700
STAR Financial Bank	(260) 467-5500
State Bank and Trust Co.	(419) 783-8950
State Bank of Lizton	(317) 994-5115
Truist Bank	(336) 733-2000
United Fidelity Bank, FSB	(812) 424-0921
WesBanco Bank, Inc.	(304) 234-9419
Woodforest National Bank	(832) 375-2505

Iowa

Name	Telephone
Rating: A	
Bank 1st	(563) 422-3883
Citizens First National Bank	(712) 732-5440
Farmers Trust & Savings Bank	(319) 668-2525
First State Bank	(641) 843-4411
Iowa State Bank	(515) 288-0111
Iowa State Bank	(712) 662-4721
Iowa Trust and Savings Bank	(641) 437-4500
Liberty Trust & Savings Bank	(563) 785-4441
Midwest Heritage Bank, FSB	(515) 278-6541
New Albin Savings Bank	(563) 544-4214
Pinnacle Bank	(641) 752-2393
Waukon State Bank	(563) 568-3451
Rating: A-	
Blackhawk Bank & Trust	(309) 787-4451
Boone Bank & Trust Co.	(515) 432-6200
Breda Savings Bank	(712) 673-2321
Bridge Community Bank	(319) 895-8200
Chelsea Savings Bank	(319) 444-3144
Citizens Savings Bank	(319) 462-3561
Citizens State Bank	(712) 324-2519
Decorah Bank & Trust Co.	(563) 382-9661
Farmers & Merchants State Bank	(515) 462-4242
Farmers Savings Bank	(641) 752-2525
Farmers Savings Bank & Trust	(319) 478-2148
Farmers State Bank	(319) 377-4891
Farmers State Bank	(515) 295-7221
Farmers State Bank	(641) 424-3053
Farmers Trust and Savings Bank	(641) 562-2696
First Bank Hampton	(641) 456-4793
First Central State Bank	(563) 659-3141
First Citizens Bank	(641) 423-1600
First National Bank	(605) 482-8293
First National Bank, Ames, Iowa	(515) 232-5561
First Security Bank	(712) 881-1131
First Security Bank-Sleepy Eye	(507) 794-3911
First State Bank	(641) 527-2535
First State Bank	(515) 832-2520
Great Southern Bank	(417) 895-5234
Heartland Bank	(515) 467-5561
Hills Bank and Trust Co.	(319) 679-2291
Iowa State Bank	(515) 295-3595
Lee County Bank	(319) 372-2243
Leighton State Bank	(641) 628-1566
Manufacturers Bank & Trust Co.	(641) 585-2825
Maquoketa State Bank	(563) 652-2491
Mount Vernon Bank and Trust Co.	(319) 895-8835
Northeast Security Bank	(563) 578-3251
NorthStar Bank	(712) 362-3322
Northwestern Bank	(712) 737-4911
NSB Bank	(641) 423-7638
Ohnward Bank & Trust	(563) 852-7696
Pilot Grove Savings Bank	(319) 469-3951
Readlyn Savings Bank	(319) 279-3321
Savings Bank	(712) 957-6815
Security National Bank of Omaha	(402) 344-7300
Security National Bank of Sioux City, Iowa	(712) 277-6500
Security Savings Bank	(515) 352-3333
Security State Bank	(712) 446-3324
Security State Bank	(515) 295-9501
Solon State Bank	(319) 624-3405
South Ottumwa Savings Bank	(641) 682-7541
St. Ansgar State Bank	(641) 713-4501
Templeton Savings Bank	(712) 669-3322
United Bank and Trust Co.	(641) 456-5587
United Bank of Iowa	(712) 364-3393
Victor State Bank	(319) 647-2231
Washington State Bank	(319) 653-2151
West Iowa Bank	(515) 887-7811
Rating: B+	
American Savings Bank	(319) 882-4279
American State Bank	(641) 342-2175
Atkins Savings Bank & Trust	(319) 446-7700
Audubon State Bank	(712) 563-2644
Availa Bank	(712) 792-3567
Bank of America, N.A.	(704) 386-5681
BankFirst	(402) 371-8005
Bellevue State Bank	(563) 872-4911
BTC Bank	(660) 425-7285
CBI Bank & Trust	(563) 263-3131
Cedar Rapids Bank and Trust Co.	(319) 862-2728
Charter Bank	(515) 331-2265
Citizens Savings Bank	(563) 427-3255
Citizens Savings Bank	(563) 562-3674
Citizens State Bank	(563) 488-2211
Citizens State Bank	(319) 465-5921
Clear Lake Bank and Trust Co.	(641) 357-7121
Community State Bank	(515) 331-3100
Community State Bank	(712) 262-3030
Corydon State Bank	(641) 872-2212
CUSB Bank	(563) 547-2040
Danville State Savings Bank	(319) 392-4261

Iowa

Name	Telephone
Dubuque Bank and Trust Co.	(563) 589-2000
F&M Bank	(402) 372-5331
Farmers Bank of Northern Missouri	(660) 947-2474
Farmers State Bank	(319) 287-3961
Farmers State Bank	(712) 376-4154
Farmers Trust & Savings Bank	(712) 747-2000
First Iowa State Bank	(641) 932-2144
First National Bank	(319) 352-1340
First National Bank in Creston	(641) 782-2195
First National Bank of Manning	(712) 655-3557
First State Bank	(641) 435-4943
First Whitney Bank and Trust	(712) 243-3195
FNB Bank	(641) 745-2141
GNB Bank	(319) 824-5431
Home Federal Savings Bank	(507) 535-1309
Home State Bank	(712) 933-5511
Home Trust & Savings Bank	(641) 732-3763
Houghton State Bank	(712) 623-4823
Iowa State Bank	(712) 439-1025
Iowa Trust & Savings Bank	(712) 852-3451
Laurens State Bank	(712) 845-2627
Liberty National Bank	(712) 224-4425
Luana Savings Bank	(563) 539-2166
Maxwell State Bank	(515) 387-1175
Maynard Savings Bank	(563) 637-2289
Northwest Bank	(712) 580-4100
Pocahontas State Bank	(712) 335-3567
Principal Bank	(800) 672-3343
Quad City Bank and Trust Co.	(563) 344-0600
Reliance State Bank	(515) 733-4396
Security State Bank	(319) 352-3500
Sloan State Bank	(712) 428-3344
State Bank & Trust Co.	(515) 382-2191
State Savings Bank	(515) 457-9533
United Bank & Trust N.A.	(641) 753-5900
Watkins Savings Bank	(319) 227-7773
Wayland State Bank	(319) 385-8189
West Bank	(515) 222-2300

Kansas

Name	Telephone
Rating: A	
CBW Bank	(620) 396-8221
City National B&T Co. of Lawton, Oklahoma	(866) 385-3444
Commerce Bank	(816) 234-2000
Farmers Bank & Trust	(620) 792-2411
Garden Plain State Bank	(316) 721-1500
Rating: A-	
Academy Bank, N.A.	(816) 472-0081
Armed Forces Bank, N.A.	(913) 682-9090
Bank of Prairie Village	(913) 713-0300
Bank of Tescott	(785) 283-4217
Bank7	(405) 810-8600
Bankwest of Kansas	(785) 899-2342
Citizens State Bank	(785) 562-2186
Citizens State Bank and Trust Co.	(785) 742-2101
Community First Bank	(913) 371-1242
Community National Bank	(785) 336-6143
Community State Bank	(620) 251-1313
Country Club Bank	(816) 931-4060
Denison State Bank	(785) 364-3131
Eastern Colorado Bank	(719) 767-5652
Exchange Bank & Trust	(913) 367-6000
Farmers & Merchants Bank of Colby	(785) 460-3321
Farmers National Bank	(785) 543-6541
Farmers State Bank	(620) 241-3090
Farmers State Bank of Aliceville, Kansas	(785) 489-2468
Farmers State Bank of Oakley, Kansas	(785) 672-3251
Fidelity State Bank and Trust Co.	(620) 227-8586
First National Bank in Fredonia	(620) 378-2151
First National Bank of Hutchinson	(620) 663-1521
First National Bank of Louisburg	(913) 837-5191
First State B&T Co. of Larned	(620) 285-6931
FirstOak Bank	(620) 331-2265
Flint Hills Bank	(785) 449-2266
Great Southern Bank	(417) 895-5234
Kaw Valley State Bank and Trust Co.	(785) 456-2021
Kearny County Bank	(620) 355-6222
Mutual Savings Assn.	(913) 682-3491
NBKC Bank	(816) 965-1400
Pinnacle Bank	(402) 434-3127
Security Bank of Kansas City	(913) 281-3165
Security State Bank	(620) 872-7224
Stanley Bank	(913) 681-8800
State Bank of Bern	(785) 336-6121
TriCentury Bank	(913) 583-3222
Union Bank and Trust Co.	(402) 323-1828
United Bank & Trust	(785) 562-2333
Western State Bank	(620) 275-4128
Rating: B+	
Adams Bank & Trust	(308) 284-4071
Alliance Bank	(785) 271-1800
ANB Bank	(303) 394-5143
Bank of America, N.A.	(704) 386-5681
Bank of Blue Valley	(913) 234-2334
Bankers' Bank of Kansas	(316) 681-2265
Central Bank of the Midwest	(816) 525-5300
CIT Bank, N.A.	(855) 462-2652
Citizens State Bank	(620) 836-2888
Citizens State Bank	(620) 345-6317
Commercial Bank	(620) 421-1000
Community Bank	(785) 440-4400
Cornerstone Bank	(913) 239-8100
Emprise Bank	(316) 383-4301
Enterprise Bank & Trust	(314) 725-5500
Exchange Bank	(308) 237-7711
Farmers and Drovers Bank	(620) 767-5138
Farmers State Bank	(785) 457-3316
Farmers State Bank	(785) 364-4691
First Bank	(620) 278-2161
First Bank Kansas	(785) 825-2211
First Commerce Bank	(785) 562-5558
First Heritage Bank	(785) 857-3341
First Kansas Bank	(620) 653-4921
First State Bank	(785) 798-3347
First-Citizens Bank & Trust Co.	(919) 716-7050
FNB Bank	(785) 890-2000
FNB Washington	(785) 325-2221
Golden Belt Bank, FSA	(785) 726-3157
Great American Bank	(785) 838-9704
Howard State Bank	(620) 374-2127
JPMorgan Chase Bank, N.A.	(614) 248-5800
Kansas State Bank	(785) 242-3600
Kansas State Bank Overbrook Kansas	(785) 665-7121
KS StateBank	(785) 587-4000
Labette Bank	(620) 784-5311
Peoples Bank	(620) 582-2166
Peoples Bank and Trust Co.	(620) 241-2100
Silver Lake Bank	(785) 232-0102
Simmons Bank	(870) 541-1000
Solomon State Bank	(785) 655-2941
Solutions North Bank	(785) 425-6721
Stockgrowers State Bank	(620) 635-4032

Kansas

Name	Telephone	Name	Telephone
Stockgrowers State Bank	(785) 256-4241		

Kentucky

Name	Telephone
Rating: A	
Cumberland Security Bank, Inc.	(606) 679-9361
Farmers Bank and Trust Co.	(270) 365-5526
Jackson County Bank	(606) 287-8484
Kentucky Farmers Bank Corp.	(606) 929-5000
Republic Bank & Trust Co.	(502) 584-3600
Stock Yards Bank & Trust Co.	(502) 582-2571
United Community Bank of W Kentucky	(270) 389-3232
Rating: A-	
Armed Forces Bank, N.A.	(913) 682-9090
Bank of the Bluegrass & Trust Co.	(859) 233-4500
Casey County Bank, Inc.	(606) 787-8394
Central Bank & Trust Co.	(859) 253-6013
Citizens Deposit Bank of Arlington, Inc.	(270) 655-6921
City National Bank of West Virginia	(304) 769-1100
Edmonton State Bank	(270) 432-3231
Elkton Bank & Trust Co.	(270) 265-9841
First Financial Bank, N.A.	(812) 238-6000
First National Bank of Grayson	(606) 474-2000
First United Bank and Trust Co.	(270) 821-5555
German American Bank	(812) 482-1314
Guardian Savings Bank, F.S.B.	(513) 942-3500
Heartland Bank	(614) 416-4601
Magnolia Bank	(270) 324-3226
Paducah Bank and Trust Co.	(270) 575-5700
Peoples Bank	(502) 477-2244
Peoples Bank MT. Washington	(502) 538-7301
Sacramento Deposit Bank	(270) 736-2212
Taylor County Bank	(270) 465-4196
Town & Country Bank and Trust Co.	(502) 348-3911
Traditional Bank, Inc.	(859) 498-0414
United Citizens Bank of Southern Kentucky, Inc.	(270) 384-2265
Rating: B+	
Bank of Clarkson	(270) 242-2111
Bank of Edmonson County	(270) 597-2175
Bank of Maysville	(606) 564-4001
Cecilian Bank	(270) 862-3294
Citizens National Bank of Somerset	(606) 679-6341
Commercial Bank	(423) 869-5151
Farmers Bank and Trust Co.	(270) 965-3106
Farmers National Bank of Danville	(859) 236-2926
First Financial Bank	(877) 322-9530
First Harrison Bank	(812) 738-2198
First National Bank of Kentucky	(502) 732-4406
First State Bank	(270) 547-2271
FirstBank	(615) 313-0080
Franklin Bank & Trust Co.	(270) 586-7121
Fredonia Valley Bank	(270) 545-3301
Independence Bank of Kentucky	(270) 686-1776
JPMorgan Chase Bank, N.A.	(614) 248-5800
Kentucky Bank	(859) 987-1795
Lewisburg Banking Co.	(270) 755-4818
Lincoln National Bank	(270) 358-4116
Meade County Bank	(270) 422-4141
PBK Bank, Inc.	(606) 365-7098
Planters Bank, Inc.	(270) 886-9030
River City Bank, Inc.	(502) 585-4600
Security Bank and Trust Co.	(731) 642-6644
Security Bank and Trust Co.	(606) 564-3304
South Central Bank, Inc.	(270) 651-7466
Springfield State Bank	(859) 336-3939
Truist Bank	(336) 733-2000
United Citizens Bank & Trust Co.	(502) 532-7392
United Southern Bank	(270) 885-0056
WesBanco Bank, Inc.	(304) 234-9419
WinFirst Bank	(859) 744-1900
Woodforest National Bank	(832) 375-2505

Louisiana

Name	Telephone
Rating: A	
First American Bank and Trust	(225) 265-2265
First National Bank of Louisiana	(337) 783-4014
FSNB, N.A.	(580) 357-9880
Rayne State Bank & Trust Co.	(337) 334-3191
Rating: A-	
American Bank & Trust Co.	(337) 948-3056
Exchange Bank and Trust Co.	(318) 352-8141
Guaranty Bank and Trust Co.	(225) 638-8621
Gulf Coast Bank	(337) 893-7733
Red River Bank	(318) 561-4000
South Louisiana Bank	(985) 851-3434
The Bank	(337) 824-0033
Rating: B+	
BancorpSouth Bank	(662) 680-2000
Bank of Sunset and Trust Co.	(337) 662-5222
BankPlus	(662) 247-1811
Beauregard Federal Savings Bank	(337) 463-4493
Citizens National Bank, N.A.	(318) 747-6000
Cottonport Bank	(318) 253-9612
Cross Keys Bank	(318) 766-3246
Evangeline Bank and Trust Co.	(337) 363-5541
Feliciana Bank & Trust Co.	(225) 683-8565
First National Bank of Benton	(318) 965-9691
First National Bank USA	(985) 785-8411
First, A National Banking Assn.	(601) 268-8998
Franklin State Bank & Trust Co.	(318) 435-3711
Guaranty Bank & Trust Co. of Delhi	(318) 878-3703
Hodge Bank & Trust Co.	(318) 259-7362
Home Federal Bank	(318) 841-1170
JD Bank	(337) 824-3424
Jonesboro State Bank	(318) 259-4411
JPMorgan Chase Bank, N.A.	(614) 248-5800
Mississippi River Bank	(504) 392-1111
Resource Bank	(985) 801-1800
Sabine State Bank and Trust Co.	(318) 256-7000
Southern Heritage Bank	(318) 339-8505
Synergy Bank	(985) 851-3341
Tensas State Bank	(318) 467-5401
Woodforest National Bank	(832) 375-2505

Nevada

Name	Telephone
Rating: A	
Bank of George	(702) 851-4200
First Security Bank of Nevada	(702) 853-0900
Royal Business Bank	(213) 627-9888
Rating: A-	
American First National Bank	(713) 596-2888
Armed Forces Bank, N.A.	(913) 682-9090
Cathay Bank	(213) 625-4791
Eaglemark Savings Bank	(775) 886-3000
East West Bank	(626) 768-6000
First Savings Bank	(605) 763-2009
Glacier Bank	(406) 756-4200
Meadows Bank	(702) 471-2265
Pacific Premier Bank	(949) 864-8000
Washington Federal Bank, N.A.	(206) 204-3446
Western Alliance Bank	(602) 389-3500
Wilmington Savings Fund Society, FSB	(302) 792-6000
Zions BanCorp., N.A.	(801) 844-7637
Rating: B+	
Bank of America, N.A.	(704) 386-5681
Charles Schwab Bank, SSB	(775) 689-6800
CIT Bank, N.A.	(855) 462-2652
Citibank, N.A.	(605) 370-6261
City National Bank	(800) 773-7100
First National Bank of Ely	(775) 289-4441
JPMorgan Chase Bank, N.A.	(614) 248-5800
Kirkwood Bank of Nevada	(702) 912-0700
Northern Trust Co.	(312) 630-6000
Plumas Bank	(530) 283-7305
Town & Country Bank	(702) 252-8777
Wells Fargo National Bank West	(702) 952-6650

New Hampshire

Name	Telephone
Rating: A-	
Camden National Bank	(207) 236-8821
Lowell Five Cent Savings Bank	(978) 452-1300
Rating: B+	
Bank of America, N.A.	(704) 386-5681
Bank of New England	(603) 894-5700
Cambridge Trust Co.	(617) 876-5500
Eastern Bank	(617) 897-1100
JPMorgan Chase Bank, N.A.	(614) 248-5800
Ledyard National Bank	(802) 649-2050
NBT Bank, N.A.	(607) 337-6416
Partners Bank of New England	(207) 324-2285
Provident Bank	(978) 834-8555

New Jersey

Name	Telephone
Rating: A	
Bessemer Trust Co.	(212) 708-9100
Metro City Bank	(770) 455-4989
Pacific City Bank	(213) 210-2000
Parke Bank	(856) 256-2500
Rating: A-	
AMG National Trust Bank	(303) 694-2190
Armed Forces Bank, N.A.	(913) 682-9090
Cathay Bank	(213) 625-4791
Cenlar FSB	(609) 883-3900
Cross River Bank	(201) 808-7000
CTBC Bank Corp. (USA)	(424) 277-4612
NewBank	(718) 353-9100
TrustCo Bank	(518) 377-3311
Unity Bank	(908) 730-7630
Wilmington Savings Fund Society, FSB	(302) 792-6000
Rating: B+	
Bank of America, N.A.	(704) 386-5681
Bank of Princeton	(609) 921-1700
Bryn Mawr Trust Co.	(610) 581-4839
Citibank, N.A.	(605) 370-6261
First IC Bank	(770) 451-7200
Firstrust Savings Bank	(610) 238-5001
Habib American Bank	(212) 532-4444
Hanmi Bank	(213) 382-2200
Israel Discount Bank of New York	(212) 551-8500
JPMorgan Chase Bank, N.A.	(614) 248-5800
Lakeland Bank	(973) 697-2000
Lusitania Savings Bank	(973) 344-5125
Peapack-Gladstone Bank	(908) 234-0700
State Street Bank and Trust Co.	(617) 786-3000
Sumitomo Mitsui Trust Bank (U.S.A.) Ltd.	(201) 420-9470
Truist Bank	(336) 733-2000
William Penn Bank,	(215) 269-1200
Woori America Bank	(212) 244-1500

New Mexico

Name	Telephone
Rating: A	
First American Bank	(575) 746-8000
First National Bank	(575) 437-4880
First New Mexico Bank	(575) 546-2691
First New Mexico Bank of Silver City	(575) 388-3121
First New Mexico Bank, Las Cruces	(575) 556-3000
Valley Bank of Commerce	(575) 623-2265
Western Bank	(575) 542-3521
Rating: A-	
AimBank	(806) 385-4441
Bank of Clovis	(575) 769-9000
Bank of Colorado	(970) 206-1160
Centinel Bank of Taos	(575) 758-6700
Citizens Bank	(806) 350-5600
Citizens Bank	(505) 599-0100
Citizens Bank of Clovis	(575) 769-1911
Citizens Bank of Las Cruces	(575) 647-4100
First Savings Bank	(605) 763-2009
James Polk Stone Community Bank	(575) 356-6601
Lea County State Bank	(575) 397-4511
New Mexico Bank & Trust	(505) 830-8100
Washington Federal Bank, N.A.	(206) 204-3446
Western Commerce Bank	(575) 887-6686
WestStar Bank	(915) 532-1000
Zions BanCorp., N.A.	(801) 844-7637
Rating: B+	
American Heritage Bank	(575) 762-2800
Bank of America, N.A.	(704) 386-5681
Century Bank	(505) 995-1200
City Bank	(806) 792-7101
CNB Bank	(575) 234-2500
Enterprise Bank & Trust	(314) 725-5500
First National Bank Texas	(254) 554-4236
First-Citizens Bank & Trust Co.	(919) 716-7050
Main Bank	(505) 880-1700
United Business Bank	(925) 476-1800
Western Bank of Clovis	(575) 769-1975

New York

Name	Telephone
Rating: A	
Alpine Capital Bank	(212) 328-2555
Amerasia Bank	(718) 463-3600
Bessemer Trust Co., N.A.	(212) 708-9100
Deutsche Bank Trust Co. Americas	(212) 250-2500
Esquire Bank, N.A.	(516) 535-2002
Fulton Savings Bank	(315) 592-4201
Metro City Bank	(770) 455-4989
Morgan Stanley Private Bank, N.A.	(212) 762-1803
Pacific City Bank	(213) 210-2000
Royal Business Bank	(213) 627-9888
Sterling Bank and Trust, FSB	(248) 355-2400
Rating: A-	
Armed Forces Bank, N.A.	(913) 682-9090
Bank OZK	(501) 978-2265
Cathay Bank	(213) 625-4791
Centennial Bank	(501) 328-4663
Citizens & Northern Bank	(570) 724-3411
CTBC Bank Corp. (USA)	(424) 277-4612
East West Bank	(626) 768-6000
First National Bank of Groton	(607) 898-5871
Genesee Regional Bank	(585) 249-1540
Maspeth Federal S&L Assn.	(718) 335-1300
Metropolitan Commercial Bank	(212) 659-0600
NewBank	(718) 353-9100
Preferred Bank	(213) 891-1188
Steuben Trust Co.	(607) 324-5010
Tioga State Bank	(607) 589-7000
TrustCo Bank	(518) 377-3311
Westchester Bank	(914) 368-9919
Rating: B+	
Bank of America, N.A.	(704) 386-5681
Bank of Greene County	(518) 943-2600
BankUnited, N.A.	(786) 313-1010
BNB Bank	(631) 537-8834
Canandaigua National Bank and Trust Co.	(585) 394-4260
Citibank, N.A.	(605) 370-6261
City National Bank	(800) 773-7100
Community Bank, N.A.	(315) 445-2282
First IC Bank	(770) 451-7200
First National Bank of Dryden	(607) 844-8141
Glens Falls National Bank and Trust Co.	(518) 793-4121
Habib American Bank	(212) 532-4444
Hamlin Bank and Trust Co.	(814) 887-5555
Hanmi Bank	(213) 382-2200
Hanover Community Bank	(516) 248-4868
Interaudi Bank	(212) 833-1000
Israel Discount Bank of New York	(212) 551-8500
Jeff Bank	(845) 482-4000
JPMorgan Chase Bank, N.A.	(614) 248-5800
Lakeland Bank	(973) 697-2000
NBT Bank, N.A.	(607) 337-6416
Northern Trust Co.	(312) 630-6000
Peoples Security Bank and Trust Co.	(570) 955-1700
Safra National Bank of New York	(212) 704-5500
Saratoga National Bank and Trust Co.	(518) 583-3114
Signature Bank	(646) 822-1500
Spring Bank	(718) 879-5000
Tompkins Trust Co.	(607) 273-3210
Watertown Savings Bank	(315) 788-7100
Wayne Bank	(570) 253-1455
Woodforest National Bank	(832) 375-2505
Woori America Bank	(212) 244-1500

North Carolina

Name	Telephone
Rating: A	
FSNB, N.A.	(580) 357-9880
Surrey Bank & Trust	(336) 783-3900
Rating: A-	
Bank OZK	(501) 978-2265
Benchmark Community Bank	(434) 676-9054
BlueHarbor Bank	(704) 662-7700
Farmers & Merchants Bank	(704) 633-1772
Fidelity Bank	(919) 552-2242
First Bank	(910) 692-6222
Live Oak Banking Co.	(910) 790-5867
Peoples Bank	(828) 464-5620
Providence Bank	(252) 443-9477
United Community Bank	(706) 745-2151
Wake Forest Federal S&L Assn.	(919) 556-5146
Rating: B+	
American National Bank and Trust Co.	(434) 792-5111
Atlantic Union Bank	(804) 327-5720
Bank of America, N.A.	(704) 386-5681
First FSB of Lincolnton	(704) 735-0416
First-Citizens Bank & Trust Co.	(919) 716-7050
JPMorgan Chase Bank, N.A.	(614) 248-5800
Morganton Savings Bank, S.S.B.	(828) 437-1426
Pinnacle Bank	(615) 744-3705
Roxboro Savings Bank, SSB	(336) 599-2137
Signature Bank	(646) 822-1500
South State Bank	(803) 771-2265
Southern Bank and Trust Co.	(919) 658-7000
Southern First Bank	(864) 679-9000
TowneBank	(757) 638-7500
Truist Bank	(336) 733-2000
Woodforest National Bank	(832) 375-2505

North Dakota

Name	Telephone
Rating: A	
Ramsey National Bank	(701) 662-4024
Security First Bank of North Dakota	(701) 794-8758
Rating: A-	
Alerus Financial, N.A.	(701) 795-3369
BNC National Bank	(602) 508-3760
Citizens State Bank of Finley	(701) 524-1921
Commercial Bank of Mott	(701) 824-2593
First Security Bank - West	(701) 873-4301
First State Bank & Trust	(701) 577-2113
First State Bank of Golva	(701) 872-3656
Liberty State Bank	(701) 464-5421
Sargent County Bank	(701) 724-3216
Stock Growers Bank	(701) 754-2226
Rating: B+	
American State Bank & Trust Co	(701) 774-4100
Bank Forward	(701) 769-2121
Bell Bank	(701) 298-1500
Bremer Bank, N.A.	(651) 288-3751
Choice Financial Group	(701) 356-9700
Dakota Community Bank & Trust, N.A.	(701) 878-4416
Dakota Western Bank	(701) 523-5803
First State Bank	(701) 847-2600
Goose River Bank	(701) 788-3110
Grant County State Bank	(701) 622-3491
Horizon Financial Bank	(701) 682-5331
Peoples State Bank	(701) 245-6407
Security State Bank, Wishek, North Dakota	(701) 452-2314
Starion Bank	(701) 223-6050
Unison Bank	(701) 253-5600

Northern Mariana Islands

Name	Telephone
Rating: B+	
First Hawaiian Bank	(808) 525-6340

Ohio

Name	Telephone
Rating: A+	
FDS Bank	(513) 573-2265
Rating: A	
Peoples Bank Co.	(419) 678-2385
Perpetual Federal Savings Bank	(937) 653-1700
Republic Bank & Trust Co.	(502) 584-3600
St. Henry Bank	(419) 678-2358
Stock Yards Bank & Trust Co.	(502) 582-2571
Rating: A-	
Buckeye Community Bank	(440) 233-8800
Citizens Bank Co.	(740) 984-2381
City National Bank of West Virginia	(304) 769-1100
Civista Bank	(419) 625-4121
Farmers & Merchants State Bank	(419) 446-2501
Farmers Savings Bank	(330) 648-2441
First Bank of Berne	(260) 589-2151
First Merchants Bank	(765) 747-1500
Guardian Savings Bank, F.S.B.	(513) 942-3500
Hamler State Bank	(419) 274-3955
Heartland Bank	(614) 416-4601
Killbuck Savings Bank Co.	(330) 276-4881
Miami Savings Bank	(513) 353-1339
North Side Bank and Trust Co.	(513) 542-7800
Ottoville Bank Co.	(419) 453-3313
Settlers Bank	(740) 373-9200
Signature Bank, N.A.	(419) 841-7773
Spring Valley Bank	(513) 761-6688
Unified Bank	(740) 633-0445
Union Savings Bank	(513) 247-0300
Rating: B+	
Bank of America, N.A.	(704) 386-5681
Commercial & Savings Bank of Millersburg	(330) 674-9015
Corn City State Bank	(419) 278-0015
Croghan Colonial Bank	(419) 332-7301
Farmers & Merchants Bank	(937) 866-2455
Farmers National Bank of Canfield	(330) 533-3341
FCN Bank, N.A.	(765) 647-4116
First Bank of Ohio	(419) 448-9740
First Commonwealth Bank	(724) 463-8555
First Financial Bank	(877) 322-9530
First National Bank in New Bremen	(419) 629-2761
First National Bank of Blanchester	(937) 783-2451
Flagstar Bank, FSB	(248) 312-5400
Greenville National Bank	(937) 548-1114
JPMorgan Chase Bank, N.A.	(614) 248-5800
LCNB National Bank	(513) 932-1414
Liberty National Bank	(419) 634-5015
Minster Bank	(419) 628-2351
Northern Trust Co.	(312) 630-6000
Osgood State Bank	(419) 582-2681
State Bank and Trust Co.	(419) 783-8950
Sutton Bank	(419) 426-3641
TCF National Bank	(952) 745-2760
Truist Bank	(336) 733-2000
Union Banking Co.	(937) 355-6511
Waterford Bank, N.A.	(419) 720-3900
WesBanco Bank, Inc.	(304) 234-9419
Woodforest National Bank	(832) 375-2505

Oklahoma

Name	Telephone
Rating: A	
Bank of Hydro	(405) 663-2214
City National B&T Co. of Lawton, Oklahoma	(866) 385-3444
Commerce Bank	(816) 234-2000
Community National Bank of Okarche	(405) 263-7491
Farmers and Merchants National Bank	(580) 227-3773
First Bank of Okarche	(405) 263-7215
FSNB, N.A.	(580) 357-9880
Payne County Bank	(405) 547-2436
Rating: A-	
BancFirst	(405) 270-1086
Bank of the Panhandle	(580) 338-2593
Bank of the West	(580) 661-3541
Bank, N.A.	(918) 423-2265
Bank7	(405) 810-8600
Exchange Bank	(918) 396-2345
F&M Bank	(405) 715-1100
First Bank	(580) 526-3332
First Bank of Owasso	(918) 272-5301
First National Bank & Trust of Elk City	(580) 225-2580
First National Bank of Fort Smith	(479) 788-4600
Great Southern Bank	(417) 895-5234
International Bank of Commerce Oklahoma	(405) 841-2100
Kirkpatrick Bank	(405) 341-8222
Liberty National Bank	(580) 351-2265
McClain Bank	(405) 527-6503
McCurtain County National Bank	(580) 584-6262
Oklahoma Bank and Trust Co.	(580) 323-2345
Oklahoma State Bank	(918) 256-5585
Peoples National Bank of Checotah	(918) 473-2237
Prime Bank	(405) 340-2775
Prosperity Bank	(979) 543-2200
Security State Bank	(580) 497-3354
Shamrock Bank, N.A.	(580) 927-2311
Sooner State Bank	(405) 381-2326
Stock Exchange Bank	(580) 256-3314
Welch State Bank of Welch, Oklahoma	(918) 788-3373
Rating: B+	
American Bank and Trust Co.	(918) 481-3000
American Exchange Bank	(405) 756-3101
Anchor D Bank	(580) 423-7541
Bank of America, N.A.	(704) 386-5681
Bank of Commerce	(918) 789-2567
Bank of Cordell	(580) 832-5600
Carson Community Bank	(918) 696-7745
Central National Bank of Poteau	(918) 647-2233
Community Bank	(918) 367-3343
Community Bank	(580) 327-5500
Fairview S&L Assn.	(580) 227-3735
First Bank & Trust Co.	(580) 255-1810
First Bank & Trust Co.	(580) 336-5562
First Bank of Thomas	(580) 661-3515
First National B&T Co. of Broken Arrow	(918) 251-5371
First National B&T Co. of Weatherford	(580) 772-5574
First National Bank	(918) 653-3200
First National Bank and Trust Co.	(405) 224-2200
First National Bank of Fletcher	(580) 549-6106
First National Bank of Lindsay	(405) 756-4433
First National Bank of Stigler	(918) 967-4665
First State Bank	(580) 623-4945
First Texoma National Bank	(580) 924-4242
First-Citizens Bank & Trust Co.	(919) 716-7050
Grand Savings Bank	(918) 786-2203
Idabel National Bank	(580) 286-7656
JPMorgan Chase Bank, N.A.	(614) 248-5800
Oklahoma State Bank	(580) 735-2545
Security First National Bank of Hugo	(580) 326-9641
Security National Bank of Enid	(580) 234-5151
Simmons Bank	(870) 541-1000
Southwest Bank of Weatherford	(580) 774-0900
State Bank of Wynnewood	(405) 665-2001
Triad Bank, N.A.	(918) 254-1444
Valor Bank	(405) 212-9800

Oregon

Name	Telephone
Rating: A+	
Pioneer Trust Bank, N.A.	(503) 363-3136
Rating: A	
Clackamas County Bank	(503) 668-5501
Riverview Community Bank	(360) 693-6650
Rating: A-	
Bank of the Pacific	(360) 537-4052
Citizens Bank	(541) 752-5161
Northwest Bank	(208) 332-0700
Oregon Coast Bank	(541) 265-9000
Pacific Premier Bank	(949) 864-8000
Washington Federal Bank, N.A.	(206) 204-3446
Washington Trust Bank	(509) 353-4204
Willamette Valley Bank	(503) 485-2222
Zions BanCorp., N.A.	(801) 844-7637
Rating: B+	
Baker-Boyer National Bank	(509) 525-2000
Bank of America, N.A.	(704) 386-5681
Banner Bank	(509) 527-3636
Columbia State Bank	(253) 305-1900
Community Bank	(541) 432-9050
First Interstate Bank	(406) 255-5000
First-Citizens Bank & Trust Co.	(919) 716-7050
JPMorgan Chase Bank, N.A.	(614) 248-5800
Lewis & Clark Bank	(503) 212-3200
Oregon Pacific Banking Co.	(541) 997-7121
People's Bank of Commerce	(541) 776-5350

Pennsylvania

Name	Telephone
Rating: A	
Haverford Trust Co.	(610) 995-8700
Parke Bank	(856) 256-2500
Rating: A-	
Citizens & Northern Bank	(570) 724-3411
Commercial Bank & Trust of PA	(724) 539-3501
Fidelity Deposit and Discount Bank	(570) 342-8281
First Columbia Bank & Trust Co.	(570) 784-1660
Honesdale National Bank	(570) 253-3355
Port Richmond Savings	(215) 634-7000
Slovenian S&L Assn. of Canonsburg	(724) 745-5000
Turbotville National Bank	(570) 649-5118
Union Savings Bank	(513) 247-0300
Unity Bank	(908) 730-7630
Wilmington Savings Fund Society, FSB	(302) 792-6000
Rating: B+	
ACNB Bank	(717) 334-3161
American Bank	(610) 366-1800
Apollo Trust Co.	(724) 478-3151
Bank of America, N.A.	(704) 386-5681
Bank of Landisburg	(717) 789-3213
Bank of Princeton	(609) 921-1700
Bryn Mawr Trust Co.	(610) 581-4839
Centric Bank	(717) 657-7727
Community Bank, N.A.	(315) 445-2282
Elderton State Bank	(724) 354-2111
Farmers and Merchants Trust Co.	(717) 264-6116
Farmers National Bank of Canfield	(330) 533-3341
First Commonwealth Bank	(724) 463-8555
First National B&T Co. of Newtown	(215) 860-9100
Firstrust Savings Bank	(610) 238-5001
Hamlin Bank and Trust Co.	(814) 887-5555
JPMorgan Chase Bank, N.A.	(614) 248-5800
National Bank of Malvern	(610) 647-0100
NBT Bank, N.A.	(607) 337-6416
Neffs National Bank	(610) 767-3875
NexTier Bank, N.A.	(724) 543-1125
Peoples Security Bank and Trust Co.	(570) 955-1700
PeoplesBank, A Codorus Valley Co.	(717) 846-1970
Philadelphia Trust Co.	(215) 979-3434
Susquehanna Community Bank	(570) 568-6851
Truist Bank	(336) 733-2000
VIST Bank	(610) 208-0966
Wayne Bank	(570) 253-1455
WesBanco Bank, Inc.	(304) 234-9419
William Penn Bank,	(215) 269-1200
Woodforest National Bank	(832) 375-2505
Woori America Bank	(212) 244-1500

Puerto Rico

Name	Telephone
Rating: B+	
Citibank, N.A.	(605) 370-6261

Rhode Island

Name	Telephone
Rating: B+	
Bank of America, N.A.	(704) 386-5681
BankNewport	(401) 846-3400
JPMorgan Chase Bank, N.A.	(614) 248-5800
Washington Trust Co. of Westerly	(401) 348-1200

South Carolina

Name	Telephone
Rating: A	
Bank of Clarendon	(803) 433-4451
Bank of South Carolina	(843) 724-1500
First Piedmont Federal S&L Assn. of Gaffney	(864) 489-6046
Palmetto State Bank	(803) 943-2671
Rating: A-	
Bank OZK	(501) 978-2265
Carolina Bank & Trust Co.	(843) 413-9978
First Bank	(910) 692-6222
First Federal Bank	(386) 755-0600
First Palmetto Bank	(803) 432-2265
ServisFirst Bank	(205) 949-0302
United Community Bank	(706) 745-2151
Rating: B+	
Ameris Bank	(404) 814-8114
Arthur State Bank	(864) 427-1213
Bank of America, N.A.	(704) 386-5681
Bank of Greeleyville	(843) 426-2161
Bank of Travelers Rest	(864) 834-9031
Bank of York	(803) 684-4249
Citizens Building and Loan, SSB	(864) 877-2054
Commercial Bank	(864) 369-7326
Conway National Bank	(843) 248-5721
Farmers and Merchants Bank	(803) 496-3430
First Community Bank	(803) 951-2265
First-Citizens Bank & Trust Co.	(919) 716-7050
JPMorgan Chase Bank, N.A.	(614) 248-5800
Oconee Federal S&L Assn.	(864) 882-2765
Pinnacle Bank	(615) 744-3705
South State Bank	(803) 771-2265
Southern First Bank	(864) 679-9000
Synovus Bank	(706) 649-4900
Truist Bank	(336) 733-2000
Woodforest National Bank	(832) 375-2505

South Dakota

Name	Telephone
Rating: A	
Pioneer Bank & Trust	(605) 717-2265
Security National Bank of South Dakota	(605) 232-6060
Rating: A-	
Dakota Prairie Bank	(605) 223-2337
First National Bank	(605) 223-2521
First National Bank	(605) 482-8293
First National Bank in Philip	(605) 859-2525
First Premier Bank	(605) 357-3000
First Savings Bank	(605) 763-2009
First State Bank of Roscoe	(605) 287-4451
First Western Federal Savings Bank	(605) 341-1203
Quoin Financial Bank	(605) 853-2473
Rating: B+	
Bryant State Bank	(605) 628-2171
Citibank, N.A.	(605) 370-6261
Department Stores National Bank	
First Bank & Trust	(605) 978-9300
First Bank & Trust	(605) 696-2265
First Fidelity Bank	(605) 775-2641
First Interstate Bank	(406) 255-5000
First National Bank in Sioux Falls	(605) 335-5200
Liberty National Bank	(712) 224-4425
MetaBank, N.A.	(605) 782-1767
Minnwest Bank	(507) 637-5731
Richland State Bank	(605) 627-5671
Security State Bank	(605) 449-4261
TCF National Bank	(952) 745-2760

Tennessee

Rating: A

Name	Telephone
Citizens Bank	(615) 735-1490
Citizens Bank	(423) 543-2265
Citizens National Bank	(865) 453-9031
Elizabethton Federal Savings Bank	(423) 543-5050
First Bank and Trust Co.	(276) 889-4622
FSNB, N.A.	(580) 357-9880
Republic Bank & Trust Co.	(502) 584-3600
Truxton Trust Co.	(615) 515-1700

Rating: A-

Name	Telephone
Andrew Johnson Bank	(423) 783-1000
Bank of Cleveland	(423) 478-5656
Bank of Lincoln County	(931) 433-1708
Bank of Marion	(276) 783-3116
Bank of Waynesboro	(931) 722-2265
Citizens B&T Co. of Grainger County	(865) 828-5237
Citizens Bank	(615) 374-2265
Citizens Community Bank	(931) 967-3342
Commercial Bank & Trust Co.	(731) 642-3341
Farmers Bank	(615) 325-2265
Financial Federal Bank	(901) 756-2848
First Federal Bank	(615) 446-2822
First Financial Bank, N.A.	(812) 238-6000
First Jackson Bank, Inc.	(256) 437-2107
First National Bank of Manchester	(931) 728-3518
First National Bank of Oneida	(423) 569-8586
First National Bank of Pulaski	(931) 363-2585
First Volunteer Bank	(423) 668-4509
Peoples Bank	(731) 858-2661
Peoples Bank & Trust Co.	(931) 728-3381
Peoples Bank of East Tennessee	(423) 442-7262
Peoples Bank of Middle Tennessee	(931) 684-7222
Putnam 1st Mercantile Bank	(931) 528-6372
Security FSB of McMinnville	(931) 473-4483
ServisFirst Bank	(205) 949-0302
Tennessee State Bank	(865) 453-0873
United Community Bank	(706) 745-2151
Wilson Bank and Trust	(615) 444-2265

Rating: B+

Name	Telephone
BancorpSouth Bank	(662) 680-2000
Bank of America, N.A.	(704) 386-5681
Bank of Crockett	(731) 663-2031
Bank of Frankewing	(931) 363-1796
Bank of Gleason	(731) 648-5506
Cadence Bank, N.A.	(800) 636-7622
CapStar Bank	(615) 732-6400
CBBC Bank	(865) 977-5900
Citizens Bank of Lafayette	(615) 666-2195
City National Bank	(800) 773-7100
Commercial Bank	(423) 869-5151
First Century Bank	(423) 626-7261
First Citizens National Bank	(731) 285-4410
First Community Bank of East Tennessee	(423) 272-5800
First Community Bank of Tennessee	(931) 684-5800
First Farmers and Merchants Bank	(931) 388-3145
First National Bank of Eastern Arkansas	(870) 633-3112
First National Bank of Middle Tennessee	(931) 473-4402
First National Bank of Tennessee	(931) 823-1261
First Vision Bank of Tennessee	(931) 454-0500
FirstBank	(615) 313-0080
First-Citizens Bank & Trust Co.	(919) 716-7050
Guaranty Bank and Trust Co.	(662) 247-1454
JPMorgan Chase Bank, N.A.	(614) 248-5800
Legends Bank	(931) 503-1234
Mountain Commerce Bank	(865) 694-5725
Pinnacle Bank	(615) 744-3705
Planters Bank, Inc.	(270) 886-9030
Renasant Bank	(800) 680-1601
Security Bank and Trust Co.	(731) 642-6644
Simmons Bank	(870) 541-1000
Southern Bank of Tennessee	(615) 758-6600
Synovus Bank	(706) 649-4900
Truist Bank	(336) 733-2000
Trustmark National Bank	(601) 208-5111
Union Bank & Trust Co.	(931) 823-1247

Texas

Name	Telephone
Rating: A+	
Citizens 1st Bank	(903) 581-1900
Rating: A	
Austin Bank, Texas N.A.	(903) 586-1526
Bessemer Trust Co., N.A.	(212) 708-9100
Citizens National Bank at Brownwood	(325) 643-3545
Commerce Bank	(956) 724-1616
Commercial National Bank of Brady	(325) 597-2961
Community Bank	(903) 236-4422
Crockett National Bank	(210) 467-5391
Crossroads Bank	(361) 293-3572
Falcon International Bank	(956) 723-2265
First Financial Bank, N.A.	(325) 627-7200
First State Bank of Bedias	(936) 395-2141
First State Bank of Odem	(361) 368-2651
FSNB, N.A.	(580) 357-9880
International Bank of Commerce	(956) 765-8361
International Bank of Commerce	(956) 547-1000
International Bank of Commerce	(956) 722-7611
Mason Bank	(325) 347-5911
Metro City Bank	(770) 455-4989
Muenster State Bank	(940) 759-2257
Sanger Bank	(940) 458-4600
Security State Bank & Trust	(830) 997-7575
Tejas Bank	(432) 943-4230
Texas Community Bank	(956) 722-8333
Texas State Bank	(325) 949-3721
TexasBank	(325) 649-9200
Trinity Bank, N.A.	(817) 763-9966
ValueBank Texas	(361) 888-4451
Waggoner National Bank of Vernon	(940) 552-2511
Rating: A-	
AimBank	(806) 385-4441
American First National Bank	(713) 596-2888
American National Bank of Mount Pleasant	(903) 572-1776
Amistad Bank	(830) 775-0295
Armed Forces Bank, N.A.	(913) 682-9090
Arrowhead Bank	(325) 247-5741
Bank of DeSoto, N.A.	(972) 780-7777
Bank of Texas	(432) 221-6100
Bank OZK	(501) 978-2265
Bank7	(405) 810-8600
BOC Bank	(806) 373-1720
Brenham National Bank	(979) 836-4571
BTH Bank, N.A.	(903) 763-2264
Buckholts State Bank	(254) 593-3661
Capital Bank of Texas	(830) 876-5221
Cathay Bank	(213) 625-4791
Central National Bank	(254) 776-3800
Citizens Bank	(806) 350-5600
Citizens Bank of Las Cruces	(575) 647-4100
Citizens Bank, N.A.	(325) 695-3000
Citizens State Bank	(936) 398-2566
Citizens State Bank	(979) 885-3571
Citizens State Bank	(325) 468-3311
City National Bank of Sulphur Springs	(903) 885-7523
City National Bank of Taylor	(512) 671-2265
Coleman County State Bank	(325) 625-2172
Comerica Bank	(214) 462-4000
Commonwealth Business Bank	(323) 988-3000
Community Bank & Trust, Waco, Texas	(254) 753-1521
Community National B&T of Texas	(903) 654-4500
CommunityBank of Texas, N.A.	(409) 861-7200
Cowboy Bank of Texas	(972) 435-2131
East West Bank	(626) 768-6000
First Command Bank	(888) 763-7600
First Community Bank	(361) 888-9310
First National Bank	(806) 659-5544
First National Bank of Albany	(325) 762-2222
First National Bank of Bastrop	(512) 321-2561
First National Bank of Burleson	(817) 295-0461
First National Bank of Eldorado	(325) 853-2561
First National Bank of Floydada	(806) 983-3717
First National Bank of Granbury	(817) 573-2655
First National Bank of Hebbronville	(361) 527-3221
First Savings Bank	(605) 763-2009
First State Bank	(903) 676-1900
First State Bank	(979) 648-2691
First State Bank	(806) 396-5521
First State Bank and Trust Co.	(903) 693-6606
First State Bank of Ben Wheeler, Texas	(903) 833-5861
First State Bank of Paint Rock	(325) 732-4386
First Texas Bank	(512) 556-3691
First United Bank	(806) 647-4151
Frost Bank	(210) 220-4011
Golden Bank, N.A.	(713) 777-3838
Grandview Bank	(817) 866-3316
Guadalupe Bank	(830) 792-1950
Happy State Bank	(806) 558-2265
HomeBank Texas	(972) 287-2030
HomeTown Bank, N.A.	(409) 763-1271
International Bank of Commerce Oklahoma	(405) 841-2100

Texas

Name	Telephone
Inwood National Bank	(214) 358-5281
Johnson City Bank	(830) 868-7131
Liberty Capital Bank	(469) 375-6600
Liberty National Bank in Paris	(903) 785-5555
Llano National Bank	(325) 247-5701
Marion State Bank	(830) 420-2331
Moody National Bank	(409) 632-5016
Open Bank	(213) 892-9999
Pegasus Bank	(214) 353-3000
Peoples Bank	(806) 794-0044
Peoples State Bank	(830) 683-2119
Pinnacle Bank	(817) 810-9110
PlainsCapital Bank	(214) 525-9000
Pointbank	(940) 686-7000
PromiseOne Bank	(678) 385-0800
Prosperity Bank	(979) 543-2200
Roscoe State Bank	(325) 766-3311
Round Top State Bank	(979) 249-3151
Schertz Bank & Trust	(210) 945-7400
Security State Bank	(830) 334-3606
Security State Bank	(806) 481-3327
Shelby Savings Bank, SSB	(936) 598-5688
State National Bank of Big Spring	(432) 264-2100
T Bank, N.A.	(972) 720-9000
Texas Bank and Trust Co.	(903) 237-5500
Texas Bank Financial	(817) 596-9998
Texas Exchange Bank, SSB	(817) 297-4331
Texas Financial Bank	(325) 869-5511
Texas First Bank	(409) 948-1990
Texas Republic Bank, N.A.	(972) 334-0700
Titan Bank, N.A.	(940) 325-9821
Tolleson Private Bank	(214) 252-3033
Washington Federal Bank, N.A.	(206) 204-3446
West Texas National Bank	(432) 685-6500
WestStar Bank	(915) 532-1000
Yoakum National Bank	(361) 293-5225
Zions BanCorp., N.A.	(801) 844-7637

Rating: B+

Name	Telephone
Amarillo National Bank	(806) 378-8000
American Momentum Bank	(979) 774-1111
American National Bank of Texas	(972) 524-3411
Anahuac National Bank	(409) 267-3106
Austin Capital Bank SSB	(512) 693-3600
Austin County State Bank	(979) 865-4200
BancorpSouth Bank	(662) 680-2000
Bandera Bank	(830) 796-3711
Bank and Trust, SSB	(830) 774-2555
Bank of America, N.A.	(704) 386-5681
Benchmark Bank	(972) 673-4000
Big Bend Banks, N.A.	(432) 729-4344
Brazos National Bank	(979) 265-1911
Broadway National Bank	(210) 283-6500
Burton State Bank	(979) 289-3151
Cadence Bank, N.A.	(800) 636-7622
Cendera Bank, N.A.	(903) 965-7755
Central Bank	(832) 485-2300
Charles Schwab Bank, SSB	(775) 689-6800
Charter Bank	(361) 241-7681
CIT Bank, N.A.	(855) 462-2652
Citibank, N.A.	(605) 370-6261
Citizens National Bank of Crosbyton	(806) 675-2376
Citizens National Bank of Hillsboro	(254) 582-2531
Citizens State Bank	(903) 322-4256
Citizens State Bank	(979) 596-1421
City Bank	(806) 792-7101
Commercial Bank of Texas, N.A.	(936) 715-4100
Commercial National Bank of Texarkana	(903) 831-4561
Community National Bank	(830) 426-3066
Community National Bank	(432) 262-1600
Dilley State Bank	(830) 965-1511
Ennis State Bank	(972) 875-9676
Falls City National Bank	(830) 254-3573
Farmers State Bank	(254) 729-3272
Fidelity Bank of Texas	(254) 755-6555
First Bank & Trust	(806) 788-0800
First Bank and Trust of Memphis	(806) 259-3556
First IC Bank	(770) 451-7200
First Liberty National Bank	(936) 336-6471
First National Bank of Alvin	(281) 331-3151
First National Bank of Aspermont	(940) 989-3505
First National Bank of Bellville	(979) 865-3181
First National Bank of Bosque County	(254) 932-5345
First National Bank of Central Texas	(254) 772-9330
First National Bank of Dublin	(254) 445-4400
First National Bank of Evant	(254) 471-5531
First National Bank of Hughes Springs	(903) 639-2521
First National Bank of Huntsville	(936) 295-5701
First National Bank of Livingston	(936) 327-1234
First National Bank of McGregor	(254) 840-2836
First National Bank of Shiner	(361) 594-3317
First National Bank of Stanton	(432) 756-3361
First National Bank of Winnsboro	(903) 342-5275
First National Bank Texas	(254) 554-4236

Texas

Name	Telephone
First State Bank	(940) 549-8880
First State Bank	(940) 665-1711
First State Bank of Burnet	(512) 756-2191
First State Bank of Uvalde	(830) 278-6231
First Texas Bank	(512) 863-2567
First Texoma National Bank	(580) 924-4242
FirstBank Southwest	(806) 355-9661
First-Citizens Bank & Trust Co.	(919) 716-7050
Fort Hood National Bank	(254) 532-1026
Frontier Bank of Texas	(512) 281-1500
Guaranty Bank & Trust, N.A.	(903) 572-9881
Hanmi Bank	(213) 382-2200
Hondo National Bank	(830) 426-3355
Horizon Bank, SSB	(512) 637-5730
Independent Bank	(972) 562-9004
Industry State Bank	(979) 357-4437
Jacksboro National Bank	(940) 567-5551
Jefferson Bank	(210) 734-4311
JPMorgan Chase Bank, N.A.	(614) 248-5800
Legend Bank, N.A.	(940) 872-2221
Lone Star National Bank	(956) 984-2991
Lytle State Bank of Lytle, Texas	(830) 709-3601
NewFirst National Bank	(979) 543-3349
NexBank SSB	(972) 934-4700
Northern Trust Co.	(312) 630-6000
Pearland State Bank	(281) 485-3211
Perryton National Bank	(806) 435-9641
Sabine State Bank and Trust Co.	(318) 256-7000
Sage Capital Bank	(830) 672-8585
Santa Anna National Bank	(325) 348-3108
Simmons Bank	(870) 541-1000
Southside Bank	(903) 531-7111
SouthStar Bank, S.S.B.	(361) 596-4611
Southwest Bank	(432) 552-5000
Southwestern National Bank	(713) 771-9700
Spirit of Texas Bank, SSB	(936) 538-1000
Spring Hill State Bank	(903) 759-0751
State Bank of De Kalb	(903) 667-2553
State Bank of Texas	(972) 252-6000
Stockmens National Bank in Cotulla	(830) 879-2331
Sundown State Bank	(806) 229-2111
Texas Brand Bank	(214) 219-0003
Texas Security Bank	(469) 398-4800
TexStar National Bank	(210) 659-4000
Truist Bank	(336) 733-2000
Trustmark National Bank	(601) 208-5111
UBank	(936) 639-5566
VeraBank, N.A.	(903) 657-8521
Wallis Bank	(979) 478-6151
Wells Fargo Bank South Central, N.A.	(713) 802-2717
Woodforest National Bank	(832) 375-2505
Woori America Bank	(212) 244-1500
Zavala County Bank	(830) 374-5866

Utah

Name	Telephone
Rating: A+	
Green Dot Bank	(801) 344-7020
Optum Bank, Inc.	(866) 234-8913
Rating: A	
Altabank	(801) 756-7681
Bank of Utah	(801) 409-5000
Central Bank	(801) 375-1000
LCA Bank Corp.	(435) 658-4824
Morgan Stanley Bank, N.A.	(801) 236-3600
State Bank of Southern Utah	(435) 865-2300
UBS Bank USA	(801) 741-0310
Rating: A-	
BMW Bank of North America	(801) 461-6500
Brighton Bank	(801) 943-6500
D.L. Evans Bank	(208) 678-8615
First Electronic Bank	(801) 572-4004
Glacier Bank	(406) 756-4200
Home Savings Bank	(801) 523-3878
Pitney Bowes Bank, Inc.	(801) 832-4440
Rock Canyon Bank	(801) 426-0150
Utah Independent Bank	(435) 529-7459
Washington Federal Bank, N.A.	(206) 204-3446
WebBank	(801) 456-8350
Zions BanCorp., N.A.	(801) 844-7637
Rating: B+	
Bank of America, N.A.	(704) 386-5681
Celtic Bank	(801) 363-6500
EnerBank USA	(801) 832-0700
Finwise Bank	(801) 545-6000
Grand Valley Bank	(435) 654-7400
Holladay Bank & Trust	(801) 272-4275
JPMorgan Chase Bank, N.A.	(614) 248-5800
Marlin Business Bank	(888) 479-9111
Sunwest Bank	(714) 730-4444
WEX Bank	(801) 568-4345

Vermont

Name	Telephone
Rating: A-	
TrustCo Bank	(518) 377-3311
Rating: B+	
Community Bank, N.A.	(315) 445-2282
Ledyard National Bank	(802) 649-2050
NBT Bank, N.A.	(607) 337-6416

Virgin Islands of the U.S.

Name	Telephone
Rating: B+	
United Fidelity Bank, FSB	(812) 424-0921

Virginia

Name	Telephone
Rating: A	
Bank of Southside Virginia	(434) 246-5211
Calvin B. Taylor Banking Co.	(410) 641-1700
First Bank and Trust Co.	(276) 889-4622
Metro City Bank	(770) 455-4989
National Bank of Blacksburg	(540) 951-6205
Surrey Bank & Trust	(336) 783-3900
Rating: A-	
AMG National Trust Bank	(303) 694-2190
Armed Forces Bank, N.A.	(913) 682-9090
Bank of Charlotte County	(434) 542-5111
Bank of Marion	(276) 783-3116
Benchmark Community Bank	(434) 676-9054
Citizens and Farmers Bank	(804) 843-2360
Citizens Bank and Trust Co.	(434) 292-8100
City National Bank of West Virginia	(304) 769-1100
EagleBank	(240) 497-2075
Farmers & Merchants Bank	(540) 864-5156
Fidelity Bank	(919) 552-2242
First Bank	(540) 465-9121
Lee Bank and Trust Co.	(276) 546-2211
Virginia National Bank	(434) 817-8621
Rating: B+	
American National Bank and Trust Co.	(434) 792-5111
Atlantic Union Bank	(804) 327-5720
Bank of America, N.A.	(704) 386-5681
Bank of Clarke County	(540) 955-2510
Chesapeake Bank	(804) 435-1181
Citibank, N.A.	(605) 370-6261
Essex Bank	(804) 419-4329
Farmers and Miners Bank	(276) 546-4692
Farmers Bank	(757) 242-6111
Farmers Bank of Appomattox	(434) 352-7171
First-Citizens Bank & Trust Co.	(919) 716-7050
FVCbank	(703) 436-4740
Hanmi Bank	(213) 382-2200
Highlands Community Bank	(540) 962-2265
John Marshall Bank	(703) 584-0840
JPMorgan Chase Bank, N.A.	(614) 248-5800
MainStreet Bank	(703) 481-4567
MVB Bank, Inc.	(304) 367-2602
Pinnacle Bank	(615) 744-3705
Shore United Bank	(410) 822-1400
Sonabank	(804) 528-4754
South State Bank	(803) 771-2265
Southern Bank and Trust Co.	(919) 658-7000
Summit Community Bank, Inc.	(304) 530-1000
TowneBank	(757) 638-7500
Truist Bank	(336) 733-2000
Woodforest National Bank	(832) 375-2505
Woori America Bank	(212) 244-1500

Washington

Name	Telephone
Rating: A	
1st Security Bank of Washington	(800) 683-0973
Bessemer Trust Co., N.A.	(212) 708-9100
Cashmere Valley Bank	(509) 782-2624
Riverview Community Bank	(360) 693-6650
Security State Bank	(360) 736-0763
Sterling Bank and Trust, FSB	(248) 355-2400
Timberland Bank	(360) 533-4747
Rating: A-	
American Continental Bank	(626) 363-8988
Armed Forces Bank, N.A.	(913) 682-9090
Bank of the Pacific	(360) 537-4052
Cathay Bank	(213) 625-4791
Coastal Community Bank	(425) 257-9000
Commencement Bank	(253) 284-1800
East West Bank	(626) 768-6000
Glacier Bank	(406) 756-4200
Kitsap Bank	(360) 876-7834
Northwest Bank	(208) 332-0700
Pacific Premier Bank	(949) 864-8000
Peoples Bank	(360) 715-4200
UniBank	(425) 275-9700
Washington Federal Bank, N.A.	(206) 204-3446
Washington Trust Bank	(509) 353-4204
Zions BanCorp., N.A.	(801) 844-7637
Rating: B+	
Baker-Boyer National Bank	(509) 525-2000
Bank of America, N.A.	(704) 386-5681
Banner Bank	(509) 527-3636
Columbia State Bank	(253) 305-1900
Community Bank	(541) 432-9050
Community First Bank	(509) 783-3435
First Interstate Bank	(406) 255-5000
First-Citizens Bank & Trust Co.	(919) 716-7050
Islanders Bank	(360) 378-3658
JPMorgan Chase Bank, N.A.	(614) 248-5800
Lamont Bank of St. John	(509) 648-3636
Northern Trust Co.	(312) 630-6000
Pacific Crest Savings Bank	(425) 670-9600
Sound Banking Co.	(253) 588-0100
Twin River Bank	(208) 746-4848
United Business Bank	(925) 476-1800
Washington Business Bank	(360) 754-1945
Wheatland Bank	(509) 458-2265
Yakima Federal S&L Assn.	(509) 248-2634

West Virginia

Rating: A-

Name	Telephone
Bank of Monroe	(304) 772-3034
Citizens Bank of Weston, Inc.	(304) 269-2862
City National Bank of West Virginia	(304) 769-1100
Clay County Bank, Inc.	(304) 587-4221
Clear Mountain Bank	(304) 379-2265
Mountain Valley Bank, N.A.	(304) 637-2265

Rating: B+

Name	Telephone
Community Bank of Parkersburg	(304) 485-7991
Fayette County National Bank of Fayetteville	(304) 574-1212
First-Citizens Bank & Trust Co.	(919) 716-7050
JPMorgan Chase Bank, N.A.	(614) 248-5800
MVB Bank, Inc.	(304) 367-2602
Summit Community Bank, Inc.	(304) 530-1000
Truist Bank	(336) 733-2000
Union Bank, Inc.	(304) 758-2191
WesBanco Bank, Inc.	(304) 234-9419
Williamstown Bank, Inc.	(304) 375-6262
Woodforest National Bank	(832) 375-2505

Wisconsin

Name	Telephone
Rating: A+	
Bank of Alma	(608) 685-4461
Bank of Prairie Du Sac	(608) 643-3393
Rating: A	
Bank of Mauston	(608) 847-6200
Charter Bank	(715) 832-4254
Farmers State Bank Hillsboro	(608) 489-2621
First National Bank of Bangor	(608) 486-2386
Intercity State Bank	(715) 359-4231
National Exchange Bank and Trust	(920) 921-7700
Northwestern Bank	(715) 723-4461
Oregon Community Bank	(608) 835-3168
WaterStone Bank, SSB	(414) 761-1000
Waukesha State Bank	(262) 549-8500
Rating: A-	
Advantage Community Bank	(715) 654-5100
American National Bank-Fox Cities	(920) 739-1040
Apple River State Bank	(815) 594-2351
Badger Bank	(920) 563-2478
Bank of Deerfield	(608) 764-5411
Bank of Lake Mills	(920) 648-8336
Bank of Wisconsin Dells	(608) 253-1111
BLC Community Bank	(920) 788-4141
Bluff View Bank	(608) 582-2233
Bonduel State Bank	(715) 758-2141
Capitol Bank	(608) 836-1616
Citizens Bank	(262) 363-6500
DMB Community Bank	(608) 846-3711
Farmers State Bank of Waupaca	(715) 258-1400
First Citizens State Bank	(262) 473-2112
First Community Bank	(608) 868-7644
First National Bank of River Falls	(715) 425-2401
Hometown Bank	(920) 907-0788
International Bank of Amherst	(715) 824-3325
John Deere Financial, F.S.B.	(608) 821-2000
Johnson Bank	(262) 619-2700
Nekoosa Port Edwards State Bank	(715) 886-3104
Oostburg State Bank	(920) 564-2336
Peoples Community Bank	(608) 795-2120
Shell Lake State Bank	(715) 468-7858
State Bank of Newburg	(262) 675-2306
Wolf River Community Bank	(920) 779-7000
Rating: B+	
Bank of Brodhead	(608) 897-2121
Bank of Cashton	(608) 654-5121
Bank of Milton	(608) 868-7672
Bay Bank	(920) 490-7600
Black River Country Bank	(715) 284-9448
Bremer Bank, N.A.	(651) 288-3751
Citizens State Bank of Loyal	(715) 255-8526
Clare Bank, N.A.	(608) 348-2727
Community First Bank	(608) 375-4117
Cumberland Federal Bank, FSB	(715) 822-2249
First National Bank at Darlington	(608) 776-4071
First-Citizens Bank & Trust Co.	(919) 716-7050
Flagstar Bank, FSB	(248) 312-5400
Great Midwest Bank, S.S.B.	(262) 784-4400
Headwaters State Bank	(715) 547-3383
Home Federal Savings Bank	(507) 535-1309
Hustisford State Bank	(920) 349-3241
JPMorgan Chase Bank, N.A.	(614) 248-5800
Nicolet National Bank	(920) 430-1400
Northern State Bank	(715) 682-2772
Northern Trust Co.	(312) 630-6000
Oak Bank	(608) 441-6000
Paper City Savings Assn.	(715) 423-8100
Partners Bank	(715) 659-2430
Peoples State Bank	(715) 842-2191
Pineries Bank	(715) 341-5600
Richland County Bank	(608) 647-6306
River Falls State Bank	(715) 425-6782
Royal Bank	(608) 462-8401
Starion Bank	(701) 223-6050
TCF National Bank	(952) 745-2760
Tri City National Bank	(414) 761-1610
TSB Bank	(920) 269-7777
WNB Financial, N.A.	(507) 454-8800
Woodford State Bank	(608) 325-7766

Wyoming

Name	Telephone
Rating: A	
RSNB Bank	(307) 362-8801
Wyoming Bank & Trust	(307) 632-7733
Rating: A-	
AMG National Trust Bank	(303) 694-2190
Bank of Commerce	(307) 324-2265
Bank of Star Valley	(307) 885-0000
First State Bank	(308) 632-4158
FirsTier Bank	(308) 235-4633
Glacier Bank	(406) 756-4200
Lusk State Bank	(307) 334-2500
Pinnacle Bank - Wyoming	(402) 697-5990
Points West Community Bank	(970) 686-0878
Zions BanCorp., N.A.	(801) 844-7637
Rating: B+	
ANB Bank	(303) 394-5143
Bank of Jackson Hole	(307) 733-8064
Converse County Bank	(307) 358-5300
First Interstate Bank	(406) 255-5000
Hilltop National Bank	(307) 265-2740
Jonah Bank of Wyoming	(307) 237-4555
Rocky Mountain Bank	(307) 739-9000

Section III

Rating Upgrades and Downgrades

A list of all

U.S. Commercial Banks and Savings Banks

receiving a rating upgrade or downgrade
during the current quarter.

Section III Contents

This section identifies those institutions receiving a rating change since the previous edition of this publication, whether it be a rating upgrade, rating downgrade, newly-rated company or the withdrawal of a rating. A rating upgrade or downgrade may entail a change from one letter grade to another, or it may mean the addition or deletion of a plus or minus sign within the same letter grade previously assigned to the company. Ratings are normally updated once each quarter of the year. In some instances, however, an institution's rating may be downgraded outside of the normal updates due to overriding circumstances.

1. **Institution Name** The name under which the institution was chartered. A company's name can be very similar to, or the same as, that of another, so verify the company's exact name, city, and state to make sure you are looking at the correct company.

2. **New Safety Rating** Weiss rating assigned to the institution at the time of publication. Our ratings are designed to distinguish levels of insolvency risk and are measured on a scale from A to F based upon a wide range of factors. Highly rated companies are, in our opinion, less likely to experience financial difficulties than lower rated firms. See *About Weiss Safety Ratings* for more information and a description of what each rating means.

3. **State** The state in which the institution's headquarters or main office is located.

4. **Date of Change** Date that rating was finalized.

Rating Upgrades

Name	State	Date of Change
Rating: A+		
Bank of Alma	WI	06/29/20
Pioneer Trust Bank, N.A.	OR	06/29/20
Rating: A		
Alliance Bank	IN	06/29/20
Amerasia Bank	NY	06/29/20
Bank of Advance	MO	06/29/20
Bank of Hemet	CA	06/29/20
Citizens National Bank at Brownwood	TX	06/29/20
Community State Bank	IN	06/29/20
Community State Bank	CO	06/29/20
First General Bank	CA	06/29/20
First National Bank	NM	06/29/20
Independence Bank	MT	06/29/20
Iowa State Bank	IA	06/29/20
Republic Bank & Trust Co.	KY	06/29/20
Security First Bank of North Dakota	ND	06/29/20
Surrey Bank & Trust	NC	06/29/20
Tejas Bank	TX	06/29/20
Trinity Bank, N.A.	TX	06/29/20
Vermilion Valley Bank	IL	06/29/20
Wood & Huston Bank	MO	06/29/20
Rating: A-		
Bank of Elgin	NE	06/29/20
Bank of Star Valley	WY	06/29/20
Bankwest of Kansas	KS	06/29/20
Bloomsdale Bank	MO	06/29/20
BNC National Bank	AZ	06/29/20
Bonduel State Bank	WI	06/29/20
Bridge Community Bank	IA	06/29/20
Camden National Bank	ME	06/29/20
Capital Bank of Texas	TX	06/29/20
Casey County Bank, Inc.	KY	06/29/20
Centier Bank	IN	06/29/20
Chino Commercial Bank, N.A.	CA	06/29/20
Citizens Bank	WI	06/29/20
Citizens Bank of Edina	MO	06/29/20
Citizens Bank of Weston, Inc.	WV	06/29/20
Citizens Community Bank	TN	06/29/20
City National Bank of West Virginia	WV	06/29/20
Coleman County State Bank	TX	06/29/20
Colorado Bank and Trust Co. of La Junta	CO	06/29/20
Commercial Bank & Trust of PA	PA	06/29/20
Community First Bank	KS	06/29/20
Exchange Bank of Missouri	MO	06/29/20
Farmers & Merchants State Bank	IA	06/29/20
Farmers State Bank of Hartland	MN	06/29/20
First Bank	NC	06/29/20
First Bank of Berne	IN	06/29/20
First National Bank of Gordon	NE	06/29/20
First National Bank of Litchfield	IL	06/29/20
First Palmetto Bank	SC	06/29/20
First Security Bank - Canby	MN	06/29/20
First Security Bank-Sleepy Eye	MN	06/29/20
First State Bank of Campbell Hill	IL	06/29/20
First State Community Bank	MO	06/29/20
Frederick Community Bank	IL	06/29/20
Fresno First Bank	CA	06/29/20
Guadalupe Bank	TX	06/29/20
Guardian Savings Bank, F.S.B.	OH	06/29/20
Homestead Bank	NE	06/29/20
Ireland Bank	ID	06/29/20
Janesville State Bank	MN	06/29/20
Kirkpatrick Bank	OK	06/29/20
Lee Bank and Trust Co.	VA	06/29/20
Meadows Bank	NV	06/29/20
Merchants Bank of Indiana	IN	06/29/20
Mission Bank	CA	06/29/20
NBKC Bank	MO	06/29/20
Northern Bank & Trust Co.	MA	06/29/20
Oostburg State Bank	WI	06/29/20
Peoples Bank	KY	06/29/20
Pointbank	TX	06/29/20
Preferred Bank	CA	06/29/20
Premier Bank	NE	06/29/20
Rock Canyon Bank	UT	06/29/20
Security State Bank	IA	06/29/20
Shelby County State Bank	IL	06/29/20
St. Clair State Bank (Inc.)	MN	06/29/20
State Bank	MI	06/29/20
State Bank of Danvers	MN	06/29/20
SunMark Community Bank	GA	06/29/20
T Bank, N.A.	TX	06/29/20
Texas Bank Financial	TX	06/29/20
Turbotville National Bank	PA	06/29/20
Unified Bank	OH	06/29/20
Union Bank of Mena	AR	06/29/20
WebBank	UT	06/29/20
West Gate Bank	NE	06/29/20
Rating: B+		
Arkansas County Bank	AR	06/29/20
Bank Forward	ND	06/29/20
Bank of Edmonson County	KY	06/29/20
Bank of Hillsboro, N.A.	IL	06/29/20
Bank of Jackson Hole	WY	06/29/20
Bank of Milton	WI	06/29/20

Rating Upgrades

Name	State	Date of Change
Bank of New England	NH	06/29/20
Bippus State Bank	IN	06/29/20
CBBC Bank	TN	06/29/20
Century Bank and Trust	MI	06/29/20
Charter Bank	TX	06/29/20
Charter West Bank	NE	06/29/20
Citizens Bank of Georgia	GA	06/29/20
Citizens State Bank	IA	06/29/20
Commercial Bank of Texas, N.A.	TX	06/29/20
Community Bank of the Midwest	KS	06/29/20
Falls City National Bank	TX	06/29/20
Farmers and Merchants State Bank	NE	06/29/20
Farmers State Bank	IA	06/29/20
Farmers-Merchants Bank of Illinois	IL	06/29/20
First Century Bank, N.A.	GA	06/29/20
First Colony Bank of Florida	FL	06/29/20
First Community Bank of East Tennessee	TN	06/29/20
First Heritage Bank	KS	06/29/20
First National B&T Co. of Broken Arrow	OK	06/29/20
First National Bank in Howell	MI	06/29/20
First National Bank of Hughes Springs	TX	06/29/20
First National Bank of Stigler	OK	06/29/20
First National Bank of Waseca	MN	06/29/20
First State Bank	ND	06/29/20
Fowler State Bank	CO	06/29/20
Friend Bank	AL	06/29/20
Garrett State Bank	IN	06/29/20
Goose River Bank	ND	06/29/20
Great American Bank	KS	06/29/20
Guaranty Bank and Trust Co.	MS	06/29/20
Hodge Bank & Trust Co.	LA	06/29/20
Houghton State Bank	IA	06/29/20
Independent Farmers Bank	MO	06/29/20
Jonah Bank of Wyoming	WY	06/29/20
Kinmundy Bank	IL	06/29/20
Lake Bank	MN	06/29/20
LCNB National Bank	OH	06/29/20
Merchants and Planters Bank	MS	06/29/20
Metropolitan Bank	CA	06/29/20
Morton Community Bank	IL	06/29/20
MRV Banks	MO	06/29/20
Nebraska State Bank and Trust Co.	NE	06/29/20
NewFirst National Bank	TX	06/29/20
Northpointe Bank	MI	06/29/20
Oak Bank	WI	06/29/20
Opportunity Bank of Montana	MT	06/29/20
Park State Bank	MN	06/29/20
People's Bank of Commerce	OR	06/29/20
Piedmont Bank	GA	06/29/20
Platinum Bank	MN	06/29/20
Plumas Bank	CA	06/29/20
PrimeSouth Bank	GA	06/29/20
Relyance Bank, N.A.	AR	06/29/20
Resource Bank	LA	06/29/20
Richland County Bank	WI	06/29/20
Roundbank	MN	06/29/20
State Bank	CO	06/29/20
Stockmens Bank	CO	06/29/20
Sutton Bank	OH	06/29/20
Synergy Bank	LA	06/29/20
Triad Bank, N.A.	OK	06/29/20
Unison Bank	ND	06/29/20
United Bank	AL	06/29/20
Valor Bank	OK	06/29/20
VeraBank, N.A.	TX	06/29/20
Watertown Savings Bank	NY	06/29/20

Rating: B

Name	State	Date of Change
American Bank of the North	MN	06/29/20
Bank of Bolivar	MO	06/29/20
Bank of Commerce	KS	06/29/20
Bank of Rantoul	IL	06/29/20
BankCherokee	MN	06/29/20
Century Bank	MS	06/29/20
Ciera Bank	TX	06/29/20
Citizens Bank	MO	06/29/20
Citizens Bank & Trust Co.	MN	06/29/20
Citizens First Bank	WI	06/29/20
Columbus Bank and Trust Co.	NE	06/29/20
Columbus State Bank	TX	06/29/20
Community Bank	KS	06/29/20
Community State Bank	WI	06/29/20
Connection Bank	IA	06/29/20
Cornerstone Bank	MO	06/29/20
Delta Bank	LA	06/29/20
Dime Bank	PA	06/29/20
Dundee Bank	NE	06/29/20
EvaBank	AL	06/29/20
Farmers & Merchants Savings Bank	IA	06/29/20
Farmers & Merchants State Bank	WI	06/29/20
Farmers and Merchants State Bank	MN	06/29/20
Farmers Bank, Frankfort, Indiana, Inc.	IN	06/29/20
Farmers State Bank & Trust Co.	LA	06/29/20
Farmers State Bank of Munith	MI	06/29/20
First Capital Bank	TN	06/29/20
First Federal Savings Bank	IN	06/29/20
First Midwest Bank of Poplar Bluff	MO	06/29/20
First National Bank of Anson	TX	06/29/20
First Southwest Bank	CO	06/29/20
First State Bank	TX	06/29/20

Appendix

RECENT BANK FAILURES
2020

Institution	Headquarters	Date of Failure	At Date of Failure	
			Total Assets ($Mil)	Safety Rating
First State Bank	Barboursville, WV	4/06/2020	152.40	E- (Very Weak)
Ericson State Bank	Ericson, NE	2/14/2020	113.02	C- (Fair)

2019

Institution	Headquarters	Date of Failure	At Date of Failure	
			Total Assets ($Mil)	Safety Rating
City National Bank of NJ	Newark, NJ	11/1/19	142.5	E- (Very Weak)
Resolute Bank	Maumee, OH	10/25/19	27.1	E+ (Very Weak)
Enloe State Bank	Cooper, TX	5/31/19	36.5	C (Fair)

2017

Institution	Headquarters	Date of Failure	At Date of Failure	
			Total Assets ($Mil)	Safety Rating
Washington Federal Banks for Savings	Chicago, IL	12/15/17	166.4	A (Excellent)
Farmers & Merchants State Bk of Argonia	Argonia, KS	10/13/17	34.2	E- (Very Weak)
Fayette County Bank	Saint Elmo, IL	05/26/17	34.8	E- (Very Weak)
Guaranty Bank (MHC)	Milwaukee, WI	05/05/17	1,010.0	E- (Very Weak)
First NBC Bank	New Orleans, LA	04/28/17	4,740.0	E- (Very Weak)
Proficio Bank	Cottonwood Heights, UT	03/03/17	80.3	E- (Very Weak)
Seaway Bank and Trust Co	Chicago, IL	01/27/17	361.2	E- (Very Weak)
Harvest Community Bank	Pennsville, NJ	01/13/17	126.4	E- (Very Weak)